MEXICAN AMERICANS

MEXICAN AMERICANS

The Ambivalent Minority

PETER SKERRY

Harvard University Press

CAMBRIDGE, MASSACHUSETTS   LONDON, ENGLAND

This Harvard University Press paperback is published by arrangement with The Free Press, a division of Simon & Schuster Inc.

First Harvard University Press paperback edition, 1995

Library of Congress Cataloging-in-Publication Data
Skerry, Peter.
   Mexican Americans: the ambivalent minority / Peter Skerry.
      p.   cm.
   Includes bibliographical references.
   ISBN 0-674-57262-9
   1. Mexican Americans—Politics and government.   2. Mexican
Americans—Texas—San Antonio—Politics and government.   3. Mexican
Americans—California—Los Angeles—Politics and government.
4. United States—Politics and government—1945–1989.   5. United
States—Politics and government—1989–1993.   6. San Antonio (Tex.)—
Politics and government.   7. Los Angeles (Calif.)—Politics and
government.   8. United States—Ethnic relations.   9. San Antonio
(Tex.)—Ethnic relations.   10. Los Angeles (Calif.)—Ethnic
relations.   I. Title.
E184.M5S57   1993
323.1'16872073—dc20   92-46317
                                                              CIP

Table 4.7 is adapted from *The Politics of San Antonio: Community, Progress, & Power*, edited by David R. Johnson, John A. Booth, and Richard J. Harris; by permission of the University of Nebraska Press. Copyright 1983 by the University of Nebraska Press.

To the memory of my father,
who taught me how to talk to strangers

CONTENTS

ACKNOWLEDGMENTS

At various stages in the evolution of this book, I benefited from the guidance of three different mentors. The original idea emerged several years ago from a lunchtime chat at Nathan Glazer's kitchen table. To Nat, who has read and reread numerous versions of the entire manuscript, as well as edited and re-edited several articles that tested out various aspects of my argument, I am indebted not only for the generosity he has shown me over the years, but the high standards of intellectual openness and honesty he has set for all of us who think and write about controversial public policy issues.

At the critical middle stage, when projects such as this one easily lose direction (and their authors lose hope), Gil Steiner was (and has been ever since) a source of support and guidance for which I will always feel, quite simply, blessed.

Finally, James Q. Wilson has been there from first to last with scholarly as well as practical advice, including help finding institutional and financial resources. To Jim, of course, political scientists, indeed all social scientists, owe a debt for the example of his economy and clarity of exposition and his intellectual rigor.

To be sure, the assistance of these mentors would have been for naught without the scores of activists, community organizers, local observers, staffers, politicians, and public officials—Anglos and blacks, as well as Mexican Americans and other Latinos, in San Antonio, Los Angeles, and throughout Texas and California—willing to talk with a stranger from back East who showed up one day asking lots of questions. To get answers to those questions, I promised anonymity to all those interviewed. Now, after some years of questions and answers, several "informants" have become friends. A few have read and commented on various versions of the manuscript. Others have spent enormous amounts of time talking with me about Mexican-American politics. Many, I fear, will be annoyed that I have not repaid them by at least mentioning them here. I hope they will understand that I still feel bound by my original pledge of anonymity.

Yet there is one instance in which I will break that pledge. I do so in part to acknowledge the special debt I owe Willie Velásquez, but also to take note of his tragically premature death at the age of 44. I first met Willie when he was teaching a course on Mexican-American politics at the Institute of Politics at Harvard's Kennedy School of Government. Willie not only offered a stimulating course, but encouraged me to come down to San Antonio and learn more. I did, and in fact I spent my first few weeks in San Antonio camped out in the offices of the organization he founded, the Southwest Voter Registration Education Project. I remained in frequent contact with Willie until his untimely death in 1988. I am under no illusion—and would seek to dispel any such notion on the part of my readers—that Willie would agree with or endorse all that I argue in this book. But I think that he would agree with some of it, and in general would find the questions I raise to be the important ones. More to the point, I wish Willie were still around to argue about the final product over a few beers at the Esquire.

Fortunately, there are debts of a more collegial nature about which I am not constrained to be silent. An early conversation with Martín Sánchez Jankowski was particularly enlightening. When I was doing fieldwork in Los Angeles, a meeting with Leo Estrada, now a colleague at UCLA, was extremely helpful. Toward the end of the project, Fernando Guerra was generous in sharing the results of his own research with me. At the very end, Ruy Teixeira provided some timely help with statistics.

For reading and commenting on the entire manuscript, I am indebted to Jim Reichley and Bob Asahina. For tackling various sections or versions of the manuscript, I want to thank Barry Chiswick, Frank del Olmo, Father Tom Gannon, Mark Goldberg, Robert Goldwin, Bob Katzmann, Herb Kaufman, Michael Novak, and Kent Weaver. David Riesman was generous with his time in commenting on articles whose arguments found their way into this final product, and he was enormously supportive throughout the project.

I also wish to thank the institutions and individuals who have provided material support to this endeavor at various stages in its history. I begin with Marshall Robinson and Peter De Janosi, both formerly of the Russell Sage Foundation, which provided the initial grant for this research. Also helpful at Russell Sage were Byron Shafer and Hugh O'Neill. The Earhart Foundation subsequently provided a modest but timely grant. Upon completing my initial field research, I spent a year at the Brookings Institution, where as the Hartley Research Fellow in Governmental Studies I benefited from the suggestions of Paul Peterson. I then became a research fellow at the American Enterprise Institute, where, thanks to Chris DeMuth, I spent three enjoyable and productive years. During my tenure at AEI, my work was supported by the Lynde and Harry Bradley Foundation.

For support of a less tangible but nevertheless critical nature I have others to thank: Dickey Wilson, for her good cheer and ready help with computers; Mae Churchill, for her hospitality and probing, sometimes scathing questions; Ray Valdivieso, for frank and honest discussions; Joanne Bickel, not just for reading and commenting on the entire manuscript with gusto, but for her constant encouragement; and Linda Chavez, for her friendship, loyalty, and grit.

I am also fortunate to have had at various times the help of several interns and research assistants, including Robert Geist, Matt Grimes, Eric Rhodes, Mike Hartman, Stuart Spencer, and Anil Kakani. In a pinch at the very end, Stephanie Wilshusen was extraordinarily helpful. Similarly indispensable has been the help of staff at the Bureau of the Census, as well as the librarians at Brookings, especially Susan McGrath, and at AEI, Evelyn Caldwell.

At The Free Press I have benefited from the skillful ministrations of not one but two editors, Peter Dougherty and Bruce Nichols; from the seemingly boundless patience and know-how of my production editor, Loretta Denner; and from the wise counsel and friendship of The Free Press's prime mover, Erwin Glikes.

To my friend Roland Marandino I am grateful for innumerable kindnesses.

Finally, I thank my wife, Martha, without whom nothing would be possible.

PART ONE
Introduction and Overview

❰1❱

The Primacy of Politics

W hen I began the field work for this book a few years ago, I traveled to Corpus Christi. This heavily Mexican-American city on the South Texas coast is home to Dr. Hector García, a practicing physician and longtime political activist. Dr. García is renowned throughout the Southwest as the moving force behind the American G.I. Forum, a Mexican-American veterans' organization founded just after World War II in response to incidents such as the refusal of a small-town Texas funeral home to wake a Mexican-American serviceman.[1]

In Dr. García's waiting room I met a young Mexican American who had just completed his first semester at Yale and was home for the Christmas holidays. He had dropped by to pay his respects to the doctor and, like me, was waiting for him to finish with the afternoon's patients. In the course of conversation, I explained my project, and the young man was soon relating his own experiences in local politics. On a more personal note, he began talking of the importance he attached to his Mexican heritage. Since he had grown up 150 miles from the Mexican border, I assumed this fellow was more or less fluent in Spanish. So, when I happened to inquire, I was surprised to hear him suddenly lower his voice. No, he replied, he did not speak Spanish, but he considered the language a critical part of the Mexican culture he fervently wanted to hold onto. And for this reason, I was assured, he would see to it that his future children

3

would learn Spanish before English. At that point, Dr. García emerged from his office, and we parted. So I never had the chance to ask this fellow how he intended to teach his children a language he himself did not speak.

Similarly vivid in my mind are the countless conversations about U.S. immigration policy that I have had with Mexican Americans of varied backgrounds and political orientations. Seldom in the course of such exchanges have my interlocutors failed to remind me that "We were here first," or that "This was our land and you stole it from us." Even a moderate Mexican-American politician like former San Antonio mayor Henry Cisneros sounds the same theme in a national news magazine:

> It is no accident that these regions have the names they do—Los Angeles, San Francisco, Colorado, Montana. . . . It is a rich history that Americans have been led to believe is an immigrant story when, in fact, the people who built this area in the first place were Hispanics.[3]

Echoing the strident claims of Chicano activists during the 1960s, such assertions today confirm the fears of many Americans that bilingual education programs are not—as Mexican-American leaders often claim—intended to move Spanish-speaking children into the American mainstream, but rather to maintain a distinct culture and language. Many Americans similarly regard bilingual ballots not as a matter of voting rights, but as a device concocted by Mexican-American leaders to maintain control of their people in isolated barrio (neighborhood) enclaves.

Morris Janowitz, the distinguished University of Chicago sociologist, has been one of the few academic observers to give voice to such anxieties:

> Mexicans, together with other Spanish-speaking populations, are creating a bifurcation in the social-political structure of the United States that approximates nationality division. . . . Thus, the presence of Mexico at the border of the United States, plus the strength of Mexican cultural patterns, means that the "natural history" of Mexican immigrants has been and will be at variance with that of other immigrant groups. For sections of the Southwest, it is not premature to speak of a cultural and social irredenta—sectors of the United States which have in effect become Mexicanized and therefore, under political dispute.[4]

Or, as the question is often put to me, "Don't we have in the Southwest today the makings of our own Quebec?"

My short answer to this query is no. Those drawn to the Quebec analogy would do well to note that despite their separatist rhetoric, Chicano activists in the heady 1960s typically argued not for secession from the

United States, but for a vaguely defined self-determination (influenced
by then fashionable notions of community control) within the existing
political framework. Reincorporation of the American Southwest into
Mexico was certainly not advocated.[5] More generally, the widespread suspicion that the growing Mexican-American community either cannot, or
will not, become part of mainstream America is simply not sustained by
the evidence.

In this book I argue that Mexican Americans present a much more
complicated, though nevertheless troublesome, scenario. Look again at
my encounter in Corpus Christi. At first glance, that young man articulated just those sentiments that many Americans find alarming. Yet his
experience also points to the enormous absorptive capacities of American society. For even in a relatively small and remote place like Corpus
Christi, a few hours by car from the Mexican border, this young Mexican American lacked sufficient opportunity to learn Spanish. Moreover,
my observations throughout the Southwest, as well as other available
data, confirm that his experience is typical of many Mexican Americans.
In the impoverished Rio Grande Valley, right next to the Mexican border, a prominent Mexican-American physician and Democratic activist
expressed dismay that his grown children "think like Dallas Republicans." And in the barrios of Los Angeles, a persistent complaint is that
Mexican grandmothers who speak little English have a hard time com-
municating with their grandchildren, who speak no Spanish.[6] At the
same time, I heard young Mexican Americans repeatedly criticize their
parents for raising them to be strangers to their Mexican heritage.[7] Indeed, I argue that precisely because absorption into the mainstream is
for many Mexican Americans so thoroughgoing and rapid, it frequently
results in a backlash, especially among the young and well educated who,
like the Yale student from Corpus, want desperately to preserve their
heritage.

Fears of a Quebec in the Southwest are not only wrong-headed, they
can also be tinged with a cranky nativism.[8] But they do express, however
ineptly or offensively, justifiable concerns that Mexicans will somehow
fail to keep the social contract that has long obtained between American
society and its constituent groups—in other words, that Mexicans are different from European immigrant ethnic groups. And given the propen-
sity of even moderate leaders like Henry Cisneros to remind Anglos that
Mexicans were here first, such anxieties cannot simply be dismissed as ir-
rational.

Yet this is precisely what our political and intellectual elites (Professor
Janowitz to the contrary notwithstanding) have done. Even when their

black allies have on occasion expressed alarm at the growing numbers of Mexicans in our cities, liberals have not been moved. Indeed, when such concerns lead to proposals for more restrictive immigration policies, liberals consistently oppose them. Their stance here reflects a view of immigrants as victims of economic or political oppression who merit compassion and help. And consistent with this perspective, the one concern liberals do express is that these newcomers will experience discrimination and be relegated to a burgeoning underclass.

Just like liberals, conservatives have for the most part welcomed Mexican immigrants and looked with favor upon the growing Mexican-American community. Yet conservatives have done so for very different reasons. For neo-conservatives, Mexicans have been seen as reinforcements in the battle for traditional values. For more market-oriented and libertarian conservatives, these immigrants have been viewed as workers whose energies and ambitions will be channeled into productive economic endeavors. Thus, conservatives—with the glaring and relatively recent exception of spokesmen such as Patrick Buchanan[9]—have been hopeful where liberals have been worried and expressed fears of an emergent Hispanic underclass.

What is remarkable here is how both liberals and conservatives have been fundamentally oblivious to politics, mistakenly assuming that Mexican-American political endeavors will straightforwardly mirror social and economic trends. Liberals have focused on obstacles to the economic and social advancement of Mexican Americans, consequently assuming they will become part of a coalition for progressive change. Conservatives, for their part, have admitted no such obstacles, therefore assuming that social and economic advancement will, as proved true for most European immigrant groups, either obviate the need for political mobilization or channel Mexican-American politics in a moderate or even conservative direction.

Both scenarios are too simplistic. In this book I argue that the challenges posed by the growing population of Mexican Americans are, to a degree widely unappreciated, fundamentally political in nature. To a large extent, the nagging questions on the minds of ordinary Americans can be easily—and affirmatively—answered. The overwhelming evidence is that yes, Mexican immigrants and their offspring will learn English; and yes, they will go to Dodger games at Chavez Ravine and pledge allegiance to the Stars and Stripes. Yet these are not the critical questions. For, having learned English, will Mexican Americans then demand, as many already do, special rights for Spanish? And having "joined the mainstream," will Mexican Americans see themselves as individual citizens or as members of an oppressed racial group? The critical question is therefore not *whether* Mexicans will become Americans, but *how*—on what terms?

My argument is that these terms will be very different from what most observers now envision. The Quebec-style separatism that many fear is simply not in the cards. But neither is the classic pattern of ethnic politics exemplified by European immigrants. While I will present evidence indicating there is good reason to believe that Mexican Americans will advance socially and economically, I will also argue that it is not clear that these gains will be sufficient to satisfy the aspirations of Mexican Americans—or to allay the fears of other Americans that this group will prove a net burden on this society. Much will hinge on the criteria used to evaluate the extent and pace of Mexican-American advancement. And these criteria have been critically shaped by the fundamental changes in our political institutions wrought since the civil rights challenges of the 1950s and 1960s. Unlike the political institutions in place during the last great wave of immigration, those in place today are tutoring Mexican Americans to define themselves as a victimized group that cannot advance without the help of racially assigned benefits.

But this book is more than a critique of Mexican-American leaders wedded to an unfortunate and divisive post-civil-rights political strategy. After all, these leaders are working within a political system largely not of their own making. Indeed, their efforts point to the problematic nature of contemporary political institutions. In recent years, shelves of books have been written on the decline of our political parties; the emergence of political consultants and pollsters; the greater role of the mass media and resultant increases in the cost of campaigns; increased reliance on bureaucracies and the courts to achieve unpopular goals; and the delocalization and consequent nationalization of American politics. Yet however familiar this litany may be, no one has seriously addressed the implications of these changes for the integration of the poorly educated, tradition-oriented immigrants arriving here today. In the chapters that follow, I explore those implications for Mexican Americans—and for Americans generally. Therefore, while this book offers a critique of prevailing Mexican-American political strategies, it also offers a critique of what Anthony King has called "the new American political system."[10]

Because the opportunities and incentives held out by this new American political system are at odds with our enduring self-image as a nation of immigrants, the likely scenario for the foreseeable future is a confusing amalgam of racial claimant politics leavened with the rhetoric of classic immigrant politics. On this point, another vignette from the field is instructive. Willie Velásquez was a native of San Antonio and a veteran of Chicano activist politics in South Texas. In 1974 he founded the Southwest Voter Registration Education Project. Over the next decade, Velásquez visited hundreds of Mexican-American communities throughout the Southwest, with the result that his name and that of his organization became synonymous with registration efforts not just among Mexican Americans but among Hispanics generally. In the mid-1980s I accompanied Velásquez and his staff on several such organizing trips, including one to the Rio Grande Valley. On the drive back to San Antonio one Sunday night, after two days of steady meetings and visits with local activists and elected officials in towns like Weslaco, Mercedes, and Donna, Velásquez was eager to reflect on the weekend's efforts. We had met in my hometown of Boston, and he knew of my Irish-Catholic roots there. So, pumped up by the enthusiastic reception he had just been afforded, he exclaimed: "Gee, Pete. Wasn't this just like the Irish in Boston, back in the 1800s?" To which I responded: "Sure, Willie. But the Irish never had any help from the Voting Rights Act, did they?"

This exchange was the essence of my ongoing dialogue with Willie Velásquez, right up to the time of his tragically premature death from cancer at the age of 44 in 1988. As a fair-minded observer and a shrewd political operative, Velásquez had learned from his activist days in the 1960s that emphasizing to Anglos the differences between them and Mexicans had its limits. More to the point, he was aware that depicting Mexican Americans as an immigrant group served to legitimate and garner support for his efforts—hence his analogy between the Boston Irish and the Mexicans of South Texas.

Yet Velásquez was also prepared to work with the materials at hand to advance his political objectives. And in post-1960s America, those materials are, by and large, the laws and institutions established to secure the civil and political rights of black Americans. Notable among these is the Voting Rights Act, which Velásquez knew well, having been one of the many advocates to persuade Congress in 1975 that Mexicans and other Hispanics should be afforded the same extraordinary protections and benefits that legislation provided black Americans. Toward that end, Velásquez and others argued that Mexicans, like blacks, have been the victims of systematic racial discrimination.[11]

Can Mexican Americans have it both ways? Should they? If their experience is in many respects similar to that of typical immigrant groups, then what entitles them to the same protections that the nation has, with considerable reluctance and controversy, given to blacks in recognition of the debilitating effects of slavery and Jim Crow? Simply to raise the question is to risk denunciation for fomenting racial discord. Yet it is a question that black Americans themselves have raised.[12]

And, like it or not, the critical, overriding question regarding Mexican-American politics *does* concern race. Will Mexican Americans define themselves as traditional ethnic immigrants or as victims of racial discrimination? Velásquez is not the only leader to invoke both perspectives. The same pattern was evident during the 1988 presidential campaign, when Mexican-American leaders who had long argued that their people merited affirmative action protection eagerly identified Michael Dukakis's Greek immigrant background as similar to their own.

The confusion is intellectual as well as political. Take, for example, the work of University of Chicago sociologist Marta Tienda. In an otherwise meticulous and thoughtful study, *The Hispanic Population of the United States,* co-authored with Frank Bean of the University of Texas, Tienda sketches the historical experience of Mexican Americans in the Southwest:

> As Chicanos lost their land, their social mobility became blocked, and this eventually led to a deterioration of their social position vis-à-vis Anglos. Racism was employed to pursue economic interests . . . ; *although Mexicans are white, their brown skin and indigenous features encouraged racism and discrimination by the Anglo majority.*[13](My emphasis)

This passage typifies the genuine quandary many Mexican Americans face: if they have "brown skin and indigenous features," then how can they be characterized as "white"? And if they are "white," then why have they been subjected to "racism and discrimination"?

Similarly revealing has been the verbal confusion following the 1991 incident in which Los Angeles police officers were caught on videotape brutally beating a 25-year-old black motorist named Rodney King. Throughout that spring, and during the riots that followed the April 1992 acquittal of the four officers most directly involved, the local and national media consistently reported that all four officers were "white."[14] Yet one of the four was Theodore Briseno, described by the *Los Angeles Times* as the son of a man who was "half-Latino" and as having himself been "teased about his Latino heritage by *white* friends in high school" [15] (my emphasis). Yet in its news columns and editorials the *Times* has—with this notable exception—consistently referred to Briseno as one of "the whites" [16] who assaulted King. Indeed, in the continuing furor over this incident, Briseno's ethnic background has been almost universally overlooked.[17]

Why in one context is Briseno considered nonwhite, and in another white? Community leaders in Los Angeles may have been concerned about exacerbating already strained relations there between Mexican Americans and blacks. But the rest of us have had no such excuse for not trying to sort out the confusion. Consider, for example, the somewhat convoluted efforts of those concerned to forge a nonwhite racial identity for Mexican Americans in the face of considerable counterevidence. As two young Berkeley social scientists (one Latino, one black) recently wrote in *PS*, the quarterly magazine of the American Political Science Association:

> Most Latinos do not identify themselves as nonwhite as evidenced by the popularization of the term "Hispanic." . . . Most Latino politicians have historically promoted a white identity for Latinos and this has contributed to a lack of interest in building "rainbow" coalitions. In addition, the complexity of the Latino racial identity has made it difficult to mobilize Latinos along the lines of one racial political consciousness as has been the case with blacks. The racial complexity notwithstanding, the majority of Latinos are nonwhite, and the prospects for coalition building with blacks will be enhanced if they are properly perceived as people of color.[18]

As for many Mexican Americans, they remain undecided even when they are not confused. In the words of one college student, described as "a fair-complexioned Chicano" by researchers with the Diversity Project at the University of California at Berkeley, "because I don't look as Latino as other people, I'm marginal, could go one way or another."[19]

That many Mexicans "could go one way or another" is not lost on blacks. As one young minister with an African Methodist Episcopal congregation in Los Angeles wryly observed to me, "Latinos can walk the Anglo walk and talk the Anglo talk." Giving the same point more of an edge, a black community leader described the dilemma facing Mexican Americans: "Latinos can't make up their minds whether they're a minority."[20] Taking my cue from this observation, I have entitled this book *Mexican Americans: The Ambivalent Minority.*

"Ambivalent" certainly describes the state of mind of many young Mexican Americans, including my acquaintance in Corpus Christi and the Berkeley undergraduate just quoted. Yet because the situation in which Mexican Americans now find themselves is not simply a youthful identity crisis, I use the word here to suggest something more. Indeed, for individuals like Willie Velásquez, ambivalence is a rational response to the mixed signals being sent out by today's political institutions.

WHEN IS A MINORITY A "MINORITY"?

The word "minority" is much more freighted with meaning than it used to be. For as the new American political system has offered Mexican Americans increased incentives to define themselves in racial terms, "minority" has come to denote just such a victimized racial claimant group in both popular and scholarly usage. The controversy surrounding this development has been intense, and one result, as recently noted by Nathan Glazer, is that "the conception of 'minority' is so muddled that there is considerable dispute over just who we mean."[21]

⟨ The beginning of wisdom here is to appreciate how the various meanings of "minority" have changed in response to social and political exigencies⟩ University of Chicago sociologist Louis Wirth, who first popularized the term, defined "minority" loosely as virtually any group—ethnic, linguistic, religious, or racial—that is differentiated from and subordinated to a society's dominant group.[22] Relying on this definition, Charles Wagley and Marvin Harris included in their 1958 book, *Minorities in the New World,* studies of Indians in Brazil and Mexico, Negroes in Martinique and the United States, French in Canada, and Jews in the United States.[23] Such an inclusive view has undoubtedly contributed to the popular tendency to use "ethnic group" interchangeably with "minority group."

Ironically, the one stipulation laid down by Wirth—that "minority" does *not* refer to a group's numerical size, but to its subordinated status[24]—is widely ignored in popular usage.⟩This tendency is undoubtedly fueled by the attentiveness to numerical minorities that the Framers of the Constitution built into the American political system.

In any event, it is only recently that "minority" has taken on its present, more restrictive, racial meaning. For example, although there are many fewer Greeks in the United States than blacks, the former are not typically referred to as a "minority." Contemporary usage is illustrated in a recent *Washington Post* article about the 1990 census: "Demographers predict that by the year 2060, minorities will outnumber whites."[25] Conversely, "white" has become, according to researchers at Berkeley's Diversity Project, "a residual category meaning either not Black, not Asian, not Chicano/Latino, etc. . . . meaning 'without color.' "[26] Thus, one hears the frequent observation that blacks, Asians, and Latinos are making California "a minority majority" state.[27]

But more than just being "people of color," minorities are understood to have experienced systematic racial discrimination. An echo of this perspective can be heard in the remarks of a white undergraduate talking about intergroup relations on the Berkeley campus: "minorities haven't had the same opportunity for education as white people."[28] Even more to the point, minority groups are now understood to have been forcibly incorporated—or "colonized"—into American society by the dominant whites.[29] Moreover, the minority's subjugated status is assumed to have been sanctioned in law. Finally, there is the presumption that even after such explicit discrimination has ended, minority group members are sufficiently burdened by their history that they deserve special help and consideration. As social scientists Joan Moore and Ralph Guzman have put it:

> For Americans, the word "minority" evokes the image of a people with long-standing grievances. It implies a moral claim on American society and, probably, a potential for political action and civil disruption.[30]

The prototype for this view of a minority as a victimized racial claimant group is obviously black Americans. Indeed, this new conception of the term reflects the success blacks had during the 1960s in getting their plight defined as a public policy priority. Concomitantly, as Americans focused on their race problem, they came to view whatever problems other groups experienced in a different light. Thus, as "minority" came to mean "racial minority" exclusively, Wirth's original conception of any group subordinated by nationality, language, or religion, in addition to race, no longer held. Consequently, Jews, many of whom still undoubtedly consider themselves a minority, are not so viewed under the new dispensation. Neither are Gypsies or Louisiana Cajuns. But Native Americans clearly are.

The European immigrants that formerly shared minority status with blacks and Native Americans, but did so on the basis of nonracial criteria, are typically referred to now as "ethnics" or "ethnic groups." Thus, minority groups are characterized by racial criteria, ethnic groups by cultural criteria.[31] More to the point, because ethnics were not conquered, enslaved, or otherwise colonized by American society, but immigrated here voluntarily, they have no special claims on the American conscience—nor are they inclined to make any.[32] This does not mean that ethnic groups, particularly as recent immigrants, have never experienced prejudice or discrimination, but it is nothing like the systematic racial discrimination sustained over generations that minorities have endured. In part, this is because the cultural characteristics that demarcate ethnic groups (language, religion, dress) are mutable, whereas racial characteristics are not. As a result, ethnic group members—particularly descendants of the first arrivals—have the option of leaving, or not identifying with "their group."

As Michael Walzer points out, ethnic identity in a pluralistic society is fundamentally a matter of individual choice—not necessity.[33]

Thus, ethnic and minority groups are distinguished by critical subjective differences. Focusing on the voluntary or involuntary nature of their contact with American society, anthropologist John Ogbu delineates this difference well. Of what I refer to here as "ethnic" groups, he says:

> Immigrants generally regard themselves as "foreigners," "strangers" who came to America with expectation of certain economic, political, and social benefits. While anticipating that such benefits might come at some cost—involving discrimination and other hardships—the immigrants did not measure their success or failure primarily by the standards of other white Americans, but by the standards of their homelands. . . . Even when they were restricted to menial labor, they did not consider themselves to be occupying the lowest rung of the American status system. . . . they saw their situation as temporary.[34]

Referring to immigrants as "voluntary minorities," Ogbu contrasts them with "involuntary minorities," of whom he notes:

> There were no expectations of economic, political, and social benefits. Resenting their initial incorporation by force, regarding their past as a "golden age," and seeing their future as grim in the absence of collective struggle, they understood that the American system was based on social class and minority conditions. While refusing to accept white denigration, the common white belief that they were biologically, culturally, and intellectually inferior to whites, their own thoughts and behaviors were not entirely free from the influence of such denigration and belief.[35]

This evolving conceptualization of ethnic and minority groups obviously has important political implications. But this in turn means that usage is hardly the exclusive domain of specialists, which only compounds the confusion. For while the terminology evolves in scholarly discourse, laymen struggle to find ways of talking about the problems arising from group differences in everyday life. At the same time, lay usage struggles to catch up with terminological changes that reflect shifts among political elites. As a result, one sometimes hears, as I indicated earlier, the terms "ethnic" and "minority" used interchangeably. Or they get combined, as in "ethnic minority." "Language minority" is another formulation that confounds the cultural and racial distinction I'm describing.[36] But in such cases, what is critical is that the word "minority" is being used to secure status as a victimized claimant group.

Additional confusion arises because these analytic categories are confounded in real life. Indeed, minority group members typically do not share only racial characteristics, but cultural characteristics as well. Thus, American blacks, whose cultural traits are certainly as distinctive as their racial characteristics, are not infrequently referred to as an ethnic group.[37] Though hardly incorrect, this designation for blacks is inconsistent with the framework presented here.[38]

Quite aside from such terminological and conceptual confusion, it is not always obvious into which category a group should be placed—or, even more important, should place itself. Take, for example, the situation of Asian Americans. Asians originally came to the United States under exploitative contract labor schemes and experienced virulent racial prejudice and discriminatory legal sanctions. The Chinese Exclusion Act of 1882, one of the first restrictive immigration laws passed by Congress, not only completely cut off immigration from China, but also deprived Chinese immigrants already here of the right to become citizens.[39] Japanese immigrants subsequently encountered similar treatment. A 1922 Supreme Court ruling deemed a Japanese-born immigrant ineligible for citizenship on account of his race; and the Immigration Act of 1924 effectively prohibited immigration from Japan.[40] Finally, Japanese Americans were of course interned in prison camps during World War II. Few other groups have experienced such extreme treatment at the hands of Americans. Perhaps not surprisingly, then, some Asian Americans have advanced minority group claims.[41] And to some extent they have been successful, for Asian Americans are one of the five groups explicitly protected under the Voting Rights Act. Yet Asians are so residentially dispersed that the Act is seldom invoked in their behalf. Meanwhile, the millions of Asians who have arrived here in recent decades have experienced nothing even remotely comparable to the barriers encountered by their predecessors. As a result, most Asian Americans appear to see themselves as a typical ethnic group[42]

In *City Limits*, his extended essay on urban politics, Paul Peterson observes:

> Color changes the character of ethnic politics. The visibility of the minority group is much greater, and therefore group members are assimilated into the larger society more slowly and more painfully. . . . As a result, minority group politics has taken a more virulent form than older forms of ethnic politics.[43]

But the Asian case suggests the need for a reformulation of Peterson's point, for color can, but does not always, change ethnic politics. Similarly, a history of involuntary immigration or systematic racial oppression may be a necessary condition for the emergence of minority politics, but it is not a sufficient one. For contrary to Peterson's implicit assumption, there is nothing automatic or preordained about minority politics. Whether or not a group makes minority claims on the polity results in part from its own strategic choices. And such *political* choices are not automatically determined by a group's social and economic choices.[44]

In this regard, it is striking that in recent years some blacks have exercised such political choice and attempted to move away from the dominant minority perspective. For example, the newly appointed school superintendent of Montgomery County in suburban Washington, D.C., the first black ever to hold that position, recently told his principals that he had a "bitter resistance to the characterization 'minority' and 'minority students' because its sets them aside, it makes them something special. It puts them outside the mainstream . . . [and] perpetuates barriers against children."[45] Similarly, recent moves by leaders like Jesse Jackson to change the designation "black" to "African American" reflect a more general effort to reorient the group's self-image away from that of a victimized racial claimant and toward a positive identification with its ethnic and cultural heritage.[46]

ARE MEXICAN AMERICANS A MINORITY?

Where do Mexican Americans fit into this schema? There can be little doubt that the dominant institutions of contemporary American society define them as a minority group. One of the earliest manifestations of this perspective emerged during the 1967 congressional hearings on bilingual education. At that time Senator Ralph Yarborough of Texas, principal sponsor of the Bilingual Education Act, argued that bilingual programs were appropriate for Mexican Americans because, unlike other non-English-speaking groups in the United States, they had not come here voluntarily but had been conquered and "had our culture imposed on them."[47]

Nongovernmental institutions are equally disposed toward designating Mexican Americans a minority. A good example is *Daedalus*, the prestigious journal of the American Academy of Arts and Sciences. In a special issue entitled "American Indians, Blacks, Chicanos, and Puerto Ricans," editor Stephen Graubard asserts:

> It is obvious that these four peoples—the "victims" of conquest—men and women who did not choose America, who have long suffered exclusion and discrimination because of their origins, live overwhelmingly in conditions substantially different from those common to other groups in the United States.[48]

Similarly, the editors of the *Harvard Educational Review* describe a special issue of their journal, entitled *Facing Racism in Education*, as having articles from contributors who "represent those groups who have historically been the targets of racism in the United States: Asian Americans, Blacks, Latinos, and Native Americans."[49] Not coincidentally, these are the groups covered by the Voting Rights Act, as well as affirmative action efforts generally.

Against this backdrop of official and unofficial designation as a minority group emerges the significance of the pervasive, but little noted, practice of treating Mexican Americans, and Latinos generally, as a racial group. For example, in a recent article entitled "California's Coming Minority Majority," political scientists Bruce Cain and Roderick Kiewiet unhesitatingly describe Hispanics as "nonwhite."[50] Similarly, the *1991 Green Book*, the overview of federal entitlement programs issued annually by the House Ways and Means Committee, presents data on Head Start enrollments by "race" under the categories: American Indian, black, white, Asian, and Hispanic.[51] And this is just a more detailed version of the typology—"whites, blacks, Hispanics"—now routinely seen in newspapers, government reports, opinion polls, and even scholarly journals.

But this typology poses several largely unexamined problems. The most obvious is that, as the Census Bureau keeps reminding us, "Hispanic" is an ethnic, not a racial designation. Because Hispanics can be of any race, whites, blacks, and Hispanics are not mutually exclusive categories. To deal with this problem, careful researchers and writers specify "non-Hispanic whites, non-Hispanic blacks, and Hispanics." But even this formulation continues to foster the mistaken notion that "Hispanic" (or "Latino")* is a residual racial category.

Of still greater import is the fact that classifying Mexican Americans as racially nonwhite conflicts rather dramatically with how they see themselves. Indeed, in the 1990 census 50.6 percent of Mexican Americans identified themselves as "white." Only 1.2 percent said they were "black." At the same time, 46.7 percent of Mexican Americans claimed to be neither white nor black, but "other race."[52] Moreover, the corresponding data from the 1980 census indicate that Mexican Americans are increasingly less likely to identify themselves as "white" and more likely to opt for "other race" (see Table 1–1). Such evidence certainly challenges the

---

* In this book I will follow the lead of the National Council of La Raza and use the generic terms "Hispanic" and "Latino" interchangeably. See Raul Yzaguirre, *State of Hispanic America 1991: An Overview* (Washington, D.C.: National Council of La Raza, 1992), 1.

TABLE 1.1
Mexican-American Racial Self-Identification (in Percent)

Racial Self-Identification	1980			1990		
	National	California	Texas	National	California	Texas
"White"	53.2	47.7	62.1	50.6	45.2	58.3
"Black"	1.8	0.5	0.4	1.2	1.2	0.8
"Other race"*	45.0	51.9	37.5	48.2	53.6	40.9

Source: U.S. Census, unpublished data tabulated by the Census Bureau.
Note: *Includes data from additional, numerically small categories, such as "American Indian."

uncritical eagerness with which even prominent academics classify Mexican Americans (and Latinos generally) as racially distinct from the white majority, even as it confirms my view that Mexican Americans are ambivalent, poised between defining themselves as an ethnic group and a minority group.

One reason why mainstream elites have so readily designated Mexican Americans a minority is that Mexican-American elites are so intent on this perspective. This is certainly true of Mexican-American academics, who typically view themselves as part of a colonized people.[53] As for political leaders, Rodolfo de la Garza's research concludes: "Chicano elites consider racism to be a defining characteristic of the Chicano experience that continues to plague them today."[54]

Yet it has not always been thus. For much of this century, Mexican-American leaders assiduously distinguished their group from blacks and, indeed, argued that Mexican Americans were white. Describing the work of an organization called the Coordinating Council for Latin-American Youth in Los Angeles during World War II, historian Mario T. García notes:

> Council members shunned identification as a minority. For them the concept of a minority meant separation. After all, the ideology of wartime America stressed the equality of all Americans. To label someone a minority . . . stigmatized them as different and made them defensive. . . . The Council focused on ethnic rather than racial discrimination. Ruiz [the leader of the Council], for example, refused to discuss Mexican Americans on the basis of race. He insisted that Mexicans were white and hence no different from other ethnic groups such as the Irish, Italians, or Germans.[55]

Twenty years later, in the mid-1960s, a massive study funded by the Ford Foundation reported similar resistance among Mexican Americans to being referred to as a minority.[56]

How is this fundamental reorientation of Mexican-American leadership views to be explained? Indeed, how are we to interpret the ironic outcome that in the past, when Mexican Americans were more likely to be treated like a racial minority, they sought protection by denying any racial distinctiveness; while today, when they experience dramatically fewer such racial barriers, their leaders are intent on defining them as a minority?

In part, today's leaders are reacting to what they regard as the naive self-deception and shameful opportunism of their predecessors, who not only rejected any commonality with blacks, but even denied their own Indian ancestry—thereby falling into a familiar pattern among Mexicans on both sides of the Rio Grande.[57] Yet the question remains. What explains the very different perspective of today's leaders?

MEXICAN AMERICANS IN
SAN ANTONIO AND LOS ANGELES

In this book I address this question by examining structural changes in the political system within which Mexican-American leaders must now operate. Many of these changes are traceable to fundamental, long-term developments in our advanced industrial society, but others stem more immediately from the transformations wrought by the civil rights movement and its progeny. I have already indicated the importance of the Voting Rights Act, to which I will devote some attention. Of additional interest will be Washington-based lobbying groups such as the National Council of La Raza and the Mexican American Legal Defense and Educational Fund (MALDEF), particularly their roles in the immigration policy debate. I argue that it is in the national political arena where the incentives for Mexican Americans to define themselves as a minority group are most evident. More precisely, it is where Mexican Americans feel the most intense competition from blacks. As an official with the National Council of La Raza once confided to me, his organization feels compelled each January, when the National Urban League comes out with its report on the state of black America, to produce a similar report stressing the problems of Mexican Americans.

Closely related to these developments at the national level are changes in state and local political institutions. To get at these, I compare Mexican-American politics in San Antonio and Los Angeles, where starkly different regimes highlight the transformation our political institutions generally have undergone. Like many things in Texas, San Antonio is struggling to change nowadays. But to a large extent, we find there what used to be common in our cities: a politics rooted in personal loyalties, reinforced by party identification and, especially, by favors and patronage. Los Angeles, on the other hand, has a strong civil service tradition, nonpartisan elections, and a preoccupation with issues. Very much at the cutting edge of political trends today, Los Angeles is the quintessentially reformed city, the embodied ideal of turn-of-the-century Progressive reformers who sought to eliminate precisely the kind of patronage-based ward politics so much in evidence in San Antonio. In essence, San Antonio harkens back to our Jacksonian past, while Los Angeles points to a possible, if not inevitable, political future.

This is the most compelling reason for comparing these metropolitan areas. But there are others. Within several hours' drive of the Mexican border, both lie well within the historic bounds of Mexican life in the Southwest—unlike Denver, Chicago, or other such cities with substantial Mexican populations. Yet neither Los Angeles nor San Antonio has the eccentricities of a border town like El Paso or San Diego; or Mexican-American communities of such relatively recent origin as Houston or Dallas. Finally, both cities are key sites in states where Mexican-American voters represent targets of opportunity in statewide as well as national political contests.

Thus, San Antonio and Los Angeles have long been paired as the two leading centers of Mexican-American life. In 1926, when the publisher of San Antonio's *La Prensa*, at the time the Southwest's leading Spanish-language newspaper, wanted to start a second publication, the obvious outlet for his ambitions was Los Angeles, where *La Opinión* is still a thriving daily.[58] Similarly, in the mid-1960s, when the Ford Foundation funded the Mexican American Study Project, the most comprehensive such study ever undertaken, the focus was a comparative analysis of San Antonio and Los Angeles—described by Leo Grebler and his Project colleagues as "these two 'capital cities' of the Mexican-American population."[59]

Further enriching this comparison is the fact that these two cities have been the sites of similar community organizing efforts. In the early 1970s, a San Antonio native named Ernesto ("Ernie") Cortes, having recently completed a training course at Saul Alinsky's Industrial Areas Foundation (IAF) in Chicago, returned to his hometown and began organizing its West Side barrio. Having achieved impressive results with Communities Organized for Public Service (COPS), Cortes then moved to Los Angeles's Eastside barrio, where he started the United Neighborhoods

Organization (UNO). COPS and UNO thus present a unique opportunity to compare efforts at building and maintaining neighborhood-based political organizations among Mexican Americans in two different contexts.

And as it turns out, the relative success of these organizations parallels the larger pattern of Mexican-American political outcomes in these two metropolitan areas—indeed, in these states. For just as Mexican Americans in San Antonio and Texas have been more successful at politics than their counterparts in Los Angeles and California, COPS has been more effective than UNO.

This finding strikes many as surprising. Most observers assume that a disadvantaged group like Mexicans would do better in California, where they have suffered relatively little racial subjugation and experienced substantial socioeconomic mobility. It is therefore all the more unexpected that Mexican Americans there have tended to engage in strident minority politics. By contrast, in Texas, where historically Mexican Americans have come closest to being treated like a racial caste, their politics has been much more accommodative and in the familiar ethnic mold.

Why, for example, is racism a more salient issue among Mexican-American leaders in California than in Texas?[60] Why do Mexican Americans in California typically use the racial designation "whites" to refer to the dominant group, while their counterparts in Texas routinely use the cultural designation "Anglos"? In the same vein, why do Mexican Americans in California identify themselves as "white" less often than Mexican Americans in Texas (see Table 1–1)?

Explaining these paradoxical outcomes is at the heart of this book. And doing so will shed light not only on Mexican-American politics in these two specific contexts, but on the broader and more fundamental question of how the new American political system is encouraging Mexican Americans to define themselves as a minority group.

THE MINORITY CASE:
FAMILIARITY AND CONTEMPT

Admittedly, such encouragement has taken hold in part because there is much in the historical experience of Mexican Americans that differentiates them from European immigrants. As Mexican Americans themselves never tire of pointing out, their Spanish and especially Indian ancestors were present in what is now the American Southwest long before the forebears of most Americans arrived on the North American continent. As Luis Valdez—playwright, founder of El Teatro Campesino, and director of the hit film *La Bamba*—has written "No Statue of Liberty ever greeted our arrival in this country, and left us with the notion that the land was free, even though Mexicans and Indians already lived on it."[61] Or as ordinary Mexican Americans have put it to me less portentously: "We did not have to cross an ocean to get here."

When they say this, Mexican Americans are in part suggesting that because it is easier to immigrate here from Mexico, doing so requires less commitment and therefore may involve more equivocation than immigrating from Europe. But this is a dubious notion in light of the evidence that about one-third of immigrants who arrived here earlier this century ultimately returned home.[62] Nevertheless, Mexican Americans do regard themselves as fundamentally different from European, or Asian, immigrants to this country.

One source of this sense of uniqueness is the continuity that Mexicans experience when they come to the United States. For such immigrants to the American Southwest, there are no radical changes in climate or geography. And though the point can be wildly exaggerated, there are even continuities in architecture, language, ranching culture, and of course history.[63] With such long-lived and visible bonds to the region, Mexican Americans enjoy a bracing sense of being on their own turf that is simply not true of, for example, the Poles in Chicago or the Irish in Boston. As political scientist Walker Connor puts it:

> The knowledge that the region was once Mexican has a psychological dimension, inspiring a special sense of a historically derived right to live in the region, a right that immigrants from an overseas ancestral homeland cannot feel . . .[64]

Another reason why Mexican Americans feel unique is of course the long and troubled history between the United States and Mexico. If wars with Japan and Germany had adverse effects on ethnic Japanese and Germans living here, then it is reasonable to expect that generations of tensions and outright hostilities with Mexico—especially the war that led to the conquest of the Southwest—have also left their mark. That Americans tend to ignore this history is reflected in the wry Mexican saying: "Americans never remember; Mexicans never forget." What Mexicans never forget is that in 1848 they lost half of their national territory to their northern neighbor.[65]

But more than just with the memory of military defeat, Mexicans have had to cope with the overwhelming economic and cultural presence of the United States.[66] How this sense of national humiliation has affected Mexicans who have settled here is difficult to say. But it seems undeniable that Mexican Americans, particularly those living in the Southwest close to their homeland, have been stigmatized by the poverty of Mexico. To be sure, many ethnic groups in this country have at one time or another endured similar burdens. Still, the situation has been uniquely onerous for Mexican Americans, whose defeated homeland with its persistent problems has long stood in such stark and proximate contrast to the United States. Mexican-American disaffection with their homeland can certainly be inferred from the fact that Chicano activists have, as I noted earlier, never actually argued for reincorporation of the conquered territories with Mexico.[67]

Yet the legacy of the past involves more than embarrassment. Mexican Americans also harbor deep resentments about the way they have been treated in this country. Many Mexican Americans have endured virtual caste status in the rural towns and ranches of the Southwest. Early this century in Gonzales County, Texas, Mexican contract laborers were chained to posts and guarded by men with shotguns.[68] Along the border at McAllen, Texas I have heard gruesome tales about Texas Rangers early this century terrorizing the locals by driving around town with a dead Mexican draped on either fender. The context of such stories is what historian David Montejano describes as "a virtual war zone" in the Rio Grande Valley during World War I. At that time, the resistance of Texas Mexicans to the changes wrought by Midwesterners introducing commercial farming into the region frequently culminated in violence. Anglo fears of insurrection were fueled by the turmoil in revolutionary Mexico, where schemes to reconquer the Southwest were sufficiently salient for Germany to seize upon them as the basis of a proposed anti-American alliance (in the infamous Zimmermann telegram). And when Northern Mexico became the staging area for raids across the border that resulted in the deaths of American citizens, Mexicans began to be perceived as an internal enemy.[69] Commenting on the violence in the region at the time, a *New York Times* editorial observed that "the killing of Mexicans without provocation is so common as to pass unnoticed."[70] Historian Walter Prescott Webb reported that between 500 and 5,000 Mexicans were killed in the Rio Grande Valley during this period, compared to 126 Americans.[71]

Is it any wonder that as late as the mid-1960s Mexican Americans in the Southwest routinely downplayed their ties to Mexico and referred to themselves as "Latin Americans" or "Spanish-speaking Americans"? More recently, I heard echoes from this violent era in anecdotes told by Mexican Americans whose parents and grandparents got caught up in the many border skirmishes. Even fresher were memories of Mexican-American citizens swept up in government-sponsored repatriation efforts, which during the Depression actually reduced the Mexican-born population in the United States from 639,000 in 1930 to about 377,000 in 1940.[72]

As for the more recent past, Mexican Americans in South Texas relate how, until a generation or so ago, they were routinely assigned to "the Mexican school in town."[73] In Los Angeles, middle-aged Mexican Americans tell how they used to be permitted into municipal swimming pools only on designated days; or how, after the Second World War, restrictive covenants kept returning Mexican-American servicemen from buying houses in certain subdivisions.[74] In the mid-1950s, Operation Wetback, conducted by the Border Patrol under the direction of a retired army general, succeeded in sending hundreds of thousands of illegal immigrants (and many of their United States-born children) back to Mexico—in the process outraging many Mexican-American citizens who were stopped and asked for proof of citizenship.[75] Such memories linger. As a city official in Los Angeles put it, he can still hear his grandmother from El Paso saying "gringo" with such contempt that "it sounded as if she were clearing her throat of phlegm."

Of course, many groups in America have similarly painful memories. Told and retold, such stories not only serve to remind individuals of gains that have been made, they also nurture the collective identity that groups often struggle to maintain. In this process, facts often get distorted. Yet regardless of their accuracy, the accounts I heard throughout the Southwest were voiced so frequently that they are clearly part of the Mexican-American folk consciousness. So, the indignities of the past are not forgotten. Indeed, they are kept alive whenever the Immigration and Naturalization Service mistreats—or merely stops to question—a Mexican-American citizen in the course of pursuing illegal immigrants. And for Mexican Americans, quite unlike for immigrant groups of European origin, this history and its retelling nurture a minority-group identity.

THE ETHNIC CASE:
NEWCOMERS WITH DREAMS

Still, there is much to support the argument that Mexican Americans are an immigrant ethnic group. It might well begin with the fact that at the close of hostilities between Mexico and the United States in 1848, Mexicans comprised at most 4 percent of the population of the Southwest— or about 80,000 people.[76] Since this was only about 1 percent of Mexico's population at the time, very few Mexican Americans today can trace their lineage back to that conquest. The vast majority are either immigrants themselves or the descendants of immigrants who arrived here in one of the various waves that have swept across the border since the turn of the century. As Tienda and Bean conclude:

> The idea, then, that Mexican Americans must be viewed as different from other national origin groups who have immigrated to the United States because they are a conquered people instead of voluntary immigrants seems hard to justify in light of these statistics.[77]

Further support for the immigrant ethnic interpretation is found in the work of historian David Montejano, who demonstrates how immigration has significantly shaped the Mexican-American experience. As he points out, "the web of labor controls" on Mexicans in South Texas—vagrancy laws, pass systems, and other such efforts to restrict the mobility of Mexican workers—was never very tightly or effectively organized, precisely because continuous infusions of pliant immigrant labor from Mexico rendered severe controls superfluous.[78] In this important respect, the situation of Mexican Americans in the Southwest has been fundamentally different from that of blacks in the South.

It is therefore not surprising that some Mexican Americans have been able to "pass." To be sure, their numbers have varied greatly according to time and place. But certainly in recent decades the evidence is striking. Intermarriage data, for example, reveal that Mexican Americans marry outside their group at rates comparable to those exhibited by European immigrants earlier this century.[79] Mexican Americans certainly marry outside their group at rates dramatically higher than those for black Americans.[80] Similarly, residential mobility studies reveal that Mexican Americans differ markedly from blacks in following the classic immigrant pattern of gradual movement up and out of initially settled urban enclaves.[81]

Thus, it is with some justification that those familiar with Mexican Americans often compare them to Italians in this country. Both groups have arrived for the most part as uneducated rural villagers who brought with them a profound distrust of change and an abiding respect for the old ways.[82] Centered around kinship ties, this deep-seated traditionalism has resulted in an uneasiness and distrust toward all that lies outside the family orbit. For both Mexicans and Italians this has meant a certain distance from our public institutions—even from the Catholic Church.

THE MEXICAN-AMERICAN MOSAIC

Yet, however convincing the case for either the ethnic or the minority perspective, neither is decisive. Consider the multilayered symbolism of the

Alamo. Generations of Anglo Americans have been taught to view this old San Antonio mission as the symbol of fierce Texan pride and heroism in the face of Mexican despotism. Meanwhile, internalizing this history, many Mexican Americans have come to see the Alamo as the symbol of their status as a conquered people. Yet, lost in the mists of the not-so-distant past is the fact that Mexicans actually fought and died alongside Anglos at the Alamo. As historian Montejano emphasizes: "Texas independence was brought about through an alliance of the newcomer Anglo colonists and the established Texas Mexican elite."[83] Indeed, the remains of this alliance lie together in a crypt in San Antonio's San Fernando Cathedral—a curious resting place for a Scotch-Irish frontiersman like Davy Crockett, who named his son after the Methodist John Wesley.[84]

Further evidence that Mexican Americans disagree among themselves about whether they are an ethnic or a minority group can be seen in the continuing debate over how they should be identified—what researchers twenty years ago called "the Battle of the Name."[85] Still quietly raging, this battle has several fronts: "Chicano" came into vogue during the 1960s and continues to be used by activists and young people espousing the minority perspective; "Latino" is popular in Los Angeles, where it links Mexican Americans with the growing Central American population; "Hispanic" is a generic term viewed by many Mexican Americans as an ill-conceived label concocted by federal bureaucrats, but also used freely by barrio political entrepreneurs when it suits their purposes; "Mexicano" is often used interchangeably with "Mexican" and is frequently heard in South Texas, where the bonds of community and tradition remain strong; and finally, "Mexican American," the most widely used and least controversial term, is especially popular among older or more mainstream-oriented members of the group.[86]*

Some of this profusion of labels reflects the ambivalence discussed earlier. Yet the group's diverse origins also play a role. For how Mexican Americans see themselves fitting into American society depends greatly on which Mexican Americans one asks. "Some of us have been here for three hundred years, some for three days." I have heard this observation over and over from the scores of Mexican-American political and com-

---

*In this work, I use the term "Mexican American" to refer both to ethnic Mexicans who are American citizens and to Mexican nationals who have settled, legally or illegally, in the United States. Given this broad usage, the term "Mexicans" will occasionally be used as shorthand for Mexican Americans, much as one might use "Italians" to refer to Italian Americans. But for the most part, "Mexicans" will refer to recent arrivals from Mexico who have not yet become Mexican Americans. On a few occasions, typically when data limitations do not permit me to speak with precision of Mexican Americans, the generic "Hispanics" or "Latinos" will be used. In each instance, the context will clarify the exact meaning.

munity leaders with whom I have spoken. More than most oft-repeated formulas, it merits consideration.[87]

In New Mexico, for example, the descendants of Spanish colonists, who have long constituted the state's elite, call themselves "Hispanos," thereby emphasizing their European heritage and differentiating themselves from their Mexican-American cousins.[88] After the Franciscan friars established a mission in San Antonio in 1718, the first settlers to arrive were from Spain's Canary Islands. Less exclusionist than their counterparts in New Mexico, the descendants of these settlers have long since melded into the city's Mexican-American community, which claims the heritage of the Canary Islanders as part of its own.[89] That Mexican-American heritage, in San Antonio and throughout the Southwest, draws importantly on the various Native American peoples with whom Spanish settlers came in contact. Choosing to emphasize this facet of their past, some Mexican Americans therefore claim indigenous origins on the North American continent.

Many other Mexican Americans are descended from the generations of campesinos (farm laborers) who have, over the years, left Mexico to avoid political turmoil and economic hardship. Many of these have complicated personal histories of moving back and forth between Mexico and the United States. Still other Mexican Americans are descendants of middle-class exiles who crossed the Rio Grande during the revolutionary upheavals at the beginning of this century.

There has also been much migration within the United States. Some Mexican Americans for whom the mining areas of Southern Arizona or the ranches of New Mexico were home, subsequently moved to California. For others the journey was from South Texas to Chicago. Then, too, there has been much movement between rural and urban areas, as families pursued employment from one setting to the other. Today, most Mexican-origin households—about 91 percent—are in urban areas, and Mexican Americans seem eager to shed their rural past.[90] Indeed, this development seems to have contributed to the diminished stature of the United Farm Workers union among Mexican Americans in the 1980s.

Yet another facet of the Mexican-American mosaic is the large number of Mexican Americans who have lived and raised families in the United States, but who have never become citizens. Some are eligible, but have not sought citizenship for complicated personal reasons. Many others have simply been ineligible because of their illegal status. In any event, Mexicans have had one of the lowest naturalization rates of any group of immigrants in America.[91]

Still another source of diversity, of increasing importance today, is the cleavage between Mexican Americans who have been here long enough to put down roots, and the hundreds, perhaps thousands of Mexican immigrants arriving daily. As these newcomers disrupt established Mexican-American neighborhoods and place growing demands on already strained municipal services, the clash of interests between them and working- and lower-middle-class Mexican Americans becomes increasingly evident.

THE PRIMACY OF POLITICS

Thus, neither history nor contemporary socioeconomic trends alone can resolve the confusion as to whether Mexican Americans are an ethnic or a minority group. Instead, the choice now facing Mexican Americans—indeed, all Americans—is fundamentally a political one. And the resolution of this question must come, if at all, through the workings of our political system.

Yet an appreciation of this fact is strikingly absent from the debates prompted by the growing number of Mexicans, and Latinos generally, in our midst. I have already discussed this oversight on the part of both liberals and conservatives in the ongoing immigration debate. Indeed, it reflects a more general tendency to reduce politics to social and economic determinants that pervades much of our public discourse.[92] This tendency derives in part from the populist strain in our political culture that refuses to see politics as anything other than a straightforward matter of administration. And in a curious way, it has been reinforced in recent years by the affirmative action ethos that seeks to equate political outcomes with the social and economic characteristics of protected groups. Furthermore, postwar social science in America has tended to reduce politics to an epiphenomenon of economic and social forces, and to assume that political actors exert no unique or independent force on society. Clearly, this view represents an inversion of ancient philosophy's perspective that the political regime defines and gives shape to society—not the other way around. In this book I attempt to strike a balance between the political determinism of the ancients and the socioeconomic reductionism of the moderns.

Such a balance is particularly important in any study of ethnic or minority politics. For, as Nathan Glazer and Daniel Patrick Moynihan observe in *Beyond the Melting Pot*, what makes sociological or economic sense for a group does not necessarily make political sense.[93] Contrary to the pervasive notion that politics merely reflects ethnic or racial dynamics, it also shapes them, influencing how groups see themselves and how others see them. With the modern state touching so many different facets of economic and social life, this influence is all the more important.

And yet, as I have been stressing, the role of political institutions has been largely ignored in the ongoing discussions of how the millions of immigrants who have arrived here in recent years will be absorbed into American society. Such discussions invariably begin with obeisance to the enormous changes in our economic institutions since the last comparable wave of immigrants at the turn of the century. With good reason, a great deal of attention is paid to the problems facing unskilled, poorly educated immigrants in today's advanced industrial economy. Yet almost nothing is said about the problems facing such newcomers in a political system that has changed just as drastically as our economy.

When this nation last experienced massive immigration, there existed an array of institutions—churches, community newspapers, labor unions, public schools—that self-consciously socialized newcomers into American life. Prominent among these was the urban political machine. It is easy to romanticize the machines and overlook the fact that they did not always undertake the task of socialization as effectively or as eagerly as sometimes asserted today. Nevertheless, as Morris Janowitz has persuasively argued, political machines were among the institutions that did help bridge the gap between the face-to-face, primary groups (such as families and neighbors) that defined the world of immigrants and the wider society's complex web of impersonal, bureaucratic institutions. Today, these bridging—or mediating—institutions are imperiled or nonexistent, not least because our old assumptions about how to socialize immigrants have been challenged by notions of cultural pluralism.[94]

The Alinsky community organizations mentioned earlier—COPS in San Antonio and UNO in Los Angeles—are contemporary examples of such mediating institutions. My analysis will highlight the obstacles such institutions face in contemporary America. But as the functional equivalent of the now defunct machines, COPS and UNO also suggest how newcomers used to be integrated into our political system. They therefore offer an interesting and important contrast to the way the new American political system encourages Mexican Americans to define themselves as a minority group.

In sum, this book is about the political assimilation of Mexican Americans in late twentieth-century America. Up to now I have avoided this habitually misused word—"assimilation"—which has become part of the liturgy of our civil religion. Academic and popular commentators alike debate whether this or that group will "assimilate," as if this were a smoothly synchronized process whose various dimensions proceeded in lock-step fashion. In particular, such discussions typically assume that the social, economic, and cultural assimilation of Mexican Americans necessarily results in their political assimilation—which is invariably interpreted as traditional ethnic politics.

My research underscores that assimilation is a process whose many dimensions do not unfold in neat, linear fashion.[95] Even when successful along the nonpolitical dimensions, assimilation can be problematic politically. Thus, while it is tempting to argue that for the overwhelming majority of Mexican Americans today, present and future opportunities loom larger than past grievances, social and economic advancement are never so secure or certain that individuals are not tempted to blame their own frustrations, real or apparent, on injustices visited on their forebears. Moreover, progress always extracts a price, and while most Mexican Americans appear to believe the price is worth paying, many do not. Indeed, a substantial number of Mexican Americans clearly perceive upward mobility to be one more step in a long process by which their people have been deprived of a distinctive culture and identity.

On the social-psychological level, there is nothing new or extraordinary going on here. After all, most newcomers have experienced dilemmas similar to, if not exactly the same as, those Mexican Americans are now negotiating. What is new and extraordinary are the incentives offered by contemporary political institutions to transform such personally painful experiences into minority group grievances.

Indeed, one means Mexican Americans now have of advancing themselves—of pursuing the American dream—is to take advantage of the racially designated benefits afforded them. Quite apart from the burdens of history or individual discontents, minority claim-making is an obvious and accepted way to get ahead. Thus, it is often the most socially, economically, and culturally assimilated Mexican Americans who espouse the fiercest opposition to "assimilation." And in this mode, assimilation results in minority, not ethnic politics. To reformulate what I asserted at the beginning of this chapter, the critical question is not *whether* Mexicans will assimilate, but *how*, and on what terms? Indeed, we must recognize that defining themselves as a minority group may be the way this new wave of immigrants assimilates into the new American political system.

This book grows out of almost twenty months of field work in the Southwest, primarily but not exclusively in San Antonio and Los Angeles. The bulk of my time in these two cities was during 1983 and 1984, and I have subsequently maintained contacts and made further visits. I have inter-

viewed scores of politicians, activists, community leaders, and local political observers. Although I focus here on Mexican Americans, I have
also talked with many Anglos and blacks willing to share their perceptions
of Mexican-American politics. My interviews have been conducted
anonymously to ensure maximum cooperation in a realm that involves
not only individual and group interests, but also individual and group
identities.

In addition to interviewing, I have spent much of my time as an observer, and occasional participant-observer, of Mexican-American politics in action. I have spent many hours in community meetings; political
rallies; campaign headquarters and outposts; parish meeting halls;
lawyers' and politicians' offices; bars, restaurants, and after-hours hang-
outs; city council meetings; Community Development Block Grant hearings; neighborhood storefronts; voter registration drives; political
conventions, including the 1984 Democratic National Convention;
county courthouses; cluttered kitchens; a noisy childcare center; backyard barbecues; a judge's private chambers; a printer's shop; and a margarita-tasting contest.

My analysis of Mexican-American politics proceeds as follows: The
second chapter offers an overview of San Antonio's social, economic, and
political context and how Mexican Americans are situated in it. The third
chapter presents a similar overview for Los Angeles. The fourth exam-
ines political outcomes for Mexican Americans—voter registration,
turnout, appointments, public employment, elected officials, and leaders—in these two cities, and in Texas and California generally. That constitutes Part One.

In Part Two (chapters 5 through 8), I examine four styles of Mexican-
American politics: two that have grown increasingly uncommon—
"friends-and-neighbors" and "organization" politics—and two that are
more consonant with contemporary trends—"elite-network" and
"protest" politics. I relate the dynamics of each style to the specific social, economic, and political context for Mexican Americans in these two
very different locales and, more important, to my overriding concern with
the choice between immigrant ethnic and racial minority politics facing
Mexican Americans. Central to this part of my argument is a thoroughgoing analysis, in chapters 5 and 6, of Alinsky community organizing efforts in San Antonio and Los Angeles.

In Part Three, I step back and examine the broader developments in
our nation's political institutions that impinge on that choice. To establish a baseline against which to gauge these developments, chapter 9 ex-
amines survey data on Mexican-American views on various issues. This

analysis identifies a gap between Mexican-American leaders and their rank and file. More than the expected cleavage between elites and nonelites, this gap reflects the institutional changes that are the focus of this book. Indeed, increased reliance on survey data is one of those changes, and as I explore at the end of chapter 9, this trend ill suits a group, such as Mexican Americans, that is not fully integrated into American society.

Chapter 10 places the new American political system in a broader sociological and cultural context and shows how, in the absence of mediating institutions which used to advance the political integration of disadvantaged groups, that system now poses obstacles to Mexican Americans. I then look at efforts to overcome these barriers and argue that they foster a short-sighted and divisive strain of racial minority politics. In chapter 11, I conclude by responding to various criticisms of my perspective. In that vein, I return to the key issue of immigration and the increasingly audible concerns about our capacities as a nation today to absorb as many immigrants as the record numbers who arrived here during the first decades of this century.

❦2❧

San Antonio

Getting Ahead and Getting Even

I n recent years the most prominent national symbol of Mexican-
American political achievement has been Henry Cisneros, the mayor
of San Antonio from 1981 to 1989. The first Mexican American to take that
office since 1842,[1] and the first Mexican-American mayor of any major U.S.
city, Cisneros is an appealing young politician who had been skillfully courting the national media even before his 1983 appointment to the Kissinger
Commission on Central America, and his 1984 interview as a possible running mate for presidential candidate Walter Mondale. In 1989 marital
problems led to Cisneros's decision to withdraw from public life and not
seek reelection. Yet throughout that ordeal his popularity with Texans—
Anglos and Mexicans alike—remained high. Today, Cisneros continues to
be the nation's pre-eminent Mexican-American—indeed, Hispanic—political figure, as evidenced by his having been President Clinton's first Hispanic appointee (as Secretary of Housing and Urban Development).

Cisneros's image has been that of a young, Harvard-educated technocrat leading a growing Sunbelt city (the nation's tenth largest, local boost-
ers never tire of saying) into the twenty-first century. Strikingly competent
and articulate, he earned a master's degree at Harvard's Kennedy School
of Government, then subsequently received a doctorate in urban administration from George Washington University.

Of much greater interest to many Texans, however, is Cisneros's bachelor's degree from Texas A&M, earned in 1968 when few Mexicans got to call themselves "Aggies." As for being a spokesman for Hispanics, it is interesting to note that when first elected to the San Antonio City Council in 1975, Cisneros was the candidate of the Anglo establishment and received a higher proportion of Anglo than Mexican votes cast.[2] As for Cisneros's being a Democrat, it is worth quoting Elliot Richardson, for whom he worked as a White House Fellow in the Nixon administration:

> I hoped Henry would become a Republican when he worked for me. I thought he might have become one. Frankly, I had not become conscious he wasn't a Republican until I noticed his party identification in connection with the Kissinger Commission.[3]

Cisneros continues to be identified with his hometown almost as vividly as the Alamo. Yet, as I will presently demonstrate, he is really more *in* than *of* San Antonio politics.

San Antonio may be the nation's tenth largest municipality, but with a metropolitan population of 1.3 million, according to the 1990 census, it ranks thirtieth among metropolitan areas.[4] To be sure, it was long the leading city of Texas. As late as 1930, it boasted the state's tallest building and was, in fact, still the largest city in Texas.[5] But by 1934, when the young Lyndon Johnson married Claudia Taylor at St. Mark's Episcopal Church on Travis Park, San Antonio was already being eclipsed by Houston and Dallas.[6] And thence began a period of less than impressive economic growth from which the city is still struggling to emerge.

As a result, San Antonio has long suffered from a second-city—more precisely, a third-city—complex. Indeed, Henry Cisneros's special genius as mayor was to bridge the deep chasm between Anglos and Mexicans in San Antonio by personifying the collective aspirations of his hometown. So bound up with those aspirations did Cisneros become that, for more than a year, the local media sat on the story about his extramarital affair until in the fall of 1988 it was finally broken and led to his withdrawal from politics.

A BIG SMALL TOWN

In the words of one union leader, San Antonio is "a big small town." It is very much a city of neighborhoods with which residents identify intensely. This is particularly true for Mexican Americans, for whom the parish tends to be the focal point of community life. A Mexican American on the city council, asked about her background, describes herself as a product of Christ the King parish, where she went to church and school and where her parents still live. A young Mexican-American barber struggling to build his business at a suburban shopping center, asked where he grew up, immediately mentions St. Timothy's parish. It is similarly revealing that Cisneros, easily the city's most cosmopolitan Mexican-American politician, still lives in the same neighborhood of modest bungalows in Sacred Heart parish where he grew up. Indeed, Cisneros has raised his family in the same house where his immigrant grandfather, having arrived in San Antonio in 1926, raised his family.[7] And for Mexicans and Anglos alike, it is striking that, on Sunday mornings in San Antonio, church services are the primary focus of seemingly everyone's attention.

This small-town ethos was impressed upon me when a young Mexican-American woman recently elected to public office refused to be interviewed over lunch. It turned out she was willing to talk to me, but for fear of starting rumors, she would meet only if accompanied by a female friend. San Antonio is the kind of community where a sense of continuity and stability keep people mindful of their place in the social order. Unlike Houston—or Los Angeles, certainly—San Antonio has not experienced the kind of explosive growth that overwhelms established mores and institutions.

As my lunch-date anecdote suggests, an important bulwark of San Antonio's small-town traditionalism is the Mexican-American community there. Opinion surveys repeatedly demonstrate Mexican Americans to be more committed to traditional values than the general population.[8] This seems particularly true in San Antonio, where the Mexican-American population is relatively stable and rooted. To be sure, the city has frequently experienced substantial immigration from Mexico. Yet it is striking that in 1980* only 11.5 percent of Hispanics in metropolitan San Antonio were foreign-born, compared to 28.4 percent in Houston and 24.6 percent in Dallas–Fort Worth—and 45.6 percent in Los Angeles.[9] In other words, a relatively small segment of the Mexican-American community in San Antonio has been subject to the destabilizing influences inevitably resulting from transnational migration.

Nevertheless, in both absolute and relative terms, the number of Mexicans in San Antonio has over the decades steadily increased. From 1970 to 1990, for example, the Hispanic population grew 92 percent.[10] But such growth has been due more to natural increase and migration from the small towns and ranches of South Texas than to immigration from across the border. Indeed, in 1980 more than four-fifths of San Antonio

---

* Here and elsewhere in this book the latest data will be cited. When, as in this instance, 1980 census data are used, it is because 1990 data for the relevant variables are not yet available.

Hispanics were born in Texas.[11] This influx further reinforces traditional values in San Antonio. In the same vein, among Hispanic immigrants there, regardless of where they come from, the evidence indicates relatively high numbers of family groups, as opposed to single adult migrants.[12] Such factors undoubtedly help explain why San Antonio has had, at least until quite recently, few problems with youth gangs and one of the lowest crime rates among large U.S. cities.[13]

AN ECONOMIC BACKWATER

Underlying San Antonio's small-town traditionalism is a long history of sluggish economic growth. To be sure, from 1950 to 1990 the metropolitan area grew almost 150 percent. But by Sunbelt standards, such an increase is below average.[14] With evident but nevertheless suggestive exaggeration, one scholar describes San Antonio as a "pre-industrial city."[15]

Even when it was the largest city in Texas, San Antonio lacked a dynamic economy. As Robert West, a prominent local entrepreneur and oilman, puts it:

> Historically, San Antonio has always been unprogressive from the economic standpoint. The city was not endowed with basic resources for economic growth. Dallas and Houston were. Houston had its seaport, its oil, its gas; Dallas, its farmers and crossroads commerce and East Texas oil. For San Antonio to grow economically would have required aggressive farsightedness, and the local leaders discouraged that.[16]

Those local leaders were notoriously cautious about promoting economic growth that might undermine their status or power. For example, in the 1930s, Henry Ford contemplated building an auto assembly plant in San Antonio, but was discouraged by a business establishment fearful that labor unions would put an end to cheap Mexican labor.[17] Of more recent vintage is the Frito episode: the corn chip was first developed in San Antonio in the early 1950s, but when expansion capital could not be found locally, Frito-Lay relocated to Dallas.

A developer who moved to San Antonio from Dallas in 1963 describes the situation at that time: "In those days, San Antonio was a little kingdom run by a small group of people who controlled all commerce and development."[18] By a decade later, a rift had opened between this stodgy old guard and a younger, more aggressive generation of entrepreneurs, with whom Cisneros was allied when he rode into the mayor's office in 1981. But the city's past has continued to weigh heavily on its future prospects, as highlighted in a 1980 issue of *Texas Business* magazine, the cover of which posed the question: "Is San Antonio finally waking up?"[19]

Today, San Antonio's business environment is much more open and diverse, but the fact that not one Fortune 500 firm makes its home there underscores the city's continuing difficulties.[20] Hindered as ever by remoteness from major national markets, it still lacks a strong industrial base and remains heavily dependent on military expenditures, as it has from its origins as a frontier outpost. Indeed, San Antonio's five major military installations constitute one of the nation's largest military complexes outside Washington, D.C.[21] About 10 percent of all air force military personnel serving in the continental United States are currently based in San Antonio.[22] With more than 18,000 nonmilitary employees, Kelly Air Force Base employs more civilians than any other U.S. air force base.[23] It is hardly surprising, therefore, that San Antonio's largest employer is an insurance company serving active and retired military officers.[24]

The Bureau of Labor Statistics reports that in 1987 a scant 9.1 percent of metropolitan San Antonio's civilian, nonagricultural labor force was employed in manufacturing—compared, for example, to 18.3 percent in Dallas–Fort Worth. Meanwhile, government accounted for 19.2 percent of San Antonio's nonagricultural employment—compared to 10.5 percent in Dallas–Fort Worth—and was the city's third largest sector after services and trade, both of which are driven by San Antonio's heavy reliance on tourism.[25]

As a result, per capita personal income in San Antonio in 1990 was $15,517, well below the national figure of $18,696.[26] Moreover, the Department of Commerce projects that by the year 2000 per capita income in San Antonio will have slipped further behind the national average.[27] But even this may prove too optimistic. For while this projection takes into account the vulnerability of the region's low-wage industrial base to competition from abroad, it does not consider the impact of impending post-Cold War military cutbacks.

AT THE BOTTOM OF THE HEAP

In such an economic environment, prospects for Mexican Americans have never been very good. During the Depression San Antonio was one of the few cities in the United States that failed to provide general relief to its indigent population.[28] Until well after World War II, Mexican Americans lived in squalor on the city's West Side, where it was not unusual for seventy-five people to be crowded into a single "corral," or series of huts built around a courtyard with a well and outdoor privy. In the late 1940s San Antonio had the nation's highest tuberculosis rate among cities over 100,000. As a result, the Mexican death rate was almost four times that of Anglos, and nearly three times that of blacks.[29] In the 1960s, the substandard housing and muddy, unpaved streets of West Side barrios so resembled Latin American shanty towns that the area was used as a training site for Peace Corps recruits.[30]

This is not to say that Mexican Americans have experienced no gains whatsoever. There is evidence that even during the latter decades of the nineteenth century, Mexicans experienced some upward occupational mobility—not as much as European immigrants, but more than blacks. More recently, during the 1970s there has been modest intragenerational as well as intergenerational mobility among Mexicans, but again not as much as among Anglos.[31]

Of late, Mexican Americans in San Antonio have made particular gains in education. In 1960 the median number of school years completed by Mexicans age 25 and over was 5.7, compared to 10.0 for all San Antonio residents. In other words, Mexican educational attainment was 57 percent that of the total population.[32] By 1970, the median figure for Mexicans was 7.4 years, compared to 11.5 for all residents, placing Mexicans at 64 percent of the overall level. By 1980, Mexicans had reached 81 percent: 10.0 years compared to 12.4 years.[33] But though greatly narrowed, the remaining gap means that in 1980 only 41.3 percent of Mexicans over 25 had graduated from high school, compared to 62.7 percent of the total population. And only 5.1 percent of Mexicans over 25 had completed four or more years of college, compared to 17.2 percent of all San Antonians.[34]

Further, there is evidence that occupational returns on equivalent amounts of education have been less for Mexicans than for Anglos in San Antonio. It is not clear, however, whether this is due to the inferior quality of schooling received by Mexicans, or to discrimination by employers.[35]

Thus, San Antonio's wealth continues to be spread unevenly across its population. With a weak manufacturing sector, growth has tended to result in low-skill jobs in services and tourism or high-skill jobs in, for example, medicine, for which positions Mexicans are generally not well prepared. This imbalance is revealed in the geography of the metropolitan area, with growth having concentrated around the pleasant hills on the predominantly Anglo North Side.

In any event, Mexican incomes lag well behind those of Anglos. In 1990 the per capita income for "whites"* in Bexar County was $13,310; for Hispanics $7,309. And while 16.6 percent of whites in 1990 were living below the poverty line, 29.2 percent of Hispanics were.[36] Because, as pointed out earlier, relatively few Mexicans in San Antonio are foreign-born, such disparities cannot be attributed to the disadvantages experienced by immigrants from Mexico. Nor can this income gap be discounted in proportion to the subjective benefits immigrants from Mexico typically experience in the United States.

Robert West, the oilman quoted earlier, observes of San Antonio's old elite: "It was to their advantage to put the Mexican American down and keep him there, and they did."[37] And while one might more evenhandedly conclude that the region's blessing and its curse has been the cheap Mexican labor on which it has grown dependent, Mexican Americans are certainly not inclined to put it so dispassionately.

Indeed, the pervasive sentiment among Mexican Americans in San Antonio is that their poverty is due not to their own failings, but to Anglo machinations. To be sure, there have always been prominent Latino families who mingled and intermarried with the Anglo elite.[38] The offspring of one such union was Bryan Callaghan II, mayor and San Antonio's first important machine politician. With fluent Spanish and a mother, Concepción Ramón, descended from the region's original settlers, Callaghan developed a loyal following among Mexican Americans at the turn of the century.[39]

For that matter, there has long been a sizable, stable Mexican-American middle class. Seeded in part by emigrés from the Mexican Revolution earlier this century, this highly visible stratum has, as I will discuss in a later chapter, provided the community with stable institutions and effective leadership.[40]

But if Mexican Americans have never quite been leveled to an impoverished mass, they have, just as the oilman says, a strong sense of having been kept in their place. Drawing on their own experiences or those of their parents and grandparents, they willingly retell the familiar stories of going to separate and inferior schools, worshiping at the back of churches, being excluded from Anglo neighborhoods by restrictive covenants, or seeing their World War II veterans refused burial in public cemeteries.[41] On the other hand, such discriminatory practices, however offensive and humiliating, were typically enforced informally

---

* I use quotation marks here to draw the reader's attention to the fact that white and Hispanic—contrary to the way they are often used—are not mutually exclusive categories. Indeed, as I noted in chapter 1, most Hispanics describe themselves as racially white.

and not enshrined in law (as they were for blacks in Texas). As a result, these barriers to Mexican advancement were frequently porous and negotiable.

PRIDE AND RESENTMENT

In any event, in recent years such blatant barriers have virtually disappeared. Yet attitudes, not to mention social and economic structures, are slow to change, and interaction between Mexicans and Anglos remains delimited. Since 1960, for example, there has been a steady if modest decrease in the residential concentration of Hispanics relative to Anglos in San Antonio. Nevertheless, in 1980 fully 57 percent of Hispanics would have had to move for the group to be evenly distributed across the city's census tracts (see Table 2.1). In fifty-nine central cities across the nation the average such figure for Hispanics in 1980 was 45 percent.[42]

By a different measure of residential concentration—the probability that Hispanics live in a census tract with Anglos—there has been virtually no change in San Antonio since 1970. In 1980 this probability was .28, compared to an average in sixty metropolitan areas of .64. Such indices rank San Antonio among the metropolitan areas in the Southwest where Hispanics are the most residentially concentrated—surpassed only, on some measures, by the border town of El Paso.[43]

A similar picture emerges with regard to the concentration of Hispanics in San Antonio's public schools. During the 1986–1987 school year

TABLE 2.1
Residential Concentration of Hispanics Relative to Anglos as Measured
by Dissimilarity Index (D-Index)[*]

	1960	1970	1980
Los Angeles (central city)	.574[a]	.510[b]	.611[c]
San Antonio (central city)	.636[a]	.603[b]	.571[c]

Note: [*] Defined as the percentage of Hispanics who would have to move in order for the group to be evenly distributed across census tracts.
Sources: [a] Leo Grebler et al., *The Mexican-American People* (New York: The Free Press, 1970), 275. [b] M. M. Lopez, "Patterns of Interethnic Residential Segregation in the Urban Southwest: 1960 and 1970," *Social Science Quarterly* 62 (1981): 53. [c] Douglas Massey and Nancy Denton, "Suburbanization and Segregation in U.S. Metropolitan Areas," *American Journal of Sociology* 94 (1988): 602–604.

in the San Antonio Independent School District, the metropolitan area's largest, no Hispanic students were in majority Anglo schools and 75 percent were in 90–100 percent non-Anglo schools. Only 7 percent of the students in the school of the typical Hispanic student were Anglos. As research by Gary Orfield demonstrates, such measures place San Antonio among the top three large school districts in the nation for concentration of Hispanic students.[44]

Perhaps the most revealing social indicator is intermarriage. In 1973 (the latest year for which data are available), only 16 percent of all Mexicans who married in Bexar County, for which San Antonio is the county seat, chose partners outside their group. This number was just two percentage points higher than a decade earlier. Such figures are comparable to exogamy rates among Italians and Poles in Buffalo during the 1930s.[45] They might, therefore, be interpreted positively as a sign that Mexican Americans will assimilate into the American mainstream much as European immigrants have done. Or, these data might be regarded as a sign of group cohesion. But in the context of South Texas, such figures underscore the persistent sense Mexicans there have of isolation and subordination.[46]

Yet at the same time, Mexicans in San Antonio have a sense of being on their own turf. As one Mexican-American courthouse politician declared, "I'm a sixth-generation Texan, and I've never felt I'm an outsider." From the city's Main Plaza, modeled after the *jardínes* (open spaces, literally "gardens") around which Mexican towns are built; to the Alamo, whose establishment as a Franciscan mission in 1718 marks the founding of San Antonio; to the string of other missions that stretches along the San Antonio River; the reminders are many that this region was once part of Mexico. The last of these riverside missions, Espada, has been restored by the National Park Service. Located on the grassy banks of the muddy stream just beyond the suburban sprawl at the metropolitan area's southern edge, Espada offers a glimpse of the quiet Mexican village that San Antonio once was.

Quite aside from such historical cues, Mexican Americans feel at home in San Antonio on account of their numbers. As of 1990, they constituted about 56 percent of the city's population and 48 percent of the metropolitan area's.[47] Such ties are reinforced by San Antonio's status as the leading city of South Texas and the Rio Grande Valley, where the concentration of Mexicans is even heavier and from whence so many Mexicans have migrated north to San Antonio. Moreover, these bonds are sustained by the substantial penetration of San Antonio print and broadcast media throughout the region.[48]

But it has not always been thus. Texas historian and San Antonio resident T. R. Fehrenbach notes that in 1876 San Antonio's assessor reported 17,314 inhabitants: 5,630 "Germans and Alsatians," 5,475 "Americans," and 3,750 "Mexicans."[49] By 1930, after substantial immigration, the Mexican-stock population of San Antonio was still only one-third.[50] Emphasizing that Mexico's inability to populate its northern frontier caused it to recruit Anglo settlers from the United States into Texas, Fehrenbach maintains that the roots of Latino culture in the region are actually rather shallow.[51] Arguing against this interpretation, writers such as Carey McWilliams see the influence of Mexican culture in Texas as pervasive, not the least example being a way of life built up around open-range cattle ranching and made possible by a climate and terrain that Texas shares with vast stretches of Northern Mexico.[52] Indeed, today these enduring features of the physical environment combine with demographics to make Mexicans feel very much at home in the region.

Yet as suggested in chapter 1, the sense of turf among Mexican Americans in a place like San Antonio is double-edged. A bucolic mission village on the outskirts of town may be a pleasant reminder of the region's Hispanic heritage, but the Alamo in the center of the city stands as a secular pantheon of Texas heroes: Anglos with names like Crockett, Bowie, and Travis, whose sacrifices paved the way for Mexico's ultimate defeat a few days later at San Jacinto and, consequently, the founding of the Texas Republic.

Thus, San Antonio is not just the cradle of Mexican history and culture in Texas; it is also the crucible in which was forged the fierce Texas pride that persists to this day as something just shy of nationalism. But Mexican Americans, most of them not far removed from the tradition-oriented, honor-based culture of their homeland, are also proud.[53] And for them the history of Texas is less glorious. As one widely respected Mexican-American community leader asserts, the Alamo was a nagging insult to him when he was growing up, a constant reminder that Anglos were seen as heroes and that "my people were not worthy"—even though, as I noted in chapter 1, Texas Mexicans died defending the Alamo against Santa Anna's troops.

Mexican Americans, then, regard this revered landmark as a symbol of their status as a conquered people—"a people living under the shadow of the Alamo," as historian David Montejano puts it.[54] For a period in the 1960s and early 1970s, such sentiments led to angry separatist rhetoric. During that period San Antonio was a center of Chicano activism, focused largely around the Raza Unida Party. But by the late 1980s, even the most extreme elements among Mexican Americans had abandoned such efforts.

Yet Mexican-American resentments continue to be an important force in San Antonio politics. And though usually submerged, they occasionally break through the surface. For example, each April the whole town gets involved with the Fiesta de San Jacinto, a week of parades, beauty pageants, and parties commemorating the victory of Texans over Santa Anna. A leading sponsor is the San Antonio Cavaliers, an elite group of prominent Anglos, whose public appearances in resplendent uniforms complete with swords keep alive the memory of the fallen heroes of the Alamo. Each year the group crowns one of their number as "King Antonio" to lead the citywide festivities. But in the spring of 1983, COPS, the powerful Mexican-American community organization, had apparently had enough. When interviewed on the NBC "Today" program, the organization's president denounced the Cavaliers as a "racist organization" reminiscent of the days when San Antonio was "a colonial society." This is hardly the kind of national exposure sought by a city heavily dependent on tourism and eager to attract outside investment. But it is precisely the kind of rhetoric that political entrepreneurs can use to tap the lingering bitterness of many Mexican Americans.

The politics of resentment is sometimes practiced by even the most cautious Mexican-American politicians. Throughout his career Cisneros has been a marvel of moderation, never even flirting with Chicano activism. But as a young city councillor in 1976, he could be heard championing the West Side in the harsh rhetoric of confrontation. At a particularly tense council session, an Anglo businessman tried to justify price increases by the city-owned utility. Councillor Cisneros shot back, "Mr. Dement, it's people like you who had their boot on the neck of my people for generations."[55]

Equally revealing is the observation, years later, of the target of this outburst: "Nowadays, Henry and I laugh about that night, but I'll tell you something; at that moment, Henry Cisneros was as close to leading a Raza Unida–type revolt as I ever saw. My wife was in the audience and she was scared to death. I don't mind telling you I was scared myself."[56]

Such exchanges point to the defining characteristic of San Antonio's social and political landscape. Though the city has seen the arrival of a surprising variety of other groups—French, Germans, Italians, Greeks, Poles, and of course the Scotch-Irish Presbyterians who figured prominently among the original settlers, and remain an important pillar of the city's elite—these various groups have melded into an amorphous "Anglo" category that stands in contradistinction to "the Mexicans." The primacy of this Anglo-Mexican cleavage is so overwhelming that San Antonio's black community, about 7 percent of the city's population, is easily overlooked. Indeed, in light of all the attention afforded Mexicans, it is interesting to note that blacks have experienced much greater social isolation than Mexicans in San Antonio. And although blacks there are more educated than Mexicans (which is true of the two groups generally), they have lower per capita income and a higher poverty rate.[57]

"PANZITA POLITICS"

San Antonio's modest growth and small-town traditionalism have therefore contributed to the creation of a cohesive Mexican-American community with a strong identity. Central to that self-image is the notion that Mexican Americans have been kept down by an equally close-knit, and certainly more powerful, Anglo elite—a view that has had important and largely beneficial implications for the eventual political advancement of Mexican Americans. As one observer describes the situation in San Antonio:

> The once totally segregated Hispanic community is slowly dispersing, moving into the northwestern section of the city and into suburban areas. The leadership base and networks created for survival during the era of segregation, however, have not been dissipated. These networks make San Antonio one of the best organized and most effective Hispanic communities in the Southwest.[58]

But recent political gains were preceded by decades of efforts to ensure that "Meskins," as they were contemptuously called, wielded little power—as if their poverty, migratory labor patterns, and low naturalization rates were not already sufficient to achieve the same result. The devices used included poll taxes, burdensome candidate filing fees, and restrictive voter registration procedures—and, when necessary, intimidation and violence.[59]

Though rendered powerless by design as well as by circumstance, Mexican Americans were not totally excluded from the political process. For at various times local as well as national Democratic candidates found it advantageous to mobilize the Mexican vote. On such occasions various "West Side *jefes* [chiefs, bosses]" were provided with the necessary funds, or "walking around money," to get their families, friends, neighbors, and subordinates to the polls. Poll taxes were paid en masse. Political signs and literature were distributed. Block walkers were paid. Campaign rallies were organized. On their way into the voting booths, the illiterate were provided with strings tied with knots, indicating where their x's should be put on the ballot. Poll watchers kept a careful eye on things to make sure the Mexicans voted as they were told. Election supervisors would routinely violate the law and enter voting booths, which in any event were not always provided.[60] And as anyone familiar with Lyndon Johnson's 1948 election to the U.S. Senate is aware, it was not at all unusual for precinct ballot boxes to disappear—only to reappear miraculously at the appropriate time with just enough votes to decide the outcome.

For their involvement in these efforts, Mexicans were meagerly rewarded. Though the *jefes'* expenses were generally adequately covered, they rarely got to run for office themselves. As for the mass of Mexican-American voters, they seldom got more than the beer and tamales provided at rallies. Indeed, the phrase "beer and tamales" has entered the Texas political lexicon as a sardonic allusion to the days when the Mexican vote could be had cheaply. A few loyal supporters may have gotten patronage jobs with the city or county. Others may have gotten some groceries to get them through a particularly lean spell. Not surprisingly, Mexican-American politicians today refer to this as "*panzita* [stomach] politics."

Such political relationships partook of the hierarchical social relations that characterized—and in some ways still characterize—the vast expanse of South Texas, where, as we have seen, many Mexicans in San Antonio have their roots.[61] Robert Caro, in his biography of Lyndon Johnson, describes how these relations preserved the "near-feudalistic" Mexican custom of "dependence on a local leader, the *patrón* or *jefe*." On the great ranches of South Texas such as the King Ranch, "*el patrón* was often the ranch owner," writes Caro. Not only was he an employer, the *patrón* was also a "lord protector" whose word was regarded as law.[62] In this context, it is not surprising that Mexicans voted as they were told.

In rural Texas counties, Mexican-American registration and turnout rates have often been higher than in San Antonio itself.[63] Yet such participation is obviously not to be confused with real power or political sophistication. Indeed, these practices have probably helped to perpetuate habits of passivity or indifference toward politics among many Mexican Americans. Nonetheless, Mexican Americans were thereby involved, however marginally, in the political process. As one San Antonio politician put it: "While blacks were not allowed to vote, Mexican Americans *were voted.*" Indeed, unlike blacks, Mexicans in Texas were not subjected to the infamous regime of "white primaries" that was struck down by the

Supreme Court in 1944.[64] As Clifton McCleskey, perhaps the leading student of Texas politics, observes:

> Unlike Negroes, they [Mexican Americans] were never officially barred from the Democratic primaries, though local rules and informal discouragement sometimes stood in their way. . . . Thus in some respects Mexican Americans have traditionally had a place in Texas politics long denied to blacks.[65]

Consequently, many Mexican-American politicos today acknowledge that by being "voted," their people learned some rudimentary yet valuable political lessons.

POSTWAR REFORM

San Antonio politics has long been marked by patronage and corruption. This was true in the last century, and it was certainly true during the period from 1914 to 1951, when the city had commission government. Under this regime, individual commissioners were elected to head the various municipal departments. With hiring prerogatives unhindered by civil service regulations, these commissioners had enormous scope to build up their own political organizations.[66]

Years of disgruntlement and efforts to change this system finally came to fruition after World War II. Complaints were heard not so much from Mexican Americans as from the Anglo business establishment. By 1951 reformers had pushed through a new city charter that replaced commission government with a nonpartisan council-manager system. Grouped under the banner of the Good Government League (the GGL), these business-oriented reformers completely dominated San Antonio politics for an entire generation. From 1955 to 1975, seventy-seven out of eighty races for city council were won by the GGL, which recruited, endorsed, and financed candidates for these at-large seats.[67]

The GGL's success at the polls was matched by its efforts to clean up city hall, efforts that led to a marked reduction in patronage and corruption. Sustained by the League's invincible political organization, the weak mayor-strong city manager regime gave San Antonio nearly two decades of reasonably efficient, professional municipal government. As described by historian Fehrenbach, the GGL was "the longest-lasting 'reform' movement in American urban history."[68]

In the years since its demise, however, the GGL has suffered much criticism, especially from Mexican Americans. Even for many Anglos, these initials have come to symbolize the bad old days when much in San Antonio smacked of a Third World country, with Mexicans the passive and dependent substratum. In the words of one former city manager: "In those days twenty families ran San Antonio." The count may not be exact, but the Anglo elite was tiny. They attended the same church, the First Presbyterian or Saint Mark's Episcopal; they socialized at the San Antonio Country Club; and, most important, economic, social, and political power came together in their hands. Key businessmen protected their interests directly by chairing appointive public boards dealing with vital matters like water, zoning, and redevelopment.[69] And for many years this confluence of powers was embodied in one man, Walter McAllister: businessman, founder of San Antonio's oldest and largest savings and loan, longtime civic leader, moving force behind the GGL, and mayor from 1961 to 1971.[70]

McAllister's power reached beyond city hall, as evidenced by the colorful slice of local political lore known as the "black hand campaign." Reportedly directed from the basement of McAllister's bank, that 1966 effort got its name from a television commercial that depicted the venerable Bexar County courthouse being engulfed by a sinister black hand. With such tactics the GGL successfully prevented a coalition of Anglo and Mexican liberals from gaining a three-man majority on the county commissioners court—and, not coincidentally, kept control of the local antipoverty program in safe hands.

Under the GGL regime, the political returns to Mexican Americans continued to be meager. Some health and sanitation problems were addressed, but for the most part municipal services and infrastructure in Mexican neighborhoods were neglected.[71] Relatively few of the appointees to key boards and commissions were Mexican Americans. Still, the GGL was not totally deaf to the group's political aspirations. Its virtually unbeatable slate for the eight at-large city council seats usually included a Mexican American or two, although these were typically small businessmen or minor professionals who did not live in the West Side barrio. Regardless of their intentions or abilities, such individuals inevitably owed more to their Anglo sponsors than to their Mexican constituents.

But eventually things began to change. In the late 1960s, the GGL began showing signs of weakness, especially among Mexican Americans. In West Side precincts where Mayor McAllister had once registered outright majorities, he was losing four to one. In 1967 a Mexican-American attorney won a city council seat without the GGL endorsement.[72] Then in 1973, for the first time in its history, the GGL's mayoral candidate lost. By 1974, in the words of two local journalists, "the city was in chaos. The Good Government League . . . was in shambles."[73]

In 1975, when Henry Cisneros first ran for political office, he was endorsed by the GGL for a city council seat. He was one of only three GGL candidates to be elected, and the only Mexican American backed by the League who won. In the at-large election he received 56 percent of the Anglo votes but only 41 percent of the Mexican-American votes.[74] Such was the level of sentiment against the GGL among Mexican Americans.

The causes of the GGL's demise were several. Having dominated San Antonio politics for a generation, its leaders got older, lost their steam, and even began to die out. A new generation of challengers emerged, not only from the increasingly assertive Mexican-American community, but also from a disgruntled group of businessmen and developers no longer willing to follow the lead of the status-quo-oriented downtown business establishment. In fact, it was the candidate of these combined forces who successfully challenged the GGL's candidate for mayor in 1973.

OUTSIDE SOURCES OF CHANGE

One factor contributing to the GGL's problems were Anglo newcomers, with no loyalties to the old regime, moving into growing suburban fringe areas that were then annexed by the city. Yet there were more fundamental outside forces impinging on San Antonio that contributed to these political developments, especially among Mexican Americans.

The most amorphous but nevertheless critical factor was the social and political ferment of the 1960s, whose effects were important even in a place as traditional and remote from cosmopolitan influences as San Antonio. For example, farmworker organizing drives in South Texas, culminating in late summer 1966 in a dramatic "March on Austin" by striking workers from the Rio Grande Valley, stimulated political interest and involvement among many young Mexican Americans.[75] And, of course, looming in the background of such events was the energizing effect of the black civil rights movement. Indeed, as the sixties unfolded, "Negroes" became "blacks," and "Mexican Americans" became "Chicanos."

More concretely, local observers credit federal antipoverty programs like Model Cities with helping to foster a more assertive Mexican-American electorate in San Antonio.[76] Around the same time, the Ford Foundation began funding Mexican-American groups pushing for social and political change in the Southwest. In 1968 the Mexican American Legal Defense and Educational Fund (MALDEF), modeled directly on the NAACP Legal Defense and Educational Fund, was set up in San Antonio by the foundation.[77] By 1972, MALDEF had successfully challenged the multi-member state-representative district for Bexar County and thereby gained single-member districts, which facilitated the election of several new Mexican-American legislators.[78]

In this period the Ford Foundation also funded various Chicano activists in and around San Antonio, including a group that attained national notoriety with the political takeover of Crystal City, a rural town about an hour's drive southwest of San Antonio. Such activities soon aroused the ire of local congressman Henry B. González, who delivered repeated tirades against Chicano activists and their foundation sponsor on the floor of Congress.[79] Ford soon began supporting less controversial projects. For example, in 1974 it was instrumental in establishing the San Antonio-based Southwest Voter Registration Education Project (SVREP), which has played a critical role in mobilizing Mexican-American voters in San Antonio. Indeed, SVREP has become the principal voter registration operation for Mexican Americans throughout the Southwest and the nation.

By the early 1970s, other outsiders began influencing events in San Antonio. The Campaign for Human Development of the National Conference of Catholic Bishops funded COPS, the Alinsky community organization mentioned in chapter 1 that has become a major force in San Antonio politics.

Finally, a critical external stimulus materialized in July 1976, when the Department of Justice threatened the city of San Antonio with a Voting Rights suit for annexing Anglo suburbs and thereby diluting Mexican-American voting strength. Confronted with a long court battle, the city council opted for the obvious alternative: single-member districting. A charter revision was narrowly approved by the electorate, with overwhelming support from Mexican-American voters.[80]

The new charter provided for a city council composed of ten members, each elected from a district, and presided over by a mayor, elected at-large. In 1977 the first municipal election under this regime resulted in five Mexican-American councillors. Since that time, there have never been fewer than four Mexican Americans on the city council.

"EVERY MAN FOR HIMSELF"

By the mid-1980s the turbulence of two decades had subsided. Chicano activists had long since dropped out of sight, typically involved either in small businesses or Democratic Party politics. Today the COPS organization is still a key actor in San Antonio politics, but has moderated the confrontation tactics that contributed greatly to the turmoil of the earlier period. As for the GGL, it is defunct. Yet no successor has emerged to impose order on San Antonio politics.[81] As I will discuss in chapters 5 and 6, COPS does provide a good measure of organizational discipline among Mexican Americans. But it scarcely dominates local politics the way the GGL did. And the introduction of single-member city-council districts has contributed to the fragmentation and unruliness of a body that the GGL had reduced to passive unanimity.

These developments in nonpartisan municipal politics are mirrored in Democratic Party politics, whose focus today in San Antonio is, as it has been for generations, the Bexar County courthouse. As one former Bexar County judge reminisced: "The Governors of Texas used to govern through the courthouses." Periodically, the courthouse would come under the rule of a powerful boss, capable of gaining the upper hand over the egos and ambitions of the various elected officials working there. In recent years, however, the courthouse has experienced no such cohesive force. Today, it houses several extremely independent political entrepreneurs, who spend much of their time battling one another for the public's attention. As for the Democratic Party, which has managed to maintain control of the courthouse despite steadily increasing inroads by Republicans, one ambitious young elected official described being a Democrat in Bexar County as "a vague idea." A veteran of various state and local campaigns, he went on to observe that "the Party doesn't exist," because there's no one to say to the various politicians, "Look, you assholes, pull this thing together."[82]

Or, as a seasoned journalist said of contemporary politics in San Antonio, "It's every man for himself." This situation is reflected in the Bexar County Democratic Committee being reduced to a battleground among the various officeholders. One young Mexican-American politician described San Antonio politics as a huge game with countless overlapping arenas and concluded that he or any other aspiring politico must be "a real gamesman," always on his toes and ready to seize opportunities as they arise. This view of the local political landscape is shared by most others. As one courthouse insider observed, "Politics in Bexar County is like a circus. Everybody is always doing something."

Of course, the decentralized nature of American politics is such that similar comments could be made about many other cities. Yet San Antonio politics is even more chaotic than most—in sharp contrast, as I will demonstrate in the next chapter, with the situation in Los Angeles. This follows from the fact that Texas politics has long been quite rambunctious. In the past, intense schisms developed between conservative and liberal factions within the dominant Democratic Party. More recently, the emergence of the Republican Party has altered these dynamics, for viable Republican challengers mean that Democratic factions can no longer wage all-out primary battles with no concern for general election contests. Texas Democrats learned this the hard way in 1978 when Dolph Briscoe lost the Democratic gubernatorial primary and then sat out the general election, permitting Bill Clements to become the state's first Republican governor this century, and only the second in Texas history.[83] At the same time, the Republicans have drawn many conservatives away from the party of their forebears, with the result that ideological schisms have moderated among Democrats and are much more intense between Democrats and Republicans.[84]

Nevertheless, these developments have occurred while local party organizations around the nation have visibly weakened, resulting in a politics focused on personalities and candidates. Parallel developments throughout Texas have contributed to the kind of free-for-all now seen in San Antonio. Thus, the chaotic politics of ideological factions bemoaned by V. O. Key in *Southern Politics* more than a generation ago has been partially supplanted by the equally chaotic politics of candidate-centered factions.[85]

With the old barriers to their political participation removed, aspiring Mexican-American politicos in San Antonio now have countless opportunities. Not yet overwhelmed by costly direct-mail and media efforts— once again, a sharp contrast with Los Angeles—politics in San Antonio is relatively inexpensive. Moreover, there are a variety of minor elective offices with small jurisdictions, campaigning for which requires little cash, but a healthy supply of family, friends, or supporters willing to walk precincts, hang signs, and distribute handbills. In addition, school board seats and constable or justice of the peace posts offer modest salaries and patronage opportunities. Such elected positions then serve as bases from which to run for higher offices with broader jurisdictions. And without a candidate screening committee, the weak Democratic County Committee has little means of controlling who enters the primaries for these offices.

As a result, there exists relatively easy access to an array of elective offices where novices can learn important political skills. Newcomers and outsiders—some qualified, many not—can and do enter the fray with ease. Indeed, a virtual unknown with no money, no outside help, and minimal experience can get elected to the state legislature from San Antonio by tirelessly walking precincts with his wife and kids.

Such a system works to the advantage of Mexican Americans, who lack financial resources but not the social networks that are critical to this kind of neighborhood-based politics. In the West Side barrio, I heard of individuals getting talked into running for office by friends and relatives, sitting around the kitchen table one night drinking beer. Indeed, the opportunities in San Antonio politics are such that if a young person remains in the shadow of some older politician for too long, people begin to question his mettle. For example, an individual from humble West Side origins faithfully served for almost ten years as an aide to a lackluster Mexican-American state representative. Considered by most observers as superior in intelligence and probity to his boss, this fellow's reputation showed signs of wear by the time he finally did decide to run for office. Many wondered out loud why he had waited so patiently in the wings for so many years.

No such qualms were ever voiced about Henry Cisneros, whose career is testimony to the new openness of San Antonio politics. After several years in Washington and Cambridge, Cisneros returned home in 1974 and within several months had won a seat on the city council. Six years later, at the age of 33, he was elected mayor.

THE EVOLUTION OF REFORM

Despite the GGL's demise, its reform legacy is still very much in evidence around city hall. The powerful city manager hires and fires not only key department heads, but also the meager staffs afforded elected officials. For example, members of the mayor's small staff are answerable to the city manager. Such an arrangement helps ensure the strict observance of nonpartisanship in municipal government. Indeed, for fear of violating the city charter, municipal employees generally abstain from political activities, even outside of work. For their part, elected officials tend to avoid direct links with party politics, which is quite distinct from municipal politics. Thus, it was only after having served on the city council for six years and in the mayor's office for almost two that Cisneros aggressively identified himself as a Democrat. His low partisan profile was so effective that, as mentioned earlier, his mentor, Republican Elliot Richardson, was not sure of Cisneros's party affiliation until sometime in 1983.

Nonpartisanship in San Antonio municipal government is also assured by a civil service system that is widely regarded as highly effective. The city charter has been interpreted as actually prohibiting elected officials from telephoning municipal departments on behalf of constituents. All such business is supposed to be channeled through the city manager's office. And while single-member districting has created political pressures causing city councillors to make such calls, this practice is still viewed by many observers as a worrisome charter violation.

Other recent developments have reinforced the reform spirit of the charter. Particularly during Cisneros's tenure, the mayor, a formally weak official with only one vote on the city council, emerged as an influential broker among competing interests in a suddenly more pluralistic polity.[86] Another change has been the expansion of the city's professional staff. In the late 1970s a Budget and Research Department was created to deal with the growing demands on municipal government. These came from state and federal authorities, but also from Mexican Americans stirred by the COPS community organization. During Cisneros's tenure as mayor city staff continued to grow larger and more professional, resulting in sharp tax increases that in turn led to a successful tax reduction movement.

Similar, though far less dramatic, changes have been evident in county government. The courthouse is quite different today from what it was twenty years ago, when county jobs were obtained on strictly political terms. Recalling the old regime, courthouse veterans describe a clear division of labor between the elected officials or their high-level appointees, few of whom tended to their official responsibilities, and their underlings, who were expected to keep up with the day-to-day business of issuing auto licenses, receiving taxes, and serving summonses. At election time, all county employees were expected to go out and toil for the politician who headed their department. Pretty secretaries were often expected to be helpful in ways less directly tied to the election cycle. And with the arrival of a new elected official, employees were completely vulnerable to dismissal. The spoils system reigned supreme.

By the 1980s the courthouse had changed. In some instances the discretion of elected county officials had been curtailed by the state legislature. Notable here was the reform of local taxing authorities across Texas. Whereas the county tax assessor-collector once enjoyed virtually unlimited discretion in assessing the property values on which taxes were calculated, a new law required all assessments to be 100 percent of market value, thereby eliminating much of the assessor's political power.

As at city hall, professionalization has been evident at the courthouse. For example, the Bexar County Commissioners Court—a powerful body with combined legislative, executive, and judicial functions—now relies on a professional administrator to brief its five elected members on issues and to set the agenda for their meetings. Originally paid with federal funds, this official now receives a county paycheck. This is a minor development that could easily be reversed by the court, but it is symptomatic of changes in county government in San Antonio.

Another such symptom is the appointment of a county roads administrator. Historically, the power of county commissioners in Texas has rested on their control of the budget for building and repairing county roads in their districts. Even today in rural counties, commissioners are most readily found, not in the courthouse, but at the district roadhouses where most of their business is transacted.[87] Although Bexar County has not been run in this fashion for some time, roads remain an important source of patronage for Bexar County commissioners.

So the creation of a unified road administration is significant. By setting up this post the county commissioners have ceded some of their power. But they have also gained some advantages: administratively, relief from burdensome duties; politically, a whipping boy toward whom constituent complaints can be deflected. Again, this is a minor development that nevertheless suggests an important courthouse trend toward reform.

Finally, civil service has also come to the courthouse. A response to the threat of unionization, the county's civil service is far less entrenched than the city's. There are still plenty of dodges around it, which is why one city hall veteran said of the county, "I'm glad they're there. They make us look good." Nevertheless, civil service has limited some of the prerogatives of courthouse elected officials.

STILL A TRADITIONAL POLITY

Despite all these changes, San Antonio remains a remarkably traditional polity. Things may not be as blatant as in the days when Lyndon Johnson, a young congressional secretary, sat in a local hotel room passing out five-dollar bills to Mexicans instructed to vote for Maury Maverick.[88] But San Antonio politics is still marked by venality and corruption.

A minor but nevertheless revealing example involves Cisneros, whose salary as mayor was $4,040 a year (a figure that has remained fixed by the city charter since 1951).[89] To supplement her husband's meager salary, Cisneros's wife worked as a public relations officer for a local Mexican-American businessman and political contributor—a job considered to be a sinecure by most San Antonians who were aware of it. Such an arrangement might raise eyebrows in some cities. But in San Antonio no one, including the press, considered it worthy of note. After all, the wives of many politicians there benefit from similar arrangements.

More serious are the many instances of outright payoffs in Bexar County. A certain amount of this activity is evident in most local politics. But in San Antonio it sets a pervasive tone. State representatives and senators are held in especially low esteem. Of one Mexican-American state

senator, I was told repeatedly, "If you want him to introduce some legislation, don't even approach him unless you have $10,000." Other state
and county elected officials are commonly known to receive inordinately
large contributions from various interests. One statewide officeholder
was recently quoted, "Don't shake my hand, put money in it." Of a particularly colorful but hardly atypical Mexican-American lawyer and former elected official, one San Antonio politico discreetly observed, "He
puts an awfully high price on his services." And though city hall is generally less tainted by such corruption, it seeps in there as well. In one
episode a local energy company was widely understood to have bribed a
city councillor into changing his vote.

Moreover, San Antonio's politics is still driven by patronage and favors.
As a former Democratic county chairman tellingly put it, "You should
never underestimate what constitutes a favor." And again, there is evidence of this kind of politics even at city hall. For while there are strictures on political activities by those employed directly by the city, there
are none on those working at private agencies with whom the city sub-
contracts for services. Thus, a Mexican-American city councillor who
championed public funding of private Latino arts programs relied on
them as a source of patronage. Indeed, he used their employees as volunteers, who spent many a Saturday driving around town in their pickup
trucks putting up campaign signs.

Traditional politics also persists in San Antonio's municipal courts.
While county and state judges are elected to the bench, municipal court
judges are appointed by the city council. These appointments typically
go to loyal supporters of the councillors, or to veteran politicians facing
retirement and collecting old debts. Appointees then have the opportunity to demonstrate their gratitude to their benefactors in their discreet
handling of traffic and parking citations. Municipal judges aspiring to
some higher, and therefore elective, bench keep computer lists of the
friends and constituents thus "processed." With enough accumulated
chits, these judges can get themselves named to one of the frequent va-
cancies on the higher courts. A system Mexican-American lawyers and
politicians have learned to work to their advantage, it is frequently attacked by outraged (typically Republican) Anglos.

But the bastion of traditional politics remains the courthouse, a fact
suggested by the physical differences between it and city hall. The latter
is a four-storey, rectangular wedding cake of a building, whose white sand-
stone, terracotta trim, lush plantings, and palm trees offer the crisp, clean
image appropriate to a Sunbelt city. The interior is lit brightly, if harshly,
with hastily installed fluorescent fixtures. Each floor is crammed with of-

fices that are tiny cubicles, divided and subdivided as the city has strained
to keep up with the changes thrust upon it. Yet city hall is remarkably
quiet and devoid of activity, except on those occasions when a controversial issue is before the council or, a few years back, when the national
media periodically descended on Mayor Cisneros.

By contrast, the turreted Romanesque courthouse looms with medieval solemnity over San Antonio's Main Plaza. The somber red sand-
stone of its exterior echoes the dimness of its interior, full of shadowy
recesses. The Mexican-tiled floors are dirty and dulled by years of heavy
traffic. The broad corridors are lined with wooden benches where the
old, the accused, the dependent, the confused—even the hopeful and the
affluent—wait to complete their business with the State of Texas through
its agent, Bexar County. The crowds milling in these corridors include
those transacting routine business like paying taxes, registering autos, or
probating wills. Others, however, come as supplicants in search of special help. As an administrative arm of the state, with no written charter
of its own such as the city enjoys, the county has through the generations
developed its own, often obscure ways of doing business. Administrative
discretion is the coin of the realm and knowledge of the courthouse's arcane mores, gained after years of experience, is at a premium.

Traditional politics also lives on in the courthouse's hiring practices. As
mentioned earlier, civil service has come to Bexar County. Yet the commissioners court appoints the members of the civil service board and ap-
proves its budget, underscoring the observation of a courthouse insider:
"There's no way all those politicians are going to give away all their power
to hire and fire people." Indeed, county officials routinely circumvent
civil service with schemes that would be familiar to Chicagoans, including temporary appointments and multiple pay scales for similar jobs. In
addition, there are large sectors of county government not covered by
civil service. For example, the staffs of county and state judges—who, it
should be remembered, are elected to office—are exempt; so are the
staffs of the county commissioners. As a close observer of Texas government and politics concludes: "By and large, county government is the last
unchallenged stronghold of the spoils system."[90]

In this regard, the Bexar County district attorney's office is notable.
Described by a local lawyer as a "political whorehouse," the office has
scores of positions not subject to civil service. It has traditionally attracted
ambitious lawyers eager to learn the arcane ways of the courthouse and
willing, for this privilege, to undertake the political chores of their boss,
who is up for election every four years.

Most notable of all, in these terms, is the office of the county sheriff.

In addition to the many deputies, clerks, and process-servers hired by the sheriff at his discretion, there are dozens of volunteer deputies who contribute their time and services in return for the camaraderie and satisfactions of involvement in quasi-official law enforcement efforts. Similar to a volunteer fire department, this arrangement hardly strikes a blow for professionalism. But it does offer the county's chief law enforcement officer the opportunity to develop strong community ties. And these translate into considerable political muscle. As one San Antonio journalist put it: "A U.S. Senator might go say hello to the county judge or commissioner when he's in town, but he goes to cut deals with the sheriff." Thus it is not surprising that when the Bexar County Democratic Committee holds a margarita-tasting contest fund-raiser, the sheriff's margaritas are voted the best.

An additional facet of traditional politics in Bexar County has been the perquisite enjoyed by elected officials of performing marriage ceremonies for a fee. This has been a particularly lucrative sideline for the county judge, justices of the peace, and other judges—many of whom admit to having earned in this way thousands of dollars beyond their regular salaries. For a cut of the marriage fee, county employees would steer starry-eyed couples to particular officials. Thus, it has been not at all uncommon for official proceedings to be interrupted for marriage ceremonies. From the politician's perspective, this was of course an opportunity to make money, but also to become part of a memorable event in the lives of two young voters. Keeping careful records of those for whom they tied the knot, officials would not hesitate later on to pull the strings—if only to send Christmas cards to such potential supporters.

At least this was how things worked up until the late 1980s, when reformers, typically Republicans intent on ending generations of Democratic control of the courthouse, attacked such practices and got them prohibited. Their success here and against other such traditional courthouse practices is a useful reminder of the changes that will inevitably affect even Bexar County—albeit at the unacknowledged price of sundering ties between local political institutions and the social fabric of San Antonio.

GETTING AHEAD AND GETTING EVEN

Long before Mexican Americans were able to get in on the action, San Antonio had established a political tradition lively enough to be renowned throughout Texas, itself renowned for political high jinks. As a community organizer who has worked in both San Antonio and Los Angeles remarked, "Politics in Los Angeles is a deadly serious business that people don't really enjoy. But in San Antonio they have a good time at it."

In this respect San Antonio is reminiscent of Boston, another city where ethnic attachments were not (for much of this century) greatly attenuated by economic growth; and where, as a result, politics has been energized by the synergistic challenges of getting ahead and getting even. For if politics is fun, it can also be profitable, as the pervasive corruption in San Antonio suggests. For Mexican Americans there today, the politics of aspiration and the politics of resentment converge. After all, one man's ambition is another man's greed. This is not to say that all public officials in San Antonio, Anglo or Mexican, are dishonest. It is to suggest that politics there is a rowdy arena where generations of built-up frustrations and newfound hopes get played out.

Another parallel between San Antonio and Boston is that in both cities political competition within and between groups has gone unrestrained by any overarching political organization.[91] Contrary to popular myth, Boston has never had a machine. Rather its politics was long dominated by personality- and turf-based factions. In the glory days earlier this century, the wags had it that Boston's machine had "one moving part"— Mayor James Michael Curley. The demagogue Curley mismanaged the city's finances and alienated its banking and business elite from municipal affairs for at least a generation. This development contributed to Boston's prolonged economic stagnation—which, as I have already suggested, played a role in maintaining the city's tight ethnic enclaves. As a result, Boston's ethnic groups have exhibited a provincialism extreme even for Northeastern ethnic strongholds, which was all too evident in the furor over busing in the mid-1970s.

Whether San Antonio faces a similar fate remains to be seen. The emergence of a Cisneros suggests perhaps not. Yet since he left office in 1989, two mayoral elections have failed to produce a Mexican-American successor to Cisneros. There is certainly no Mexican-American elected official in San Antonio, or Texas generally, of his prominence—or soon likely to achieve it. In the meantime, only COPS, the powerful community organization that will be scrutinized in Part Two, appears capable of providing the sustained leadership necessary to overcome the factionalism and venality that, despite its vigor, afflict Mexican-American politics in San Antonio.

❦ 3 ❧

Los Angeles
Moving In, Out, And Up

S an Antonio's small-town traditionalism stands in sharp contrast to the cosmopolitanism of Los Angeles, the nation's second largest metropolitan area. Quite aside from being the center of the world's entertainment industry, Los Angeles has of course emerged as a hub of financial and business activity in the huge Pacific Basin.

To one interested in Mexican Americans, the contrast between the two cities is perhaps most glaring on Sunday mornings. In San Antonio, churchgoing is still very much part of the lives of Anglos and Mexicans alike. There simply aren't many alternatives on a typical Sunday morning. Local religious programs typically preempt television-network news programs. In Los Angeles, however, climate, geography, and social mores all conspire to lure people away from the churches and onto the freeways, which even on Sunday mornings are crowded with Angelenos intent on enjoying their day of rest. A round of golf on the municipal course in Montebello; a family outing to the Whittier Narrows Recreation Area; a trip down the coast to Laguna Beach: these are typical Sunday activities for a good number of Mexican Americans in Los Angeles.

For the loyalty of Mexican Americans in San Antonio, the Catholic Church competes with folk beliefs, anticlericalism, and fundamentalist Protestantism. In Los Angeles the Church contends with all these, plus secularism. To be sure, secular forces are evident in Texas, but in South-

ern California they are pervasive, and sustained by an aggressively hedonistic life-style that is for many a virtual substitute religion.[1]

While San Antonio is a big small town struggling to get bigger, Los Angeles is a huge metropolis refusing to stop growing—despite an emergent slow-growth backlash. Both cause and symptom of this growth is the
region's ever-expanding Mexican population. In 1960 about 9 percent of
metropolitan Los Angeles was "Spanish surnamed" individuals, virtually
all of whom were Mexicans. By 1980 about 28 percent of the metropolitan area was Hispanic. As of 1990, four years after enactment of the restrictive Immigration Reform and Control Act, Hispanics constituted
about 38 percent of the metropolitan population. In absolute numbers,
the Hispanic population just about doubled from 1970 to 1980—from
about 1.05 million to about 2.07 million.[2] By 1990 there were more than
3.35 million Hispanics in metropolitan Los Angeles—about three-fourths
of whom were of Mexican origin. Insofar as Mexican Americans (or other
Hispanics) are concerned, therefore, Los Angeles in the 1990s is hardly
the same city it was in the 1970s, much less the 1960s.

In one respect, however, Los Angeles has not changed. In their 1970
study, *The Mexican-American People*, Leo Grebler and his colleagues described Los Angeles as "a place for newcomers" and San Antonio as "a
place of oldtimers."[3] Still, whereas Grebler's newcomers were often from
elsewhere in the Southwest, most subsequent arrivals have come directly
from Mexico.[4] Indeed, from 1970 to 1983 about 550,000 immigrants
from Mexico, the overwhelming majority illegals, settled in Los Angeles
County. Nearly 200,000 more arrived in the rest of Southern California.[5]
The Immigration Reform and Control Act of 1986 (IRCA) curtailed illegal immigration somewhat during the late 1980s. But by the early 1990s
illegal immigration was approaching pre-IRCA levels. Indeed, it has been
estimated that as of 1990 two-thirds of all Hispanics in Los Angeles
County had arrived since 1970.[6]

Mexicans are not the only ones arriving in substantial numbers in Los
Angeles in recent years. In fact, they constitute less than half of the nearly
1.2 million immigrants (legal and illegal) that the Urban Institute estimated settled in Los Angeles between 1970 and 1983. The remainder included close to 150,000 other Latinos and more than 300,000 Asians.[7]
The result is a metropolitan region of extraordinary diversity, which further distinguishes Los Angeles from San Antonio.

In any event, the Mexican presence in Los Angeles today is much more of a foreign immigrant phenomenon than in San Antonio. As mentioned in the previous chapter, 46 percent of Hispanics in metropolitan Los Angeles in 1980 were foreign-born, compared to only 12 percent in San Antonio.[8] While local level data for 1990 have not yet been released, the available state-level data indicate that this difference between these two metropolitan areas did not fundamentally change during the 1980s. As a result, much more Spanish is heard on the streets of East Los Angeles than on the West Side of San Antonio. Indeed, surveys consistently reveal that Los Angeles has a significantly higher proportion of Spanish-dependent individuals than San Antonio.[9] This is why the Spanish-language daily, *La Opinión*, has been thriving in Los Angeles, while its sister publication in San Antonio, *La Prensa*, has long since been defunct.[10] And as the enormous flood of Mexican immigrants has continued, East LA, along with the other barrios scattered across the metropolitan region, has taken on an increasingly foreign air. Posters, billboards, and store signs are all in Spanish, and merchants fill the streets with Latin music blaring from loudspeakers. At parish fiestas, lottery jackpots are advertised in pesos; and to accommodate the many illiterates, bingo is played not with numbers and letters, but with animal pictures. In the bars and restaurants of Boyle Heights, bedraggled youngsters go from table to table pleading with people to buy novelties like those found in the stalls of Tijuana. Outside on the sidewalks, their mothers, often with infants in their arms, stop passers-by and beg for money. In San Antonio, such vivid reminders of daily life in Mexico are much less in evidence.

Perhaps most telling is the scene any Sunday at the old mission church adjacent to the original pueblo at Olvera Street. While their assimilated cousins pursue Southern California's good life, thousands of Mexican immigrants stream into Our Lady Queen of the Angels Church. La Placita, as it is popularly known, conducts masses continuously from 6:30 A.M. to 7:00 P.M., all in Spanish. Many are filled to the point where the crowds spill out the front entrance onto Sunset Boulevard. And as that famous thoroughfare begins its long trek west toward the Pacific through places like Hollywood and Beverly Hills, one cannot help but think of the social and cultural distance these immigrants have yet to negotiate.

Inside the compound formed by the church and its rectory, one might as well be in Mexico. No word of English is heard, and woe to any Anglo clergy not at ease speaking Spanish. The atmosphere is that of a bazaar, with merchants hawking Coca-Cola and *pan dulce* (pastry) and activists collecting signatures against immigration restriction. A sign advertises that the downstairs cafeteria is serving, among other favorites, *menudo*, a spicy tripe stew.

Several times each Sunday, hundreds of parents carrying unbaptized infants are crowded into a cool, dark chapel in the church basement. To escape the commotion outside, the doors are sealed. Only then, above the din of the wailing infants, does the priest attempt a short sermon about the Church's teaching on baptism and then administers the sacrament en masse. Upstairs in the main church, parishioners of all ages, mostly female, press constantly in and out of the small chapels on the side aisles, lighting votive candles and reverently caressing the statues of the saints. After mass, when each wave of worshipers recedes, old women with red plastic pails hobble through the pews picking up litter with their bare hands.

As a kind of regional shrine, La Placita is an extreme case, but it is illustrative of what can be seen at Catholic churches in East LA and other Mexican enclaves in the metropolitan region. Such scenes of immigrant life are much rarer among the more settled Mexican Americans of San Antonio. Yet the way of life in San Antonio is in many respects more traditional—more Mexican—than in Los Angeles.[11] This was evident in Grebler's 1970 study, which found Mexican Americans in San Antonio to be less achievement- and more family-oriented than their counterparts in Los Angeles,[12]

To be sure, the hundreds of thousands of immigrants arriving in Los Angeles have brought with them the traditional values of rural villages and small towns left behind in Mexico.[13] But in Southern California such values have few places to take root and sustain themselves. Moreover, they stand in stark contrast to the pervasive, even intrusive American mainstream. Thus, in Los Angeles these newcomers face a choice between two quite disparate alternatives, with very little in between. In San Antonio, on the other hand, a distinct Mexican-American subculture has had more opportunity to develop and lodge itself in strong community institutions.

THE BARRIO OF BARRIOS: EAST LA

La Placita sits at the edge of downtown Los Angeles, across from Union Station and the main post office. The site of the original pueblo that became the city of Los Angeles, this area is now close to the garment factories and rooming houses where many Mexican immigrants live and work. Yet it is actually quite removed from what has come to be the center of Mexican-American life in Los Angeles, the barrio of East LA.

East LA is a huge, amorphous area lying a few miles east of the downtown business district and separated from it by a sunbaked no-man's-land of railroad tracks, high-tension wires, and a wide swath of concrete that was once the gravelly bed of the Los Angeles River. Immediately east of the river, on a broad flood plain, crowded in among the warehouses, can be found a few public housing projects, whose residents are Mexican. But East LA really doesn't begin until the terrain climbs up an escarpment at the top of which sits Boyle Heights. The barrio then extends north toward Lincoln Heights and Highland Park; and from there east toward the hills around California State University at Los Angeles, beyond which lie affluent enclaves like Pasadena and San Marino. But for its greatest extent, East LA spreads out to the south and east beyond the Los Angeles city limits and into unincorporated Los Angeles County, onto a plain that eventually becomes the vast San Gabriel Valley, an expanse of blue-collar and middle-class suburbs that have attracted growing numbers of Mexican Americans. Indeed, from 1980 to 1990 the Hispanic population of the Valley increased by almost 50 percent.[14]

Vast though it is, East LA is only one of several major concentrations of Mexicans in metropolitan Los Angeles. In places like Pacoima in the east San Fernando Valley remnants of old migrant labor camps have developed into distinct Mexican communities.[15] More recently, communities several miles south of downtown, like South Gate and Bell, which used to be home to working-class whites, have become centers of Mexican life. A similar growing Mexican presence is found in the Wilmington–San Pedro area around Los Angeles harbor.[16] And there are many other such enclaves.[17]

It is only in recent decades that East LA itself has been so heavily Mexican. In Boyle Heights, the many abandoned synagogues on the side streets off Brooklyn Avenue are reminders of the Jewish population that lived there until after World War II. As recently as the mid-1960s, remnants of earlier Japanese and Russian communities could be found in East LA.[18] In adjacent areas like Highland Park and Eagle Rock, some survivors of the Dust Bowl migration into Southern California—the Okies—remain, but are inexorably being displaced by Mexicans. Elsewhere in East LA, Mexicans have moved into what used to be Armenian neighborhoods.

Nevertheless, throughout the postwar period of Mexican population growth in all parts of the metropolitan region, East LA has remained the symbolic heart of the Mexican-American community in Southern California. This was "the barrio" where Robert Kennedy campaigned with César Chávez in the spring of 1968. This was where Walter Mondale came in 1984 to gain the support of Mexican-American politicos. So, too, was it the mandatory port of call for both Michael Dukakis and George Bush in 1988.

Walking about East LA, one comes upon street after street of tiny bungalows, fronted by small plots of grass and separated by barely enough space for a car and a chain-link fence. Glancing down the narrow driveways, the casual visitor will observe small garages. But closer scrutiny reveals that these have typically been converted into living quarters, and that an additional dwelling is sometimes found right behind the main house, in what used to be the backyard. Such accommodations may have originally been intended for the owner's elderly parents or recently married children—another manifestation of the strong family ties among Mexican Americans. But with the flood of immigrants, Mexican-American homeowners have gradually become landlords.

As the newcomers crowd into these modest but once-stable neighborhoods, they bring old habits inappropriate to their new environment. As one Mexican-American city employee still living in East LA observed, "These guys straight from the rancheros think nothing of stooping down and relieving themselves at the curb." Less offensive but nevertheless bothersome is the noise of several groups crammed into one house, never settling down all at once because everyone works different hours; or the parking problems caused by overcrowding, leading renters to park on what were once plots of grass. Then there is the eager entrepreneur who opens a vegetable stand on his front porch.

The renters themselves face other problems. Even rent shared with others can be an overwhelming burden without steady work. Congested living quarters increase the likelihood of domestic disputes. Individuals apprehended by the Immigration and Naturalization Service (INS) may suddenly disappear. And in general, illegals encounter more difficulties than those normally experienced by legal immigrants. Then, too, individuals and families often pick up and leave to live with relatives elsewhere, or perhaps return to Mexico. Having put up with such nuisances, a landlord may decide to go back to renting to relatives. Or a relative may need a place to stay, and strangers must be asked to leave, or perhaps threatened with a visit from the INS. Even if a landlord tolerates all these problems, his neighbors who are still resident owners may not. As a result, the more established Mexican Americans—the working- and lower-middle-class homeowners raising families—have been pushed out of East LA. In most parishes in the area, such families are now an endangered species.

But note that East LA is not the port of entry. The most recent arrivals from Mexico are found in rundown buildings near the garment district, adjacent to downtown, or in various parts of South-Central Los Angeles. For these immigrants the bungalows of East LA represent the next stage in the struggle for advancement. A rental in Boyle Heights might be the first step, to be followed by several moves to the east or south, into progressively more comfortable neighborhoods where assimilated Mexican-American families are found in increasing numbers. Indeed, this pattern undoubtedly helps explain why East LA, unlike Hispanic neighborhoods in South-Central and in particular the Pico-Union district, did not erupt in riots after the Rodney King verdict in April 1992.

MOVING IN, OUT, AND UP

Thus, East LA is not a place where people settle down and establish community ties. Indeed, community organizers working there have been struck by the population flux in and out of the neighborhoods. Religious professionals* working in the parishes make the same point and refer to the people they serve as "transients." One young priest working with the organizers attributes the difficulty of their endeavor to the fact that one-fourth of the families in his parish move away every three months.[19] He speaks with such precision because every three months the parish mails out packets of contribution envelopes. And every three months one-fourth are returned undelivered, because the addressees have disappeared. Yet these stacks of returned envelopes actually underestimate movement into and out of the parishes, for it is the more settled families who manage to connect up with churches in the first place.

To be sure, the situation in East LA is extreme. The Urban Institute, relying on 1980 census data, estimated that only 7.2 percent of Hispanics in East LA live in owner-occupied housing, compared to 65.2 percent in Pacoima and 39.6 percent in the harbor district.[20] Yet few Mexican enclaves in Los Angeles can be characterized as stable communities. The *Los Angeles Times*, for example, estimates that in the metropolitan region there are 200,000 "garage people," almost exclusively Hispanics, living in illegally converted garages with little or no plumbing, heating, or windows and with extension cords to nearby houses for electric power.[21]

These social dynamics come clearly into focus when compared with San Antonio. For example, in 1985 only 37 percent of Hispanics in met-

---

* This term includes both diocesan and religious priests, as well as nuns and members of monastic orders. It typically refers to Catholics, but in some contexts may refer to Protestants and members of other faiths.

ropolitan Los Angeles lived in their own homes, compared to more than 58 percent in metropolitan San Antonio.[22] Other indicators present a similar picture. The 1980 census reports that 42 percent of Hispanics (over the age of 5) in metropolitan Los Angeles were living in the same house they had five years before; in San Antonio the figure was 59 percent.[23] Similarly, 43 percent of Hispanics in Los Angeles in 1980 were born in California.[24] By contrast, 83 percent of Hispanics in San Antonio that year were born in Texas.[25] Finally, the fact that San Antonio has for some time attracted more immigrant families (as opposed to single, adult migrants) than other cities similarly suggests that Hispanics are less atomized and more rooted there than in Los Angeles.[26]

In some respects, such transience, or geographic mobility, is nothing new for Californians—Anglos or Mexicans. In no decade since California joined the Union in 1850 has a majority of the state's population growth resulted from natural increase.[27] The difference today, of course, is that foreigners represent a dramatically larger proportion of the influx. Among Mexicans specifically, Los Angeles has long attracted migrants from across the Southwest: from the copper mines of southern Arizona, the barrios of El Paso, the ranches and border towns of South Texas, the villages of New Mexico, and the parishes of San Antonio—as well as Mexican nationals from across the border. And as historian Ricardo Romo points out, most Mexicans who arrived in Los Angeles during the early decades of the century did not immediately break out of the migrant labor stream and settle down; rather they moved back and forth between urban and rural settlements.[28] Furthermore, in the 1950s and 1960s, many Mexican neighborhoods were torn up and their residents dispersed by massive freeway and redevelopment projects like Dodger Stadium, which completely eliminated an old barrio in Chavez Ravine, just north of downtown.[29]

For most groups, the geographic mobility, even rootlessness, for which Southern California is renowned has also meant social and economic mobility. Although this has not always been true for Mexicans there, they have nevertheless fared much better in recent decades than their cousins elsewhere in the Southwest. Again, the contrast with San Antonio is particularly striking.

During the 1960s, for example, Los Angeles offered Mexicans much greater opportunities for advancement than San Antonio. The overwhelming evidence for this claim comes from the Grebler study, which assembled a variety of indices to compare the socioeconomic situation of

Mexicans in these two cities. Some were quite mundane, but revealing: while only 1 percent of Mexican households in Los Angeles in the mid-1960s lacked hot water, 26 percent in San Antonio did; and while three-fourths of Mexicans in Los Angeles had telephones in their homes, only 56 percent in San Antonio did.[30] Other indices were more conventional: while 15 percent of Mexicans in metropolitan Los Angeles had family incomes of less than $3,000, over 43 percent in metropolitan San Antonio did.[31] In the end, Grebler concluded:

> It is clear from the recent history of Los Angeles and San Antonio as milieus for the Mexican-American population, and from the educational attainment, the incomes, and especially the occupational distribution of the survey respondents, that social isolation of the minority people is far greater in the Texas metropolis, as is their poverty.[32]

Focusing on this social isolation, Grebler and his colleagues found—across generational and income lines—much greater "ethnic exclusiveness" in San Antonio.[33] For example, 55 percent of Mexican survey respondents in San Antonio had exclusively Mexican friends, compared to half that figure in Los Angeles. One-third of the children of the San Antonio respondents had exclusively Mexican-American schoolmates, compared to 10 percent in Los Angeles.[34] Summing up the evidence, Grebler observed, "San Antonians remain far more confined to members of their own group, Angelenos have far more social relations with Anglos."[35]

Another such indicator dealt with residential patterns. As Grebler put it:

> San Antonio is a far more segregated city. The 1960 census shows only about 10 percent of the Mexican Americans in Los Angeles living in census tracts that were more than three-quarters Mexican, as compared with more than half the Mexican-American San Antonians.[36]

Subsequent data confirm this finding. Thus, Table 2.1 indicates that although from 1960 to 1970 the residential concentration of Mexicans in both cities decreased, the decline in Los Angeles was somewhat greater, despite greater growth of its Hispanic population. In any event, in 1970 Mexicans in San Antonio were still more residentially concentrated than their counterparts in Los Angeles.

One final indicator is intermarriage between Mexicans and non-Mexicans in the two cities. In 1963, over 25 percent of Mexicans who married in Los Angeles County did so outside their group. Moreover, with the passage of time in the United States and improved occupational standing, Mexican Americans were increasingly likely to marry outside their group. Indeed, Grebler reported that in Los Angeles County in 1963 it was more likely that a third-generation Mexican American would marry an Anglo than a first- or second-generation Mexican American.[37]

There are no subsequent intermarriage data for Los Angeles. But in 1974 the exogamy rate among Mexicans in California, obviously heavily weighted by trends in Los Angeles, was 34 percent.[38] This was more than double the rate in San Antonio at that time—16 percent—a figure that had barely moved in a decade. With such findings at hand, Grebler concluded:

> Contemporary Los Angeles is far less hostile to Mexican Americans and offers much greater economic opportunity than do most of the other large Southwest metropolitan communities.[39]

Such conclusions are confirmed by what I have heard in the field. Mexican Americans who grew up in Los Angeles during the 1950s and 1960s typically complain to me that they were encouraged by their parents and teachers to "act like whites," and consequently were raised with little knowledge of their culture and language.[40]

Yet if there is little doubt that in the recent past Los Angeles offered much greater opportunities to Mexicans than San Antonio, the same case may be harder to make today. For as noted earlier, the massive Mexican immigration of the last ten or fifteen years has made the Los Angeles of the 1980s and 1990s quite different from that of the 1950s and 1960s. Quite aside from whether Southern California can sustain recent levels of economic growth, there is good reason to believe that the assimilation of a group that represented 9 percent of the metropolitan population in 1960 would be much less problematic than that of a group representing 38 percent in 1990.[41]

To be sure, there are signs Mexicans are continuing to assimilate into the mainstream. Hardly atypical are the remarks of a dismayed young Mexican-American priest, complaining about families in his East LA parish who have "forgotten their roots;" or who remember just enough to celebrate their daughters' *quince años*,* but then complain about illegal immigrants from Mexico: "I pay my taxes. Why should I pay for them?" Similarly revealing are the laments of Mexican-American politicians in Los Angeles. Having come of age politically in the 1960s, they express

---

* A young woman's fifteenth birthday, marking the passage from childhood to adulthood and typically celebrated by Mexican-American families with a special mass and an elaborate party or reception. For an ethnographic analysis of the *quince años* in one Mexican-American community, see Ruth Horowitz, *Honor of the American Dream: Culture and Identity in a Chicano Community* (New Brunswick, NJ: Rutgers University Press, 1985), pp. 52–55, 243.

frustration that their past efforts are largely unappreciated by the up-coming generation, which in their view faces relatively few barriers. As one such politico remarked over drinks one afternoon, young Mexican Americans today assimilate so fast that they lose touch with their heritage and political history; consequently, "There's no way to make them feel guilty."

How do such anecdotes square with the reality of rapidly growing bar-rios all over Southern California? Table 3.1 presents worrisome data on the residential concentration of Hispanics in Los Angeles. From 1970 to 1980 the residential concentration of Hispanics in metropolitan Los An-geles increased dramatically, while in San Antonio it actually declined slightly. By 1980, in fact, the concentration of Hispanics in the two cities was roughly equal.

Yet this change in Los Angeles has been driven by immigrants from Mexico. Moreover, the available research confirms that in Los Angeles and other metropolitan areas, Hispanic socioeconomic advances trans-late into residential *de*concentration and integration, which sharply dis-tinguishes Hispanics—Mexicans in particular—from blacks. Summing up the evidence for Los Angeles, a study from the Rand Corporation con-cludes:

> The degree of residential segregation between Anglos and Latinos is di-rectly related to the proportion of immigrants in the Latino community and to the average socioeconomic levels of Latinos. The higher the pro-portion of native-born and the higher the status of Latinos, the more in-tegrated Latinos and Anglos are. Moreover, unlike the patterns for blacks, an influx of Latinos into an area does not appear to precipitate an outflow

TABLE 3.1
Residential Concentration of Hispanics Relative to Anglos as Measured by Dissimilarity Index (D-Index)*

	1970	*1980*
Metropolitan San Antonio (SMSA)	.591	.572
Metropolitan Los Angeles (SMSA)	.468	.570

Note:
*Defined as the percentage of Hispanics who would have to move in order for the group to be evenly distributed across census tracts.
Source:
Douglas Massey and Nancy Denton, "Trends in the Residential Segregation of Blacks, Hispanics, and Asians: 1970–1980," *American Sociological Review* 52 (1987): 815–816.

of Anglos. Thus, with increasing exposure to U.S. society and continued upward mobility, Latinos blend into the larger society.[42]

Or as Joan Moore and Harry Pachon, two leading students of Hispanic affairs, observe:

> The degree of Hispanic [residential] segregation has been studied only since 1960, but there are strong indications that Hispanic patterns are unlike the black-white pattern and more closely resemble those of European immigrants.[43]

For this reason sociologists Frank Bean and Marta Tienda use the term "voluntary segregation" when explaining Mexican-American residential patterns.[44] Indeed, the difference between the black and Mexican patterns is so great that it is seriously misleading to apply to the latter the term "segregation," which of course connotes the racial exclusion uniquely experienced by black Americans. Hence my preference for the term "residential concentration."

Another encouraging sign of Los Angeles's continuing capacity to absorb newcomers is the evidence on English acquisition. In the late 1970s Professor David López concluded from a study of over 1,100 Mexican households in Los Angeles, "were it not for new arrivals from Mexico, Spanish would disappear from Los Angeles nearly as rapidly as most European immigrant languages vanished from cities in the East."[45] Similarly, an analysis of 1980 census data by the Rand researchers quoted above found that in California, English proficiency among Mexican immigrants and their offspring improved markedly over time. Indeed, these researchers reported that nearly half the permanent immigrants from Mexico speak good English. Moreover, their native-born children are mostly bilingual, with more than 90 percent proficient in English. As for the grandchildren of Mexican immigrants, more than half speak English only.[46] To be sure, since 1980 Los Angeles has been inundated with Spanish-speaking immigrants, such that the 1990 census reveals that 50 percent of Hispanics in Los Angeles County do not speak English "very well."[47] But if previous patterns of language assimilation prevail, then these individuals—and certainly their offspring—will learn English.

Here again, my field research confirms such findings. By the mid-1980s, about four out of five Sunday masses in East LA were in Spanish. Yet in parish after parish religious professionals reported battles over language between newcomers and established residents, whose own immigrant parents and grandparents had struggled with English. No wonder the Mexican-American priest quoted earlier was dismayed that many of his parishioners had lost touch with their roots. Moreover, many Mexican-American politicians and activists in Los Angeles speak little or no Spanish. Typical was a 1984 campaign in which the adept Anglo who represented East LA on the city council seized every opportunity to use his fluent Spanish against two young Mexican-American challengers, both of whom had been raised in East LA but neither of whom could speak Spanish.

Further evidence of continued social and economic assimilation is found in the educational attainment data. Table 3.2 provides median education levels for Hispanics and the total population (age 25 and over) of metropolitan Los Angeles and San Antonio from 1950 to 1980. These data demonstrate once again that for most of the postwar period, Hispanics had greater opportunities in Los Angeles than in San Antonio. Table 3.2 also confirms a point made earlier in the San Antonio chapter: the city's Hispanics have made enormous gains in education, not only relative to the total population there, but also relative to Hispanics in Los Angeles. In 1980 the median number of school years completed by Hispanics in San Antonio was 10.0, compared to 10.2 in Los Angeles. But these figures are misleading, since they include the huge immigrant population with which Los Angeles has had to cope. With about 550,000 poorly trained and educated Mexican immigrants having arrived in Los Angeles County between 1970 and 1983, it is remarkable that the educational attainment figure for Hispanics not only did not decline, but increased marginally.

TABLE 3.2
Median School Years Completed by Hispanics in San Antonio and Los Angeles (SMSAs 1950–1980)

	1950	*1960*	*1970*	*1980*
Metropolitan San Antonio	4.5* (.49)**	5.7 (.57)	7.4 (.64)	10.0 (.81)
Metropolitan Los Angeles	8.2 (.68)	8.9 (.74)	9.8 (.79)	10.2 (.80)

Notes:
*Number of years.
**Ratio of median Hispanic educational attainment to median attainment of entire metropolitan population.
Sources:
Joan W. Moore and Harry Pachon, *Hispanics in the United States* (Englewood Cliffs, NJ: Prentice-Hall, 1985), 67; and Joan W. Moore, *Mexican Americans* (Englewood Cliffs, NJ: Prentice-Hall, 1976), 68.

Income levels are one final indicator of Hispanic economic assimilation in Los Angeles. According to the 1990 census, 29.2 percent of Hispanics in San Antonio fell under the poverty line, compared to 22.9 percent in Los Angeles.[48] And as Table 3.3 indicates, in 1989 Hispanics in Los Angeles earned markedly more than their counterparts in San Antonio. Here again, the superior position of Hispanics in Los Angeles is all the more remarkable in view of the huge influx of unskilled, poorly educated newcomers. Moreover, analyses of such data reveal that there has been income and occupational mobility between the immigrant and subsequent generations among Mexicans in Los Angeles.[49] To be sure, intergenerational mobility among Mexican Americans does not reveal a uniformly positive pattern. Among other concerns, we cannot be sure that whatever mobility has been evident up to now can be sustained in the future—particularly under conditions of continued mass immigration. I will touch upon some of these issues in chapter 10. But certainly the evidence confirms that Mexican Americans in Los Angeles have consistently enjoyed marked social and economic mobility relative to their cousins in San Antonio.

"¡ES PARAÍSO!"

Such mobility—geographic, social, and economic—has had a significant impact on politics in Los Angeles and indeed throughout the state. In his history of California politics, *Dancing Bear*, journalist Gladwin Hill attributes Governor Pat Brown's 1966 upset loss to Ronald Reagan to the thousands of newcomers who had arrived in California during the 1950s and 1960s, thereby transforming the electorate Brown had faced when

TABLE 3.3
1989 Measures of Hispanic Income in the San Antonio and Los Angeles Metropolitan Areas

	Mean household income	Per capita income
Metropolitan San Antonio (Bexar County)	24,968	7,309
Metropolitan Los Angeles (Los Angeles County)	33,586	8,066

Source: 1990 Decennial Census, Summary Tape File 3; tabulated by Texas and California State Data Centers.

first elected eight years earlier.[50] Alternatively, political scientists confirm the not surprising finding that geographic mobility has a negative impact on voting.[51]

Among Mexicans, geographic mobility has been one of many factors contributing to weakened communal attachments. Compared to their San Antonio cousins, Mexicans in Los Angeles lack strong identification with their neighborhood or parish. Immigrants may flock to Sunday mass, as at La Placita, but East LA religious professionals complain of the number of "unattached families" without ties to any community institutions, religious or secular. Similarly, Alinsky organizers trained to work with indigenous institutions and leaders complain that parishes in East LA are devoid of the rich organizational life—the parish councils, Holy Name Societies, Choir Societies, Guadalupanas*—so evident in San Antonio.

For illegal immigrants struggling with a foreign language, transience, and economic survival, low levels of community involvement are understandable.[52] Among more established Mexican Americans, obstacles or disincentives to participation in civic affairs may be less evident, though several will be examined here. One source of weak communal ties among Mexicans generally in Los Angeles is the palpable lack of a sense of turf, which their counterparts in San Antonio so clearly enjoy. For despite Southern California's long and distinctive Hispanic heritage, Mexicans are not especially at home there. As noted earlier, East LA still bears the traces of previous ethnic influxes. Mexican neighborhoods in Los Angeles have about them a feeling of ethnic succession reminiscent of cities back East. A curious observation, perhaps, in light of the pervasive view that ethnicity is of little importance in California. But compared to San Antonio, Mexicans in Los Angeles are much more caught up in a long-term process of absorption into a new and alien environment.

This is true not only on the neighborhood and parish level, but also on the broader civic plane. Missing for Mexicans in Los Angeles are historical landmarks, like the Alamo or San Fernando Cathedral, which visibly link Mexicans to the day-to-day life of the metropolis. The throne of the archbishop for what is now the largest Catholic diocese in the nation is housed in St. Vibiana's Cathedral, hidden away on downtown's skid row. That Vibiana is not a Spanish name itself points to the gulf between the Church and Mexicans in Los Angeles. Nor is there any citywide tradition comparable to San Antonio's weeklong annual Fiesta, however double-edged that celebration of Texan valor may be for Mexican Americans. In-

---

* A women's parish-level service organization devoted to Our Lady of Guadalupe, patron saint of Mexico.

stead of pervading the city, as it does in San Antonio, the Mexican heritage exists at the margins of Los Angeles's civic life. Officially acknowledged and even preserved, as with the old pueblo at Olvera Street, Mexican culture and institutions are encapsulated and overwhelmed by the dominant Anglo culture.

Along with this weaker sense of turf, Mexicans in Los Angeles also lack the anger toward Anglos that in San Antonio is so bound up with the group's identity. Chicano activists in Los Angeles acknowledge this, and complain that the climate and "laid-back lifestyle" make it difficult to arouse their people to political action. Or as an Alinsky organizer familiar with both cities puts it, "There just isn't the edge to Mexican politics in Los Angeles that there is in San Antonio."[53] As I will explore in subsequent chapters, this factor contributes importantly to the relative lack of Mexican-American leadership in Los Angeles.

Immigrants themselves seem relatively content. In an exhaustive longitudinal study of Latino immigrants in the United States, Alejandro Portes and Robert Bach found that despite frustrated occupational aspirations and some perceived discrimination, Mexican immigrants are overwhelmingly satisfied with life here—a finding consistently reported in numerous other studies.[54] Indeed, barrio activists complained to me of the frustrations trying to organize immigrants, whether legal or illegal. But the situation was described most aptly by a middle-aged Mexican-American homeowner in East LA, citing the typical response when he urges his neighbors to join the community organization in which he is active:

> Why should I join your organization? Where I came from I had no toilets, no streets, and no sidewalks. Here I have a nice house and all those things. ¡Es paraíso!

If there is anger among Mexicans in Los Angeles, it is to be found among Chicano activists. Stymied by the complacency of the barrio, these typically well-educated individuals are also resentful of the price they feel they have paid for social and economic advancement in this Anglo-dominated society. The result, as I will examine in the chapter on protest politics, has often been impulsive, sometimes destructive political behavior.

REFORM POLITICS:
AN OCTOPUS WITHOUT TENTACLES

Lack of turf and anger are not the only impediments to the political organization of Mexican Americans in Los Angeles. One must also consider the metropolitan region's political culture and structure. Earlier this century, in the period leading up to the First World War, California underwent perhaps the most thoroughgoing overhaul of its political institutions of any state in the Union. A reform movement led by Progressives like Hiram Johnson successfully sought to end the Southern Pacific Railroad's stranglehold on the state's politics. Their objective was to eliminate the organizational basis of the railroad's statewide political machine, aptly described and named in Frank Norris's novel *The Octopus*. To undermine the hold of railroad lobbyists on the state legislature, the executive branch was strengthened. But the primary target of Progressive reformers, in California and elsewhere, was the political parties, the domination of which gave the Southern Pacific a rock-solid political base up and down the social hierarchy of the vast state. Party nominating conventions were replaced by primary elections. Candidates were permitted to compete for the nomination of more than one party in the same primary. In general elections, party labels were stricken from the ballots. And at the local level, the role of the parties was eliminated altogether, with all municipal and county elections made nonpartisan.

Civil service was also part of the reform agenda. Like their counterparts in the burgeoning cities of the Midwest and East, California Progressives were simultaneously alarmed by the emergence of patronage-based political machines among the immigrant laboring classes and convinced of the power of expert knowledge. But unlike their counterparts back East, the California Progressives were extraordinarily successful. Not only did they loosen the grip of the Southern Pacific on California politics, they virtually eliminated the possibility of political machines developing.[55]

The legacy of such reforms is still evident today. The weakened political institutions fashioned by the Progressives have, along with increased demands for services, created a vacuum filled by huge bureaucracies that have taken on lives of their own. Government agencies in Los Angeles are notoriously well insulated from elected officials, and local government has alternately been praised for its professionalism and denounced for inattention to the will of the people. (We are obviously now in the latter mode.) One paradoxical result has been the notorious careers of various Los Angeles police chiefs, whose independence from elected officials has allowed them to use the post as a base from which to launch their own political careers. In response, Mayor Bradley has over the years complained about the constraints on his powers to discipline bureaucrats, and has joined various city councillors in calling for measures to increase control by elected officials over department heads. Thus, the furor over Police Chief Daryl Gates's role in the Rodney King incident and the subsequent riots has been the latest installment in a long-standing debate over the merits of the city's rigid civil service system.[56]

By contrast, few public servants in San Antonio have ever been criticized for their overzealous pursuit of bureaucratic or professional prerogatives; the occasional complaints one hears there about unresponsive bureaucrats are typically directed at the very idea of civil service. But in Los Angeles, where one hears frequent gripes about "the bureaucracy," the unquestioned civil service norm remains beyond reproach.

The difference between these two regimes is even manifested physically. As described earlier, the sprawling, turreted Bexar County courthouse looms over one end of San Antonio's Main Plaza, its shadowy interior bustling with activity that is an extension of the downtown traffic just outside. The Los Angeles County Hall of Administration, by contrast, is a huge, polished blank box sitting amidst freeways, parking lots, and a pleasant but deserted public park. Inside, its marble-walled corridors gleam under antiseptically bright lights, and in the empty coolness one hears on a typical day little but the hum of air conditioning.

The number and type of electoral opportunities available under these two regimes are also quite different. Whereas in San Antonio there is an elaborate hierarchy of elective posts, including many easily contested minor offices with small constituencies, elective offices in Los Angeles are limited to a few high-visibility positions with large jurisdictions, campaigning for which requires substantial resources. Even on the Westside, where raising money may not be a problem, opportunities are so limited that the politicians there are in electoral gridlock, waiting (for the most part patiently) for colleagues to move up or out, thereby freeing up a precious political commodity—an elective office. As one Westside politico told the Los Angeles Times, "If you think the freeways are crowded, look at the political pathways."[57] This situation could partially be attributed to the huge scale of the City and County of Los Angeles, but it is much more fundamentally a legacy of the Progressives, for whom the short ballot limiting the number of elective offices was another way of making government more efficient and professional.

Today in Los Angeles, one of the lowest rungs on the electoral ladder is a seat on the school board. The second largest in the nation, the Los Angeles Unified School District actually encompasses more territory than the City of Los Angeles itself.[58] Until 1982 all seven seats on the board were contested at large. Since then, however, the LAUSD has been carved up into seven single-member districts. Yet getting elected remains a formidable undertaking. Each of the seven districts has a greater population than a state assembly or even a city council district. In 1983, when the smallest district had more than 510,000 residents, a young Mexican American spent about $160,000 getting elected to a school board seat paying $12,000 a year. Today, the average size of these seven districts has grown to more than 601,000.

With fifteen single-member districts—each with less than two-fifths the number of residents in each LAUSD district—a seat on the Los Angeles City Council would appear to be more within reach of Mexican Americans. Yet quite the opposite has been the case. For most of this century the council was simply unattainable for the city's Mexican Americans. Prior to 1985, only one Mexican American had served on the council this century (Edward Roybal from 1949 to 1962).[59] From 1962 to 1985 no Mexican American sat on the council. As I will argue in chapter 10, there are many reasons for this hiatus, but certainly one major obstacle has been the enormous resources necessary to mount a campaign. In the mid-1980s even a lackluster effort for a council seat cost in excess of $200,000. About the same amount of money was then necessary for a competitive assembly race.[60] By the early 1990s, a contested California state senate race might well cost the candidate as much as $700,000—more than the cost of running for Congress in the same territory.[61] By contrast, in San Antonio in the mid-1980s, a city council race cost about at most $100,000. Indeed, as I pointed out in the previous chapter, a political novice can get himself elected to the Texas House of Representatives from San Antonio with minimal cash and a concerted effort walking the district each night with his wife and children. Moreover, for his hotly contested and successful first mayoral bid in 1981, Henry Cisneros raised $247,000—about the cost of a state assembly or city council campaign in Los Angeles.[62]

Finally, the most powerful elective post in Los Angeles has been the least accessible. The five-person county board of supervisors presides over a land area nearly four times larger than the State of Rhode Island.[63] And with about 8.9 million residents in 1990, Los Angeles County has a larger population than forty-two states. Exercising both legislative and executive powers, these five supervisors preside over a $12 billion-plus budget and are easily the most powerful elected officials in all of Southern California. Chosen from a single-member district for a four-year term, each supervisor represents about 1.8 million individuals—aside from statewide elected offices, the largest constituencies in California.[64] Such numbers make county government in Los Angeles like no other in the nation. One of the few comparable jurisdictions would be Harris County (Houston) Texas, whose four county commissioners represent districts with only two-fifths as many residents as the districts of their Los Angeles counterparts.[65] Such huge jurisdictions mean that serious candidates for the Los Angeles board must typically raise between $1 million and $2 million.[66] Consequently, the average tenure of county supervisors in the post–World War II period has been fourteen years; they typically retire or die in office.[67] Since 1960, only three incumbents have been defeated for reelection.[68] In any event, no Spanish-surnamed individual served on the board from 1875 to 1991,[69] at which time, as I will discuss in chapter 10, a Voting Rights suit led to the election of City Councillor Gloria Molina to the board.

In the early 1970s, this lack of entry points into the political arena led to an effort to carve a separate Mexican-American municipality out of the huge segment of the East LA barrio lying within unincorporated Los Angeles County. In a strategy later followed by the Los Angeles homosexuals who succeeded in incorporating the City of West Hollywood, Mexican-American politicos and activists felt the need to create a manageable enclave where political skills and leadership could be developed. At that time, practically the only such forum available was the East Los Angeles Junior Chamber of Commerce, which functioned as the de facto training ground for several Mexican politicians. Pragmatic politicos were mindful of the advantages of controlling their own municipal budget and visible political base, and Chicano activists were eager to implement their separatist agenda. Together these two groups might have prevailed, but they were opposed by Mexican-American homeowners who feared that the proposed municipality's weak economic base would result in higher property taxes.[70]

Exacerbating these structural barriers to entry into Los Angeles politics, for Mexicans or any other group, has been the centralization of power in Sacramento. In the late 1970s this development was fueled by Proposition 13, the property-tax limitation measure that resulted in increased state funding of services previously financed at the local level.[71] And during the 1980s, of course, this trend was reinforced as federal budgetary constraints shifted more and more burdens to the states.

In California, the state assembly has been at the center of these events. And critical to its institutional development was Jesse Unruh, who as assembly speaker in the late 1950s transformed that position into one of major importance statewide. Before Unruh, the speaker was a cipher easily elbowed aside by well-organized lobbyists plying their trade directly with individual legislators. As journalist Lou Cannon has pointed out, this situation emerged in the vacuum created when the Progressives dismantled the state's political parties. To make legislators less susceptible to lobbyists, Unruh doubled his colleagues' salaries and increased their perks. And to reduce dependence on lobbyists for information, he increased the size and quality of assembly staff. In essence, Big Daddy (as he was known in those days) professionalized the California Assembly—though not so much that he, or subsequent speakers, would lose control of its members.[72]

The principal means of that control, not surprisingly, has been money. The extraordinary costs of political campaigns in California are, of course, legendary. It was, after all, Speaker Unruh who said, "Money is the mother's milk of politics."[73] And he knew whereof he spoke. As speaker, he interposed himself between lobbyists and legislators, collecting funds from the former and channeling them to favored assembly colleagues.

Through most of the 1980s and into the 1990s, Unruh's successor as speaker, Willie Brown, has also been a powerful figure, controlling millions distributed to politicians throughout the state. As a result, decisions about running for office are determined more by an individual's ties to the speaker and key elected officials in Sacramento than his or her ties to the jurisdiction to be represented. Reflecting these political realities, general election winners in 1982 assembly races received over 92 percent of their contributions from out-of-district sources. Indeed, two successful candidates that year received 100 percent of their campaign funds from outside their districts.[74] Subsequent research suggests this trend has continued.[75]

Yet these dynamics are hardly confined to assembly races. Indeed, a good example of how the California system functions is the ascendance of Nancy Pelosi, who in a 1987 special election won the seat representing San Francisco's 5th congressional district. Pelosi had never run for office before, but as a former Democratic Party fund-raiser, she had the support of party insiders and elected officials. As Congressional Quarterly's *Politics in America* puts it, "When she began her campaign for the House, Pelosi was more familiar to national Democratic activists than to San Francisco voters."[76] Nevertheless, she was able to beat a strong grassroots opponent.

Thus, there is a definite Sacramento tilt to Los Angeles politics. Yet at the same time much of the money driving the process statewide comes from Los Angeles. Indeed, the concentrations of wealth in the metropolitan region are enough to attract fund-raisers from around the nation.[77] When accompanied by limited electoral opportunities, the effect locally is to drive up campaign costs even further.

A good example is the 1982 campaign of former Students for a Democratic Society (SDS) activist Tom Hayden. To win a seat representing Santa Monica in the state assembly, Hayden spent slightly more than $2 million, about two-thirds of which came from his then wife, actress Jane Fonda. Considering Hayden's access to the enormous resources of the film and entertainment industry, one might well ask whether his campaign was a symptom or a cause of the high cost of politics in Los Angeles.

Heavy reliance on electronic media, especially television, contributes substantially to the high cost of campaigns in California. Yet in many local contests television is frequently too costly to be used efficiently. In Los Angeles, campaigns that are not city- or countywide seldom use television. But they do rely heavily on direct mail, which accounts for the preponderance of expenditures in such local campaigns.[78] Indeed, in recent years computer-targeted direct mail has been developed into a political art form by such Los Angeles politicians as Congressmen Henry Waxman and Howard Berman—the so-called Waxman-Berman machine.

Direct mail contributes not only to the high cost of politics in Los Angeles, it also feeds an already highly issue-oriented political environment. Here again, the stage was set generations ago by California Progressives, whose reforms were based in part on the judgment that political parties hindered rational debate about issues. At the same time, the Progressives' commitment to direct democracy led them to advocate reliance on initiatives and referenda in state and local elections.

To a large extent the Progressives were correct in their analysis and successful in their efforts. For without strong party organizations that invariably try to hold themselves together by blurring issues, California politics has become very issue-oriented. Further contributing to this development have been the media, which have moved into the information vacuum created by the dismantling of the parties. Playing a critical role in these developments has been the *Los Angeles Times,* which has not only helped create this highly issue-driven polity but to a remarkable extent also determines which issues go on the agenda. And now computerized direct mail reinforces these tendencies by permitting politicians to address narrowly targeted voter groups while minimizing the risk that contradictory positions will get exposed in high-visibility media.

BLACKS, JEWS, AND MEXICANS

The critical political resources in Los Angeles today are therefore issues and money. Mexican Americans lack both. Much better situated are Jews and blacks. Jews tend to be issue-oriented liberals willing and able to contribute to candidates who defend their interests and champion their causes. Blacks lack financial resources but identify themselves, and are identified by others, with the issues on the liberal agenda.[79]

Indeed, blacks and Jews, respectively about 11 and 6 percent of the metropolitan area's population,[80] have joined in a long-lived coalition, personified by five-term mayor Tom Bradley. To be sure, there have in recent years been tensions in Los Angeles between blacks and Jews over racial quotas. The Rev. Jesse Jackson's relationship to Louis Farrakhan has further strained relations, with Bradley caught very much in the middle. Indeed, the mayor managed to offend both coalition partners by, on the one hand, failing to repudiate the anti-Semitic black Muslim and, on the other, subsequently refusing to endorse Jackson's presidential candidacy.[81] Black disaffection with Bradley has also been evident in two unsuccessful gubernatorial efforts. In 1982 the mayor's razor-thin loss to George Deukmejian was attributed to modest black turnout; in 1986 turnout for Bradley among Los Angeles blacks was even lower.[82] Though badly weakened by the defeat of city council allies (one of them in the black district Bradley himself had represented for a decade on the council) in the 1987 elections, Bradley managed two years later to get reelected to a fifth term—albeit by a slim, 51 percent majority against what should have been token opposition.[83]

Meanwhile, Mexicans remain on the sidelines and have yet to position themselves to be part of any new governing coalition. Blacks and Jews may look to Mexicans for support on specific issues, but the group's reputation for low turnouts and bitter factionalism means they are viewed as unreliable allies.

Jews are also wary of the social conservatism of this overwhelmingly Catholic group. In the mid-1960s the Grebler study found Mexican-American parents in both Los Angeles and San Antonio stressing that the schools teach their children *"la disciplina* [discipline]."[84] Two decades later, similar values were in evidence when a young Mexican American who had run unsuccessfully for the Los Angeles School Board confided to me that his conservative positions on school discipline and sex education alienated many otherwise sympathetic "Westside Jews."[85]

Abortion is a potentially more divisive issue. Opinion surveys consistently reveal Jews to be the most pro-choice group in America. Mexicans, on the other hand, are decidedly uneasy about abortion. They are in fact one of the least pro-choice groups.[86] Yet as I will explore in chapter 9, Mexican Americans are not generally very visible or vocal in their opposition to abortion. Nevertheless, the issue looms as a real source of strain between the two groups.

Despite such points of tension, Jews and Mexicans in Los Angeles have long-standing ties. In the 1950s and 1960s, Mexican-American political breakthroughs were due largely to the resources and skills of Jewish sponsors. This was true of Edward Roybal's election to the city council in 1949, and of his subsequent move to Congress in 1962.[87] The other rising Mexican-American star of that era was Enrique ("Hank") López. López's unsuccessful bid for California secretary of state in 1958, the second Mexican-American statewide candidacy in the twentieth century, was initiated and advanced not by Mexican Americans but by a Los Angeles-based group of liberals and Jews. A similar coalition was behind the 1967 election of a Mexican-American college professor, Dr. Julian Nava, to an at-large seat on the Los Angeles School Board.[88] And in 1982, the renowned Waxman-Berman organization played an important role in the election to Congress of San Gabriel Valley politician Matthew Martínez.

Yet such recent efforts by individual politicians or businessmen belie the fact that as a group, Jews in Los Angeles today may be less invested in Mexican Americans than ever. The major Jewish organizations do little more than sponsor interethnic dialogues or joint trips to Jerusalem and Mexico City, activities which one Jewish leader describes as "embarrassingly naive." This same individual asserted that Jews know of or care about Mexicans only insofar as they are domestics or garment workers.

This disengagement may derive from Jewish frustrations. As a result of recent strains in the Jewish-black coalition, some Jews in Los Angeles are clearly tempted to regard Mexicans as a new minority partner that might help revive the glory days of the civil rights era. But there is too much evidence to the contrary. Despite the best efforts of Chicano activists, most Jews realize that Mexicans are not another racial minority group like blacks. A television producer said a mouthful one day when she observed, "Hispanics just aren't hip." Or as a member of Mayor Bradley's inner circle put it, denouncing the venality of local Mexican-American politicians, "The problem with Mexican Americans is they aren't a cause the way blacks are."

For their part, Mexican Americans in Los Angeles are extremely wary of Jews. The former, as I have already indicated, are decidedly uncomfortable with the liberal positions Jews typically take on social issues. Moreover, one discerns among Mexican Americans echoes of anti-Semitism similar to what one hears from blacks.[89] At a minimum, there is a widespread concern among Mexican Americans in Los Angeles about remaining independent of Jewish interests—albeit while bemoaning, as I will discuss shortly, the special attention Jews have bestowed on blacks.

Of much greater concern are relations between blacks and Mexicans in Los Angeles. In the mid-1960s the Grebler study presented survey data revealing Mexican Americans to be unenthusiastic about social contact with blacks.[90] In that same period, other survey research found that Mexican Americans in Los Angeles reacted as negatively to the Watts riot as Anglos did.[91] Then in 1969, Mexican-American voters cast the majority of their ballots against City Councillor Tom Bradley when he challenged conservative mayor Sam Yorty. Four years later Bradley's more moderate—and successful—challenge to Yorty succeeded in capturing a bare majority of the Mexican-American vote.[92]

Two decades later, Mexican-American voters may have grown more comfortable supporting Bradley as mayor, but overall relations between the two groups are more strained than ever—and likely to grow worse. Since the War on Poverty, Mexican Americans have complained that blacks have gotten more than their fair share of federal program benefits. More generally, Latinos have long resented black resistance to their being included under the provisions of the Voting Rights Act or the 1991 Civil Rights Act. Such strains within the civil rights coalition have typically gone unnoted by outsiders. But they broke out into full public view in the spring of 1990, when Latino groups threatened to pull out of the Leadership Conference on Civil Rights because the organization's black and labor members were unsupportive of arguments that sanctions on employers hiring illegal immigrants written into the Immigration Reform and Control Act of 1986 had resulted in discrimination against Latinos generally.[93]

Today at the local level in Los Angeles, such tensions manifest themselves in Latino complaints about the overrepresentation of blacks (based on their population) in public sector jobs. Indeed, the data confirm this charge, if not necessarily the frequently heard claim that blacks have an unfair advantage on civil service exams because they face no language barrier.[94]

As the 1992 riots made clear, for their part, blacks in Los Angeles feel under siege on several fronts. For example, relations between blacks and Asians, especially Koreans, whose entrepreneurial efforts in black neighborhoods are daily sources of annoyance and embarrassment, are more tense than those between blacks and Latinos. Yet the more pervasive and serious threat comes from Latinos, especially Mexicans, whose already large numbers continue to increase in areas such as South-Central, where the rioting began.[95]

Blacks in Los Angeles complain that Mexican immigrants are taking jobs away from them.[96] Such charges are widely disputed,[97] but what cannot be challenged is that blacks feel themselves to be at a competitive disadvantage to Mexicans. Also not subject to dispute is the fact that such immigrants are moving into traditionally black neighborhoods in South-Central Los Angeles, crowding several families into single-family dwellings, and consequently dispersing long-established black neighborhoods. In the process Mexicans are putting their own stamp on what were once regarded as specifically black institutions. For example, Martin Luther King County Hospital, built in the wake of the Watts riot, now has a predominantly Latino clientele and staff and is frequently cited as a facility that has been "taken over" by Latinos.[98] Not surprisingly, the area's recently retired county supervisor, an astute Anglo politician who for years skillfully catered to his black constituents, hired Mexican-American aides. In the same neighborhoods, Alinsky organizers trying to build a multiethnic community organization have encountered difficulties with language issues and other points of contention between blacks and Latinos, Central Americans as well as Mexicans.

Such strains have emerged dramatically in Compton, a separately incorporated municipality just south of Watts. Compton's predicament is evident as one drives down narrow rutted streets of shabby bungalows, fitted with security grates and laundry spread to dry on bushes (as one finds in any Latin American country). The county courthouse in downtown Compton has more security—metal detectors, guards, plexiglass shields—than the average airport. Once a blue-collar white suburb, Compton turned black and is now experiencing a massive influx from Mexico. In 1990, enrollment in the public schools was about 41 percent black and 57 percent Hispanic, which represents a substantial Hispanic increase in just a few years. With a murder rate higher than the City of Los Angeles, Compton's Latino merchants, many of whom speak little English, have banded together to hire security guards for protection. The result, according to staff at the Los Angeles regional office of the U.S. Civil Rights Commission, has been frequent clashes between these hired thugs and black vandals. Local religious professionals report that battles between black and Latino youths are routine. Indeed, such conflicts break out sporadically throughout the metropolitan area. Yet almost miraculously—and much to the wonderment of law enforcement officials—black and Latino gangs avoided direct confrontation during the 1992 riots.

Away from the streets, in the halls of government, black and Mexican elected officials in Los Angeles enjoy extremely good relations. But these reflect the accidents of personal history and, as I will explore later, the politicians' lack of accountability to their constituents. In any event, during the 1980 redistricting, the conflicts that inevitably emerged between the two groups were quite subdued—in no small measure because state assembly speaker Willie Brown, who is black, had the political sense to appoint as chair of the redistricting committee East LA assemblyman Richard Alatorre. And while Mexican Americans in Los Angeles gained an assembly and two congressional seats, blacks lost none.

The more recent 1990 redistricting has gone somewhat less smoothly. For while the black population shrank in relative size, the Hispanic population—absolutely and relatively—has continued to grow. Because this growth is driven by high fertility and illegal immigration, it will be some time before Hispanics translate their numbers into actual voting strength, thereby providing a much-needed buffer between black and Hispanic political aspirations. Nevertheless, as Mexican-American leaders well know, their population numbers do get figured into redistricting calculations, which rely on census data that the Constitution requires to include "persons," not just legal residents or citizens. As a result, at least one black on the Los Angeles City Council has complained about the possibility of being redistricted out of his seat on account of "wetbacks." Yet on balance the 1990 redistricting has been remarkably free of rancor.

This burgeoning population presents heady opportunities for a group long relegated to the sidelines by its relatively small size—and by the political successes enjoyed by blacks quite disproportionate to their numbers. Indeed, Mexican-American leaders tend to have an exaggerated sense of confidence, even arrogance, as they look at the demographic tidal wave on which they find themselves and assume it will give them an easy ride to financial and political success. But some are not so sure. As Danny Villanueva, president and general manager of Spanish-language television station KMEX in Los Angeles, warned in 1985: "Numbers are like opium. Our leaders look at them and say that, by 1990, we're going to be 20 or 30 million people, and therefore, we will have power."[99] Genuine political power will, of course, await political mobilization. But in the interim, Mexican-American leaders will also have to convince Anglo elites, especially liberal Jews, that their group's problems make them worthy of special attention—a task made no easier by the powerful assimilative processes described earlier, to say nothing of the inevitable comparisons with blacks.

It is this *political* competition between blacks and Mexicans for the support of Anglo liberals that in the years ahead will be as important, if not more so, than the economic competition that has to date received so

much attention.[100] For as Mexican-American leaders in Los Angeles rue-
fully observe, "There is only room for one minority in this town." This rivalry makes Mexican-American politics in Los Angeles quite different
from that in San Antonio. Indeed, it offers Mexicans in Los Angeles, and
throughout California, much stronger incentives to define themselves as
a racial minority group. These incentives could result in coalition efforts
between blacks and Mexicans, but as I have indicated, they might also result in severe strains between the two groups.

THE ALATORRE-TORRES CLIQUE:
MORE PARACHUTES THAN GRASSROOTS

The high entry costs into Los Angeles's competitive political arena have
placed a small group of Mexican-American insiders in a highly strategic
position. State Senator Art Torres and City Councillor Richard Alatorre,
both career politicians from East LA, form the nucleus; the rest include
staff aides and other officeholders, who tend to be former aides whose
careers have at one time or another been advanced by Alatorre and Torres. At various points over the past decade the group has included Alatorre, Torres, an aide to Torres who also served on the Los Angeles School
Board, and a former aide to Alatorre who went on to the state assembly.
Former UAW official and now congressman Esteban Torres should be
mentioned here as an Alatorre-Torres ally, though hardly a protégé. Notably excluded from this list is recently retired East LA congressman Edward Roybal, whose longevity provided him with a base independent of
Alatorre and Torres. Indeed, in recent years Roybal and, in particular, the
director of his Los Angeles district office succeeded in getting Roybal's
daughter, Lucille Roybal-Allard, elected to the state assembly and subsequently to Congress. Over the years they also provided critical support
to former assemblywoman and city councillor Gloria Molina, particularly
in her recently successful bid for the county board of supervisors.
Roybal and his coterie thus emerged as a counter to the Alatorre-Torres
group. So the latter is hardly the only locus of political activity among
Mexicans in Los Angeles, but it is very visible and quite typical in its
operations.

Through their contacts in Sacramento and elsewhere in the state, Alatorre and Torres have access to the substantial resources necessary to run
for political office. And although the growing middle and upper-middle
classes have in recent years made fund-raising among Mexican Americans somewhat more fruitful, most political money for Mexican candidates still comes from non-Mexicans. Such reliance on outside money is

hardly unique to Mexicans, but as I will explore in the next chapter, for a group still struggling to attain political maturity, problems of dependency and accountability inevitably arise. In any event, without the support of the Alatorre-Torres group, or one of the other East LA gatekeepers, few, if any, Mexican Americans could contemplate waging a credible campaign for even the lowliest office in Los Angeles.

One of the more salient characteristics of the group is its clannish exclusivity. Members refer to it among themselves as *"la familia* [the family]"; but to an outsider trying to learn about it, it resembles nothing so much as an exclusive high school social clique. My perception is echoed in the comments of several Mexican-American women who left the group because they felt excluded from the action by their male colleagues, and who denounced as "prom queens" the few women who stayed on with the men. Both expressions hark back to the East LA neighborhoods from which many clique members come. As an Anglo official of the California Democratic Party observed, "They all grew up together." Taking advantage of postwar educational opportunities not available to their parents, some clique members went to local colleges together, where they continued to see one another and, in a few cases, dated the same women. As they settled down and started their own families, they made one another *compadres.**

Nevertheless, it would be a mistake to think of the Alatorre-Torres clique as strongly rooted in the neighborhoods. In a community so much in flux—and consequently with such weak institutions—one could hardly expect otherwise. Indeed, I will argue later that the clique's power depends heavily on the lack of organizational life in East LA and other Mexican neighborhoods.

That Mexican-American politics in Los Angeles has relatively weak community roots was suggested more than two decades ago by the Grebler study, which found that low-income Mexicans in Los Angeles were half as likely as their San Antonio counterparts to get help from kin about how to deal with problems at city hall.[10] More recently, research by the Southwest Voter Registration Education Project indicates that Mexican-American adult citizens are more likely to participate in politics in San Antonio—especially in such relatively demanding activities as attending meetings and working in campaigns—than in East LA.

My own fieldwork confirms such survey findings. For example, in San Antonio Mexican-American politicians equip squads of loyal followers

---

* Literally "coparents." For a fuller explanation of this special type of godparent relationship in Mexican culture, see page 133.

with distinctive caps and T-shirts and send them out in borrowed pick-up trucks to post signs on neighborhood lawns. Indeed, as I will explore in a subsequent chapter on friends-and-neighbors politics, such activities actually grow out of athletic teams sponsored by Mexican-American politicians in San Antonio. By contrast, the Los Angeles clique eschews such efforts, and devotes the bulk of campaign resources to computerized direct-mail operations. Even bumper stickers are relatively rare in local races in Los Angeles. Yet just such paraphernalia and hoopla help draw volunteers into campaigns, especially among less affluent and unsophisticated constituents. In fact, as I will discuss later, the Alatorre-Torres clique has at times avoided relying on campaign volunteers.

There are many other indicators of these weak community ties. I have already remarked on the definite Sacramento orientation of Mexican-American politics in Los Angeles. Similarly suggestive is the fact that some of the elected officials representing East LA maintain their sole local offices in the downtown business district. But because East LA is some distance from downtown LA, barrio residents needing to see these elected officials face either traffic jams and parking expenses (if they have a car), or an exceedingly time-consuming journey (if they take the bus).

It is also striking that in San Antonio Mexican-American politicians are at pains to "work the churches" and make visible efforts to attend Sunday masses. Yet their Los Angeles counterparts don't even go through the motions. Neither do they identify with specific neighborhoods. Members of the clique are viewed, by Mexicans as well as Anglos, as vaguely representing the vast expanse of East LA, not distinct areas within it. In fact, few if any Mexican-American politicians actually reside in East LA. Instead, they live in places like South Pasadena, immediately adjacent to the barrio but suburban, affluent, and predominantly Anglo.

In this regard, a minor incident is revealing. A Chicana activist who was unsuccessfully trying to get the attention of Alatorre decided to confront him at his home. But unable to determine his exact address, she was forced to scrutinize the mail boxes in a huge apartment complex perched on the hills overlooking East LA. Because Alatorre's apartment was listed in his wife's name, the search would have been in vain, except that the woman happened to spot Alatorre in the parking area. This vignette stands, of course, in striking contrast with San Antonio, where neighborhoods are critical features of the social and political landscape, and Mexican-American politicians have deep and visible ties to specific parishes.

Predictably, Mexican-American politicos in Los Angeles have a distinct carpetbagging mentality. In countless conversations about potential contenders for various offices, I never once heard mention of whether the individuals in question had any ties to the districts they were maneuvering to represent. For example, a Mexican-American woman serving as vice chair of the state Democratic party was rumored to be a potential challenger to an incumbent assemblywoman, an Anglo with a growing Mexican-American constituency in the San Gabriel Valley. Although the district was some twenty miles to the northeast of the Mexican woman's home base in Long Beach, not a single person I talked to considered this anything more than a technicality. It was simply assumed that the challenger would move. The critical question was whether she would get the backing of the Alatorre-Torres clique and, by implication, assembly speaker Willie Brown.

According to their own staff and supporters, several Mexican-American officeholders in Los Angeles have been "parachuted" into the districts they now represent. Since 1982 Congressman Esteban Torres has represented an increasingly Mexican swath of blue-collar suburbs southeast of downtown Los Angeles. As an aide on that 1982 campaign put it, "Torres knew as much about his congressional district at first as he knew about Maui [Hawaii]." Or as a clique staffer said to me, with youthful braggadocio that he could do a better job representing "*la gente* [the people, folk]": "None of these guys here has any community base."

Finally, it is significant that, unlike San Antonio, recruitment into Los Angeles politics is typically not through neighborhood or civic activities or other means of building up a community base. Rather individuals enter politics primarily through the narrow gate of staff work for elected politicians. In such positions the politically ambitious develop the contacts with party officials, political consultants, *and* funders so critical to campaigning in California.[102]

Nor is this likely to change soon, despite much recent talk of resurgent "grassroots" politics in California. Upon closer examination, that resurgence can be traced back not to the grassroots, but to the politicians who initiate such activities for their own ends. Appearing around election time and then quickly disappearing, these efforts lack any organizational life between elections that would allow them to develop independently of their politician-creators. As such, they are the most recent example of a long history of politician-dominated citizen organizations in California.

With such weak community ties, one would expect the Alatorre-Torres clique to be subject to challenge. And it is. Metropolitan Los Angeles is simply too big, its economy too dynamic, its social structure too diverse for one small group, however strategically situated, to totally dominate

Mexican-American politics there. As I will discuss in subsequent chapters on elite-network and protest politics, the clique faces opposition from many quarters: the growing number of young Mexican-American professionals, Mexican-American political entrepreneurs in the Republican Party, disaffected Mexican-American women who were once part of the clique, and leftist Chicano activists. But as I will demonstrate, the nature of the political system in Los Angeles is such that these challengers themselves lack strong community bases. Nevertheless, they have engaged the clique in nasty brawls that have given Mexicans there, as elsewhere, a reputation for infighting and fragmenting their already meager vote.

Yet compared to San Antonio, Mexican-American politics in Los Angeles is strikingly well ordered and predictable. The high entry costs have imposed a relative discipline by means of which the clique, with its access to the necessary resources, has often been able to force a consensus as to which Mexican American will run for office. In essence, Mexican politics in Los Angeles is, like politics in California generally, highly specialized and professionalized.

A lawyer who has worked for the Mexican American Legal Defense and Educational Fund (MALDEF) in both cities observed that political wounds are much slower to heal in San Antonio than in Los Angeles. As an example, he noted that the rift between Mexican-American supporters of Jimmy Carter and Ted Kennedy in the 1980 nomination battle was still an issue in San Antonio several years later, while in Los Angeles any such differences were quickly forgotten. As he put it, "They play for keeps in San Antonio."

They play for keeps in San Antonio because politics there is so rooted in the Mexican community that neighborhood passions and rivalries inevitably infect the process. In Los Angeles, by contrast, Mexican-American gatekeepers such as the Alatorre-Torres clique insulate the process from the inevitable swings of community sentiment. The result is a politics cleansed of many, though hardly all, of the petty emotions and venalities so evident in San Antonio; but it is also a politics of insiders, inward-turning and isolated from the social flux that churns about them.

❧ 4 ❧

Paradoxical
Political Outcomes

What did the Voting rights Act actually sut do?

T he previous chapters suggest that Mexican Americans have been
more successful at politics in the harsh socioeconomic environment
of San Antonio than in the more benign context of Los Angeles. Such a
conclusion will undoubtedly surprise many readers. After all, the barriers to political participation facing Mexican Americans in Texas were critical in persuading Congress in 1975 to bring Hispanics throughout the
state under coverage of the Voting Rights Act—whereas at that time
Hispanics in only a few California counties (not including Los Angeles)
gained coverage.[1]

Nevertheless, Mexican-American politicos typically regard their colleagues from Texas as the most experienced, skillful, and successful in the
nation. Occasionally, New Mexicans make a bid for this status. But between Californians and Texans, there is no question that it belongs to the
latter—a fact that arouses reactions from begrudging admiration to jealous scorn on the part of Mexican Americans in California. I am reminded
of the Los Angeles politico who related that when he served in the Carter
administration he always found the Mexican-American politicians from
Texas to be his most resolute and astute allies. More motivated by envy
were the remarks of Richard Alatorre's associates when Henry Cisneros
was being considered as a possible running mate for Walter Mondale in
1984: instead of applauding the success of the Texan, they cavalierly dis-

missed him as a "lightweight." For their part, Mexican-American politicos from Texas look upon their California cousins with some wariness and
see them as soft and co-opted, more interested in getting paid than getting elected.

In this chapter, I will scrutinize the evidence on Mexican-American
political outcomes in San Antonio and Los Angeles, and in Texas and
California more generally. That evidence reveals that Mexican Americans
in San Antonio and Texas have indeed been more successful in politics
than their counterparts in Los Angeles and California for quite some time.
In fact, Mexican Americans in Texas were doing better than their
California cousins in 1975, the year Texas was brought under the Voting
Rights Act. Having established that Texas has been a more hospitable political environment, I will then examine various explanations why this
should be so. In so doing I will challenge the reductionist tendency to interpret political outcomes as straightforwardly reflecting social and economic dynamics.

Any discussion of the outcomes of political processes must be undertaken with caution. Politics is an enterprise that thrives on ambiguity,
and outcomes are perhaps its most nebulous and ambiguous aspect.
Moreover, as I examine several different indices for Mexican Americans,
it will become apparent that one researcher's outcome is frequently another's input or resource. Yet despite these caveats, the evidence does
confirm the commonsense impressions of Mexican-American politicos
with regard to the relative success of their colleagues in Texas and
California.

VOTER TURNOUT:
NUMBERS AREN'T EVERYTHING

Frequently used as an outcome measure, voter turnout data are worth
examining first—in part, because they appear to challenge the commonsense view just described. Table 4.1 presents the only available turnout
figures for eligible Mexican Americans in San Antonio and Los Angeles.
As these extremely limited data indicate, in two out of three general elections Mexican-American turnout was actually greater in Los Angeles.

These metropolitan-level data are hardly conclusive, but state-level
data also seem to challenge the notion that Texas has proved a more fer-
tile political environment for Mexican Americans than California. The
time-series data in Figure 4.1 (see also Table 4.2) reveal that from 1974
to 1988, Mexican-American turnout in the November election has gen-

TABLE 4.1

Turnout (in Percent) of Eligible[†] Mexican-American Voters in San Antonio and Los Angeles in Selected General Elections

	San Antonio	Los Angeles
1964[a]	38.1 (603)[††]	49.9 (949)
1986[b]	°26.5 (160)	45.4 (259)
1988[b]	49.4 (167)	47.6 (107)

Note:
[†]Eligibility denotes citizen, 18 years or older. [††]Numbers in parentheses are unweighted Ns. °Difference between values for these two metropolitan areas for the designated year is significant at the 95% confidence level.
Sources:
[a]Leo Grebler et al., *The Mexican-American People* (New York: The Free Press, 1970), 564–565. For 1964, San Antonio refers to San Antonio City while Los Angeles refers to Los Angeles County. [b]U.S. Bureau of the Census, Current Population Survey (November 1986 and November 1988), unpublished data tabulated by Survey Research Center, University of California at Berkeley. For 1986 and 1988, data are for metropolitan San Antonio (SMSA) and metropolitan Los Angeles (PMSA).

erally been higher in California than in Texas—though the gap between the two states has been narrowing and in two years (1976 and 1988) turnout in Texas was apparently higher.

So there is some evidence that Los Angeles and California have been the more hospitable political environment for Mexican Americans. But quite aside from the limitations of these data, it is not evident how they are to be interpreted. I have thus far examined these turnout figures as a political outcome measure, but as suggested earlier, they might also be regarded as an input measure.[2] For example, they could be treated as an indicator of political effort, in which case one would presumably want to take into account the generally lower socioeconomic status of Mexican Americans in Texas. Calvo and Rosenstone have done precisely this and demonstrate that, when demographic variables are controlled, Mexican Americans in Texas are actually 7 percent *more* likely to vote than their counterparts in other Southwestern states, including California.[3]

Such findings point to the reason why Mexican Americans have, in fact, been more successful politically in San Antonio and Texas than in Los Angeles and California. The relevant consideration is not simply turnout, but political effort, and beyond that, political efficacy—about which the data we have thus far looked at tell nothing. To get at this question, Mexican Americans must be examined in the overall political environment within which they compete. Specifically, Mexican-American polit-

FIGURE 4.1

Turnout (in Percent) of Eligible° Mexican-American Voters in Texas and
California (November 1974–November 1988)

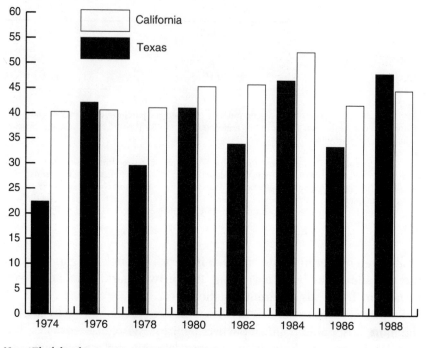

Note: °Eligibility denotes citizen, 18 years or older.
Source: U.S. Bureau of the Census, Current Population Survey (November 1974–November 1988),
unpublished data tabulated by Survey Research Center, University of California at Berkeley.

ical effort must be compared with that of other groups. Once again, the
metropolitan-level data are limited and inconclusive. Table 4.3 presents
turnout data for Mexican Americans, non-Mexican Americans, and blacks
in Los Angeles and San Antonio for general elections in 1986 and 1988
(the only years for which such data are available). In 1986 the turnout
gaps between Mexican-American and both other groups were greater in
San Antonio than in Los Angeles. In 1988, by contrast, those gaps were
greater in Los Angeles.

At the state level, we find additional evidence that Mexican Americans
have been more politically efficacious in Texas than in California. Figures
4.2 and 4.3 compare graphically Mexican-American voter turnout with
that of non-Mexican Americans and blacks in California and Texas general elections from 1974 to 1988. Those data, tabulated in Table 4.4, re-

TABLE 4.2
Turnout (in Percent) of Eligible[†] Mexican-American Voters in Texas and California (November 1974–November 1988)

	Texas	*California*
1974	*22.7 (597)[††]	40.2 (573)
1976	42.0 (612)	40.8 (546)
1978	*29.8 (568)	41.1 (516)
1980	41.0 (722)	45.3 (573)
1982	*34.2 (694)	45.7 (626)
1984	*46.1 (674)	52.6 (602)
1986	*33.6 (739)	41.8 (516)
1988	47.6 (715)	44.5 (307)

Note: [†]Eligibility denotes citizen, 18 years or older. [††]Numbers in parentheses are unweighted Ns. *Difference between values for these two states for designated years is significant at the 95% confidence level.
Source: U.S. Bureau of the Census, Current Population Survey (November 1974–November 1988), unpublished data tabulated by Survey Research Center, University of California at Berkeley.

veal that Mexican Americans in California, unlike their counterparts in Texas, have voted much less than their competitors. While in both states eligible blacks and non-Mexican Americans vote in higher proportions than eligible Mexican Americans, the gaps have been consistently higher in California. In other words, these data suggest that one reason why Mexican Americans in California have been less successful in politics than their cousins in Texas is that they have had stiffer competition.

Such voting data are suggestive, but they fail to reveal other factors that undermine the political efficacy of Mexican Americans in California. For example, because Mexican Americans there are more likely to marry outside the group and are more residentially dispersed than their Texas cousins, they are also less cohesive politically. Moreover, because these data include only individuals eligible to vote, they exclude from consideration a huge segment of the Mexican-American population: noncitizens. Particularly evident in Los Angeles and California, these ineligibles are another factor contributing to the political weakness of Mexican Americans there.

Table 4.5 reveals that in 1988, while Mexican Americans constituted 20.3 percent of all voting-age Texans, they were only 12.9 percent of the electorate that November. Of this disparity, 50 percent was accounted for

TABLE 4.3
Voting Turnout Gaps between Mexican Americans, non-Mexican Americans, and Blacks in the San Antonio and Los Angeles Metropolitan Areas[†] (November 1986 and November 1988)

	1986		1988	
	San Antonio	Los Angeles	San Antonio	Los Angeles
A. Percentage of eligible[††] non-Mex. Ams. voting	°49.9 (263)[†††]	64.0 (2154)	64.6 (235)	71.4 (840)
B. Percentage of eligible blacks voting	42.8 (18)	60.3 (295)	59.4 (22)	68.6 (124)
C. Percentage of eligible Mex. Ams. voting	°26.5 (160)	45.4 (259)	49.4 (167)	47.6 (107)
Gap between non-Mexican Americans and Mexican Americans (between A and C)	23.4	18.6	15.2	23.8
Gap between blacks and Mexican Americans (between B and C)	16.3	14.9	10.0	21.0

Notes: [†]Data are for the San Antonio SMSA and the Los Angeles PMSA. [††]Eligibility denotes citizen, 18 years or older. [†††]Numbers in parentheses are unweighted Ns. °Difference between values for these two metropolitan areas for designated year is significant at the 95% confidence level.
Source: U.S. Bureau of the Census, Current Population Survey (November 1986 and November 1988), unpublished data tabulated by Survey Research Center, University of California at Berkeley.

by noncitizens. In California that same year, Mexican Americans represented 16.9 percent of those old enough to vote, but only 6.8 percent of the November electorate. Fully 71 percent of the disparity in California was accounted for by noncitizens.

The impact of noncitizens is even more dramatic at the metropolitan level. Table 4.6 demonstrates that in 1988, while Mexican Americans constituted 24.4 percent of the voting-age population of metropolitan Los Angeles, they were 9.1 percent of the electorate that November. About three-fourths of this disparity was due to noncitizens. By contrast, Mexican Americans constituted 49.1 percent of the voting-age population in metropolitan San Antonio, and 39.6 percent of the November elec-

FIGURE 4.2

Voting Turnout Gaps (in Percent) between non-Mexican Americans and Mexican Americans in Texas and California (November 1974– November 1988)

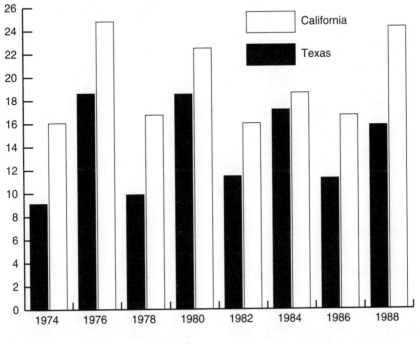

Source:
U.S. Bureau of the Census, Current Population Survey, (November 1974–November 1988), unpublished data tabulated by Survey Research Center, University of California at Berkeley.

torate. But only 24 percent of this disparity was due to the presence of noncitizens.

Because they are based on census surveys that understandably do not gain much cooperation from Mexicans here illegally, these data actually understate the impact of voting-age ineligibles on Mexican-American political strength. And that impact is not due merely to the simple dilution of the group's numbers. For as I will explore later in this chapter, these large numbers of nonvoters exacerbate the already considerable difficulties facing those attempting to organize Mexican Americans politically. Moreover, the impact of these nonvoters is intensified by the extensive efforts under the Voting Rights Act to create Hispanic districts. Due to the presence of so many noncitizens, such districts inevitably have few

TABLE 4.4

Voting Turnout Gaps between Mexican Americans, Non-Mexican Americans, and Blacks in Texas and California (November 1974–November 1988)

		1974	1976	1978
A. Percentage of eligible[†] non-Mex. Ams. voting	CA	*56.2 (7171)[††]	*65.6 (7182)	*57.8 (7270)
	TX	31.8 (3998)	60.7 (3981)	39.7 (3800)
B. Percentage of eligible blacks voting	CA	*51.2 (564)	*57.5 (620)	*51.4 (552)
	TX	24.4 (542)	49.2 (526)	30.7 (456)
C. Percentage of eligible Mexican Americans voting	CA	*40.2 (573)	40.8 (546)	*41.1 (516)
	TX	22.7 (597)	42.0 (612)	29.8 (568)
Gap between non-Mexican Americans & Mex. Ams. (between A & C)	CA	16.0	24.8	16.7
	TX	9.1	18.7	9.9
Gap between blacks & Mexican Americans (between B & C)	CA	11.0	16.7	10.3
	TX	1.7	7.2	0.9

Note:

[†]Eligibility denotes citizen, 18 years or older.

[††]Numbers in parentheses are unweighted Ns.

*Difference between values for these two states for designated years is significant at the 95% confidence level.

Source: U.S. Bureau of the Census, Current Population Survey (November 1974–November 1988), unpublished data tabulated by Survey Research Center, University of California at Berkeley.

TABLE 4.4—*Continued*

1980	1982	1984	1986	1988
°67.8 (7245)	°61.7 (7185)	°71.2 (6681)	°58.5 (5955)	°68.7 (3618)
59.5 (3983)	45.6 (4081)	63.2 (3745)	44.8 (3488)	63.5 (3598)
°59.3 (641)	°58.5 (553)	°69.1 (568)	°53.8 (466)	°65.4 (263)
42.9 (503)	40.9 (503)	57.0 (452)	44.0 (459)	52.7 (468)
45.3 (573)	°45.7 (626)	°52.6 (602)	°41.8 (516)	44.5 (307)
41.0 (722)	34.2 (694)	46.1 (674)	33.6 (739)	47.6 (715)
22.5	16.0	18.6	16.7	24.2
18.5	11.4	17.1	11.2	15.9
14.0	12.8	16.5	12.0	20.9
1.9	6.7	10.9	10.4	5.1

FIGURE 4.3

Voting Turnout Gaps (in Percent) between Blacks and Mexican Americans in
Texas and California (November 1974–November 1988)

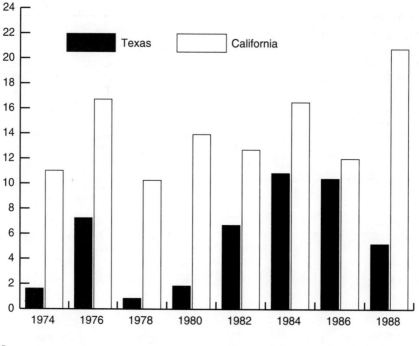

Source:
U.S. Bureau of the Census, Current Population Survey (November 1974–November 1988), unpublished data tabulated by Survey Research Center, University of California at Berkeley.

actual voters. As I will elaborate in chapter 10, such districts are in effect
rotten boroughs that not only raise concerns about the accountability of
those elected from them, but also draw additional attention to already
low levels of voting among Mexican Americans, thereby reinforcing the
group's image of political weakness.[4]

A SHORT DIGRESSION ON
(STATISTICAL) CONTROL FREAKS

Focusing on differential rates of political participation typically arouses
anxieties that invidious comparisons are being drawn across groups. In
response, social scientists frequently attempt to explain such disparities
by means of statistical exercises that control for relevant variables.

TABLE 4.5

Noncitizenship and Mexican-American Registration and Voting Percentages in Texas and California
(November 1988)

	Texas	*California*
A. Mex. Ams. as % of individuals 18 years or older	°20.3 (4825)†	16.9 (4917)
B. Mex. Ams. as % of citizens 18 years or older	°16.6 (4418)	9.3 (4021)
C. Mex. Ams. as % of registered voters	°14.5 (2645)	6.8 (2621)
D. Mex. Ams. as % of electorate	°12.9 (2639)	6.2 (2611)
Gap between A and D	7.4	10.7
Percentage of gap due to noncitizenship	50	71

Notes: †Numbers in parentheses are unweighted Ns. °Difference between values for these two states is significant at the 95% confidence level.
Source: U.S. Bureau of the Census, Current Population Survey (November 1988), unpublished data tabulated by Survey Research Center, University of California at Berkeley.

TABLE 4.6

Noncitizenship and Mexican-American Registration and Voting Percentages in the San Antonio and Los Angeles Metropolitan Areas†
(November 1988)

	San Antonio	*Los Angeles*
A. Mex. Ams. as % of individuals 18 years or older	°49.1 (443)††	24.4 (1357)
B. Mex. Ams. as % of citizens 18 years or older	°46.8 (413)	13.2 (976)
C. Mex. Ams. as % of registered voters	°44.6 (236)	10.3 (657)
D. Mex. Ams. as % of electorate	°39.6 (235)	9.1 (652)
Gap between A and D	9.5	15.3
Percentage of gap due to noncitizenship	24	73

Notes: †Data are for the San Antonio SMSA and the Los Angeles PMSA. ††Numbers in parentheses are unweighted Ns. °Difference between values for these two metropolitan areas is significant at the 95% confidence level.
Source: U.S. Bureau of the Census, Current Population Survey (November 1988), unpublished data tabulated by Survey Research Center, University of California at Berkeley.

A prominent example is the work of Raymond Wolfinger, who in a study of voter turnout in California declares that the "turnout rate of Hispanics seems to lag a bit, but the size of the gap is vastly exaggerated . . ."[5] Wolfinger goes on to assert "Once they are registered to vote, Hispanics go to the polls at nearly the same rate as non-Hispanics."[6] By controlling for intervening variables, Wolfinger manages to reduce the gap in predicted turnout rates between Hispanics and non-Hispanics in California in 1986 to only two percentage points: 55 to 57 percent.[7]

Using the same techniques on a different data set, Carole Uhlaner and her colleagues reach similar conclusions. Arguing against cultural explanations of group differences in voter participation, Uhlaner concludes that statistical controls on several intervening variables "fully account for lower Latino participation rates" in California in 1984[8] and, indeed, that "ethnicity per se has no independent effect" on differential participation rates.[9]

Such analyses offer useful insights into group differences. They are built on a familiar and plausible hypothesis: if education, income, and other socioeconomic variables were equalized across groups, would not political participation rates also be equalized? Yet this approach has its limits. For example, Wolfinger's analysis reveals, as have many others, that once education, income, and other such intervening variables are controlled, blacks actually have a higher predicted turnout rate than whites. Yet having demonstrated this, Wolfinger has nothing to say about why it is so.

More to the point, such approaches tell us nothing about why such group differences in education, income, and similar variables exist in the first place. Indeed, the causes of such variables are treated as exogenous to these models. Nevertheless, important assumptions about these socioeconomic variables and their causes creep into these analyses. In particular, the statistical exercise of equalizing group differences in education and the like gratifies the normative assumption that such group differences are illegitimate or temporary, amenable to melioration with the appropriate policies or, perhaps, the passage of time. In contemporary America such assumptions have enormous and perhaps irrefutable appeal. My point is simply that in the types of analyses described here they remain assumptions, unarticulated and seldom scrutinized.

Thus, we begin with the question: If Mexican Americans were like everyone else, wouldn't they vote like everyone else? But an equally valid question—are Mexican Americans like everyone else?—is seldom squarely posed, much less answered. Consider, for example, naturalization rates. As I have already indicated, noncitizenship is an important factor in the low levels of Mexican-American voting. The approach taken by Wolfinger and Uhlaner verifies this datum and then asserts that if Mexican Americans became citizens at the same rate as other groups, then much of the voting gap between them and others would disappear. Yet the fact remains that naturalization rates have long been lower for Mexicans than for other immigrants.[10] Why is this? Will it change with time? The models employed by Wolfinger and Uhlaner not only fail to answer such questions, they subtly imply that such persistent differences will fade away.

Similar questions can be raised about Mexican-American education, income, and occupational levels. By assuming that these are exogenous to the phenomenon being analyzed, the approach taken by Wolfinger and Uhlaner can foster the impression that, over time, Mexican Americans as a group will inevitably exhibit socioeconomic characteristics similar to those of other Americans. But this impression is questionable and misleading, particularly under conditions of continued mass immigration of relatively poor and uneducated newcomers from Mexico.

Perhaps most fundamentally, such models are by themselves inadequate for a complete understanding of the ongoing dynamics of Mexican-American politics. For they obscure the commonsense perception that residents of Mexican-American neighborhoods (especially in Southern California) do not vote in numbers proportionate to other groups and communities. Politics is, above all, an endeavor dealing in perceptions: those of the gubernatorial candidate who knows he cannot expect even the strongest East LA politician to deliver many votes for his campaign; or those of the White House aide described earlier, who knew that his strongest political allies were from Texas, not California. It is worth emphasizing that the persistent perception of those on the ground—who cannot, and do not wish to, control for intervening variables—is that Mexican Americans are weak politically.

OFFICEHOLDING:
LESS THAN MEETS THE EYE

Compared with voter turnout, political officeholding seems a fairly reliable and straightforward index of political strength. And when the political efficacy of Mexican Americans in San Antonio and Texas is measured by the number of offices to which they have been elected, it appears much greater than that of their counterparts in Los Angeles and California. The embodiment of this assertion is of course Henry Cisneros, whose eight-year mayoral reign (1981–1989), though marred at the end by personal problems, verged on the triumphant. Still the most prominent Mexican

American in national public life, Cisneros's stature is unrivaled by any Mexican-American elected official in Los Angeles, much less California.

Granted, Cisneros was the first Mexican-American mayor of San Antonio elected since 1842. Indeed, with no Mexican American as yet succeeding him, Cisneros remains the only Mexican-American mayor of modern San Antonio. But Mexican Americans have captured many other major offices in that city. In 1978, for example, Albert Bustamente, the son of South Texas farmworkers, was elected county judge—the chief elected and administrative officer of Bexar County—and held that office until 1984, when he was elected to Congress. Two years after Bustamente was first elected county judge, a Mexican American was elected to the important, patronage-laden post of county sheriff. Mexican Americans have also been elected to such countywide posts as county clerk and tax assessor-collector. Then there are the scores of Mexican Americans elected in recent years to other local offices: justices of the peace, constables, city councillors, county commissioners, and school board members. By the time Cisneros became mayor, Mexican-American officeholding had reached 80 percent of parity with the group's proportion of the population (see Table 4.7, which does not even include school board members).[11]

To be sure, this figure reflects substantial gains during the previous decade. But it would be a mistake to overlook the significant level of officeholding enjoyed by Mexican Americans in San Antonio for some time before that. For example, in 1970 Mexican Americans had achieved more than 50 percent of parity in officeholding (see Table 4.7). Even during the heyday of the Anglo-elite-dominated Good Government League in the 1950s and 1960s, Mexican Americans won important elective offices. In 1955 Henry B. González ran countywide and got elected to the State Senate. Six years later he went to Congress, becoming the nation's first Mexican-American congressman. Also in 1955 Albert Peña was elected as one of four Bexar County commissioners, and he, too, went on to become a nationally prominent Mexican-American leader.

Finally, throughout this period, Mexican Americans were consistently being elected to the city council. Indeed, the number of such Mexican-American officeholders steadily increased throughout the postwar era, averaging overall about one out of four council members.[12] To be sure, most of these were allied with the Anglo elite. But not all of them were, especially after the GGL came under challenge in the late 1960s. In any event, it would be incorrect to depict Mexican Americans during this period as completely powerless.[13]

For Los Angeles, by contrast, it would hardly be worth assembling such data (see Table 4.8). By the early 1990s, there were two Mexican Americans

TABLE 4.7
Mexican-American Elected Officeholding in Metropolitan San Antonio (Selected City and County Posts)

Office	1970[a]		1981[a]		1992	
	Percentage Mexican Americans	Index of Representation*	Percentage Mexican Americans	Index of Representation	Percentage Mexican Americans[b]	Index of Representation[c]
Mayor & city councillors	26%	.50	45%	.84	45%	.81
County commissioners	13	.29	50	1.08	60	1.21
Other county officials**	17	.37	30	.65	40	.80
Higher judicial officials***	17	.37	10	.22	43	.87
Minor judicial & law enforcement officials****	38	.84	53	1.14	38	.76
State legislators & senators	23	.51	40	.86	50	1.01
All officials	23	.51	37	.80	45	.91

Notes: *Ratio of percentage of Mexican-American elected officials to percentage of Hispanics in total population. A value approaching zero indicates extreme underrepresentation; a value of 1.0 indicates perfect parity of officeholding with population. **Includes sheriff, county clerk, tax assessor-collector, treasurer, surveyor, district clerk, and district attorney. ***Includes district judges and county court-at-law judges. ****Includes constables and justices of the peace.

Sources: aJohn A. Booth, "Political Change in San Antonio, 1970–1982: Toward Decay or Democracy?" in David R. Johnson et al, eds., *The Politics of San Antonio: Community, Progress, and Power* (Lincoln, NE: University of Nebraska Press, 1983), 198. [b]*Texas State Directory*, 35th edition (Austin, TX: Texas State Directory, Inc., 1992). Pre-November 1992 data. [c]1990 census data used for Hispanic population figure.

TABLE 4.8
Mexican-American Elected Officeholding in Metropolitan Los Angeles (Selected City and County Posts)

Office	1970		1980		1991	
	Percentage Mexican Americans[a]	Index of Representation*	Percentage Mexican Americans[a]	Index of Representation	Percentage Mexican Americans[a]	Index of Representation[b]
Mayor and city councillors	0%	.00	0%	.00	13%	.31
Other city officials**	0	.00	0	.00	0	.00
County Supervisors	0	.00	0	.00	20	.53
Other county officials***	0	.00	0	.00	0	.00
LA school board members	14	.96	0	.00	14	.38
State legislators and senators	2	.15	9	.33	12	.32
All officials	3	.17	5	.19	12	.32

Notes: [a]Ratio of percentage of Mexican-American elected officials to percentage of Hispanics in total population. A value approaching zero indicates extreme underrepresentation; a value of 1.0 indicates perfect parity of officeholding with population. **Includes city attorney and controller. ***Includes county assessor, sheriff, and district attorney.

Sources: Fernando J. Guerra, "The Career Paths of Minority Elected Politicians: Resemblances and Differences," in Shirley Williams and Ted Lasher, eds., *Ambition and Beyond: The Career Paths of American Politicians* (Berkeley, CA: Institute of Governmental Studies Press, forthcoming). [b]1990 census data used for Hispanic population figure.

among the fifteen persons sitting on the Los Angeles City Council, each elected from single-member districts. There was similarly one Mexican American representing one of seven districts on the Los Angeles School Board. But all three of these individuals were quite new to their positions. Indeed, this was the high-water mark for Mexican Americans in Los Angeles in the twentieth century. A few years earlier, at the very beginning of the 1980s, there had been no local Mexican-American elected officials in Los Angeles. Indeed, for a generation, from 1962 to 1985, there were no Mexican Americans on the city council. Before that time, Edward Roybal, the first Mexican American to sit on the council in the twentieth century, served from 1949 to 1962, when he was elected to Congress.

At the county level, Mexican Americans have done even worse. Not only has no Mexican American ever been elected Los Angeles sheriff or district attorney, there have been virtually no Mexican-American candidates for these posts. Most glaring has been the absence for more than a century of Mexican Americans on the powerful Los Angeles County Board of Supervisors. Indeed, it was only in 1991, by virtue of a controversial Voting Rights suit that will be scrutinized in chapter 10, that a Mexican American was elected to the board.

The bright spot for Mexican-American officeholding in Los Angeles has been at the state legislative level. It was, after all, as state assemblymen that clique leaders Richard Alatorre and Art Torres began their electoral careers in the early 1970s. And over time they have been able to get some of their staffers and allies elected to other legislative posts in Sacramento. But such gains have hardly made up for the overall dearth of Mexican-American officeholders in Los Angeles.

Statewide, the contrast is less dramatic. Nevertheless, Mexican Americans have captured more elective offices in Texas than in California. The overall numbers presented in Table 4.9 reveal part of the picture. Accounting for about 26 percent of the population of Texas in 1991, Hispanics held 7.3 percent of all elective offices there. By contrast, accounting for approximately the same proportion of California's total population, Hispanics there held only 3.2 percent of elective posts.[14] Put another way: Texas, with 19.4 percent of all Hispanics in the nation, accounts for 46.9 percent of all Hispanic elected officials; while California, with 34.4 percent of Hispanics, accounts for only 14.7 percent of Hispanic elected officials nationally.[15]

Table 4.9 also reveals that back in 1973 Mexican-American officeholding in Texas, adjusted for population, was greater than in California.

TABLE 4.9

Hispanic Elected Officeholding in Texas and California in 1973 and 1991

	1973		1991	
	Texas	California	Texas	California
Number of Hispanic elected officials	565[a]	231[a]	1969[a]	617[a]
Hispanic elected officials as % of all elected officials	2.3[b]	1.3[b]	7.3[a]	3.2[a]
Ratio of % of Hispanic elected officials to Hispanic % of total population	.13	.09	.28	.12

Sources: [a]1991 National Roster of Hispanic Elected Officials (Washington, DC: National Association of Latino Elected Officials Educational Fund, 1991), viii and x. [b]Derived from data in U.S. Bureau of the Census, Census of Governments: Popularly Elected Officials (Washington, DC: GPO, 1968, 1978, 1990).

Indeed, if the specific kinds of offices held by Mexican Americans over time are scrutinized, it is evident why they have long been perceived as doing better in Texas. Statewide races illustrate the point. In the late 1970s two Mexican Americans were elected to minor state executive offices in Texas.[16] In 1986 a Mexican American was elected (with 49 percent of the Anglo vote) to a seat on the Texas Supreme Court.[17] That same year District Court Judge Roy Barrera, Jr., was the Republican nominee for attorney general. Although Barrera lost to the Democratic incumbent, he was heavily supported by Anglo Texans.[18] Indeed, Barrera was only the latest in a series of Mexican Americans whom Texas Republicans have, since the mid-1960s, nominated to run for statewide office.[19]

For their part, Texas Democrats have been slower to put Mexican Americans on statewide tickets. Before his withdrawal from politics in 1989, Cisneros was widely regarded as a strong candidate for either governor or U.S. senator. In 1991, Democratic state representative Lena Guerrero was appointed to the Texas Railroad Commission by Governor Ann Richards and was favored to win election to the post in 1992—at least until the press caught her falsifying her educational credentials. In any event, a few months earlier in November 1990, Dan Morales, Guerrero's Democratic colleague in the Texas House, was elected attorney general, from which post two recent gubernatorial candidates have been launched.

In California, by contrast, no Mexican American has been elected to statewide office this century. Indeed, there have been some bitterly disappointing defeats. In 1986, for example, State Supreme Court Justice Cruz Reynoso lost his appointment when his seat came up for voter approval. With the exception of the quixotic gubernatorial campaign of Mario Obledo, whose 1982 bid for the Democratic nomination was supported by few if any Mexican-American leaders, the Reynoso race was the closest any Mexican American in California has come to statewide electoral politics in recent years. Prior to that, the last Mexican-American statewide candidacy was writer-lawyer Enrique "Hank" López's losing race for secretary of state in 1958. Moreover, as California enters the last decade of the twentieth century, there are few if any Mexican-American politicians who are perceived as potential statewide candidates. State Senator Art Torres, for some time the most obvious such choice, has been plagued by personal problems that have apparently eliminated him from that arena.[20]

Finally, it is at the state legislative level that the electoral successes of Mexican Americans in Texas are most evident. As Tables 4.10 and 4.11 reveal, in 1993 not only is the absolute number of Mexican-American legislators much higher in Texas than in California (thirty-two versus eleven), so too is the percentage of legislators who are Mexican-American—17.7 percent versus 9.2. Moreover, Mexican-American state legislators in Texas work together as a much more cohesive and effective caucus than their counterparts in California.[21]

With Hispanics constituting roughly similar proportions of the total population of each state, this disparity cannot be ascribed to population differences. To be sure, some of the disparity is traceable to the recent growth in the numbers of Hispanics in California ineligible to vote. But as Tables 4.10 and 4.11 also show, the superior record of Mexican Americans in Texas is no recent phenomenon. Whether relying on absolute numbers, percentage of state legislators who are Mexican American, or this percentage adjusted for Hispanic population in the state, Mexican Americans have long been much stronger in the state legislative arena in Texas than in California. Moreover, these successes were achieved in the face of much greater obstacles to the group's political participation. As Grebler remarked when he and his colleagues found a similar disparity between Texas and California in the late 1960s:

> Texas, with a Spanish-surname population about as large as California's, shows a far more favorable picture—despite the fact that Texas ranks far lower than California on almost any yardstick of socioeconomic position for this group, despite the fact that its social system generally is more hos-

TABLE 4.10
Hispanic State Legislators in California (Selected Years, 1930–1993)

Year	Number	Percent of legislature	Hispanics as percent of total population	Representation index[†]
1930	0[a]	0.0%	6.5%	0.00
1942	0[a]	0.0	6.9°	0.00
1950	0[b]	0.0	7.2	0.00
1952	0[a]	0.0	7.6°	0.00
1960	0[b]	0.0	9.1	0.00
1962	2[a]	1.7	9.7°	0.18
1964	1[a]	0.8	10.2°	0.08
1966	0[a]	0.0	10.8°	0.00
1967	0[c]	0.0	11.0°	0.00
1968	1[a]	0.8	11.3°	0.07
1970	2[a]	1.7	11.9	0.14
1972	5[a]	4.2	13.4°	0.31
1973	5[d]	4.2	14.1°	0.30
1974	8[b]	6.7	14.8°	0.45
1976	6[a]	5.0	16.3°	0.31
1978	6[a]	5.0	17.7°	0.28
1979	9[d]	7.5	18.5°	0.41
1981	7[d]	5.8	19.9°	0.29
1983	7[b]	5.8	21.4°	0.27
1984	7[e]	5.8	22.1°	0.26
1985	7[e]	5.8	22.8	0.25
1986	7[e]	5.8	23.4°	0.25
1987	7[e]	5.8	24.0°	0.24
1988	7[e]	5.8	24.6°	0.24
1989	7[e]	5.8	25.2°	0.23
1990	6[e]	5.0	25.8	0.19
1991	7[e]	5.8	26.5	0.22
1993	11	9.2	27.9°	0.33

Notes:
[†]Ratio of Hispanic percentage of state legislature to Hispanic percentage of total state population.
°Interpolations (in 1993, extrapolation) of census population data.
Sources:
[a]Fernando V. Padilla, "Chicano Representation by Court Order: Impact of Reapportionment," in Richard Santillan, ed., The Chicano Community and California Redistricting, Vol. I (Claremont, CA: The Rose Institute of State and Local Government, Claremont Men's College, 1981), 98. [b]Joan Moore and Harry Pachon, Hispanics in the United States (Englewood Cliffs, NJ: Prentice-Hall, 1985), 185. [c]Leo Grebler et al., The Mexican-American People (New York: The Free Press, 1970), 561. [d]John A. Garcia, "The Voting Rights Act and Hispanic Political Representation in the Southwest," Publius 16 (1986): 58. [e]National Roster of Hispanic Elected Officials (Washington, DC: National Association of Latino Elected Officials Educational Fund): 1984, xi; 1985, xi; 1986, xiii; 1987, xv; 1988, xiv; 1989, vi; 1990, vii; 1991, viii.

TABLE 4.11
Hispanic State Legislators in Texas (Selected Years, 1930–1993)

Year	Number	Percent of legislature	Hispanics as percent of total population	Representation index[†]
1930	1[a]	0.6%	11.7%	0.05
1942	3[a]	1.7	12.7°	0.13
1950	0[b]	0.0	13.4	0.00
1952	1[a]	0.6	13.7°	0.04
1960	7[b]	3.9	14.8	0.26
1962	6[a]	3.3	15.1°	0.22
1964	8[a]	4.4	15.4°	0.29
1966	11[a]	6.1	15.8°	0.39
1967	10[c]	5.5	15.9°	0.35
1968	12[a]	6.6	16.1°	0.41
1970	12[a]	6.6	16.4	0.40
1972	12[a]	6.6	17.3°	0.38
1973	14[d]	7.7	17.8°	0.43
1974	15[b]	8.3	18.2°	0.46
1976	19[a]	10.5	19.2°	0.55
1978	20[a]	11.0	20.1°	0.55
1979	21[d]	11.6	20.5°	0.57
1980	22[d]	12.2	21.0	0.58
1981	21[d]	11.6	21.2°	0.55
1983	19[b]	10.5	21.7°	0.48
1984	25[e]	13.8	21.9°	0.63
1985	23[e]	12.7	22.1	0.57
1986	23[e]	12.7	22.8°	0.56
1987	25[e]	13.8	23.5°	0.59
1988	25[e]	13.8	24.1°	0.57
1989	25[e]	13.8	24.8°	0.56
1990	27[e]	14.9	25.5	0.58
1991	25[e]	13.8	25.9	0.53
1993	32	17.7	26.7	0.66

Notes:
[†]Ratio of Hispanic percentage of state legislature to Hispanic percentage of total state population.
°Interpolations (in 1993, extrapolation) of census population data.
Sources:
[a]Fernando V. Padilla, "Chicano Representation by Court Order: Impact of Reapportionment," in Richard Santillan, ed., *The Chicano Community and California Redistricting,* Vol. I (Claremont, CA: The Rose Institute of State and Local Government, Claremont Men's College, 1981), 98. [b]Joan Moore and Harry Pachon, *Hispanics in the United States* (Englewood Cliffs, NJ: Prentice-Hall, 1985), 185. [c]Leo Grebler et al., *The Mexican-American People* (New York: The Free Press, 1970), 561. [d]John A. Garcia, "The Voting Rights Act and Hispanic Political Representation in the Southwest," *Publius* 16 (1986): 58. [e]*National Roster of Hispanic Elected Officials* (Washington, DC: National Association of Latino Elected Officials Educational Fund): 1984, xi; 1985, xi; 1986, xiii; 1987, xv; 1988, xiv; 1989, vi; 1990, vii; 1991, viii.

tile to Mexican Americans, and despite voting procedures that militate against its minority populations.[22]

For decades before the 1960s, when such obstacles were arguably far worse, Mexican Americans in Texas were still winning legislative seats that, however few in number, were simply beyond the reach of their California counterparts. As one student of the subject observes:

> Historically, California Chicanos have had less representation in the state legislature than the Chicanos of any other of the five southwestern states. . . . In fact, there were no Chicanos at all elected to the lower house from 1904 through 1962, nor were any elected to the state Senate from 1912 to 1974.[23]

Mexican Americans in California finally made the breakthrough into the state legislature in the 1960s. But as Table 4.10 also demonstrates, they have only recently improved on the gains of the 1970s. Again, this contrasts with Mexican Americans in Texas, who have over the same period been steadily increasing their number of legislative seats.

Of course, such comparisons of numbers of Mexican-American office-holders across jurisdictions must be made with care. Above all, one must be sure that the offices being compared are commensurable. Quite apart from differences in the energy and character of the individuals occupying equivalent offices, one must take into account whether, for example, a seat on the Los Angeles City Council is equivalent in importance to one on the San Antonio City Council. Certainly a seat in the well-paid, full-time California State Assembly should not be equated with one in the poorly paid, part-time Texas House of Representatives, which meets in regular session for not more than 140 days once every two years.[24]

A second consideration is whether the seats in question represent jurisdictions with equivalent numbers of nonvoters. As I have already indicated, there are proportionately many more illegals and noncitizens in Los Angeles and California than in San Antonio and Texas. Officeholders representing large numbers of people who cannot vote are bound to command less attention than those with constituents who vote. Such rotten boroughs become devalued—which is precisely what has happened to many heavily Hispanic districts in Los Angeles.

A third consideration is whether the offices being compared represent single-member or at-large jurisdictions. Politicians elected from the former may not have put together such diverse and strong coalitions as politicians elected from the latter. On the other hand, Mexican Americans elected at-large have often been sponsored by dominant coalition partners whose interests may conflict with those of the barrio.

Such considerations are precisely why some researchers seek alternative measures of representation. For example, in their study of black and Hispanic politics in ten Northern California cities, Rufus P. Browning and his colleagues explicitly reject representation as gauged by numbers of elected officials in favor of "political incorporation," which they define "as the extent to which group interests are effectively represented in policy making."[25]

This shift from *numerical* to *effective* representation serves as a reminder that group interests do not necessarily depend on the ethnic or racial background of officeholders. Indeed, the research evidence on this point is rather clear. For instance, a recent study of thirty-five large urban school districts found no relationship between the presence of Hispanics on school boards and educational outcomes for Hispanic students. That study did find a modest but statistically significant relationship between Hispanic school board members and numbers of Hispanic teachers. But this relationship was far less significant than that between Hispanic population and numbers of Hispanic teachers.[26]

In the classic study in this literature, Peter Eisinger found that while there was some positive relationship between black civil service employment in forty-three U.S. cities in the mid-1970s and the presence of a black mayor, there was no relationship between black employment and black city councillors. Similar to the study just cited, the strongest predictor of black municipal employment was the percentage of blacks in the population.[27]

Such findings are not news to Mexican-American politicos, who readily admit that the ethnic background of elected officials is less important to them than the degree of access they have to those officials. At least this is what Mexican-American leaders say in private. In public, of course, they not only demand more Mexican-American elected officials, they also make rather grandiose claims about what can be expected of these officials. Not untypical is the testimony of Professor Richard Santillan of the Rose Institute at Claremont Men's College before the California Advisory Committee to the U.S. Commission on Civil Rights, in the midst of the 1980 redistricting:

The lack of [Hispanics on the city council] has denied Chicanos in the City of Los Angeles the right to influence public policy, educational policy and community resources which would result in social, economic and educational upward mobility. When we look at the years of completion in high school . . . at unemployment . . . at the median income . . . at the poverty [level], . . . they all fall far behind in the Latino [community].[28]

There is a simple explanation for such rhetoric: In a complicated and often intractable world, the number of Mexican-American elected officials is a tangible, achievable goal whose attainment can be readily measured. In other words, elective posts have become one of the goods that Mexican-American leaders can deliver to their people. Though clearly reinforced by the logic of affirmative action, this development is also sustained by the commonsense reasoning that sees the number of individuals from a group elected to office as a rough-and-ready guide to its political success. But as the foregoing suggests, it is not sufficient to limit the present analysis of Mexican-American political outcomes to this single index.

JOBS, JOBS, JOBS

One alternative is suggested in the studies just cited—namely, a group's ability to secure public sector jobs. And according to this index, once again Mexican Americans in San Antonio and Texas have done much better than their counterparts in Los Angeles and California.

Indeed, it is striking how long Mexican Americans in San Antonio have had a substantial share of public sector jobs. As far back as 1960, 38 percent of public sector jobs in metropolitan San Antonio were held by Mexican Americans, a figure which approximated their share of the population at that time.[29] By 1973, employment levels of Mexican Americans in San Antonio city government remained close to parity, approximating their proportion of the area's work force as well as overall municipal salary levels. To be sure, the percentage of Mexican Americans employed as professionals lagged behind such aggregate figures, but they nevertheless constituted 29 percent of the city's professional employees.[30]

Even in San Antonio's patronage-riddled public schools, Mexican Americans did not do badly. For example, during the 1976–1977 school year 27 percent of elementary and secondary teachers in the San Antonio Independent School District were Hispanic, while 69 percent of the students were. These numbers undoubtedly reflect the lag between increasing enrollment of Mexican-American youngsters and the less rapid turnover of non-Hispanic teachers hired under the old regime. Still, it is worth noting that at that time Hispanics constituted 34 percent of the SAISD's principals, coveted positions known to be highly susceptible to political pressure.[31]

Comparable data for Los Angeles in the 1960s have not been obtained, but there are data for California and Texas that sustain the inference that

Mexican Americans were doing much better in San Antonio than in Los Angeles at that time. In 1960 Mexican-American males, relative to their share of the total workforce, were substantially underrepresented in California's public sector, and slightly overrepresented in Texas's. Most of this advantage enjoyed by Texas Mexicans was traceable to their disproportionate share of federal jobs, particularly at San Antonio's several large military installations. Moreover, despite their lower average educational attainment, Mexican Americans in Texas were *not* heavily concentrated in low-wage public sector jobs.[32]

During the 1970s Mexican Americans still did better in Texas than in California. Indeed, a multiple-regression analysis of public sector employment in 93 Southwestern municipalities from 1973 to 1978 found that Hispanic municipal employment was higher in Texas than in California.[33]

By 1983, Hispanics in Los Angeles were still not making a strong showing. Constituting close to 30 percent of the city's population, they accounted for only 14.5 percent of its municipal workforce. Their presence in the county work force around this same time was only marginally better.[34]

More recently, during the 1990–1991 school year Hispanics made up more than 63 percent of the students, but only 12 percent of teachers and administrators in the Los Angeles Unified School District.[35] By contrast, in the San Antonio Independent School District that same year, Hispanics constituted 80 percent of the students and about 53 percent of the teachers and 40 percent of the principals.[36]

To be sure, Los Angeles was experiencing massive immigration throughout the 1980s, and as I have already argued, it is not entirely fair to use such immigration-driven population figures as criteria by which to evaluate Mexican-American progress. Nevertheless, immigration has hardly alleviated the long-standing underrepresentation of Mexican Americans in public sector employment in Los Angeles and California.

LEADERSHIP: THE TEXAS EDGE

Of all the indices of Mexican-American political advancement, the most straightforward has already been mentioned in earlier chapters: the amount and quality of leadership that has come out of San Antonio and Texas, particularly South Texas. I have mentioned Albert Peña, Henry B. González, and Henry Cisneros, all three of whom have played nationally important roles in Mexican-American politics. But there are many others. This is not to say that no leaders have emerged from Los Angeles and California; Edward Roybal and César Chávez come readily to mind. Yet over the years, the number and diversity of nationally known leaders and organizations spawned in Texas easily outstrips the competition in California.

Take, for example, the generation that came of age during the 1960s. A focal point of Chicano activism in the Southwest at that time was St. Mary's University in San Antonio. After earning a master's degree in political science there, José Angel Gutiérrez helped found the Raza Unida Party and then gained national prominence as leader of the Chicano political takeover of Crystal City, the small South Texas town where he had grown up.[37]

One of Gutiérrez's fellow activists at St. Mary's was Willie Velásquez, mentioned earlier as the founder of the Southwest Voter Registration Education Project (SVREP). Still based in San Antonio, SVREP has been the primary force behind increasing Mexican-American voter registration levels throughout the Southwest. SVREP continues to sponsor registration efforts in all states of the region, and its polling and research activities have been a major source of information on Mexican-American voting patterns. Since its founding in 1974, Southwest Voters, as it has come to be known, has conducted more than 1,000 drives in over 200 communities in fourteen states. It deserves credit for most of the increase in Hispanic voter registrations nationally over the past fifteen years.[38]

A less activist-oriented leader is attorney Vilma Martínez. A carpenter's daughter who could not speak English when she started school in San Antonio, Martínez served as general counsel and president of the Mexican American Legal Defense and Educational Fund (MALDEF) from 1973 to 1983.[39] Now practicing law with a prominent Los Angeles firm, Martínez has served as a member and chair of the Board of Regents of the University of California and continues to be an influential member of the MALDEF board. From these bases, Martínez played a key role in organizing opposition to immigration reform legislation during the 1980s.

MALDEF itself was founded in San Antonio in 1968 by a local Mexican-American attorney, with funding from the Ford Foundation. With its headquarters subsequently moved to San Francisco, and with offices in San Antonio, Los Angeles, Denver, and Washington, MALDEF has emerged as perhaps the preeminent organizational voice of Mexican Americans in the national arena. Along with Martínez, it was at the center of Mexican-American opposition to the Simpson-Mazzoli immigration legislation and subsequent reform efforts.[40]

In its early days, while still headquartered in San Antonio, MALDEF was headed by a Harvard-educated attorney by the name of Mario Obledo.[41] Obledo later left Texas to become secretary of Health,

Education, and Welfare in the administration of California governor Jerry Brown, from which post, as I have already mentioned, he launched an unsuccessful bid for the governorship of his adopted state. Obledo then went on to head the League of United Latin American Citizens (LULAC), from which platform he, too, figured prominently in the opposition to immigration reform.

As it turns out, MALDEF is perhaps the most visible of several Mexican-American organizations started in South Texas. LULAC itself was founded in Corpus Christi in 1929. Begun as a nonpartisan effort among middle-class Mexican Americans who (as their name suggests) sought improvement of their status through assimilation, LULAC has endured on the local level largely as a civic organization, while on the national level its leaders have pursued a more activist agenda. LULAC remains one of the few nationally visible Mexican-American membership organizations.[42]

Another such stalwart is the American G.I. Forum, also founded in Corpus Christi, in 1949. The Forum reflected the aspirations of Mexican-American veterans who, after serving in World War II, found the familiar barriers to their advancement back home unacceptable. The founder of the Forum was Dr. Hector García, the prominent physician mentioned in chapter 1. A World War II combat surgeon, García was spurred to action when a mortuary in the small Texas town of Three Rivers refused to accept the body of a Mexican-American serviceman killed overseas. From this beginning, García built the nation's largest Mexican-American membership organization, reaching its peak in the mid-1960s when García's longtime ally, Lyndon Johnson, was in the White House. Today, the American G.I. Forum remains a presence in Mexican-American communities around the nation.[43]

Another source of leadership dates back to the 1920s, when a wave of political agitators and intellectuals flowed into South Texas from revolutionary Mexico. Among these was a self-educated pamphleteer and printer, José Romulo Munguía y Torres, who arrived in San Antonio in January 1926 after fleeing the regime of General Obregón. Munguía's wife and four children soon followed, and at the age of 41, he found work at *La Prensa*, then the leading Spanish-language newspaper in the Southwest. *La Prensa* had been founded in 1913 by Ignacio Lozano, another political refugee from Mexico; and by the time Munguía arrived, the paper was home to many others—such as the editor, Leonides González, the father of future congressman Henry B. González.[44]

As for Lozano, he left San Antonio in the 1920s to establish a sister publication in Los Angeles, *La Opinión*. *La Prensa* eventually ceased publication in the early 1960s, and *La Opinión*, down to a circulation of about 13,000 in the mid-1970s, almost met the same fate.[45] But with the recent flood of Mexican and Central American immigrants into Los Angeles, *La Opinión* now boasts a circulation of more than 96,000 and is the largest Spanish-language daily in the Southwest. Until recently, the paper's publisher was Ignacio Lozano, Jr., son of the founder and a prominent Southern California Republican who served briefly as ambassador to El Salvador under President Ford.[46] Lozano has also served on the boards of the Bank of America and MALDEF. And although *La Opinión* was bought by the Times-Mirror Company in 1990, Lozano's children, José and Monica, are today actively involved in publishing the paper. Such are the Texas origins of one of Southern California's leading Mexican-American families.

As for Romulo Munguía, he remained in San Antonio, where he established a printing business, aided by his two sons, Rubén and Romulo. Today the Munguías not only print fliers for local businessmen and politicians, they also dispense valued political advice. In this respect they carry on the fading but honorable American tradition of the republican printer-pamphleteer, personified by Ben Franklin. Among the politicians who have benefited from the Munguías' counsel is their nephew, Henry Cisneros, who grew up around the corner from the printing shop, and learned some of his earliest lessons there at the scene of many a West Side political intrigue. It is hardly surprising that when Cisneros first ran for office, his uncle Rubén Munguía helped secure the endorsement of the GGL.

San Antonio has also nurtured Mexican-American leadership in the Catholic Church. In the late 1960s and early 1970s, San Antonio was the center of activity for a national caucus of Latino priests, PADRES. Among other endeavors, this group advanced the career of Patricio Flores, archbishop of San Antonio since 1978. The son of a farmworker family, Flores became the nation's first Mexican-American bishop when appointed auxiliary bishop of San Antonio in 1970. Over the years Flores has supported efforts from farmworker organizing campaigns to the Alinsky community organization COPS; today he is the preeminent spokesman for Mexican-American issues in the U.S. Conference of Catholic Bishops.

With COPS, we return to the generation of leaders who emerged in South Texas during the 1960s. For the founder of that organization is yet another San Antonio native. Raised near one of the mission churches along the San Antonio River, Ernesto Cortes, like Cisneros and Velásquez, graduated from Central Catholic High School. Also like Cisneros, Cortes graduated from Texas A&M at a time when "Aggie" was more or less synonymous with "Anglo." While a graduate student in economics at the University of Texas at Austin, Cortes became involved in Chicano activist causes, then worked in antipoverty programs in San Antonio, and eventually moved to the Midwest to train as an Alinsky community organizer.

In the early 1970s, Cortes returned to his hometown and organized COPS. Since then, he has extended his efforts to Los Angeles, Houston, Fort Worth, Dallas, Austin, El Paso, and the Rio Grande Valley. Cortes has gained recognition not only from Mexican Americans throughout the Southwest, but also from such quarters as the MacArthur Foundation, which granted him one of its "genius awards" in 1983. An editor at the *Texas Monthly* recently described Cortes as "the most powerful Mexican in Texas."

Gutiérrez, Velásquez, Martínez, MALDEF, Obledo, LULAC, García, the G.I. Forum, Lozano, González, Munguía, Flores, and Cortes—the list is impressive. I mentioned earlier that there are certain parallels between San Antonio and Boston. Perhaps most striking is that, like Boston and Massachusetts, San Antonio and Texas have been net exporters of political talent.

SAVED BY THE VOTING RIGHTS ACT?

After perusing the evidence and concluding that Mexican Americans have done much better politically in San Antonio and Texas than in Los Angeles and California, how do we explain this disparity?

One possible factor is the Voting Rights Act (VRA). As mentioned earlier, the political barriers confronting Mexican Americans in Texas were the primary evidence offered for expanding the VRA to Hispanics in 1975. From that date forward, Hispanics throughout the state have come under the Act's provisions. Meanwhile, Hispanics in California did not receive comparable coverage until 1982, when a series of amendments effectively brought the entire state, indeed the entire nation, under the VRA. (Before the 1982 amendments, the only covered jurisdictions in California were four rural counties.)[47] Given this history, it is only logical to ask: How much of the difference in outcomes between Texas and California is attributable to the differential impact of the VRA?

Most observers conclude that the Act has had a decided impact on increasing the number of Mexican-American officeholders throughout Texas.[48] Indeed, as mentioned earlier, the threat of a Voting Rights suit caused the San Antonio City Council to shift from at-large to single-member districts—a shift that has resulted in a council with an entrenched

Mexican-American plurality. Similarly, a VRA suit in Houston led to a re-organized city council and a gain of seats by Mexican Americans.[49]

In California, the VRA has in recent years been responsible for a few dramatic developments, but their long-term implications remain unclear. In Los Angeles, in particular, Mexican-American breakthroughs onto the city council and the county board of supervisors clearly would not have been scored without Section 2 of the Voting Rights Act. Yet as I will explore in chapter 10, these gains may be more apparent than real. Among other factors, large numbers of illegals and noncitizens in Los Angeles and California generally make it particularly difficult to draw Hispanic-voting-majority districts. The end results are typically rotten boroughs whose occupants have correspondingly small political bases. Under such circumstances the VRA may, to repeat a distinction drawn earlier, enhance the *numerical* but not the *effective* representation of Mexican Americans.

The evidence therefore leads to an obvious but typically overlooked conclusion: the greater impact of the VRA in Texas reflects the preexisting political strength of Mexican Americans there relative to their counterparts in California. For what gets lost in the controversies over the creation of Hispanic majority districts is that the VRA cannot *will* Mexican-American political power into being. The most that the VRA can accomplish, in either Texas or California, is to facilitate Mexican-American political endeavors. The Act has been so effective in Texas only because there was something to facilitate.[50] (In this regard, it is worth noting that in the mid-1970s, when COPS was making significant strides in San Antonio, the organization actually debated within its own ranks whether VRA-induced single-member districts would advance or hinder the political aspirations of Mexican Americans there.) Here again, it is critical to recall that Mexican Americans enjoyed greater political successes in Texas than in California long before the Act was implemented. All the VRA did was take the lid off a pot that was already boiling, and allow Mexican Americans in Texas to achieve their political potential.[51] In California, by contrast, the fundamental factors contributing to Mexican-American political advancement have been much less in evidence. The lid may have been taken off, but there is not much cooking.

POPULATION:
THE EXPLAIN-BY-NUMBERS APPROACH

What are the factors contributing to a group's political strength? With regard to the difference between Mexican Americans in San Antonio and

Los Angeles, the factor most frequently cited is population. The argument typically goes, "Sure, Mexicans are more successful politically in San Antonio; there are more of them there."

Yet this explanation is highly problematic. In its own terms, it fails to explain why Mexican Americans in Los Angeles have had so much less political clout than sheer numbers would predict. Nor does population alone explain why, earlier this century, Mexican Americans constituted a sizable proportion of San Antonio's population but nevertheless lacked substantial political power. In the same vein, one is reminded of V. O. Key's finding that in the late 1940s it was precisely in those areas of the South where blacks predominated numerically that they were weakest politically.[52]

Nor does population explain much about the divergent political outcomes for Mexican Americans in Texas and California generally. This was true in the 1960s, when Mexican-American population differences between the two states failed to account for the vastly superior political position of Mexicans in Texas. And it is true today, when with roughly equivalent population shares in both states, Hispanics in Texas are still more successful.

Particularly with regard to Mexican Americans, population data must be scrutinized carefully. Large numbers of noncitizens can, as I have already indicated, skew comparisons of political outcomes across jurisdictions. Similarly relevant for a group including so many immigrants are the effects of social and geographic mobility. Residential patterns must certainly be taken into account.

Because such considerations are fairly obvious, one would assume that they effectively undercut heavy emphasis on population to explain Mexican-American political outcomes. Yet that emphasis persists, for several reasons. First, it is sustained by a body of social-science literature (some of which I cited earlier) that consistently identifies minority population as a strong—often the strongest—correlate of minority political outcomes in U.S. cities.[53] From such research it is frequently, and improperly, concluded that population is not just a correlate but a cause of minority political outcomes.

Reinforcing such leaps of logic is the social-science reductionism criticized earlier, which interprets political processes and outcomes as reflections of social and economic dynamics. In recent years this perspective has gained wider currency from affirmative action efforts, which have helped propagate the notion that there ought to be a correspondence between group population shares and economic and political outcomes.

To be sure, there is a relationship between a group's relative size and its political power. But this relationship is hardly direct. Instead, it is mediated by many other factors. Population should be seen as a limiting factor, in the sense that it obviously correlates with Mexican-American political success, but cannot by itself explain or account for that success. Certainly, groups that fall below certain obvious population thresholds cannot get attention in most political arenas. But even for a large group, numbers are a latent resource that becomes relevant only when the group is politically mobilized. And numbers by themselves do not automatically lead to mobilization.

To extend the boiling pot analogy: citing Mexican-American population in San Antonio as a sufficient explanation for the group's political strength is like saying that the amount of steam one can produce is due to how much water is available. In one sense, of course, this is true: without water, there can be no steam; and the more water available, the more steam can be produced. Water here is the limiting factor. But it is not the critical factor. No matter how much water is available, one cannot produce steam without energy. Overlooked in mere comparisons of Mexican-American population numbers are the energy factors that turn population "water" into political "steam."[54]

SOCIAL STRUCTURE:
IRONING BOARDS AND ELITES

As the foregoing discussion suggests, attempts to explain political outcomes by population figures lead naturally toward considerations of social structure. The chapters on San Antonio and Los Angeles have already touched on the effects of social structure on Mexican-American politics: specifically, how the stable community ties of San Antonio are more conducive to political endeavors than the geographic and social mobility of Los Angeles. This point will emerge again in chapter 6, where I compare Alinsky community organizing in the two cities. But it is worth considering here for the light it sheds on political outcomes.

Much of the mobility of Mexican Americans in Los Angeles is attributable to immigrants, most of whom are illegals. Not only do these noncitizens dilute the political strength of Mexican-American numbers, they exacerbate the already formidable obstacles to organizing the group in Southern California.

For example, large numbers of such immigrants create severe, if little-noted, problems for those mounting voter registration drives. Veteran organizers and political operatives explain that door-to-door canvassing (as opposed to a stationary, "on-site" approach) is the best way to register new voters. Talking with people in their homes is said to afford more opportunities to convince people to register than does approaching them on a street corner as they hurriedly go about their errands. Organizers also claim that gaining entrance to a home provides clues that can be used to persuade the residents not only to register but, once registered, to get out and vote. And, if a canvasser can literally get a foot in the door, he or she will likely find other members of the household eligible to register.[55]

Well known to any door-to-door salesman, these tricks of the trade have proven successful in countless voter registration drives across the nation—especially in those conducted in Mexican-American communities in Texas by the Southwest Voter Registration Education Project (SVREP). Yet they have not worked well in Southern California. On the contrary, in precincts where the number of illegal immigrants and noncitizens rivals or exceeds the number of potential voters, door-to-door registration drives resemble the proverbial hunt for a needle in a haystack. Even when a potential registrant is located, the odds are low that he or she will live in a household with many other eligible voters. Not surprisingly, the search soon becomes as tiresome as it is inefficient—and expensive.

As a result, voter registration coordinators in Los Angeles have abandoned door-to-door campaigns in favor of wholesale on-site approaches. Making a virtue of necessity, they stumbled on an attention-getting symbol for their efforts when they had their workers set up ironing boards at busy East LA shopping malls and intersections. By the mid-1980s, even UNO (United Neighborhoods Organization), the East LA Alinsky group committed to community organizing on the basis of face-to-face relationships, went wholesale and resorted to ironing boards after several disappointing failures with door-to-door campaigns.[56]

The available evidence indicates that such efforts have been fairly effective at registering substantial numbers of Mexican Americans, and that most of those registered have turned out to vote in the next election.[57] Yet because such efforts are not part of a larger strategy of building strong political organizations, these effects quickly dissipate, resulting in the perception that Mexican Americans in Los Angeles must keep running just to stay in place. In other words, the campaigns are strictly one-shot affairs. Among the highly mobile Mexican Americans of Southern California, new cohorts keep coming of voting age, newcomers keep arriving from other jurisdictions, and registered individuals keep moving within jurisdictions without re-registering. Without the continuity offered by organizational ties, the only solution is to set up the ironing boards all over again—and then to mount subsequent get-out-the-vote drives.

Needless to say, such recurrent efforts require fresh infusions of resources. What may in the first instance have looked like a cheap and efficient means of bringing individual citizens into the political process
begins looking less so. As with religious revivals, the fervor needed to raise
more and more resources can engender a certain cynicism among the
populace—especially in light of the inevitable abuses that occur. In this
regard, it is surely no accident that the originator of the ironing-board approach, organizing wizard Marshall Ganz, went on to work with former
governor Jerry Brown at the California Democratic Party and then lost
his job when Brown accused him of spending too much on voter registration.[58] Likewise, it is not surprising that Senator Alan Cranston's recent
brush with financial scandal stemmed in part from his mismanagement
of voter registration funds.

For these reasons, Mexican-American voter registration drives in Los
Angeles have the reputation of being something of a farce. All too frequently, they have amounted to little more than perfunctory exercises
carried out to justify the funds raised by political entrepreneurs. Among
political insiders, there are persistent complaints that the numbers of new
registrants are exaggerated, and that those actually registered do not necessarily turn out to vote. As one lawyer associated with MALDEF described the situation, "voter registration is the hustle of the eighties." By
the 1990s, of course, funding for voter registration had long since dried
up, and the hustle had lost its bustle.

Residential patterns are another relevant aspect of social structure. As
discussed earlier, Mexican Americans in San Antonio have been much
more residentially concentrated than their cousins in Los Angeles. This
general pattern appears to hold for Texas and California generally. For
while 52 percent of Texas's Hispanics are located in 20 percent of that
state's congressional districts (as of 1992), 51 percent of California's
Hispanics are in 27 percent of its districts.[59]

Like population, residential patterns are frequently cited as an explanation of the differences between Mexican-American political outcomes
in these two jurisdictions. But once again, the critical factor is not arith-
metic, but social structure. What residential concentration points to is the
relatively sharp social—and economic—cleavage between Mexican
Americans and Anglos in San Antonio and Texas. As described earlier,
there is an angry edge to intergroup relations there lacking in Los Angeles
and California. It is this lingering resentment, this sense of having been
treated unfairly, that provides the energy behind the "steam" so evident
in Mexican-American politics in Texas.

There is one final social-structural factor that should be taken into account when explaining the superior political outcomes of Mexican Americans in Texas, especially the state's preeminence as a crucible of leadership. Absolutely critical in this regard have been Mexican-American elites capable of sustaining institutions that channel the energies welling up within the community toward constructive ends.

In the nineteenth century, such leadership came from the descendants of San Antonio's original settlers. Given the rigid class barriers characteristic of Hispanic societies, it would be easy to exaggerate the benign influence of such an elite.[60] Nonetheless, historian T. R. Fehrenbach points to San Fernando Cathedral's imposing gothic tower, completed in 1873, as evidence of the vitality of the city's Hispanic elite during the last part of the nineteenth century. As he describes it:

> Although the Canary Island families and other descendants of the Spanish *pobladores* [settlers] no longer ruled the town, they knew who they were, and they knew each other. They held minor offices and formed a necessary infrastructure between the dominant "Americans" and the Spanish-speaking working classes.[61]

By the early decades of this century, more middle-class leadership was emerging.[62] Filling its ranks were the families of the Mexican political exiles described earlier: the Lozanos, the Gonzálezes, the Munguías. Down through the years, such families have provided the leadership and sustained the institutions needed to bridge the gap between resentment and aspiration still evident among Mexican Americans in Texas today.

POLITICAL STRUCTURE:
VITALITY VERSUS VACUUM

Yet these social-structural factors do not by themselves explain the political success of Mexican Americans in San Antonio and Texas. Moreover, the most obvious factors—political structure and culture—are the least appreciated. Consider, for example, the evidence on public employment discussed earlier. That Mexican Americans have secured more public sector jobs in Texas than in California can be explained by several non-political factors. Chief among these is the pressure that South Texas's stagnant economy has long placed on the public sector to provide jobs.

But this economic difference is only part of the story. Indeed, the political differences between these two states are critical. The public sector in Texas has been more responsive to such pressure, for the simple reason that it has relied much more on patronage than California has. Yet if it is by now self-evident to the reader that California, the quintessentially reformed polity, is suffused with the civil service ethos, this fact is ignored in many of the studies cited above.

A similar point can be made about officeholding. One obvious reason why there are so many more Mexican-American officeholders in Texas than in California is simply that Texas has more elective offices. With less than three-fifths of California's total population, Texas has 254 counties, compared to California's 52. Moreover, in California counties the number of elective posts typically includes five county supervisors, a sheriff, a district attorney, and an assessor. In Texas, county posts are much more numerous. As we have already seen in San Antonio, these typically include the county judge, four county commissioners, a sheriff, a county attorney, a district attorney, a county clerk, a tax assessor, a treasurer, and numerous district judges, justices of the peace, and constables. In the state legislative arena, a similar pattern is evident: California has 120 seats; Texas 181. As for statewide elective officials, California has 16; Texas 30.[63]

It would be incorrect to say that analysts examining Mexican-American political outcomes at the state level never acknowledge that Texas has more elective offices than California. But the difference is typically presented as a given, as though it were the work of God or nature, not man. Seldom, if ever, acknowledged is the connection between the multiplicity of elective offices in Texas and the state's Jacksonian political culture. Texas's many minor, overlapping political posts and jurisdictions may be an administrative nightmare, but they also reflect a persistent political tradition that insists ordinary citizens are capable of governing—and wisely. By the same token, California's streamlined roster of elective officials reflects that state's Progressive political tradition, with its deliberate emphasis on the short ballot, professional administration, and centralized authority.

It is therefore not as paradoxical as it seems that Mexican Americans in Texas have displayed leadership abilities far superior to those of their California cousins. The former are products of a political system whose myriad offices, however minor or inconsequential, have presented countless opportunities where political skills could be learned and perfected. The latter are products of a regime explicitly designed to prevent politically weak and unsophisticated groups from ever gaining such skills.

To be sure, alternative political formations have emerged to fill the vacuum created by reformers in California. I have already described the Alatorre-Torres clique. Another such development is the sponsored candidacy. In a regime that requires substantial resources to run for a relatively small number of offices and that is also sensitive to pressures that all groups be represented, one inevitable result is the candidacy of individuals from resource-poor groups sponsored by outsiders. Not surprisingly, political advances thus made are often more apparent than real.

Throughout the postwar era, Los Angeles has seen numerous sponsored Mexican-American candidates. The first was Edward Roybal. Elected to the Los Angeles City Council in 1949 from a district in which Mexican Americans were a distinct numerical minority, Roybal received critical support from Jewish and other liberals. Subsequently, Hank López, Julian Nava, and most recently Congressman Matthew Martínez have been similarly sustained by outside resources.

Admittedly, there is nothing new or unique about sponsored candidacies. Indeed, there is a certain inevitability about such developments in democratic politics. In San Antonio, for instance, Mexican-American candidates were routinely backed and endorsed by the GGL. Yet undoubtedly because such sponsorship was in plain view, few illusions about what was going on were possible. In Los Angeles, by contrast, the role of sponsors has been much less obvious, and the result has often been artificially raised expectations followed by bitterness and frustration.

For example, in 1962 when Roybal went to Congress and vacated the city council seat he had occupied for thirteen years, he was succeeded by a black. Years later, there were still recriminations from that episode echoing within the Mexican-American community that Roybal had sold out his people to "the blacks and the Jews."[64] In the event, it was over twenty years before a Mexican American regained a seat on the council. And during that period, Roybal's tenure at city hall stood as a painfully visible benchmark of what Mexican Americans in Los Angeles had won—and then lost.

Hank López's 1958 candidacy for secretary of state is another such episode. As mentioned earlier, López lost. But more to the point, he was the only Democrat on the statewide ticket that year to do so. Whether attributable to the inadequacies of the candidate or to the prejudices of his ticketmates or California voters generally, there was an undeniably premature quality to López's candidacy. And, once again, the outcome was bitterness and frustration for Mexican Americans in California.

Then there is Julian Nava, elected to the Los Angeles School Board in 1967. A Harvard-trained historian and college professor, Nava ran a successful at-large campaign in the huge Los Angeles Unified School District at a time when Mexican Americans constituted only about 15 percent of the metropolitan population. Not surprisingly, his candidacy was made viable by the support of Anglo liberals, again including many Jews.[65] When Nava quit the school board in 1979 to become the Carter administration's ambassador to Mexico, his seat met the same fate as Roybal's: it went to a non-Mexican American. Nava's lack of stature and influence within the Mexican-American community was underscored upon his return from Mexico, at which time he was unable to find a job—in a political environment where Mexican-American insiders have no trouble taking care of their own. Nava was so bitter that he announced his plight to the national media.

Julian Nava is perhaps the best illustration of how counterproductive such sponsored candidacies have been for Mexican Americans in Los Angeles. Not only was the spectacle of Nava's joblessness embarrassing to him personally and to Mexican Americans generally, his tenure on the school board was marred with recriminations that by now sound familiar. As one Mexican American complained, with considerable justification, "The truth is that East LA didn't elect Julian; the [San Fernando] Valley and Westside did."[66]

Sponsored candidacies are one reason why Mexican-American politics in Los Angeles has been marked by so many episodic individual careers. How else to explain why, in a political system that is exceedingly difficult to break into, there have been so many Mexican Americans who have gotten elected, served for a while, and then dropped out of public life?[67] Apart from the frustrations and disappointments described here, this pattern suggests that officeholding among Mexican Americans in California represents even less political strength than a straightforward reading of the numbers would indicate. Many of these candidates and officeholders have been, to say the least, premature.

Such are the problems presented by a regime long ago designed to prevent the development of working-class, neighborhood-based political institutions. Without the means of building enduring organizations, Mexican Americans in California have had to hang their aspirations on individuals, many of whose careers have been short-lived or otherwise disappointing. The resulting lack of continuity has in turn hindered the transfer of leadership skills from one generation to the next. To be sure, in recent years the Alatorre-Torres clique indicates the emergence of more long-lived political relationships. But as I will explore at length in Part Two, this style of politics also holds limited promise for the mass of ordinary Mexican Americans.

PART TWO

Four Styles of
Mexican-American Politics

❦ 5 ❧

Friends-and-Neighbors
Politics and the
Need for Organization

O ne obvious explanation of the paradoxical political outcomes highlighted in the previous chapter is the great difference in economic
and social mobility experienced by Mexican Americans in these two different contexts. In San Antonio, fewer opportunities for individuals have
resulted in greater emphasis on advancement through collective political
effort. In Los Angeles, greater social and economic opportunities for individuals have reduced some of the pressure on politics as a means of
group advancement, to say nothing of depriving the group of potential
political leaders. In Albert Hirschman's terms, Mexican Americans in Los
Angeles have been more likely to exercise "exit"—as opposed to "voice"
or "loyalty"—than their counterparts in San Antonio.[1]

Yet this explanation is too simple. One problem with Hirschman's perspective is that it reduces political outcomes to a simple function of social and economic processes—and neglects the independent effects of
political institutions on those outcomes. Moreover, Hirschman's framework explains nothing about the paradox at the core of this study: the fact
that in the relatively benign context of Los Angeles, Mexican Americans
have pursued racial minority politics; while in the harsher context of San
Antonio, their politics has been more akin to immigrant ethnic politics.
In the next four chapters, I intend to highlight this critical difference be-

tween San Antonio and Los Angeles (and Texas and California), and focus on the role played therein by political institutions.

In general, my argument will be that in San Antonio, the social and communal resources that Mexican Americans enjoy in relative abundance (in part traceable to their diminished opportunities) have been channeled into political relationships and organizations yielding political successes—recognition, patronage, offices—that serve to moderate the deep-seated resentments Mexican Americans in South Texas have built up over generations. In Los Angeles, by contrast, such social and communal resources (already much weaker than in San Antonio) have been further disadvantaged by a regime where neighborhoods are not well integrated into the political system, and where money, media, issues, and highly paid professionals—media consultants, political consultants, pollsters—dominate the process. In such a regime, the advantage goes heavily to those elements in the Mexican-American community capable of capturing the attention of dominant elites. In the broader context of California and national politics, this pattern of advantage affords disproportionate influence to those Mexican Americans inclined to define their group in racial minority terms.

FRIENDS-AND-NEIGHBORS POLITICS: STRAIGHT UP FROM THE ROOTS

Friends-and-neighbors politics is the dominant style of politics among Mexican Americans in San Antonio. Its essence is captured in the scene, mentioned in chapter 2, of a group of middle-aged Mexican Americans sitting around a kitchen table drinking beer and talking one of their number into running for the local school board. From such settings emerge the highly volatile, disorganized efforts that characterize much Mexican-American politics in San Antonio.

The phrase "friends-and-neighbors politics" comes of course from V. O. Key's *Southern Politics*, the classic study of the fluid, faction-ridden politics of the post–World War II South. Focusing on the dynamics of one-party politics at the state and national level, Key emphasized the localistic tendencies that at that time hindered the development of statewide political organizations in the South.[2]

In this study, I focus on a related but slightly different facet of friends-and-neighbors politics: its thoroughgoing grounding in the face-to-face, primary group ties that loom so large in the day-to-day lives of Mexican Americans in San Antonio. Other observers might refer to this as neighborhood or grassroots politics. Although these terms capture the organic social basis of Mexican-American politics in San Antonio, I prefer not to use them because their overuse, in a variety of contexts, has reduced them to imprecise and empty rhetoric.

Friends-and-neighbors politics is simultaneously nurtured and constrained by the primary group ties in which it is immersed. On the one hand, participants derive considerable rewards from the sociability, fellow-feeling, and recognition that come from association with people one knows well. But as I will also demonstrate, the noninstrumental nature of such relationships not only exacerbates the difficulty of organizing them toward collective ends, but leaves them subject to intense emotional fluctuations. And this is why such solidary incentives alone are found wanting, and are typically supplemented by material incentives—favors, jobs, payoffs—all of which are much in evidence in San Antonio.[3] Yet because these material incentives are supplemental, the dominant characteristic of friends-and-neighbors politics is the infighting and factionalism that follow from the demands placed on face-to-face, primary-group ties.

In San Antonio, the limits of this style of politics are highlighted by the word *compadre*, which literally means "cofather." This is a traditional Mexican institution that, to varying degrees, survives among Mexican Americans today. In essence, to be someone's *compadre* is to be the godfather (*padrino*) of his or her child. Yet as the term suggests, the emphasis here is less on the relationship between the godparent and the child than between the godparent and the natural parent. The *compadre* (or *comadre*, in the case of a woman) may be a blood relation. But he is frequently not, in which case he becomes a fictive kin.[4] The *compadre* relationship can therefore be seen as one means whereby a culture that places a high value on the family and its self-sufficiency hedges its bets by expanding family boundaries beyond their natural limits.

But what does all this have to do with politics? In a close-knit, tradition-oriented setting such as San Antonio, political ties among Mexican Americans typically grow out of personal relationships. But those relationships are frequently unstable, subject to arguments and bickering, and often do not endure. As a result, the political landscape in the barrio is littered with sundered ties, and one repeatedly hears Mexican-American politicos there observe, in the course of explaining their relationship to some political foe, "He's my *compadre*, but I haven't spoken to him in years."

In the overview of San Antonio, I remarked on the Bexar County sheriff's volunteer deputy force, which gives this elected official a strong political base and also affords his department strong community ties. Yet this happy circumstance raises questions: Are these volunteers, coming together for camaraderie and fellowship, officially part of the county's law enforcement effort? And to the extent they are agents of Bexar County, what are the limits of their liabilities and responsibilities? Because such questions lack unambiguous answers, they suggest another critical facet of friends-and-neighbors politics: its blurring of social and political relationships. More to the point, the sheriff's volunteers represent a throwback to a period when strict accountability and professional standards were not demanded of law enforcement agencies. Indeed, this volunteer deputy force resembles the volunteer fire departments that politicians in antebellum New York City used as political bases, which were later incorporated into Tammany ward organizations. As Amy Bridges notes in her study of the origins of machine politics in New York, such politicians, who were the immediate predecessors of the machine bosses, tried "to give primarily social organizations like gangs and social and civic organizations like militia and fire companies a partisan role."[5]

A related dimension of friends-and-neighbors politics is how its practitioners fail to distinguish between private and public roles. This tendency is evident in my description of how employees in the Bexar County district attorney's office are expected to campaign for their boss as well as perform their official duties. It could also be seen in my account of the perquisites enjoyed by courthouse officials who, up until quite recently, have earned substantial extra income for themselves by performing marriage ceremonies.

A good example of friends-and-neighbors politics not yet mentioned is a group based on San Antonio's South Side. "The Three Panchos," as they have sometimes been called, include Congressman Frank Tejeda, State Senator Frank Madla, and City Councillor Frank Wing ("Pancho" is Spanish for "Frank"). Tejeda, a Berkeley-educated lawyer, is the group's leader. Madla is a former teacher and former member of the board of the South San Antonio Independent School District. Wing, a whiz at the city's budget processes, is a systems specialist at the huge South Side military base. Along with Tejeda's reputed relative, who has served as an elected constable; his cousin, who has been elected county commissioner; their allies on the local school boards; and their relatives; the Three Panchos—also known simply as the Tejedas—are probably the most effective friends-and-neighbors political grouping in San Antonio. Yet they too are subject to the vicissitudes of this style of politics. For Frank Wing has recently broken with the Tejedas, and now there are only Two Panchos.

The Panchos' constituency has been composed primarily of the hard-working, socially conservative people among whom they grew up. These of course include Mexican Americans, largely working-class families that are sometimes referred to as "brownnecks," but also Anglos of similar socioeconomic status, who once predominated on San Antonio's South Side. The Panchos have been particularly skillful at courting Anglo Baptists, who for example strenuously oppose the legalization of pari-mutuel horseracing and state-run lotteries. Although the Panchos are Democrats, their attentiveness to such constituents means they have remained aloof from their more liberal Democratic colleagues in Bexar County. As one member of the group puts it, "We don't want Mexican-American liberals telling us how to run the South Side."

The Panchos' successes are all the more striking in light of its members' history as Chicano activists during the 1960s. Their strength stems from the fact that they all grew up together on the South Side. In fact, many of their parents grew up together in the same neighborhoods and, for example, fought together in World War II. The Panchos and their peers played basketball together as teenagers (indeed, they still do); and as one political opponent complained, came of age living and breathing politics together, attending meetings and then going for coffee and talking late into the night. In essence, the Panchos are the core of a teenage gang that has matured and been absorbed into San Antonio politics. Such a pattern is, once again, reminiscent of New York and other American cities in the nineteenth century.[6] What is significant is that in San Antonio, the energies of such social formations are still being channeled so directly into politics.

The conduit for those energies on the South Side has been a baseball league organized by the Panchos. With funds raised from local businessmen and other backers, they have established teams in each parish and supplied youngsters with jerseys, caps, and equipment. With parents involved as spectators and as coaches, the Panchos have provided hard-pressed families with an inexpensive means of recreation and at the same time have of course built up extensive social networks on which their political endeavors flourish.

In an era when even San Antonio has experienced—at least in the last year or two—gang violence, such efforts have considerable merit.[7] The Tejedas are certainly not reluctant to claim that they are providing a valuable social service. Yet it is not clear whether their efforts, though with undeniably strong community ties, can successfully address the kinds of social problems that San Antonio is beginning to face. In any event, reformers, typically Anglo Republicans, whose courthouse aspirations I

have already described have begun attacking the Tejedas' baseball league
as a manipulation of children for political ends.

The Tejedas of course have other means of securing their community
base. During a recent campaign, they rented a neighborhood house, con-
veniently located right next to a freeway, and used it as a field headquarters where signs got assembled and campaign workers provisioned.
Having won the election, the Tejedas turned that house into a "district
office" that is a cross between a community center and a club house. On
any given weekend, one or more of the Panchos, their lieutenants, and
local residents can be found there celebrating the birthday of the daughter of one of their supporters, or just having a barbecue. Such get-
togethers are as much social in nature as political, with grandmothers arriving with gifts or perhaps a favorite dish. Some of the adults may be discussing politics, but others are likely talking about problems their kids are
having in school. At such informal gatherings of family, friends, and neighbors, speeches are certainly not made.

SCHOOL DISTRICT POLITICS:
THE EMERGENCE OF POWER BASES

Perhaps the purest and most revealing manifestation of friends-and-
neighbors politics in San Antonio is in the school districts. Bexar County
is carved up into fifteen independent school districts, each with its own
elected school board and administration. With some 60,000 students in
average daily attendance, the San Antonio Independent School District
is the largest, but its jurisdiction is almost exclusively the West Side barrio. There are several other majority Mexican-American districts with
much smaller student populations. Indeed, their small size has made
school districts highly accessible bases for political aspirants. School
board presidents strike deals with politicians and are dubbed "political
powerhouses" and "West Side warlords" by local observers. For example,
the former superintendent of the Edgewood Independent School District, José Cardenas, went on to establish a consulting firm specializing in
helping schools implement and evaluate bilingual education programs.
The firm has also provided computerized data services to individual
politicians and advocacy groups. Another firm member, Blandina
("Bambi") Cardenas Ramirez (no relation to José), became assistant secretary of HEW in the Carter administration and then a member of the
U.S. Civil Rights Commission.

The importance of school districts to Mexican-American politics in San
Antonio is underscored by the Barrera family. Roy Barrera, Sr., is a well-

connected attorney who grew up in the modest Lakeview area. As first a member of, then president of, and finally counsel to the Board of the Edgewood Independent School District during the 1950s, Barrera developed a political base in Lakeview. Barrera also established himself in a lucrative law practice. In 1972 he waged an unsuccessful campaign for the San Antonio City Council. Prior to that effort, in 1968, he had been appointed Texas secretary of state by Governor John Connally.[8] Like Connally, Barrera came to move in Republican circles. He has nevertheless remained a Democrat, and as such headed "Democrats for Connally" when the former governor sought the Republican presidential nomination. Perhaps not surprisingly, then, in 1983, when the son of fellow Texan James Baker was charged with possession of marijuana, Barrera was his attorney.

During the same period, Barrera's son, Roy, Jr. ("Little Roy"), was appointed a district judge by Republican governor Bill Clements. In November 1982, young Barrera stood for election to his judicial post and topped the Republican ticket in Bexar County, actually running ahead of Governor Clements. Having grown up in an affluent neighborhood on San Antonio's North Side, Barrera received substantial Anglo support. But he also benefited from his father's home base, gaining the endorsement of the young liberal Democrat who was president of the Edgewood School Board. In 1986 Barrera Jr. ran unsuccessfully as the Republican nominee for Texas attorney general, but having won more Mexican-American votes than any other Republican running statewide in Texas—including Ronald Reagan—in at least a decade, Barrera's political star is still rising.[9] It is no surprise, though undoubtedly an exaggeration, that *Washington Post* columnist David Broder has dubbed Barrera as "Cisneros's Republican rival."[10]

In recent years the most visible—many would say the most notorious—symbol of school politics in San Antonio was the president of the board of the San Antonio Independent School District, Dr. William Elizondo. Democratic activists admit to having relied on Dr. Elizondo, an optometrist, to get out the Mexican-American vote by sending his pupils home with carefully worded pamphlets urging their parents to vote for candidates "supportive of education." Yet this is surely the least controversial of the doctor's many such *"movidas,"* routinely exposed on the front pages of local newspapers.

None of this is new for San Antonio, or for Texas. School districts there have long been important bases for Anglo politicians—going back to the days when schools, especially in rural areas, were among the largest local employers. It is probably no coincidence that Lyndon Johnson's first real job was as a schoolteacher in Cotulla, Texas—a predominantly Mexican town sixty miles from the Mexican border.[11] Nor is it an accident that the controversy over the Chicano activist takeover of Crystal City focused largely on school board elections.[12] In the 1960s, school officials were still unhindered by civil service requirements, and they wielded considerable power. They controlled the letting of lucrative contracts for school construction, insurance, and supplies. And, because each independent district had the authority to assess and then tax real estate, they could also offer political favors in the form of reduced assessments and tax abatements. Armed with information about delinquent taxes, many school district insiders were well positioned to make a killing buying up property for back taxes.

Today, statewide reforms have deprived independent school districts of much of their taxing authority. Yet their political role seems scarcely diminished. Civil service has still not come to the schools. School officials have unlimited discretion over the hiring of scores of clerical and service personnel. As a result, many politicians' wives work as secretaries in the schools, and many loyal foot soldiers are janitors. Teacher aide positions are viewed as patronage plums. Teachers themselves are apparently less likely to be hired for political reasons, and they do have tenure rights. But these hardly assure desirable assignments or promotions. Indeed, advancement into well-paid administrative posts is highly political. As the superintendent of a predominantly Anglo school district in San Antonio put it: "Administration is where the political shenanigans go on." Veteran teachers complain, "The kids aren't the problem. It's the administrators." It is therefore not surprising when a former Mexican-American activist, state senator, and then political appointee in the Carter administration ends up as an elementary school principal in the Edgewood District; or that his wife is a bilingual education administrator in the San Antonio District. These being the stakes, teachers and other school employees understandably respond when asked to buy tickets to a politician's fundraiser or work on his phone bank.

But the opportunities in school politics do not end there. Relatives and allies of school board members who own land benefit from decisions about where schools will be built. One longtime observer reports that kickbacks on contracts are routine. Another reports that it is not uncommon for contracts to be let out to firms recently established by friends and relatives of school board members. Nor is it unusual for a politically savvy architect to get three separate fees for designing three schools—all with identical plans. Another school insider points out that because insurance rates are heavily regulated by the state, board members are left with considerable discretion as to who gets such contracts. Finally, one of the most lucrative plums in school politics is a retainer as legal counsel to one or more school boards. Several San Antonio lawyers, including Roy Barrera ,Sr., have built small empires from such beginnings. Not surprisingly, these positions have been the object of rancorous battles, especially in the larger districts.

Such opportunities explain why during the 1960s much of the political activity among Mexican Americans in San Antonio occurred around school board elections. At a time when citywide races for at-large council seats put Mexican Americans at a disadvantage, the large number of relatively small school districts permitted them to capitalize on their population concentrations in specific areas.

This ferment was reflected in the landmark *San Antonio v. Rodriguez* school finance case. Initiated in 1968 in behalf of the parents of Mexican-American schoolchildren in various San Antonio school districts, the suit was soon joined by other parties, including the aforementioned José Cardenas, who had recently been named superintendent of the Edgewood District. Their charge—that the Texas school finance system unconstitutionally discriminated against minority children in property-poor school districts across the state—was ultimately rejected by the U.S. Supreme Court.[13] That 1973 decision was a stunning blow to the plaintiffs' legal counsel, the fledgling Mexican American Legal Defense and Educational Fund.[14] But the political forces pushing for reform were not turned back, and subsequently shifted to the Texas legislature, where Mexican Americans have been at the center of efforts throughout the 1980s and into the 1990s to overhaul the state's school finance system.

During this period, more and more Mexican Americans have been drawn into school politics. Some districts have been battlegrounds between once-dominant Anglos and members of the emergent group. In other districts Mexican Americans have completely taken over school boards, which have then typically been beset by factional infighting. As a result, school politics has a reputation for being quite vicious. One Mexican-American politician with extensive ties to the schools observes, "school politics can screw you." An Anglo city councillor sees school politics as destructive of its participants, and notes that very few board members—Anglos or Mexicans—are able to move on to higher elected offices.

At first glance, this discouraging assessment may seem surprising. The relatively low costs of entering the fray in San Antonio's many small districts, and the clear rewards of victory, would seem to make school boards ideal launching pads for political careers. In practice, however, easy entry means that school politics attracts many amateurs lacking the skills necessary to moderate conflicts over the division of spoils. Such conflicts

are intensified when the participants are Mexican Americans just beginning to flex their political muscles after a long period of Anglo domination. For many Mexican Americans, the schools offer teaching jobs that
represent the first step out of the blue-collar world of the barrio. For the
more ambitious, there are tempting administrative positions with high
salaries and status. One school superintendent stresses how large a school
principal's salary looms for an upwardly mobile Mexican American with
few other means of earning a comparable income in San Antonio's sluggish economy.

Many successful Mexican-American politicians know all this firsthand:
a good number of them are former teachers who parlayed their visibility
in the community, perhaps as a football coach or bandleader, into elective office. It is noteworthy, however, that very few of these more successful politicians started off as elected school board members. Instead,
they have relied on their ties to the districts without getting caught up in
the bitter infighting. Such politicians know that their former colleagues
make good campaign workers, in part because teachers have a good deal
of free time. The politicians also know that teachers generally develop interpersonal and communication skills that blue-collar workers may lack;
yet they are not so educated or elevated in status that they are likely to
alienate or threaten working-class voters.

Thus, school districts have emerged as important bases for Mexican-
American politicians in San Antonio. In particular, there is a nexus between school districts and Mexican-American state legislators, whose
low-pay and part-time status leave them with little visibility or power. The
school districts provide these legislators with significant patronage not
otherwise available to them. In turn, the legislators vote on legislation of
critical importance to teachers. One Mexican-American state senator was
said to have had thirty-eight relatives on the payroll of the San Antonio
Independent School District. Perhaps exaggerated, such comments nevertheless capture the essence of the situation.

Yet school politics is not driven exclusively, or perhaps even primarily,
by venality and the desire for power. Strong community loyalties also
come into play. As suggested by the rituals surrounding Friday night football games across the state, schools in Texas are the focus of almost pri-
mordial communal sentiments. And because many of the school districts
in San Antonio grew up around small, well-defined communities subsequently annexed by the city, the schools often represent the last link to a
cherished past. Especially where Mexicans have been gradually crowding out the residents of former Anglo enclaves, school politics is particularly rancorous. According to a veteran politico and participant in one

such situation, "the battle in Harlandale [Independent School District] was not just over patronage, but basically over the definition of the community."

Finally, education speaks to the aspirations Mexican Americans, after generations of social isolation and despair, have today for their children. As one Anglo politician in San Antonio puts it, "education is today the gut issue among Mexican Americans—how to get out of the West Side." These aspirations were certainly evident in the *Rodriguez* case, and in the support Mexican-American organizations in San Antonio and across the state gave subsequent school finance and other education reform proposals.

This intense involvement in the schools is one reason why, despite long-standing concerns about the quality of their children's education, Mexican Americans in San Antonio have never seriously entertained solutions like busing or consolidation with wealthier Anglo districts. As one of the "West Side warlords" observes, such policies would undermine some of the most important political bases that Mexican Americans have developed.

ORGANIZATION POLITICS: MACHINE POLITICS, PROPERLY UNDERSTOOD

Criticized as corrupt and venal, friends-and-neighbors politics is often disdainfully dismissed as "patronage politics." Ironically, this usage reduces "patronage" to a mere monetary relationship, when its root is of course "patron," whose denotation of an authority relationship is an important dimension of friends-and-neighbors politics to which I now turn. Implicit in the face-to-face, primary-group ties in which friends-and-neighbors politics is immersed are the status and authority relations that naturally obtain among individuals, and that are particularly evident in a tradition-oriented setting like San Antonio: relations between parent and child, community leader and neighbor, or perhaps priest and parishioner. In many contexts this hierarchical dimension may not be particularly salient. But in others it is very much in evidence.

Take, for example, a not atypical scene in the Bexar County Courthouse. An elderly Mexican-American woman, stooped over and wrapped in a shawl, waits patiently on a bench outside the county judge's office. She is having problems paying this month's rent. When the old woman finally gets the chance to explain her situation, the judge pulls out his wallet and hands her a few bills. Next on the bench, a middle-aged couple are distraught over their teenage son's behavior in school. The judge consoles them and urges them to come back with their son, to whom he will deliver a lecture on responsibilities to one's family. Whatever their problems and however long they have to sit, such constituents know that this man will help them in some way: a phone call to another official, a word of advice, a small loan.

This variant of friends-and-neighbors politics has sometimes been called deference politics or, alternatively, the politics of "personal fealty."[15] In Texas it is often referred to as *patrón* politics. By whatever name, this style of politics is a vestige of the hierarchical social relations of South Texas ranching culture, in which social, political, and economic power were typically wielded by a single individual or elite. The multidimensional role of the *patrón* (or *jefe*) has in the past been played by Anglos as well as Mexicans. Today, Mexican Americans who practice *patrón* politics shame and enrage their younger, more educated colleagues, who regard it as a throwback to the days when Mexicans sold their votes for "beer and tamales." It is certainly difficult to imagine a politician like Henry Cisneros playing this role. Although he has enormous appeal to the humblest Mexican Americans, this self-styled technocrat simply does not wield that kind of authority; nor did the largely symbolic powers of the mayor's office afford him the opportunity to distribute such benefits to individual supplicants. Nonetheless, *patrón* politics persists in San Antonio, particularly at the county level, where elected officials still exercise considerable discretion, and where large numbers of Mexican Americans remain disposed, by cultural tradition and low socioeconomic status, to rely on personal relationships with public officials for help with any number of life's problems.

Patrón politics is relevant to my analysis because the hierarchical relationships which characterize it highlight an important source of the discipline necessary to overcome the fragmentation and factionalism of friends-and-neighbors politics. In the United States this discipline has, at least in the past, been provided by the political machine, which took the strong primary group ties of ethnic neighborhoods and reoriented them toward the goals of a larger, more impersonal organization, which is after all the connotation of the word "machine." The more stable, instrumental relationships that characterize political machines are achieved by reliance on material inducements, which are more easily marshaled and managed than the solidary incentives of friends-and-neighbors politics. Indeed, while friends-and-neighbors politics relies primarily on solidary incentives, supplemented by material inducements, the political machine relies on precisely the opposite mix of incentives.[16]

Quite unlike friends-and-neighbors politics, the machine is not a naturally occurring political formation, but the result of human artifice and convention. In other words, political skill and leadership are necessary to forge the relationships of friends-and-neighbors politics into a machine. Political machines have consequently been relatively rare in American politics. Indeed, the organizational cohesion and hierarchical authority on which machines depend have been continuously undermined by the centrifugal tendencies of our decentralized political system. As a result, the friends-and-neighbors style has been much more common, indeed pervasive, than the political machine.

Despite these fundamental differences, friends-and-neighbors politics and political machines have been confused in the public mind. In part this is because both styles flourished in the same kind of close-knit ethnic communities. And as I will explore below, both styles are similarly inattentive to issues and substantive political outcomes. Further compounding the confusion has been the reliance of both styles on incentives—personal ties, favors, jobs, money—indiscriminately and disdainfully lumped together by reformers as "patronage," on whose misleading connotation I have already commented.

More generally, "machine" is perhaps one of the most misunderstood words in the American political lexicon, applied haphazardly to all variety of political formations: from the personal following of a patronage-wielding demagogue like Boston's James Michael Curley, to the sophisticated computer-targeted direct-mail operation of Los Angeles congressmen Henry Waxman and Howard Berman, to the citywide political organization put together by a figure like Chicago's (first) Mayor Daley. Of these, only the last is a machine in the strict sense of the term: a political organization encompassing a major political jurisdiction—an entire city or state—that transcends the personal ties and ambitions of its individual participants.

For all these reasons, I prefer to avoid the term "machine politics" and use instead the more generic term "organization politics," which captures the essential point, as expressed by James Q. Wilson, that "the machine was the supreme expression of the value of organization."[17] This more generic term will permit me to explore Alinsky community organizations in San Antonio and Los Angeles that are not, properly speaking, political machines but that are in many respects—particularly with regard to the discipline and order they seek to impose on Mexican-American politics—quite similar to them.[18]

To some, it may seem curious to place these Alinsky organizations in the same category with the Daley machine, particularly since Richard Joseph Daley and Saul David Alinsky were longtime political antagonists in their native Chicago, where Alinsky began his labor and community-organizing efforts back in the 1930s. In light of Alinsky's well-deserved reputation for staging highly disruptive demonstrations, any parallels between his and Daley's political styles may seem particularly far-fetched. Nevertheless, I argue here that Alinsky community organizing has evolved in a direction that now makes it the functional equivalent of the virtually defunct political machines.

THE METHOD OF ALINSKY ORGANIZING[19]

As mentioned earlier, Communities Organized for Public Service (COPS) and the United Neighborhoods Organization (UNO) were both started in the 1970s by Ernesto Cortes, a community organizer trained in the techniques developed by the late Saul Alinsky and now promulgated by the Industrial Areas Foundation (IAF), the umbrella group set up by Alinsky in 1940. The most noted, and deplored, of these techniques are noisy protests and confrontations. Yet outside observers, particularly if they have had to tangle with such groups, overlook the fact that Alinsky organizers resort to confrontation not merely to promote group solidarity or to get media attention—the usual protest goals—but to build and maintain their organizations. Moreover, confrontation is only one of several different tactics on which these organizers rely. Today in San Antonio, COPS spends more time quietly negotiating with private and public officials than loudly confronting them. In strategy sessions and weeklong training retreats, Alinsky organizers teach recently recruited leaders that there is a time to confront and a time to back off—in Alinsky jargon, a time to "polarize" and a time to "depolarize." Indeed, organizers sometimes complain that leaders are "too confrontational" and lack more subtle political skills in dealing with adversaries. Specifically, organizers teach that precisely because today's enemy may well be tomorrow's ally, negotiation and compromise are as critical to the art of politics as confrontation.

To be sure, Alinsky organizers typically express the kind of contempt for politicians that one hears from activists. On the other hand, they do not disdain all politicians. For example, organizers read and discuss books about Mayor Daley and the Chicago machine, not necessarily as one would study a role model, but as one would seek to understand a worthy adversary. In any event, these organizers certainly do not see themselves as protest leaders, whom they dismiss as "sixties movement types" incapable of building and sustaining organizations.

The first thing Alinsky organizers do upon arriving in a community is conduct brief interviews—"one-on-one's"—with as many people as possible. In thirty-minute sessions, organizers seek to discover two things: the issues on people's minds that might serve as organizing foci and, even more important, the community's "natural leaders." From the organizer's perspective such individuals can not only be trained to lead the organization, they also provide the "networks" whose numbers will build up its ranks.

By its very nature, then, Alinsky organizing is predicated on full-blooded, face-to-face relationships. This is why organizers encourage their leaders to avoid, whenever possible, shortcuts like telephone canvasses or in-house newsletters. Such concerns explain why Alinsky and his followers have typically worked best with homeowners in stable working- and lower-middle-class neighborhoods. Such communities inevitably have problems around which to organize, but also strong primary group ties and viable institutions with which to work. Seldom, if ever, have Alinsky organizers worked with the poorest and most destitute populations.

In San Antonio and Los Angeles, Alinsky organizers have attempted to use the bonds of neighborhood, parish, and ethnic group to build organizations that then focus these typically affective, nonrational ties on achieving rational goals. Organizers emphasize that a community organization is not one organization but "an organization of organizations." This reflects the Alinsky dictum that a community organization must be rooted in a functioning community whose relationships and institutions antedate it. Clearly at odds with orthodox leftist perspectives that assume the necessity for external agents to impose order and direction on an atomized mass, the Alinsky view, with evident roots in Aristotle, depicts the organizer as perfecting and giving shape to a set of diverse, organic social formations. As these organizers put it, "All organizing is reorganizing what's already there." In the past, Alinsky organizations have typically been stitched together out of union locals, block associations, and civic and church groups.[20] Today, COPS and UNO are made up almost exclusively of Catholic parishes. Other Alinsky organizations rely more heavily on Protestant and, in a few instances, Jewish congregations. Some organizations have been experimenting with local chapters affiliated with university campuses and unions. But the backbone of Alinsky organizing efforts among Mexican Americans remains Catholic parishes.

Another hallmark of Alinsky organizing is its aggressive rejection of abstract appeals, whether to middle-class ideals of civic virtue, left-wing ideologies, or ethnic or racial identities. Organizers adopt a pragmatic, almost opportunistic stance that distinguishes (in their terminology) between the vaguely defined "global problems" typically addressed by activists and the narrow "winnable issues" of immediate concern to those being organized. "Self-interest" is a much overworked phrase in Alinsky circles. Yet it is definitely the starting point for the organizers' concentration on mundane, concrete issues—whether the need for storm drains or lower insurance rates.[21]

Consider the situation of an Alinsky organizer who comes across a middle-aged housewife with a husband and several children, all crowded into a rundown house on San Antonio's West Side. Mrs. Juarez begins to get involved in COPS activities in her parish. She soon expresses interest in housing issues, especially a provision of the Community Development Block Grant program that provides for the razing of substandard owner-occupied homes and their replacement with completely new structures. Entire blocks of such single-family houses have been built in some West Side parishes.

By this time, the organizer has figured out what Mrs. Juarez is after. As he puts it matter-of-factly, "Mrs. Juarez wants a house." The organizer neither denies her motive nor embellishes it with elaborate ideological trappings. He simply takes her self-interest as a given. According to the Alinsky maxim, the organizer is taking the world "as it is, not as it ought to be."[22] But though careful not to confuse the "ought" with the "is," the organizer is not willing to leave the world as he finds it. Nor is he content to leave Mrs. Juarez's self-interest unchallenged. He is definitely not prepared to indulge it, as did welfare-rights organizers in the 1960s when they traded their members' involvement in boisterous demonstrations for increased AFDC (Aid to Families with Dependent Children) benefits.[23] For Alinsky organizers see themselves as teachers, and as such they regard Mrs. Juarez's efforts to gain a new house as the first step on the road to her self-interest being broadened to include that of the organization as well.

Paraphrasing de Tocqueville's formulation about "self-interest properly understood,"[24] Alinsky organizers distinguish between "self-interest" and "enlightened self-interest." Despite their talk of building a community organization by focusing on issues of immediate self-interest, they actually have a much more subtle, long-range process in mind. For organizers understand that an individual's self-interest is not necessarily obvious or self-evident; above all, it is highly subjective and therefore malleable, amenable to deliberation and refinement.[25]

So, self-interest is not just an organizing gimmick. It is an ethos that suffuses the day-to-day functioning of Alinsky organizations. In dealings among themselves, leaders are expected to approach one another on the basis of mutual self-interest. *"Quid pro quo"* is a phrase they hear continually from the organizers. And while the needs of the organization may occasionally be invoked to get someone to act, leaders are far more likely to bargain with one another for help in, say, producing a large turnout for a meeting. If a leader fumbles, the organizer will sit her down and ask: "Mrs. Garcia, why should Mrs. Rodriguez come over to help you on this drainage issue? Her parish doesn't need drainage projects. What's in it for her and her local?"

Thus does bargaining pervade Alinsky organizations: leaders bargain with their chapter members and with organizers for recognition within the organization; organizers bargain with leaders over their salaries. Indeed, in an organization built around the self-interest of volunteer members and leaders, the self-interest of paid organizers is taken very seriously. Gone are the days when Alinsky organizers were quixotic troublemakers willing to thrive on low pay and long hours.

Today the hours may still be grueling, but the pay is a bit more respectable. An entry-level organizer may start off with an annual salary as low as $22,000, but can move up to a lead organizer position paying from $38,000 to as much as $50,000. A few senior organizers draw even higher salaries. Alinsky organizers take their work very seriously and regard themselves as professionals.[26] They dress accordingly: at leadership training sessions male organizers wear ties and sports jackets. Unlike organizing efforts such as Massachusetts Fair Share or ACORN, both with roots in 1960s student activism, Alinsky projects do not typically recruit recent college graduates willing to live from hand to mouth.[27] Alinsky organizers are typically in their forties and have families and children. Late-night beer-drinking strategy sessions are something these people associate with their younger "movement days." Quite a few of these organizers are religious professionals; some are ex-seminarians. Strikingly, very few are veterans of the New Left or its offshoots.

Self-reliance is the concomitant of the Alinsky emphasis on self-interest. The frequently invoked "Iron Rule" is: "Don't do for people what they can do for themselves." At a weeklong leadership institute for trainees from around the country, not a single name tag is to be seen: participants are expected to find out about one another on their own initiative.

Self-reliance is most evident in the way Alinsky organizations raise money. COPS and UNO, for example, shun government funding. This policy was apparently maintained even when Sam Brown, director of ACTION in the Carter administration, was willing to fund Alinsky organizations, as he did other community organizing efforts. These organizations have influenced—in some cases quite successfully—the flow of public funds to favored projects, but such resources have not typically been sought for the direct subvention of the organizations themselves.

In this as in other respects, COPS and its sister organizations share Alinsky's contempt for government-subsidized activism—in the 1960s he denounced the War on Poverty as "political pornography."[28] Also like Alinsky, who long ago brandished the phrase "welfare colonialism," these organizers criticize government social programs for fostering dependencies that stifle the innate political capacities of poor communities.[29] They hardly favor dismantling the welfare state, but they are skeptical of many assumptions undergirding it. As one organizer put it, "You know, Reagan is about 30 percent right."[30]

Convinced that early Alinsky projects like the Community Service Organization (CSO) in California and The Woodlawn Organization (TWO) in Chicago went astray when they accepted government funds,[31] these organizers today look warily even at support from private foundations.[32] As mentioned earlier, COPS, UNO, and their sister organizations have typically gotten off the ground with seed grants from the Catholic Church's Campaign for Human Development. But these have generally been limited to three years, after which the organization is expected to fend for itself.

Organizers have tried to turn this "necessity" into a virtue. For example, COPS leaders are responsible for raising the organization's budget, currently about $150,000 annually. Of this sum, approximately one-third comes from the dues assessed on each parish chapter. A substantial portion of the remainder is raised by soliciting advertising from local businesses in the organization's annual "adbook." Since the book has a very limited printing and virtually no advertising value, this is in essence a pretext for soliciting financial support from precisely those parties with whom COPS has often found itself in an adversary relationship. Indeed, the organization's critics have sometimes denounced this undertaking as "extortion." Nevertheless, the adbook has proved successful financially. COPS leaders speak with considerable, though perhaps exaggerated, justification when they proudly declare, "We don't owe our money to anyone except ourselves." To drive home the point, a favorite Alinsky ploy has been to make an occasional show of returning a contribution that, as one organizer put it, "reeks of charity rather than an exchange between equals."

Yet the adbook campaign is also intended to contribute to leadership development. COPS organizers know that their leaders, for the most part unsophisticated Mexican Americans from humble origins, find it difficult to solicit funds from San Antonio's leading citizens. But the organizers also know that having to sell the organization in person to local notables builds up the leaders' confidence in themselves and in COPS.[33] As a result, these organizations avoid the defensiveness of protest groups, whose insularity typically convinces members of the uncompromising hostility of their adversaries.

This notion of leadership development is fundamental to Alinsky organizing. Just as with the self-interest of new members, these organizers are not content to take a hands-off attitude toward those whom they refer to as "natural leaders." Indeed, as I have already indicated, Alinsky organizers make no bones about the fact that a large part of their job is teaching. In contrast with New Left-inspired community organizers, these people are not smitten with egalitarian notions of participatory democracy. Whether in daily strategy sessions or weekend training retreats, leaders are constantly being coached and critiqued on their writing and speaking style, their political judgments, their public demeanor. It is fascinating to watch an organizer who a few moments earlier was relentlessly haranguing a befuddled federal bureaucrat sit down with his leaders and patiently explore with them what went well in the meeting and what did not. "Mentor" is a word heard frequently in these circles, and as one organizer explains, "All that organizing really is is being a good teacher." In essence, organizers give their leaders intense tutorials in the nature of politics that would arouse the envy of many a political science graduate student.

The authoritative role played by organizers has a significant impact on the recruitment of leaders. Because organizers expend considerable time and energy working with them, leaders tend to find their involvement with these organizations quite stimulating. Unaccustomed to the sort of attention they receive, leaders typically experience marked personal growth. A few clearly find it the most rewarding experience of their lives.[34] But at the same time, these leaders, who are after all unpaid volunteers, must be willing to put up with the organizers' demanding, sometimes harsh treatment (as when one organizer, a nun, criticized a leader's public demeanor by saying she was "too fat"). For those who have a lot to learn, the bargain may seem a reasonable one. But for those with broader horizons and opportunities, it may not. As a result, the leaders of COPS and UNO have been, with a few exceptions, working- and lower-middle-class Mexican-American housewives with limited career prospects. These organizations have a much tougher time attracting college-educated Mexican Americans, especially well-educated men.

From the Alinsky perspective, being a good teacher most definitely does not mean being a good friend. In order to challenge and push leaders, organizers are expected to maintain a certain distance. As one organizer puts it to his trainees "good teachers don't care if you like them or not." Another describes the ideal bond between organizer and leader: ". . . a love-hate relationship . . . the leaders should be relieved to hear the organizer is being reassigned to another project." Indeed, one leader says of the organizers, "Sometimes we could just kill them." In some cases there are real tensions, even animosities between leaders and organizers. In any event, maintaining a detached, businesslike relationship with leaders is another facet of the professionalism Alinsky organizers very self-consciously bring to their work. This concern explains why organizers routinely spend only two to three years at a time with any one organization.

On the other hand, given the enormous amounts of time organizers and leaders spend together, maintaining this professional distance is sometimes not easy. A not atypical situation arises when an admiring leader invites the organizer home for dinner. Knowing it might be better to politely refuse, but also feeling awkward about declining previous invitations, the organizer accepts, on condition they talk business after dinner. But when the leader's daughter and son-in-law show up, the evening suddenly becomes a purely social event. When this happened to one COPS organizer, he expressed great frustration and emphasized how accepting the leader's hospitality compromised his ability to be as demanding of her as necessary—particularly because Mexican Americans do not casually invite outsiders into their homes.[35]

As teachers, organizers regard instilling in leaders this sense of professional distance as central to their efforts. According to the frequently repeated Alinsky dictum, leaders must "learn to separate the public from the private." As I have indicated, one weakness of friends-and-neighbors politics is that its practitioners confound the public and the private. Organizers see this problem every time one of their leaders invites a sympathetic state bureaucrat home to dinner, or asks a politician who has been helpful on some issue to a COPS victory celebration. Indeed, organizers warn against such gestures, reminding members that the private realm of friends and family operates on fundamentally different principles from the public realm of business and politics. More specifically, organizers carefully draw the distinction between the diffuse, unconditional relationships of private life with the role-segmented, reciprocal relations of public life. Yet they do not teach that one sphere is superior to the other, merely that each has unique dynamics that must not be confused.

And this is what politicians do instinctively when they address leaders by their first names or compliment them on their new hairdos. By deliberately blurring the line between the public and the private, organizers emphasize, politicians seek to gain advantage over political novices.[36]

As a result, Alinsky leaders conduct their affairs with a self-consciously businesslike bearing. They refuse to address others, or to be addressed, on a first-name basis. They are insistent upon starting meetings on time, and never hesitate to scold tardy politicians or corporate executives and remind them that community leaders are also busy people. Dispensing with preliminary small talk, these leaders proceed abruptly to the business at hand, and then just as abruptly adjourn the session. To individuals on the receiving end of such treatment, it seems curiously rigid and a bit bizarre. But that's because they've never heard an Alinsky organizer lecture on separating the public from the private. Nor have they heard organizers teach leaders how to maintain control of situations by doing the unexpected, "by going outside the experience of your opponents."[37] Even so, leaders admit to having a hard time getting used to acting in ways that they consider downright rude.

Members are continually reminded of the public dimension of their activities, and urged to "test their friendships" by involving fellow parishioners and neighbors. In some instances, organizers admit, long-standing relationships may be strained, but this is the price of building an organization. As these housewives become leaders and spend more and more time with the organization, this price may also include renegotiating relationships with their families, who often prefer that their wives and mothers simply stay at home. For women who admit (as most of these leaders do) to never having been out of town without their husbands, going to New York for a two-week IAF training session—typically over their husbands' strenuous objections—is a major turning point in their lives.

The same principles obtain inside these organizations. Organizers encourage members to deal with one another in a professional manner. A visitor notices an air of brisk efficiency about the organization's office. Members typically address one another, as well as their opponents, by surname; and tend not to socialize with one another. These organizations are definitely not conceived of as fellowships bound by all-inclusive loyalties against a hostile environment. In other words, they are certainly not what James Q. Wilson refers to as "redemptive organizations."[38]

The context within which these lessons get taught are the confrontations with businessmen and politicians for which Alinsky and his disciples are justifiably notorious. In all such "actions," as organizers refer to them, a key objective is to build up the confidence of politically unsophisticated members by demonstrating to them—and their opponents—how *as a group* they can exercise control over, and even humiliate, public figures to whom *as individuals* they would likely defer.

As one San Antonio politician describes it: "Their game is to make you feel inadequate." That game often involves gimmicks that underscore the organization's detachment from the commotion it creates and its members' refusal to be awed by public figures. A sense of humor to leaven typically tense confrontations is consequently critical to an Alinsky organizer's bag of tricks. A good example is an event that never actually took place. Rochester, New York has long been noted for its philanthropic tradition and civic-mindedness. Arriving there in 1965, Alinsky found himself being ignored by the city's elite—until he let it be known that his people would be holding a bean supper and then attending the symphony en masse. The mere threat of this "stink-in" got Alinsky the attention he wanted.[39]

To create drama around an action, Alinsky organizers routinely reduce complicated public policy issues to simple conflicts between good and bad individuals. Indeed, organizers deliberately fasten onto such personalized targets in order to draw unsophisticated members into the intimidating and confusing world of politics.[40] Here again, a sense of humor, in the form of ridicule, is a key weapon in the Alinsky arsenal. When COPS challenged the policies of the San Antonio Water Board, it focused its attack on the appointed chairman, one of the area's leading real estate developers. To sustain its charge of a basic conflict between this individual's business interests and his official responsibilities on a public body making critical decisions affecting developers, COPS nicknamed its target "bwana," thereby focusing attention on the contrast between his carefully crafted image as a progressive community leader and his penchant for extravagant African safaris.

Many observers dismiss such Alinsky tactics as mere stunts to gain media attention and raw emotional appeals to tap pent-up frustrations. These aspects of the confrontations cannot be denied. Yet there is more to them. Just as with their appeals to material self-interest, Alinsky organizers do not merely indulge base sentiments, but use them to draw individuals into a process that seeks to teach about what Cortes calls "the art of public discourse and political argument." Moreover, the better-established and more successful Alinsky organizations now show signs of abandoning the more egregiously simplistic tactics on which they have undeniably relied.

Punning on their term for a confrontation or demonstration, Alinsky organizers continually remind their members, "the action is in the reaction." That is, the action is a means of producing a response with which the organization must then deal. And after every action there is an "evaluation," in which the organizer assesses the performance of the participants. Sometimes the evaluation is just a hurried meeting of organizers and key leaders on the steps of city hall after a session with the mayor; other times it is more leisurely and deliberative. One way or another there is always some kind of reflection on what the organization has just done. Indeed, organizers describe the evaluation as the most important part of every action.

To officials who have been publicly harassed and humiliated by an Alinsky organization, this interpretation may seem overly sympathetic or downright incorrect. Yet all Alinsky actions are carefully planned and orchestrated events. Large public meetings are typically patrolled by a team of highly visible "floor captains" capable of dealing with disruptive members of the audience. Woe to the inspired soul who stands up out of turn and presents a personal complaint, or compliment, to the politicians present; he or she is quickly muzzled. Such sessions are also assigned a "press committee," which attends to representatives of the fourth estate. At meetings directly sponsored by the organization, designated members are responsible for escorting politicians and other guests, making sure they don't do too much politicking on the way to the podium, and then "debriefing" them on the way out to get their reactions to the proceedings. Leaders, who typically pose pointed, yes-or-no questions to the guests, are carefully rehearsed in advance. Organizers rely heavily on role-playing techniques, which are seen as a teaching device to get them to reflect on the motivations and perspectives of their adversaries.

Moreover, organizers make no bones about getting the best possible performances out of their leaders. As one organizer observes, "We teach political drama, and an action is a good one-act play." Given their familiarity with the mores of the Catholic Church, Alinsky organizers are quick to draw analogies between political theater and religious liturgy. As a nun working with COPS puts it, "All politics relies on ritual—on liturgy. And such liturgy teaches people about the world as it should be."[41]

Despite such attention to drama, all this careful planning often results in meetings that are reduced to dull formalities. A skeptic might conclude that the annual COPS convention, at which the organization's officers are elected, resembles a session of the old Supreme Soviet. Participants know their parts; there are few surprises; and votes are mechanical, with generally preordained results.

Yet this too is by design. For, as organizers explain, the leaders' energies should be focused on participating in premeeting planning and post-meeting evaluation. Indeed, leaders are taught that good political operatives reach agreements with opponents in advance of any public meetings. Public votes should then be pro forma ratifications of prior deals. Thus, the hallmarks of a good Alinsky meeting are simplicity and brevity. These are critical, the organizers emphasize, because nothing alienates prospective members more than long-winded sessions where nothing gets accomplished.

THE GOALS OF ALINSKY ORGANIZING

These very features, of course, might be indicative of manipulative, antidemocratic tendencies within Alinsky organizations. At a minimum, there is the potential for leaders to become dependent on their organizer-mentors. Signs of such dependence are certainly evident. But this seems unavoidable, since organizers see themselves as teachers and focus on leadership development in small, private group sessions appropriate to that task.

Yet such concerns about Alinsky methods are substantially lessened when the objectives or goals toward which they are directed are examined. Because these organizations lack well-defined or formal goals, this can be a frustrating exercise. Despite, for example, considerable rhetorical commitment to family, neighborhood, and parish,[42] the preoccupation of Alinsky organizers with process and the maintenance of their organizations obscures the substantive goals toward which their efforts are directed. It may therefore be easier to get a handle on these community organizations by specifying goals they do *not* have.

To begin, Alinsky organizations cannot fairly be identified with any established political program or perspective. For example, they are frequently taken to be leftists, but as I have already emphasized, they are not. Alinsky always pinned the label "radical" on whatever he said or did, but this was very misleading. Though he sometimes drew on the leftist lexicon, his rhetoric was fundamentally populist. Alinsky's willingness to work with Communists at times, and his vehement criticism of anti-Communists, should not be allowed to obscure his own rejection of communist doctrine.[43] Alinsky certainly never saw himself as engaged in a Marxian class struggle. He was a radical only in the sense that his confrontational tactics violated the comity of interest-group politics. His goals were never radical, which is why he was reviled by leftists—and why he always returned the compliment.

Alinsky's heirs at COPS and UNO are similarly disdainful of leftists, which has nevertheless not prevented them from being red-baited.[44] As noted earlier, very few Alinsky organizers today are refugees from, or admirers of, the New Left. Although leaders are trained to be suspicious of politicians and businessmen, class envy and antagonism are not part of the curriculum. The problem with leftists, according to one organizer, is that they always "try to resolve the tension between the world as it is and the world as it ought to be." The utopianism of leftists offends these hard-headed pragmatists.[45]

For that matter, Alinsky was similarly critical of liberals.[46] Alinsky organizers today also get embroiled with liberal sympathizers, whose offers of help and support make excellent targets for organizations of lower-middle-class homeowners in need of a good fight and a sense of self-reliance. The Alinsky critique of liberals is not merely tactical, however. From this perspective, the quintessence of liberalism is the War on Poverty, whose self-deluded paternalism never faced up to the hard realities of grassroots politics. One organizer made the connection explicit when in a leadership training session he traced the origins of the War on Poverty back to Lyndon Johnson's early association with Congressman Richard Kleberg, whose family's King Ranch in South Texas embodied the *patrón* values of a Mexican hacienda.

Consistent with their rhetoric extolling neighborhood and family, Alinsky organizers are particularly disparaging of what they regard as contemporary liberalism's preoccupation with individual rights, which they insist are of fundamental importance but must nevertheless be balanced against communitarian concerns. Although they steer their organizations away from the controversial social issues, organizers, when pressed, generally prove unsympathetic to the standard liberal positions on drugs, abortion, and pornography. Discussing these issues, one organizer refers with some disdain to "the ACLU problem."

This does not mean Alinsky organizations won't work with liberals when it suits their purposes. Indeed, some of their best friends are liberals. But such allies are regarded with considerable skepticism. A good example is MALDEF, with whom Alinsky organizers have worked on a variety of issues, including school finance reform in Texas. In spite of such cooperation, organizers have doubts about such legal strategies. In part, this reflects a gut sense that the quickest way for an organizing drive to lose momentum is to get bogged down in complicated legal proceedings. But this view also reflects the more general Alinsky critique of what organizers regard as elitist, top-down reform that would bestow benefits and rights on the powerless without teaching them the political skills necessary to secure these for themselves.[47]

The Alinsky emphasis on process over substance is particularly evident when organizers tell members: "Issues don't really matter." Indeed, the *idée fixe* of Alinsky and his heirs is that issues are only the means to the end of building up and maintaining "the organization." Organizers consequently disdain single-issue efforts and insist upon building multi-issue organizations that subsume a variety of interests and therefore do not depend for survival on any one problem or concern.[48]

In the same vein, Alinsky organizations do not run their own candidates for political office. Indeed, nonpartisanship is a critical aspect of their self-image, and they similarly refuse to endorse specific individuals for elective offices. In the case of COPS and UNO, this stance flows partly from the close ties of these organizations to the Catholic Church, which is obviously restricted in its political activities. But it also derives from the concern to buffer the organization from the manipulations and vicissitudes of individual politicians. And though on occasion stretched to its limits, this independence is generally maintained—which often means other political actors are not always eager to work with these organizations.

Of central importance to this study, Alinsky organizations do not pursue ethnic or racial goals. To be sure, with exclusively Mexican-American memberships, COPS and UNO derive considerable cohesiveness from the social glue of ethnic ties: a common history of deprivation and a shared cultural heritage. In the day-to-day life of the organizations, solidarity is clearly fostered by a prayer to the Virgin of Guadalupe at the beginning of an action, or a Mexican folksong sung at a *pachanga* (party).

Yet for all the vitality and cohesion it affords these organizations, this common heritage is merely a backdrop to their day-to-day operations. This is not to say that members are urged to deny or downplay their heritage; it is so much a part of their lives that it can't help but play a role. Yet ethnic pride or consciousness is not the raison d'être of these organizations. Their antiseptic names—Communities Organized for Public Service and United Neighborhoods Organization—suggest this immediately. It follows that Alinsky organizers are disdainful of Chicano activists and other practitioners of the politics of ethnic or racial consciousness. Since most of these organizers are not Mexican Americans, this should perhaps not be surprising. But more fundamentally, broad affirmations of "Chicanismo" are not compatible with the concrete, "winnable" objectives pursued by Cortes and his colleagues. Nor are they compatible, as I will explore later in this chapter, with the commitment of Cortes and his colleagues to building, whenever possible, community organizations made up of diverse ethnic, racial, and religious groups.

Nevertheless, to their adversaries these organizations have not always seemed untainted by the politics of ethnic consciousness. For example, in its early days in San Antonio, when relatively few Mexican-American officials were available as targets, there was inevitably an ethnic edge to COPS actions. The organizers certainly did all they could to tap generations of discontent among Mexicans there. Yet even if they hadn't, South Texas history would have made that edge inevitable. Paradoxically, that history means that organizers in San Antonio have not typically had to cast their actions in explicitly ethnic terms.

Thus, COPS and UNO (the latter to a lesser extent, for reasons I will explore below) have not focused on explicitly ethnic issues. In San Antonio, the early battles were for drainage systems, street pavements, and sidewalks; in Los Angeles, lower auto insurance rates. More recently, COPS has pursued better housing, improved police protection, economic development, and education reform; UNO has put many of these same items on its agenda, along with a successful effort to increase the minimum wage in California. Conspicuously absent from this list are the issues typically associated with Mexican Americans in recent years: U.S. policy in Central America, bilingual education, and immigration. Again, these are the kind of "global issues" that Alinsky organizers reject as "unwinnable."

Perhaps most revealing of how ethnic identity is handled in these organizations is the way leaders are taught to deal with Mexican-American officials. Because ethnic pride is not emphasized, the steadily increasing number of Mexican-American public figures has posed few problems. Organizers certainly do not fire up members by denouncing adversaries who happen to be Mexican-American as "*vendidos* [sell-outs]." On the contrary, they teach the same lesson as when the targets were primarily Anglos: that politicians are by definition untrustworthy and require constant scrutiny.

This is not to say that a figure like Cisneros has presented no difficulties for COPS organizers in San Antonio. Mexican Americans are like other groups in their craving for recognition and acceptance by the mainstream. Naturally, they responded enthusiastically to Cisneros, whose success confirmed their own aspirations. As mayor he was therefore able, on several critical issues, to appeal to the barrio over the heads of COPS leaders. Conversely, despite its renunciation of ethnic political posturing, COPS's de facto status as the organized voice of Mexican Americans in

San Antonio allowed Cisneros to use the organization to extract concessions from Anglo elites.

Language use further reveals how these organizations deal with ethnic identity. Spanish can be an important part of day-to-day life in the stable Mexican-American neighborhoods targeted by Alinsky organizers. While many residents may speak little or no Spanish, they can usually understand it. Recent immigrants, of course, mean fresh infusions of Spanish monolinguals. And among the elderly, many able to get along with English feel more comfortable with Spanish, particularly at large meetings where complicated issues are being discussed. Nevertheless, at COPS's tenth anniversary convention the two-and-a-half-hour proceedings were almost entirely in English, causing many older members to grow restless and leave early. Yet organizers teach that "English is the language of power" and insist that English proficiency is a must for anyone aspiring to a leadership position.

A cynic might say this emphasis on English reflects the simple fact that most Alinsky organizers, including some of the Mexican Americans among them, are not native Spanish speakers. For that matter, many leaders, who tend to be younger and more assimilated than rank-and-file members, are not so fluent that they feel at ease speaking Spanish in public. Yet in this area, as in others, Alinsky organizers are entirely pragmatic. Although major public events are primarily in English, they won't hesitate to introduce Spanish to embarrass or confuse an adversary who speaks none. Moreover, a good deal of Spanish can be heard at routine organizational meetings of COPS and UNO. At the beginning of sessions, those present might be asked what language they feel most comfortable with. Either key segments are conducted entirely in Spanish, or separate groups are set aside with bilingual members providing simultaneous translation. At the parish level, entire meetings may be in Spanish. Recent arrivals from Mexico are hardly their primary targets, but as immigration levels have skyrocketed, Alinsky organizers have inevitably had to adapt and learn Spanish. Leadership training sessions are sometimes conducted in Spanish. Nevertheless, members are continually reminded of the fundamental importance of English.

I mentioned earlier that Alinsky organizations do not run their own candidates for elective office and in fact maintain a nonpartisan status. Yet these organizations obviously do not hesitate to exercise influence over politicians. Indeed, this is a primary goal of Alinsky organizing.

Even more than "self-interest," "power" is the most overworked word around these organizations.[49] Leaders are repeatedly told that their aim is to build "a power organization." I can still hear the piercing twang of COPS's lead organizer, a nun from East Texas, telling a Mexican-American housewife who had acted diffidently before a leading Anglo businessman: "Mrs. Velásquez, you're a leader of this organization. You're a *power person*, just like he is." Or as another organizer declared at a leadership training session: "Power is such a good thing that everybody should have some of it."

This straightforwardness about acquiring power is something else that distinguishes Alinsky organizers from their New-Left-inspired counterparts. For example, in his book about the upcoming generation of political leaders, *Changing of the Guard*, journalist David Broder discerns among the community organizers he talked to, who were typically former SDS and welfare-rights activists, a "genuine discomfort with the idea of exercising real power."[50] Broder may confuse discomfort with disingenuousness, but these very different attitudes toward power are nevertheless striking.

Within Alinsky organizations, such Machiavellian pronouncements on power serve several functions. On the one hand, they impart a certain seriousness of purpose to the organization's activities, and thereby help instill pride and confidence among members. But more important, such pronouncements have shock value. They offend otherwise sympathetic liberals, whose denial of the realities of political rule always riled Alinsky. These pronouncements also get the attention of the target population, stable working- and lower-middle-class homeowners whom organizers see as hamstrung by middle-class proprieties.

Yet once these organizations amass some power, the question persists: to what ends will it be directed? Of course, the same question (and the same not completely satisfactory answers) arise with regard to many political organizations. What, for example, are the goals of the Democratic Party—other than to elect Democrats and thereby perpetuate the organization? In fact, there are several respects in which Alinsky organizers resemble the politicians for whom they express such disdain: in particular, their pragmatic, sometimes opportunistic approach to issues and their emphasis on process and organizational maintenance.

Still, these organizers differ from politicians in important ways. Not unrelated to their almost obsessive honesty about power, a discernible zeal, or sense of mission, is evident in the work of these individuals. And, however moderated by the practical concerns of maintaining a political organization, this moralistic strain once again confounds any straightforward assessment of their values and goals.

Nevertheless, we can safely impute to Alinsky and his heirs a goal that is implicit in the building and maintenance of their organizations: moving their members into the mainstream of American life, which from their perspective is necessarily achieved through politics. This stance is suggested by the Pledge of Allegiance with which meetings begin; by the distinctive red, white, and blue logo and bunting that lend COPS meetings the air of a Fourth of July celebration; and by the attitude of these organizations toward ethnic identity. Most important of all, Alinsky organizations do not define themselves in opposition to their environment. To be sure, they are critical of what they regard as the excessive individualism and consumerism of contemporary America, not to mention the impoverishment of our political life. But nothing about them smacks of the conventicle or sectlike haven from the outside world.[51] Competition and conflict among members are taken as givens. Indeed, the competitive egoism of the wider society is built into these community organizations.[52]

Although the exclusion of various groups from the mainstream feeds a certain moralism among Alinsky organizers, they are not motivated by a sweeping critique or condemnation of American society. Always careful to distinguish the "is" from the "ought," they are basically seeking a piece of the pie for themselves and their members. As a COPS vicepresident, a housewife married to a San Antonio police sergeant, declared to the 7,000 members at the organization's tenth anniversary convention in 1983, "COPS will be the Chamber of Commerce of the barrio." Indeed, that leader has since left COPS and taken an executive position with one of the real estate developers with whom the organization has repeatedly tangled. More recently, she was appointed to an open seat on the San Antonio City Council. Such noncontroversial goals have not always been evident to those on the receiving end of the confrontation tactics used by these organizations, but they have been clear enough to the leftists who have consistently lambasted Alinsky and his followers. Certainly in San Antonio today, COPS has become so much a part of the political scene that it must worry about losing its edge.

In fact, the men and women who work with Alinsky organizations report that their efforts have shifted away from "organizing against" toward "organizing for" and that they are now "more concerned with governance." For as they have emerged as established political actors, these organizations play an increasingly visible role in getting other political actors to focus on broad issues beyond the immediate concerns of their members. And as more and more of their resources are spent in putting issues like education and job training on local, state, and even national agendas, these organizations are finding that they must play an important follow-through role in the implementation and oversight of innovative programs for which they have successfully lobbied. This development suggests that the dictum "issues don't really matter" is increasingly inappropriate. Despite their continuing and obvious preoccupations with process and, as one organizer puts it, "teaching politics," the essentially reformist, arguably social democratic goals of these organizers have become more and more apparent—to them as well as to outside observers. Thus, these Alinsky organizers may be committed to building "power organizations," but the power of which they speak so freely is hardly without purpose—however difficult it is at times to specify.[53]

BEYOND ALINSKY THE FATHER

Much of what I've been describing here is classic Alinsky, developed by the master during a lifetime of labor and community organizing. But a good deal of it has been formulated by Alinsky's followers since his death in 1972. Taken as a whole, this body of practical knowledge is maintained, refined, and passed on in a kind of oral tradition through training sessions and consultations. As a result, Alinsky's writings, including his two books *Reveille for Radicals* and *Rules for Radicals*, are incomplete guides to the work of his heirs in San Antonio and Los Angeles today.

As mentioned in chapter 1, the institutional framework for this work is the Industrial Areas Foundation (IAF). Founded by Alinsky in Chicago in 1940 with funds from department-store heir and philanthropist Marshall Field III, the IAF was the peripatetic Alinsky's institutional base for more than three decades.[54] In the late 1960s, when Alinsky was absorbed with writing and speaking responsibilities, the IAF was taken in hand by his associate Edward Chambers, a former Catholic seminarian. Today, the IAF is headquartered just outside New York City, and as executive director, Chambers maintains a network of about thirty IAF-sponsored community organizations in several states, including (in addition to California and Texas) New York, New Jersey, Maryland, Tennessee, and Arizona. So, while the IAF has been particularly successful among Mexican Americans in the Southwest, it sponsors organizations—consistent with its rejection of the politics of ethnic or racial consciousness—in a variety of settings: among urban blacks as well as suburban whites, Protestants and Jews as well as Catholics.

Though many individuals and groups lay claim to Alinsky's legacy, the organizers grouped under the IAF banner are his lineal descendants. But it would be a mistake to see them as dutiful disciples following the dictates of the master. Ernesto Cortes, for example, met Alinsky only twice, and was not particularly fond of his abrasive manner. Another IAF organizer recalls, without much warmth, meeting Alinsky at a training session, questioning one of his statements, and being promptly thrown out of the room.

Thus, it is not surprising that Cortes and company have been willing to rework Alinsky's method. An obvious example is the eight-member IAF Cabinet, a kind of steering committee made up of Cortes, Chambers, and six other veteran organizers. This collective leadership arrangement (through which decisions are arrived at consensually) replaced Alinsky's one-man, charismatic regime. Chambers has similarly sought to regularize the relationship between IAF headquarters and affiliates like COPS and UNO. In the old days, Alinsky's people would be dispatched to a city, put together an organization within a fixed time period, and then leave. The inevitable result was that groups like The Woodlawn Organization in Chicago, or FIGHT in Rochester, would soon displace the organizers' goals with their own. Chambers's solution has been to require local organizations, as a condition of their contract with the IAF, to keep its personnel permanently on staff. An IAF-trained organizer therefore typically works a two- or three-year rotation in one location, moves on to another assignment, and is replaced by another IAF organizer. Not only has this helped the IAF exert considerable influence over its local affiliates, it has enabled it to recruit new organizers with the promise of places to train and eventually employ them. And as indicated earlier, this has been part of a conscious effort to make organizing a respectable career, to professionalize it.

The most important innovation, however, concerns the IAF's fully elaborated relationship with the Catholic Church. To be sure, Chambers, Cortes, and company have also been developing ties to various Protestant denominations and individual Jewish congregations. Such activities reflect a self-conscious effort to build organizations within which the values and interests of diverse groups are represented. Yet this goal is pursued less out of a commitment to some abstract notion of tolerance or inclusiveness than out of a strategic choice such as would be made by a political party seeking to broaden its constituency. This goal also reflects the IAF's concern to build organizations within which its members will learn political skills from grappling with the interplay of such diverse interests.

Nevertheless, there is a unique and long-standing relationship between the Catholic Church and the IAF. When Alinsky started out in the 1930s as an organizer with the CIO in the Back of the Yards section of Chicago, his target population, immigrant workers in the downright Dickensian meatpacking industry, was overwhelmingly and fervently Catholic. Of course, the strong religiosity of the working class has never prevented leftists from ignoring or denouncing the Church. But in this respect, once again, Alinsky was different. From early on, he saw the Church as a source of financial backing and moral legitimacy for his efforts. By the late 1930s he had secured the help of Bishop Bernard Sheil—a union sympathizer, founder of the Catholic Youth Organization, and aide to Cardinal Mundelein. With Sheil at his side, Alinsky approached the pastors of the various ethnic parishes in the Back of the Yards. A short time later, Bishop Sheil introduced Alinsky to Marshall Field III, who bankrolled the IAF for its first two years, beginning in August 1940.[55]

After that, Alinsky's ties to the Church broadened. In the 1950s his investigation of racially troubled Chicago neighborhoods for Cardinal Stritch led to the formation of The Woodlawn Organization. Indeed by the end of that decade, this son of Russian Jewish immigrants was viewed with suspicion by black Protestant ministers as the front man for the Catholic takeover of Chicago.[56] It was during this period that Alinsky first encountered Father John Egan, an activist priest who was highly visible in the battle against the conservative Cardinal Cody. When Alinsky's associates established several new community organizations in Chicago during the 1960s, Catholic parishes figured prominently in them.

For Alinsky's heirs, this close working relationship with the Church has deepened and intensified. As I have indicated, the Church's social action arm, the Campaign for Human Development, provides critical seed grants for IAF organizing projects. And as I will explore below, the San Antonio and Los Angeles dioceses have served (to varying degrees) as infrastructures that sustain the day-to-day efforts of IAF organizers.

These closer ties represent a qualitative change from Alinsky's day. Whereas Alinsky relied on other institutions besides the Church as organizational bases, Chambers and his colleagues rely more heavily, though not exclusively, on it. Moreover, they have developed this relationship to the point where the Church is more than a useful collection of buildings and warm bodies. It is an indispensable source of moral and spiritual authority, particularly among Mexican Americans, whose relationship to the Church may be suffused with ambivalence but is nevertheless marked by a degree of respect and awe afforded no secular institution.

As a result, Catholic (and other) religious professionals have been deeply involved with both COPS and UNO from the beginning. These

individuals have been leaders, organizers, or merely occasional participants. COPS at one time had two vice-president posts reserved for clergy.
More recently, these have been replaced with a clergy caucus within the
organization. In San Antonio, one extremely vocal and committed parish
priest played a key role in the early days of the organization. At one point
he aspired to become president of COPS, but was dissuaded for fear of
linking the organization too directly with the Church. In Los Angeles, as
I will explore later, there have been complaints that priests in particular
exert too much influence on UNO.

Whatever their specific roles, religious professionals generally have
been valuable as highly visible symbols linking these organizations to the
Church in the minds of Mexican-American parishioners. On a day-to-day
level, most meetings or actions benefit from the visible presence of a Roman collar. But with or without a priest or other religious professional,
organizational activities typically begin with a prayer. As one organizer
explains, "This helps keep everyone present honest—the politicians, the
organizers, the leaders, and the members. A good prayer helps keep
things in the proper perspective."

Indeed, prayer can put the organization's adversaries on the defensive.
This was evident at a meeting between leaders from one of San Antonio's
poorest parishes and one of the city's biggest developers. Few of the
COPS members present spoke English, and their spokesman, a laborer
in his mid-thirties, arrived at the 4 P.M. meeting in his overalls directly
from work. The organizer then asked the smartly dressed Anglo businessman and his two aides to wait in one corner of the barren parish hall,
while the COPS contingent formed a circle in another corner and prayed
in Spanish. By this time, the three Anglos appeared bemused and ill at
ease, while the parishioners, bolstered by the sense that praying had
evened the odds, seemed less intimidated by their visitors. The meeting
then proceeded, haltingly, in Spanish and English. At the end of an hour,
the parishioners had what they wanted: a written agreement that a nearby
parcel of land would not be developed so as to threaten the residential
character of their neighborhood.

For many disgruntled young religious professionals, part of the IAF's
appeal is the interest in theology shown by the organizers, an interest
that can be traced back to Cortes. There is no evidence that Alinsky, a
self-described agnostic Jewish radical, saw his religious views, or lack of
them, challenged by years of working with Catholics.[57] But the same cannot be said of Cortes. Twenty years ago, when he first went into the Mexican-American parishes of San Antonio, Cortes organized exclusively
around political issues. But he and his colleagues were gradually drawn

to theological concerns. They now read and discuss theology—Catholic, Protestant, and Jewish—among themselves and encourage their leaders to do likewise. Cortes has helped San Antonio's Archbishop Flores with major pastoral letters. At training sessions, papal encyclicals are analyzed, and lectures are scattered with references to writers such as Reinhold Niebuhr, Karl Rahner, and the contemporary theologian Gregory Baum. From such discussions the IAF has developed a series of Bible study classes to encourage members to reflect on the spiritual life of their congregations. It is striking that priests involved with IAF speak of Cortes with enormous respect. One young Jesuit in San Antonio marvels at how "this layman" has challenged him and his colleagues theologically.

These activities may in some respects resemble the *comunidades de base* extolled by liberation theologians in Latin America, but the IAF's overall perspective should not be confused with such efforts. For while these organizers make use of insights they derive from liberation theology, they are also critical of those who systematically apply its Marxist categories to the United States. As one organizer puts it, "liberation theology confuses the City of Man with the City of God."[58]

Nor are such IAF efforts mere manipulation or opportunism, although they may appear that way to outsiders—a category that includes many Mexican-American churchgoers who resent how Cortes and his colleagues have politicized their parishes, as well as the Mexican-American politicians who accuse them of using the Church to "lead our people around like sheep." Even supporters of these organizations express discomfort with their reliance on the influence clerics typically wield over Mexican Americans. At times, IAF organizing does come close to reducing religion to social reform: for example, when a zealous young minister stands up at a meeting and speaks of "the theological assumptions underlying high utility rates in Texas"; or when the participants in a collective action mistake a rush of group energy for "a spiritual experience"; or when a leader tells a priest, "Father, you'll have to choose between your parish and COPS."

It is, of course, difficult to judge motives in this realm. IAF organizers do take full advantage of their close ties to the Church. Yet while one might disagree with the way they mix politics with religion, it is for the most part difficult to doubt the organizers' sincerity. For many their efforts grow out of the Catholic ethos and heritage they share with their Mexican-American members. At any rate, IAF organizing does *not* smack of the pandering to local mores typical of deracinated intellectuals trying to ingratiate themselves with "the people."

THE CATHOLIC INFLUENCE:
ORGANIZATIONAL ETHOS

In some ways, the Catholic social tradition is of more help to these organizers than the explicitly religious or moral teachings of the Church. In
purely institutional terms, the Catholic Church is the locus of an organizational ethos to which a Saul Alinsky would understandably be attracted.
More specifically, the Church is a source of traditionalist, communitarian values that organizers can use to countervail the individualism of
American culture. Thus, at outreach meetings where parishioners are
first approached, organizers read passages from the Bible that emphasize
the communitarian values in Paul's Epistles and in the ancient image of
the Church as the mystical body of Christ.

The importance of these institutionalized cultural patterns has been
apparent when the IAF has sought to organize black Protestant congregations. Those efforts have resulted in some successes—for example, the
BUILD (Baltimoreans United in Leadership Development) organization
and East Brooklyn Congregations in New York[59]—but many disappointments as well. The fact is that black congregations are more difficult to
organize than Catholic parishes. Blacks have never been especially receptive to the ministrations of outsiders, particularly in San Antonio and
Los Angeles, where those outsiders are strongly identified with Mexican
Americans, whom blacks understandably regard as competitors. But just
as problematic is the organizational ethos of Protestant, particularly evangelical, congregations.

Consider the strategic situation of a Baptist minister. Employed directly by his congregation, he is answerable to no higher denominational
authorities. The size of his congregation, hence his status and salary, is
set not by territorial boundaries but by the limits of his energies and skills
as a fund-raiser, counsellor, spiritual adviser, politician, and preacher. This
is clearly why religious broadcasting has long been dominated by just such
clergy, accustomed as they are to operating without hierarchical organizational constraints. A Baptist preacher may or may not be a charismatic
leader. But he is—he must be—an entrepreneur.

By contrast, a Catholic priest is the classic organization man. His salary
and status are determined primarily by his rank in the world's oldest hierarchical institution. His assignment to a parish comes from his superiors in that hierarchy, not from the parishioners themselves, who have little
say in the matter. The priest's aspirations are therefore shaped more by
the need to gain the support of Church officials than to accommodate the
faithful. Finally, his efforts are moderated by the awareness that the

parish, a territorial jurisdiction with fixed boundaries, was there before he arrived and will be there after he is called to a new assignment.

For community organizers, the implications of these different dynamics are enormous. As entrepreneurs, Baptist ministers are understandably jealous of whatever power and influence they wield over their congregations. And among black clergy, who play such an important role in the community, the stakes are even higher. A Catholic nun trying to get black ministers involved in an IAF project in South-Central Los Angeles pinpoints the problem: "Their egos are involved." Such individuals are likely to be suspicious of anyone, whether another black minister or a white community organizer, who talks of making their congregation part of some larger organization.

Conventional wisdom has long considered black ministers easy to organize. Yet the history of the civil rights movement suggests otherwise.[60] So does practical experience. In San Antonio politicians routinely make payments to the churches of key black ministers. These "contributions" vary in amount; the privilege of addressing the congregation on a Sunday morning just before the election is obviously not as costly as an outright endorsement from the preacher. One Mexican-American county official reports with grim humor that he "bought a new roof for one East Side church." COPS has similarly tried to ingratiate itself with an influential black minister by securing his appointment to the IAF board. My point is not that such ministers are by nature more venal than other clergy, but that as entrepreneurs, they are understandably accustomed to being compensated for their efforts, particularly those they perceive as risky.

By contrast, a Catholic priest enjoys the security of being part of a two-thousand-year-old multinational corporation that shows no signs of going bankrupt. Of course, a priest may therefore grow so indifferent or lazy that he fails to cooperate with organizing efforts in his parish. This is, in fact, a frequent complaint of IAF organizers. Yet a priest is much less likely than a Baptist preacher to resist out of fear of being swallowed up by a larger enterprise. Moreover, a priest is much less likely to view other priests as direct competitors for his congregation. For all these reasons, Catholic priests are generally easier to organize than their Baptist or many of their other Protestant colleagues. This is particularly true when the diocesan hierarchy supports such efforts. Indeed, among many Protestant denominations there is no comparable authority to whom an organizer might appeal. As one nun summed up the IAF's difficulties with black preachers, "There's no bishop to lead the way."

After decades of relying on the material and organizational resources of the Catholic Church, Alinsky efforts have in some respects come to resemble the Church organizationally. It is difficult to know whether Alinsky and company originally sought out the Church because they were drawn to its organizational ethos, or whether they came to share it after long association. Alinsky's highly pragmatic style suggests his organizing methods were simply influenced by the situational imperatives of working in Catholic neighborhoods. Alinsky's successors at the IAF, as I have indicated, have had more organic ties to the Church. Still, any straightforward analysis of what "caused" what is impossible. All one can say is that down through the years discernible organizational affinities have developed between the Catholic Church and the IAF.

Two examples emerge from the above comparison of the situations of Baptist ministers and Catholic priests: territoriality and diversity. Unlike Protestant congregations, whose members may have widely scattered residences but share a denominational choice, Catholic parishes are composed of all those residing within their boundaries. Tracing back to when the Church exercised political as well as spiritual authority, the parish is a territorial jurisdiction based on the assumption that religion is not a matter of individual choice. In contemporary America this assumption is obviously not valid. But the parish system retains its territorial dimension, and thereby articulates with that dimension of political parties and community organizations. It is certainly no accident that precinct and ward boundaries have often coincided with parish boundaries. Moreover, territoriality distinguishes community organizations from trade unions and may thereby account for the former's arguably stronger and certainly more enduring ties to the Church.

Territorially defined parishes also imply diversity, in the sense that all those Catholics residing in the parish have no choice as to which church to attend. On the other hand, a Baptist or similarly constituted Protestant congregation implies uniformity, in the sense that those who belong to any given church have freely chosen to join together in religious observance. Over the centuries the Catholic Church has developed institutional forms to deal with the greater diversity of its membership. The inevitable conflicts among groups as well as individuals have obviously not always been resolved. Yet by and large, accommodation and mediation have been fundamental to the history of the Catholic Church. By contrast, Protestants have exhibited the opposite tendency and have typically settled disputes by schism and separation.

Thus, Alinsky organizations reflect the Catholic ethos when they strive to avoid the uniformity of opinion and interest characteristic of the single-issue group. As *community* organizations, their memberships are supposed to reflect the full array of interests in the community. Competition and conflict among members are consequently taken as the norm. As noted earlier, all trappings of the conventicle, or sect of the like-minded, are rejected. Indeed, Alinsky and his followers have sought to build into their organizations the competitive egoism of "the world as it is."

Just as COPS transforms the diverse interests of individual leaders into identification with the organization as a whole, the Catholic Church continually negotiates the differences among varied religious and theological perspectives. And just as IAF organizations interpose themselves between Mexican-American voters and politicians, the Catholic Church mediates between its adherents and God. By contrast, Protestant congregations, especially Baptists and similarly organized denominations, are not interposed between their members and God, but are conceived of as aggregations of individuals each with his or her own direct relationship with God. But this emphasis on unmediated religious experience then creates tremendous competitive pressures among individual believers. For without a priest to interpret and, as it were, adjust the diverse religious experiences of the various members, Protestants tend to be anxious about who has the best—the most authentic—relationship with God. Because it is relatively easy to leave one Protestant congregation for another, individuals sort themselves out into groups of like-minded believers. The characteristic dynamic among Protestants is thus fragmentation and uniformity; among Catholics mediation and diversity.

One way the Catholic Church has dealt with diversity is through decentralization. As articulated by Pope Pius XI in his encyclical *Quadragesimo Anno*, the principle of subsidiarity asserts that, in earthly institutions, "it is an injustice, a grave evil and a disturbance of right order for a larger and higher organization to arrogate to itself functions which can be performed efficiently by smaller and lower bodies."[61] Thus, a global institution like the Catholic Church has often afforded considerable discretion to local authorities having the most intimate knowledge of their own problems. As a result, the inevitable conflicts that arise within and among the Church's diverse jurisdictions have frequently been contained, and relatively few institution-wide schisms have developed.

A pertinent example of subsidiarity in practice is the discretionary authority parish pastors have over the language of church services. In Los Angeles, for example, Spanish-language masses have been the cause of intense conflicts between recently arrived Mexican immigrants and established Mexican Americans, who often speak little or no Spanish. By avoiding broad policy declarations that would only exacerbate the controversy, Church officials allow these tensions to be worked out within individual parishes.

Subsidiarity is also operative in Alinsky organizations. Consistent with the IAF dictum that these are "organizations of organizations," there is explicit emphasis on promoting ferment in the local parish chapters. Parish leaders are encouraged to work on local neighborhood issues, and thereby to develop their own political bases. Sometimes this means local chapters embarrass the larger organization, as when a COPS leader worked with her neighbors to reopen a parish school that organizers and diocesan officials felt should have remained closed. In general, however, organizers accept such developments and don't try to keep track of everything happening in the parishes. In their view, this allows them more time and energy to devote to broader organizational and long-range strategic concerns.

Of course, permitting lower-level decisionmaking implies a strong sense of hierarchy within the organization as a whole. This is certainly true of the Catholic Church. It is also true of IAF community organizations, which have clear lines of authority. Consistent with their role as teachers, the organizers are unquestionably in charge. There is a "lead organizer," who in turn answers to superiors within the IAF network. Working under him or her usually is a "number two organizer." Both may have trainee organizers working with them. While the number two typically works in the field with local parish chapters, the lead focuses on organizational strategy and works with key leaders. Presumably because of their heavy investment in leadership development, organizers seem not at all hesitant to identify which leaders are—and are not—worth their time. They speak openly of "primary," "secondary," and "tertiary" leaders. Such rankings generally parallel the organization's own hierarchy, a series of ascending jurisdictional levels, each with its own elected officers.

Still another facet of the Catholic Church's organizational ethos absorbed by IAF organizations can be seen in their strongly corporatist nature. One facet of traditional Catholic social doctrine, tracing back to Aquinas and ultimately Aristotle, is the medieval notion of community as "an assemblage of morally integrated minor groups," a community of communities (in Latin, *communitas communitatum*). Social theorist Robert Nisbet refers to this as "the plural community" and contrasts it with the modern notion of community as an aggregation of individuals held together by their relationship to a single sovereign authority.[62] IAF organizations, as I have just indicated, similarly see themselves as "organizations of organizations." What this means is that individuals cannot join COPS or UNO directly, but only through membership in local parish chapters. This may seem a fine distinction, but it carries a very concrete message. For if one wishes to join the organization but does not live in a member parish, one must go out and organize another local chapter.

Another way in which IAF organizations are structured to reinforce the notion that the parish, not the individual, is the basic unit, can be found in their encouragement of competition among parishes. At planning sessions for actions, parish leaders are assigned quotas for the number of members they will turn out. At large organizational sessions, such as quarterly area meetings or annual conventions, members arrive with their local chapter on parish buses and are seated together as units. Such rallies begin with a roll call of the parishes, giving each chapter the opportunity to make its presence felt. Not coincidentally, this also permits organizers to see how well parish leaders delivered on their quotas. For although the ability to produce warm bodies is not the only leadership criterion, it is an important one.

Parish identity is also reinforced, for example, through COPS's role in the Community Development Block Grant (CDBG) program. Early each spring, at the start of the CDBG funding cycle, COPS instructs its member parishes to draw up "wish lists" of projects that meet program guidelines. Because funds are targeted primarily for public goods such as drainage systems, street pavements, parks, and libraries, this initial step encourages members to look beyond their individual interests. But this is not to say the process is marked by calm disinterest. For during the subsequent three months, the competition and bargaining back and forth within the organization are fierce. As one organizer put it, "Just put some seed on the sidewalk and watch the pigeons fight over it." Indeed, chairing the COPS CDBG committee is such a frustrating and consuming task, few members have been willing to volunteer for it. As a result, the same man—a meat processor who worked nights and was therefore free during the day—held the position for years.

As the parish lists get passed up the organizational hierarchy, local leaders have the opportunity to build up their bases by pushing projects of particular interest to their members. Yet if they wish to advance within the larger organization, leaders are also obliged to address the concerns of other parishes. Like any good politician, the aspiring COPS leader has to balance CDBG priorities in his local against those in other chapters. And on occasion, projects in the parishes of key leaders get left out of the final CDBG package submitted for pro forma city council approval. In this manner, COPS encourages leaders simultaneously to build upon and to transcend the primary group ties of neighborhood and parish.

The internal struggles over CDBG funds do not appear to have hurt

COPS. While there has been grousing about certain parishes being favored in the process, none have actually quit the organization. This is obviously because COPS has controlled the CDBG process in San Antonio; its proposal has invariably been the basis of the city council's final package. Individual parishes therefore recognize that they stand to benefit more as part of the organization, even though their pet projects are sometimes put off to subsequent years. Thus, the entire CDBG process has ended up reinforcing organizational as well as parish identity.[63]

The subordination of individual ambitions to organizational goals is also evident in the collective leadership principle. Similar to the IAF cabinet, the elected leaders are expected to function as a collegium, reaching decisions through discussion, persuasion, and bargaining with one another. And when they meet with outsiders, leaders typically do so in small groups. This is how solicitations for the adbook described earlier in this chapter are handled. Similarly, leaders do not meet with politicians or businessmen individually, but as part of a group delegation. In such ways are the anxious bolstered by their colleagues, and the ambitious hindered from developing individual ties with outsiders.

IAF's policy of not endorsing political candidates also speaks to an emphasis on the well-being of the collectivity over and above the ambitions of individual leaders. It avoids, for example, divisive internal battles over endorsements of leaders who might use the organization as a launching pad into electoral politics. Collective leadership has been promoted by limitations on the amount of time an individual can serve as president of an IAF organization, thereby making more difficult the domination of any one leader. Such limitations also help promote the circulation of new blood, as it encourages the organizers to do what they should be doing anyway—seeking out and developing new leaders.

Finally, the collective leadership regime provides an arena where organizers can keep an eye on promising (or troublesome) individuals. And because aspiring leaders recognize the need to gain the support of the lead organizer in particular, they also get imbued with the notion of bringing along new leaders.

This scenario is admittedly not always followed. Leaders and organizers alike can get caught up in the demands of the moment and overlook the need to develop new leaders. And while no one is supposed to dominate the executive board, the organizer often does. Swell-headed leaders are particularly prone to losing sight of the collective leadership idea. One organizer recounted the following exchange: "I was invited to have breakfast with the Mayor," boasted the president of COPS. "No you weren't, COPS was," snapped the vice-president. "Yes," replied the president, "and I am COPS." Such remarks reveal that, however elusive it may be, collective leadership is an acknowledged norm within the IAF. Undoubtedly in response to such tensions, COPS has subsequently eliminated the positions of president and vice-president in favor of a true collective leadership regime of co-equal officers, or "co-chairs."

THE CATHOLIC INFLUENCE: PHILOSOPHICAL AFFINITIES

Underlying such constraints on individual drives and ambitions, on which any viable organization depends, are deeper philosophical affinities between IAF principles and Catholic social thought. Perhaps the most unexpected and suggestive such link is the long friendship between Alinsky and neo-Thomist philosopher Jacques Maritain.

As an exile from his native France during World War II, Maritain met Alinsky while lecturing at the University of Chicago. The two remained close personal friends for the rest of their lives. When Maritain returned home, he tried to interest De Gaulle in the organizer's work as a means of countering the looming threat of communism in postwar France. Later, as French ambassador to the Holy See, Maritain introduced Alinsky to Archbishop Montini of Milan, later to become Pope Paul VI. In the late 1950s Montini was concerned about communist inroads among the workers of his diocese. There were discussions with Alinsky about starting a project in Milan, and later talks with officials from the Vatican and the Italian government.[64] Nothing ever came of these, though the circle was completed almost two decades later in 1978, when Archbishop Flores was pictured prominently in the San Antonio diocesan newspaper giving a COPS button to Pope Paul for his blessing.

But what did this agnostic Jewish radical and the Catholic theologian have in common? In the course of battling against collectivist ideologues and individualist liberals, Alinsky came up with a middle way that parallelled Maritain's efforts to sensitize traditional Catholic social doctrine to the individualism of modern life and to respond to twentieth-century statism and totalitarianism. The practical outcome of the philosopher's efforts—Christian democracy, "the third way"—has much in common with Alinsky's community organizations.[65]

The IAF's views on power similarly track Catholic social doctrine. I noted earlier how organizers unabashedly declare their pursuit of power. Implicit here is the notion that power is not some evil drive in man to be suppressed or denied. But neither is it necessarily a good. Quoting neo-Thomist theologian Karl Rahner at a leadership training session, one organizer draws a parallel between sex and power, and observes that both in themselves are morally neutral and can be put to either good or evil ends.

The IAF's interpretation of self-interest is similarly "Catholic." The Protestant ethic, as analyzed of course by Max Weber, is "this-worldly as-ceticism."[66] In politics this ethic has often led to the denial of individual self-interest and its transcendence through appeals to civic virtue, to collectivist ideologies, or to the teachings of selfless charismatic leaders. By contrast, Catholic social teaching (to be sure, more in Europe than in America) has tended to be more realistic and tolerant of human frailty. Rejecting extreme views of human depravity (Calvin) or of human perfectibility (Marx), Catholicism opts for a middle range in which individual needs and wants are taken as natural traits that can be put to either good or evil ends.[67]

Finally, Catholic social doctrine regards individual self-interest as a morally neutral given that can be directed toward good ends through reason, reflection, and mediation. Yet it does not expect the individual to accomplish such a task all by himself. The IAF takes a similar view: just as the individual's soul cannot be saved without the help of the institutional Church, his self-interest cannot be enlightened and refined without the help of the community organization.

⁌ 6 ⁍

Obstacles to
Organization Politics

T he preceding discussion of Alinsky organizing is no mere intellectual exercise. The organizations that Ernesto Cortes and his IAF colleagues have built in communities across the Southwest constitute one of
the most intriguing and enduring developments in contemporary Mexican-American politics. The oldest of these are COPS in San Antonio and
UNO in Los Angeles. Both were started up during the 1970s by Cortes
himself and have over the years been staffed by many of the same organizers.

Yet these two community organizations have fared very differently. As
the previous chapter indicates, IAF organizers have an impressive, well-
thought-out method for dealing with the factionalism of friends-and-
neighbors politics. The decentralized nature of American politics has long
exacerbated such factionalist tendencies and, contrary to much of our
lore, made it difficult to build strong political organizations. Still, some
settings have been more hospitable than others for organization politics,
and this is certainly true today for the IAF. San Antonio and Los Angeles
present two extremes, with the former self-evidently optimal and the latter much less so.

COPS AND UNO:
A STUDY IN CONTRASTS

For almost two decades, COPS has been one of the most powerful political actors in San Antonio, a household word in all parts of the city. Entire neighborhoods have been transformed by the drainage works, parks,
housing, and other highly visible projects for which the organization le-
gitimately claims credit. Like all organizations, COPS has had its ups and
downs, defeats as well as victories. But locally, it has certainly rivaled the
nationally visible Henry Cisneros for attention. Insofar as it has been on
the scene before, during, and after his tenure as mayor, the organization
is arguably the single most important political development among Mexican Americans in San Antonio. Indeed, as the first and most successful
of several IAF organizations across the state, COPS represents the most
important political development among Mexican Americans in Texas. No
doubt that explains why, when President Reagan came to town to celebrate the Cinco de Mayo, COPS was offered several coveted podium tickets—which, in typical Alinsky fashion, were promptly but respectfully
turned down in a show of self-assertion and independence.

    In Los Angeles, by contrast, UNO has managed to achieve consider-
able recognition and visibility, but nothing comparable to COPS's accomplishments and stature. UNO emerged on the scene in the late 1970s
with an impressively quick victory over high auto insurance rates, but then
struggled for much of the 1980s to be identified in the media as other
than a nameless "East LA community organization." An organizer who
has worked with both UNO and COPS offers a revealing insight. In Los
Angeles he got used to his phone calls not being returned and his requests
for meetings turned down. He notes that in the mid-1980s UNO had still
not quite recovered from an incident at city hall a few years earlier, when
Mayor Bradley bristled at the organization's tactics, declared that "this is
my house," and then walked out of the meeting. Later working with
COPS, the organizer marveled at how he could pick up the phone and
get through to anyone in San Antonio, from bank presidents to the mayor.

    In recent years UNO has, with the help of several other IAF organi-
zations subsequently launched in the metropolitan region, managed to
secure an undeniable niche in the political firmament, particularly among
the city's corporate and media elites. To do so, UNO and its affiliates have
relied on substantial turnouts for rallies and conventions organized
around issues like crime, drugs, and education. These events have been
impressive by Los Angeles—or any other—standards. But they have been
mounted at the expense of parish-level organizational development. And

despite them, UNO is still not taken very seriously by the politicians, who know that it speaks largely for nonvoters. Indeed, the accomplishments of UNO and COPS are sufficiently disparate that there has been occasional rivalry between the two organizations, and a certain defensiveness on the part of UNO leaders and organizers toward their San Antonio counterparts. Yet the root of this disparity lies not so much with the individuals involved as with the contexts within which they must operate. Indeed, it is hard to imagine a more daunting challenge to IAF community organizers than contemporary Los Angeles.

Composed of about twenty-five local chapters in Catholic parishes on the West and South Sides of San Antonio, COPS's members are stable working- and lower-middle-class Mexican-American homeowners. It was only after a decade of successful operation that COPS even attempted to organize various West Side public housing projects (referred to as "*los courts*"), where the poorest and most dispirited Mexican Americans struggle to get by. Alinsky efforts among such populations have generally not been very successful.

Down through the years men have been involved in COPS, but its leadership has been dominated by middle-aged housewives whose volunteer efforts in the organization have typically grown out of prior civic or PTA activities. Of COPS's six presidents, only one, the first, has been a man. The organization's foot soldiers are elderly Mexican Americans. Through the years these elderly have always been ready to board the church buses that pick them up at parish senior centers and carry them to demonstrations or meetings. As a result, COPS has been capable of consistently turning out hundreds of people on very short notice. For its annual conventions a few thousand members typically turn out. On the occasion of its tenth anniversary convention in 1983, 7,000 faithful gathered at the Hemisfair Arena to hear politicians, including Texas governor Mark White, sing the praises of COPS.

Yet COPS does a lot more than stage rallies. In general, Mexican-American homeowners with a clear stake in their parishes form the backbone of the organization. It was at these families that Cortes directed his efforts when he began organizing in 1972. For years they had been complaining of conditions that made their neighborhoods look like Third World slums. The torrential rains that sweep across South Texas not only turned the clay soil of unpaved West Side streets to peanut butter, they resulted in serious flooding. Heavy property damage was compounded by occasional fatalities—including children caught in flash floods on their way to or from school. And while Mexican-American neighborhoods, crowded onto the low-lying plains of the region, struggled with such "natural" calamities, affluent Anglo neighborhoods nestled on the wooded hills on the North Side of town remained quite literally high and dry. Cortes's first achievement was to focus the accumulated anger and resentments of generations of Mexican Americans on to this day-to-day, physical manifestation of their situation. After years of failure by Chicano activists to rouse the West Side with leftist slogans or racial appeals, Cortes succeeded in organizing around mud and floods.

In those early days, COPS developed its aforementioned reputation for disruptive, though never violent or uncontrolled, confrontations with leading Anglo politicians and businessmen. One of the organization's first targets was Tom Frost, a local banker whose great-grandfather arrived in Texas from Alabama in 1855 and eventually parlayed a merchandising business into one of South Texas's leading banks.[1] As a symbol of the city's Anglo elite, Frost was the obvious target on which to focus the anger of Mexican-American housewives and homeowners. So, when he refused to follow up on his first meeting with COPS, the organization promptly staged a "change-in" at the downtown office of the Frost National Bank, with hundreds of Mexican Americans changing their pennies into bills and then back into pennies. Frost eventually conceded to COPS's demands, thereby handing the fledgling group one of its first victories.

At city hall, COPS began asking questions to which no one had answers: How many sidewalks needed repair? What size and age were the water mains in the various neighborhoods? A city council long accustomed to dispatching its public business with a brief meeting one morning a week was suddenly embroiled in raucous all-day, all-night sessions dominated by COPS. Armed with well-researched facts and figures, Cortes and company earned the begrudging respect of their adversaries, who still acknowledge, "COPS does its homework." Packing meetings with busloads of boisterous members, the organization's signature gesture has been to depart en masse right after completing its business, leaving the council to continue its deliberations in an eerily empty chamber.

From its inception, COPS has pursued an electoral strategy, registering voters and getting them out on election day. The fulcrum of the organization's power has been the city council, where considerable influence is exercised over the four or five councillors in whose districts the organization has a presence. Especially critical to COPS has been its virtually total control over the city's Community Development Block Grant (CDBG) process, through which the organization has been able to direct millions of federal dollars to projects in its member parishes—ranging from street improvements, to recreational facilities, libraries, and even (as we've seen) new private housing.

Consistent with the IAF policy described earlier, COPS never endorses candidates for public office. Yet the organization does signal its preferences to members by issuing score cards with responses to the yes-or-no questions posed to candidates at "accountability nights." Most public figures in San Antonio have appeared at these public forums when summoned by the organization.

Now that it is an accepted feature of the San Antonio political landscape, COPS relies much less on disruption. Indeed, the organization now spends as much time negotiating as demonstrating. In recent years, Cortes—making the point to his leaders that in politics there are no permanent enemies or friends—has even boasted that former adversary Tom Frost is one of the organization's staunchest allies. Indeed, Frost now chairs the committee overseeing implementation of an innovative job training program that Cortes and his IAF colleagues developed and for which they have secured local, state, and federal funding.[2]

In short, COPS appears at times to have been co-opted. The business and political leaders of San Antonio, having initially fought this obstreperous newcomer, have learned not only to tolerate it, but to include it in their deliberations. Mayor Cisneros, for example, skillfully used the organization to bolster his profile as an honest broker between the Anglo establishment and the Mexican-American community. City officials have come to rely on the organization's domination of the CDBG program as a way of ordering what might otherwise be a chaotic scramble for federal funds. Finally, private developers have discovered how helpful the organization can be. For example, a participant in a federally subsidized economic development project reports that COPS paved the way for the venture with an innovative plan to include housing for the inner-city residents who otherwise would have been displaced by the project.[3]

Naturally, COPS organizers are aware of the dilemma facing them. Concerned to maintain the organization's stance as outside critic, they have decided against participating in many civic efforts. Yet Cortes and his colleagues also realize that to fulfill the aspirations of their members, the organization must continue to play a prominent role in San Antonio politics. It remains to be seen whether the once ferocious COPS can be tamed without becoming toothless and declawed—especially when it loses significant battles, as in the late 1980s it failed to head off a tax limitation campaign, and did not succeed in blocking a favored project of Mayor Cisneros, a downtown stadium complex (the Alamodome). Up until a few years ago, COPS supporters might have derived some perverse satisfaction from the constant criticism of local politicians who privately reviled the organization's iconoclastic methods and its refusal to give them recognition for their efforts. Mexican-American politicians in particular felt upstaged and abused by the organization. But today as COPS approaches its twentieth anniversary, even this dynamic has changed, as this mature organization now routinely works with and shares credit with politicians, bureaucrats, and businessmen it once kept at arm's length.

In Los Angeles, by contrast, Mexican-American politicians have typically saved their venom for Chicano activists, and have long viewed UNO as harmless. As one Mexican-American officeholder explains his strategy for dealing with the organization and its accountability sessions, "The trick is to say 'yes' to everything." Whereas COPS has been able to punish politicians at the polls, UNO has been able, at best, to embarrass them before the media. In this way, UNO has sometimes functioned more like a protest group—for which it has consequently earned the enmity of Los Angeles's highly visible Chicano activists, who resent the competition. With many members who are either illegals or noncitizens, UNO has not been heavily involved in electoral politics. It has sponsored only a few modest voter registration drives; and, as the above quote suggests, it has had only limited success with accountability nights. Indeed, one organizer admits that candidates and officials on occasion fail to show up. Not surprisingly, UNO has not wielded much influence over significant funding sources such as Community Development Block Grants.

These shortcomings are especially disappointing in light of UNO's impressive start. In the late summer of 1976, three years after launching COPS, Cortes left his hometown and moved his family to Los Angeles. With the support of the archdiocese's auxiliary bishop, Juan Arzube, and a seed grant from the Campaign for Human Development, Cortes hoped to duplicate his San Antonio success in East LA. At first it looked as though he might do so around the unlikely issue of auto insurance rates.

Though hardly a gut issue like the mud and floods of San Antonio, auto insurance rates were the issue that, after scores of one-on-one interviews in the parishes, struck Cortes (in typical Alinsky fashion) as "winnable." Regulated by state officials in Sacramento, insurance rates presented an opportunity to use the symbolic importance of East LA against then governor Jerry Brown, who had been actively courting Mexican Americans. Cortes began staging demonstrations charging the governor's insurance commissioner with permitting insurance rates that discriminated against barrio residents. The media attention threatened to embarrass Brown, and the commissioner finally agreed to investigate UNO's claims. Eventually, an insurer was found willing to underwrite policies for substantially less than the prevailing rates. UNO negotiated rate reductions for those with East LA zip codes, and further reductions for members of UNO parishes, who signed up for the program as they came out of Sunday mass.

All this transpired a little more than two years after Cortes's arrival in Los Angeles. In such a difficult place to organize, it was a real coup. Yet many of the factors contributing to this initial splash contained the seeds of problems which have plagued UNO ever since. An IAF insider familiar with the complex Sacramento proceedings into which UNO was drawn, involving many different pieces of legislation, admits that "we had no business up there," and that the victory had been due largely to "smoke and mirrors." Like other Mexican-American political endeavors in Los Angeles that I will examine, success for this young organization was more apparent than real.

Within a few years UNO was struggling, and by the mid-1980s, it had still not equaled that first victory. By then there were nominally eighteen local chapters, one Episcopal, and seventeen Catholic parishes, scattered around East LA—a figure that represented a decline from a few years earlier. Most of these had ceased to function, except as mere paper organizations. There were few, if any, regular local chapter meetings; there were only about five genuinely active parishes; and whatever organizational activity there was occurred at the central office. Members typically described the situation in their home parish as "back to where it was when UNO first started."

Indeed, it was during this period that East LA saw its biggest controversy in years—and UNO was only marginally involved. In 1984 a group called the Mothers of East Los Angeles organized protests against a new state prison scheduled to be built in their neighborhood. Led by a parish priest with no ties to UNO or the IAF, these Mexican-American housewives and homeowners took on Governor Deukmejian, Assembly Speaker Willie Brown, and several Mexican-American elected officials—and stopped the prison. Resembling UNO in tactics and constituency, the Mothers of East Los Angeles revealed the organization to be less than dominant in East LA.

Nonetheless, UNO could claim to represent a larger, more enduring constituency than most such rivals; it had long been able to turn out substantial crowds of several thousand East LA residents for key events. Two days before the 1984 California presidential primary, UNO and its sister organization, the South-Central Organizing Committee (SCOC), assembled in a church parking lot some 7,000 people to be addressed by Walter Mondale, Gary Hart, and Jesse Jackson. In a state where a political rally has been defined by political consultant Robert Shrum as "three people gathered in front of a television set,"[4] this was not an insignificant achievement. It was undoubtedly one of the largest, if not *the* largest, such gathering any of the three Democrats had seen in California that spring.

Three years later, UNO celebrated its tenth anniversary convention in the Shrine Auditorium, with the help of SCOC and a newly formed third organization, the East Valleys Organization (EVO). Yet with all three organizations present, the turnout was the same as three years before (about 7,000 people), a figure that was still impressive but that hardly indicated substantial growth at the grassroots.[5]

UNO and its IAF affiliates—including a fourth organization begun in 1988, Valley Organized in Community Efforts (VOICE)—have continued to turn out large crowds for issue-oriented events. In October 1990 they participated in a business-elite dominated coalition for education reform, culminating in a rally with 15,000 people in the LA Sports Arena.[6] Such efforts have resulted in some undeniable victories for the IAF in Los Angeles. Long before the 1992 riots focused attention on liquor sales in South-Central Los Angeles, the IAF succeeded in getting liquor licenses in the area restricted. Several hazardous-waste sites in East LA have either been closed or stopped at the planning stage. The organizations played an important role in the establishment of an innovative gang intervention program. In 1987 they initiated a campaign that persuaded the California Industrial Welfare Commission to raise the minimum wage. More recently, UNO and its affiliates have put together a complicated funding package for low-income housing modeled on a successful effort, Nehemiah Homes, engineered by an IAF organization in Brooklyn. Unfortunately, implementation of the Nehemiah West plan has been stymied by IAF opponents, and no housing has as yet been built.

Many of these victories have actually been won in Sacramento, where these IAF groups have typically worked in coalitions dominated by other, weightier organizations. Reminiscent of the "smoke and mirrors" surrounding UNO's effort to cut insurance rates, such successes at the state capital reflect carefully chosen shots more than real political clout. As one organizer puts it, "We've dibbled and dabbled in various legislative pieces up in Sacramento." Los Angeles is admittedly a huge arena in which to operate. But even taking this difference of scale into account, all of UNO's efforts in Southern California have netted it nothing comparable to the changes wrought by COPS in San Antonio, where entire neighborhoods have been visibly transformed by the organization.

The fact is that the huge rallies on which the IAF has built its reputation in Los Angeles have diluted its sense of purpose and mission there. As the much smaller routine meetings and assemblies of the four constituent organizations indicate, these media-oriented mega-events attract large numbers of people who are not committed members. More to the point, the means relied upon to pull in such large numbers undercut some basic principles of Alinsky organizing. As one organizer notes, "Delivering [attendance quotas] is different from developing [leaders]." Yet it is not clear what alternatives the IAF has in Los Angeles, given the obstacles to neighborhood-based organizing that exist in that setting.

OBSTACLES TO
ORGANIZING IN LOS ANGELES

Given the substantial population of illegal immigrants and noncitizens in the parishes where UNO and some of its affiliates operate, it is hardly surprising that the large number of Spanish monolinguals there should be an obstacle to IAF efforts. In San Antonio, where there are proportionately fewer Spanish monolinguals, language can still be an impediment to communication between generations. But this is a minor problem, one that people are used to dealing with in their families and neighborhoods. In addition, the Spanish language is part of the social glue that helps define and bind together Mexican Americans vis-à-vis Anglos in San Antonio—even for those who don't feel entirely at ease speaking it. Using Spanish in this way, COPS has found it to be as much an asset as a liability in organizing.

In Los Angeles, Spanish is much more of a barrier dividing two different social groups: the increasing numbers of recent arrivals, and the decreasing numbers (in East LA at least) of assimilated Mexican Americans. As I noted earlier, there has been considerable dissension in East LA parishes over the use of Spanish. Indeed, in parish after parish, religious professionals tell of older residents and newcomers battling over which language is to be used at mass, or about how much Spanish is to be used at parish functions. At a meeting with her pastor, one slightly exasperated Mexican-American nun sighed, "Thank God we don't have any Vietnamese." As I have already mentioned, by the mid-1980s most Sunday masses in East LA were in Spanish. And the battle continues, even as it shifts from East LA, where there are fewer and fewer assimilated Mexican Americans, to other parts of the metropolitan region.

Not surprisingly, these tensions have surfaced within UNO itself. Most of the organization's public meetings are conducted in both languages: first a segment in English, then one in Spanish. All written materials are also bilingual. And to reach out to the Spanish speakers, many of the organization's private sessions are in Spanish.

Yet such accommodation has its price. Some members, repeating the motto that "English is the language of power," express resentment at the Spanish speakers. And this points to a fundamental problem for UNO. In a huge metropolis like Los Angeles, the organization must use the media to communicate its concerns to the wider populace. Its leaders have tended, therefore, to be relatively assimilated, articulate Mexican Americans capable of stepping into this role. Yet such individuals have had evident problems gaining the confidence of the growing numbers of the unassimilated in East LA. The effectiveness of such leaders depends in part on their ability to speak Spanish, but many have to struggle with the language and find the whole business an annoying chore. One leader (whose own father's English was, she recalls, limited to "Hi, boy" and "Fill 'er up") admits that despite her "better instincts," she sometimes says to herself, "Oh, why can't they just learn English?" For some time UNO was able to finesse these problems, but its continued efforts to adapt to Spanish speakers cannot necessarily overcome—and may actually exacerbate—this widening social cleavage. Indeed, one UNO organizer expresses the fear that soon all the remaining middle-class, assimilated families will be driven out of East LA and, therefore, out of the organization. Such concerns have obviously been an impetus to starting affiliated organizations, particularly in suburban areas where such assimilated Mexican Americans have settled.

Heavy reliance on Spanish tends to subvert time-tested Alinsky techniques. After all, those carefully planned confrontations rely on pacing and surprise to demonstrate to outsiders and members alike that the organization is in control of events. But the necessary tension is lost when the proceedings lumber along first in one language, then in another. The inevitable tedium bores members and gives adversaries more room to maneuver.

The obvious alternative is for members to learn English, which the available evidence indicates they eventually will.[7] But this is a long-term solution that does not address the immediate crush of immigrant monolinguals. In any event, organizers, for fear of being distracted from their primary objective, resist getting directly involved in running English-language classes. Thus UNO faces a dilemma: on one side, the situational realities of organizing Mexicans in Los Angeles; on the other, the IAF's assimilationist orientation.

But the language obstacle is only the beginning. In San Antonio, the bonds of family, neighborhood, and parish have been critical to the success of a method that refashions primary group ties and community institutions. In Los Angeles, by contrast, the "transience" of Mexican immigrants (it should be recalled that this is the organizers' term, not mine) and the mobility—geographic, social, and economic—of Mexican Americans make these bonds difficult to establish, let alone refashion.

Cortes's experiences upon arriving in East LA in 1976 are illustrative. As he had done in San Antonio, Cortes started off by visiting the various Catholic parishes to see who among the religious professionals might support his efforts and, more important, refer him to key parish leaders. Yet to Cortes's surprise, the priests and nuns could point to few such individuals. Indeed, the parishes were devoid of the rich organizational life on which COPS has thrived. Several parishes had no functioning parish councils, the post-Vatican II innovation affording laity the opportunity to advise their pastors. Also missing were the usual church groups where lay leadership develops. Only a couple of parishes operated senior centers, which have been used so effectively by COPS.

More recently, after years of record levels of immigration from Mexico, the situation in the parishes is no better. But appearances can be deceptive. Take the example of Our Lady of Victory, a tiny parish in the heart of East LA, squeezed between the San Bernadino Freeway and the Union Pacific Railroad tracks. On any Sunday the services attract crowds of immigrants greatly outnumbering the few Mexican-American families still living in the neighborhood. Despite parishioners who are continually on the move, and who may attend services intermittently at best, the parish manages to put on its annual *jamaica* (festival). This three-day event features talent shows, rock bands, a professional sound system that gets the attention of the entire neighborhood, carnival games and rides, and every variety of homemade Mexican food. With the sale of beer and lottery tickets, as much as $25,000 typically gets raised, making the *jamaica* the parish's major fund-raising event.

Yet however much this scene, or others like it at La Placita, reveal the Catholic Church to be a focus of newcomers' traditional values, the fact is that in Los Angeles the Church has weak roots in the day-to-day lives of Mexican Americans—especially among recent immigrants. As it turns out, the *jamaica* is not only Our Lady of Victory's biggest effort; it is virtually the parish's only effort. There is almost no other organizational activity in the parish; no parish council, no Holy Name Society, no Guadalupanas, no Choir Society. And the *jamaica* came about only through the strenuous personal efforts of the pastor, a burly Italian from New York City.

As a result, Cortes and his successors have been forced to assign religious professionals a disproportionate role as leaders in the struggling organization. Priests and nuns began interviewing potentially supportive parishioners and became highly visible at UNO actions. As one of Cortes's colleagues has pointed out, "having as many Roman collars at actions as possible" was also Cortes's response to the local hierarchy's lack of enthusiasm for his efforts. In the short run this approach proved highly successful, for religious professionals, especially priests, have special influence over tradition-oriented Mexican immigrants. Indeed, as another organizer put it: "If a collar isn't involved, the parishioners won't follow." But as such comments also suggest, the legacy of this strategy has been a tendency for clergy to dominate the organization, a problem I will return to later.

UNO's difficulties are further compounded by the extraordinary assimilative processes evident in Los Angeles. If, as I have indicated, the collective leadership principle is sometimes put to the test in San Antonio, it is often overwhelmed in the porous, co-optive environment in which UNO operates. I have already described class and language differences between UNO leaders and the rank and file. These leaders have also tended to be more articulate, sophisticated, and politically experienced than their San Antonio counterparts, for the most part housewives whose family concerns drew them into civic affairs. While both sets of leaders have similar working- and lower-middle-class backgrounds, UNO leaders have been more likely to be unmarried and employed or otherwise involved in endeavors outside the home. As a result, UNO leaders are less dependent on the organization for advancement and personal growth. The organizers therefore have a harder time wielding authority over them. When a former president of UNO rebuked an organizer for not being sufficiently demanding of leaders, he replied: "I'm afraid if I get too tough with the ladies, I'll scare them away."[8]

Because social boundaries between Mexicans and Anglos are more blurred in Los Angeles than in San Antonio, UNO cannot rely on the resentment that is so much a part of Mexican-American identity in Texas. For instance, at a typical UNO meeting, where the Los Angeles County sheriff was to be grilled about gang problems, the leaders failed (in IAF jargon) "to pin him" with a single tough question. Indeed, as the session limped to a conclusion, they ended up posing with the sheriff for photographs and inviting him for coffee and cookies. Such goings-on would be unimaginable at any COPS actions, where law enforcement officials get treated with a brusque efficiency, leaving no time for cookies or cameras.

On another occasion, having formed an alliance with California school superintendent William Honig to increase education funding, UNO invited him for a publicity-generating tour of several East LA schools. If COPS had sponsored such an event, Honig would have been kept at a critical distance and members continually reminded that he was merely a temporary ally. Instead, UNO leaders declared Honig to be "our friend" and turned the occasion into what a sympathetic *Los Angeles Times* reporter familiar with Alinsky techniques deplored as "a love-in."

Not all UNO actions have been love-ins, as the above-mentioned confrontation with Mayor Bradley attests. But organizers themselves point to a palpable lack of anger among Mexican Americans in Los Angeles. One nun who worked first in Los Angeles and then in San Antonio remarked on the negative sentiments that she felt directed at her as an Anglo by COPS members, but never by UNO members.[9] Another organizer familiar with both cities cited a major meeting between UNO and several local corporate leaders. During the session an irascible oil executive announced to the organization's leaders, "I'm an immigrant, too." He subsequently asked them, "Are you the kind of Mexicans that clean up after themselves?" To the organizer's astonishment, the UNO leaders silently let the comments pass. He knowingly observed: "COPS leaders would have been crawling all over the guy."

THE CATHOLIC CHURCH: AN EMBATTLED BARRIO INSTITUTION

Critical to the different fortunes of these two Alinsky organizations has been the support each has received from the local Catholic hierarchy. But consideration of this factor must be preceded by a digression on the broader relationship between the Catholic Church and Mexican Americans.

The conventional wisdom sees the Church as a key barrio institution. Certainly the Sunday morning scenes described here reinforce this perception. Indeed, many Mexican-American leaders are embarrassed by the Church's hold on their people. Yet the Church's perceived strength is relative to the weakness of competitors for the loyalties of Mexican Americans in an era—and a region—marked by weak political parties and a moribund labor movement.[10] Compared to the historical ties between the Catholic Church and many European immigrant groups, those between Mexicans and the Church are tenuous.[11]

To begin, the four-and-a-half centuries of the Church's presence in Mexico pale in comparison to its two millennia in Europe. Moreover, the Church in Mexico has never been identified with national aspirations as it has, for example, in Ireland or Poland. Indeed, a strong current of anticlericalism was institutionalized by the revolution earlier this century, and despite recent conciliatory moves by the Salinas regime, that current continues to exert a fundamental influence on Mexican life. Local priests may exercise considerable personal authority, but obedience to them does not necessarily translate into loyalty to the Church as an institution. Meanwhile, politicians in Mexico City remain intensely distrustful of the Church and have long endeavored to contain its influence and visibility.[12]

Reflecting these weak institutional ties, the faith Mexican immigrants bring with them to the United States is typically untutored and mixed with persistent folk beliefs and superstitions. At least, this is how many Catholic religious professionals in the United States see it. One Mexican-American priest described his people as "catechumens," a term from the early Christian era referring to pagans still in the process of conversion. Parishes routinely conduct adult confirmation classes for the many individuals who never received proper instruction as teenagers. One Irish nun, working with elderly Mexicans in a working-class parish near downtown San Antonio, used the phrase "baptized pagans" and then motioned toward a corner of the room where a wizened old woman wrapped in a shawl fervently stroked a statue of the Virgin. In the lower-middle-class neighborhood where Henry Cisneros grew up (and still lives), one emerges from Sacred Heart Church to see roosters strutting about under a hand-painted sign advertising the services of a folk healer, or *curandero*. As a nun working in the parish observes, the sign is strategically placed to attract clients as they stream out of Sunday mass.

The response of the Catholic Church in the American Southwest has rarely done much to strengthen such weak ties. For generations the region was mission territory. As a result, there were few formally organized parishes, and traveling priests paid infrequent visits to widely dispersed communities.[13] The first parish on San Antonio's West Side was not actually founded until the beginning of this century, and many of the parishes in COPS today were missions until quite recently. Even today, quite aside from the perennial shortage of Mexican-American priests, many Southwestern dioceses have remarkably low ratios of priests to parishioners generally.[14] Moreover, parishes are typically poor and unable to build parochial schools on the scale practiced in Catholic dioceses back East.[15]

Yet a more developed infrastructure would not necessarily have bridged the gap between Mexicans and the U.S. Catholic Church. Because they have brought few clergy with them, Mexican immigrants have typically found the Church here in the hands of Irish or Irish-American priests, nuns, and brothers whose austere Catholicism (as perhaps the above-quoted remarks indicate) does not resonate well with Mexican culture. Many of the poorest Mexicans remain unchurched. For "*los pobres* [the poor]" who feel unworthy or ashamed to come inside the church for services, one West Side parish in San Antonio maintains a special outdoor chapel. Many religious professionals, Mexican as well as Anglo, have tried to reach out, but such efforts have not been enough to overcome the deep-seated sentiment among Mexican Americans that the Church is somehow not entirely theirs.

As a result, Mexican-American relationships with the Church tend to be episodic. A frequent complaint of clergy is that Mexicans come to them only in time of need or crisis: when a destitute mother cannot feed her children or, more routinely, when a couple want to get married or baptize a newborn. Mexican Americans themselves admit this; one elderly man, a former union activist in San Antonio, chuckled: "I'm a b-and-b Catholic—just baptized and buried." To some extent such weak ties reflect ambivalence toward the institution, but they also reflect the personalistic orientation of Mexicans. A family may develop a bond with a particular priest, who then gets transferred to a different parish. Or there may be a falling out with a priest over plans for a wedding. In either case, the family may simply stop going to church.[16]

One result of such episodic relationships is that financial contributions are low. In the poorest parishes, even those attending mass do not necessarily offer donations. A typical complaint of clergy is that a family not seen for a year suddenly appears and requests a mass to celebrate their daughter's *quince años*. Much money is then spent on an elaborate cotillion, but the church, it is said, receives only a pittance.[17]

To deal with such problems, dioceses may require those seeking the sacraments to meet rather strict requirements. Couples wishing to get married must register six months in advance and attend classes. Parents, and sometimes godparents, must register in advance and receive religious instruction before their infants can be baptized. While it is true that in theory all Catholics are obliged to satisfy such requirements, they are more likely to be rigorously enforced in heavily Mexican dioceses. As an aide to the archbishop of San Antonio acknowledged, such strictures indicate this is a group not well schooled in its faith.

But beyond ambivalence and ignorance, the heritage of Mexican anticlericalism persists in America as indifference, lack of respect, and even hostility. In San Antonio, walking with a young, bearded Mexican-American priest through a dilapidated housing project two blocks from his church, I was struck by the cold stares his friendly greetings earned him from the young men hanging out on the corner. Or at the *jamaica* described earlier, private security personnel were posted around Our Lady of Victory's parking lot, and an armed guard accompanied the pastor as he went from booth to booth collecting the proceeds. The reason for these precautions was explained quite matter-of-factly by one parishioner running a ring-toss booth: local gangs are always nearby, waiting for a chance to pull off a robbery.

As Mexican Americans assimilate and move into the middle class, there is some evidence that they become more involved in the institutional life of the Church.[18] But there is also reason to believe that many other upwardly mobile Mexican Americans will pull even further away.[19] The best educated and most successful are often uneasy with the traditionalism of Catholicism, particularly as practiced in the barrio. Even an UNO leader expresses embarrassment at the organization's members being "hung up on the authority of the *padrecito.*"* In many instances such embarrassment shades into anticlericalism, which is never far from the surface. As one young San Antonio politico with a degree from the University of Texas remarked: "Have you ever noticed that the priest lives better than anybody else in the barrio?"

These various currents come together in the challenge posed by Protestantism. Protestant denominations have long maintained a presence in the barrio. In the mid-1960s, about 5 percent of Mexican Americans in San Antonio and Los Angeles were Protestants.[20] By the early 1980s this figure had doubled to about 10 percent, an increase apparently traceable to the impressive growth of fundamentalist sects.[21] Typically housed in run-down storefronts, these congregations keep very much to themselves, and not much is known about them. They appear to cater to the poorest and least-assimilated barrio residents.[22] Spanish is virtually the only language spoken. Like their Anglo and black counterparts, these fundamentalists vehemently reject social or political re-

---

* A term of affection meaning "little father," used here with sarcasm.

form and emphasize individual salvation. Indeed, their rigid strictures for daily living (no gambling, drinking, or smoking) seem to appeal to immigrants caught in an alien and disorienting environment—all the more so because the puritanical lessons are taught by ministers who are Latino, not Anglo. Usually quite small, these sects also offer an intimacy and fellowship that are often missing in typically larger, more impersonal Catholic parishes.

The competition from these fundamentalists is felt keenly in the parishes. One can sit in the crowded waiting room in the rectory of Our Lady of Guadalupe in San Antonio and hear gossip about who has "just turned Protestant," attending services at the storefront around the corner and forbidding their children to play with Catholic cousins. Vehemently anti-Catholic, these sects make much of parish fund-raisers where beer is sold and bingo played. Political activities such as COPS and UNO are similarly anathema to these groups.

The Catholics respond in kind. It is difficult to find a priest in San Antonio or Los Angeles with a good word about the storefront ministers in his parish, though most admit never having had any contact with their competitors. The hierarchy is very concerned about the growth of these sects and upset by their aggressive anti-Catholicism. In San Antonio, the archdiocese has launched its own television station as a countermeasure. And in Washington, D.C., the U.S. Conference of Catholic Bishops has taken official note of the fundamentalist challenge among Mexicans and Latinos generally.[23]

Indeed, none of these difficulties has been lost on the Church. Nor have any of the opportunities, since Latinos represent its fastest-growing segment in the United States. Responses range from alternative liturgies incorporating Mexican folk music to Pope John Paul II's 1987 tour of the Southwest. Yet even the latter revealed problems: turnout for the pope in the heavily Mexican-American cities he visited, including both San Antonio and Los Angeles, was much lower than the American bishops had anticipated.

A TALE OF TWO HIERARCHIES

The Church has also tried to respond to problems by appointing Latino bishops. Most visible of these has been Patricio Flores, appointed auxiliary bishop of San Antonio in 1970, and archbishop in 1978. Near the top of Flores's agenda has been COPS. Indeed, his enthusiastic support has greatly distinguished the situation of Alinsky organizers in San Antonio from that of their counterparts in Los Angeles—at least during the organization's formative years and before the arrival of Bishop Roger Mahony in Los Angeles.

COPS actually got started under the sympathetic regime of Flores's predecessor, Archbishop Francis Furey. In fact, Flores's elevation to the archbishop's throne was aided by a COPS letter-writing campaign. And under Flores the community organization has flourished. His visible and enthusiastic backing has opened up parish resources to the organization. As already mentioned, parish buildings are routinely used for COPS meetings, and parish buses take members to and from actions. In many instances, organizers have persuaded pastors to pay the dues assessed on each parish chapter directly out of operating revenues.

Moreover, the archbishop routinely shares the aura of his office with COPS. He appears in the diocesan newspaper with its leaders and speaks at its annual convention. But going well beyond ceremonial and symbolic support, his administrative decisions have made clear to San Antonio priests that participation in COPS will not hurt their careers. Indeed, key posts in the chancery are now held by priests who were, or still are, active in the organization. As one Mexican-American politico noted, "All the priests that used to be on the outside raising hell are now insiders at the chancery."

But Archbishop Flores has done more than absorb individual priests sympathetic to COPS into the diocesan hierarchy. For instance, he established a spin-off of the community organization within the hierarchy. The Office of Parish Development was headed by priests trained in Alinsky tactics and seasoned in organizing battles. The Office was staffed principally by ex-COPS officers, who traded in their positions as volunteers with the organization for jobs as full-time, paid employees of the archdiocese. Working out of the chancery, they organized parishes in remote, heavily Mexican areas of the region—rural towns south of San Antonio like Crystal City, Uvalde, and Carrizo Springs.

Although the Office of Parish Development was subsequently closed, it provided support at a critical juncture in the mid-1980s by helping the IAF expand its base beyond San Antonio. Moreover, this operation provided additional rungs on the organizational ladder for COPS leaders to climb. In this way skills learned at considerable expense to the organization were put to use in ways that did not undermine it. After all, working for the diocese helped reduce the ever-present possibility that COPS leaders would pursue independent political careers—a development that could compromise the organization's carefully crafted nonpartisan stance, as well as engender internal political battles.

In fact, this very situation has now arisen. For as already indicated, a former COPS leader, contrary to the wishes of her old colleagues in the organization, has recently been appointed to the San Antonio City Council. Less problematic for the organization has been the much less visible but influential role played by another former COPS leader serving as education adviser to Texas governor Ann Richards. Such individual achievements underscore the success of COPS. But they also point to the problems that come with success, and consequently to the critical function of the Office of Parish Development, which would not have been possible without Flores's cooperation.

Archbishop Flores is actually the latest in a series of liberal bishops attentive to the needs of Mexican Americans in San Antonio. Despite his very different personal style, Flores's immediate predecessor, Archbishop Furey, shared Flores's social-action orientation during his decade-long reign. Similarly, Furey's predecessor, Archbishop Robert Lucey, was known as "the pink bishop" for putting his diocese at the forefront of social change in Texas, for nearly three decades from 1941 to 1968. A union sympathizer who supported farmworker organizing efforts in the Rio Grande Valley in the 1960s, Lucey was friendly with Lyndon Johnson and threw the Church behind San Antonio's principal community-action agency, which was in fact headed by a diocesan priest.[24]

During this same period in Los Angeles, by contrast, James Francis Cardinal McIntyre set a tone of immovable conservatism. Although he retired as archbishop in 1970, McIntyre's imprint on the archdiocese of Los Angeles lasted well into the 1980s. Still referred to by some Catholic liberals as "little Hitler," McIntyre is renowned for his combative defense of hierarchical prerogatives during a period when the Church and American society were both undergoing drastic changes. Not only did he stubbornly refuse to implement liturgical and administrative reforms advocated by Vatican II, he drew a bright line between religion and politics. Whereas Archbishop Lucey encouraged priests to get involved in the civil rights movement and union-organizing efforts, numerous stories still circulate in Los Angeles about the punishment meted out by McIntyre to priests who, even in that environment, continued to be involved in union or other liberal causes.

Such accounts are confirmed by Grebler, whose survey found that during the mid-1960s pastors of Mexican-American parishes in Los Angeles were dramatically less likely to be involved in civic, neighborhood, or protest activities than their counterparts in San Antonio.[25] Not only did McIntyre refuse to support 1960s activist causes such as the farmworker strikes or grape and lettuce boycotts, he actively opposed them—as when he called in police to eject Chicano protesters from midnight mass at St. Basil's Church on Christmas Eve, 1969.

In the wake of that incident (which will be examined in relation to Chicano protest politics, in chapter 8), Timothy Manning succeeded McIntyre as archbishop. A pietistic figure who moved quickly to be conciliatory wherever his predecessor had been combative, Manning implemented the Vatican II reforms that McIntyre had scorned, including a priests' senate affording rank-and-file clergy an official arena in which to respond to their superiors.

As for Mexican Americans, Manning made several overtures. Soon after his appointment, he met with representatives of *Católicos por La Raza* (Catholics for the People), the group that had staged the protest at St. Basil's. In 1972 Manning named the archdiocese's first Latino auxiliary bishop, Juan Arzube. At about the same time, Manning led a group of Mexican Americans on a pilgrimage to the Shrine of Our Lady of Guadalupe just outside Mexico City.

Despite such gestures, tensions soon reemerged between the chancery and many laity, as well as religious professionals. The change at the top notwithstanding, certain fixtures from McIntyre's tenure remained as key members of Manning's staff. Foremost among these was Msgr. Benjamin Hawkes, vicar general of the archdiocese and pastor of St. Basil's (in whose rectory the retired McIntyre continued to live). Like McIntyre, Hawkes entered the priesthood after a career in business, and he knew how to put those skills to good use, maintaining highly centralized control over diocesan finances.

But more than a tightfisted administrator, Hawkes also earned a reputation as a bureaucratic intriguer. Rumored to be the inspiration for the wheeling-and-dealing monsignor in John Gregory Dunne's novel *True Confessions*, Hawkes possessed extensive knowledge of the Church bureaucracy which enabled him to fill the vacuum left by the aloof Manning.[26] As administrator of the ambitious building program of one of the largest dioceses in the United States, Hawkes developed ties with wealthy Catholic businessmen, to whom he was occasionally linked in controversies over the misuse of Church funds. Perhaps this is why, although the archdiocese can proudly say that every parish, including the poor parishes of East LA, has its own school (a goal that impoverished San Antonio has long since abandoned), this achievement became tainted with the public image of churchmen more concerned with bricks and mortar than with people.[27] As a *Los Angeles Times* editorial writer, a Catholic, said of Hawkes: "He must look out from the pulpit at St. Basil's and see a sea of checkbooks."

As for religious professionals involved in politics, both Anglo and Mexican-American politicians and activists confirm that under Manning, political activity continued to be discouraged, though much less aggressively. Until well into the 1980s, no one accused the Catholic Church in Los Angeles of fostering the political advancement of Mexican Americans.

Indeed, under Manning new tensions emerged between Mexican Americans and the hierarchy. Bishop Arzube did not prove to be an especially forceful advocate, and the fact that he was Ecuadoran engendered resentments. In the late 1970s Manning himself skirmished with Mexican-American activist religious professionals. Subsequently, in the summer of 1984, the chancery aroused a storm of protest over its decision to close a Catholic high school near East LA with which Mexican Americans had come to identify strongly. Their sense of betrayal was exacerbated by the fact that the building was being sold to a Hong Kong-based developer planning to demolish it. Also contributing to the furor was the archdiocese's surprise announcement of its intentions during the third week in July, when virtually every major Mexican-American politician in town was away at the 1984 Democratic National Convention in San Francisco. The immediate response was a long-distance phone call between Manning and State Senator Art Torres that quickly degenerated into a shouting match with the prelate remonstrating with Torres, a Baptist, over his pro-choice position on abortion. Subsequent community meetings, and the intervention of the Los Angeles City Council, eventually forced the archdiocese to change its plans. But the episode did little to bridge the persistent gap between the hierarchy and Mexican Americans in Los Angeles.

Thus, by the mid-1980s, when Manning was about to retire as archbishop, his episcopate was regarded by many as essentially a continuation of his predecessor's, despite obvious differences in style and temperament between the two men. Religious professionals and laity alike passed on stories about shady dealings at the chancery. The attitude of many was typified by the mild-mannered pastor of an East LA parish who dismissed Manning and his entourage as "a bunch of Republicans" who socialized with wealthy businessmen and offered the poor palliative services—at best.

UNO AND THE CHURCH:
A LUKEWARM EMBRACE

Given this history of high-handed bureaucratic rule, it is not surprising that for much of its existence UNO has not been enthusiastically supported by the Los Angeles hierarchy. When the initial inquiries were made in the mid-1970s about setting up an IAF organization in the diocese, the chancery resisted. Archdiocesan officials were eventually maneuvered into permitting the IAF into their domain, in part because doing otherwise would have meant turning down large seed grants from sympathetic religious orders and the Campaign for Human Development, which Manning himself had been instrumental in establishing.[28]

Another reason why the hierarchy accepted UNO, however reluctantly, was that few, if any, of the individuals identified with the IAF effort had been involved with the activist protests of the late 1960s and early 1970s, including the debacle at St. Basil's. It was also true that, while McIntyre and Manning hardly shared the IAF's vision for the Catholic Church, there were nonetheless a number of important issues that the IAF could be counted on *not* to raise. In a period of drastic and swift liberalization of both laity and religious professionals within the American Catholic Church, the conservative hierarchy of Los Angeles did not have to fear challenges from UNO on issues like abortion, women's ordination, or nuclear weapons. Indeed, these are precisely the kinds of "global issues" toward which the IAF's indifference earns it the label "opportunistic" from activists.[29]

Nevertheless, there is an obvious and basic antagonism between conservative churchmen like McIntyre and Manning on the one hand, and IAF organizers on the other. There was, in fact, a long-standing personal feud between Alinsky and McIntyre, going back to 1968 when the organizer characterized the cardinal as "an un-Christian, prehistoric mutton-head."[30]

The relationship between UNO and Manning was never that rancorous, but it was chilly. One UNO leader described the chancery's attitude toward the organization as "benign indifference." Others saw downright hostility. One young priest insisted that Hawkes discouraged powerful friends like Peter O'Malley, owner of the Los Angeles Dodgers, from making contributions to UNO. Other leaders told of priests being rebuked by the chancery for working with the organization. On one occasion, UNO joined forces with a pastor charging that the expansion of a local tortilla factory would disrupt the neighborhood. The owner of the *tortillería* got the chancery to intervene and exerted pressure on the pastor to desist; and lacking the confidence to defy the chancery, UNO unilaterally withdrew—a decision that, in the words of one of the priest's colleagues, "left him hanging." Eventually the pastor had a nervous breakdown and was relieved of his duties.

It's hard to judge the accuracy of such accounts, but the frequency with which they are related reveals UNO's sense of powerlessness vis-à-vis Manning's hierarchy—which tolerated but did not encourage the organization. Unlike Archbishop Flores, who has allowed himself to be personally identified with COPS, Manning almost never appeared with UNO. Under his regime few, if any, priests active in UNO were promoted into the upper echelons of the chancery; and no diocesan Office of Parish Development was established in Los Angeles to afford former UNO leaders the opportunity to create new IAF organizations. Given UNO's weak position, it is no wonder the organization kept a low profile during the mid-1980s when Manning's successor was being chosen, for fear its support of a particular candidate would backfire. As it turned out, the organization's preference, Bishop Roger Mahony of Stockton, was selected. But here again, UNO's strategy contrasts strikingly with COPS's vigorous letter-writing campaign on behalf of Flores.

The consequences of this lack of support from the Los Angeles hierarchy have been enormous. Outside the channels of power at the chancery for much of its existence, UNO has had a difficult time raising local chapter dues. For without the archbishop's active support, it has been difficult to persuade pastors to pay dues directly out of their Sunday collections, as has been done in many COPS parishes. Instead, UNO parishes have raised dues through time-consuming activities like fiestas, which organizers resent as sapping energy from their primary mission. UNO's weakness has also meant that local chapters have been proprietary about funds they raise, and have frequently withheld dues to bargain with the organizers. Even pastors sympathetic to UNO have resorted to such tactics. This maneuvering obviously exacerbates the organization's problems. And because, unlike COPS, UNO has had no control over CDBG or comparable funding, its ability to discipline members has been further diminished.

UNO's outsider status has caused additional problems when it has sought the support of diocesan priests, who have been trained in the diocese and expect to spend their entire careers there. Such clerics obviously tend to be more concerned with their standing at the chancery than at UNO headquarters. Moreover, most parishes in East LA are staffed by nondiocesan priests, reflecting the aforementioned historical pattern of the Church relying on missionary orders to minister to Mexicans. The organization has consequently come to rely heavily, though not exclusively, on religious order priests (typically Missionhursts, Oblates, and Claretians) whose education is broader and outlook more cosmopolitan than that of diocesan priests, and who are also less directly under the control of the archbishop.

But this reliance on religious order priests has created problems for UNO. Over the organization's protests, religious priests have been routinely reassigned by their orders, with the result that parishes active under their tutelage suddenly drop out of the organization. And independence from the chancery has also meant independence from UNO, with individual religious priests taking the opportunity to build up sizable personal followings within UNO. Indeed, as I have already suggested, there have been numerous complaints both inside and outside the organization about the undue influence wielded by its priest-leaders. The result has been entrepreneurialism of the sort I attributed in the previous chapter to Protestant ministers, which only further weakens UNO.

Consider the case of Fr. Luis Olivares, a member of the Claretian order and for many years pastor of Our Lady Queen of the Angels Church (La Placita), whose overflow crowds were described earlier. Before he was forced into retirement by AIDS, Olivares would boast of the ten to twelve thousand worshipers at his church every Sunday. He sounded like a politician talking about his political base—and well he might, for La Placita doesn't just attract immigrants. It is famous among Mexican Americans throughout the Southwest. On a typical weekday, for example, the office staff can be overheard making arrangements for a couple coming in from Arizona to have their infant baptized.

Olivares (referred to by one organizer, half in jest and half in awe, as "Large Louie") is probably the most popular priest ever involved with UNO, and would get a rousing hand whenever introduced at organizational meetings and public gatherings. He claimed the title of "Mr. UNO," but also enjoyed considerable visibility in the Los Angeles media for his involvement in a variety of other causes. For example, when the archdiocese moved to close down the popular East LA high school mentioned above, Olivares showed up to say mass at the protest rally. He often made La Placita's facilities available to César Chávez; he allowed Marxist union activists on church grounds to solicit signatures against immigration restriction; and he declared his church a sanctuary for Central American refugees and other illegal immigrants. And when President Daniel Ortega and his Sandinista colleagues visited Los Angeles, Olivares hosted a prayer breakfast for them.[31]

Such activities often resulted in phone calls from UNO leaders, rebuking Olivares for not clearing his participation with the organization. Because Olivares was so strongly identified with UNO, organizers frequently criticized his involvement in what they disparagingly refer to as "movement causes." In addition, his freelancing and cultivation of a personal following flouted the IAF collective leadership principle. But because UNO needed him more than he needed UNO, Olivares got away with pursuing his personal agenda. When the organization staged important rallies, Olivares was typically called upon to turn out his followers and given a prominent role in the proceedings.

Not surprisingly, such powerful priests have gotten involved in internal UNO elections.[32] In one critical contest, Olivares himself delivered a sizable block of votes to the woman who was elected president. Her opponent was supported by another powerful priest, who subsequently refused to cooperate with the winner. The second priest's continued efforts at sabotage ended only when he was reassigned by his order and went to San Antonio to head the Office of Parish Development.

The extraordinary influence of such clerics has also hindered UNO's efforts at developing lay leaders, who tend to feel overshadowed and demoralized by figures like Olivares. Of one UNO president, an organizer observed: "Gloria had a hard time filling Olivares's shoes." Other leaders have imitated the freelancing style of their priest-mentors. For example, one UNO officer and protégé of the reassigned priest violated a cardinal IAF rule when she went to a meeting with a member of Mayor Bradley's inner circle of advisers by herself, without any other UNO leaders present. When rebuked by members of the organization's executive board, this articulate young woman, unmarried and pursuing a career in addition to her duties as an UNO officer, shot back: "What's wrong with it? Father Pedro did it all the time." This incident underscores a point made earlier: the opportunities available to Mexican Americans in Los Angeles make lay leaders, as well as priests, less dependent on the organization for personal growth and advancement, thus making it harder for UNO to maintain organizational discipline.

This problem is one facet of a larger one: UNO's lack of success in moderating the moralism of participants. In the previous chapter I suggested that the moralistic streak that distinguishes Alinsky organizers from politicians gets tempered by the organizers' commitment to the day-to-day needs of the organization. For religious professionals, especially young

Catholics suffused with the high-minded social reformism against which Reinhold Niebuhr warned liberal Protestants more than a generation ago, moralism is an even greater temptation.[33] When the IAF encounters such individuals—including adherents of liberation theology, as well as Marxists—it views them warily, but nevertheless takes them in, reasonably confident that its methods will turn them around.

The emphasis on diversity within IAF organizations facilitates the inclusion of such individuals. But once in the organization, they are subjected to intense socializing forces. Over time, two possibilities arise: either they are so entrenched in their moralism that they cannot function successfully in the highly pragmatic atmosphere of Alinsky organizing, or they are absorbed into the enterprise and gradually weaned from their moralistic politics. The opportunity to participate in an ongoing political organization offers such individuals the chance to develop by testing their ideals against reality and, consequently, to channel their moral energies into constructive political endeavors.

For this process to work, however, the community organization must be disciplined, cohesive, and capable of delivering the goods, psychologically and materially. COPS meets these requirements, but UNO has had difficulty doing so. With few rewards or sanctions to dispense, the latter is relatively powerless to prevent moralistic religious professionals from pursuing their own political causes. Moreover, because UNO is so dependent on clerics like Fr. Olivares to deliver their followers, controversial issues that Alinsky organizers would ordinarily dismiss as "unwinnable"—such as American policy in Central America or the plight of illegal aliens—get foisted on the organization.

Such problems have been both cause and effect of the Los Angeles hierarchy's grudging attitude toward UNO. Here as elsewhere, weakness engenders weakness. Yet the situation has been changing. In 1985 Cardinal Manning retired and his successor, Roger Mahony, appeared intent on making up for lost time. Notably, the diocesan financial affairs so long dominated by Msgr. Hawkes (who died shortly after Manning's retirement) were turned over to lay professionals. Although a conservative on issues like abortion, homosexuality, and the ordination of women, Mahony is a liberal on social welfare and economic issues. As bishop of Fresno in the 1970s, for example, he served as chairman of Governor Jerry Brown's Agricultural Labor Relations Board.[34]

Shortly after arriving in Los Angeles, Mahony instituted a five-year, multimillion-dollar program to improve Church ties with Hispanics.

Launching the effort at a rally in Dodger Stadium, the archbishop declared in Spanish to the 50,000 present, "Los Angeles is your home, the Catholic Church is your home, and I am your pastor."[35] Shortly before being named cardinal, Mahony reveled in the excitement created by Pope John Paul II's 1987 visit to Los Angeles and made sure Latinos figured prominently in it.

Not surprisingly, Mahony has been extremely supportive of UNO, which, as mentioned earlier, quietly supported his elevation to the archbishopric and has certainly been useful in reaching out to Latinos. In sharp contrast to his predecessor, Mahony appears frequently at UNO and other IAF functions, and lends the authority of his position to their efforts in innumerable ways. For example, diocesan priests have definitely gotten the message that working with the IAF will not hurt their careers. Yet the cardinal is mindful of other constituencies in Southern California. For example, during that 1987 visit he engineered a historic papal address to the assembled notables of the entertainment industry at Universal City. In other words, Mahony is a sophisticated and skillful public figure who, while supportive of UNO and its affiliates, has his own agenda and is not about to give them the blank check that Archbishop Flores has given COPS in San Antonio.[36]

LOST IN LOTUS LAND

Yet even with Cardinal Mahony's support, UNO and other IAF organizations in Los Angeles face daunting obstacles in a political system so inimical to neighborhood-based politics. In San Antonio, COPS has found vulnerable targets in the dozens of public officials elected from many different jurisdictions, large and small. At its outset, the organization also benefited from the demise of the GGL. Able to move into the resulting electoral vacuum, COPS also took advantage of the institutional void due to the underdeveloped state of local governmental structures resulting from the GGL's regime of informal, but centralized power. Additionally advantageous to COPS was the advent in 1977 of single-member districting of the San Antonio City Council.[37]

By contrast, Los Angeles has presented UNO and its IAF affiliates with a less porous, more monolithic political system. The fact that the city elects fewer public officials from much larger jurisdictions suggests that UNO needs to be larger than COPS. But as I have already indicated, UNO has fewer members, both absolutely and relative to the size of the metropolitan area within which it operates. Further diluting UNO's clout is the fact that its member parishes are scattered astride the boundary between the City of Los Angeles and unincorporated Los Angeles County. As a result, a large proportion of the organization's few thousand members have no municipal political arena in which to make their presence felt. Instead, they get swallowed up in one or another of the huge county supervisorial districts. Thus, the sheer scale of the metropolis overwhelms the community organization. As one organizer complains: "We just can't compete with Hollywood, or with Lockheed, or with the aerospace industry." Another organizer emphasizes: "You just don't feel you can effect any change or make any impact in Los Angeles. . . . There are so many players. . . . I've been here for four and a half years, and I'm still meeting new players."

Compounding such difficulties is a well-entrenched bureaucracy whose unyielding nature UNO organizers understand all too well. They frequently complain about the difficulties of pushing city, or for that matter county, administrators to implement the programs they have successfully advocated. One organizer describes his predicament: "They [the bureaucrats] have a very different kind of self-interest from politicians. They are there, secure in their jobs, and really don't have to respond to you if they don't want to." Such comments are seldom heard from these organizers' counterparts in San Antonio.

Along with this impervious bureaucracy, UNO organizers are up against what they perceive as an elusive power structure. They stress how difficult it has been to find visible targets in Los Angeles's private sector. As a result, they explain, UNO's early efforts focused on drawing attention to the so-called Committee of Twenty-Five, a low-profile group that included such key corporate leaders as William French Smith.

It is difficult to judge UNO's perceptions here; trained to target individuals vulnerable to personalized confrontation, Alinsky organizers are predisposed to power elite scenarios. Yet one need not accept the *film noir* image of a sunlit land of lotus-eaters ruled by conspirators lurking in the shadows to recognize that the economic and political powers-that-be in Southern California are rather faceless. This was driven home to me while talking with an aide to Mayor Bradley. Pondering a question about his boss's heavy investment in a certain issue, the young politico confided, "You know, you never know who the Mayor is fronting for." Certainly when compared with a place like San Antonio, where even today a relatively small, identifiable elite controls the city, a huge metropolis like Los Angeles exhibits complex power relations difficult to fathom.

Yet if power in Los Angeles tends to be faceless and remote, it is also co-optive. It is striking, for example, that IAF veterans consider UNO's initial campaign to lower auto insurance rates as having succeeded too easily. They claim this was in part because the Los Angeles corporate establishment was too accepting of the community organization. Indeed, organizers note that the private sector has typically been more cooperative toward UNO than the public sector. Several leaders cite the lack of a single major battle between UNO and the corporate establishment as an important reason why the organization has not made greater strides. Certainly, in recent years UNO and its affiliates have been working closely with corporate leaders to build support for issues such as education.

REACHING OUT INSTEAD OF DOWN

But more than just co-optation, UNO's relationships with corporate and business elites reflect the organization's efforts to do what other political actors in Los Angeles have done: reach *out* to build relationships with potential allies in the metropolitan region and Sacramento, instead of reaching *down* to build up their community base. As will be evident in the next chapter on elite-network politics, these Alinsky organizers work much harder than Los Angeles politicians at practicing genuine grassroots politics. Yet the fact remains, their efforts are stymied by the obstacles and disincentives to neighborhood-based politics so evident throughout California.

In this regard, Cortes's calculations upon first arriving in Los Angeles are instructive. He knew political targets would be difficult to find in East LA. Art Snyder, the crafty Anglo who represented the area on the Los Angeles City Council, was entrenched in the parishes as an anomaly: a practitioner of something resembling traditional ward politics who, by skillfully servicing constituents, had managed to prosper amidst the thoroughly reformed politics of Los Angeles. He had UNO outorganized on its own turf before the community organization even got off the ground. As an IAF veteran familiar with those early days put it: "Every time we even thought about making an issue of a needed stop sign or traffic light, Snyder got word of our plans through his networks in the parishes and moved on them." To take on Snyder would have been to polarize Cortes's prospective base.

Yet Snyder was the only target UNO had the remotest chance of influencing. Because the Los Angeles School Board was at that time elected at large in a jurisdiction actually larger than the City of Los Angeles, the upstart community organization could do little in that arena. And as I have already indicated, UNO had no prospect of leverage on the county's five-person board of supervisors. In any event, the liberal Democrat whose supervisorial district included East LA had been quietly supportive of Cortes's efforts.

By contrast, auto insurance rates looked promising. Yet as I have indicated, the issue led Cortes away from the parishes in East LA and toward Governor Jerry Brown, the media, and the state legislature in Sacramento. Since then, UNO has continued to organize at the parish level, but also to operate in Sacramento. For example, in the mid-1980s the organization participated in a coalition to increase Los Angeles's share of state education funds, and to secure passage of a state bond issue for new school construction. With area schools inundated with the children of hundreds of thousands of immigrants, this was a popular issue with the *Los Angeles Times* and state legislators. And as we've seen, UNO worked closely with State Superintendent of Public Instruction Bill Honig, who was forging a statewide coalition for education reform and presenting himself as a spokesman for education nationally.

To the extent that Honig, a statewide elected official, harbored further political ambitions, an organization like UNO, representing thousands of parents who may not be citizens but whose children nevertheless need decent schools, was useful—but only as a symbol, not for its electoral clout. Hence Honig's walking tour of East LA schools, mentioned earlier. By hitching a ride on such media events, UNO has won much-needed visibility. But such events have also, as I shall explain below, subverted IAF organizing techniques and may have actually weakened UNO's community base.

Again, comparison with COPS is instructive. The San Antonio organization has also been involved with education issues at the state level. In the mid-1980s it was a key supporter of the controversial education reform package that came out of Governor Mark White's Select Committee on Public Education, headed by H. Ross Perot. But unlike UNO, COPS took on this challenge only after building up a statewide base. Indeed, by the beginning of the 1990s, there were IAF organizations in San Antonio, the lower Rio Grande Valley, Eagle Pass, El Paso, Fort Bend, Austin, Fort Worth, and Houston, as well as exploratory sponsoring committees in several other cities. Operating under the umbrella of the Texas IAF Network, which has a permanent staff and headquarters in Austin, these organizations are capable of bringing hundreds, indeed thousands, of members (who are predominantly but not exclusively Mexican Americans) to the State Capitol. With that kind of clout, Texas IAF has played an important role in any number of issues affecting low- and moderate-income Texans: including public utility rates, education, health care, and most recently job training. Challenging though these issues are, Texas IAF has been tackling them from a position of strength gained by its solid community base. The contrast could not be more stark with UNO—which, as mentioned earlier, is tackling even more difficult social problems, such as gang violence, but with a much weaker base.

Even at the local level, UNO and its IAF affiliates have reached out, instead of down. The large issue-oriented rallies on which they have relied to maintain their visibility in the huge metropolis are a case in point. To attract such numbers, these organizations rely less on the parish-based leaders whom they continue to seek out and develop than on elite allies willing to endorse and, in effect, advertise an event. Such changes in the usual IAF organizing process can also be seen in the dependence of these organizations on entrepreneurial priests—and in the support lent to the IAF by Cardinal Mahony, whose own penchant for such events has more than once resulted in his presiding over huge mass assemblies at Dodger Stadium.[38] The IAF's elite strategy in Los Angeles is further revealed in its courting of corporate, business, and political leaders, who lend critical, visible support to these assemblies. Finally, this strategy is evident in the good relations the IAF has built up with the media in Los Angeles, particularly with the *Los Angeles Times*. With the endorsement of this and other media, IAF rallies have attracted numbers clearly in excess of the membership of the four organizations.

The IAF in Los Angeles has reached out in one other significant way. I have already alluded to the three affiliated organizations that have been spun off from UNO. With SCOC in South-Central Los Angeles, Valley Organized In Community Efforts (VOICE) in the San Fernando Valley, and the East Valleys Organization (EVO) in the San Gabriel and Pomona valleys, the IAF has managed to spread itself throughout Los Angeles County. But it has spread itself rather thin.

SCOC illustrates the difficulties the IAF has had making inroads among blacks in Los Angeles. When the organization was founded in 1981, South-Central constituted the city's black core, subsuming the better-known Watts district. But during the 1980s South-Central was inundated by Hispanic immigrants, who now constitute more than half the area's population. It was with this population mix that South-Central achieved its recent notoriety as the epicenter of the 1992 riots.

SCOC began with a core group of a few black Episcopal and several black Catholic churches. It was from these congregations that the organization's leadership emerged. Indeed, many of these same leaders are still on the scene, which indicates not only a lack of organizational vitality but also the fact that the organization has never been able to break into the mainstream black churches—the Methodists, Baptists, and Pentecostals. IAF organizers have encountered resistance in such congregations, not only on account of the organizational dynamics described in the previous chapter, but also on account of animosities and suspicions toward outsiders—nonblacks—coming in and presuming to direct black political efforts. The dearth of black organizers in the IAF network obviously contributes to this problem.

Despite such obstacles, in the mid-1980s SCOC scored some victories with campaigns demanding increased police patrols and restrictions on liquor licenses at neighborhood stores—efforts which have received renewed attention in the aftermath of the recent riots.[39] Also in the mid-1980s the organization expanded southward into Compton and established an alliance with the bishop of the Christian Methodist Episcopal (CME) Church. But here, too, appearances proved deceptive. A recently established black denomination, the CME Church was a newcomer to Los Angeles—a fact that only underscored SCOC's continuing inability to break into the mainstream black churches. Moreover, by this time the organization had, for a variety of interpersonal and political reasons, succeeded in arousing the outright animosity of political leaders such as Mark Ridley-Thomas (now on the Los Angeles City Council) and then assemblywoman Maxine Waters (now in Congress).[40]

Compounding these problems have been the demographic changes just mentioned. With the more upwardly mobile blacks leaving South-Central, SCOC was left with those blacks most difficult to organize—and with newly arrived Hispanic immigrants, whose challenges to Alinsky techniques I have already identified. Tensions between the two groups have not made the task any easier. Faced with such obstacles, it is hardly surprising that SCOC has, as I will explore below, followed UNO in modifying Alinsky methods in order to gain media attention in the vast Los Angeles basin.

The IAF's other expansion efforts in Los Angeles highlight obstacles of a different sort. EVO and VOICE are based in suburban areas, with members not only more middle-class but also less likely to be Hispanic, Catholic, or black. Indeed, VOICE boasts three synagogue-based local chapters (whose active members include the parents of actor Richard Dreyfuss), a chapter at a Jewish social service agency, and another at a local college. Such chapters obviously add the diversity sought by the IAF— a not inconsequential commodity in Southern California these days; they also offer a potential supply of articulate spokesmen and leaders. But, given the cleavages already identified within UNO between assimilated Mexican Americans and more recent arrivals, one must question how effective such middle-class leaders can be across all four organizations. More important, one must wonder how amenable such individuals will be to the rigors of IAF leadership training. Merely to ask these questions is to underscore the difficulties the IAF has been having with its more natural constituencies in less affluent parts of Los Angeles.

Such expansion efforts have been hindered by a problem of perennial concern throughout the IAF network: the scarcity of talented organizers. In Los Angeles this problem has been exacerbated by the perception, among some leaders at least, that the IAF's heavy investments in Texas have been at the expense of its efforts in Southern California. The validity of such claims is difficult to assess. On the one hand, the importance of maintaining a vital presence in the largest Mexican-American community in the United States has translated into an undeniably serious commitment by the IAF in metropolitan Los Angeles. On the other hand, UNO leaders have at times felt neglected. They point to the so-called "Texas Strategy" as evidence that the IAF has focused on that state. They also point out that Cortes left Los Angeles after only two years (sooner than expected for an organizer starting a new effort), and returned to his home state to launch a new organization in Houston. UNO leaders complain that after his departure they had to battle with the IAF to get good staff assigned to them. The response from IAF headquarters was (as it is to all local organizations): "Grow your own organizers." But for the many reasons noted, this has been particularly difficult to do in Los Angeles. As a result, attempts to develop organizers from within UNO's ranks have led to several disappointments and, at times, high staff turnover.

Most IAF organizations have probably had similar difficulties. And it may be unfair for UNO leaders to fixate on Cortes's premature departure as a sign of the IAF's lack of commitment in Southern California. Nevertheless, some continue to argue, as one leader put it, "We don't have a local boy who made good . . . we don't have anyone who really feels it in the gut [the way Cortes does]." Certainly for many in UNO—as for most other political actors in Los Angeles—the successes of their Texas counterparts rankle. Indeed, at times UNO leaders have seemed angrier toward the IAF than toward the public figures they are trained to confront.

To cite just one example: A priest involved with UNO recounts an occasion when Cortes flew into town to meet with reporters from the *Los Angeles Times*. One of several such sessions Cortes and UNO were having with the paper, the meeting was an opportunity not only to secure for the organization much-needed media exposure, but also to upbraid individual reporters for their poor coverage of East LA. But as newspapers are wont to do, the *Times* focused on personalities rather than on organizations: one outcome was a feature-length article about Cortes—and his fellow Texan, Cisneros. As a result, some UNO leaders came away from the episode feeling frustrated and angry that their efforts, and the organization generally, had been relegated to the background. Instead of bolstering organizational morale, this media attention exacerbated sentiment within UNO that it was being neglected by the IAF.

UNO AND THE MEDIA:
SEDUCED AND UNDERMINED

It is hardly coincidental that the above episode involves the *Los Angeles Times*, arguably the most powerful political actor in Southern California. For in such a huge metropolitan region, with its highly mobile population and weak political parties and governmental institutions, the media—print and electronic—play a particularly important role. It is, of course, a commonplace that the media are critical to the political life of Los Angeles, and California generally. The image has been etched in the public mind of candidates who spend most of their time raising money for television ads, and who consequently have meager incentives for direct contact with voters.

But from the perspective of a community organization that has had to struggle to make itself visible, a somewhat different picture emerges. UNO's problem has obviously not been raising money for media time, but simply attracting media attention. Los Angeles is a huge and daunting place. Quite aside from its importance as the center of the entertainment industry, the metropolitan region is itself the second largest media market in the nation. Among those drawn to Los Angeles, therefore, are journalists eager to make it big.

In this highly competitive environment, journalists are aggressive and adversarial. So, even when UNO attracts their attention, they can be difficult to deal with. One organizer describes the problems UNO has had managing the media according to established IAF techniques. Apparently, if too many conditions or strictures are laid down, Los Angeles journalists have been known to pack up and leave. On the other hand, organizers admit that, as a group representing the heart of the barrio, UNO has enjoyed attention and even a certain sympathy from some media, especially from various Mexican-American journalists in the metropolitan area. These journalists come to the organization for "the Mexican-American view" on various controversies and issues. But this attention, organizers complain, has often been episodic and lackadaisical. They cite the difficulty of getting reporters to come out to East LA to cover stories, particularly those from the *Times*, who face a 3:00 P.M. deadline. But even if they are successful, organizers note that stories about UNO don't always make it past the editors.

UNO's problems with the media come into focus when contrasted with the situation of COPS, which has long enjoyed extensive, at various times daily, coverage in the local media. As it happens, the San Antonio media have not always been particularly sympathetic to the Alinsky organization. Nor has COPS been able to rely on the sympathies of Mexican-American journalists, of whom there have been surprisingly few in San Antonio. In any event, organizers familiar with both cities claim that COPS has encountered far more hostility from the media than has its sister organization in Los Angeles.

Yet this hostility has rarely translated into searching scrutiny of COPS. Virtually all San Antonio politicians and journalists report that the local media are remarkably passive. The city's two dailies, one a Hearst and the other a Murdoch paper, depend heavily on the wire services for hard news. As one Mexican-American city councillor put it, "To find out what's going on in the world, we have to read the *Wall Street Journal*." As for local events, neither paper offers much hard-hitting, investigative coverage. Indeed, one COPS organizer aptly observes that the media express very little curiosity about the organization. The frequent attention it does get is repetitive and offers little analysis. Over the years, all the issues and controversies in which COPS has been involved have been dutifully reported, but one searches through piles of old clippings in vain for articles probing beyond the obvious. For example, there have been no efforts to examine possible improprieties arising from COPS's political activities and its support from the Catholic Church. In this "big small town," the media obviously plays a much less significant political role than in a huge metropolis like Los Angeles. In addition, with its strong base in Mexican-American neighborhoods and parishes, COPS is substantially less dependent on the local media than UNO. Both factors, along with the attention it commands as a major political actor, account for COPS having a much easier time managing the media than its counterpart in Los Angeles.

Thus, media attention has been simultaneously more critical and more problematic for UNO. Nonetheless, the organization has managed to get itself noticed. Indeed, its initial outing with the auto insurance issue suggests what can be accomplished through clever manipulation of the right issue at the right time. Still, as mentioned earlier, UNO struggled for some time to be identified in the media as other than a nameless East LA community organization. By the late 1980s, with the help of its IAF affiliates, the organization had moved well beyond that stage and today enjoys considerable media visibility and recognition. As mentioned above, these organizations have developed extremely good relations with the *Los Angeles Times*, which now routinely praises and supports their efforts. But, however critical such recognition may be in the huge metropolis, it also contributes to the softening of Alinsky principles and methods.

The essence of Alinsky organizing, it should be recalled, is the transformation of the informal, primary group ties between friends and neighbors into the instrumental ties binding members of a formal organization. As explained in the previous chapter, the initial stage of an organizing drive requires months of interviews in order to surface likely issues and potential leaders. Subsequently, there are many hours of meetings and consultations in which members are taught basic organizational and political skills. The key to these efforts is the intense mentor-pupil relationship between organizers and leaders.

Not only is this tedious, time-consuming process of little interest to the media; it can be easily subverted by their presence. Now, as we've seen, Alinsky organizations do seek out confrontations with public figures that succeed in attracting the media. But media attention is not the primary objective of such actions. Rather, such confrontations are intended to create confusion and commotion, over which the organization can demonstrate its mastery to nonmembers and members alike. Carefully planned and then evaluated, these actions are designed to teach members about their collective power to influence events. In addition to being a means of communication, the media are among the political actors to be influenced. So their presence is useful to the organizing effort. But it is not essential.

A strong organization like COPS succeeds in physically controlling the media present at its actions. Adhering to the Alinsky methods described earlier, COPS relies on carefully trained and rehearsed floor captains to make sure that reporters, or any other outsiders, do not roam about unattended. By contrast, a weak organization like UNO has difficulty exerting such control. Lacking a well-disciplined membership, it tends not to field floor teams capable of preventing aggressive journalists, particularly television reporters and their camera crews, from creating their own commotion by scurrying about, interviewing whatever public officials are present. If not contained, such activities quickly cause UNO members to feel like onlookers, not participants, at their own meetings. Likewise, when news photographers succeed in getting public officials (such as the cookie-eating county sheriff described earlier) to pose for photos with UNO leaders, the tension on which Alinsky confrontations depend for dramatic effect is seriously undercut. And when the media are left free to conduct noisy interviews, the post-action evaluations used by organizers as teaching sessions get seriously disrupted.

An aggressive, unmanaged media corps also creates problems by singling out specific individuals as spokesmen for the organization. Fr. Olivares is a prime example. Similarly harmful to organizational cohesion are the numerous occasions when the media approach individual leaders for comments on issues on which UNO has not taken an official position. In COPS, such inquiries are typically channeled through the organizational hierarchy. But in the less disciplined UNO, press inquiries get handled more haphazardly. It is understandable that the organization would want to take advantage of such opportunities, but by permitting individual leaders to respond to the media on their own, UNO runs obvious risks. This practice also puts the organization in the position of passively responding to media initiatives, ceding significant control over its own agenda and image. At the same time, the status and power of those singled out for attention are enhanced, thereby further undercutting the IAF principle of collective leadership.

An awareness of the corrosive effect of the media has led IAF organizers generally to keep a low profile. As good "organization men," Cortes and his colleagues long avoided media exposure so as not to overshadow their leaders, or the community organizations themselves. Throughout COPS's first decade, Cortes, though well known by reputation in San Antonio, was an extremely elusive figure who refused to give interviews and avoided having his picture taken.

But as the episode over Cortes's interview with the *Los Angeles Times* indicates, this policy has changed. For example, at COPS's tenth anniversary convention Cortes addressed the 7,000 members present—the first time he had ever delivered a formal address to the organization in public. At about the same time, Cortes was awarded a coveted MacArthur Fellowship. More recently, he has been the focus of a two-hour PBS program hosted by Bill Moyers. These changes reflect a deliberate decision by the IAF to give its organizers more visibility and recognition.

Yet as the ill-feeling generated by Cortes's interview also suggests, increased attention to the media runs the risk that these community organizations may be diverted from their objectives. A sign that something has been wrong within UNO is the frequent observation that members turn out for big meetings only when they know the media will be there. As UNO leaders have complained repeatedly, "Everyone wants to be on television." Meanwhile, routine meetings of the parish chapters, where the real work of the organization is supposed to occur, have gone largely unattended. The presence, or absence, of the media is too simple an explanation of UNO's attendance problems, but the frequency with which it has been offered by leaders is certainly suggestive. So, too, is the fact that no such complaints have been heard from COPS leaders in San Antonio.

More serious problems develop when organizers begin building actions around the media. Here again, there have been numerous examples within UNO. When the first question that an UNO organizer asks about an action is, "Were the media there?", the dynamic at work is sharply at odds with Alinsky methods. But given the enormous power of the media in Los Angeles, it is hardly surprising that IAF organizers incline toward the view that whatever happens at actions is not intrinsically important, but matters only insofar as it gets reported or broadcast. As one organizer, referring to the *Times*'s afternoon deadline, observed with grim irony, "If it doesn't happen before 3:00 P.M. in LA, it doesn't happen."

A telling example of this dynamic arose when an UNO leader took charge of the planning for one of the organization's few accountability sessions with local politicians. When the event was over, the organizer complained, "There were no pictures or set-ups the TV cameras could capture." The leader pleaded guilty to the charge, but pointed out that instead of focusing on media pictures, she had been concerning herself with leadership development, trying to structure the session to give the other leaders maximum opportunity to confront the politicians.

Similar problems are evident with UNO's walking tours of East LA. For example, as the above-described tour with Superintendent Honig was ending, the press corps literally pushed UNO leaders aside and began peppering Honig with questions, many of which departed from the subject at hand: increased funding for school construction. Under like circumstances, COPS would have asserted control, either by whisking the official away or by requiring that questions be asked through its moderator. But UNO allowed things to proceed to the point where Honig was asked about school prayer and responded by criticizing some recent Supreme Court decisions. At that point, the organizer winced: here was a commentary newsworthy enough to eclipse the issue of education funding, not to mention UNO itself.

UNO has conducted many other such tours of East LA neighborhoods for groups like the American Jewish Committee, as well as for individual politicians and government officials. The appeal of such events for UNO has been the opportunity for media exposure depicting itself and other political players working together on issues of mutual concern. It is understandable that UNO would seek to promote itself in this manner. Nevertheless, these tours go against the basic Alinsky idea of building up group solidarity and leadership through confrontation—not conviviality —with officialdom. Undoubtedly this is why a subsequent organizer vowed "no more walking tours."

The most vivid example of how preoccupation with the media undermines IAF methods arose, not with UNO, but with its sister organization, SCOC. As part of its aforementioned campaign to limit liquor sales in the South-Central district, SCOC deliberately staged a media confrontation. By prior arrangement with a local television station, three of the organization's leaders confronted the president of a retail liquor dealers' association, in front of a neighborhood store that SCOC charged with abusing its liquor license. Under other circumstances, these would have been the ingredients for a classic Alinsky confrontation. But this event, broadcast live on a late-afternoon news program, was controlled not by SCOC, but by the TV reporter asking the questions. As a result, there was no opportunity for the carefully planned sequence of action, reaction, and evaluation around which Alinsky organizers teach their members the fundamentals of politics. And because the three leaders were the only representatives of the organization present, there was no opportunity for the membership to feel its collective power.

There was, however, a crowd present—of idle teenagers drawn both to the tension of the scene and to the expensive television equipment. For a while it looked as though a free-for-all was brewing between the mostly white television crew and the teenagers, who were black. In the end, the debate ceased, the outsiders departed, and the crowd dispersed. But once again, a struggling Alinsky group had bought media exposure at the price of ceding control over an event which did little to actually build up the organization, and which could have developed into a nasty incident.

Yet beyond these considerations, the most important impact of the media on IAF organizations in Los Angeles is their tendency to encourage Mexican Americans to view themselves as a racial minority. In great measure, the media's affinity for this perspective reflects their heady experience as active participants in the civil rights movement. But it also reflects more fundamental institutional predilections: a bias toward the underdog, ingrained cynicism about established institutions, and an attraction to the sensational or dramatic. Working under these constraints, not to mention the pressure of deadlines, journalists accept the surface validity of the proposition that Mexican Americans are "our second minority group." To do otherwise would require probing into the subtleties of the Mexican-American experience, an historical and imaginative exercise that journalists seem to have neither the time nor the inclination to undertake. Instead, they pick up on the obvious differences between Mexicans and the American mainstream: low income and educational levels; substandard housing; overcrowded schools. These are the stuff of newspaper and television accounts of the barrio.

When held up as evidence of the contrasting situation of blacks and whites, such journalistic staples have considerable validity. But when offered as insights into barrio life, they neglect the critical subjective dimension of the Mexican immigrant who, with an eye to the situation of friends and relatives back home, declares that he has arrived in *"paraíso."* But even when immigrants express less positive sentiments, journalists making forays into the barrios tend to exaggerate their significance and ignore how the passage of time ameliorates some of the difficulties immigrants undeniably experience—or how their children become the focus of their aspirations.

Not surprisingly, UNO responds to such cues from the media. Understandably, organizers are frequently tempted to say what they think journalists want to hear, as in a press briefing where an organizer recites a litany of problems in East LA, gradually building to the climax of warning his audience: "We're sitting on a tinder box!" It might be argued that the 1992 riots proved that organizer to be prescient—except for the fact that East LA proved virtually immune to the disturbances. My point is that the organizer was exaggerating well beyond the evidence at hand in order to hold the attention of the media.

The establishment of SCOC is a different response to similar media cues. With both black and Latino members, the organization has afforded the IAF the opportunity of tapping into the black-liberal coalition that has long dominated Los Angeles politics. Yet fitting Mexican Americans into the minority-politics mold will not be easy. A few black leaders of SCOC who happen to speak Spanish have been featured at UNO meetings, but such gestures do not resolve the persistent tensions between blacks and Mexicans within SCOC itself.

A more subtle response is UNO's transformation into an all-purpose spokesman for Mexican Americans in the metropolitan area. As mentioned above, the media frequently go to UNO in search of "an Eastside story." This contrasts with COPS in San Antonio, where despite being much less curious and aggressive, the press and television nevertheless approach COPS as a political actor of consequence, rather than as a voice representing the Mexican-American community (although it is certainly that). The result is quite different from what I've described with UNO, precisely because COPS takes the Mexican-American identity of its members as a given. It does not seek to focus or heighten that identity so much as to transcend it, just as members are urged to transcend other primary group ties.

But with UNO, a very different dynamic obtains. The prevalence of the view, among the media and elsewhere, that Mexican Americans are a racial minority reinforces the notion that Mexican-American identity cannot be transcended. After all, this view assumes that racial discrimination will not permit Mexican Americans to leave their caste status behind. Because media attention accrues to UNO primarily as a representative voice of a racial minority, the struggling organization becomes wedded to that perspective. Gradually, group identity moves into the foreground: while the prosaic name "United Neighborhoods Organization" avoids any emphasis on group identity, the more commonly used, Spanish-sounding "UNO" does the opposite. And in its promotional literature, UNO describes itself as "Hispanics organized for power," a group-oriented characterization that one does not hear from "Communities Organized for Public Service" in San Antonio.

In sum, UNO has difficulties doing what COPS does, which is to provide a bridge between Mexican Americans and the wider society. Instead, it seeks media attention at the price of being pigeonholed as a kind of minority protest group—which, ironically, makes it look weaker and less effective than it really is. Few political actors in Los Angeles could turn out thousands of people for the rallies described earlier. But because many of its members are known to be illegal immigrants or noncitizens, and because political observers in Los Angeles are cynically attuned to media politics, UNO often fails to distinguish itself. As a result, the city's politicos—Anglo and Mexican-American alike—see the organization as marginal. As a key aide to Mayor Bradley put it, "UNO is just another protest group." Thus perceived, UNO must rely all the more on media attention, at the expense of building up its base in the neighborhoods.

⟨7⟩

Elite-Network Politics

The Clique and Its Challengers

In Los Angeles, Mexican-American politics has, as I have already noted, been dominated in recent years by the Alatorre-Torres clique, which is composed of a few officeholders and their key staffers. Local observers typically refer to this as "the East LA machine," but nothing about this ring of political insiders resembles the classic ethnic political machine, or its latter-day equivalent, the IAF community organizations just discussed. Neither does the clique resemble friends-and-neighbors politics. What it does exemplify is the distinctive style of politics that I refer to as elite-network.

"Network" refers to the structural dimension of this style of politics, and will be explored below. "Elite" refers to the clique's exclusivity and weak community ties, in contrast to the relative social diversity and community base of both friends-and-neighbors and organization politics. As already indicated, the Alatorre-Torres clique is adept at coordinating the efforts and promoting the advancement of a few political professionals, but not at organizing large numbers of politically unsophisticated Mexican Americans.

The low level of community involvement in the clique's campaigns is a case in point. To be sure, this is a general characteristic of Los Angeles politics, but it is particularly true of Mexican-American politics there. For example, in the summer of 1984, when the clique decided to wage a cam-

217

paign to unseat Art Snyder, the Anglo then representing East LA on the city council, the entire effort was managed on a day-to-day basis by a young aide on full-time loan from State Senator Art Torres's office. He was joined afternoons, evenings, and weekends by other staffers and their spouses, but none of the paraphernalia that traditionally draws volunteers into a campaign was in evidence. Indeed, the only volunteers were a handful of *paid* "volunteers" who worked phone banks run out of the downtown offices of supporters. That was the whole organization.

Now there are several reasons why such a campaign would fail to attract volunteers. Most obvious, the economically marginal have little time or inclination for civic or political affairs. This is certainly true of the immigrants crowding into the neighborhoods of East LA. It is also true of the upwardly mobile Mexican Americans in the working- and lower-middle-class suburbs of the San Gabriel Valley, where relatively low levels of voter registration suggest that here, too, the pursuit of economic opportunity takes precedence over politics.[1] Moreover, there is in Mexican culture specifically, and Latino culture generally, a strain of cynicism toward activities in the public realm outside the confines of the family.[2] Still, as we have seen in the case of IAF organizing in Texas, such obstacles to Mexican-American political participation are not insuperable. There must be something beyond the situation of the rank and file to explain why the clique fails so completely to enlist volunteers.

One possibility is that in a milieu characterized by paid volunteers and well-paid staff aides, politically inclined amateurs are much less likely to donate their time and services, particularly if economically pressed and accustomed to viewing politics as a path of individual advancement. Precisely this scenario is described repeatedly by Mexican-American politicos from Texas who have worked on campaigns in Los Angeles, or elsewhere in California. Such individuals almost uniformly report that their California cousins have forsaken grassroots politics and been co-opted by big-spending campaigns.

For example, the experience in Los Angeles of the San Antonio-based Southwest Voter Registration Education Project (SVREP) is instructive. As discussed in an earlier chapter, SVREP's remarkable success in Texas has not been replicated in California, in part because of the high concentrations of illegals and rapid mobility there. But another reason is simply that SVREP has had difficulty finding campaign operatives willing to work for its modest stipends. In especially sharp contrast to South Texas, where SVREP has found it fairly easy to bring Mexican Americans together to work on voter registration drives financed on a shoestring and involving large numbers of volunteers whose enthusiasm often gave the efforts the air of a cause, SVREP has found Southern California a hard row to hoe. In the spring of 1984, after years of haggling and false starts, SVREP succeeded in mounting a modestly successful registration drive in East LA. Significantly, this effort was managed by a full-time coordinator who was on leave from then assemblyman Alatorre's staff and was paid the equivalent of his usual income. Even so, the coordinator complained about his salary, and several times threatened to quit. Also, having to pay for staff positions that in other drives were typically filled by volunteers, SVREP ultimately spent several times more in East LA than it ever had anywhere else in the Southwest.[3]

Compelling though such factors may be, they do not fully explain why the Alatorre-Torres clique does not attract—and, indeed, does not seem to want—volunteers. The latter statement may sound extreme, but the fact is, clique members make it very clear that they view nonpaid political workers with considerable uneasiness. Indeed, they express outright disdain for genuine volunteers, whom they regard as prone to enthusiasms about specific issues and therefore unpredictable and difficult to handle. From this perspective, paying volunteers is a compromise. Unlike regular volunteers, paid volunteers can be used intensively and then let go with minimal prospects of their coming back to collect on any debts.

   The lack of anything resembling patronage in Los Angeles politics has not only made it difficult for Mexican-American politicians to involve large numbers of constituents; it has positively discouraged them from doing so. For if the prospect of substantial material benefit can bring an individual into the political process, the threat of its withdrawal will not only keep that individual involved, but involved in ways pleasing to his or her benefactor. Conversely, without such inducements, a politician's ability to influence or discipline a constituent is greatly diminished. Paying "volunteers" is not the same, in this respect, as large-scale, labor-intensive patronage politics. Thus, the clique spends enormous amounts of money, but most of it is devoted to capital-intensive campaign technologies.

FROM THE AMATEUR DEMOCRAT
TO THE PROFESSIONAL DEMOCRAT

As indicated earlier, the cost of campaigns in California, particularly at the local level, is driven primarily by computer-targeted direct mail. This fact of political life is sometimes viewed as a response by politicians to overarching economic or technological imperatives. But just as important, perhaps more so, is the impact of California's highly issue-oriented electorate. State-of-the-art computerized mailings conducted by California campaign consultants permit politicians to address narrowly targeted groups of voters without relying on high-visibility media campaigns or public forums. From the politician's perspective, this approach has the great appeal of reducing the risk that contradictory positions will be exposed, or that voters will come together physically and thereby become aware of their collective interests and strengths.[4] In essence, computerized mail eases the lot of the politician by contributing to the atomization of the electorate, thereby reducing its ability to organize for political ends.

To be sure, Mexican Americans do not fit the stereotype of the issue-oriented California voter. The typical Mexican American, assuming he is a citizen and therefore eligible to vote, seems more concerned with the economic well-being of his family than with politics. At least, this is what can be deduced from the experience of earlier immigrant groups and from low voter registration levels among Mexican Americans. Or as one Mexican-American politico in Los Angeles puts it, "Your average Mexican is preoccupied with making his payments on the Chevy."

Still, Mexican-American politics in Los Angeles is not completely devoid of issues. As I will discuss later, social issues like abortion, gay rights, and feminism are salient for some Mexican-American voters. Through their unions, other Mexican Americans are focused on labor issues. Finally, highly visible Chicano activists succeed in placing issues like bilingual education, U.S. policy in Central America, and immigration on the agenda.

Thus Mexican-American politics in Los Angeles mirrors, however faintly, the issue-oriented political culture of California in general. In this culture, issue voters tend to possess the organizational and financial resources to command the attention of politicians. And although politicians have traditionally juggled diverse and even warring constituencies with fungible material benefits, it is a lot more difficult to juggle several groups of voters all pressing a candidate to take mutually contradictory positions.

Nevertheless, California politicians have grown quite adept at dealing with issue voters. For example, in *The Amateur Democrat* James Q. Wilson chronicles the rise and fall of the California Democratic Council (CDC), an unofficial caucus of issue-oriented liberals within the Democratic Party. By the late 1950s the CDC had succeeded in electing several of their own candidates to statewide office. But soon the CDC-endorsed officeholders began distancing themselves from their former associates, whose positions on various issues were proving to be liabilities. Eventually, these elected officials took legislative steps to weaken the influence of such unofficial groups within the state's political parties.[5]

Similar dynamics were evident among Mexican Americans during the same period. The CDC itself made few gains within the group, but throughout the 1950s and into the early 1960s, Mexican Americans in California had their own issue organizations, notably the Community Service Organization (CSO) and the Mexican American Political Association (MAPA).[6] Indeed, these two groups were important to the political fortunes of Ed Roybal when as a young man, originally from New Mexico, he first got involved in Los Angeles politics. But according to veterans of the successful campaigns electing Roybal first to the Los Angeles City Council in 1949 and then to Congress in 1962, he moved quickly after taking office to "defang" the organizations that helped put him there.

In general, the contest between California politicians—Anglo or Mexican—and issue activists seems to have been won by the former. As various observers have noted, the state's regime of weak political parties primarily benefits officeholders, not, as many reformers argued, "the people." Indeed, in California today, the two major parties are seen as subservient to the will of elected officials. Since the demise of the CDC, politicians have had to make more and more room for pollsters, media consultants, direct-mail wizards, issue experts, and other specialists. Yet the circles of power and influence in California politics remain remarkably small. To be sure, frequent initiatives and referenda, such as the controversial Proposition 13, have come to symbolize California politics. But such outbursts of plebiscitary democracy are best understood as occasional, and spasmodic, responses to a political system increasingly in the hands of insiders and experts. The recent passage of a statewide initiative imposing term limits on officeholders is of course evidence of both voter outrage at this regime and of the process Californians have come to rely on as a remedy for their frustrations.

Thus, the modus operandi of the Alatorre-Torres clique reflects the broader political dynamics in Los Angeles and California. Specifically, I have been describing a process of specialization and professionalization by which politics becomes more and more an insiders' game. The complex, informal ties of dependence and reciprocity that in more traditional settings have bound politicians to their constituents have been drastically simplified and formalized. The result is a politics cleansed of the petty emotions and venality so evident in San Antonio, but also a politics increasingly turned in upon itself and insulated from the surrounding social flux.

One manifestation of this phenomenon is the decided Sacramento orientation of politics in Los Angeles. I have already described the centralization of power in the state capital. Much of this is associated with the emergence of the assembly speaker as a powerful office and the concomitant growth of a well-staffed, highly professionalized state legislature. For many legislators from Los Angeles the demands of the job and the sheer physical distance between the two cities have led them to move their families to Sacramento, returning to their districts primarily on weekends.

For Mexican-American legislators from Los Angeles, the pull of Sacramento seems to be even greater. On the one hand, their relatively unorganized, passive constituents place few demands on them. On the other, their political sponsors and their own ambitions focus their attention on Sacramento. As one leading member of the clique admits, the necessity of spending so much time in Sacramento is one reason why Mexican-American legislators have been so slow to build up their bases in Los Angeles.

Hence the pattern described earlier, in which the earliest and most visible gains of Mexican Americans in Los Angeles have been state assembly and congressional seats. In 1980 the only major Mexican-American elected officials in metropolitan Los Angeles were state legislators and congressmen—all of them Democrats. Later in the decade, two Mexican Americans captured seats on the Los Angeles City Council. Yet, significantly, both were former state legislators. Having for the most part replaced Anglo politicians, these elected officials have been cited as evidence of the progress made by Mexican Americans in recent years.

Yet it should be clear by now that such gains reflect less the political mobilization and organization of Mexican Americans than the advances of individual Mexican-American politicians, particularly within state Democratic party circles. Take, for example, the leader of the clique and Los Angeles's preeminent Mexican-American politician, Richard Alatorre. Born and raised in East LA, Alatorre was 46 in December 1985, when he became the second Mexican American this century to serve on the city council. The political base that permitted Alatorre to win this seat was his East LA assembly district, which he had represented for more than a decade. Like a great many California state legislators today, Alatorre began his career as an aide to a state legislator—a liberal Democrat, Wally Karabian, who in the late 1960s represented parts of

East LA in the State Assembly. Karabian, now a Los Angeles lawyer with a successful private practice, remains a close adviser to Alatorre and other Mexican-American politicians whose careers he helped launch.[7]

But the main impetus behind Alatorre's rise was someone with few, if any, ties to East LA: California assembly speaker Willie Brown. As a recently elected assemblyman in 1974, Alatorre supported Brown's first unsuccessful bid for assembly speaker and was relegated to the backbenches by Brown's successful opponent, Leo McCarthy. There Alatorre languished until 1982, when Brown, who is from San Francisco and himself a protégé of Congressman Phil Burton, launched a successful bid for the speakership. Alatorre was originally committed to the candidacy of fellow Angeleno, Assemblyman Howard Berman, a labor lawyer and liberal Democrat from the San Fernando Valley, whose longtime association with West Los Angeles politician Henry Waxman has already been mentioned. But when Brown decided to enter the contest, he persuaded his old friend from the back of the chamber to switch his vote. As it turned out, Alatorre's vote proved critical to Brown's success.[8]

As speaker, Brown appointed Alatorre chair of the assembly committee handling the 1980 redistricting.[9] Then in 1984, again presumably through the good offices of Speaker Brown, Alatorre was named chair of the strategic Credentials Committee at the Democratic National Convention. But perhaps the most important outcome of his alliance with Brown has been Alatorre's position in the extensive fund-raising network that each of Brown's predecessors since Jesse Unruh in the 1960s has developed as a power base. In this regard, Alatorre's role was double-faceted. On the one hand, he raised funds for the leadership's coffers and, in the words of one Mexican-American politico, was frequently "bagman for the speaker." But at the same time, Alatorre was in a position to fill a few bags for his Mexican-American colleagues in the clique.

In the same vein, Torres, who grew up with Alatorre and served with him in the state assembly, became state senator for East LA in part through the Willie Brown connection. Having joined with Alatorre in providing decisive support for Brown's speakership bid, Torres then benefited from the new speaker's help in gaining access to the enormous resources necessary for a bitter, but successful, campaign to unseat a veteran Mexican-American state senator. Then in 1984, with few political accomplishments to his name, Senator Torres was nonetheless given the highly visible post of chief spokesman for the Mondale presidential campaign in California. Much smoother and more articulate than Alatorre, Torres is seen as nonthreatening to Anglo voters, and despite well-publicized personal and marital problems, he has been considered perhaps the best prospect for statewide office from among this generation of Mexican-American politicians.

Apart from these individual gains, the clique as a whole benefited tremendously from the 1980 legislative reapportionment. As chairman of the Assembly Committee on Elections and Reapportionment, Alatorre was able to hold onto his own seat, as well as those of two other Hispanic assemblymen in Los Angeles County. Moreover, by fighting off threatened incumbent Democrats and outraged Republicans, he managed to increase the number of assembly districts likely to elect Hispanics. One lawyer with the Mexican American Legal Defense and Educational Fund, which was actively involved in the push for more Hispanic seats, declared himself "shocked, favorably, by the plan. For the first time in the history of the California legislature, Hispanics have made gains from an assembly reapportionment plan."[10]

Similar results emerged through the good graces of Speaker Brown's political mentor, San Francisco congressman Philip Burton, whose masterful redistricting effort created two new Hispanic congressional districts in metropolitan Los Angeles. As the *Congressional Quarterly*'s Alan Ehrenhalt puts it: "In California, the two new Hispanic House members—Esteban Torres and Matthew (Marty) Martínez—owe their presence largely to Philip Burton."[11] Although neither one of these has been clearly within the Alatorre-Torres clique, the process by which their districts were created reveals the debts owed by Hispanic officeholders to their Democratic Party sponsors, and more generally, the dynamics of elite-network politics in California.

SOME DEBTS FALL DUE

One payment on such debts has been the pro-choice stance of members of the clique and other Mexican-American politicians in Los Angeles. As I will explore more thoroughly in a subsequent chapter on issues, Mexican Americans can at best be described as uneasy with the pro-choice position. Yet it is just about impossible to find a Mexican-American Democrat in Los Angeles who is not pro-choice. Their position on abortion has therefore placed these Mexican-American leaders in some uncomfortable situations.

One such was a bitter 1982 battle in which then assemblyman Art Torres successfully challenged veteran legislator Alex Garcia for the latter's state senate seat. Fighting for his political life, Garcia focused relentlessly on his liberal young opponent's pro-choice record. Years later, Torres's staffers had vivid memories of that aspect of the campaign, and volunteered that they still felt extremely vulnerable on their pro-choice stance. Although other clique members have not been confronted so directly with it, the abortion issue makes them similarly skittish.

More to the point, their pro-choice position is one more reason why clique members neglect building up their community base. This fact of political life was driven home to me one afternoon in a pleasant lounge adjacent to a municipal golf course, perched on a hill above the San Bernadino Freeway. As I have indicated in an earlier chapter, Mexican-American politicians in Los Angeles—unlike their counterparts in San Antonio—tend to avoid the Catholic parishes in their districts. After months of asking why this was so, I nodded as a key member of the clique recited the usual explanations. Then, almost parenthetically, he added: "Besides, we don't go into the churches because you always run the risk of stirring up the right-to-lifers."

Another debt payment owed by the clique involves voter registration campaigns. In this critical but widely overlooked realm, substantial disincentives to community-based politics are once again evident. I have already cited several obstacles to registering Mexican Americans in Los Angeles. An important one remains: the resistance of the Alatorre-Torres clique itself. As I indicated earlier, it was not until 1984, after years of setbacks, that the Southwest Voter Registration Education Project conducted a successful campaign in Los Angeles. To gain the grudging cooperation of clique members for that effort, Southwest Voters had to embarrass them with planted newspaper stories about low registration levels in their districts and then had to fund an alternative drive conducted by UNO. Lending critical support to Southwest Voters at that time were then assemblywoman Gloria Molina and then deputy mayor Grace Montanez Davis. A longtime activist and reigning grande dame of Mexican-American politics in Los Angeles, Davis was apparently motivated by genuine concern for her community. So was Molina, but she was also eager to outmaneuver the clique, whose members had been making loud noises that her assembly district had one of the lowest voter turnout rates in the state. In any event, the two women served as the drive's co-sponsors and were effective troubleshooters for the many obstructions thrown up by clique members.

One concession SVREP granted Alatorre and Torres was to exclude a young Mexican-American upstart by the name of Steve Rodriguez (whose efforts against the clique will be explored later in this chapter) from any role in the nonpartisan registration effort. Another concession was the designation of an Alatorre aide as drive coordinator, who was, as noted earlier, paid a handsome salary. But to keep him and his bosses honest, Southwest Voters made sure that outside consultants of its choosing were on hand.

Meanwhile, a different scenario was developing out in the suburban San Gabriel Valley. There, the key Mexican-American elected officials, Congressman Esteban Torres and Assemblyman Charles Calderon, initially agreed to permit Southwest Voters to mount a campaign in their districts, whose population was divided fairly evenly between Anglo and Mexican-American voters. Early in 1984, target areas were identified, a paid coordinator named, and grants processed. But as soon as word of the drive got about, local Anglo Democrats began to protest vehemently. One particularly nervous assemblywoman with an increasingly Mexican-American district immediately took her case to Speaker Willie Brown. The Mexican-American politicians, never enthusiastic about SVREP's plans, backed down quickly and quietly. As an aide observed at the time, "We have too many Anglo friends in the Valley to go about things like Southwest Voters would like us to." The drive was never officially canceled. The funds were spent; the coordinator paid. But no Mexican-American voters were registered.

Mexican-American politicians in Los Angeles clearly have a different agenda from Southwest Voters. To satisfy corporate and foundation sponsors, Southwest has the relatively straightforward goal of increasing the number of Mexican Americans registered to vote. Critics say that this objective does not always include increasing the number of Mexican Americans who actually do vote. Still, in South Texas and other areas of the Southwest, the organization's goals have for the most part coincided with those of local Mexican-American politicians and activists, who welcome SVREP's expertise and resources.

But in Southern California the situation has been more complicated. First, Mexican-American politicians there suffer from a second-city complex. As noted earlier, San Antonio is unique in the number of nationally prominent Mexican-American leaders and organizations it has produced. One result, as seen repeatedly, is that Mexican Americans in Los Angeles are prone to feeling outdone by their country cousins from Texas. From their perspective, Southwest Voters and particularly its leader, Willie Velásquez, are just more outsiders from San Antonio competing for attention and resources.

But more than bruised egos, Mexican-American politicians in Los Angeles have concrete interests dictating their lack of cooperation with

SVREP. Ensconced in safe districts, members of the clique, like any similarly situated politicians, have no incentives to go out and register more Mexican-American voters. Indeed, as I have been arguing, heavy debts to their Democratic Party sponsors give these Mexican-American politicians every reason *not* to mobilize more voters in their districts.

For the fact is that Democratic Party leaders in California are profoundly ambivalent toward Mexican Americans. Lip service is paid to the importance of Mexican-American interests. Safe Mexican-American districts are carved out. But, as Bruce Cain makes clear in his study of the 1980 assembly redistricting, party leaders are primarily concerned with maximizing Democratic seats, not maximizing Mexican-American seats (or votes).[12] California Democrats may be rhetorically committed to increasing the number of Mexican-American voters, but they are also concerned that the demands of such voters would conflict with those of other party constituencies. Even committing resources to register Mexican Americans is dicey for the Democrats, for many of those most likely to vote, once registered, will vote Republican. The ambivalence of California Democrats was evident in 1984 when a one-dollar bounty was offered for every new registered Democrat. Without the front-end commitment of resources critical to getting a serious registration effort off the ground, this scheme was not taken very seriously by Mexican-American activists. Moreover, many who took the party up on its offer complained that the bounties were not promptly paid.

Thus, in Los Angeles today there are few incentives for Mexican-American officeholders to undertake the arduous task of organizing their districts. Indeed, the enormous disparity between their debts to Anglo sponsors and to Mexican-American residents leads these officeholders to encourage passivity among their constituents, who are of more use as bodies to be counted than as voters to be courted.

CONNECTIONS AND CADRES:
THE FARM SYSTEM

The foregoing speaks to the "elite" aspect of elite-network politics. Equally important is the "network" dimension. Network, of course, suggests a set of interconnecting relationships reaching out in many directions with no sharply defined boundaries. And as the word "net" implies, a network is spread thin and lacks organizational height or depth.

I borrow this term from Hugh Heclo, who writes of "issue networks" in the making of federal policy in Washington. In contrast to the image of rigid and exclusive iron triangles, Heclo notes, "it is almost impossible to say where a network leaves off and its environment begins."[13] The ethos of these networks is collegiality, as opposed to bureaucratic or hierarchical control. Because Heclo is describing the relationships among a specific set of issue experts and policy entrepreneurs, the parallel with Mexican Americans in Los Angeles is not exact. Yet the broad image of an amorphous, flat entity, as opposed to a more traditional organizational hierarchy, is quite apt.

Up to now, of course, I have emphasized the clannishness and exclusivity of the Alatorre-Torres operation, which is after all what the word "clique" suggests. But this is the view from below, from the neighborhoods of East LA. Viewed from Sacramento, the clique is not clannish at all. On the contrary, it is involved in a variety of interconnecting relationships. The clique may not have roots reaching down into Los Angeles, but it has plenty of branches extending widely across the state.

The obvious impetus for this statewide orientation is the Sacramento tilt of Los Angeles politics. Clearly, the members of the clique have accumulated substantial debts to their benefactors in the Democratic Party, most notably Brown. And Brown has not been reluctant to collect on those debts. In the name of party unity, he has (at least up until the campaign finance reforms enacted by recent referenda) required members of the assembly Democratic caucus to contribute to his kitty. Legislators grumble about "being dunned by the speaker," in the words of one observer. They also resent having to lend their staffers to far-flung campaigns targeted for special attention by the speaker. Yet they know if they help with "the problem," as one party official describes the task of maintaining Democratic control of the assembly, they will get desired committee appointments, staffing, and other perquisites. Besides, helping the leadership authorizes individual legislators to go into fund-raising with a vengeance. No one expects them to turn over all the proceeds to the speaker, so helping him means helping themselves. As indicated earlier, the typical assemblyman raises the lion's share of his funds from outside his own district.[14]

Another way to help oneself in Sacramento is to develop ties with other caucus members across the state. After all, speakers have been known to fall from power. So, while it is expedient to keep the present one happy, it is also prudent to be prepared when his number is up. Mexican-American legislators, like their Anglo counterparts, spend part of their resources helping colleagues to stay in Sacramento, and part helping promising aspirants to get there. So, when Gloria Molina was a state assemblywoman and was then (as now) eager to build up her feminist credentials, she supported an Anglo school board member from Long Beach making her first bid for an assembly seat. Similarly, a Mexican-American assemblyman from the San Gabriel Valley, mindful of the political clout of the Armenian community in Southern California, committed himself to a young Armenian running for the same Long Beach seat.

With relatively quiescent constituents and safe seats, Mexican-American legislators are particularly well situated to play this Sacramento-based game of reaching out beyond their own districts. Inevitably, many of those to whom they reach out will not be Mexican Americans. Such alliances have the obviously beneficial effect of drawing Mexican-American elected officials into the mainstream of California politics. Yet they also foster the dynamic mentioned earlier in connection with UNO: instead of reaching *down* into their own districts to build up their home bases, Mexican-American officeholders are encouraged to reach *out* across districts to build up their statewide party base.

If the structural flatness of the Alatorre-Torres clique points to its shallow roots in the neighborhoods of Los Angeles, this same feature also suggests the clique's lack of organizational hierarchy. Here again, the clique contrasts with both the classic ethnic machine and IAF community organizations. Lacking a base in the multifaceted, face-to-face community ties that get rationalized by organization politics, clique members deal with one another in a highly contractual way, based primarily on their calculations as self-interested professionals. And by "professionals," I don't mean in the sense of doctors or lawyers, but political insiders who know no other means of earning a living, and whose ties to one another are fundamentally instrumental, drained of personal loyalty, affection, or organic authority. Nor are clique members bound by ties of ethnic or race consciousness. They certainly do not see themselves as part of a movement or cause. Some members of the clique may have gone to school together and even occasionally refer to themselves as "*la familia*," but they are colleagues more than friends. In this sense, relations among clique members perhaps may resemble those among political pros heading a political machine, or the enforced formality among IAF leaders and organizers. But it is essential to recognize that a machine, or an IAF organization, is a true hierarchy, with followers as well as leaders. The elite network is not.

The instrumental, or careerist, nature of the ties holding the clique together are perhaps most evident among its second generation members. Typically in their thirties, these individuals come from somewhat more diverse backgrounds than their elders. Unlike the elders, these younger members may not have grown up in the same neighborhoods or attended the same schools. But they are similar in usually being the first in their families to attend college; in attending local institutions for the most part; and in having begun working with the clique as interns or summer employees while still in school. Also like their elders, they typically did not pursue advanced or professional degrees. For example, very few clique members, young or old, are lawyers. For these sons and daughters of working- and lower-middle-class families, politics itself has been the path of upward mobility. For example, a young staffer proudly observes that, whereas his parents (a salesman and a housewife) have never been to downtown Los Angeles's Biltmore Hotel, he has been there for political functions three or four times within the last few months. Or, as another member of the clique, born in Mexico, declares, with the panache of someone who has just figured something out for himself, "Politics is a career accelerator."

Jobs thus play a particularly important role in keeping the clique together. For if patronage—in the classic sense of jobs distributed on the basis of political criteria in sufficient numbers to sustain a rank-and-file organization—does not exist in Los Angeles today, there is nevertheless a supply of jobs, contracts, and similar benefits for a few political insiders. Such benefits—staff positions, consulting contracts, commission appointments—are naturally limited in number because they are of use almost exclusively to the politically initiated.

This applies *a fortiori* to Mexican Americans, who are even less well positioned than the average Angeleno to take advantage of such political rewards. A well-connected Mexican-American businessman might get a contract with a state agency; a political operative might be appointed a consultant to the state assembly; or a young Mexican American with political experience and a master's degree in public administration might get named as an aide to the director of the Rapid Transit Board. But such positions are obviously ill-suited to the talents and training of the vast majority of Mexican Americans in Los Angeles.[15]

The same can be said of the political rewards available through the private sector. For example, a former aide to Congressman Ed Roybal has been an executive with a construction firm involved in a huge freeway project. He was able to place in that firm a young Mexican-American woman with a master's degree from Harvard's Kennedy School who had worked for a Mexican-American assemblywoman. Another Mexican-American woman, a mother of five in her forties, got involved with "Chicana" politics. She resumed her education and eventually obtained an MPA degree from the University of Southern California. Through her political connections, the woman landed a public affairs job at United

Way, a position which her Mexican-American sponsors anticipated would afford them entrée to establishment funding sources. Similar public affairs and community relations positions in large corporations such as Carnation or Hunt-Wesson Foods have served as political bases for well-connected Mexican Americans. From such posts they distribute corporate contributions to the many nonpartisan activities, whether an obscure Latino child care center or the very visible MALDEF, with which their highly partisan Mexican-American colleagues are involved.

Compared to peers not involved in politics, younger clique members enjoy jobs that are moderately well-paying, relatively secure, and quite exciting. One such individual, who had been loaned to Ted Kennedy's 1980 presidential campaign, explained that there was no way apart from politics that someone with his modest background and experience would have enjoyed such opportunities. As a result, clique members soon reach a point beyond which they have few appealing career alternatives. Those with political ambitions remain in the clique with the reasonable expectation that they will be tied into the political and financial networks—and eventually permitted to run for office. As it happens, there is a fairly well-established pecking order within the Alatorre-Torres clique regarding which staffers will run for which offices.

In essence, Alatorre and Torres have developed a farm system: an orderly and efficient means of recruiting, training, promoting, and disciplining political cadres. Although, as I will describe presently, there are inevitably tensions and rifts within the ranks, the clique is relatively cohesive, staffed by young Mexican-American politicos eagerly but patiently waiting in line for their turn to run for political office. Certainly this picture bears very little resemblance to the free-for-all I have described in San Antonio.

Of course, the image of a farm system does not suggest that the clique is a collegium of similarly situated professionals. Alatorre and Torres do succeed in imposing order and discipline on Mexican-American politics in Los Angeles, but it is crucial to note that their power to do this does not flow from any personal authority or respect enjoyed in the community, but from their access to critical resources—appointments, jobs, and especially campaign funds. Whether through Sacramento lobbyists or Los Angeles-based interests, their access to the huge amounts of money necessary to run for office in Los Angeles, and California generally, gives Alatorre and Torres strategic influence over which Mexican Americans enter into the political arena.

An excellent example of this power is the 1983 election to the Los Angeles School Board. Several Mexican-American candidates emerged for a newly created East LA seat. Torres and Alatorre called a "community forum" to which all candidates and their supporters were invited. At that open meeting, each candidate had the opportunity to speak and answer questions. Opinion was divided as to who was the best candidate to challenge the longtime Anglo incumbent. If anything, Larry González, Senator Torres's young aide who emerged as the choice of the forum and went on to be elected to the board, was generally regarded as among the weaker prospects. But the backing of his boss—and the financial resources implicit in that support—compelled all but one of the other candidates to get behind González.

In the spring of 1985, there was a similar meeting at Steven's Steakhouse, the scene of frequent political intrigues in East LA. At that closed session, clique members gathered to decide who among them would run for—and doubtless win—the seat from which the veteran city councillor Art Snyder was finally being forced to resign. Not surprisingly, Alatorre successfully seized this opportunity to become the first Mexican American on the Los Angeles City Council in a generation. As a participant at the Steakhouse meeting explains, "Richard was able to get the rest of us to go along with his running not because we love him, but because he's got the money."

CHALLENGERS TO THE CLIQUE

I have thus far discussed the Alatorre-Torres clique as if it were the only example of elite-network politics among Mexican Americans in Los Angeles. But it is certainly not. Indeed, as I have already indicated in my overview of Los Angeles, the clique's weak community roots virtually assure the emergence of challengers—albeit, challengers whose roots are not much stronger.

For instance, challengers are emerging from the small but visible stratum of well-credentialed Mexican-American professionals in Los Angeles. Unlike clique members, who regard politics as their means of mobility, these individuals have acquired advanced degrees and achieved social and economic mobility quite independently of politics. Some have been temperamentally disinclined toward politics; others have been pursuing career opportunities away from Los Angeles. In any event, there is a group of young Mexican Americans (lawyers, doctors, accountants, and business executives) who owe the Alatorre-Torres clique nothing, and who now (whether from greed, ambition, guilt, group pride, or civic-mindedness) feel increasingly drawn to politics.

A lawyer with a prestigious downtown firm, or an MBA at Northrop or some other defense contractor, is simply not dependent on the clique as are its aspiring junior members. Moreover, a graduate of a distant, elite university who returns to Los Angeles and finds his less cosmopolitan classmates already embarked on political careers, is going to be less willing to queue up in the clique's farm system. Such individuals find it fairly easy to get themselves appointed to the many city and county commissions. A few have obtained positions that could lead into electoral politics, such as one young partner from a downtown law firm who was appointed by Mayor Bradley to the highly visible Police Commission, which post has led to a continuing relationship with the mayor and his inner circle of advisers, who obviously see advantages in bolstering Mexican Americans independent of the clique. Much to the clique's dismay, such independent professionals have been able to get their own allies appointed to posts once held by members of the clique.

Yet such challengers face considerable obstacles. Even their sponsors in the Bradley administration admit that these Mexican-American professionals tend to be "Westside Mexicans" lacking even a semblance of a community base among their own people. Not surprisingly, the social and economic mobility enjoyed by these professionals has typically been at the expense of ties to their old neighborhoods. Another consideration, cited by the challengers themselves, is that running for office means sacrificing handsome incomes that their modest origins won't let them easily abandon. As a result, many of these Mexican-American professionals have been content with honorific appointments and occasional advisory positions. But in time, it is likely that some will seek elected office, and clashes with the clique will inevitably follow.

Some of these individuals will find outlets for their ambitions as Republicans. As one such young lawyer, recently returned home with a degree from Harvard Law, put it, "The line is shorter over here." And for him it was: after a couple of unsuccessful efforts at an assembly seat in a heavily Democratic district, he was appointed to a judgeship by Governor Deukmejian. In this regard, Mexican Americans in Los Angeles today are reminiscent of Italian Americans back East two or three generations ago. For example, as depicted by Robert Dahl in his classic study of New Haven politics, *Who Governs?*, Italians who felt shut out of Democratic Party politics frequently became Republicans.[16]

It remains to be seen, of course, how substantial Republican inroads among Mexican Americans will be. Exit polls show that President Reagan may have gotten as much as 42 percent of the Hispanic vote in California

in 1984.[17] In 1988 George Bush did marginally less well than his predecessor among Hispanics.[18] But it is one thing to vote for a Republican president, or governor, and quite another to identify oneself as a Republican.
Still, there are quite a few Mexican Americans willing to do just that.

Yet the story does not end there. The Mexican Americans from business and professional backgrounds who are typical Republican converts
are motivated not by ideology or principle so much as by personal ambition. One remarkable implication of this unremarkable fact is that few
Mexican-American Republicans are eager to run for office. For many, as
I indicated above, holding public office would mean an unacceptable cut
in income. And even for those who turn to Republican politics for material gain, the goal is not usually elective office, but the relative ease and
security of an appointive position. In any event, the best way for a recent
Mexican-American convert to prove himself to GOP stalwarts is to run
for office. But those who do so rarely expect to win. And they're usually
right, given the still considerable allegiance of Mexican-American voters
to the Democratic Party (particularly at the local level), and the still discernible reluctance of Republican activists to support Mexican-American
Johnnies-come-lately. Given these dynamics, Mexican Americans who do
run for office as Republicans often end up being rewarded for their efforts with the appointive post they sought in the first place. Everyone is
happy, but the ranks of Mexican-American Republicans aspiring to elective office are thereby depleted. And without such a growing cadre, it will
likely be a while before Republicans establish a vital presence among
Mexican Americans.

A different sort of challenger to the clique, albeit a rather weak one,
is Congressman Matthew (Marty) Martínez. I mentioned Martínez earlier as the beneficiary of Congressman Phil Burton's artful and highly partisan 1980 redistricting. But unlike his fellow beneficiary Esteban Torres,
whose election to Congress—once the district was drawn—received substantial help from the clique, Martínez is completely outside its orbit and
instead heavily indebted to the Waxman-Berman organization. Thus,
while Congressman Torres and the rest of the clique supported Mondale
in the 1984 presidential primary, Martínez followed the lead of Waxman
and Berman and went with Gary Hart.

THE MEANING OF
LOU MORET'S SMILE

Challengers to the Alatorre-Torres clique were much in evidence one sti-
fling August evening at a candidates' forum sponsored by the Latina Po-

litical Assembly, a group of Mexican-American women created by then assemblywoman Molina. Brought together shortly before a 1984 special election were all three candidates for the one seat on the Los Angeles City Council representing the East LA barrio: the Anglo incumbent, Art Snyder; Steve Rodriguez, a young urban planner and political novice who had single-handedly challenged Snyder when no other Mexican American would; and Lou Moret, candidate of the Alatorre-Torres clique, belatedly joining the fray to teach the upstart Rodriguez a lesson.

Also evident that evening were various weaknesses of Mexican-American politics: emotionalism, exaggerated personal loyalties, lack of discipline. Crammed into the small, un-airconditioned auditorium at East LA's Plaza de la Raza were a couple of hundred hot, impatient spectators not bashful about expressing their opinions. At various points, candidate Rodriguez jeered at his many detractors, while his mother jumped up from the audience, vociferously defending her son. Another Rodriguez supporter, a cheery plump woman, pranced about taunting the other two candidates and their loyalists. Assemblywoman Molina scurried about the room serving cold drinks to the many elderly people present suffering from the heat. As for the moderator, Antonia Hernández, a young attorney with the Los Angeles office of MALDEF (who has since become the organization's president and general counsel), her stern but tiny voice was no match for the chaos. Neither was her shoe, which had been forced into service as a gavel.

Meanwhile, on the dais, next to his two opponents, gazing down on the commotion, was the immensely calm, almost beatific visage of Lou Moret. The smug smile which never left his face that evening was the expression of a man who expected only to profit from the confusion all about him.

Yet at the same time, Moret's smile was partly bravado. For also revealed at that meeting was the clique's meager hold on political power in Los Angeles. Until his scandal-clouded departure from public life in 1985, Snyder was a symbol of Mexican-American political impotence in the city. First elected in the early 1970s, Snyder had successfully fended off numerous Mexican-American opponents.[19] This candidates' forum was just another reminder that the inability of Mexican Americans to unite behind a single challenger would once again mean victory for their Anglo nemesis.

The man defying the Alatorre-Torres clique, and upsetting the modus vivendi it had worked out with Snyder over the years, was Steve Rodriguez. Rodriguez grew up in El Sereno, a solidly working- and lower-middle-class district nestled against the hills on the northeastern edge of East Los Angeles. Parts of El Sereno resemble the barrio—rows of bungalows separated by narrow driveways and chainlink fences, interrupted now and again by small apartment buildings. But parts of it, especially the more recently settled neighborhoods in the hills, look downright suburban, with stylish ranch houses set amidst carefully tended lawns and terraced gardens. This is the type of area that a French Canadian television producer, visiting Los Angeles in order to film a documentary on "Chicanos," carefully kept out of his viewfinder. But it is also where Steve Rodriguez, an urban planner with the City of Los Angeles, and his wife, Gloria, a public school teacher, decided to raise their family.

Thus El Sereno is not exactly "the barrio," but Rodriguez could say that he was a life-long resident of East LA and a product of its schools. With a master's degree from UCLA, he is also typical of that segment of postwar Mexican Americans in Southern California who graduated from high school and went to college in pursuit of opportunities that had not been available to their parents. And like many other young, upwardly mobile Mexican Americans in the region, Rodriguez had never been involved in politics or community affairs. Indeed, his single claim on the public's attention was that his young family had been chosen to host President Jimmy Carter for an overnight stay in their home in the spring of 1980.

No one in Los Angeles seems to know how or why the Rodriguez family was selected for this honor. At least no one in the Alatorre-Torres clique, several of whose members were Carter administration appointees, will admit to knowing. Back in 1980 no one had ever heard of Steve Rodriguez. But after weeks of media attention—before, during, and as much as a year after the presidential visit—the result was clear: an obscure city bureaucrat and his attractive young family had been transformed into minor celebrities.

With the kind of media coverage that few local politicians, Anglo or Mexican American, could afford to buy, Rodriguez was suddenly in an excellent position to end-run the Alatorre-Torres clique. After a year of seasoning in Washington on a fellowship at the Department of Housing and Urban Development, Rodriguez returned home and reestablished his presence by launching a voter registration drive in East LA. By the spring of 1983 he felt ready to take on Snyder.

Snyder was a natural target. Over the years the shrewd politician had put together a coalition of conservative Anglos, typically survivors of the Dust Bowl migration who had settled in the northern end of the 14th councilmanic district; and middle-aged and elderly Mexican Americans concentrated in the more southerly Boyle Heights, Lincoln Heights, and Highland Park districts. Snyder was the closest thing Los Angeles had to a classic ward politician. He never missed an opportunity to praise the culture of his Mexican-American constituents, and unlike both Mexican-American challengers, he could do so in fluent Spanish. Snyder also backed up his words with actions. Even his Mexican-American detractors described the councilman as a moving force behind the construction of Plaza de la Raza, a Mexican-American cultural center and park in East LA. But the key to Snyder's enduring success was his well-deserved reputation for ensuring the delivery of all variety of mundane public services to his constituents.

His ability to get things done at city hall, however, frequently entangled Snyder in questionable, if not illegal, dealings. Throughout his career, he was involved in a spate of scandals ranging from drunk driving to corrupt business practices that would have quickly undone a less skillful, if more honest, politician. Working to Snyder's advantage was the fact that his Mexican-American supporters saw the two sides of his public persona reinforcing one another: they attributed his effectiveness as their champion to his craftiness and underhandedness. One middle-aged Mexican-American housewife, working on a phone bank at Snyder campaign headquarters, echoed the sentiments of many East LA residents when she said in praise of the councilman, "Let's face it. To be a good politician, you've got to be a bastard." Indeed, Mexican Americans tend to expect little of politicians and the public realm they inhabit; the private sphere of family life is where serious emotional investments are made. By ensuring that the trash got collected, vacant lots cleared, street lights repaired, and neighborhood children provided with parks and swimming pools, the unsavory Snyder instinctively engaged his Mexican-American constituents' deep-seated cynicism in behalf of their concerns for their homes and families.

It was among the younger, better-educated Mexican Americans that Snyder had real problems. To them, this conservative Anglo's skill at delivering concrete and symbolic rewards to his intensely loyal barrio supporters smacked of the *patrón* politics they wanted to believe had long since passed. Unable to express anger publicly at their elders for playing the stereotypical role of passive, subservient Mexicans, young Mexican Americans in Los Angeles compensated by heaping abuse on Snyder.

But quite apart from the style of politics Snyder represented, his critics resented his prolonged presence on the Los Angeles City Council as *the* elected voice of East LA. Typical were the remarks of a Mexican-

American aide to Mayor Bradley. Acknowledging Snyder's skills as a politician, and his record of providing services to East LA residents, this young man nevertheless insisted that he had to be replaced. Precisely because there were no Mexican Americans on the city council, he noted, Snyder was continually being thrown up by Anglo corporate and civic leaders as proof that Mexican Americans were politically backward. Even while admitting that access to a politician, regardless of his ethnic background, is more important to Mexican Americans than merely electing one of their own to office, this individual could not avoid the painful conclusion that "Snyder had become a symbol of the Anglo who outsmarts the sleepy Mexicans."

As fellow professionals, members of the Alatorre-Torres clique were too admiring of Snyder to be outraged by him. On a few occasions they had tried to challenge him, but were soundly defeated. Besides, Snyder had been smart enough to cut them in on various deals (a few of which were later the subject of scandal). By the early 1980s, when Steve Rodriguez was first emerging as a challenger, the clique had reached an accommodation with Snyder. As late as the spring of 1984, various clique members were still describing the councilman as "a good friend."

Thus, when Rodriguez challenged Snyder in 1983, he was taking on the Mexican-American political establishment as well. Yet the clique was slow to take his challenge seriously. At the time the clique was preoccupied with getting its candidate elected to the Los Angeles School Board. But more fundamentally, members of the clique simply didn't think this upstart Rodriguez had a chance against the crafty Anglo who had humbled them so many times.

So, Steve Rodriguez startled everyone in the spring of 1983 when he came within a hundred or so votes of forcing Snyder into a runoff election. A prolonged recount battle did not change the outcome, but it did maintain Rodriguez's visibility in the media. In the end, Rodriguez was able to launch a recall petition that resulted in the August 1984 special election.

In this second campaign, Rodriguez attracted the support of many Mexican Americans outside the clique: a few militant trade unionists; several university-based activists, a few of whom were still uncomfortable with electoral politics; and many young, educated Mexican Americans who typically had been raised in Los Angeles, gone off to college and perhaps graduate school, and were then pursuing careers in business and the professions. Like Rodriguez himself, these supporters had not devoted much time or energy to electoral politics, and they now felt excluded from the process by the Mexican-American political establishment.

From such ranks the Rodriguez campaign drew dozens of eager volunteers who manned phone banks and walked precincts. With a $200,000 budget raised with the help of a wealthy Mexican-American wholesale grocer, and the likes of actor Ed Asner, this was hardly a shoestring operation. Indeed, that kind of money allowed Rodriguez to hire professional campaign managers affiliated with Tom Hayden's Campaign for Economic Democracy, who knew how to run phone banks, voter registration drives, and computerized mail programs. Still, with Rodriguez's wife and kids pitching in to help, and his mother offering volunteers home-cooked enchiladas, his campaign exuded the enthusiasm of the cause that it was.

By this time the clique had begun to take Rodriguez more seriously. Disdain turned into denunciation of this "Mexican preppie," this "elitist who hasn't paid his dues." Once Rodriguez had forced Snyder into the recall election, clique members realized that this persistent upstart was threatening their entire farm system.

Throughout the spring of 1984, there were rumors the clique would run someone against both Snyder and Rodriguez. Finally, in June, Lou Moret announced his candidacy. Mentioned earlier, Moret is an important but not very visible member of the clique—the insider's insider. Despite his French surname, he is Mexican-American, from a lower-middle-class, East LA family. Like Alatorre's, Moret's career was mentored by Wally Karabian, a lawyer from the politically potent Armenian community in Montebello, adjacent to East LA. As an assemblyman in the early 1970s, Karabian suddenly found himself with several new precincts in East LA, thanks to redistricting. One summer he hired Moret, still in college at the time, to manage a voter registration drive in those neighborhoods. After graduation, Moret went on to a series of full-time staff jobs, first with Karabian and then with members of the emergent Mexican-American clique. During the Carter administration, he went to Washington where he had a couple of political appointments in the Department of Commerce. His only claim to fame there was a minor scandal, exposed by the *Washington Post*, involving government contractors and Las Vegas showgirls. Shortly thereafter, Moret returned to Los Angeles, where his friends in the clique secured him a prized slot on the city's five-man Public Works Commission. Chaired at that time by a member of Mayor Bradley's inner circle of advisers, the Commission oversees millions of dollars of construction contracts, and is one of the few municipal commissions paying its members substantial salaries.[20]

As the consummate insider, Moret had never actually run for office and had little or no name recognition in East LA. What he did have was access to the resources available to the clique. So when Moret announced his candidacy for the city council barely two months before election day, he already held the bulk of the approximately $250,000 he was to spend on the campaign. This permitted Moret's staff to boast that his funding came from within the Mexican-American community, though in fact most of it came through Alatorre's Sacramento contacts.

Immediately after the announcement, scores of Moret posters—many more than are usually seen in Los Angeles campaigns—popped up on buildings all over East LA. As noted earlier, Moret's campaign was managed on a day-to-day basis by a young aide loaned from Torres's office, and assisted by other clique staffers and their spouses, as well as by the handful of "paid volunteers." The heart of the campaign was a computerized mail operation that sent out a series of expensive glossy brochures (all in English) targeted separately to Mexican-American and Anglo voters. These were supplemented with television spots, virtually unprecedented for a local race in Los Angeles's expensive media market, in which Moret appeared with a prominent Anglo elected official.

Thus, the bloodlessly professional Moret campaign had none of the amateurish energy of the Rodriguez effort. On Saturdays just before the election, Moret headquarters felt like a savings bank on a midweek morning, while the Rodriguez storefront was teeming with confusion and enthusiasm. Rodriguez and his wife would pump up volunteers with pep talks about the justice of finally putting a Mexican American on the city council, echoing their campaign slogan: "¡Es nuestro tiempo!"

By contrast, soft-spoken Moret would ramble on to staffers about his wife's pregnancy, or his determination not to regain the fifteen pounds he had lost walking precincts. Yet, despite such a lackluster effort, devoid of any community involvement, Moret ended his two-month campaign by capturing about 47 percent of the meager turnout. Rodriguez, who had been campaigning continuously for almost two years, received about 53 percent of the vote. But Rodriguez's slim victory was for naught, since in the recall election held that same day, Snyder won handily and held on to his city council seat.[21]

In the end, Snyder spent about $300,000 to beat back the recall effort. As noted above, Moret spent about $250,000; Rodriguez about $200,000. It is hardly news that an incumbent was able to raise this kind of money. Nor, in light of what we have seen of the Alatorre-Torres clique, should it be surprising that Moret was able to match Snyder almost dollar for dollar. More unexpected, perhaps, is the amount that Rodriguez's rag-tag coalition was able to put together. The effort was costly, though. Despite all the free media coverage he was able to generate, Rodriguez's two-year crusade against Snyder required taking a leave from his city job and relying on his wife's salary as a teacher to support their family. Both he and his parents went into considerable personal debt, including second mortgages on their homes. And in return for such sacrifices, the brash outsider did only marginally better at the polls than the smug insider Moret. Such was the grip of the Alatorre-Torres clique on East LA politics.

Finally, it is worth noting that Snyder's campaign combined the professionalism and resources of Moret's with the energy and community involvement of Rodriguez's. At Snyder's Boyle Heights campaign office, one heard much more Spanish spoken than at Moret or Rodriguez headquarters. On weekday mornings the Snyder office was full of middle-aged and elderly Mexican Americans, many of them housewives, phoning their neighbors and urging them to vote for "Art." Each one had a story to tell about how Snyder had solved some neighborhood problem that had stymied other officials.

With the exception of a few stray young Mexican-American Republicans, brimming with conservative ideological zeal, Snyder's campaign totally lacked the crusadelike feel of the Rodriguez effort. Instead, his supporters evidenced the quiet, almost stony pride typical of more tradition-oriented, less assimilated Mexican Americans. Very much in evidence in San Antonio neighborhoods, this pride often coincides with a stubborn, undemonstrative religious faith. So it was not surprising that as the polls closed on election day, Snyder's chief aide and campaign manager, Ross Valencia, a dapper man in his fifties and a veteran of many East LA political battles, gathered together the volunteers at the Boyle Heights office and had them join hands in prayer. This utterly unselfconscious gesture, the like of which was not to be seen at Moret or Rodriguez headquarters, is perhaps the most revealing indication of the difference between Snyder's core constituency and those of his two opponents. Ironically, neither Mexican-American candidate had as strong a community base as the Anglo *"patrón,"* Art Snyder.

THE CHICANA CHALLENGE

Steve Rodriguez ran against the clique a few more times, but never with quite the same verve or enthusiasm. He eventually faded from view and retreated to his job with the City of Los Angeles's Department of Planning. In the meantime a much more enduring challenger to the clique emerged from within its own ranks. This should be no surprise. Precisely because clique members have known one another so long, "they know one another's dirt," as one politico puts it. And given the limited opportunities for those—Mexicans or Anglos—seeking office in Los Angeles, it is hardly surprising when a young clique member, describing the scene from the inside, observes: "All these guys are on top of one another."

The most serious breach within the clique is traceable to Gloria Molina: former assemblywoman, former city councillor, and currently Los Angeles County supervisor. The first Mexican American since 1875 to sit on the Board of Supervisors, the most powerful elective body in Southern California, Molina has now been catapulted to national prominence. In 1992, for instance, she was named national co-chair of the Clinton campaign.

Unlike many of her clique colleagues, Molina started off working in community-based organizations. But soon afterward, she began a series of staff jobs for politicians that by the late 1970s had led her, along with several of her clique colleagues who went to Washington to serve in the Carter administration, to a job in the White House. Upon her return to California and before she ran for the state assembly, Molina worked for Assembly Speaker Willie Brown as his chief deputy for Southern California.[22]

The daughter of an immigrant laborer, Molina is smart, articulate, and can work a crowd in an appealing manner that her male colleagues in the clique should envy. Although she attended college, she never actually obtained her bachelor's degree—a fact that surprises many of her fans in the Democratic Party. Molina's story is typical of the benefits the clique has to offer a few Mexican Americans from humble origins. Yet her story has its own revealing twist. Back in 1982 Molina was, like many of her colleagues, not unreasonably looking forward to the day when she would succeed one of her mentors in office. Yet when Assemblyman Art Torres decided to run for the State Senate that year, Molina's claim on his vacated seat was summarily rejected by several clique members in favor of a male aide to Alatorre, who had also been working his way up in the farm system. With the backing of Torres, his wife, Yolanda Nava—a local television personality—and a group of female Mexican-American activists with whom she was long affiliated, Molina decided to challenge Alatorre's candidate.

The result was a Democratic primary brawl with Torres, Molina, and their many female supporters pitted against Alatorre's candidate and his predominantly male following. This was hardly the first (or last) dispute to arise within the clique, but it was certainly the most bitter—and the most public. The male candidate, Richard Polanco, implied in subtle and not-so-subtle ways that Molina, an attractive young woman in her thirties who at the time was unmarried, led an abnormal private life. Molina responded in kind with charges that Polanco, a likeable but less-than-savory product of an East LA housing project, was in default on child support payments to his divorced wife. In the event, Molina won and became the first "Chicana," as she and her female loyalists refer to themselves, to sit in the California Assembly.[23]

Subsequently, in 1985, when Alatorre ran successfully for the Los Angeles City Council, the scramble for his vacated Sacramento post pitted Polanco against Assemblywoman Molina's candidate. On that occasion Polanco won, but not without another intense and bitter battle. Then, in 1987, when Molina ran for a newly created Hispanic seat on the Los Angeles City Council, she once again confronted the clique and its male candidate, Los Angeles School Board member Larry González. Molina won that contest and became the first Chicana to sit on the Los Angeles City Council, where she served until 1991. At that point she ran successfully for the newly created Hispanic seat on the Los Angeles County Board of Supervisors. Once again, it came down to a battle between Molina and the clique's candidate, this time State Senator Art Torres, Molina's one-time ally against Polanco.

Although the rigors of Los Angeles politics have helped to avoid the kind of free-for-all evident among Mexican Americans in San Antonio, such skirmishes have created the widespread impression in Southern California of disarray among Mexican-American politicos there. Many of the participants in the original brawl between Molina and Polanco are still barely on speaking terms. During the 1992 California presidential primary, this rift caused problems for the Clinton campaign. Subsequently referring to the infighting between Molina and Alatorre, the *Los Angeles Times* pointed to the city's "deeply divided Latino establishment" as the cause of businessman Peter Ueberroth's stalled effort to appoint prominent Latinos to the board of Rebuild LA, the organization he put together at the behest of Mayor Bradley in the aftermath of the spring 1992 riots.[24]

But more than merely breaking with the clique, Gloria Molina has developed a political style discernibly different from the elite-network politics I have been describing here. To some extent Molina was forced into a different political posture by the heavy-handed treatment of her male colleagues. But it is also true that Molina has long practiced a more open and inclusive politics than "the guys."

For example, in the early 1970s Molina was a founding member of a Mexican-American women's organization, Comisión Femenil Mexicana

Nacional. Later in the early 1980s, as I have already indicated, Molina was one of the few Mexican-American leaders in Los Angeles to help the Southwest Voter Research Education Project get started in the region. Similarly, as I also mentioned above, Assemblywoman Molina organized the Latina Political Assembly.

But perhaps the most revealing example of Molina's political style was her involvement in a controversy over the siting of a state prison in East Los Angeles. In the mid-1980s, Governor Deukmejian and Assembly Speaker Willie Brown pushed through legislation authorizing construction of a new state prison in Molina's East Los Angeles district. Widely regarded as reflecting his displeasure with Molina, Speaker Brown eventually brought in her old rival, recently elected assemblyman Richard Polanco, to press for the East LA prison. What these politicians had not counted on was the outrage their proposal provoked from residents of near-by neighborhoods. Indeed, a parish-based organization, the Mothers of East Los Angeles, made up of local residents and homeowners reminiscent of UNO's membership, appeared and staged demonstrations vehemently opposing the prison, which was never built.

Not surprisingly, Molina positioned herself at the head of this crusade. Since this episode, Molina has continued to work with the Mothers of East Los Angeles, as well as more typical Chicano activist and protest groups. Particularly during her tenure on the city council, Molina emerged as an urban populist denouncing the schemes of bureaucrats and developers who, she warned through the media, would no longer have a free hand to disrupt neighborhoods as they did a generation ago when they crisscrossed East LA with freeways or built Dodger Stadium on the ruins of Chavez Ravine.

In this stance Molina has had the opportunity not only to defend her powerless constituents, but also to challenge and embarrass her fellow politicians. Molina has done this in the state assembly, on the city council, and now on the county board of supervisors, where she has championed reform of the powerful and antiquated machinery of county government. Among her targets have been the pay and perquisites of her fellow supervisors, as well as of top county administrators.

A local journalist refers to Molina as a "professional outsider."[25] Others refer to her as "the unyielding crusader," "the unwavering advocate."[26] Whatever the label, Molina's political posture as the defender of an oppressed minority has afforded her some credence among Chicano activists in Los Angeles, who have long since dismissed Alatorre and Torres as a bunch of "businessmen" whose "constituency is money." Her stance has also brought Molina the support of Anglo elites, particularly those who regard her as a minority leader who will be a vigorous ally on behalf of various progressive causes. The *Los Angeles Times* endorsed her candidacy to the city council and to the board of supervisors, on which body she is viewed by the paper as the sparkplug of reform.[27] And starting with her first tempestuous assembly race, Molina has received considerable support from Westside liberals and feminists. The latter—locally, statewide, and nationally—have been enthusiastic contributors to Molina's campaigns. And she has in turn been a staunch supporter of the feminist agenda.

These differences between Molina and the clique can be seen readily in her successful campaign for the county supervisorial seat, in which her principal opponent was State Senator Art Torres. With the endorsements of most local and state elected officials (including Mayor Tom Bradley), and most of the unions (including those representing county employees), Torres was the moderate, establishment candidate, who in fact did better than Molina in those parts of the huge supervisorial district in the suburban San Gabriel Valley. Outspending Molina more than two-to-one, Torres relied on an expensive, highly professionalized Sacramento-based political consultant to run his campaign. Yet with the support of the *Times* and enthusiastic, issue-oriented volunteers, Molina won with 55 percent of the vote.[28]

Nevertheless, these differences should not obscure the fundamental similarities between Molina and the clique. In the contest just described, it was frequently noted that Torres and Molina had many of the same supporters, who agonized over their choice.[29] Indeed, as Molina herself admitted on numerous occasions, there were no serious differences on the issues between her and Torres. There were certainly no differences between them—or between Molina and any other clique members—as to claiming racial minority status for Mexican Americans.

Thus, Molina is very much a creature of the same regime as her adversaries in the clique. Like them, she has benefited from racially gerrymandered seats contested in special elections in which turnouts were low and financial resources at a premium. To contest the newly created Hispanic seat on the city council in 1987, Molina, like her clique opponent, had to move into the district. Each candidate spent in excess of $200,000 for a special election in which only 12,000 votes were cast, representing one-third of registered voters in the district that already had the lowest registration in the city. In one precinct only seventeen votes were cast.[30] In the 1991 special election to become Los Angeles's first Latino county supervisor in more than a century, Molina and Torres together spent more than $1.5 million.[31] One of the most expensive elections in the county's history,[32] this money was spent on professional phone banks, paid precinct walkers, computer-targeted mailings, and absentee ballot efforts. Yet once again, all these resources resulted in a turnout of only 23 percent of registered voters.[33]

Despite her own efforts to increase voter registration among Hispanics, such low turnouts are highly functional for Molina. Like her clique competitors, she has had to make her way in a capital-intensive and issue-oriented political system with constituents who are poor and politically quiescent. A key participant in Molina's 1982 assembly campaign characterizes the working-class Mexican Americans residing in that district as "totally useless as far as the campaign was concerned." Even more than most California politicians, therefore, Molina—like her clique competitors—must rely on outside resources. Much of these, as I have already noted, come from Anglo feminists and other cause-oriented liberals. Indeed, the aide just quoted above reports that in Molina's 1982 assembly battle fully 70 percent of her funds came from women and women's groups outside the district.

Such debts create particular problems for Molina. On a personal level many of the women who have worked with Molina express considerable uneasiness with the views of the Anglo, particularly Jewish, feminists on whom they have depended heavily for support. These Chicanas point out that they could never bring themselves to join organizations like NOW. Indeed, they are reluctant to call themselves feminists. And with regard to abortion, they admit to serious reservations about the pro-choice position they publicly espouse. Summing up the differences these Chicanas see between themselves and their Anglo feminist allies, one Molina confidante states: "We don't hate our men."

Yet regardless of the personal views of the young Mexican Americans who have rallied around Gloria Molina, they all understand that her outspoken advocacy of this and other such liberal causes puts her very much at odds with her socially conservative Mexican-American constituents. Thus, there is a definite connection between the stridency of Molina's positions on potentially volatile social issues and the quiescence of her constituents. Indeed, the latitude she has enjoyed to pursue what one of her staffers refers to as "elite issues" is premised on the passivity of those she represents. Gloria Molina may be outside the clique, but she also partakes of elite-network politics.

The fact is that despite her outsider stance, Molina is herself part of an elite network. In addition to the feminist allies I have already mentioned, she has been supported by officeholders tied into the Westside-based "Waxman-Berman machine." Her network also has included Congressman Ed Roybal, who has consistently supported Molina's electoral bids. Indeed, Roybal's longtime chief district aide was the unofficial, behind-the-scenes manager of Molina's supervisorial campaign. Molina's debts to Roybal have been such that when she gave up her assembly seat to run for the city council in 1987, she (along with the Alatorre-Torres clique, in a rare show of unity) endorsed his daughter as her successor in Sacramento. Lucille Roybal-Allard, a political novice who had never run for office, was then elected to the assembly in another special election that was managed by Molina's trusted political consultant. (In the manner of elite-network politics, Roybal-Allard was not living in the working-class district she sought to represent, but in suburban Pasadena. To establish residence in the district, she rented an apartment there.)[34] At the same time, Molina has supported the candidacies of other Mexican-American aspirants. As indicated above, she unsuccessfully opposed the clique's candidate for Alatorre's old assembly seat with one of her own. A few years later, Molina successfully supported that same individual to succeed her on the city council. And most recently, in the June 1992 primary she and her campaign consultant secured the Democratic nomination of the young Mexican-American assemblyman who was then elected to succeed retiring congressman Ed Roybal.

Another critical element in Molina's network is the Mexican American Legal Defense and Educational Fund (MALDEF). Molina is a personal friend of MALDEF's Los Angeles-based president and general counsel, Antonia Hernández, another Mexican-American woman who has battled with male colleagues.[35] Consistent with her advocacy-oriented stance, Molina sits on the MALDEF board of directors. More to the point, she owes her seat on the board of supervisors to MALDEF, which played a highly visible role in the litigation that brought about creation of the Hispanic majority supervisorial district that Molina now represents. Even more critical to Molina's political fortunes is the role played by MALDEF as architect of the new district boundaries. For in substantially adopting the organization's proposal, the federal district court opted for a district that included not only the Pico Rivera community where Molina grew up, but the neighborhoods where the antiprison Mothers of East Los Angeles were strong. Certainly among Mexican-American politicos in Los Angeles the final district was widely—and among supporters of Art Torres, angrily—viewed as reflecting MALDEF's bias toward Molina.

Similarly, the MALDEF district failed to include the San Gabriel Valley suburb that was the home base of Sarah Flores, a Mexican-American Republican who ran against both Torres and Molina in the first round of the nonpartisan supervisorial election. Flores had started working in county government as a young secretary. Thirty-four years later she was a high-level aide to the crusty, conservative county supervisor Pete Schabarum. A moderate Republican with a broad base of support among the residents and officeholders of the San Gabriel Valley communities with which she had worked over the years, Flores decided to run for county supervisor when her boss announced that he would not seek reelection.[36] In June 1990, Flores won the primary with a plurality and was well positioned to defeat the second-place Anglo in a runoff. But that contest never happened, for the day before Flores's primary victory, a federal district judge ruled that the existing supervisorial lines conspired against the election of a Hispanic to the board of supervisors. Though his ruling was seemingly proved incorrect by the next day's events, Judge David Kenyon invalidated the June primary results and ordered new elections in a redrawn district in which Hispanics constituted a majority of registered voters.[37] Even though this new MALDEF-created district excluded three-fourths of the old district in which she had run so well, Flores continued her campaign for supervisor with strong backing from conservative incumbents on the board. Flores ultimately placed third, five points behind Torres, in what became a race among four Hispanics.[38] That Molina and Torres bested a candidate with such strong, broad community ties is eloquent testimony to the dominance in Los Angeles of the elite-network style through which both Molina and Torres have come to power.

Elite-network politics is not without its critics in Los Angeles. For example, when a university-based activist predictably dismisses Mexican-American politicians as unrepresentative of the community and removed from the day-to-day problems of their constituents, he speaks with considerable justification. Or when an aging Chicano activist now working for the federal government says of Alatorre, "Richard's constituency is money," he is talking less about corruption than about Alatorre's preoccupation with Sacramento lobbyists rather than with voters. Or when another activist bolsters his position by pointing to the low voter registration levels in districts represented by the clique, he is simply stating the facts.

Nor are such barbs confined to activists; politicians routinely aim them at one another. For instance, one (admittedly biased) source declares

Molina's assembly district "the safest district in the state." Pointing to the low registration and turnout in that district, this same source concludes that Molina "doesn't even have to show up to win." In the bitter battle between Torres and the middle-aged Mexican American he succeeded as state senator, the latter sent out glossy mailers accusing Torres of abandoning his district by moving his family to Sacramento. Recently, Alatorre disparaged (not without some justification) the Molina-backed candidate for Roybal's seat, noting, "He is the so-called community candidate, but he ain't from the community."[39] And Alatorre and Torres have themselves been dismissed—by a seasoned Mexican-American politico working in Mayor Bradley's office—as "operators" whose attentiveness to lobbyists for well-heeled interests such as racetrack owners have precluded their providing vigorous leadership.

Needless to say, such comments can be heard about politicians in any community. Yet their sheer frequency with regard to Mexican-American officeholders in Los Angeles suggests that, quite apart from their accuracy, they have taken on a reality of their own. At a minimum, such comments coming from a variety of sources indicate that Mexican-American politicians are hardly looked up to as champions of their people.

One might have hoped that the election of Alatorre and Molina to the city council would have reoriented the attention of the clique more in the direction of Los Angeles, and perhaps even strengthened their ties to the Mexican-American community. But it has not, because geographic proximity is hardly as critical as the nature of governmental institutions—which in Los Angeles, as I have been arguing, lack solid grounding in the social structure of the metropolis.

In sum, there is a real problem with the credibility and strength of Mexican-American elected officials in Los Angeles and California generally. A regime so dominated by political elites that it lacks solid social bases risks its legitimacy among all sectors of society, but particularly the economically and socially marginal.[40] At a time when Angelenos and Californians generally are experiencing great disaffection with elected officials who seem out of touch with their constituencies, Mexican Americans are likely to be as disaffected as anyone—perhaps more so, because their disappointed hopes in newly elected officials feed what is already a deep current of cynicism about politics.

❦ 8 ❦

Protest Politics
Symbolism and Symbiosis

W hether due to temperament or force of circumstance (or both), Gloria Molina has developed a somewhat more cosmopolitan version of elite-network politics than the Alatorre-Torres clique. Her articulate support of various liberal causes has allowed her to reach out further than "the guys" to a more sophisticated, issue-oriented body of supporters. Faced with the same constraints as her clique competitors, Molina must seek support either from the traditional interest groups—unions, developers, trade associations; or from more issue-oriented groups—environmentalists, feminists, and Chicano activists. While both may provide critical financial resources to wage the expensive campaigns necessary in Southern California, the more issue-oriented groups also offer opportunities for youthful volunteers dedicated to "progressive" causes. Compared to the clique, Molina has relied less on money and more on volunteers. With regard to Chicano activists, such reliance is significant because they have played a discernible role in California that has not developed in the same way in Texas. In this chapter, under the rubric of "protest politics," I examine how, since the 1960s, such activists have followed a different path in Los Angeles from that in San Antonio. Specifically, I will explore the dynamics of interdependence between activists and Molina as well as other Mexican-American politicians in Los Angeles.

James Q. Wilson defines protest as "a process whereby one party seeks by public display or disruptive acts to raise the cost to another party of continuing a given course of action."[1] The highly committed individuals who engage in protest politics may, like practitioners of organization and elite-network politics, address specific issues, but they typically do so in a manner that subordinates them to the articulation of a broader cause, vision of the world, or ideology. Such encompassing, intangible goals are of course quite unlike the material rewards—favors, payoffs, jobs—evident in friends-and-neighbors, organization, even elite-network politics.

Moreover, protest politics in California is less concerned with bargaining to achieve concrete objectives than with venting frustrations and moral outrage. Wilson refers to such activities as "pseudo-protest" and distinguishes them sharply from the kind of protest that seeks to induce bargaining.[2] One need not accept the negative valuation that attaches to "pseudo" to see how Wilson's distinction might apply to the two contexts discussed here. In Texas, Mexican Americans protested because they felt excluded from the social, economic, and political system, and they "wanted in." Their efforts toward this goal have met with considerable success, and protest has virtually disappeared. But in the much more favorable setting of California, Mexican Americans have already gotten "in"—compared, at least, to their Texas counterparts. Deprived of the obvious barriers upon which their ideology nevertheless continues to fixate, Chicano activists in California have pursued more expressive, symbolic concerns. Lacking concrete objectives, their protest endures as dramaturgy, deriving considerable sustenance from California's political institutions and culture.[3]

As IAF organizers are prone to pointing out, protest politics does not typically result in a well-defined organizational structure. In fact, protest leaders often self-consciously avoid building organizations, for fear that such efforts inevitably detract from protest objectives.[4] In this regard, they practice the protest version of the business dictum of "staying lean and mean." This hostility to organization leads to fluidity and instability in protest politics, which is consequently often referred to as "movement" or "activist" politics. Indeed, I have already used "activist" to refer to those engaged in protest politics.

Also characteristic of this style of politics are the strong social bonds that develop among participants as they pursue their protest goals. It is certainly no accident, for example, that New Left protesters during the 1960s adopted the same theme of "solidarity" that earlier generations of leftist and union activists had sounded. Unlike with friends-and-neighbors politics, these social bonds do not begin as all-inclusive primary group ties; but they often end up as something similar. The social bonds of protest politics are certainly different from the highly conditional, role-segmented relations of elite-network or organization politics. Indeed, protest groups tend to be characterized by a camaraderie fostered by the participants' sense that their all-important political goals fundamentally challenge a hostile environment. At the extreme, that environment is perceived to be so hostile that all bargaining, compromise, and other hallmarks of "politics as usual" are spurned by protesters. This chapter will explore the paradox that such extreme variants of protest politics have been far more evident in sunny, affluent California than in hardscrabble Texas.[5]

Mexican Americans who engage in protest politics typically refer to themselves as "Chicanos" (though not all who call themselves Chicanos engage in protest politics). Such individuals subscribe to a vaguely defined ideology of "Chicanismo" that interprets the Mexican-American experience as that of a distinct race that is indigenous to the American Southwest and has been colonized by the American political and economic system. During the 1960s this admixture of Marxism and race consciousness hardened into separatism. Today, Chicano activists have long since abandoned such notions. Yet they continue to advocate policies based on the premise that as "a conquered people" Chicanos have not been, and will not be, fully assimilated into the dominant society—and therefore have special claims against the American polity not enjoyed, for example, by Europeans who immigrated here.

Like so much politics in post–World War II America, protest politics has been profoundly shaped by the civil rights movement. This is particularly true for Mexican Americans, most of whose current leaders came of age politically during the 1960s, when blacks were relying on protest politics to stir the conscience of the nation. At a time when Mexican Americans were struggling with conventional political strategies to overcome their profound sense of isolation in the Southwest, remote from the perceived centers of power and influence in the East, blacks showed them an alternative. Echoing dozens of Mexican-American leaders who talked to me of their political education in the 1960s, County Commissioner Albert Peña of San Antonio was quoted in a 1966 issue of the *Nation*:

> Last year at the President's meeting on civil rights there were 3,000 delegates. But there were only eight of us Latin Americans. Our problems were not discussed—only Negro problems. We were told consistently, "The

trouble with you is, you don't make enough noise, you don't demonstrate, you don't raise Cain enough.[6]

Or as the authors of that article concluded, albeit with some exaggeration:

The new Mexican leader studies Negro civil rights technique with a degree of attention approaching the Pentagon's study of Chinese guerrillas.[7]

More systematic evidence confirming this point has subsequently been provided in Rufus P. Browning's study of black and Hispanic politics in ten Northern California cities from 1960 to 1980. Browning and his colleagues found that Hispanic protest politics consistently occurred later than, and was stimulated directly by, black protest politics.[8]

For many of today's Mexican-American leaders, their initiation into politics was with the United Farm Workers union. Significantly, the union's charismatic leader, César Chávez, relied heavily on acts of moral witness—fasts, religious services, marches—that reflected lessons learned from the black civil rights movement. More than twenty years later, the UFW is the victim of its own success. In California, passage of the California Agricultural Labor Relations Act in 1978 secured the union's status as the legally recognized bargaining agent for farmworkers in the nation's principal agricultural state, thus hastening its evolution from social movement to interest group. This process has required forays into the cross-currents of California politics that have inevitably tarnished the union's standing among Mexicans and Anglos alike. Still, as an individual, César Chávez is viewed with reverence and awe by virtually all Mexican Americans, who see him, as one aide to Mayor Bradley put it, "as the closest thing we have to a Martin Luther King."[9]

CHICANO ACTIVISM IN TEXAS AND CALIFORNIA

Though organizing among Mexican farmworkers has been most visible and successful in California, such efforts were also mounted elsewhere, including South Texas. Indeed, Chávez's work in California touched off a wildcat strike against melon growers in the Rio Grande Valley in 1966, which culminated in an historic march from the Mexican border to the State Capitol in Austin, where farmworkers were rebuffed by then governor John Connally. Poor planning, the Texas Rangers, and imported Mexican labor all contributed to the breaking of the strike.[10]

But the UFW was not the only vehicle for Chicano activism in Texas. Historian David Montejano writes: "Although the Valley strike failed, it succeeded in catalyzing the Chicano civil rights movement in Texas."[11] An array of marches, high school boycotts, and other protests throughout South Texas inspired the founding of the Raza Unida Party by Chicano graduate students at St. Mary's University in San Antonio. Guided by what Montejano describes as a populist-nationalist program, Raza Unida cadres gained national attention in the early 1970s with their aforementioned electoral takeover of the school board and county commissioners' court in Crystal City, Zavala County—a remote agricultural community of about 10,000 inhabitants forty miles from the Mexican border that advertises itself as "the Spinach Capital of the World," and has a six-foot statue of Popeye in the center of town to prove it.[12] Although this Raza Unida effort eventually foundered on factionalism and charges of corruption, it moved Governor Dolph Briscoe to call Crystal City "little Cuba," thus alarming many Anglo Texans for years to come.[13]

The Raza Unida Party reached another high-water mark in 1972, when its gubernatorial candidate, Ramsey Muñiz, won six percent of the statewide vote. Indeed, in forty South and West Texas counties, Muñiz got 18 percent of the ballots. Adding to the weight of this vote was the fact that it came at the expense of Briscoe, the conservative Democratic incumbent, who was reelected with less than a majority—48 percent compared to his Republican opponent's 45 percent. Soon thereafter, official denunciations, more factional infighting, and the arrest of Raza Unida leaders on marijuana smuggling charges led to the dissolution of the party.[14]

During this same period, Raza Unida was also active in California. Around Los Angeles in particular, Raza Unida candidates contested various offices but were nowhere as successful as their counterparts in Texas. In 1971 a Raza Unida candidate got 7 percent of the vote in an East LA assembly race. The next year the party's candidate in another East LA assembly contest got 13 percent of the Democratic primary vote.[15] But unlike its Texas counterpart, the Raza Unida Party in California never made it onto the statewide ballot. Indeed, it collected less than a third of the 66,000 registrations required for official party status.[16]

On the other hand, Chicano activists in California were much more strident than in Texas. Commenting on activist efforts in the two states, Grebler and his colleagues noted in 1970:

> It is an interesting commentary on the regional diversity of Mexican Americans that MAPA [the Mexican American Political Association], in the comparatively open social environment of California, is at once more clearly Mexican and less disposed to seek allies outside the Mexican-American community. PASSO [the Political Association of Spanish-Speaking Orga-

nizations], on the other hand, operating in the more restrictive milieu of Texas, pragmatically adopted a euphemism for a label and proceeded to form political coalitions.[17]

Quite unlike anything in San Antonio, Los Angeles spawned the paramilitary Brown Berets, modeled after the Black Panthers. In August 1972, twenty-six Brown Berets seized Santa Catalina Island, renamed it "Aztlán* Libre," and remained there twenty-four days, at which point they were forced to leave by armed sheriff's deputies.[18] Other Chicano activists organized large-scale public school boycotts (referred to as "blowouts") and boisterous antiwar demonstrations. One of these, the National Chicano Anti-War Moratorium, held on August 29, 1970, brought together thousands of Chicanos for a march down East LA's Whittier Boulevard. The day was marked by battles between demonstrators and police, and by the death of former *Los Angeles Times* reporter Rubén Salazar, who was sitting in a bar when hit in the head by a ten-inch tear-gas canister fired by police.[19] This incident set the stage for deteriorating police-community relations and subsequent rioting in East LA.[20]

Symptomatic of the rancorous relations between Chicano activists and established authority in Los Angeles at this time were the events involving Católicos Por La Raza (CPLR). As mentioned in chapter 6, CPLR's efforts focused on the conservative regime of James Francis Cardinal McIntyre: after researching the Los Angeles archdiocese's extensive real estate holdings, CPLR began demanding that the Church fund barrio community action programs. Weeks of meetings, challenges, and unyielding responses from the chancery culminated in the aforementioned midnight melee at St. Basil's Church, on Christmas Eve 1969.

The recently completed St. Basil's is an unapologetically modern edifice in the fashionable mid-Wilshire district, whose $4 million cost indicated its importance as a showpiece for the cardinal. Regarding the church as symptomatic of the cardinal's obliviousness to the needs of Chicanos, the young militants staged a protest mass on its steps. Having completed their mass, they then tried to attend the cardinal's own mass inside and found themselves locked out. Eventually finding a way in, the demonstrators were confronted by plainclothes deputies from the Los Angeles

---

* As Luis Valdez explains: "We have been in America a long time. Somewhere in the twelfth century, our Aztec ancestors left their homeland of Aztlán, and migrated south to Anáhuac, "the place by the waters," where they built their great city of México-Tenochtilán. . . . Aztlán is now the name of our Mestizo nation, existing to the north of Mexico, within the borders of the United States." See Luis Valdez, "Introduction: 'La Plebe,'" in Luis Valdez and Stan Steiner, eds., *Aztlán: An Anthology of Mexican American Literature* (New York: Vintage Books, 1972), xxxiii–xxxiv.

County Sheriff's Office and fully outfitted members of the Los Angeles Police Department's riot squad.[21] Wielding nightsticks and mace, the armed policemen managed to expel the protesters from the church. At the end of the mass, the cardinal addressed the congregation and likened the demonstrators to the "rabble" at the foot of Christ's cross. By the time the evening was over there were several arrests. The archdiocese refused to drop charges, and eventually seven persons were convicted and sent to the county jail.[22]

When Cardinal McIntyre retired shortly after these events, his departure was shrouded in mystery, and partly attributed to his age. At the same time, the Chicano activists in CPLR could claim a good deal of credit for the specific timing of his retirement. But it would be a mistake to assume CPLR spoke for a majority of Mexican Americans in Los Angeles. The virtual disappearance of the group a short time afterward suggests that they did not. In any event, it is striking that during this period of acrimony in Los Angeles, there were no comparable tensions in San Antonio between Chicano activists and the local hierarchy.

Not unrelated to the stridency of Chicano activists in Los Angeles, and California generally, was their strong ideological orientation. The rhetoric of class conflict and pronouncements on Third World solidarity were much in evidence. In California Raza Unida activists tended to be suspicious of electoral politics, which they regarded as "reformist." When such efforts were undertaken, they were regarded not so much as a means of gaining political office, but of educating the community—of "raising the level of political consciousness."[23]

In Texas, by contrast, Chicano activism relied less on Marxist ideology and more on populist rhetoric. The Raza Unida Party there was certainly more concerned with winning elections than its California counterpart. Consequently, Raza Unida activists in Texas talked less about the Third World and more about local issues. Indeed, party leaders in Texas such as founder José Angel Gutiérrez were so concerned to build local bases that they resisted what they regarded as premature efforts to run statewide candidates and, certainly, involvements in national politics.[24]

Undoubtedly because of their pragmatism, Chicano activists in Texas long ago dropped out of sight. Certainly, the Raza Unida Party no longer exists, its former cadres having either retired from politics completely or moved, like the Tejeda gang in San Antonio, into the Democratic Party. As a result, many Mexican-American political leaders in San Antonio and Texas today are Raza Unida veterans, who invariably describe those experiences fondly as their education in "the nuts and bolts of Texas politics."[25] To be sure, the accumulated resentments from generations of tensions and animosities between Mexicans and Anglos in Texas continue to boil to the surface of San Antonio politics. But such sentiments get channeled through conventional political paths; they no longer fuel activist fires. In the process, the Democratic Party in Texas has been moved in a more liberal direction, thereby contributing to the exodus of many conservatives. But at the same time, many former Chicano activists have also moderated their political views.

In California, by contrast, an assortment of orthodox Communists, unaffiliated leftists, Marxist academics, and union militants has managed to keep the old flame alive into the 1990s. In one or two places—such as the city of San Fernando, site of the old mission church where Pope John Paul II met with the U.S. bishops on his visit to Los Angeles in 1987— Raza Unida chapters manage to survive in the hothouse of Southern California politics. Such veterans of the battles of the 1960s and early 1970s, many now well into their forties, have for the most part moderated the highly disruptive methods of their youth. But despite their small numbers, they are surprisingly visible and continue to exert influence in Los Angeles, California, and even national politics.

To be sure, these Chicano activists in Los Angeles are less suspicious than they used to be of electoral politics. In 1984, for example, they helped Jesse Jackson win 17 percent of the Hispanic vote in California's Democratic presidential primary.[26] Four years later they worked with Jackson to garner 36 percent of the Hispanic vote against Michael Dukakis.[27] By contrast, no such activist effort was visible in Texas, and in both years Jackson received smaller proportions of the Mexican-American vote: 10 percent in 1984 and 24 percent in 1988.[28] Making their presence felt on another front, Chicano activists at the California Democrats' spring 1988 convention managed, in the midst of Mexico's own tumultuous presidential campaign, to get a plank into the state party platform calling for greater democratization in Mexico.[29]

One way these activists have maintained their visibility is attacking Mexican-American elected officials. Indeed, an important political cleavage among Mexican Americans in Los Angeles today is between the politicians in the Alatorre-Torres clique and Chicano activists. The latter are of course deeply suspicious of any successful practitioners of conventional politics. They are quick to denounce clique members as self-serving opportunists with no regard for the interests of their constituents. And while such pronouncements are made with the intense disdain that only ideological leftists can summon for practical men of affairs, in Los Angeles such charges happen to resonate with the widespread perception that Mexican-American politicians lack solid community support.

Yet like the politicians they criticize, these activists also have weak community bases. This was certainly true in their heyday in the early 1970s, when, as I already indicated, their candidates were badly beaten at the polls, or their proposal for a separate Chicano municipality was overwhelmingly rejected by East LA homeowners fearful of increased property taxes. In recent years, support for Chicano activists and their causes has grown even smaller. Nevertheless, they can still call upon modest groups of loyal followers to turn out for community meetings or demonstrations—for example, getting their picture in the *Los Angeles Times* protesting the Dodgers' dismissal of Fernando Valenzuela.[30]

For their part, Mexican-American politicians in Los Angeles are just as critical of the activists. Typical is the dismissive tone of a clique member talking about "these grassroots types." Yet such scorn is mixed with some uneasiness. Back in 1971, for example, the Raza Unida candidate for state assembly may have received only 7 percent of the vote, but this was enough to stymie up-and-coming Alatorre's first bid for the seat and deliver it to his Republican opponent.[31] Widely believed to be supported by Richard Nixon's Committee to Re-elect the President as part of a broader strategy to weaken Mexican-American ties to the Democrats, this Raza Unida effort helped earn activists a reputation among Mexican-American politicos as "spoilers," even "provocateurs."

More recently, Chicano activists in Los Angeles have continued to live up to this billing. In the mid-1980s, a group of extremely ideological and obstreperous individuals took over the local chapter of the Mexican American Political Association (MAPA), fostering much dissension and contributing greatly to the decline of the organization. During the 1984 election cycle, other activists attempted to disrupt voter registration efforts from which they apparently felt excluded. And more generally in the electoral arena, Chicano activists have continued to prove capable of garnering just enough support to create, in the view of clique members, confusion in the community. One example follows upon the 1983 community forum described in the previous chapter, at which the clique engineered near unanimous support for its candidate for the Los Angeles School Board. Refusing to abide by the forum's decision, and the only Mexican-American to run against the clique's candidate, was a Raza Unida veteran who had since become a professor of Chicano studies at Cal State-Northridge. That individual did not win, but he did get 24 percent of the vote in a three-way race, thereby forcing the clique's candidate into a runoff before he could claim victory.[32]

CAMPUSES AND CAMERAS

These two different trajectories of Chicano activism can be explained by a variety of factors. To begin, the social dynamics that distinguish Los Angeles from San Antonio reinforce the more strident, ideological strain of activism there. The overwhelming size, impersonality, and transience of Los Angeles—for Anglos and Mexicans alike—certainly make life there much closer to the Marxist conception of capitalist social relations than it is in San Antonio. Such leftist perspectives gain even greater credence if one focuses on the Mexican-American neighborhoods of Los Angeles that have been inundated with immigrants for more than a decade. Compounding the effects of these social dynamics of course is the relative inaccessibility of the political system in Los Angeles. Taken together, these factors explain why survey evidence suggests that voting-age Mexican-American citizens in Los Angeles experience greater political alienation in Los Angeles than in San Antonio.[33] In any event, the raw materials for protest politics are found in relative abundance in Los Angeles. Moreover, as I mentioned earlier, the extreme transiency of Mexican-American neighborhoods in Los Angeles contributes to a political vacuum in which Chicano activists wield influence disproportionate to their meager numbers and atypical views.

Still another factor to be considered is California's renowned higher education infrastructure, in particular its extensive system of public colleges and universities. These have served as secure bases for Chicano activists pursuing their highly ideological brand of politics since the late 1960s and early 1970s, when these same institutions furnished the movement with scores of student cadres. Indeed, Mario Barrera and Carlos Muñoz stress that in California the Raza Unida Party was "largely an outgrowth of the Chicano student movement."[34] They further note that despite the relatively low numbers of Chicanos in Northern California, the first Raza Unida chapter in the state was established in Berkeley.[35]

In subsequent years, state colleges and universities in California have been safe havens for activists less as students than as professors. If Chicano activists in Texas have disappeared into the Democratic Party, in California they have largely retreated into the state's far-flung system of higher education, especially to its many Chicano studies programs.[36]

By contrast, San Antonio has an extremely underdeveloped higher education sector. Indeed, building up this sector was an important goal of the growth-oriented Cisneros. It was not until 1969 that San Antonio got its own branch of the University of Texas. As a result, the leading institutions in the city are private. The preeminent school is Trinity University, a well-endowed and selective institution founded by the Presbyterian Church. With strong ties to the city's Anglo elite, whose Scotch-Irish fore-bears settled modern San Antonio, Trinity has been slow to enroll signif-icant numbers of Mexican Americans.

The other major university is St. Mary's, a Catholic institution which has educated many of Texas's Mexican-American leaders, including, as I have already indicated, several activists. Yet these two schools, along with the city's lesser institutions of higher education, do not constitute the crit-ical mass to sustain the kind of safe haven for activists provided by the huge system of public colleges and universities in and around Los Ange-les. Moreover, when activists were visible in San Antonio, their efforts were sustained less by ties to universities than to Mexican-American elected officials and labor unions[37]—which undoubtedly accounts for the moderation and eventual absorption of activists into the mainstream of San Antonio and Texas politics.

The decisive factor in explaining the persistence and stridency of Chi-cano activism in Los Angeles is undoubtedly the role of the media. As already indicated, paid media exposure is of relatively minor impor-tance to candidates running in local contests. But to activists trying to get their message across, unpaid media attention—by making the news—is essential. I have already described the role of the media in Steve Rodriguez's brief rise to prominence. Such an episode is far less likely to occur in San Antonio, due to its relatively rooted Mexican-American pop-ulation and a porous political system that greatly reduces the political im-portance of the media.

A revealing illustration of the dynamic between Chicano activists and the media in Los Angeles involves Antonio Rodriguez. The head of a small legal clinic housed in shabby, second-floor offices in the Boyle Heights neighborhood of East LA, Rodriguez has emerged as a zealous advocate for the rights of illegal aliens. Rodriguez was born in Mexico and educated at UCLA, but he still speaks English with a discernible ac-cent. More important, he speaks fluent Marxism, which does not win him much of a following among the struggling residents of East LA. Yet his energetic efforts in behalf of illegal aliens and in Jesse Jackson's 1984 and 1988 California campaigns have earned him front-page attention in the *Los Angeles Times*, as well as frequent mention in the *New York Times*.[38]

In similar fashion, a longtime activist and Cal State-Northridge Chi-cano studies professor named Rodolfo (Rudy) Acuña became, in the late

1980s, a regular columnist for the *Los Angeles Herald Examiner* and now appears frequently in the *Los Angeles Times*, platforms that have magnified his views far beyond their prevalence among Mexican Americans in the metropolitan region.

Then there is Richard Santillán, an academic who has divided much of his professional life between the Ethnic and Women's Studies Department at California State Polytechnic at Pomona, and the Rose Institute of Local and State Government at Claremont Graduate School. A product of the Chicano studies programs at California State-Los Angeles and California State-Northridge, Santillán has written extensively on Chicano politics. Yet he has hardly contented himself with the role of detached observer. Indeed, Santillán's early activities in the Raza Unida Party have earned him the continuing suspicion of many Mexican-American politicos, who regard his affiliation with the Rose Institute, officially nonpartisan but widely understood to be Republican in orientation, as further evidence that Santillán, like other Raza Unida activists during the early 1970s, struck a deal with Republicans trying to splinter the Mexican-American vote.[39]

Santillán has since worked on campaigns for Mayor Tom Bradley. Significantly, his entrée into the Bradley camp was not through the Alatorre-Torres clique, whose ties to the mayor have not always been strong, but through then vice-mayor Grace Montanez Davis, a veteran activist whose status as the grande dame of Mexican-American politics in Los Angeles set her apart from, and somewhat above, the clique. Santillán also worked on Jesse Jackson's 1984 presidential campaign. In fact, he engineered a Jackson coup that greatly embarrassed the clique and demonstrated once again the importance of the Los Angeles media in sustaining Chicano activism.

The setting for Santillán's feat was a statewide meeting of the Mexican American Political Association (MAPA), convened on a May weekend to endorse a presidential candidate in the upcoming June (1984) primary. Founded in 1958 by the emergent postwar generation of Mexican-American leaders, MAPA was at one time an influential voice in California politics.[40] But by the 1980s, the statewide organization had been taken over and used for personal or partisan gain so many times—in the late 1960s by young militants, in the late 1970s by Mexican-American Republicans, and then in the early 1980s by the UFW in the person of César Chávez's son, Fernando—that it had become a shell.[41] More precisely, MAPA had become an arena in which various factions found it convenient to do battle.[42] In the spring of 1984 a nationally prominent Mexican-American leader, weary of the image of Mexican Americans constantly bickering

among themselves, observed that "MAPA has become one very danger-
ous organization."

Still, the MAPA endorsement is valued by candidates. It has long since
ceased to confer campaign workers or money. What it has come to mean,
almost exclusively, is media attention—for the organization as well as for
the candidates it chooses to showcase. At the local level, where it takes
about five people to stack a meeting and endorse a candidate for local office, the MAPA imprimatur is not hotly contested. But in a presidential
primary, which attracts media like a picnic does ants, the stakes for this
largely paper organization's endorsement are much higher.

Into this arena stepped Richard Santillán, on behalf of Jesse Jackson.
Due to MAPA's extremely flexible membership rules, Santillán was able
to fill the convention with Jackson supporters, their numbers exaggerated
because Mother's Day observances had prevented many MAPA regulars
("MAPistas") from making the trip to San Jose. Although Santillán was
not able to deny Walter Mondale the MAPA endorsement, he did create
enough turmoil before the reporters and television cameras so that Jackson's close second-place finish made the former vice-president look like
an embattled figure on the eve of the primary.

Back in Los Angeles, the Mexican-American political establishment,
solidly lined up behind Mondale, was livid. The clique's embarrassment
was heightened the next day, when the Monday morning edition of the
Los Angeles Times carried a front-page article on the MAPA convention
in which Santillán was quoted, declaring that "Jackson would do the best
job of bargaining on behalf of Latinos at the Democratic National Convention."[43]

Later that week, at a private get-together of key advisers and staff celebrating then assemblywoman Gloria Molina's birthday, reactions to Santillán ranged from dismissive skepticism to smoldering outrage. Some
regarded his efforts as a flash in the pan, arguing that Jackson would get
a scant 1 percent of the Latino vote in the upcoming primary. Others were
hardly so detached. They agreed that Santillán lacked any organizational
base, and that once the primary was over, he would fade quickly from
public view. But they also expressed angry bewilderment that such a "self-
appointed leader" could get front-page attention in the *Times*, thereby
fostering the misleading impression that Jackson had serious support
among Mexican Americans in California.

As it turned out, both perspectives were wide of the mark. Those coolly
dismissing Santillán's efforts seriously underestimated his candidate's
strength. For as mentioned earlier, Jackson got about 17 percent of the
Mexican-American vote statewide in the Democratic primary. And those

angered by Santillán totally missed the irony of the situation. For while they were correct in their assertions that such activists speak for only a few Mexican Americans, they ignored the weakness of their own claims to representing Mexican-American opinion.

TWO POLITIES, TWO TRAJECTORIES

The persistence of Chicano activism in Los Angeles should not therefore be explained solely by social structural factors. The metropolitan region's unique political structure and dynamics must also be considered. In this regard, the difference between Los Angeles and San Antonio is pinpointed by journalist Tony Castro:

> The difference between the Raza Unida parties in California and Colorado and the party in Texas was that the leaders outside Texas ignored the lesson of Crystal City, with its ward-style politics, and hoped that La Raza Unida's philosophy and platform would awaken the nationalism within Mexican Americans. It was on nationalism, after all, that Corky Gonzales [a Colorado-based activist] built his own movement, and the activists believed the nationalist sense of pride and belief in one's own people ought to over-ride the pragmatism of traditional politics.[44]

In light of my earlier discussion of school politics in San Antonio, it is worth noting that Raza Unida cadres in Crystal City were first able to establish themselves and build their political base by capturing control of the local school district. And while this takeover eventually degenerated into bitter in-fighting, this was the petty squabbling of friends-and-neighbors politics more than the ideological battling of protest politics. Crystal City therefore suggests that the material incentives of traditional Texas politics moderated the ideological thrust of Chicano activists there.

It is similarly worth noting that by the mid-1980s the very few remnants of Chicano activism left in San Antonio were to be found at the Guadalupe Cultural Arts Center. Still long-haired and counterculturally dressed, these activists were nevertheless municipal contractors who could be seen, at election time, driving around town in a pick-up truck posting signs for their benefactor on the city council. Like the Tejeda gang, they had been drawn into San Antonio's patronage politics.

These two trajectories for activism also have much to do with the different patterns of political recruitment in these two cities. In San Antonio, as I have noted, many of today's Mexican-American leaders began as activists in the wide-open, rough-and-tumble of local politics. But in Los Angeles, the paths into politics are so narrow and few that the present leaders of the clique were already apprenticing themselves to established politicians in the late 1960s when their activist peers were out in the streets organizing school boycotts and antiwar demonstrations. And because the number of such apprenticeships was necessarily limited, Chicano activists—unlikely in any event to play the patient insider's game—were soon locked out of the system entirely.

As a result, very few, if any, of those now involved in the clique today were ever activists. Indeed, Mexican-American politicians and Chicano activists in Los Angeles have long been shunted onto separate tracks. This might in part be attributable to the divergent social origins of the two groups. For instance, a key member of the Alatorre-Torres clique claims he was so busy working his way through college he had no time for Chicano activism. He describes his graduation from a local college in the early 1970s, when he was denounced as a sellout by other Mexican-American students for not wearing a protest armband. "Today," he notes with satisfaction, "they are all much more conservative than I will ever be."

Though suggestive, this vignette seems too self-serving to be entirely convincing. My own impression is that activists come from better-situated families than clique members, but the difference appears to be the relatively slight one between the working and the lower-middle classes.[45] A more promising explanation for this bifurcation of mainstream and activist politics among Mexican Americans in Los Angeles seems to be California's distinctive political dynamics.

Consider Governor Jerry Brown's appointment of scores of Mexican Americans to various posts in state government. One such prominent appointee observed that Brown "cleaned the streets of activists." More to the point, many of Brown's appointees had no ties to the then emergent Alatorre-Torres clique. For example, his first major Mexican-American appointment, to head the Department of Health, Education, and Welfare, the largest agency in state government, went to Texas attorney Mario Obledo. Obledo, who has since gone on to national visibility as president of the League of United Latin American Citizens (LULAC), had headed (the then San Antonio-based) MALDEF, and taught law at Harvard. But at the time of his appointment in 1975, he was largely unknown to Mexican Americans in California. And while clique members had undoubtedly heard of Obledo, they were not consulted by Brown, whose action stunned and infuriated them. According to one older clique member, ever mindful of the young staffers patiently waiting in line, Brown's actions "put out the word that you didn't have to put in your time to get somewhere." Clique members got some satisfaction later, when in 1982 they had the opportunity to refuse to support Obledo's quixotic bid for the Democratic gubernatorial nomination.

Governor Brown's motives are not difficult to fathom. Indeed, they constitute a case study in how California's weak organization politics feeds on itself and produces more of the same. Having decided to court Mexican-American voters, Brown needed to create cadres loyal to him, not to the emergent Mexican-American political establishment or their sponsors in the Democratic Party, from whom he was also keeping his distance. Brown also knew that Mexican-American politicians like Alatorre and Torres could not deliver many votes. So, the new governor did much of his courting of Mexican Americans by appearing frequently at El Adobe, the Hollywood restaurant owned by his friends Frank and Lucy Casada—aging MAPA activists with limited ties to the new generation of Mexican-American politicians. And when it came time to register voters and walk precincts in the barrios of Los Angeles, Brown relied not on local politicos but on César Chávez's UFW members, bused in from the fields.

The irony is, once again, that the activists appointed by Brown had even weaker community bases than the Mexican-American politicians he disdained. But this was of little concern to the media-conscious governor, who also knew that such weak appointees would be all the more tractable and dependent on him.

ANTAGONISTIC SYMBIOSIS

A final factor contributing to the niche Chicano activists occupy in Los Angeles is the antagonistic symbiosis between them and the Mexican-American clique. Despite the friction and downright animosity evident in episodes such as the Santillán coup in behalf of Jesse Jackson at the MAPA convention, activists generate the attention and create the pressure that the politicians cannot do by themselves. As one clique member readily admits, "There is nothing better than people out there complaining when you're trying to push an issue on the inside." Another clique member makes a similar point by noting the vulnerability of Mexican-American Republicans, who lack any such activist threat to reinforce their position within the GOP.

To varying degrees, of course, most politicians have this problem. But it is particularly conspicuous among Mexican-American politicians in Los Angeles, whose safe seats in poorly organized districts render them particularly ill-equipped to gain attention for themselves or for their constituents. Such politicians need activists in order to get taken seriously by their benefactors in the Democratic Party. By pointing over their shoulders to the "crazies" behind them, they ensure themselves a role to play.

In essence, Chicano activists enhance the opportunity for Mexican-American politicians to act as brokers to the Democratic leadership.

This dynamic is highlighted by a look at some of the issues on which activists and politicians in Los Angeles have, in effect, colluded. A good example would be the 1980 legislative reapportionment in California. In that process a group of Chicanos, mostly academics and a few lawyers, organized to press for more Chicano seats. Armed with the computer resources available to Santillán at the Rose Institute, Californios for Fair Representation combined technical sophistication with protest tactics to obtain their objectives. According to one of the participants, Californios, as the group came to be known, relied heavily on the media to project a statewide presence, though its handful of members were predominantly from metropolitan Los Angeles.[46]

Californios' principal targets were Assembly Speaker Willie Brown and Alatorre, then chair of the Assembly Committee on Elections and Reapportionment. Because of substantial Mexican-American population gains since 1970, Brown obviously anticipated pressure from that quarter during the 1980 reapportionment. This was clearly a major consideration in his choice of Alatorre to oversee the process. But, as I have already indicated, the East LA assemblyman was also the speaker's close political ally and could be entrusted with the delicate task of balancing activist demands for more Mexican-American seats with the needs of Democratic incumbents.

In the event, Alatorre seems to have flourished in this role. Pressure from the activists was at times intense, including well-publicized sit-ins at Alatorre's and Brown's offices. Participants recall a particularly acrimonious meeting at Los Angeles's Bonaventure Hotel, at which the speaker was asked to explain his widely quoted remark about Mexican Americans: "They're fine people, but if they're not registered to vote, they can't help you very much."[47] Through all this, Alatorre helped absorb a good deal of the pressure focused on Brown. At the same time, the assemblyman presided over a reapportionment that, as I indicated earlier, satisfied even the Chicano activists in Californios.

In the prolonged debate over the Simpson-Mazzoli immigration restriction legislation that raged until President Reagan finally signed a bill in 1986, one finds another case of this antagonistic yet symbiotic relationship. Left to themselves, Mexican-American politicians, particularly those at the state and local levels, would hardly have chosen to address such a difficult matter of national policy. Members of the clique publicly opposed to Simpson-Mazzoli privately admitted, "It's a complex issue and no one knows what they want." These politicians readily acknowledged that Mexican-American opinion on this question was sharply divided: that, while highly vocal activists denounced efforts to control immigration from Mexico as racist, many Mexican Americans supported it. Not limiting themselves to opinion poll data, most of the politicians I talked to cited support for immigration restriction within their own families. One assemblyman quoted a brother, a blue-collar family man, on the subject: "Hey, let's take care of the Mexicans who are already here."

Sensitivity to this perspective was even greater among Mexican-American politicians from suburban districts. In part this was due to their sizable Anglo constituencies, but it also reflected the politicians' reading of their Mexican-American constituents. Thus, Congressman Esteban Torres, representing just such a mixed district in the San Gabriel Valley, was not much in evidence in the long battle against the Simpson-Mazzoli legislation, and he was one of the first members of the Hispanic Caucus to break ranks and vote for the bill that finally passed Congress.

Thus, the impetus for the battle against immigration restriction in Los Angeles came not from the politicians, but from activists and MALDEF. The absolutely critical role of the latter will be examined in a subsequent chapter. But activists, too, played an important role in building pressure at the local level against Simpson-Mazzoli. Throughout the spring of 1984, for example, when that legislation was inching its way through Congress, activists railed against employer sanctions, insisting that such penalties against those hiring illegal aliens would lead to employment discrimination against all Latinos. In Los Angeles, the focus of their efforts became the June presidential primary. Their goal was to get the various Democratic candidates, particularly frontrunner Mondale, to denounce Simpson-Mazzoli. And in response to such pressure, clique members, who were all committed to Mondale, publicly opposed the legislation. At a Los Angeles session of the Democratic Platform Committee, chaired by Congresswoman and soon-to-be vice-presidential candidate Geraldine Ferraro, clique member Lou Moret criticized Speaker Tip O'Neill for keeping the legislation alive.

Once again, members of the clique found themselves mediating between Democratic Party allies and Chicano activists. For as one insider smugly pointed out, politicians like Mondale prefer not to bother with unreliable grassroots types when they can deal with politicians like themselves. So, by keeping up the pressure against Simpson-Mazzoli, MALDEF and the activists were putting local Mexican-American politicians at the center of an important national controversy. And as long as the pressure and the controversy were kept within bounds, thereby permitting the Mexican-American politicians to serve as reliable brokers, they were more than happy to play out that highly visible role.

Yet as the struggle continued, tensions among the various participants began to surface. One politician recounts how Vilma Martínez, former general counsel and president of MALDEF and now an influential member of its board, spent a critical strategy session haranguing those present about the importance of defeating Simpson-Mazzoli. At one point she asserted that if necessary, "We'll take to the streets." Thereupon, Martínez was reminded by the politicos that such exaggeration did not cut much mustard with them.

Tensions increased as many Chicano activists lent their support to Jesse Jackson, who came out unequivocally against Simpson-Mazzoli early in the campaign. Mondale, tied to labor unions supporting immigration restriction, continued to equivocate through the spring and into the summer, thus playing into the hands of Santillán, organizing for his aforementioned Jackson coup at the MAPA convention.

Meanwhile, an article appeared in the *Los Angeles Herald Examiner* quoting two key activists who criticized Mondale for his lack of support in the battle against Simpson-Mazzoli.[48] Both individuals—a young woman who had held several positions in Governor Jerry Brown's administration, and a wealthy grocery wholesaler who had backed various Chicano causes—had strong ties to César Chávez.

These statements were seen as provocative by the clique, because a few years earlier, during the California Assembly speakership battle, Chávez had broken with Alatorre and Torres when they backed off their original support of then assemblyman (and long-time Chávez ally) Howard Berman in favor of Willie Brown. Subsequently, Chávez went so far as to send his union members into Los Angeles to campaign against Torres's nasty but successful effort to unseat an incumbent Mexican-American state senator. Finally, though Chávez and his union were officially neutral in the presidential primary, they were generally regarded as favoring Gary Hart, who was also supported by Berman, who had by then moved on to serve in Congress with his friend and ally, Henry Waxman.

Against this backdrop, the two activists quoted in the *Herald Examiner* were immediately seen as agents of the clique's sworn enemies. That the article in question was written by a Mexican-American reporter (albeit under her married name, Linda Breakstone) added a sense of betrayal to the embarrassment clique members felt before the Mondale campaign. Once again, they were open to the charge of not being able to keep their people in line. And once again, the media seemed to be conspiring against them by giving front-page attention to otherwise obscure activists.

ACTIVISTS IN THE NATIONAL ARENA

The final stage of this dynamic between activists and politicians can be seen in the emergence of the immigration issue at the 1984 Democratic National Convention in San Francisco. In that arena, Chicano activists succeeded in making the defeat of Simpson-Mazzoli the most important—indeed, virtually the only—item on the Mexican-American political agenda. Politicians who had previously managed to sidestep or ignore the issue were suddenly at the center of efforts to defeat immigration restriction legislation.

Mayor Henry Cisneros was the prime example. During the years prior to the convention when immigration was being debated, the ambitious young politician had little or nothing to say about it. Indeed, a member of the Los Angeles clique expressed surprise at Cisneros's visibility on the issue at San Francisco, mentioning that a year earlier Cisneros had declined an invitation to come out to California to speak against Simpson-Mazzoli.

Several factors explain Cisneros's initial stance and then his switch. Although further deterioration of the Mexican economy subsequently altered the situation, in 1984 illegal immigration was not a salient issue to San Antonians, Anglo or Mexican. With a much less dynamic economy than, for example, Houston or Dallas, San Antonio at that time served principally as a stopover for illegals journeying north. Unlike Los Angeles, the city was experiencing neither the problems of massive illegal immigration, nor agitation about it by Chicano activists. In the May 1984 Texas presidential primary, for example, Simpson-Mazzoli was simply not a subject that preoccupied politically active Mexican Americans in San Antonio or, for that matter, elsewhere in Texas.

Yet as Cisneros emerged as a national political figure, the shape of the issue began to change for him. In the summer of 1983, the mayor was thrust into prominence by his appointment to the Kissinger Commission on Central America. A year later, he was being interviewed by Walter Mondale as a possible vice-presidential running mate. By the time of the San Francisco convention, Cisneros was the nation's preeminent Mexican-American politician, and as such he could hardly continue to ignore Simpson-Mazzoli. Moreover, the issue gave him the opportunity to play in the national arena the role of broker between Anglos and Mexicans that he had so successfully played in his hometown.[49]

At the convention, the drive against Simpson-Mazzoli originated among Chicano activists who were for the most part not even delegates. Highly visible were Delores Huerta of the United Farm Workers union and Mario Obledo, under whose leadership LULAC had emerged as perhaps the most recalcitrant opponent of Simpson-Mazzoli.[50] As suggested earlier, this and other positions taken by the organization, including its vocal opposition to the Reagan administration's Central American policies, were generally regarded as reflecting Obledo's personal views more than those of his approximately 5,000 middle-aged members. But that did not seem to diminish Obledo's clout on this issue at the convention.

On the Sunday afternoon before the opening day of the convention, the activist strategy emerged quickly. At a meeting of the Hispanic Caucus, delegates were urged to abstain on the first ballot. By thus embarrassing Mondale as he aimed for an overwhelming first-ballot victory, the anti-Simpson-Mazzoli forces were counting on extracting even stronger commitments from the candidate, who had continued to qualify his opposition to the legislation in an effort to placate both his union and Mexican-American supporters. On the sidelines, quietly supporting the abstention effort, were operatives of candidate Gary Hart, hoping at least to slow down the frontrunner's momentum.

The Mondale counterattack was handled by Mexican-American elected officials managing to walk a narrow line between opposition to Simpson-Mazzoli and loyalty to their candidate. Cisneros and especially State Senator Art Torres seized the initiative from the activists and out-organized them at crucial meetings of the Hispanic Caucus. Their efforts were complicated by the fact that several Mexican-American delegates from the Los Angeles area were heavily indebted to the Waxman-Berman clique, which (as I explained earlier) not only had long-standing ties to César Chávez and the UFW, but was also supporting Hart.

At a meeting on the first day of balloting, Mondale addressed the Hispanic Caucus. Although the candidate did not substantially change his ambiguous position on Simpson-Mazzoli, he managed to convince those present of his sympathy with their cause. The activists who had been pressing for an outright repudiation of Simpson-Mazzoli were thus denied a substantive victory. Yet by obliging Mondale to meet with the caucus, they did succeed in gaining national media attention for their efforts against immigration restriction. For Obledo, this was apparently enough; he ended his support of the abstention drive as soon as Mondale had finished addressing the caucus.

Later that same day, the abstentions having been kept to a minimum, Mondale got his overwhelming first-ballot victory. Still, several Mexican-

American delegates were mysteriously taken ill and were nowhere to be found during the balloting. By far the most serious illness occurred in the California delegation, where the activists and Hart forces together succeeded in producing some twenty-seven abstentions.[51]

Here again, Chicano activists clearly created brokering opportunities for Mexican-American politicians. Yet such opportunities carried risks: if Cisneros and Torres had not been able to rein in the abstention effort, they would have looked foolish before their Anglo colleagues. The stakes were especially high for the Los Angeles clique—because their leaders were so visibly identified with the Mondale campaign, because the abstention effort was strongest in their delegation, and because they had not saved Mondale from humiliation at the hands of Richard Santillán earlier that summer at the MAPA Convention. Thus, clique members leaned particularly hard on at least one Mexican-American delegate from the San Gabriel Valley who was contemplating abstention. As he reported later, they accused him of "embarrassing us in front of the Mondale people."

Mexican-American politicians know all too well that Chicano activists can be unreliable, even perverse, and that bickering with them can result in being stigmatized by colleagues in the Democratic Party as factious and politically inept. But these politicians also understand that by serving as brokers between the activists and the Anglo political establishment, they get to play a visible role that, given their meager political bases, they would otherwise be denied. Such is the political terrain that practitioners of elite-network politics have carved out for themselves in Los Angeles and California.

PART THREE

The National Perspective

❧ 9 ❧

The State of
Mexican-American Opinion

W hat do Mexican Americans want from politics? What are their
political goals? When such questions are raised, the discussion
typically turns to issues: what issues are of most concern to Mexican
Americans? Yet issues are hardly the only ends of politics. In today's
highly issue-oriented politics, this point needs special emphasis. For, as
the preceding analysis of political styles also underscores, not all those
involved in politics are pursuing specific policy objectives or well-
articulated, formal goals.

At one extreme, those enmeshed in the friends-and-neighbors politics
characteristic of San Antonio are preoccupied with face-to-face relationships and concrete material benefits to the virtual exclusion of specific
policy outcomes. Similarly, participants in organization politics tend to be
indifferent to issues and formal goals. To be sure, machine politicians pro-
fessed great concern with specific issues. Yet their fundamental concern
was the maintenance of their organizations. Alinsky organizers, as we
have seen, present a more complicated picture. For while their single-
minded pursuit of "power" leads them to be dismissive of issue-oriented
politics, their significant investments in substantive policy initiatives have
been increasingly evident. Nevertheless, the Alinsky emphasis clearly remains on nurturing the organization over advancing any one issue or formal goal.

Elite-network politics is very much concerned with formal goals and issues, although this doesn't mean that individual practitioners of this political style are any less cynical about issues than organization politicians. They certainly do not resemble Chicano activists who carry issues to extremes in pursuit of highly abstract notions of equality, justice, or perhaps revolutionary transformation. But elite-network politics is for Mexican Americans, as for other political actors in California, heavily issue-oriented. And this kind of politics poses specific problems for this relatively unsophisticated group.

Those problems also emerge when the focus shifts, as it did at the end of the previous chapter, away from local and state politics to the national arena. Having made this shift, I now intend to stay with it through the final three chapters—for the compelling reason that it is in the national political arena where the most powerful incentives encouraging Mexican Americans to pursue racial minority politics are found. To get at the dynamics of this process, I begin the present chapter with an analysis of survey data on Mexican-American opinion on various issues. One implication of my analysis is that such surveys have limited utility with a group, such as Mexican Americans, large numbers of whom are not here legally, are not citizens, or in numerous other ways are not completely integrated into the wider society. Another implication is that the gap between Mexican-American leaders and rank and file with regard to race issues like affirmative action reflects more than the expected distance between elites and nonelites. In chapter 10 I argue that this gap reflects the fundamental difficulties of mobilizing disadvantaged groups in this new American political system, which has weak mediating institutions but strong norms of participation and representation. Indeed, I explore the sociological and cultural as well as political-structural sources of these difficulties. Finally, in the concluding chapter I respond to criticisms of my perspective and relate it to the overarching and defining issue of Mexican-American politics—immigration.

Before beginning my issue-by-issue analysis of opinion survey data, prudence dictates a couple of caveats. First, any such exercise should be mindful that data on political *attitudes* are limited guides to political *behavior*. Observers have frequently pointed out that opinion surveys typically fail to measure how strongly respondents feel about one issue relative to others. And even when issue preferences are elicited, such responses are necessarily hypothetical and fail to take into account the effects of political context, organizational constraints, and leadership orientation. Indeed, my analysis of Mexican-American political styles has focused on just such factors, arguing that it is these, not simply rank-and-file opinion, that shape issues and give them salience.

Finally, one more caveat is in order. Although clear patterns can be discerned, the data presented here are often disparate, divergent, and confusing. In part, this is because many of the available polls survey "Hispanics" or "Latinos," thereby lumping Mexican Americans together with Puerto Ricans, Cubans, and other Spanish-speaking groups. I shall deal with such terminological shifts as they arise.

More fundamentally, these disparate numbers point to the profound methodological problems of polling a relatively uneducated and, as yet, largely unassimilated group. At issue here is the inchoate nature of public opinion among Mexican Americans, which in turn raises important questions about the adequacy of representation of Mexican-American interests in late twentieth-century America. I will address such concerns at the end of this chapter.

ABORTION

Abortion is undoubtedly the clearest example of how Mexican-American leaders have been constrained to take a position sharply at odds with rank and file sentiment. For while the leadership, particularly in California, is overwhelmingly pro-choice, Mexican Americans in general are decidedly uneasy with abortion.

Indeed, Mexican Americans are more opposed to abortion than Americans generally. A 1984 survey of Hispanics in California found that, while only 4 percent of "whites"* in California agreed that "by law, abortion should never be performed," fully 13 percent of Latinos agreed. And while 60 percent of whites felt "[b]y law, a woman should always be able to obtain an abortion as a matter of personal choice," only 40 percent of Hispanics felt this way.[1]

More recently, exit polls of Hispanics in California, Texas, and New Mexico conducted by the Southwest Voter Research Institute (SVRI) in November 1988 found that while only 33 percent of Anglos favor making abortion illegal except in the case of rape or incest, 41 percent of Latinos favor such restrictions. As SVRI concludes: "On the question of abortion, Mexican Americans are somewhat more conservative than the general population."[2]

---

* I use quotation marks here to draw the reader's attention to the fact that white and Hispanic—contrary to the way they are often used by pollsters—are not mutually exclusive categories. Indeed, as I noted in chapter 1, most Hispanics describe themselves as racially white.

Such views reflect a deeply ingrained social conservatism that Mexican Americans themselves will readily, and self-consciously, trace back to their strong family values. This social conservatism proves less troublesome to Mexican-American leaders on other issues. For example, Mexican Americans overwhelmingly support the Equal Rights Amendment[3]—apparently by even larger margins than non-Hispanics.[4] But the same is certainly not true of abortion.

More to the point, such survey data do not begin to convey how problematic abortion and similar social issues can be for Mexican-American politicians. Recall that Gloria Molina's challenge to the clique led to rumors that she was a loose woman, or perhaps a lesbian. That such accusations would fall on receptive ears is suggested by one painfully revealing incident. When Assemblywoman Molina discovered what she took to be the forced sterilization of poor Latino women in the Los Angeles County Hospital, she protested to the media. When her own mother saw her daughter's picture in the newspaper in connection with such a story, she reacted in horror, mistakenly concluding that Molina was advocating sterilization for women and therefore condoning sexual promiscuity.

Such sentiments are never voiced in public. Here again, deep cultural patterns are evident. For as Richard Rodriguez has observed in his memoir, *Hunger of Memory*, Mexican Americans have an extremely strong sense of privacy about family matters. Just as Rodriguez's mother could not fathom how movie stars could go on television talk shows and discuss details of their personal lives,[5] so did a veteran Chicana activist confess to me her amazement and contempt toward Anglo comrades who went about in the 1960s publicly denouncing their parents.

In a similar vein, the woman friend of a Mexican-American politico explained to me the intrafamily dynamics of abortion. If a Mexican-American girl gets in trouble, an abortion, though perhaps rare, is typically not out of the question. But whatever gets decided, the expectation is that the problem will be handled discreetly by the girl's *comadres** without her father ever knowing. From such attitudes it follows, I was told, that Mexican Americans don't consider abortion a suitable topic for public debate—regardless of the position taken. Certainly, Molina's experience with the mere mention of sterilization drives home the point.

Abortion then is not a very salient issue for most Mexican Americans, precisely because there is an inclination to regard it as a topic unsuitable for discussion in public with strangers. By the same token, when abortion

---

* Literally, co-mothers. For a brief explication of the *compadre* relationship, see above, page 133.

is raised, it can be highly volatile and explosive—as Mexican-American leaders know and dread. In the chapter on elite-network politics, I explained how this puts Mexican-American politicians in a tricky position vis-à-vis their constituents and is one more disincentive against building up strong community bases—at least in barrio parishes. But there are also risks and problems on the other side—from their allies in the Democratic Party.

These Mexican-American leaders certainly have practical reasons for keeping their objections to the feminist agenda to themselves. As one Chicana activist describes her situation, questioning the pro-choice position would offend her "natural allies." For her, the point was driven home when a fellow activist, a man who also happened to be a fervent pro-life advocate, spoke against abortion at a session of the Democratic Platform Committee, chaired in Los Angeles in the summer of 1984 by then congresswoman Geraldine Ferraro. That Chicano's "natural allies" responded by trying to relieve him of his minor party post.

Such episodes understandably feed the suspicions of Anglo liberals that Mexican Americans are not reliable allies. Yet one should not conclude that Molina or her adversaries in the clique are restive under the tutelage of their Democratic Party sponsors. The cleavage on social issues between liberal Democrats and Mexican Americans is substantial. But as long as Molina and her male counterparts can finesse such issues, and are not obliged to speak out aggressively in behalf of the liberal social agenda, they appear content to play out their role as junior partners in the California Democracy.

FOREIGN AND DEFENSE POLICY

Abortion is not the only issue in which Mexican-American leaders are clearly marching to a different drummer from their rank and file. The survey data with regard to foreign and defense policy are not as plentiful as for abortion, but they are equally suggestive. For example, a 1986 straw poll of Latino leaders across California found that only 15 percent favored increased defense spending,[6] while in an exit poll that November, 26 percent of California Latinos favored such an increase and 13 percent were undecided.[7]

Even more suggestive of a gap between leaders and rank and file in this area are the results of a *Los Angeles Times* poll of delegates to the 1988 Democratic National Convention. This survey reported that 87 percent of the Latino delegates favored decreased spending for national defense.[8] By contrast, a November 1988 SVREP exit poll of Latino voters in California, Texas, and New Mexico found that only 43 percent opposed increased defense spending.[9]

Central American policy evoked similar findings. In 1986, for instance, California Hispanic leaders were virtually unanimous in their opposition to military aid to the Nicaraguan rebels, while a much smaller segment of Hispanic voters in California—59 percent—opposed such aid.[10] Similarly, 66 percent of Hispanic voters in California, Texas, and New Mexico opposed military aid to the contras in 1988.[11]

Such numbers indicate that while U.S. intervention in Central America could hardly have been construed as a policy popular among Mexican Americans generally, it enjoyed more support among rank and file than among leaders. And apart from these numbers, it is my strong impression from interviews in the field that opposition to the Reagan policy in Central America loomed much larger and was sustained by much more ideological zeal among leaders than among rank and file. Certainly, the intensity of opposition expressed by such leaders as Mario Obledo, Tony Anaya, and Willie Velásquez at a 1988 conference at the Democratic Party's Roosevelt Center in Washington underscored substantial tolerance, and even support, of the Sandinista revolution.[12]

THE NEED FOR CONSENSUS

Mexican-American leaders may have the latitude to diverge from their rank and file on some issues. But they are seldom, if ever, free agents acting without constraints from their constituents. However poorly informed or organized those constituents may be, the leaders must at some point respond—or appear to respond—to the preferences, desires, and goals of the people they claim to represent. Not surprisingly, considerable effort is made to focus on issues that elicit agreement among most Mexican Americans. One such issue is the Voting Rights Act, overwhelmingly supported by Mexican Americans.[13] Indeed, as currently interpreted, the Voting Rights Act now leads to the creation of single-member districts that virtually assure the election of Mexican-American officeholders[14]—a goal that few, if any, Mexican Americans are likely to oppose, whatever the principled arguments of the opposition. And even though many Mexican Americans acknowledge that such officeholding does not necessarily constitute real power, they are not about to denounce or reject such efforts.

In a similar way, education and employment issues, however vaguely defined, also elicit widespread and generalized agreement. Throughout the 1980s and into the 1990s, whenever Mexican Americans and their leaders were asked about the key problems facing their community, these two sets of issues inevitably appeared at, or near, the top of the list.[15] Other issues, notably crime and drugs, also rank high—and these, too, get invoked as unifying themes.[16] But education and employment issues have probably been the most salient and consistently mentioned. Certainly, these classic bread-and-butter issues are what one would expect to be of greatest concern to a lower- and working-class immigrant population.

Yet it is easier for leaders to increase the number of Mexican-American officeholders—a result that, under prevailing interpretations of the Voting Rights Act, will follow more or less directly from increases in the Mexican-American population—than to deliver on education and employment issues. Added to the other constraints operating on these leaders, this means that emphasizing such popular and salient issues, though necessary, is not always straightforward. Indeed, education and employment issues often get conjoined with other less widely supported causes and ideas.

BUSING

The dynamic just described can be seen most clearly with busing. This issue peaked of course in the late 1970s, but it is not completely dead. Indeed, recent work by researchers like Gary Orfield emphasizes Mexican-American residential "segregation"[17] and the consequent need for metropolitan busing.[18] Yet regardless of how visible it is today, busing is an issue worth examining because it highlights important aspects of agenda formation among Mexican-American leaders.

Some leaders turned to busing in response to parental concerns about improving educational opportunities for Mexican-American children. Yet more important was the response of Mexican-American leaders to the concerns of black and liberal allies. As I have already indicated, busing has never been on the Mexican-American agenda in San Antonio, where the rewards forthcoming from such allies are relatively meager—and where Mexican-American politicians are not eager to give up the power they wield in the metropolitan area's many small school districts. On the other hand, Mexican-American leaders in Los Angeles, prodded by Chicano activists there, have at times advocated busing.[19]

Yet in both locales, anecdotal as well as opinion survey evidence has clearly and consistently demonstrated that Mexican-American rank and file are not enthusiastic about busing, or about desegregation generally.[20] Local observers attribute this antibusing sentiment to tight Mexican-American family bonds that result in an unwillingness to let children get too far from home and neighborhood. A common mid-morning sight in the barrio is mothers meeting their children at the schoolyard fence with the day's lunch. For such parents, the prospect of their children getting bused to some distant corner of the sprawling Los Angeles Unified School District is troubling. Because many barrio parents do not have cars available during the day, they typically ask how they are to reach their children in case of emergency. Such concerns have been raised when busing has been proposed to alleviate severely overcrowded schools. Indeed, Mexican Americans in Los Angeles have willingly accepted double and summer sessions to alleviate overcrowding in their neighborhood schools, rather then see their children bused into underutilized facilities in Anglo neighborhoods.[21]

It is also evident that Mexican Americans have not been enthusiastic about busing because of their attitudes toward blacks. As Grebler concluded from his 1965 opinion survey, "Mexican Americans are generally far more prejudiced against Negroes than against Anglos."[22] In private, many Mexican-American leaders today point to their group's racial animosity toward blacks. Putting it quite baldly, more than one leader has said to me, "We Chicanos are racists."

More generally, it is true that while Mexican Americans typically aspire to leave inner-city neighborhoods, they do not feel any special stigma associated with sending their children to predominantly Mexican-American schools, or with living in exclusively Mexican-American neighborhoods. For black Americans, such arrangements are weighted with the history of slavery and Jim Crow. Of course, Mexican Americans have also felt the burden of discrimination and exclusion. But for the most part, they take living among their own kind as unexceptional and natural, much as European immigrants have.

In defiance of these attitudes, and in spite of the fact that integration flies in the face of other favored initiatives like bilingual education and multiculturalism, Chicano activists in Los Angeles have nevertheless taken a pro-busing stand. Committed to an ideologically derived position on the importance of a "black-brown coalition," they have decided, in the words of one activist, that "on this issue, we have to educate our people." Needless to say, this statement implicitly acknowledges that busing and desegregation are not popular in the barrio.

In private, Mexican-American community and political leaders readily acknowledge these facts. But they have seldom done so in public. In addition to the pressure they feel from activists, Mexican-American politicians have been mindful of their liberal sponsors in the Democratic Party and have dealt gingerly with the issue: either supporting busing without enthusiasm, or quietly opposing it. In either case, the force of Mexican-American community sentiment has not been given full voice.

BILINGUAL EDUCATION

Bilingual education is another issue by means of which Mexican-American leaders attempt to respond to barrio concerns about education. But instead of identifying Mexican-American concerns with those of blacks, bilingual education differentiates them. Indeed, the protection of bilingual education programs has led some Mexican-American leaders to temper their enthusiasm for busing and desegregation efforts. In any event, bilingual education—unlike busing—enjoys a good deal of support among Mexican Americans generally. Yet there is also considerable confusion as to what Mexican Americans mean when they express support for such programs. Indeed, while bilingual education differs from other issues examined here in not presenting a cleavage between leaders and rank and file, the confusion surrounding it has been exacerbated, and even fostered, by leaders pursuing their own agendas.

Mexican-American leaders are certainly highly disposed toward bilingual education—and have been for some time. Rodolfo de la Garza interviewed 241 Mexican-American appointed, elected, and community leaders in several different cities from 1978 to 1980. Ninety-seven percent of these individuals, who constituted nearly the entire universe of Mexican-American leadership at the time, supported bilingual education "at least in principle"; and 67 percent "strongly support(ed) bilingual education, including a kindergarten–twelfth grade program."[23]

A 1983 survey of 448 Hispanic (not just Mexican-American) leaders conducted for the Hispanic Policy Development Project by Daniel Yankelovich revealed similar levels of leadership support for bilingual education. Almost three out of four of these leaders felt bilingual education to be "worth the effort." The same proportion agreed: "Bilingual programs will help Hispanic children become more employable." Finally, 71 percent disagreed with the statement: "Bilingual programs put Hispanic children at a disadvantage because they won't learn English as quickly as they might otherwise."[24]

More recent evidence from the Southwest Voter Registration Education Project indicates continued leadership support for bilingual education. In 1985 and 1986 straw polls of those attending regional leadership meetings in Texas and California revealed overwhelming support for increased spending on bilingual education programs. Only slightly more enthusiastic than leaders from other regions were those from California, who were characterized by SVREP as "almost unanimous" in their support for increased bilingual education funding.[25]

Rank-and-file Mexican Americans have similarly supported bilingual education, though by less decisive margins. A 1981–1982 survey by Southwest Voters found that 89 percent of Mexican-American citizens in San Antonio and Los Angeles agreed: "It is a good idea to have bilingual education in the schools."[26] SVREP exit polls in the 1984 and 1986 general elections in Texas found about three-fourths of Mexican-American voters supported increased funding for bilingual education.[27] In November 1988, SVREP exit polling in Texas found marginally lower support— 71 percent—for increased spending on bilingual education among Mexican Americans.[28] And in California that year, SVREP found that only 66 percent of Mexican-American voters favored bilingual spending increases.[29]

Other polls report similar levels of support for bilingual education. A 1982 survey of Hispanics in Los Angeles and New York City (which therefore included many non-Mexican Americans) by researchers at Columbia University concluded: "Only a small minority [about 10 percent] of Hispanics oppose bilingual education as a general idea."[30] A 1984 poll by researchers at Cal Tech found that 69 percent of Hispanics in California (the overwhelming majority of whom are Mexican Americans) favored "teaching non-English speaking students in their own language as well as English."[31] A 1985 Texas Poll reported that 71 percent of Mexican Americans there (compared to 39 percent of Anglos) said yes when asked: "Should schools be required to have Spanish speaking teachers available to teach children who speak Spanish in the home?"[32] Finally, a 1988 poll by the Rose Institute at Claremont McKenna College found that 67 percent of California Hispanics disagreed with the assertion: "Bilingual education does not help children learn better."[33]

At the same time, a discernible segment of Mexican Americans is hostile to bilingual education. I think of the "brown necks" described to me by a Mexican-American state legislator representing a working-class district in San Antonio: typical is the man who drives about town in his pickup truck, seeing a sign in Spanish and exclaiming: "That asshole thinks I can't speak English!" Or I think of the young father, living in a *colonia*° along the Mexican border, who reacts to the mere mention of bilingual education by insisting: "I'm an American and I want my children to learn

---

° An unincorporated subdivision to which urban residents aspiring to own their own homes are drawn by inexpensive land that developers have not been required to provide with adequate water, drainage, sewage, roads, and other infrastructure.

English." These anecdotes help explain why 41 percent of California Hispanics voted in support of a successful 1986 ballot initiative amending the state constitution to designate English the state's official language;[34] and why in an opinion survey two years later, 58 percent favored "making English the official language of California."[35] Such views may also explain why San Antonio congressman Albert Bustamente—the son of migrant farmworkers who, at the age of 9, could neither read nor write English—has opposed bilingual education.[36]

Though perhaps a minority view among Mexican Americans, resistance to bilingual education is evident when the questions posed are less general and more probing. At that point, a more complicated picture emerges. For example, a 1983 *Los Angeles Times* poll asked: "If some public school classes are taught in Spanish, do you think that helps Spanish-speaking students to learn more quickly; or do you think it hurts their education because they learn to speak English more slowly?" Only 45 percent of California Hispanics felt that such efforts help, while 34 percent felt they hurt.[37]

Nevertheless, there is also widespread popular support for the goals of bilingual education—defined either as providing temporary or transitional help to Spanish-speaking children, so that they might eventually be taught entirely in English; or as maintaining the Spanish language and Mexican-American culture. A national survey conducted in 1987 by the Educational Testing Service (ETS) found substantial support for both approaches among Mexican-American parents.[38] Similarly, the Columbia survey mentioned above found that 36 percent of Hispanic parents in Los Angeles and New York City felt that non-English-speaking children should be "taught in both Spanish and English for a few years until they can learn how to speak English," while an additional 34 percent indicated such children should be "taught in both Spanish and English throughout their education so that they can learn both languages." Only 28 percent of the Hispanic parents said that non-English-speaking students should be taught only in English—the so-called "immersion" method.[39]

In that same survey, 67 percent of Hispanic parents said children who already know English when they enter the public schools should be taught in Spanish *and* English. When asked what should be the primary goal of educating Hispanic children in both languages, 36 percent of the respondents said it was to ensure that Hispanic children do not fall behind in their education; 34 percent said it was to help preserve the cultural identity of Hispanic people; and 25 percent said both were equally important.[40] These figures led the Columbia researchers to conclude that "the majority of Hispanics support bilingual education not only for pragmatic purposes but for its contribution to the preservation of Hispanic culture."[41]

Based on a sample that includes Puerto Ricans as well as Mexicans, these findings cannot be definitive with regard to the latter. Yet their thrust is confirmed by other surveys indicating that Mexican-American parents attach considerable importance to their children being able to speak Spanish. For example, in the 1983 *Los Angeles Times* poll cited earlier, 85 percent of Hispanics in California said it was "very important" to "preserve the Spanish language for their children."[42] The 1987 ETS national survey just mentioned found that 75 percent of Mexican-American parents said it was important that their children speak Spanish well.[43] Finally, a Field survey that same year reported that 66 percent of Hispanics in California felt it was a "good thing" for immigrant groups to preserve their foreign languages.[44]

Yet it must also be noted that there is overwhelming agreement among Mexican Americans on the importance of learning English. Once again suggestive is the Columbia survey, in which 89 percent of the respondents said it was "very important" for Hispanics living in the United States to speak English well; another 10 percent said it was "important."[45] Indeed, 48 percent of the Hispanics in that survey felt the country would be better off if immigrants stopped speaking their native language.[46] Corroborating and more definitive evidence is offered by the ETS study, which reports more than 97 percent of Mexican-American parents believe it to be "very important" for their children to speak English well.[47]

More important, such attitudes appear to translate into practice. In the ETS survey, for example, more than 46 percent of the Mexican-American parents rated their ability to read, write, understand, and speak English as "not very well" or "not at all." Yet almost 87 percent of those parents rated their children's English competence as "very well" or "pretty well."[48] The Columbia survey came up with similar findings.[49] Moreover, analyses of census data cited earlier confirm that not only are Mexican-American children rapidly learning English, they are also losing Spanish.[50]

To sum up: support for bilingual education, or even for the maintenance of Spanish, should not necessarily be construed as opposition to learning English. But neither should insistence on learning English be construed as indifference or hostility to the maintenance of Spanish.[51] That learning English and maintaining Spanish are not regarded as mutually exclusive by many Hispanics is suggested by the above-mentioned Yankelovich survey, in which 83 percent of Hispanic leaders agreed: "Bilingual programs are essential in helping Hispanic children to learn

English and to do better in school"; and 63 percent agreed: "Bilingual programs are important to maintaining Hispanic traditions."[52] It would appear that Mexican Americans—along with other Hispanics, not to mention Anglos—tend to want it both ways.

Yet when Mexican Americans are presented with a choice between English and Spanish, or when that choice is somehow constrained, most seem to opt for English. For example, a 1988 Field survey asked California citizens if they "would be willing or unwilling to pay ten dollars more per year in taxes so that the public schools could teach Hispanic and Asian children in their native language if they don't know English well?" While 74 percent of Anglos were unwilling, so were a majority—51 percent—of Hispanics.[53] Even more starkly, when asked by ETS if schools should teach in Spanish if it took away from learning English, Mexican-American parents rejected instruction in Spanish nearly four to one.[54]

Striking as these findings are, they have very little impact—in part because the current debate over bilingual education is far too muddled to present Mexican Americans with any such stark choice between Spanish and English. That muddle is reflected in rank-and-file views. A little-noted finding from the survey data is that Mexican Americans, and Hispanics generally, are confused about bilingual education, and that the same individuals often express contradictory or inconsistent opinions. For example, in a 1984 poll of Spanish-surnamed registered voters in Phoenix, 70 percent agreed: "Bilingual education should be used to help children keep their native language and culture as well as learn English." But 88 percent of that same sample also agreed: "Bilingual education should be used *only to help children learn English*" (my emphasis).[55]

Similar inconsistencies were found in the Columbia study cited earlier. In that survey, 47 percent of the respondents who favored all-English immersion programs for non-English-speaking children, also favored bilingual programs for English-speaking children. And 62 percent of those who said non-English-speaking children should be in bilingual programs only until they learned English, also said that English-speaking students ought to be in bilingual programs. Finally, 55 percent of those who identified the primary purpose of bilingual education to be the prevention of non-English-speaking students falling behind in school, also said that students who already know how to speak English should be in bilingual programs.[56] Such findings led the Columbia researchers to observe:

In general the Hispanic sample had low levels of formal education. Some of the people we interviewed obviously did not understand some of the words used in the questionnaire. For example, phrases like "cultural heritage" and "cultural identity" did not have clear meaning to some of the Hispanic respondents who would ask the interviewers what these terms meant. . . . It is likely that some of the respondents did not understand the nuances of some of the questions.[57]

The ETS researchers similarly found Hispanic parents confused about bilingual education. As they noted:

There was as much "teaching" as there was gathering information concerning the three types of programs—"bilingual, transitional and immersion." Many of the concepts we were asking about are abstract, or idiosyncratic to educators and may well have "lost something in the translation."[58]

Much of this confusion is presumably due to the fact that poorly educated Mexican immigrants are more preoccupied with economic survival than with the specifics of their children's educational programs. Indeed, the ETS researchers report that about 38 percent of Mexican-American parents surveyed did not know whether or not their child's school encouraged, discouraged, or was neutral about the use of a non-English language at school.[59] Forty-five percent of Mexican-American parents did not know whether their child's school provided special help to children who spoke Spanish.[60] As a study of bilingual education in the Los Angeles Unified School District tellingly points out: "Bilingual education, in LAUSD at least, is a program initiated and shepherded by mostly middle-class Chicano activists—not barrio masses."[61]

Yet these responses may imply more than a lack of attention, information, or education. Among Mexican Americans, one discerns fundamental misgivings about the benefits—and the likely costs—of assimilation into American society. Presumably, such sentiments are similar to those of other newly arrived groups struggling to become Americans. Yet there is evidence that the struggle is especially intense for Mexicans—more so than for Asians, for example. The 1984 Cal Tech survey cited earlier found that although similar majorities of Hispanics and Asians in California reported a language other than English as their primary language, Hispanics were much more supportive of bilingual education than Asians (69 percent versus 51 percent).[62]

Similarly, the ETS study cited earlier, which surveyed Asians as well as Mexicans and other Hispanics, indicates that Asians have a much more straightforward assimilationist stance, at least when it comes to language. For example, Hispanic parents seem to attach more importance to the maintenance of Spanish than Asian parents do to their various mother tongues. Indeed, three-quarters of the Mexican Americans indicated it was "very important" to them that their children speak Spanish well, but only 53 percent of the Asians felt this way about their children speaking their mother tongue.[63]

As for attitudes toward bilingual education, 60 percent of Asian parents in the ETS survey felt that teaching in a non-English language interferes with learning English, while 43 percent of Mexican-American parents did.[64] Even more tellingly, when asked how non-English-speaking students should be taught to read and write, 67 percent of the Asian parents said "only in English," whereas just 28 percent of the Mexican-American parents so responded.[65]

This pattern persists even after various demographic and other background variables are controlled, leading the ETS researchers to conclude: "There appears to be a cultural difference between the Asian and Hispanic parents with respect to having their children maintain their native language."[66] For Mexican Americans specifically, some of this difference may be explained by the uniqueness of their experience: unlike other immigrants, Mexicans arrive here from a neighboring nation that has suffered military defeat at the hands of the United States; and they settle predominantly in a region that was once part of their homeland. As I have already noted, Mexican Americans enjoy a sense of being on their own turf that is not shared by other immigrants. This fact, along with continual infusions of new Spanish monolinguals, would arguably account for much of the resistance, if not to learning English, then to abandoning Spanish. It also helps to explain the dramatically low naturalization rates that Mexican immigrants here have exhibited over the decades.[67] On the other hand, it is worth noting that, on the language issues being discussed, Cubans and Puerto Ricans—neither of whom shares in this unique history, but both of whom have their own problematic ties to the United States—often appear to be even less assimilationist than Mexicans.[68]

Whatever its origins, this desire to retain Spanish is at odds with contemporary social dynamics, which virtually assure that Mexican immigrants—at least their children and grandchildren—will learn English and forget Spanish. This seemingly inexorable process creates intense misgivings and anxieties among many Mexican Americans, especially the more educated and upwardly mobile. Recall from chapter 1 the Yale undergraduate who, having lost Spanish himself, was determined to pass it on to his own children.

Another manifestation of such thinking can be found in a recent publication of the Southwest Voter Registration Education Project. Commenting on the 1988 general election in Texas, SVREP researchers observed:

> Texas Mexican voters were also clearly unified on the issues involving *their* language. By large margins, both Dukakis and Bush supporters favored increases in spending for bilingual education in the schools. (My emphasis)[69]

Now, it is clear that the language referred to here is Spanish. Yet SVREP researchers are stretching the point when one considers that fully 40 percent of native-born Hispanics in Texas consider English their "usual language."[70]

Such elite attitudes, however, are different from those of the rank and file. For one thing, the inconsistencies of leaders cannot be readily ascribed to lack of education or sophistication about issues of language and culture. Quite the opposite. For among university-educated Mexican Americans in particular, these issues tend to be highly salient and politically charged. Indeed, I would argue that among the Mexican-American elite, one can discern with particular clarity the ambivalence toward assimilation that, to varying degrees, is felt by the majority.

Yet it would be a mistake to reduce these elite sentiments to intellectual confusion or psychological anxiety. For the muddles over bilingual education, and language in general, have been significantly conditioned by the political context in which the Mexican-American elite operates.

As I suggested earlier, bilingual education has been important to Mexican-American leaders as an issue that differentiates their claims on the polity from those of other disadvantaged groups, especially blacks. But it is also clear that bilingual education appeals to leaders as an issue that can bring Mexicans together with Puerto Ricans, Cubans, and other Latinos.[71] Yet, in order to avoid questions that would create dissension among the diverse participants in this coalition, and also to minimize the opposition of Anglos, bilingual education advocates have kept their objectives vague. As Senator Ralph Yarborough, principal sponsor of the Bilingual Education Act of 1968, commented at the time: "Every time people ask me, 'What does bilingual education mean?' I reply that it means different things to different people."[72] More precisely, as education historian Diane Ravitch explains about the passage of that original legislation:

> Supporters of bilingual education thought that they had won a victory for preservation of non-English cultures and languages, but congressional supporters thought of bilingual education as a remedial program to help

children become literate in the English language and then join English-speaking classes.[73]

Today, this politically functional confusion persists. Take, for example, the Hispanic Policy Development Project's characterization of Yankelovich's findings on the views of Hispanic officials on bilingual education:

> The majority of our officials displayed a moderate position on the issue. Only a tiny fraction (1 percent) prefer the radical option of offering all courses in Spanish. A 75-percent majority favors the teaching of basic subjects in English, with supplementary courses in Spanish.[74]

Yet this "moderate" stance also includes what appears to be the highly controversial maintenance view. For, as indicated earlier, 63 percent of these Hispanic officials agree: "Bilingual programs are important to maintaining Hispanic traditions." Even more provocatively, 78 percent of these officials agree: "Since Hispanics are becoming a very large part of the American population, bilingual programs are equally important for Anglo children."[75]

This vagueness—which, it must be said, often verges on deception—has allowed some Mexican-American and Hispanic leaders to advance their extreme, maintenance version of bilingual education. For unlike an issue such as immigration, which commands the attention of many disparate interest groups, bilingual education is a classic special-interest issue whose advocates can wage their battles in courtrooms and agency offices without full-scale mobilization of supporters. All such advocates need is a lack of opposition, which this vagueness of goals permits. After two decades of such maneuverings by their leaders, it is no wonder that Mexican Americans—quite apart from whatever ambivalence they may feel about assimilation—are left confused about bilingual education.

RACE AND DISCRIMINATION

The preceding discussions of busing and bilingual education underscore the enormous influence of black politics on Mexican Americans. Indeed, busing and bilingual education offer obverse images of the same political dynamics. On the one hand, busing represents the efforts of at least some Mexican-American leaders (especially in Los Angeles) to articulate their group's interests as similar to those of blacks. The resulting failure points up the different socioeconomic experiences and divergent political goals of the two groups.

Bilingual education, on the other hand, is predicated on such divergence, and represents an explicit effort to distinguish Mexican-American

interests from those of blacks. Yet paradoxically, this very effort at differentiation occurs within the framework of our post-civil-rights, affirmative
action regime, in which Mexican Americans compete with blacks to carve
out special claims and group rights. Thus, it is difficult, if not impossible,
to discuss Mexican-American political goals without reference to those
of blacks.

In chapter 1, I presented the surprising evidence that despite what
their leaders say, most Mexican Americans identify themselves in the census as "white," while about 1 percent say they are "black" and the remainder put themselves in a vaguely defined "other race" category. These
findings raise questions about how Mexican Americans view their situation with regard to what is, for blacks, the critical issue: racial discrimination. An examination of the evidence indicates that, here as elsewhere,
Mexican Americans fall somewhere between blacks and Anglos.[76]

There is no better place to begin such an examination than with the
observation of Grebler and his colleagues:

> Prejudice has been a loaded topic of conversation in any Mexican-Ameri-
> can community. Indeed, merely calling Mexican Americans "a minority,"
> and implying that the population is the victim of prejudice and discrimi-
> nation, has caused irritation among many who prefer to believe themselves
> indistinguishable from white Americans. As mentioned earlier, there are
> light-skinned Mexican Americans who have never experienced the faintest
> discrimination in public facilities, and many with ambiguous surnames
> have also escaped the experiences of the more conspicuous members of
> the group. . . . Finally, there is the inescapable fact that . . . even compar-
> atively dark-skinned Mexicans—such as some consular officials or
> tourists—and also the United States-born middle-class "Spanish" could get
> service even in the most discriminatory parts of Texas a generation or two
> ago. All of these equivocations, inconsistencies and changes in the actual
> position of Mexican Americans have meant a long and bitter controversy
> among middle-class Mexican Americans about defining the ethnic group
> as disadvantaged by any other criterion than individual failures. The re-
> curring evidence that well-groomed and well-spoken Mexican Americans
> can receive normal treatment has continuously undermined either group
> or individual definition of the situation as one entailing discrimination.[77]

Subsequent research highlights the subtlety of Anglo-Mexican relations in the Southwest, particularly in Texas. In his meticulous study of
the Raza Unida takeover of Crystal City, John Staples Shockley notes that,
even in this remote South Texas town where "the Anglos were unquestionably in control of the situation," Mexicans were never completely deprived of educational opportunities or access to the political process.[78]

Indeed, Shockley emphasizes that, as of 1963 in Crystal City, "the Anglos did not rule by discrimination against all Mexican Americans in all areas."[79] He goes on to emphasize:

> Thus, the issue of racial discrimination was in several respects quite different from the more clear-cut, obvious discrimination existing in the South between Negroes and whites. . . . discrimination revolved at least as much around questions of class and of culture as of race. If the Mexicans in the community were willing and—at least as important—were able to shed their culture, then there was a good chance that they would be accepted by many Anglos in the community, at least in a number of activities.[80]

The complexity of Mexican-Anglo relations was compounded by local variation. With regard to the critical issue of segregated schools, Clifton McCleskey characterizes the situation for Mexican Americans throughout Texas:

> The segregation of Mexican-Americans from Anglo children that was practiced in Texas until after World War II was a matter of local policy rather than state-declared policy. Such was not true of the discrimination against blacks. The Texas constitution as adopted in 1876 required separate schools for white and black children . . . [81]

This pattern of wide local variation is highlighted in a recent historical monograph, *Anglos and Mexicans in the Making of Texas, 1836–1986.* Author David Montejano acknowledges that, unlike blacks, Mexicans in Texas faced no constitutionally sanctioned separate but equal policies, and that, "[a]ccording to the prevailing jurisprudence, Mexicans were 'Caucasian.' "[82] Yet throughout his study, Montejano also emphasizes "the complex character of Mexican-Anglo relations."[83] Writing of the 1930s, he offers this example: "In some counties, Mexican and Anglos were completely separate. In others, there was an easy mingling among the two 'races' and few social distinctions were drawn between them."[84]

Montejano goes on to quote an Anglo school superintendent, recently moved to a Gulf Coast town from Central Texas, whose observations bring both sides of the coin into relief:

> In Caldwell County if a Mexican tried to sit by you someone would knock him for a row of stumps. At a barbecue here I saw some old Mexicans rubbing up along against white women. They mix here like one race. You don't know how disgusting it makes you feel.[85]

Montejano then concludes:

In South Texas, then, there were a number of perplexing contrasts in human relations—"white primaries" in some places, political machines in others; segregation here, integration there; and so on.[86]

Writing from a Marxian perspective, Montejano traces such diversity in Texas to different class relations under ranching and farming modes of production. He argues that the organic, reciprocal relations of the paternalistic ranches gave way to the more rigid, oppressive relations of commercialized agriculture, which in turn were supplanted by the less formal social controls of urban Texas.[87] Whatever its etiology, this diversity of local conditions has characterized the Mexican-American experience not just in Texas, but throughout the Southwest—a point emphasized repeatedly by the Grebler study.[88]

Of course, under conditions of outright peonage such as existed in Mexico, or of systematic controls on the mobility of black labor such as were established in the antebellum South, this diversity of conditions would have limited import. But in the much more open environment of the nineteenth-century frontier or of the twentieth-century West, this diversity afforded Mexican Americans opportunities to get out from under oppressive situations—or at least to pierce the veil of what, in many instances, might have otherwise been perceived as unalterable circumstances.

The most obvious mechanism by which such dynamics came into play was the migrant labor stream. Illustrative are the recollections of a San Antonio native who related to me how, as a child, she left town each spring with her family and followed the harvest north:

> In Texas we knew whose front yard we could not enter and whose kids we could not play with. In Oregon the farmers we worked for every year let us play with their kids, and their wives came over to cook with our mothers and learned how to make tortillas. And the housing we were provided up there was better than what we had back home.

Perhaps such positive experiences can be attributed to the fact that Mexican-American farmworkers often traveled in small family groups, thus posing fewer threats to local mores than, say, large numbers of unattached males. It may also be that the temporary nature of such visits facilitated acceptance by farmers in need of the migrants' labor, and by merchants eager for their business. In any event, I heard similarly positive accounts from other Mexican Americans who had been part of the migrant stream.[89]

In his study of Crystal City, Shockley echoes such accounts, and emphasizes their implications for life in Texas upon the migrants' return:

[Because] they tended to earn higher wages and meet with less racial discrimination when they worked in the north . . . they were less susceptible
to Anglo pressure upon their return. It was more difficult for the Anglos
to attempt to acculturate or control them.[90]

Another path out of isolated Southwestern communities was World
War II mobilization. In the course of numerous conversations, many
Mexican-American veterans volunteered to me that the war had been a
positive experience. As a San Antonio lawyer and former Democratic officeholder wryly noted:

Nobody crapped on Mexicans up North. . . . Up in New Jersey a Mexican
couldn't keep the girls away. Up North we were "Latin lovers." Back in
Texas after the War we were "fuckin' Mexicans."

Another veteran, a small businessman and Republican Party activist,
claims that World War II gave him and his brothers the opportunity to
find out that "we were just another ethnic group . . . and we were just as
good and could compete with Italians from Philadelphia and Irish from
New York." During the late 1960s, the Grebler study came across similar accounts in interviews across the Southwest.[91]

Here again, the contrast with blacks is striking. When they went off to
fight fascist racism in World War II, black Americans did so in segregated
units—unlike Mexican Americans. And of course when blacks moved out
of the rural South, they were all too frequently disappointed by what they
found in the cities of the North.

This is not to say that the migrant labor stream or wartime military service were uniformly positive experiences for Mexican Americans.[92] But
such examples do indicate that, for many, there have been significant opportunities to escape the often harshly restrictive environments of the
Southwest. Mexican Americans may have harbored few illusions about
their lives on the ranches of South Texas or in the copper mines of Arizona. But experiences outside the region have offered grounds for hope
that elsewhere America was different.

Indeed, from such experiences the middle-aged San Antonio housewife described above, who went on to become a resolute and often feared
COPS leader, says she learned that "there are good Anglos and bad Anglos." A similarly revealing perspective was offered by a school board
"warlord" in San Antonio, whose family did not follow the migrant stream
but was nevertheless rather poor. Lamenting Mexican-American tendencies to boisterous factionalism, this young, college-educated politico
observed that "there seems to be one big Anglo mind out there that qui-

etly gets things done." When I asked whether I was part of that mastermind, he quickly replied, "No, you're from the Northeast."

Such patterns of individual experience and subsequent interpretation presumably explain what Grebler wrote two decades ago:

> A curious phenomenon noticed early in the research probably reflects the great milieu variations: Quite a few respondents who *have* experienced discrimination fail to generalize their resentment about it, but continue to particularize incidents and places and times.[93]

Since then, the discrimination experienced by Mexican Americans, who have increasingly concentrated in urban areas away from the oppressive circumstances of rural communities, has arguably diminished. The point is even acknowledged by advocates such as SVREP, whose researchers, in analyzing their own survey data, observe:

> Older Mexican Americans experienced explicit and harsh discrimination in almost all aspects of their daily lives, while the younger generation has faced real but, in all probability, less severe and less overt discrimination.[94]

The operative question thus becomes: how severe is the discrimination actually experienced by Mexican Americans today? Survey evidence confirms that Mexicans feel much less discriminated against than blacks. Extremely revealing in this regard is a widely cited 1970 study of blacks and Mexican Americans in Houston. Focusing on participation in voluntary organizations—which, in the case of blacks, is generally regarded as a response to racial discrimination—the authors hypothesized that since Mexican Americans as a group share "similar socioeconomic composition" with blacks, and since the two groups "have both been targets of white discrimination," Mexican Americans would also resemble blacks in their high level of participation in voluntary organizations. But discovering that, in fact, Mexican Americans in Houston participated much less than similarly situated blacks, the authors were at a loss to explain "these discrepant findings." Indeed, blinkered by their assumptions, the authors ignored their own data, which revealed that Mexican Americans in Houston experienced—subjectively and objectively—less discrimination than blacks there.[95]

More recent research confirms my point. For example, Cal Tech researchers Bruce Cain and Roderick Kiewiet found in their 1984 survey that while 42 percent of blacks in California felt blacks "get fewer opportunities than they deserve," only 23 percent of Latinos described their situation in such terms. Moreover, only 8 percent of Asians so characterized their situation.[96] In the same survey, while only 21 percent of blacks in California felt "most Americans are not prejudiced" against them, 36 percent of Latinos felt this way—and 42 percent of Asians.[97] Finally, 61 percent of blacks in this survey claimed to have "personally experienced discrimination," but only 35 percent of Latinos did.[98] Curiously, a greater proportion of Asians than Latinos—45 percent—said they had personally encountered discrimination.[99]

Still more recent evidence confirms this general pattern of difference between blacks and Mexicans on the one hand, and between Asians and Mexicans on the other. A January 1989 *Los Angeles Times* poll of Southern Californians found that while 49 percent of blacks claimed to have personally experienced at least some discrimination, only 29 percent of Latinos so claimed. And again, Latinos reported less discrimination than Asians—41 percent of whom claimed having experienced at least some. Indeed, Latinos in Southern California reported less discrimination against them than Jews did—36 percent of whom claimed to have experienced some sort of discrimination.[100] These findings do not mean that Latinos never feel discriminated against. But they do suggest that this group experiences less discrimination than other groups, blacks in particular.

AFFIRMATIVE ACTION

Even in San Antonio, where memories of Texas-style discrimination are still fresh, Mexican Americans are less preoccupied with gaining restitution for past wrongs than with taking advantage of present and future opportunities. As one politico put it:

> I don't care about whether the Anglos are willing to invite me home to dinner or let me marry their sister. All I care about is that they are willing to give us the seats on the city council that we deserve.

For Mexican Americans like him, doing well is the best revenge.

Yet when Mexican Americans say that "all we want is to be treated fair," it is not always clear what they mean. Some mean merely the chance to compete with Anglos, while others mean the more certain assurances of affirmative action quotas. However "fair" is defined, the concept is less emotionally charged for Mexican Americans than for blacks. For although they have endured segregation, employment discrimination, disenfranchisement, and other injustices, Mexican Americans have never experienced these as systematically or completely as have blacks.

More precisely, they have never experienced the extremes of intimacy and humiliation with dominant whites that blacks experienced under slavery and Jim Crow. As a result, Mexican Americans have had more social and psychic space in which to anchor themselves. They certainly seem less focused on acceptance or rejection by their "betters." In this regard, the democratic ethos of the frontier West, as compared with the aristocratic tendencies of Southern plantation culture, may have worked to their benefit.

Moreover, the knowledge that they chose to immigrate, and could choose to return home, must have softened many of the blows endured by Mexicans. Along with other immigrants in America, Mexican Americans found considerable comfort and shelter in their homogeneous enclaves. Again this contrasts with the experience of blacks, who were deprived, by slavery and segregation, of a strong sense of the appropriateness of their own distinctive institutions. As I indicated earlier, the barrio has never borne as heavy a stigma for Mexicans as the ghetto has for blacks.

Yet when it comes to estimating how these perceptions translate into policy preferences, the available evidence is scanty. In the *Los Angeles Times* poll cited above, 60 percent of blacks disagreed with the assertion: "These days you hear too much about the rights of minorities and not enough about the rights of the majority," while 49 percent of Latinos (and 42 percent of Asians) disagreed. Similarly, when asked, "Do you think the government is paying too much attention to blacks and other minority groups, or paying about the right amount of attention to them or do you think the government is paying too little attention to blacks and other minority groups?" 74 percent of blacks said "too little," while 45 percent of Latinos so replied.[101]

For such questions, the difference between black and Latino responses is not always statistically significant. But that difference invariably lies in the same direction poll after poll. Take, for example, a 1982 Field poll of English-speaking adults in California. Responding to the assertion: "Government should not make a special effort to improve the position of Blacks and minorities because they should help themselves," only 18 percent of blacks agreed, while 33 percent of Hispanics and 50 percent of "whites" agreed.[102]

The same poll asserts: "To make up for past discrimination women and members of minority groups should be given special treatment in getting jobs and places in college." While 67 percent of California blacks agreed with this position, 45 percent of Hispanics did, and only 19 percent of "whites."[103] Finally, in response to the assertion: "Business should be required to hire a certain number of minority workers and women even if this means some Whites and men would not be hired," 62 percent of blacks agreed, but only 43 of Hispanics did, and 25 percent of "whites."[104]

Later in the decade, the Field poll asked similar questions of blacks,

Hispanics, and Asians. In 1988 Field reported that while 56 percent of California blacks favored being granted "special preferences" in hiring and promotional practices, only 36 percent of Hispanics did—and 15 percent of Asians. In the same survey, 55 percent of California blacks favored being granted "special preferences" for college admission, compared to 37 percent of Hispanics and 20 percent of Asians.[105] Again, these findings do not indicate that no Mexican Americans ever seek "special preferences." Some clearly do. But most do not, and the difference between Mexican Americans and blacks clearly persists.

Turning to the evidence on Mexican-American leaders' views about preferential treatment and affirmative action, one again encounters the pattern of Mexican Americans falling between the extremes of black and Anglo opinion. In a 1988 *Los Angeles Times* poll of delegates to the Democratic National Convention, 64 percent of black delegates favored quotas to support affirmative action for minority employment, while 56 percent of Latino delegates did—and 32 percent of Anglo delegates. Conversely, only 35 percent of black delegates favored affirmative action without quotas, while 42 percent of Latino delegates took this position, and 64 percent of Anglos did.[106]

At the same time, the 1983 Yankelovich survey sponsored by the Hispanic Policy Development Project found that 57 percent of Hispanic leaders cited the "failure of the [Reagan] administration to support affirmative action programs" as a serious problem for Hispanics.[107] Taken together, these findings suggest that Mexican-American leaders are more supportive of affirmative action—quotas in particular—than their rank and file.

To be sure, the evidence for this conclusion is hardly definitive. The fact that "quotas" were not mentioned in any of the surveys of Mexican-American rank and file leaves the question frustratingly unresolved. Nonetheless, it is worth noting that only 2 percent of Hispanic delegates to the 1988 Democratic Convention opposed affirmative action in any form—compared to the much higher proportion of such opposition generally reported in Field's nonelite surveys. Such data confirm my field observations that Mexican-American leaders are out in front of their rank and file in supporting preferential treatment for their group. Moreover, it is no accident that this gap appears on an issue touching so directly on race. As we saw with busing (and will see presently with immigration), the temptation of race politics is one to which Mexican-American leaders today are extremely susceptible.

IMMIGRATION

Immigration has probably been the issue most visibly identified with Mexican Americans in recent years. And no wonder. It is arguably the most important issue facing Mexican Americans today. For not only does immigration determine the size and composition of the Mexican-American community, it also fundamentally affects the well-being of that community.

Yet the importance of immigration does not mean that Mexican-American opinion on this complicated issue is easy to characterize. Mexican Americans are like other Americans in this regard: they display a certain schizophrenia about immigrants and immigration. Indeed, there is a tendency among Mexican Americans to disapprove of immigrants generally, but to approve of those they know specifically; or to disapprove of immigrants now arriving, but to praise those already settled.[108] If anything, the unique circumstances of Mexicans in this country, along with the size of the present influx, undoubtedly cause Mexican Americans to feel such contradictory sentiments with particular intensity.

The most comprehensive poll of Hispanic attitudes about immigration was jointly undertaken in 1983 by V. Lance Tarrance and Associates and Peter D. Hart Research Associates. Sponsored by the Federation for American Immigration Reform (FAIR), the principal immigration restriction lobby, this survey was also the most controversial.

Yet many of the findings from the Tarrance-Hart survey were highly predictable. For example, Tarrance-Hart reported that a solid majority of Hispanics—74 percent—favored amnesty for illegal immigrants living here.[109] Confirmed by many other polls, this level of support for amnesty among Mexican Americans hardly seems surprising.[110]

But even such levels of support indicate something short of unanimity. Indeed, several other surveys found less solid support for amnesty. For instance, the 1984 Cal Tech survey cited earlier found that only 61 percent of Hispanics in California (most of whom are Mexican Americans) favored amnesty for illegals.[111] And in 1985, a Texas Poll posed the question: "Do you think people who come into the U.S. illegally, but have lived here seven years should be made a U.S. citizen?" Only 57 percent of Texas Hispanics (the overwhelming majority of whom are Mexican Americans) agreed.[112] Finally, November 1986 exit polls by SVREP reported that 56 percent of Texas Hispanics favored legalization of the undocumented—compared to 69 percent of California Hispanics.[113] Apart from suggesting that Texas Mexicans were more opposed to amnesty than their counterparts in California, these data underscore that there was a substantial minority of Mexican Americans opposed to amnesty for illegals.

In any event, the Tarrance-Hart poll presented additional evidence that Hispanics are favorably disposed toward illegal immigrants. For example, 71 percent favored "having the government provide free public education to the children of illegal immigrants."[114] It is interesting to note, however, that Mexican Americans living in heavily impacted areas are much less favorably disposed toward helping illegals and their children. Thus, a study of Hidalgo County, Texas (along the Mexican border), reported that "more Mexican American respondents opposed free schooling for children of undocumented workers than supported it." This is why Mexican-American elected officials along the border led the fight against efforts to compel the enrollment of such children in their schools.[115] Similar sentiments are reflected in Tarrance-Hart's finding that only 36 percent of Hispanics favored allowing illegal immigrants to receive welfare benefits, while 52 percent favored "allowing illegal immigrants to receive Medicaid."[116]

The Tarrance-Hart poll also revealed Hispanics to be less than enthusiastic about the continued immigration of illegals. Fully 57 percent agreed with the proposition:

> Some people say tough restrictions on illegal immigration are the *right* approach because illegal immigrants take jobs away from American workers and give employers a way to avoid paying decent wages. The U.S. already is having enough problems in meeting the needs of its own people, including disadvantaged and minority citizens, and we cannot afford to have the extra burden of all the people who might want to come to our country.[117]

More specifically, 47 percent of Hispanics agreed that "our laws need to be changed to be *tougher* and more restrictive on illegal immigration and illegal aliens."[118]

Here again, numerous other surveys have confirmed the thrust of these controversial findings. A 1983 poll sponsored by the Urban Institute found that 54.3 percent of Southern California Hispanics felt that "the influx of illegal or undocumented immigrants into southern California has an overall . . . unfavorable effect on the state as a whole."[119] Similarly, a 1987 Field poll reported that 53 percent of California Hispanics felt the overall effect of illegal immigrants on the state to be unfavorable.[120]

The Tarrance-Hart poll reported similar uneasiness with regard to *legal* immigration. Forty-six percent of Hispanics felt the government should admit fewer legal immigrants and refugees each year, and 37 percent even felt there should be fewer legal immigrants from Mexico.[121] And again, these findings from the much-reviled Tarrance-Hart poll have been generally confirmed by other surveys. For example, a 1983 *Los Angeles Times* poll found that fully 44 percent of Latinos in California agreed: "At the present time . . . there are too many immigrants in this country from Mexico."[122] About four years later, a Field poll found that 47 percent of California Hispanics—compared with 50 percent of Anglos—felt the number of immigrants permitted to enter this country should be decreased.[123] And in 1988, another Field poll found that 46 percent of Hispanics in California—compared to 57 percent of Anglos—reported that they were either "very worried" or "somewhat worried" in response to the statement:

> Because of immigration and other factors, the population of California is rapidly changing to include many more people of Hispanic and Asian background. Some people are worried that the changing make-up of California will make it hard to maintain American traditions and the American way of life. Others say this is not a problem and that these groups quickly adapt.[124]

More recently, a 1989 *Los Angeles Times* survey found that 60 percent of Hispanics in Southern California felt that "[a]t the present time . . . there are too many immigrants in Southern California today . . ."[125] One month later, another *Times* poll found that 45 percent of Hispanics in Los Angeles County felt there are "too many immigrants in Los Angeles today"—a lower, but not inconsiderable level of disaffection with prevailing levels of immigration.[126]

The most controversial finding of the Tarrance-Hart poll concerned Hispanic attitudes toward sanctions on employers hiring illegal immigrants. In the midst of an intense national debate in which virtually all Hispanic leaders were vehemently opposed to just such sanctions (as proposed in the pending Simpson-Mazzoli legislation), Tarrance-Hart reported that 60 percent of Hispanics favored "penalties and fines for employers who hire illegal immigrants."[127] The predictable result was a barrage of polemical and methodological criticisms of the survey.[128]

In fact, several polls did indicate much lower levels of Hispanic support for sanctions than reported by Tarrance-Hart. For example, a 1983 *Los Angeles Times* poll reported that only 34 percent of California Hispanics supported sanctions, while 57 percent opposed them.[129] A few years later, a 1986 nationwide poll by the *New York Times* similarly reported that only 34 percent of Hispanics supported employer sanctions, while 49 percent opposed them and 17 percent were undecided.[130]

Other polls suggested Hispanics were more evenly split over sanctions. For example, a November 1984 exit poll conducted by SVREP found that 42 percent of Hispanics in Texas favored employer sanctions and 40 percent opposed them, with 18 percent not sure.[131] The above-cited Cal Tech poll, undertaken right after the 1984 general election, revealed California Hispanics to be similarly split on sanctions: 40 percent in favor, 42 percent opposed, and again 18 percent undecided.[132] That such large numbers would be opposed to or undecided on a position that their leaders had made the number one priority throughout that presidential election year highlights once again the persistent gap between the Mexican-American political elite and the rank and file.

Moreover, other polls actually confirm the high level of support for sanctions found by Tarrance-Hart. For example, a 1978 poll sponsored by the Immigration and Naturalization Service, at the time headed by Mexican American Leonel Castillo, found majority support for employer sanctions among Hispanics throughout Texas. Moreover, that support increased as one got closer to Mexico: in border counties, almost 70 percent of Hispanics agreed that "a law should be passed to stop people from hiring undocumented aliens."[133] A few years later in the early 1980s, a survey in Hidalgo County, Texas found that a solid majority of Hispanics there along the Mexican border supported employer sanctions.[134]

Similarly, a 1982 Field Institute survey found that 60 percent of California Hispanics felt the government should be doing more to discourage the entry of illegal immigrants into this country; and 71 percent—compared to 76 percent of California Anglos—agreed that "severe penalties" should be imposed on employers hiring illegals.[135]

Lesser but nonetheless majority support for sanctions was reported by de la Garza in the spring of 1984. In the midst of a hotly contested race for the Democratic nomination for U.S. senator from Texas, de la Garza's survey found that 52 percent of Mexican Americans approved of sanctions.[136] About a year later—at the peak of the immigration debate—the Texas Poll revealed that 62 percent of Hispanics in the state felt that "it should be against the law to employ a person who has come into the United States without proper papers."[137] A statewide exit poll conducted by SVREP in November 1986 reported that 56 percent of Hispanics favored employer sanctions, with 35 percent opposed and 11 percent not sure.[138] Finally, in October 1987, one year after employer sanctions had been enacted into law, the Field Institute reported that 68 percent of California Hispanics approved of them.[139]

More recently, surveys conducted by Tarrance and Associates in 1989 found that 54 percent of Hispanics in Texas registered to vote approved "of the laws against employers hiring illegal aliens," while 39 percent disapproved.[140] In California about the same time, Tarrance found even higher levels of support for sanctions among Hispanics registered to vote.[141] Most recently, a 1991 Roper survey found that 58 percent of Hispanics nationally "favor . . . a law that forbids the hiring of illegal aliens," while 39 percent oppose.[142]

The opinions of Mexican Americans on immigration seem to divide along generational and social-class lines. For example, the above-cited survey of Mexican Americans in Hidalgo County, Texas found that while a majority of Mexican-American respondents supported employer sanctions, upper-income as well as third-generation Mexican Americans were more likely to support them than their less affluent and more recently arrived cousins.[143] Similarly, in the 1983 *Los Angeles Times* poll cited earlier, while only 22 percent of foreign-born Hispanics supported employer sanctions, 47 percent of native-born Latinos did.[144] And in the Tarrance-Hart poll that same year, 38 percent of Hispanic noncitizens favored sanctions, but fully 66 percent of Hispanic citizens did.[145]

A similar correlation between length of time in the United States and uneasiness about immigration is evident among Mexican Americans on other aspects of the immigration issue. With regard to amnesty, for example, 88 percent of Hispanic noncitizens in the Tarrance-Hart poll supported it, but only 70 percent of Hispanic citizens did.[146] And the 1984 Cal Tech survey reported that 74 percent of first-generation California Hispanics supported amnesty, but only 58 percent of second-generation and 49 percent of third-generation Hispanics did—compared to 44 percent of all Anglos.[147]

Now, many of these poll results must be used with caution, since (as indicated in the endnotes) they are often based on small sample sizes. Nevertheless, the fact that they all lie in the same range affords them considerable credibility. Taken together, these data indicate that, at a minimum, the level of support for sanctions and amnesty among Mexican Americans has been much higher than their leaders have let on.

THE LEADERSHIP'S OPEN-BORDERS STANCE

Whatever its precise dimensions, there was throughout the 1980s and into the 1990s a discernible and substantial uneasiness among Mexican Americans with prevailing levels of immigration. Yet such views have infrequently been articulated by Mexican-American leaders. Indeed, these leaders have, with few exceptions, advocated amnesty and opposed employer sanctions with a zeal that belies the complicated crosscurrents within their communities.

The gap between this leadership position and rank-and-file opinion is highlighted by the results of a controversial, but now forgotten, election. The 1984 Democratic nomination for U.S. senator from Texas came down to a contest between liberal state senator Lloyd Doggett and conservative congressman Kent Hance. Hance, who subsequently followed fellow Boll Weevil Phil Gramm into the Republican Party, waged a campaign that, in the midst of a heated national debate over Simpson-Mazzoli, had overtones of an anti-immigrant crusade. Yet in the June runoff, for which the Mexican-American turnout rate was actually higher than that of Anglos, the defeated Hance actually got 24.5 percent of the Mexican-American vote.[148] This showing hardly qualified Hance as a champion of Mexican Americans, but neither did it quite fit the picture painted, just before the runoff, by SVREP executive director Willie Velásquez: "If Mr. Hance wins, it will be a signal for all sorts of yahoos (of which Texas is so abundantly blessed) to run negative campaigns at the expense of the Mexican American community."[149]

With regard to amnesty, the evidence indicates Mexican-American leaders have been far more supportive of the idea than their rank and file. In a 1984 study of attitudes toward immigration among Hispanics in Texas, de la Garza reported that Hispanics there were "much less supportive of amnesty for the undocumented than are local elites from across the Southwest. Forty-nine percent of Texas respondents, compared to almost 90 percent of community leaders in California, New Mexico, and elsewhere support amnesty."[150] Similarly, the 1986 exit polls mentioned earlier indicated that while 69 percent of Latino voters in California supported amnesty,[151] surveys conducted a few months earlier indicated that it was supported by fully 86 percent of Mexican-American leaders around the state.[152]

As for employer sanctions, the persistent segment of rank-and-file support depicted above has not been echoed by the leadership. On the contrary, leaders have enthusiastically, and overwhelmingly, denounced sanctions. The most moderate opposition has apparently been in West Texas (Hance's home ground), where a 1985 SVREP straw poll of leaders found only 58 percent opposed to sanctions.[153] More typical were SVREP's findings elsewhere: in Southeast Texas at about the same time, 67 percent of Hispanic leaders opposed sanctions,[154] and in California in July 1986, 89 percent of Mexican-American leaders statewide opposed sanctions.[155]

Yet such data hardly begin to convey the intensity of Mexican-

American leaders' antagonism toward employer sanctions. One such indicator was their opposition to the Simpson-Mazzoli bill, which included employer sanctions *and* amnesty. An obvious attempt to bring those with divergent views together behind immigration reform, Simpson-Mazzoli was loudly denounced by Mexican-American leaders, whose support for amnesty was clearly outweighed by their opposition to sanctions. Thus, 78 percent of Hispanic delegates to the 1984 Democratic National Convention opposed Simpson-Mazzoli.[156] At about that time, SVREP concluded: "SVREP studies have consistently shown that the Hispanic leadership is against Simpson-Mazzoli."[157] Indeed, as indicated earlier, the summer of 1984 saw opposition to Simpson-Mazzoli emerge as virtually the only item on the Mexican-American political agenda. And two years later, as the debate over immigration was peaking, SVREP polls of Hispanic leaders in California found that 89 percent opposed sanctions and 97 percent opposed Simpson's legislation.[158]

In light of such developments, it is worth noting that this is a departure from the historic position of Mexican-American leaders on immigration. As I shall explore in chapter 10, through the mid-1960s Mexican-American leaders adopted a firmly restrictionist stance. The 1970s and early 1980s, however, were a transitional period. Immigration was on the back burner, and while leaders were certainly aware of it, they saw immigration as posing no particular problems and therefore not worth much attention. Drawing on interviews with 241 Mexican-American leaders, de la Garza noted that, as of 1982, "the undocumented worker issue . . . goes virtually unnoticed by Chicano leaders," who were more concerned with economic issues, education, and racism.[159]

When de la Garza prodded these leaders as to their views on undocumented workers, 32 percent expressed concern to provide safeguards for them, while 42 percent simply felt undocumented workers were an asset that posed no problems. He found that only 22 percent of the leaders "responded that the presence of undocumented workers adversely affected the interests of the Chicano community."[160] De la Garza concluded:

> The issue of undocumented workers, which is of such great concern to non-Chicano elites, does not concern Chicano elites. To the contrary, these leaders see no need to control the flow of undocumented workers except to protect the workers themselves. They do not see undocumented workers as contributing to the problems of the Chicano community.[161]

As the decade wore on, and the number of illegal immigrants steadily increased (with a record high of approximately 1.6 million border apprehensions in 1986), Mexican-American leaders remained fixed in their stance—even in the face of research findings indicating that Mexican Americans already settled here were competing with illegals for jobs.[162] Certainly, nothing that was said in the course of the continuing debate over immigration restriction would indicate that the leadership had significantly modified its views from what de la Garza had found at the beginning of the decade. Indeed, as leaders pointed with increasing outrage at substandard housing, inadequate barrio health-care facilities, and overcrowded schools, they seldom if ever acknowledged that solutions might at least in part be found in moderating the continuing influx of immigrants.

Additional insight into the views of Mexican-American leaders is offered by de la Garza's findings that "[a]lmost half of the respondents indicated they favored completely opening the U.S.–Mexican border."[163] Thus, 49 percent supported an "open border," while 40 percent opposed it, and 11 percent were uncertain, leaving de la Garza to conclude: "Indeed, more respondents explicitly support this radical policy option than oppose it."[164]

A few years later, even more Mexican-American leaders appeared to accept the open-borders option. At least, this was implicit in their stance, which was to oppose employer sanctions at any cost—even the loss of amnesty and, at times, their own credibility. Newspaper editors, politicians, and ordinary citizens may have expressed increasing alarm about "losing control of our borders"; but Mexican-American leaders hardly budged.[165] In fact, they appeared to rise above the fray and express satisfaction with the status quo—albeit a status quo that meant continual growth and turmoil in the barrios.

Eventually, some Mexican Americans began criticizing the leaders' tactics as dilatory and obstructionist. As de la Garza, himself hardly a staunch critic of the leaders, noted in a 1985 article:

> Elected Mexican American leaders as well as the heads of national organizations, in reaction to Simpson-Mazzoli and other immigration proposals, initiated no legislation or discussions until reform seemed imminent. This contrasts sharply with the conduct of these individuals with regard to bilingual education, voting rights, and general civil rights issues.[166]

By 1986, when passage of restrictionist immigration legislation appeared inevitable, several Mexican-American congressmen, particularly those newly elected and with substantial Anglo constituencies, quietly moderated their opposition to the Immigration Reform and Control Act (IRCA) and even ended up voting for it. But the loudest and most articulate Mexican-American voices continued to oppose the legislation, employer sanctions in particular.[167]

So, while the 1980s started out with Mexican-American leaders indifferent to immigration issues, it did not end that way. On the contrary, the battle against immigration restriction and the continuing struggle over implementation of IRCA has placed the issue squarely at the center of the Mexican-American political agenda. Yet through all this, the stance of the leadership has barely changed. Opposition to employer sanctions remains vehement. There is still little evidence of concern that the influx of illegals creates problems—either for Mexican Americans already settled here or for other sectors of American society. The dominant leadership stance remains acceptance of an open-borders policy—despite more complicated and conflicted sentiments among the rank and file.

MEXICAN-AMERICAN OPINION AND AMERICAN DEMOCRACY

This chapter began with a warning: that the survey data on Mexican Americans are confusing and even contradictory. This problem is nowhere more apparent than with regard to immigration. Yet it shows up in many other places—for example, in exit polls of the 1984 presidential election. While all the national polls showed Walter Mondale winning a majority of Hispanic votes, there was considerable disagreement as to the size of his margin. According to NBC News, Mondale won 68 percent of the Hispanic vote nationwide; Reagan 32 percent. CBS News had Mondale over Reagan 61 to 37. ABC reported an even slimmer margin: Mondale 56, Reagan 44.[168] In the 1988 presidential election there were similar though less marked inconsistencies.[169] As *Washington Post* reporter Dan Balz observed: "The variety of the findings is all the more perplexing when contrasted to exit poll findings on the white vote and the black vote, which varied only a few percentage points among the network polls."[170]

One problem with polling Hispanics is that, though a fast-growing group, they nevertheless represent a relatively small segment of the U.S. population (about 9 percent), and an even smaller proportion of the electorate.[171] It is therefore difficult, and costly, for pollsters to get a sufficiently large sample from which reliable statistical inferences can be drawn.

Another source of bias in the poll data lies in the imprecision of the label "Hispanic." Encompassing subgroups with drastically different socioeconomic profiles and political perspectives, this term has little actual sociological meaning. Yet pollsters continue to use it, because "Hispanic" has become part of our political discourse—and because focusing on the subgroups would exacerbate the problem of unreliably small samples. Moreover, because the Hispanic subgroups are clustered geographically and because pollsters, for reasons of economy, tend to cluster their respondents geographically, the task of getting a representative national sample of the disparate group we call "Hispanics" is further complicated. Thus, the observed differences in the polls cited above could simply be due to samples being skewed by greater or lesser numbers of Cubans, who vote overwhelmingly Republican.[172]

Yet these are hardly the only sources of bias in the Hispanic data. For example, similarly divergent numbers appear in polls in California and Texas, where "Hispanics" does not comprise a dramatically variegated admixture of Puerto Ricans, Cubans, Mexicans, and Central Americans, but an overwhelmingly Mexican-origin group.[173] Yet despite this relative homogeneity, the NBC News poll indicated that in Texas in 1984 Mondale beat Reagan by a margin of 65 to 35; while ABC News came up with Mondale 76, Reagan 24. In California, the numbers were even more divergent. ABC News found Mondale's margin to be 57 to 42; while NBC reported it to be 76 to 24.[174]

Moreover, there are any number of additional sources of bias in Hispanic survey data. For example, because Hispanics own proportionately fewer telephones than non-Hispanics, surveys relying on telephone interviews may be particularly prone to error.[175]

A more basic problem is language. For example, the *Los Angeles Times* found that 50 percent of Hispanic respondents in one of its statewide surveys preferred to be questioned in Spanish.[176] Yet many polls, including Mervin Field's California Poll, routinely do not employ Spanish-speaking interviewers, and consequently survey only Hispanics who speak English.

Yet even when Spanish-speaking interviewers are used, communication problems persist. As my analysis of the bilingual education data revealed, the very terms of debate may not be understood by many Hispanics. The result is a muddle of contradictory opinions. But what else could one reasonably expect when uneducated immigrants, more concerned with economic survival than politics, are asked to express their views on complex issues?

Indeed, the distinctive cultural values that these immigrants bring with them to the United States pose a series of problems for American pollsters. As I. A. Lewis of the *Los Angeles Times* Poll has observed, the extended-family structure of many Hispanic households and the tendency of Hispanic men "to speak for their wives, daughters, and other female relatives" confounds the methodological assumptions of survey researchers.[177] Thus, the very definition of what Americans refer to as "individuals" living in "households" differs from the social reality of many Hispanics.

A related difficulty concerns the transience that characterizes many Hispanic communities. Emphasized in previous chapters, this aspect of any immigrant community is heightened among Mexican Americans, whose proximity to their homeland results in increased movement back and forth between Mexico and the United States.[178]

Of course, the large number of illegal Hispanic immigrants presents still more obstacles to accurate polling. First, the presence of illegals fosters a tendency to be reticent and uncooperative with pollsters, whose samples are consequently biased.[179] Second, the large and indeterminate number of illegal immigrants renders the total population of Mexican Americans or Hispanics—from which samples are drawn and about which inferences are made—similarly indeterminate.[180]

Of course, such obstacles are part of the broader problem of polling any population that is marginal to the mainstream. Yet among Hispanics there is at the same time a quite different set of problems. For while many newcomers and others remain outside the mainstream, many other Hispanics are rapidly becoming part of it. For example, the relatively high levels of intermarriage between Mexicans and Anglos mean that deciding who is—and who is not—Mexican American is no straightforward matter. Quite aside from complicated questions as to how individuals of mixed parentage choose to define themselves ethnically, there is the sheer practical difficulty of relying on surnames to pick out Mexican Americans, or Hispanics. Slightly more than two-thirds of those who identify themselves as Hispanic have Spanish surnames, and slightly less than two-thirds of those with Spanish surnames identify themselves as Hispanic.[181] Here again, the social context in which Mexican Americans specifically and Hispanics generally function makes the task of defining the universe from which survey samples are drawn, and about which inferences are made, highly problematic.

The political implications of these methodological difficulties encountered by survey researchers are enormous. A recent study of immigrant attitudes by the National Association of Latino Elected Officials (NALEO) observes:

> Another and less well-noted consequence of having large numbers of in-
> dividuals ineligible to participate in the political process is the potential ef-
> fect on accountability of publicly elected officials, who may believe that
> they can ignore those constituents who cannot participate.[182]

This study is of course referring to the conventional forms of political participation, such as voting. Yet the accountability of public officials is also
promoted by the kind of opinion surveys discussed here, because in contemporary democracies such findings have become an integral part of the
process by which public opinion is formed and articulated. In a sense,
opinion polls have emerged as another means by which individuals and
groups "participate" in the political process.

Therefore, the confusing and contradictory data examined in this chapter serve to further weaken the political accountability of Mexican-American and Hispanic leaders. De la Garza has even gone so far as to say that
the poor quality of survey data about Hispanics results in their "partial
disenfranchisement."[183]

In one sense, the cleavages between leaders and rank and file described in this and earlier chapters are hardly surprising. Such cleavages
are, after all, intrinsic to politics. Yet for several reasons, these cleavages are particularly troublesome in the case of contemporary Mexican-
American politics.

First is the unique position of the Mexican-American leadership. On
the one hand, these leaders speak for a group that includes large numbers of individuals who are, by virtue of their illegal status, simply unable
to participate in politics. It is important to remember that this is a new
phenomenon: arriving at a time when our borders were virtually open,
earlier immigrant groups did not include large numbers of illegals. On
the other hand, Mexican-American leaders operate in a regime that has,
especially since the 1960s, become highly attuned to broadly participatory norms, particularly with regard to the representation of ethnic and
minority groups.

These circumstances put today's Mexican-American leaders in an extraordinary position. Because so many Mexican Americans do not, or cannot, participate, the means of ascertaining and representing the group's
interests are necessarily limited. Yet at the same time, the wider society
places enormous demands on Mexican-American leaders to represent
those interests. With only weak ties to their nominal constituents, who
remain in a state of political passivity, it is hardly surprising that these
leaders should rely on the resources of non-Mexican-American allies and
sponsors. Inevitably, these allies and sponsors play a role, however indi-
rect, in setting the Mexican-American political agenda.

This is not to say that the Mexican-American leadership does not set its own agenda. Clearly, it does. But as suggested by the above discussions of issues like abortion and immigration, that agenda frequently diverges from the imperfectly articulated opinions and interests of the group as a whole. Moreover, precisely because those opinions and interests are so poorly defined, the leaders' agenda becomes more important. The very vagueness and confusion reflected in the survey findings on such issues as bilingual education suggest that, however out of touch the leadership may be, their agenda is far from irrelevant to the political direction of the group as a whole. Indeed, by defining the agenda for a poorly organized and largely disenfranchised group, the leaders exert extraordinary influence over how it views the world.

❦10❧

Assimilation and
Its Discontents

T he cleavages between Mexican Americans and their leaders discussed in the previous chapter are not completely surprising. As
Mexican-American leaders would be the first to point out, leadership requires leading, which often means getting out in front of the rank and
file. Yet there is more going on here than the usual lag between leaders
and followers—or even an ideological gulf between inordinately liberal
leaders and their constituents, though some of that is evident. Indeed,
there is reason to believe that a similar gulf exists between Mexican-
American rank and file and leaders who are conservative Republicans.

In this chapter I will examine the underlying sources of such cleavages. To do so, I will step back further from my comparison of Mexican-
American politics in San Antonio and Los Angeles and situate the
dynamics I have been exploring at the local and state levels within the
broader institutional context of the new American political system. From
this perspective it is evident that several developments exacerbate the
already serious sociological, demographic, and cultural obstacles to
Mexican-American political advancement. One such contemporary development, which I will explore by way of comparison with American politics earlier in our history, is the differentiation of political from social and
economic institutions. Another development to be considered is the nationalization of American politics that has been evident for some time

now. Finally, I will examine how the increasing separation of private from public life hinders the political development of Mexican Americans at the end of the twentieth century.

While the new American political system makes it more difficult than ever for a group like Mexican Americans to make its way politically, our political culture fosters extraordinarily high expectations that all groups, but especially the poor and racially oppressed, participate in the system—or at least be represented. Highly responsive to the resulting frustrations are national elites who have launched various initiatives to advance Mexican-American representation. Yet because these elites remain oblivious to the structural factors emphasized here and insist that the primary obstacle to Mexican-American political advancement is racial prejudice, their efforts have not been very successful. Indeed, as my analysis of Mexican-American politics in Los Angeles and California suggests, such elite initiatives have often proved counterproductive, with representation achieved only in the most formal sense—and often at the expense of Mexican-American mobilization and genuine political power. In the name of racial justice, we end up with an exceptionally strident and divisive new voice in a polity already fragmented by powerful interest groups.

One result are the cleavages between rank and file and leadership identified in the previous chapter. But much more important—and little appreciated—is that the contemporary political-structural environment does not register the considerable social and economic advancement that Mexican Americans do experience. In fact, our political institutions ignore—indeed, deny—that progress. Moreover, the inevitable discontents that accompany mobility in contemporary America get emphasized and magnified by our institutions. This perspective suggests that "assimilation" does not necessarily lead to the optimal individual and social outcomes that we typically expect.

THE SOCIAL AND THE POLITICAL: A WIDENING GAP

In his magisterial treatise on American society and politics, *The Last Half-Century*, Morris Janowitz observes: "The emergence of modern society implies a historical process of a degree of separation of political institutions from economic and social structures."[1] As a result, political institutions in advanced industrial societies face a curious bind. On the one hand, the state assumes greatly increased responsibilities for the management of social and economic outcomes. Fewer and fewer decisions are made in the market, more and more in what Daniel Bell calls "the political cockpit."[2] Indeed, as Samuel Huntington argues, complex modern societies crucially depend on political institutions to create community (political community, properly speaking) that less complex, face-to-face societies simply do not need.[3] On the other hand, the specialization of functions that characterizes such societies, and helps create the need for the interventionist state in the first place, affects political institutions as well. For as these grow in size and importance, they focus increasingly on one another, and operate more and more according to their own bureaucratic dynamics. This process is reinforced by increased reliance on expert knowledge and the steady flow of tax revenues. As a result, there is a tendency for political institutions in advanced industrial societies to become insulated from the social and economic forces they seek to direct. Hence the irony that the state becomes more active and intrusive as its social base becomes more restricted.

This general tendency in advanced industrial societies has many specific manifestations. One such is the professionalization of politics. These dynamics are well described by Huntington and Nelson's insight into declining levels of political participation in developing societies:

> Socio-economic development also tends to increase the functional specificity of relationships and organizations, including those related to politics. In a traditional agrarian society, the elite and mass are presumably related to each other through diffuse ties, encompassing economic, social, religious, and political relationships. . . . The overall tendency in modernizing societies, however, is toward more specific functional relationships. To the extent that this occurs in politics, that is, to the extent that organs of political participation become distinct and specialize purely in political participation, they will become less successful at it. The expansion of political participation leads, paradoxically, to the development of a professional political class, which, by segregating political relationships from other relationships, tends to reduce or to limit political participation.[4]

In one sense, of course, political professionals have long been evident in American politics. Machine politicians once prided themselves on being "pros," disdaining reformers and other amateurs as "mornin' glories."[5] But what Huntington and Nelson are talking about is a different kind of "professional," a cosmopolitan with the educational skills and credentials of a society's dominant institutions, whose political base is less likely to be in a specific geographical community than in a large bureaucratic organization. In this sense, the professional community organizers being trained by the Industrial Areas Foundation may be viewed as transitional figures. More typical are some of the political professionals in the elite-networks of Los Angeles and California; or an even purer example, the highly trained and educated reformers who, as Daniel Patrick Moynihan has pointed out, launched the War on Poverty not from community centers and clubhouses, but from government bureaus and elite philanthropic institutions. Accordingly, Moynihan dubbed this trend "the professionalization of reform."[6]

Professionalization has an obvious benefit—namely, that it provides direction and purpose where otherwise there might be only inertia, venality, or the pursuit of power for its own sake. As Moynihan (himself part of the professionalization he chronicled) has observed, "The Irish did not know what to do with power once they got it."[7] But professionalization also involves costs—which Moynihan understands, since he has both praised and faulted the trend.[8] In Los Angeles and California, these costs include the one cited by Huntington and Nelson: decreased participation in politics. It's no accident that the term limits movement, which reflects extreme and explicit disaffection with professionalized politics, began in California. And as evidenced by elite-network politics in Los Angeles, professionalization also opens a gap between politicians and the day-to-day community life of those whom they represent.

Another way of describing the political-structural changes affecting Mexican Americans is in terms of the shift away from the representation of territorial jurisdictions and toward the representation of functional (interest) groups. In many respects Los Angeles and California have long been at the cutting edge of such developments in the United States. I noted in chapter 7 the Sacramento tilt in Los Angeles politics, and the loose ties between Mexican-American politicians there and the districts into which they get "parachuted." To some extent, of course, a shift from territorial to functional representation is visible in any modern, differentiated political system. But in California, where for generations extremely high levels of (domestic) immigration and geographical mobility have resulted in a political culture in which residents do not identify strongly with local jurisdictions, the shift has been quite marked. To some extent driven by the technological and organizational complexities of contemporary society, it has been further reinforced in California by the cost of campaigns: as indicated earlier, state assembly candidates now typically raise the preponderance of their funding from outside their districts. Finally, the influence of the media and the concomitant centralization of political power in Sacramento have further undermined the territorial basis of representation in California.

Yet this shift to functional representation should not be seen merely as a response to social and economic trends. Though clearly influenced by such developments, the shift also reflects political dynamics. Particularly in California, it is rooted in Progressive era reforms intended to forestall the development of immigrant, working-class political organizations such as had developed back East. Yet the Progressives were not simply hostile to immigrants and political parties; they were also inspired by the image of the newly powerful business corporation. As historian Samuel Hays reminds us, political parties, particularly at that time, were organized geographically to represent the interests of local, face-to-face communities. By contrast, the corporation operated over broad distances less on the basis of face-to-face bonds and more on the basis of impersonal relationships organized around functional specialization and the attainment of rational goals. The Progressives were not enthusiastic about interest group politics, but their reforms nevertheless weakened locally based political parties, de-emphasized territorial representation, and passed decision making to a higher level dominated by educated, cosmopolitan actors. It was no coincidence, Hays points out, that those elected in this more functionally oriented regime—regardless of whom they represented formally—resembled those who dominated the emergent national business culture.[9]

New Dealers, the heirs of the Progressives, pursued a similar, though not identical, agenda at the federal level. Like the Progressives, New Dealers sought to delocalize politics, but they were hardly hostile to interest groups. Moreover, Roosevelt mobilized the very immigrant, working-class voters disdained by the Progressives and included them in an unlikely coalition with elite reformers, blacks, and Southern Bourbons. This feat was achieved by establishing direct ties between emergent interest groups and federal agencies such as the Social Security Administration and the National Labor Relations Board—thereby circumventing geographically based conservative party bosses, whether in the urban North or the rural South. As Benjamin Ginsberg and Martin Shefter conclude in their recent book, *Politics by Other Means: The Declining Importance of Elections in America*: "New Deal liberals thus began the process through which the Democrats became a party grounded in governmental bureaucracies rather than local organization."[10]

Today the process is complete. In the words of political scientist Gerald Pomper, our once highly parochial, geographically based political parties have been "torn from their local roots and transformed into national bureaucratic competitors."[11] As we approach the end of the twentieth century, our national political parties are wealthier and better staffed than ever before, but they lack firm organizational bases in the face-to-face communities where people actually live and work.[12] As Ginsberg and Shefter observe, the parties

> have essentially become coalitions of public officials, office seekers, and political activists; they lack the direct organizational ties to rank and file voters that had formerly permitted parties to shape all aspects of politics and government in the United States.[13]

Concomitant with this deracination of the parties is what A. James Reichley, among others, has noted as their increasingly ideological orientation—and consistency.[14] This fact reflects a variety of developments that cannot be explored here. Suffice it to say that in the past, parties and politicians could maintain ties to the electorate with the rewards following from the camaraderie and solidarity of community-level organization, as well as the concrete material benefits of large patronage operations; but that now they must rely on pollsters, campaign finance consultants, and the media to connect them to a more scattered and educated electorate. It is hardly surprising that in this new regime images, abstractions, and ideas have come to play an increasingly dominant role.

The implications of these broad developments for our politics have been identified and criticized by many commentators. Yet few have considered what this new American political system bodes for newly arrived or emergent groups like Mexican Americans.[15] The evidence from Los Angeles and California generally, where these national political trends are very much in evidence, suggests consequences too serious to overlook.

What we see most clearly in California is the further deterioration of the link between ethnicity and geographical community—the trend Janowitz had in mind when he observed that "the deconcentration of human settlement and the increased range of daily and residential mobility have served to weaken the territorial basis of ethnic solidarities."[16] This trend may be obscured by the high visibility of rapidly growing barrios in California, but as already noted, the ties between Mexican-American leaders and those geographical communities are tenuous. Meanwhile, large numbers of upwardly mobile Mexican Americans have been dispersing throughout the state's metropolitan areas. In the context of California politics, the phrase "the Mexican-American community" is rapidly becoming an abstraction with little meaningful geographical referent.

The basis of the group's representation is largely functional, transforming Mexican Americans into an interest group.

This development may afford Mexican Americans representation they might otherwise have lacked, but it also raises several questions. The delocalization of this kind of politics arguably makes it more difficult for rank-and-file Mexican Americans to relate to the political process. Politics is certainly one more step removed from their day-to-day experiences in the neighborhoods where they live. This perennial problem with functional representation, which disproportionately affects lower socioeconomic strata, has in the past been mitigated by trade unions.[17] But in an era of diminishing union strength, this difficulty re-emerges with particular salience for Mexican Americans.

Even more problematic, it is difficult to identify what common interest, or interests, define such a large and disparate group. This is another important finding from the survey data in the previous chapter. It is certainly not self-evident what interests recently arrived illegal Mexican immigrants share with third-generation Mexican-American college graduates. These are admittedly polar extremes within the growing Mexican-American population. But in between these poles many similar questions arise.

As it turns out, Mexican Americans emerge in California as not just any interest group, but—in keeping with the dynamics of our new American political system—as one organized around an idea. That idea is that, like blacks, Mexican Americans comprise a racial minority group. This abstraction poses no problems for the ideologically oriented Chicano activists who see the world in such terms. Indeed, it is highly useful to elite-network insiders who are in need of some cogent category that subsumes the disparate population they aspire to represent. Yet this race idea is somewhat at odds with the experience of Mexican Americans, over half of whom designate themselves racially as "white," and the overwhelming majority of whom draw sharp distinctions between themselves and blacks. The resulting paradox, as we've seen, is that in Texas, where Mexican Americans have experienced something akin to racial caste treatment but have nevertheless pursued a much less racially oriented politics, they have made enormous political strides. Whereas in California, where they have experienced relatively little such racial discrimination, Mexican Americans have to a much greater extent defined themselves as a racial minority—and not prospered politically. Indeed, instead of helping them advance, such efforts have actually exacerbated the problem that any advanced industrial society would have in integrating relatively uneducated, unsophisticated newcomers into its political system.

MEDIA IMPRESSIONS AND ELITE IMPATIENCE

Central to the development of the California scenario have been the media. In terms of the delocalization of Mexican-American politics, I have already described how the media in Los Angeles contribute to the erosion of commitment to the tedious, low-profile work necessary to build and maintain Alinsky community organizations. In addition, I argued that the Southern California media encourage those organizations to emphasize the racial minority facet of the Mexican-American experience, despite the IAF's long-standing emphasis to the contrary. The larger and more powerful the media, the more they seem to feed a certain political competition between Mexican-Americans and blacks. Recall that even in San Antonio the president of COPS, when presented with the opportunity to appear on national television, denounced the city's exclusive Anglo service organization as "racist." Recall too how Mayor Henry Cisneros's stance on the discriminatory impact of immigration restriction changed when he entered the national limelight at the 1984 Democratic National Convention. Finally, recall how one leader of a Washington-based Mexican-American organization feels constrained each year, when the National Urban League comes out with its report on "the state of black America," to come up with a comparable list of grievances.

The media are willing and largely uncritical conduits for such messages because they are, like generals, fighting the last war: the struggle for black civil rights.[18] Sustained by the moral capital accumulated during the civil rights years, and fortified by Watergate and other Washington scandals, journalists, particularly those in the national media, are keen to play this role again. This predisposition, in addition to the time constraints under which they work, means that journalists tend to accept uncritically the racial minority interpretation of the Mexican-American experience offered by advocates and activists.

In their readiness to treat Mexican Americans as another racial minority, the media ignore important aspects of their experience similar to that of European immigrant groups. In particular, they reinforce in public debate a certain impatience with barrio conditions and prospects that ignores the historical experiences of other groups in American society. Thus, in a recent issue of *Time* it was observed:

> On the basis of numbers alone, the redistribution of political power is long
> overdue. . . . Despite the phenomenal growth of California's minority pop-

ulations in the past 20 years, just two blacks and one Asian have been elected to statewide office. . . . The 45 members of Congress from California include only four blacks, three Latinos and two Asians.[19]

No doubt *Time*'s readers would be surprised if reminded how long it took various immigrant groups to advance into the American mainstream. For example, the Irish, perhaps the most politically successful of all groups in America, began to enter Tammany Hall in the 1820s and 1830s, but they did not dominate it until Boss Tweed's downfall in 1871. Even so, New York did not elect its first Irish mayor until 1880. In Boston, the date was 1884; in Chicago, 1893.[20] Do such historical examples mean that Mexican Americans should expect to wait for half a century before one of their own becomes mayor of Los Angeles? No, but they do counsel a degree of patience and a sense of proportion lacking among the media as well as among many Mexican-American leaders.

Granted, the history of Mexicans in the Southwest cannot simply be reduced to that of European immigrants in America. Yet the very complexity of the Mexican-American experience, and hence of any such comparisons across groups, poses problems for the media. And once again, predisposition and resource constraints mean that such problems are resolved by pursuing the path that arouses the fewest objections, particularly from Mexican-American political elites.

The media's role in generating a "revolution of rising expectations" among the poor and marginal in developed as well as underdeveloped societies has been widely observed.[21] Much less noted has been the impatience generated by the media among mainstream Americans toward the disadvantaged, especially recently arrived immigrants. To be sure, the media are not unique in heavily discounting time when assessing the advancement of marginal groups. Indeed, this tendency reflects broader currents in elite opinion and our political culture generally.[22] Certainly the salience of racial concerns among elites in the national political arena is hardly an accident. What has been called "the nationalization of American politics" is a long-term trend driven by diverse economic and technological forces.[23] But equally significant in recent decades have been the political forces assailing states' rights on behalf of the civil rights of blacks. Indeed, the civil rights movement not only transformed our political institutions, it also had a formative, energizing impact on an entire generation of political actors, including journalists. Combine this development with the immediacy and directness of media images showing the disparity between the situation of recent immigrants and mainstream Americans, and the general impatience of elites is readily understood.

In recent years these national elites have fostered and reflected changes in our political culture to the point where any disparity between groups is seen as unacceptable—especially if it appears to be racially based. Accordingly, new norms of representation have appeared that are applicable to all groups, regardless of their level of political development. And as the state has come to permeate more and more aspects of social and economic life, these hyperpluralistic norms have come to seem more and more reasonable. With regard to Mexican Americans, as we have seen, there is now a sense of urgency that their burgeoning numbers are not reflected in the numbers of elected and appointed Mexican-American officeholders. Whereas in the past, the political obstacles facing a large, mostly immigrant group would have been tolerated or ignored, today they cannot be.

The foregoing changes have had profound effects on how Mexican Americans have engaged in politics. Consistent with the trend just described, Mexican-American politics has been nationalized. That process, itself the result of much political effort and struggle, is revealing of the dynamics I'm describing. First, Mexican-American leaders had to overcome their isolation from the rest of the nation—and from one another, divided as they were into separate communities scattered across the Southwest. Second, they had to find a way to win the attention of national elites. Here again, the catalyst was the black civil rights movement. As Grebler observed:

> Our first exploratory interviews with Mexican Americans throughout the Southwest in 1964 suggested that we were defining the Mexican-American population in a particular way—as a national minority. To a leadership involved in local and regional quarrels, this was a novel interpretation. Our definition (tentative at that time) seemed threatening to many leaders. It appeared to classify all Mexican Americans with the least acculturated people in the group. It appeared to slight traditional Mexican culture. It appeared to suggest the end of local autonomy. It implied unsettling comparisons with Negroes and their new militant tactics.[24]

Ever since, this new identity as a "national minority" has been "replacing the parochial orientation of earlier spokesmen who sought to solve individual problems in individual areas."[25] But the process has been slow, and it remains incomplete. For example, in their study of ten Northern California cities over the period 1960–1980, Rufus Browning and his colleagues found that while black protest politics was clearly part of a national movement, Mexican-American protest remained an ad hoc response to local conditions.[26] Today, virtually all Mexican-American leaders are convinced of the need for a national strategy. In fact, many express concern that their group and its problems are perceived as a regional, Southwestern phenomenon whose importance has not impinged on the national consciousness—or conscience. Indeed, this concern to project a national presence is one reason why Mexican Americans have joined with Puerto Ricans on the East Coast and Cubans in Florida in referring to themselves as "Hispanics" (or "Latinos")—albeit at the expense of blurring each group's distinctive identity.[27]

ELITE INITIATIVES:
HIGH PROFILE, LOW ACCOUNTABILITY

Fueling this process of nationalization have been efforts initiated by major foundations. Indeed, no analysis of Mexican-American politics would be complete without mention of the Rockefeller and Ford Foundations. The latter in particular has, since the 1960s, played a unique role in the evolution of Mexican-American politics. Its immense resources render Ford atypical, of course. But its very preeminence means that its perspective on Mexican-American politics has come to be shared by many philanthropic and nonprofit institutions.[28]

Ford funded the pathbreaking study of Mexican Americans by Grebler that has been referred to so frequently here. Much more visible than such scholarly efforts, however, were the foundation's support of advocacy groups in the 1960s. Much as it aided black activists seeking community control of the New York City public schools, Ford supported Chicano activists across the Southwest—including, for instance, Raza Unida Party members who led the political takeover of Crystal City, Texas. Indeed, Ford-funded activists in the region were so numerous and vocal, they aroused the ire of San Antonio congressman Henry B. González, who repeatedly denounced them and their sponsor on the floor of the U.S. House of Representatives.[29]

Delivered at a time when Congress was reevaluating the tax status of foundations, González's tirades caused Ford to pull in its horns. The headquarters of the Ford-created Mexican American Legal Defense and Educational Fund (MALDEF) was moved from San Antonio, where it had proved a particular annoyance to the congressman, to San Francisco.[30]

Ford also began supporting less protest-oriented efforts, such as voter registration drives. I have already described the social as well as the political barriers to Mexican-American voter registration. Caught between its stance as the party of the working masses and the political realities inhibiting expansion of its natural base, the Democratic Party has not done much to increase Mexican-American voter registration. Thus, it made sense for a liberally oriented foundation like Ford to step into the breach. The Southwest Voter Registration Education Project (SVREP) has certainly been one of Ford's most successful efforts among Mexican Americans. With a noncontroversial and easily evaluated objective, SVREP has caused the foundation few, if any, problems.[31]

Still, SVREP's success has not been universal. As indicated earlier, its efforts in Los Angeles have encountered many obstacles. Moreover, SVREP's singular success in Texas has been due largely to the indigenous leadership of Willie Velásquez, who began as a Ford-supported Raza Unida activist and then went on to develop a considerable base through years of political endeavors in San Antonio and throughout Texas. As argued earlier with regard to the Voting Rights Act, national elite initiatives aimed at promoting Mexican-American political advancement have been so successful in San Antonio and Texas because conditions there were uniquely ripe.

My point is that there are real limits to what such national elite initiatives can accomplish, and that whatever results are achieved come at a price. In the relatively benign and non-controversial realm of voter registration, that price has been negligible. It is nevertheless discernible. Throughout Texas and the Southwest, Velásquez's work propelled into elective office scores of Mexican-American politicians, some of whom subsequently proved unworthy of his help. In essence, these elected officials were free riders, and in the final years of his life, Velásquez was casting about for a way to exercise some accountability over them. But he didn't find it. If Velásquez's successors at SVREP attempt to hold accountable the politicians they help elect, the latter may very well turn and ask the hard question: to whom is SVREP accountable?

Without a doubt, the strongest institutional expression of the racial minority view of Mexican Americans is the Mexican American Legal Defense and Educational Fund (MALDEF). Just as the Ford Foundation viewed SVREP as analogous to its earlier voter registration efforts among blacks, so did it model MALDEF on the NAACP Legal Defense and Educational Fund. Announcing the foundation's $2.2 million startup grant in May 1968, Ford president McGeorge Bundy opined: "In terms of legal enforcement of civil rights, American citizens of Mexican descent are now where the Negro community was a quarter-century ago."[32] NAACP Legal Defense Fund executive director Jack Greenberg was appointed to MALDEF's first board of directors. Moreover, NAACP staff attorney Vilma Martínez helped prepare the initial grant application to Ford, and then served as liaison between the two public interest law firms. Martínez subsequently served as MALDEF's executive director.[33]

Though hardly the oldest Mexican-American organization in the nation, MALDEF has for almost a quarter century been the most visible Mexican-American presence in the national arena, where it has certainly generated more controversy than SVREP. The 1973 *San Antonio v. Rodriguez* litigation, which challenged the State of Texas's school finance program, was the organization's first major foray—and most notable defeat, since the Supreme Court rejected MALDEF's argument that the program violated a fundamental, constitutionally protected right to education. MALDEF had to wait a decade for a major victory, which came in 1982 when the Supreme Court upheld its argument (in *Plyler v. Doe*) that Texas public schools were constitutionally required to educate the foreign-born children of illegal immigrants. Significantly, the *Plyler* case reflected Vilma Martínez's decision to emulate the legal strategy pursued a generation earlier by the NAACP: laying the groundwork for illegal immigrants' rights litigation by focusing on the educational disadvantages of children.[34]

Yet there is a striking difference between MALDEF and the NAACP. Unlike the latter, MALDEF has never been a membership organization.[35] To be sure, MALDEF has ties to the Mexican-American professionals and businessmen who contribute to it financially and sit on its board. But it has no mass membership base among Mexican Americans. Throughout its history, MALDEF has been financially dependent on the Ford Foundation, with additional help from a handful of other major foundations, corporate sponsors, even the federal government. During the 1980s, MALDEF received from one-third to almost half of its total annual revenues from Ford alone.[36] MALDEF has been far and away the single largest recipient of all foundation grants to Latino organizations.[37]

This base of support raises questions about MALDEF's strengths and liabilities as a champion of Mexican-American interests. Its political clout was most evident in the decade-long battle that culminated in the Immigration Reform and Control Act of 1986. With headquarters in San Francisco and regional offices in Los Angeles, San Antonio, Chicago, Denver, and Washington, MALDEF was the only Mexican-American organization with the expertise and resources to wage a national campaign in Congress and the media against immigration restriction. Yet it did so without widespread grassroots support, a fact that was certainly evident to the participants in that battle, at the local as well as national level. As mentioned earlier, a group of Mexican-American politicians was particularly amused when, at a 1984 meeting in Los Angeles, Vilma Martínez threatened that if Simpson-Mazzoli were not blocked in Congress, "We'll take to the streets."

Less evident was the way in which MALDEF focused Latino opposition to Simpson-Mazzoli onto the presumed racial dimension of the issue. Indeed, MALDEF argued that the legislation's proposed sanctions on employers hiring undocumented workers would lead to employment discrimination—not just against undocumented workers, but against "all brown-skinned people." This argument may have resonated among Mexican Americans who remembered family members (including U.S. citizens) being rounded up and deported in Depression-era repatriation efforts, or in Operation Wetback during the early 1950s.[38] But it was not at the time supported by any systematic evidence. Indeed, MALDEF's charges flew in the face of research findings that employment and earnings disparities between Mexican Americans and other groups are explained as much by human capital factors, such as education and facility with English, as by discrimination at the workplace.[39] Nonetheless, those charges allowed MALDEF to tie up congressional negotiations over Simpson-Mazzoli for months at a time at various critical junctures. Although the organization did not prevail, and employer sanctions were eventually enacted into law, MALDEF managed to dilute their effectiveness and secured creation of an office within the Justice Department to investigate complaints of discrimination. Perhaps most importantly, MALDEF succeeded in defining the terms of the debate and thereby persuaded many Americans that racial discrimination was an overriding concern of Mexican Americans.

MALDEF's posture on employer sanctions is particularly striking when one considers the other possible lines of attack available to the organization. As a number of Mexican-American businessmen reminded me at the time, sanctions could have been opposed as burdensome to employers. Or Mexican-American leaders could have drawn on the argument, then being articulated by conservatives like Patrick Buchanan, that sanctions and other efforts to restrict immigration went against the American grain.[40] Completely ignoring such alternatives, MALDEF focused single-mindedly on racial discrimination—as might be expected of highly trained civil rights attorneys working for an organization modeled after the NAACP Legal Defense Fund.

Yet not only did MALDEF ignore the views of potential allies, it also ignored those of the rank and file. As already discussed, the de facto open-borders stance taken by most Mexican-American leaders, including MALDEF, is at odds with the conflicted, ambivalent views of the majority. MALDEF also disregarded the pleas of the many illegal immigrants who, according to a staff attorney in Los Angeles, called the organization daily and urged it to support Simpson-Mazzoli, employer sanctions and all, because of the bill's amnesty provisions.[41]

Now, it is arguably true that the pleas of such desperate individuals— possibly ill-informed and more than likely willing to overlook drawbacks elsewhere in the legislation—might prudently be overruled by experienced lawyers with a broader view of the needs of Mexican Americans as a whole. These matters involve political judgments that I am certainly not prepared to second-guess. Still, this example does point to the lack of mechanisms holding externally supported Mexican-American elites accountable to those whose interests they claim to represent. By the same token, such external support helps to account for some of the opinion gap explored in the previous chapter.

To be sure, the illegal immigrants for whose children MALDEF secured the right to public education presumably welcomed the organization's efforts in *Plyler v. Doe.* But because many Mexican Americans, including officeholders and homeowners concerned about higher taxes in heavily impacted jurisdictions, disagreed with MALDEF on that issue, similar questions about representativeness and accountability again arise. At a minimum, it can be said that an advocacy organization calling itself the *Mexican American* Legal Defense and Educational Fund fosters confusion and risks deception about the nature of its constituency when, as in *Plyler*, it litigates in behalf of newcomers who are not here legally, and who may have little intention of staying or becoming naturalized. In this regard, it is instructive to recall that when McGeorge Bundy launched MALDEF back in 1968, he carefully defined its mission as serving the needs of "American *citizens* of Mexican descent" (my emphasis).[42]

Accountability problems of a different sort arise in MALDEF's most recent and highly visible victory: its role in getting a Mexican American on the powerful five-person Los Angeles County Board of Supervisors. In the chapter on elite-network politics, I described the close relationship between MALDEF and Supervisor Gloria Molina. I also mentioned that supporters of Molina's opponent in that race felt that the organization had acted to benefit her. Many of these same individuals were already angry that, after refusing to join with them in their challenge to the county redistricting back in 1981,[43] MALDEF wound up getting all the credit. Though such sentiments remained beneath the surface of the general euphoria over the successful litigation and subsequent election, they were nevertheless in evidence. And for the first time, many politically active Mexican Americans in Los Angeles, who had been accustomed to

MALDEF's taking the lead on various national issues such as immigration, began wondering to whom this organization claiming to represent all Mexican Americans is in fact accountable.

My point is that there is no single, overriding Mexican-American interest that one organization can represent. Experiencing more mobility and less discrimination than blacks, Mexican Americans embody interests too diverse to be channeled into any one organization working in the highly focused way that the NAACP worked to end legal segregation. Indeed, the NAACP itself has recently lost membership and become divided as to its mission[44] If it no longer makes sense for blacks to conceive of themselves as defined by a single, overriding interest, then it arguably makes even less sense for Mexican Americans to do so.

Yet the more important question about MALDEF is not *whom* it represents, but *how* it represents them. As the work of various observers suggests, MALDEF is typical of public interest organizations, which generally lack a membership base and rely on corporate and foundation support.[45] Such third-party support allows political entrepreneurs to represent interests or groups that might otherwise be left out of the political process. This "vicarious representation," as James Q. Wilson calls it,[46] is one more manifestation of the differentiation of our political institutions from the social structure. When such entrepreneurs are environmentalists or campaign-finance reformers, questions about whose interests actually get represented are appropriate. When those being vicariously represented include illegal immigrants and noncitizens, such questions are imperative.

One characteristic of public interest law firms like MALDEF is their tendency to litigiousness. Recall that when twelve students from East LA's Garfield High School were accused by the Educational Testing Service of cheating on their Advanced Placement math exams, MALDEF's immediate response was to file suit against the Princeton-based testing conglomerate. The students' teacher, the now famous Jaime Escalante, demurred and sought other means of redress, which eventually vindicated him and his students.[47]

Such lawyerly behavior reflects a more general posture of intransigence that has been evident whenever MALDEF participates more directly in the political process. In the battle over Simpson-Mazzoli, for example, MALDEF was perceived by allies and opponents alike as purist and unwilling to compromise.[48] During this same period, I heard similar comments about MALDEF from Alinsky organizers in Texas who were

part of a coalition supporting the education reform efforts of then governor Mark White and Dallas billionaire H. Ross Perot. On several occasions
organizers expressed frustration with MALDEF's unwillingness to bargain with Texas legislators offering a compromise that included increased
state aid to local school districts. At least since MALDEF's defeat in the
1973 *Rodriguez* decision, school finance reform had been a popular issue
among Mexican-American educators, politicians, and parents. Yet
MALDEF was reluctant to settle for a compromise offer because, as one
organizer explained to me, its lawyers were already planning litigation
charging the Texas legislature with racist opposition to reform. In the end,
despite MALDEF's resistance, a compromise was worked out, and more
than a decade after *Rodriguez*, Mexican-American and other financially
pressed school districts in Texas got much needed help from Austin.

These episodes highlight the curious structure of incentives within
which MALDEF functions. In one sense the organization behaves like
any group of ambitious, well-trained lawyers. But without any members
or clients to which it is answerable, MALDEF can take a much broader,
longer view than any conventional law firm. This was of course what the
Ford Foundation had in mind when it established MALDEF. By contrast,
IAF community organizations have actual members with immediate
needs that must be responded to if their participation is to continue. Such
constraints—though frustrating to agenda-setting foundation executives
and public interest litigators—are nevertheless the basis of the accountability we typically expect of group spokesmen in a democratic society.

Implicit in this comparison of MALDEF and IAF organizations is an
important difference between functional and territorial representation.
Janowitz argues that community organizations encourage a weighing and
balancing of the diverse interests within a territorial jurisdiction, thereby
prefiguring, however imperfectly, some notion of the public interest:

> In the local community, the person and his household have the opportu-
> nity—by no means generally realized—to both internalize and aggregate
> the cost and benefits of alternative public policies. At least the aspiration
> of the public interest is not lost as a goal. Each citizen is forced to consider
> his definition of the "good community" and to confront the costs he will
> have to endure for such a social order.[49]

For Janowitz, the critical outcome is that territorial representation fosters more informal, prepolitical resolution of tensions and conflicts where
they arise—a process he refers to as "social control."[50] In essence, community organizations and other geographically based political organizations are proto-governing institutions. Some even explicitly seek to

govern. By contrast, interest groups are, in Janowitz's pithy formulation, "prepared to bargain but without aspiring to rule."[51] Unrestrained by the responsibilities of actually governing, interest groups pursue their narrow objectives unmindful of broader public concerns. Increasing in number and influence without benefit of the moderating influence of political parties, these groups ever more energetically press their demands on the state, and the result is political overload and governmental paralysis.[52] Such tendencies are only exacerbated when interest groups do not even have members to whom they must answer.

Now if elite initiatives like MALDEF genuinely advanced the political standing of Mexican Americans, then these objections would obviously carry less weight. Yet the evidence is that such legal strategies are actually counterproductive. The point has been made forcefully by Charles Hamilton about black politics:

> Instead of concentrating time and resources on being politically astute (mobilizing, bargaining, compromising), black leaders had to concentrate on being legally precise and Constitutionally alert. As useful as this training is in a political democracy, it is hardly the sort that prepares a constituency for viable *political* participation. In an important sense, then, an effective black elite developed keen legal skills (and in turn both influenced and encouraged the enforcement of American Constitutional law). But it was unable to develop those skills required for mobilizing masses and maneuvering in the political marketplace. Blacks, in other words, developed plaintiffs rather than precinct captains. And except for a few places in Northern cities like New York and Chicago, they developed legal warriors, not political ward leaders.[53]

Hamilton's point applies *a fortiori* to Mexican Americans. For the disaffection with politics that they bring with them from their homeland is reinforced by their illegal and noncitizen status in this country. In the present context, of course, such political inertness only increases pressure for the remedies of public interest entrepreneurs. Yet the vicarious representation provided does nothing about the primary causes of that inertness and arguably exacerbates it by conveying to the presumed beneficiaries the message that the fruits of politics may be had without resort to its messy processes.

THE ULTIMATE ELITE INITIATIVE: THE VOTING RIGHTS ACT

I have already mentioned the most significant elite initiative toward Mexican Americans in the national arena: the Voting Rights Act. Today, the VRA is the single strongest incentive for Mexican Americans and their leaders to define themselves as racial minority claimants. But it was not always thus. Not until 1975 was the original 1965 Act amended to designate Asians and "persons of Spanish heritage" as "language minorities" subject to the same extraordinary protections that had, until then, been afforded almost exclusively to black Americans. Indeed, as Abigail Thernstrom reveals in her meticulous study of the VRA, Mexican Americans were brought under its umbrella despite spotty evidence (advanced, not coincidentally, by SVREP and MALDEF, among others) that they had been subjected to the kind of systematic racial discrimination experienced by blacks. At the time black leaders knew better, and objected strenuously. But Anglo elites in Washington remained ignorant of the subtleties of group relations in the distant Southwest. From their viewpoint, the Mexican-American situation was analogous to that of blacks, and that was that.[54]

As this bit of history suggests, voting rights for Mexican Americans is a potentially divisive issue. Black elected officials have been heard to complain of being redistricted out of office on account of "wetbacks." Upon hearing of the benefits afforded Latinos under the VRA, a senior member of the Los Angeles City Council, of Italian descent, expressed outrage: "Italians never had such protections. Why should Latinos get it? This is un-American."[55]

But while I would argue that the VRA contributes to a generalized sense among the populace that "minorities" are getting more than their fair share, it does not seem to be the source of notable rancor or division. Consider, for example, San Antonio, where in the mid-1970s the threat of a VRA suit led to single-member districting, which increased the number of Mexican Americans on the city council. At that time a citywide referendum authorizing the shift from the Anglo-dominated at-large regime barely passed, and the vote split along group lines.[56] Several years later there was some grumbling among Anglos about this change having been imposed from the outside. But by and large, single-member districts are today a noncontroversial feature of San Antonio's political landscape. More to the point, the VRA has advanced Mexican-American political fortunes there without engendering the polarization that would have delayed or prevented the Anglo-Mexican coalition that was the basis of Cisneros's successful mayoralty.[57]

In other words, Thernstrom is correct in referring to the VRA as a "controversial policy that has somehow stirred no controversy."[58] Unlike busing, employment quotas, or even the use of Spanish in public institutions, voting rights for Mexican Americans create few victims—except the political elites directly concerned. It is certainly no accident that the complaints mentioned above come from elected officials. On the surface, then, there is nothing terribly divisive about the VRA and its role in our current regime of group rights.

Yet a closer look reveals that, for Mexican Americans at least, the VRA offers illusory and even counterproductive gains. Defining the primary obstacles to Mexican-American political advancement as racial in nature, the VRA completely ignores the demographic and political-structural factors described here.[59] Like the other elite initiatives I have discussed, the VRA is confronted by the widening gap between the social and the political experience of Mexican Americans; but like them, it doesn't close that gap so much as paper over it.

It is in Los Angeles that the full impact of the VRA can best be assessed. In 1986 the Justice Department launched a suit challenging the 1981 redistricting of the Los Angeles City Council on the grounds of inadequate Hispanic representation. Widely regarded as a Reagan administration move to embarrass Democratic mayor Tom Bradley, then running for governor, this suit led to the creation of a new Hispanic majority district, from which Assemblywoman Gloria Molina was elected to the council in 1987.

In 1988 the Republicans in Washington made another election-year effort to ingratiate themselves with Hispanics. That year, the Reagan Justice Department initiated proceedings for a similar suit, this time challenging the Los Angeles County Board of Supervisors with discriminating against Hispanics in its 1981 redistricting plan. In what was reportedly the largest VRA suit ever brought, costing the litigants in excess of $12 million, *Garza v. County of Los Angeles* resulted in the creation of a Hispanic majority district from which Molina was elected in 1991 as the first Mexican American to sit on that powerful five-person body since 1875.

In this particular episode, the role of the media is especially worthy of note.[60] The *Los Angeles Times*'s endorsement of Molina helped her overcome the superior financial resources of her principal rival, State Senator Art Torres. But of much greater relevance was the rhetoric the *Times* brought to bear on behalf of Molina. Praising the reasoning of the federal district judge who upheld the plaintiffs' arguments against the board's 1981 redistricting, the *Times* intoned:

> That kind of racial or ethnic gerrymandering is illegal under federal law and is as offensive as poll taxes, literacy tests and the other racist tactics that all-white governments used to discourage African-Americans from voting during the worst days of segregation in the Deep South.[61]

From such rhetoric one would never guess that the historical evidence brought to light in this litigation[62] revealed nothing like the treatment experienced by blacks in the South. Moreover, although the federal district judge who ruled against the Supervisors found "discrimination" within the definition of the Voting Rights Act, he found (as a federal appellate judge subsequently pointed out) no racial animus against Hispanics per se in the supervisors' 1981 redistricting effort.[63] Instead, the district judge found intense ideological competition among two liberal Democrats and three conservative Republicans, each anxious to hold onto his own seat:

> During the 1981 redistricting process, the Supervisors' primary objective was to protect their incumbencies and that of their allies. . . . The Court believes that had the Board found it possible to protect their incumbencies while increasing Hispanic voting strength, they would have acted to satisfy both objectives.[64]

However self-interested or ignoble, the supervisors sacrificed the interests of Hispanics not out of ill will or racism, but in order to hold onto their seats.

Revealingly, one day after the federal district judge determined that "an Hispanic candidate is unable to be elected to the Board under the current configuration of supervisorial districts,"[65] Sarah Flores won the primary in the First Supervisorial District with 35 percent of the total vote, including 68 percent of the Hispanic and 31 percent of the non-Hispanic vote. Moreover, with the second place finisher, a male Anglo, winning only 20 percent of the total vote, Flores was favored to win the seat.[66] Yet as noted in chapter 7, that same judge subsequently nullified these results, consistent with his initial finding that the supervisorial districts were improperly drawn.

In addition to exaggerated rhetoric, the *Times* also displayed the ahistorical impatience described earlier. Typical was the observation of reporter Richard Simon: "Latinos make up one-third of the county's population, but no Spanish-surnamed person has been elected to the powerful board since 1875."[67] Simon's facts are correct, but he seriously misleads his readers by implying that for generations a substantial segment of the county's population had been denied representation. For as I have already demonstrated, throughout most of this century the Mexican-origin population of Los Angeles was significantly smaller than it is today.

This same perspective was much in evidence the night Gloria Molina won her county supervisor's seat. In a celebratory article entitled, "In 30

Years, History Comes Full Circle from Roybal to Molina," *Los Angeles Times* columnist Bill Boyarsky quoted Molina:

> This victory should have been celebrated 30 years ago. That is why I want to dedicate this victory to Congressman Ed Roybal. They stole the election from him 30 years ago.[68]

As the article explains, Molina was referring to a 1958 supervisorial contest that then city councillor Roybal initially won by 393 votes, but that after four recounts and some apparent chicanery, he subsequently lost. What the article does not explain—thereby reinforcing Molina's claim that her victory compensated for injustices against her people—is that Roybal ran in a district in which only 23 percent of the population (not voters) were Hispanic, at a time when Hispanics constituted only 9 percent of the county's population.[69]

Assertions such as these, repeated over and over by sympathetic media commentators, reveal the power of the historical claim made by Mexican Americans that "we were here first." The statement is true for some, but it scarcely leads to the conclusion that the entire group's present meager economic and political resources are the result of racial oppression.

We need not deny past injustices to see that there are problems with the Mexican-American claim to racial minority status. The most obvious is that the overwhelming majority of the Mexican-origin population in Los Angeles County are either immigrants or the offspring of immigrants. Indeed, about two-thirds of all Hispanics now living in the county have arrived within the last twenty years.[70] And most of these have been illegal immigrants. It is in fact probable that a majority of Hispanics in Los Angeles at the time of the 1980 redistricting were not citizens.[71] Yet when it is argued that Mexican Americans have been excluded from the political process, these simple facts are completely ignored. The plaintiffs' briefs and even the judges' opinions in the *Garza* case are full of references to vague "demographic factors" to which the supervisors were supposed to respond. But in these documents one is hard-pressed to find the words "immigrant" or "immigration." Nor is there any acknowledgment that the supervisors' response was conditioned by the fact that only 32 percent of Hispanics in the county in 1980 were even eligible to register and vote.[72]

This concatenation of vague misconceptions was in full view when the *Los Angeles Times* endorsed Molina. As the editors pronounced, "The supervisors opted in 1981 to protect their own incumbencies by diluting the potential voting strength of the county's 3 million Latino residents."[73]

Quite aside from the fact that in 1981 there were only 2 million Latinos in Los Angeles County, this 3 million figure (the county's Latino population in 1990) ignores the huge proportion of Latinos who cannot vote due to their age or legal status. Under these circumstances it is downright misleading to talk of "the potential voting strength" of 3 million Latinos. Committed to the view that the supervisors engaged in "racial gerrymandering," the *Times* simply refuses to address the primary sources of the dilution of the Latino vote in Los Angeles.

Similarly ignored in the *Garza* controversy has been the residential mobility of Mexican Americans. Because compactness is one of the criteria to be considered in drawing districts, a widely dispersed group greatly complicates the process. This has certainly been the case with Hispanics in Los Angeles County. To design a Hispanic majority district there, demographers focused on what they called "the Hispanic Core," an area composed of 229 contiguous census tracts, all but three of which had a majority of Hispanics. The Core contained 81 percent of all census tracts in the county with Hispanic population majorities in 1980, and 72 percent of its total population was Hispanic. Barely 27 percent of these Core Hispanics were voting-age citizens. But more to the point at hand, Hispanics in Los Angeles have dispersed such that the Core contained only 40 percent of the total Hispanic population in the county, and just 36 percent of all citizen voting-age Hispanics.[74]

Thus, drawing Hispanic majority supervisorial districts in Los Angeles County is no easy task. Indeed, in 1981, when Mexican Americans constituted 28 percent of the county population, it was simply not possible to draw a supervisorial district with a Hispanic voting majority.[75] Significantly, none of the experts for the plaintiffs or defendants in the *Garza* case ever argued otherwise. Even the Chicano activists who in 1981 single-handedly challenged the supervisors' redistricting plan never asked for such a district. Instead, they sought two "influence districts" in which Hispanics would hold less than a voting majority, but would nevertheless have the potential either to elect one of their own to the board or to exert significant clout over whoever did get elected.[76]

Moreover, throughout the 1980s creating a Hispanic-voting-majority district remained problematic, with demographers and political scientists disagreeing as to exactly when in the decade it was feasible.[77] When the new district was finally created by order of the courts in 1990, Hispanics constituted 71 percent of its population and 59 percent of its voting-age citizens, but just 51 percent of its registered voters.[78]

For all these reasons, it is no wonder that MALDEF hesitated for almost a decade before bringing suit against the supervisors. As already mentioned, the organization declined to join forces with Chicano activists in 1981 when they challenged the county redistricting plan.[79] Even after the 1982 amendments to the VRA made such suits easier, MALDEF was still reluctant to risk the enormous resources required. In the end, the catalyst was the Reagan Justice Department. Having been preempted by Justice in the 1986 Los Angeles City Council redistricting case, MALDEF could not afford to sit out a second round. So, when Justice began threatening the Board of Supervisors in 1988, MALDEF launched its suit in the midst of ongoing negotiations between the county and the feds. Shortly thereafter, Justice joined the suit.[80]

ROTTEN BOROUGHS AND THE NUMBERS GAME

On the surface, *Garza* was an enormous victory for MALDEF. Yet the gain may be far less substantial than touted. Highly revealing in this regard is the disappointingly low turnout for the historic election that resulted in Molina's victory. Only 23 percent of those registered voted in the runoff between her and Art Torres.[81] Although Molina ran a more grassroots campaign than her clique opponent, it is not easy to overcome the disincentives to neighborhood-based politics in Los Angeles—even with the help of the Voting Rights Act and the federal courts. Indeed, it may be particularly difficult to do so with such help—which is, after all, highly consonant with elite-network politics.

A more salient datum from this election is that out of approximately 1.8 million residents in the newly created First Supervisorial District, only 88,102 votes were cast—less than 5 percent of the total population.[82] The simple fact is that this new Hispanic district does not have many residents eligible to vote. For example, when it was created, the First District had 707,651 voting-age citizens, while the predominantly Anglo Third District had 1,098,663.[83] Thus, a vote in the First weighs much more than in the Third. This curious development arises because the federal courts have interpreted the one-person-one-vote principle as mandating districts roughly equal in total population—not in eligible voters. When laid down by the Supreme Court in *Reynolds v. Sims*, this principle was based on the assumption that equipopulous districts contain correspondingly equal numbers of electors. Yet today, under conditions of mass immigration, this assumption is often wrong.[84]

The same mistaken assumption underlies the creation of city council and other districts under the VRA. Such constituencies, packed with large and growing numbers of individuals unable to vote, increases the number of Latino elected officials in metropolitan Los Angeles. But these gains do not translate into commensurate political power. These officeholders are certainly not viewed by their Anglo colleagues and allies as capable of delivering large blocks of voters—quite the contrary. We are reminded, again, that legalistic efforts to advance Mexican-American political interests are subject to inherent constraints that cannot be overridden by impatient elites. Unfortunately, this homely truth has been obscured in the struggle to jump-start Mexican-American politics.

Here, too, such efforts may actually hinder Mexican-American political advancement. By concentrating noncitizens in highly visible districts, the problem of low Latino political participation is highlighted, and the stereotype of Latinos as politically passive and indifferent is reinforced. At the same time, by fostering the impression that significant political power is being acquired, pressure for more substantive gains is reduced. And while advocates argue that an increase in the number of Mexican-American officeholders raises the level of rank-and-file political involvement, the evidence from Los Angeles suggests otherwise. For with large and growing numbers of constituents ineligible to vote, Latinos elected from these districts experience relatively little home-grown opposition. The resulting political vacuum makes it all the more likely that these elected officials respond more to the politicians or advocacy groups responsible for the creation of their districts than to those whom they formally represent. As we saw in connection with voter registration efforts in Los Angeles, these Mexican-American officeholders not only fail to encourage voter participation, they actually discourage it. Like any officeholders, they are not eager to expand the numbers of those who might put demands on them. Moreover, they have every reason to avoid getting caught between their often conservative Mexican-American base and their typically liberal Democratic allies.

In essence, these Latino districts represent a new type of "rotten borough." The term could not be more appropriate, since it harkens back to an era when standards of voter participation and officeholder accountability were far less rigorous than today. The irony, of course, is that these rotten boroughs follow from today's more demanding standards. The result is that we have increased Mexican-American representation, but only in the most formal and delimited sense.

Even more disturbing is how the VRA seduces Mexican-American leaders into playing a numbers game with ever-increasing populations of politically passive constituents. These rotten boroughs may not provide Mexican-American officeholders with powerful positions, but they do provide them with secure political bases. The trouble is that, having struck this bargain, the officeholders succumb to its logic. On the one hand, they get used to the passivity of their many nonvoting constituents. On the other, in a dynamic social and political system, they cannot rest content with their relatively weak positions. Like all political actors, they seek more influence. But they know all too well the difficulties facing them if they try to expand their voting base. So they opt for the easier and safer route of relying on the increasing overall number of Latinos. The continuing influx of newcomers from Mexico—illegal and legal—answers this need quite neatly.

As suggested earlier, such high levels of immigration are not necessarily in the interests of Mexican Americans generally. Economically, there is evidence that immigrants undercut Mexican Americans, especially those at the lower end of the wage scale.[85] And politically, immigrants present the array of problems I have been addressing. Immigrants generally are not easy to organize for political goals in any case, and immigration at the levels we have been seeing creates so much instability and transience that the task becomes far more difficult. Large numbers of illegal immigrants only further complicate matters.

For all these reasons, Mexican-American leaders used to be wary of immigration from Mexico. De la Garza reports that during the 1950s and 1960s, "Mexican American leaders were among the most vociferous of the opponents to continued Mexican immigration."[86] Given the complicated and continuing ties between Mexicans on both sides of the border, this position was often arrived at reluctantly. But for two decades after World War II, organizations such as LULAC and the American G.I. Forum nonetheless argued for restricted immigration from Mexico, on the grounds that large numbers of newcomers would undermine the social and economic position of Mexican Americans struggling into the American mainstream. As educator and political activist George I. Sanchez argued in 1966:

> Time and time again, just as we have been on the verge of cutting our bi-cultural problems to manageable proportions, uncontrolled mass migrations from Mexico have erased the gains and accentuated the cultural indigestion.[87]

It was not long afterward that a momentous shift occurred in leadership views toward immigration. As noted in chapter 9, today's Mexican-American leadership is overwhelmingly in favor of adopting a de facto open-borders stance, while Mexican Americans generally seem as sharply divided as ever.[88] There is certainly no voice comparable to Sanchez's objecting to the present influx of immigrants to be heard among Mexican Americans today.

The critical factor that accounts for this widely ignored sea-change is, it seems clear, the Voting Rights Act and similar initiatives that now reward Mexican-American leaders not for their group's political clout at the polls, but for its population totals at census time.[89] The affirmative action logic that now pervades our political culture means that steadily increasing numbers of Mexican immigrants readily translate into demands for steadily increasing quotas for Latino employees and Latino majority electoral districts. Thus, Mexican-American leaders have not only acclimated to immigration from Mexico at high levels, they have in fact become dependent on it as the source of their visibility and influence[90]—particularly as compared to blacks, who these leaders have been continually reminded are "the nation's largest minority."

There have been some notable nonparticipants in this numbers game, including César Chávez's United Farm Workers union and the IAF. The former's position on immigration has flip-flopped over the years. Owing its initial successes to the cessation of the Bracero contract labor program in 1964, the UFW has long understood the competitive threat that cheap immigrant labor poses to its organizing efforts. Yet the fact that many of its members are themselves recent immigrants has made it difficult for the union to draw a sharp line at the border.[91] For its part, the IAF has certainly taken no public stand against immigration; in fact, it has recently begun exploring efforts (in Dallas, for example) to focus specifically on organizing immigrants. Nevertheless, this is not a stance the IAF has arrived at blithely, and at various points individual organizers have expressed concerns about the negative impact of continued immigration on their efforts. In both cases, concerns about the impact of high levels of immigration on Mexican-American communities are fueled by the self-interested need to maintain organizations. The contrast with other Mexican-American leaders, who typically lack such organizational bases in their communities, could not be more glaring.

At least as applied to Mexican Americans, the Voting Rights Act smacks of a legalistic quick fix that refuses to acknowledge the real obstacles to the group's political advancement. As such, the VRA satisfies the demands of an impatient society more concerned that the disadvantaged be formally represented than that their actual influence or power be enhanced. We seem unable even to wait for new immigrants to settle in and adapt to their new home—much less to build political institutions—before we declare them to be victims of a regime that fails to include them.

But on a much more concrete level, the VRA benefits various political elites. Most obviously, it has advanced the careers of Mexican-American leaders whose electoral opportunities have been significantly expanded by it. It has also fostered the affirmative action logic whereby Mexican-American leaders generally can press their special claims as the spokesmen and representatives of an aggrieved racial minority whose numbers happen to be growing. Yet the dynamic that makes these leaders dependent on continuing high levels of immigration in fact weakens the group politically—and perhaps economically. Thus, the political fortunes of Mexican-American leaders are at odds with the political and organizational strength of Mexican Americans as a group. As a result, the Voting Rights Act not only fails to address the gap between social and political institutions confronting Mexican Americans today, it arguably exacerbates it.

But Mexican-American elites are hardly the sole beneficiaries of this regime. VRA-mandated districts also reassure concerned Anglo elites that Latinos are getting represented. More specifically, these rotten boroughs speak to the specific needs of Democratic Party leaders in California and elsewhere. Quite aside from the objective difficulties and expense of organizing Mexican Americans under the conditions I have been describing, Democrats are not eager to mobilize new voters whose demands might further complicate the problems of putting together winning coalitions.[92] Rotten boroughs allow party leaders to avoid this risk while at the same time responding to Mexican-American demands for representation.

Charles Hamilton's work on black politics is once again extremely pertinent. In a seminal article written at the end of the 1970s, Hamilton sought to explain the decline in black political participation and power in New York City.[93] He did so by identifying a curious political dynamic he called "patron-recipient politics," which he traced back to the War on Poverty and then contrasted with the "patron-client politics" of the old urban ethnic machines. Of direct relevance to my analysis of Mexican-American politics is the distinction Hamilton draws between the impersonal, one-directional nature of patron-recipient ties and the multifaceted, face-to-face relationships that characterized the ethnic machines. Hamilton observes:

The party official provided favors, divisible benefits, jobs for the constituents. In return, grateful constituents gave their votes on election day.
. . . At all times, both patron and client clearly understood the basis of the
relationship: *quid pro quo*. . . . The recipient receives from the patron and
is asked to do nothing *but* receive the benefits. . . . The client becomes a
political actor; the recipient remains a political nonactor.[94]

As Hamilton emphasizes, the patron-recipient tie, because it is fleet-
ing and transient, lacks the organizational dimension that characterizes
the patron-client relationship:

The patron expects to service a revolving recipient group, which becomes
one measure of the patron's viability: the numbers of *different* recipients
served. This is so, because the basis of the relationship is the recipient's
needs, not necessarily the patron's resources. Presumably, that need can
be met. Therefore, it is not expected that a permanent or even long-term
relationship be developed between the patron and the recipient. Again,
unlike the patron-client association, it is hoped that the particular patron-
recipient relationship will be ephemeral and transitory. It is difficult, therefore, to perceive a viable, sustained political foundation being built upon
such an orientation.[95]

Lacking strong organizational bases, practitioners of patron-recipient
politics resort, when necessary, to protest tactics. Once again, no lasting
relationships between leaders and rank and file are forged. Finally,
Hamilton argues that patron-recipient politics—quite contrary to the intentions of those who often support it—depoliticizes its intended beneficiaries. Although he does not put it in such terms, patron-recipient
politics fosters the political equivalent of welfare dependency.

Hamilton's analysis of patron-recipient politics is, if anything, more
relevant to an understanding of Mexican-American than black politics—
because, due to the various cultural and structural factors I have been examining, Mexican Americans are more prone to political passivity than
blacks. Moreover, Hamilton highlights the particular symbiosis between
elite-network and protest politics so evident in Los Angeles and national
politics. Finally, his analysis puts into perspective the implicit strategy of
Mexican-American political elites who, contrary to what their critics typically charge, are not concerned to organize or control an insulated barrio constituency, but rather to represent—vicariously—a continually
expanding body of constituents to whom they have only the most tenuous ties.

THE FABLE OF THE CRABS

National elites intent on removing obstacles to the political advancement of Mexican Americans have ignored still another dimension of the rationalizing process that results in the separation of political from social structures in advanced industrial societies. This dimension, which overlays the social-political divide like a palimpsest, concerns the distinction between the private and the public. As political economist Albert Hirschman explains, the need to make this distinction is characteristic of modern societies:

> The "unblushing confusion" of the public and private spheres, which was given quite properly the more neutral term "patrimonialism" by Max Weber, prevailed in most countries up to the nineteenth century and is still today in evidence over broad areas of the globe. . . . Nevertheless, the separation of the two spheres has been proclaimed in the West, and it has become an aspiration elsewhere as well.[96]

This "unblushing confusion" is nowhere more evident than in Mexico itself, so it's hardly surprising that Mexican immigrants bring it with them across the border. And just as a tendency to confound the private and the public persisted among prior immigrant groups with premodern values, so does it persist in the culture of Mexican Americans. That is why IAF organizers focus on teaching leaders "to separate the private from the public": negotiating the passage from the primary group ties of family and friends to the instrumental relationships of the wider society is *the* fundamental challenge facing Mexican Americans—with implications for their political, as well as their social and economic progress.

The evidence from San Antonio and Texas lends particular credence to this statement. For in San Antonio, we saw how the dense social networks of the Mexican-American community nurture an open and spirited politics. But at the same time, the powerful family and neighborhood ties that foster friends-and-neighbors politics also infuse that politics with the passions inevitably infecting close-knit communities. Conflicts between personal loyalties and the instrumental demands of public life become pervasive, and it is only through the extraordinary efforts of skilled community organizers that a larger, more overarching organization like COPS comes into being.

By the same token, Henry Cisneros and the other nationally prominent Mexican-American leaders out of San Antonio are typically not products of its countless personal and turf rivalries. Many of those leaders have been exported, or have found a national audience. Indeed, it is arguable that to succeed in politics, San Antonio's best and brightest have gone outside the city. Thus, San Antonio demonstrates the irony that the primary group ties that are the greatest political resource of Mexican Americans are at the same time their greatest liability.

The same tendency toward infighting is evident, to varying degrees, in Mexican-American communities throughout the Southwest, including Los Angeles. Indeed, it is a problem that Mexican Americans themselves volunteer in conversation. When asked to elaborate, virtually every one of the scores of Mexican Americans I have talked with cited infighting as a group cultural trait, related to a strong sense of individual and group pride. Many pointed to the Mexican-American political lexicon, which is full of folklore about such matters. For example, one politico offered this wry summation of the fierce pride felt by Mexicans in general: "We Mexicans are so proud, we forget what we're proud of." Another elected official explained the concept of *"orgullo falso,"* or false pride, which he described as a macho trait that "mothers instill in their children to defend themselves against jealous friends and neighbors." As for the disposition to envy, *"la envidia,"* it is the most common explanation given for the group's factionalism. As one Mexican-American politician in San Antonio summed it up: "If I can't have it—a horse or a woman—no one can."

This pattern of feuding and bickering is reminiscent of rural village cultures more generally, to judge by the observations of peasant life in Italy and France by Edward Banfield and Laurence Wylie.[97] Moreover, it is conveyed in a fable volunteered, sooner or later, by almost every Mexican American with whom I have discussed politics. The tale is of a fisherman with a bucket full of crabs for bait. A neighbor comes along and notices the crabs trying to escape by building themselves into a pyramid up the side of the bucket. "Aren't you afraid they'll get out?" asks the neighbor. "No," replies the fisherman. "They're Mexican crabs. Every time one of them gets near the top, the others knock him down."[98]

Mexican pride finds individual expression in the cult of machismo.[99] But it finds even stronger group expression in another group cultural trait that can impede advancement: the ideal of the cohesive, self-sufficient family that disdains the help of outsiders. This ideal, though frequently breached in practice, is evident in the conservative strain revealed in Mexican-American attitudes toward social welfare programs.[100] It has also served Mexican Americans well in recent years, when liberals and conservatives alike have come to extol family values. Picking up such cues from the mainstream, both leaders and ordinary Mexican Americans point with pride to the central role family plays in their lives—claims that are confirmed by demographic and especially ethnographic evidence.[101]

In an era when the basic social unit is threatened and seems at times to be unraveling, such findings about Mexican Americans are heartening. Yet strong families and family values are not an unmixed blessing. I indicated in chapter 5 how they can hinder the development of political organizations.[102] In a different vein, strong families can seriously hinder the social and economic advancement of individuals. Writing of his own struggle to get out of Harlem, black economist Thomas Sowell recounts how his otherwise supportive family could not accept his desire to succeed at one of New York City's competitive academic high schools, and how he ultimately had to defy them in order to realize his ambitions.[103]

In San Antonio, these cultural crosscurrents swirling about the family are very much in evidence. As members of a proud ethnic group, Mexican Americans there boast of their strong family values; but as school administrators and judges enforcing truancy laws, Mexican Americans complain that their people are frequently lax about school attendance. These community leaders explain that the poor and recent immigrants are particularly prone to distrust institutions outside their immediate families, even those run by Mexican Americans. The impact of such attitudes is intensified by economic hardship, which causes parents to acquiesce when young boys prefer work and earning money over going to school, while their sisters help out with the chores at home, sheltered from the threatening American youth culture.[104] As Cisneros elaborates on this dynamic:

> Hispanics are predominantly poor. They come from rural areas where there's no tradition of higher education, and their social patterns and mores are a disincentive. Fathers are very protective of their daughters and don't want them to leave home. The males are supposed to go to work to help the family or into the military.[105]

Nor is such behavior limited to the unambitious. A revealing vignette is recounted in the recent book (and film) about acclaimed East Los Angeles math teacher Jaime Escalante. When a student drops out of his trigonometry class, Escalante pays a visit to her parents. Recent immigrants from Mexico, the couple are running a restaurant west of downtown Los Angeles—an apparent American success story. Yet when their daughter's homework interferes with her responsibilities at the restaurant, where her math skills are desperately needed, they decide she must leave Escalante's demanding class. Their decision is reversed only after the teacher pleads with them—and threatens to report them to the child labor authorities.[106]

Another cultural obstacle to Mexican-American advancement, especially in politics, is the pattern of humility and deference to authority that has persisted for generations, often in tandem with a smoldering resentment that finds few constructive outlets. Mexican behavior tends to oscillate between strong primary group controls and individualistic outbursts; Mexican culture has a highly emotional strain that moves between sullen passivity and sudden passion, whether joyous singing and dancing or violent fighting. These traits are not conducive to sustained collective action. As the journalist Alan Riding writes: "The Mexican is not a team player."[107]

I realize that this cultural perspective is controversial. Smacking of "blaming the victim," and suggesting that not all barriers to Mexican-American advancement are external to the group, such explanations are certainly not voiced publicly by Mexican-American leaders. Typical were the remarks of a Cisneros campaign adviser, who described in great detail the feuds raging on the West and South Sides of San Antonio and then warned, "If you quote me, I'll deny it."

The irony is that these leaders give more credence to cultural explanations than is warranted. There is no doubt, for example, that San Antonio's fragmented political system contributes to the factionalism of Mexican-American politics there. Conversely, the more professionalized and less neighborhood-based politics of Los Angeles imposes relative discipline on Mexican-American infighting there.

Yet the difference between San Antonio and Los Angeles is only relative. Indeed, as I have already indicated, Mexican-American politics in Los Angeles is characterized by intense feuding between Gloria Molina and her feminist-oriented supporters and Richard Alatorre and the rest of the male-dominated clique. Similar gender-related schisms have arisen in organizations such as the Southwest Voter Registration Education Project and MALDEF, where in 1987 former New Mexico governor Tony Anaya led a divisive and unsuccessful effort to oust the young female attorney heading the organization.[108] Similarly, in San Antonio in the early 1980s, a Mexican-American woman had to battle just about every Mexican-American male politico in town in her ultimately successful bid for a city council seat.

Here again, such strife owes much to the rigid, traditional attitudes many Mexican-American men, particularly those from working- and lower-middle-class backgrounds, display toward women, especially Mexican-American women with political ambitions. And while the singular bitterness and longevity of the split in Los Angeles owes much to the specific personalities involved, at its root is the heavy-handed treatment afforded Molina by her male colleagues in the clique.

But such infighting should not be explained exclusively in cultural terms. Particularly in Los Angeles, it has been fueled and exacerbated by the substantial resources available to Molina and her Chicana supporters from Anglo feminists. So, here again, cultural tendencies interact with, and are conditioned by, social, economic, and political structures.

THE ROLE OF MEDIATING INSTITUTIONS

Earlier in this century, American institutions played an important role in changing immigrant values similar to those brought here today from the villages of Mexico. Such institutions performed this task by providing opportunities for newcomers to learn to behave like Americans, but without cutting them off from their native languages or heritages. Thus, Janowitz depicts public schools as having offered immigrants and their children "a bridging institution from the local residential neighborhood to the larger metropolis, to the larger society, and to the nation-state."[109]

This insight derives from Janowitz's intellectual forebears at the University of Chicago. In the aftermath of World War I, when the advocates of "Americanization" were insisting that the only way to incorporate immigrants into American society was through the rapid and complete elimination of all traces of foreign languages and customs, pioneering sociologists like Robert Park offered a dramatically different perspective. What they saw in immigrant communities were not unassimilable lumps, but peasants who, though still enmeshed in the enveloping group life of transplanted European villages, were nevertheless in the early stages of a long process through which they would eventually learn to act as individuals in a society characterized by complex, impersonal ties. As Park and his colleague Herbert Miller observed in their 1921 book, *Old World Traits Transplanted*:

> The apperception mass of the immigrant, expressed in the attitudes and values he brings with him from his old life, is the material from which he must build his Americanism. It is also the material we must work with, if we would aid this process. Our tools may be in part American customs and institutions, but the substance we seek to mold into new forms is the product of other centuries in other lands. . . . A wise policy of assimilation, like a wise educational policy, does not seek to destroy the attitudes and memories that are there, but to build on them.[110]

To drive home their point, Park and Miller noted how the United States government had successfully relied on immigrant organizations to sell Liberty Bonds during World War I.

In this same period, Park's Chicago colleagues, William Thomas and Florian Znaniecki, published their classic study, *The Polish Peasant in Europe and America*. In this monumental 1,800-page work, the authors concluded that mutual-aid and self-help societies helped Polish immigrants cope with the challenges of America by subjecting their face-to-face communal ties to the rational calculation necessary to function in modern society. Thomas and Znaniecki describe a life insurance plan offered by a Polish-American organization:

> It should be realized that the function of this business side of the Polish-American institutions is not to create a bond between the members—the real bond is the satisfaction of the "social instinct"—but only to stabilize and extend a social cohesion which otherwise would manifest itself only irregularly and within narrower limits. In a word, mutual insurance is not a basis of association but of organisation. It gives a minimum of rational order to those social relations which are the essential factor of the racial cohesion of American Poles.[111]

From this perspective, such immigrant organizations were critical to assimilation because they partook of both the old and the new. They relied on Old World customs and traditions to function as a primary group, providing the whole person with an identity and social solidarity. Yet they also took those primary group ties and used them to build an institution addressing the specific needs of immigrants in America, where the lack of continuity and strong traditions left them facing new and daunting choices. Such institutions subtly transformed the old into the new by modifying and elaborating primary group ties without abruptly sundering them.

The specifically political dimension of this process is captured by Huntington in his treatise on political development:

> The distinguishing characteristic of a highly institutionalized polity . . . is the price it places on power. . . . If the society is modern and complex, with a large number of social forces, individuals from any one of the social forces may have to make extensive changes in their behavior, values, and attitudes in the process of acquiring power through the political institutions of society. They may well have to unlearn much which they have learned from family, ethnic group, and social class, and adapt to an entirely new code of behavior.[112]

The obvious parallel is with the "unlearning" fostered by IAF. Indeed, it is striking how Alinsky organizers echo Huntington when, mindful of the cultural values their Mexican-American members bring with them, the organizers seek to reorient those values in accordance with the goal of organization-building. (It is worth noting that Alinsky organizers emphasize that all groups have some sort of "unlearning" to undergo. For example, they point to the need for middle-class individuals to overcome ingrained habits of politeness before they can be effective IAF leaders.) Step by step, organizers teach their members that politics is about power, and that to obtain power they must learn to distinguish the private from the public.

In this sense, Alinsky organizations are, in Janowitz's formulation, "bridging institutions." Yet because in chapter 5 I used the word "mediation" to describe the accommodation of diverse interests that occurs within IAF organizations, and attributed that mediating function to the influence of the Catholic Church, I prefer to call IAF organizations "mediating institutions."[113] The phrase does more justice to the complex transformation—the social alchemy—that actually occurs when the strong primary group ties of Mexican-American culture are blended with, and altered by, the instrumental ties of an impersonal political organization.

The point is amply illustrated by the ways in which COPS takes the rich group life of Mexican Americans and gives it a shape that both rescues it from personality and turf disputes and subjects it to the discipline of effective organization politics. Typical is the way COPS deals with Mexican-American infighting and pride. However much commotion COPS creates with its "actions," they are always planned in advance and executed with care and precision. When the organization has had its say before an official body and then leaves en masse, it cleverly manages to disrupt and show discipline at the same time. Such tactics directly address the defensiveness of Mexican Americans about their infighting. At the same time, COPS reinforces group pride with its stance of rugged self-sufficiency. "Never do for others what they can do for themselves," the IAF "Iron Rule," applies inside and outside the organization. Leaders are taught to bargain and compete for power with one another; the organization rejects government subsidies; the focus stays on barrio economic development; and irksome would-be contributors get their donations unceremoniously returned. In all these ways, COPS sustains its members' pride while also allowing them to demonstrate group cohesion to potentially disdainful Anglos.

Likewise, COPS organizers do not deny or reject the strong family loyalties of Mexican Americans. Instead, they appeal directly to such sentiments by concentrating on issues of immediate relevance to the welfare and self-interest of families. They take family feelings as a given, and then use them to build the organization, which in turn subjects such feelings to its discipline. For example, a mother's individual desire for a new house is bound up with her family's needs, but it is also used to build her attachment to COPS. When she becomes a leader, the role she plays in dividing up Community Development Block Grants serves to broaden her feelings of self-interest from an exclusive focus on the needs of her family to identification with the needs of their parishes and of the organization. In essence, these organizational dynamics prefigure the public interest, much as Janowitz would have it.

Moreover, IAF tactics have been particularly effective in jostling humble Mexican Americans in San Antonio out of old patterns of deference to authority and suppressed resentment. The clear lines of authority within COPS have great appeal for Mexican Americans. At the same time, the organization uses its authority to require members to act on their resentment. By transforming complicated issues of public policy into personalized conflicts between Mexican-American housewives and individual members of the Anglo elite, COPS taps into the anger that Mexican Americans only intermittently reveal to themselves, much less to their Anglo "betters." Yet the discipline and authority of the organization also channel that anger in a highly structured, and therefore constructive, direction. COPS engages in the politics of resentment, but only as a stepping-stone to the politics of aspiration.

In sum, IAF organizing seeks out what Mexican Americans have to offer: their pride, their desire for self-sufficiency, their strong sense of family and neighborhood, their respect for authority and their anger. The organization then informs and refines these raw materials in a way that resonates with another Mexican-American cultural trait that I have not yet discussed: cynicism about politics. IAF's rejection of abstract appeals to civic duty or political ideology, and its emphasis on self-interest, are particularly well-suited to a group whose roots in the rural villages of Mexico are still evident. Today, circumstances are changing rapidly, but a long history of near caste status in the Southwest has kept older attitudes alive—particularly among the working- and lower-middle classes, where IAF has focused its efforts.

"Unlearning" this cynicism is perhaps the most important lesson that IAF teaches. In essence, the lesson concerns the proper ends of politics. Along with cynicism, Mexican Americans also incline toward moralism, particularly when social issues such as abortion or pornography, or even mundane matters like corruption, surface. These contradictory traits also derive from the family-centeredness of Mexican-American culture—specifically, the tendency of Mexican Americans to confound family values with political goals. The difference between these two realms may be clear to the upper-middle-class reader, but it is not to the San Antonio meat processor or housewife who projects the everyday world of the family on to the unfamiliar world of politics. The result is not merely factionalism, but moralism unmindful of the limits of politics. And when those limits are encountered again and again, moralism turns to cynicism.

As Plato teaches through the character of Thrasymachus in *The Republic*, the cynic who rejects the idea of justice as a sham, a smokescreen for power, is typically the disillusioned moralist whose high ideals have been frustrated by political reality.[114] In contemporary America, this cynicism-moralism dialectic appears frequently in the lower-middle class, whose aspirations feed middle-class pretensions but whose insecurities foster working-class cynicism. This social class dynamic is reinforced among Mexican Americans, whose cynicism is fed by memories of the past, but whose optimism is fueled by the opportunities of today.

Successful IAF organizing presents Mexican Americans with a resolution of this dialectic: political and ethical realism, which derives from the Catholic natural law tradition as expounded in this era by Jacques Maritain and John Courtney Murray.[115] To barrio moralists outraged by abortion on demand, for example, IAF teaches that disillusionment will result if political objectives are shaped exclusively and directly by family values. To cynics convinced the gringo can't be beaten, IAF teaches that he can, but only if Mexican Americans are prepared to make the difficult passage from the private to the public—to venture, and to act, outside the close-knit families and neighborhoods where they feel most secure.

THE IMBALANCE BETWEEN THE PRIVATE AND THE PUBLIC

As institutions that mediate between the private and the public, IAF organizations manifest characteristics of both spheres. COPS, for example, plays a key role in the public life of San Antonio, while self-consciously imposing the rigors of the wider society's competitive individualism onto Mexican-American primary group relations. Yet the organization's status in the community is ambiguous. It wields considerable political power, but unofficially, as a private voluntary organization whose leaders are not paid. Meanwhile, COPS's paid organizers tend to stay in the background. Although it has effectively controlled the spending of millions of public dollars, the organization itself has not been the recipient of public funds. And as COPS organizers have met with success and acceptance, they have struggled to avoid becoming too integrated—co-opted, they would say— into the official, public life of San Antonio and, indeed, Texas. Thus, COPS is a hybrid, with both public and private facets. Fitting neatly into neither sphere, it is in a state of dynamic tension, a delicate balance maintained through the prudent efforts of the organizers.[116]

In her classic work, *The Death and Life of Great American Cities*, Jane Jacobs identifies a similar characteristic of urban institutions generally. She notes: "Formal public organizations in cities require an informal public life underlying them, mediating between them and the privacy of the people of the city."[117] As likely spots for such informal public life, Jacobs cites certain sidewalk areas and neighborhood stores. The specific virtue of such venues is that they allow individuals to overcome urban anonymity on a circumscribed basis so that their privacy is not completely sacrificed or threatened. As Jacobs puts it:

> A good city street neighborhood achieves a marvel of balance between its people's determination to have essential privacy and their simultaneous wishes for differing degrees of contact, enjoyment or help from the people around.[118]

Because their responsibilities inevitably lead to intrusive questions and full disclosure, formal public organizations cannot typically perform this delicate task. Jacobs adds that one enemy of this balancing act is "togetherness," or forced intimacy. At one time in vogue among urban planners, such notions sought to extend the private sphere beyond its natural limits, and not surprisingly ended up with city dwellers retreating totally into private life for refuge.[119]

But threats to informal public life do not come solely from well-meaning elites. They also come from below. Jacobs quotes a community organizer working with public housing tenants in New York City:

> These projects are not lacking in natural leaders. . . . They contain people with real ability, wonderful people many of them, but the typical sequence is that in the course of organization leaders have found each other, gotten all involved in each others' social lives, and have ended up talking to nobody but each other. They have not found their followers. Everything tends

to degenerate into ineffective cliques, as a natural course. There is no normal public life. Just the mechanics of people learning what is going on is so difficult. It all makes the simplest social gain extra hard for these people.[120]

These remarks clarify why IAF leaders are discouraged from inviting organizers home for dinner; why organizers avoid having meetings in private homes; and why members are expected to address one another as "Mr." or "Mrs." One is tempted to view such methods as primarily concerned with coaxing Mexican Americans out of their family and neighborhood relationships and into the broader public realm. But these methods are also intended to protect the organization from the sheer strength of those relationships—to keep it from being overwhelmed to the point of degenerating into a social club or exclusive clique.

All mediating institutions share this double-faceted nature; otherwise they could not perform the delicate balancing act between the private and public. But this same quality renders mediating institutions extremely fragile. I refer not only to their internal dynamics, but to their vulnerability to external criticism and attack. A case in point is the Alinsky community organization's lineal forebear—the political machine. Of this nearly extinct species, Theodore Lowi has observed: "Sociologically, the Old Machine was a combination of rational goals and fraternal loyalty."[121] In other words, the machine partook of both public and private realms.

In her study of the origins of machine politics in antebellum New York, Amy Bridges explains how straddling the private-public divide created problems by blurring the image of this political organization and its leader, the boss:

> Despite his ascendancy, the boss remains an elusive figure, sometimes denounced as a demagogue, rogue, or thief, at other times lauded as a Robin Hood, defender of the immigrant, and cultural symbol of the political triumph of the common man. The Fernando Wood who was the "friend of the working man" was also a demagogue, the open-hearted William Tweed an embezzler, the efficient Mayor Daley a power broker. When account is taken of the social forces among whom the boss mediated, the compromises he orchestrated, and the city he governed, it can be recognized that ambiguity is fundamental to the boss and the machine he organized. The ties of the boss to the dangerous classes and to the respectable element were equally strong, and his autonomy from each of them equally important to his continued ascendancy. The institutional arrangements of machine politics organized social force, political faction, dominant group, and government.[122]

Such subtleties were, of course, lost on the boss's contemporaries. Where today we may see functional ambiguities, reformers saw only sinister shadows obscuring a figure who not only wielded more power than duly elected officials, but did so hidden from public view. And today where we may see political parties as mediating institutions linking private interests to government, reformers saw only the will of the people being perverted by unseen middlemen making deals in the proverbial smoke-filled rooms.

Earlier this century, native-born Americans, steeped in classical liberalism's ideal of the rational individual, were repulsed by an immigrant politics based on nothing more, in their view, than tribal loyalties and the buying and selling of votes. They regarded immigrants as literally corrupting republican virtues and institutions. Only a level-headed few like Park and his University of Chicago colleagues saw that although American institutions were being changed by the immigrants, so too were the immigrants themselves being transformed. Indeed, the Chicago school perceived that immigrant institutions like the machines were the means by which uneducated peasants were learning how to become Americans.

In our own era, mediating institutions fare no better. Arguably, they fare worse. Today's affluent, educated citizens demand more and more openness and accountability of all institutions. With the resulting scrutiny, especially under the bright lights of the media, the shadows in which mediating institutions perform their vital functions are less and less acceptable, or even possible.[123]

An important factor here is the increased emphasis on individual rights in our political culture. Of particular significance have been the successful claims of women and racial minorities that institutions such as political parties, social clubs, and private schools have discriminated against them. The long-term impact of such efforts has been a gradual redefinition of the private sphere. Whereas it was once conceived of as the realm of individual and associational prerogatives over and against those of the state,[124] the private sphere is now seen as comprised largely of the aggregated rights of individuals. Even the family is cast in terms of contractual relationships among individuals.[125]

This reduced conception of the private sphere has, not coincidentally, been accompanied by an expansion of the public. It is certainly no accident that the challenge to institutional prerogatives in the name of individual rights has been led by participants who refer to themselves as *public* interest lawyers. More to the point, the challenge to private institutions has been governmental, and the public sphere has expanded along with government generally.

Still, this reconceptualization of the private and the public antedated public interest law. It can be traced back earlier this century, when government began expanding its reach by engaging private organizations—for example, trade unions and business associations—in behalf of its objectives. Whether private organizations thereby benefited from official recognition or actual government subvention, they paid for it with their autonomy.[126] As a result, more and more "private" organizations are so in name only. And though the distinction between public and private has in that sense grown murky, there can be no doubt that the public (that is, governmental) sphere has expanded at the expense of the private.[127] Moreover, given the rationalizing tendencies of government bureaucracy, it is increasingly difficult—if not downright impossible—to be "semi-public." Indeed, the merest governmental tie is now sufficient grounds for public regulation of what were once regarded as private associations. For example, tax-exempt status is now considered tantamount to an actual fiscal grant, and the "recipient" organization is fully subject to governmental regulation.[128] The end result is that a very bright line has been drawn between an inclusive public realm of formal, organizational efforts and a private sphere of individual rights.

That line will not be an easy one for Mexican Americans to cross. In the first place, today's intensely individualistic culture corrodes the primary group ties that could be the basis of organized political action. Second, whatever such ties Mexican Americans manage to sustain get devalued in the formalized, professionalized realm of contemporary politics. More than ever, there is a need for mediating institutions to provide venues within which Mexican Americans can learn—and unlearn—what they must in order to advance politically.

The irony, of course, is that the decline in mediating institutions is matched by the rising demand for representation discussed earlier. The unmediated gap between the public and the private therefore creates a tension that demands resolution. One possible response, which I have not explored, is charismatic leadership. The great exemplar of such leadership is, of course, Martin Luther King, Jr. His powerful, direct appeals to ordinary blacks helped overcome the quarreling among turf-conscious ministers in which the civil rights movement had become mired.[129] In a similar though less dramatic way, César Chávez became what Mexican Americans call "our Martin Luther King" by seizing upon the personalism of Mexican-American culture and building a movement on the intense bonds that farmworkers and other Mexican Americans felt with him. Elements of charismatic leadership can also be discerned in Henry Cisneros's surmounting the factionalism of friends-and-neighbors politics in San Antonio. An appealing young leader in whom his people have invested their hopes for acceptance and advancement, Cisneros has embodied the aspirations every Mexican-American mother has for her sons. Though not of Chávez's renown, the young leader's bond with his people is such that his picture is found in West Side homes alongside that of the Pope and the Kennedys.

The problem with charismatic leadership is the same as its strength: its personal basis, which leaves followers open to disillusionment, either with the original leader, whose human foibles emerge over time, or with his would-be successors, who never quite live up to his example. Fortuitous and undependable, charismatic leadership is highly unstable. Very seldom do its intense, direct bonds get transferred or institutionalized into something more rational and enduring.

A more general and pervasive effort to close the gap between the public and the private is to remake the public in the image of the private. This response to a fundamental dilemma of political life traces back to Plato's *Republic*, in which the *polis* was to be recast as a family. It is also implicit in the rhetoric and actions of utopians and revolutionaries who set about restructuring society by simultaneously abolishing the private sphere and reconstituting the public in its image. Faint—very faint—echoes of this same tendency can be heard in the exhortations of politicians such as Governor Mario Cuomo that we ought to conceive of our nation as a family.

Among Mexican Americans, this impulse to close the public-private gap has typically found voice in protest politics. It is certainly implicit in activist demands for public affirmation and governmental support for Chicanos as a racial minority. Typically arguing that their people either cannot or will not be integrated in the American mainstream, these activists insist that the mainstream adapt itself to them. In essence, they argue that barrio values be brought into the public sphere unmediated.

ASSIMILATION AND ITS DISCONTENTS

This stance is not without merit. Assimilation into American life has never been quick or painless, for any group. In a variety of realms—not just political, but also social, economic, and cultural—Mexican immigrants and especially their children and grandchildren must negotiate the difficult passage from the private to the public sphere. Becoming part of the American mainstream comes at a price, and some Mexican Americans now believe that price is too high. Chicano activists have taken the lead by questioning the very goal of assimilation, often dismissing it as not only unattainable but undesirable.

In the ensuing debate over whether or not Mexicans and other groups are, or should be, integrating into American society, "assimilation" is typically characterized as a one-dimensional, linear process that results in societal consensus. Yet it is no such thing. As I argued in chapter 1, assimilation must be considered in its various and distinct dimensions. And given the transformations in our political system that I have been examining, the *political* assimilation of Mexican Americans is critical, because it is in that realm where the predictable discontents and frustrations accompanying social, economic, and cultural assimilation are being transformed into the divisive demands of race politics. The resulting irony is that for Mexican Americans political assimilation has increasingly come to mean defining themselves as a racial minority.

The beginning of wisdom here is to reject the romantic notion that immigration to America is a uniformly positive experience that most peoples of the world would readily undertake, if given only half a chance. Though buoyed by hopes and aspirations, immigrants have also viewed the endeavor with uncertainty, a sense of loss, even dread. We know, for example, that Mexican immigrants today are uneasy with the impact of America's individualistic, at times hedonistic culture on their family-oriented way of life.[130] Similar fears were evident more than half a century ago, when, as former *New York Times* reporter Nicholas Gage relates about his immigrant family, his father, a Greek villager, came to the United States but delayed for years sending for his family out of fear that America would corrupt the morals of his young daughters. Indeed, it was only after Communists had overrun their village and murdered his wife that Gage's father relented.[131] Seldom was coming to America seen simply as the first step on the glorious road to political liberty and social and economic advancement. Otherwise, the extent of return of immigrants to their homelands would not have been as great as it was.[132]

Certainly, this sense of painful disorientation is conveyed by historian Oscar Handlin in the title of his classic study of immigration to America, *The Uprooted.*[133] Still more cogent is the image painted by playwright William Alfred of his great-grandmother, an Irish immigrant with whom he lived in Brooklyn as a child:

> Although she always used to say she had no desire to return to Ireland to live, she lived out of a trunk to her dying day, and taught her children to do the same. . . . When, over eighty, she died in the early thirties, it did not seem strange six months afterward to receive a clipping from an Irish newspaper, which read: "Died in Exile: Anna Maria Gavin Egan."[134]

Yet, despite such travail, most immigrants (at least those who decide to stay) have generally been content with their new lives. Within a decade or two of their arrival, immigrants match the earnings of individuals in their national origin group who are native-born and have similar earnings characteristics.[135] However difficult the struggle, their situation in America is typically an improvement over where they came from—and where their friends and relatives remain. And, of course, immigrants look to the future, with their hopes and energies invested in their children. As anthropologist John Ogbu writes:

> Immigrants will often compare their situation in the United States with what they have known or what their peers are experiencing "back home." When making such comparisons, they find encouraging evidence to believe that they will enjoy greater opportunities in the United States for themselves or for their children.[136]

And the children of immigrants do well. Indeed, as a group the second generation not only outperforms their parents,[137] but actually achieves overall socioeconomic parity with the native population.[138] In fact, sociologists David Featherman and Robert Hauser report that second-generation males actually enjoy "somewhat greater socioeconomic success than men born to native parents."[139] Nevertheless, the children of immigrants are not always secure in their success. Memories of struggle and poverty die hard.[140] And life in the American mainstream may seem anemic—as well as anomic—to those who grew up in tight-knit families and cohesive neighborhoods. Typically caught between their parents' world and the wider society, the second generation may not know quite where they fit in. Of himself, William Alfred observes: "I myself, till well on in my twenties, felt that Ireland, which I had never seen, was my true country."[141] Alfred may be an extreme case, but the immigrants' sense of loss often gets passed on to their children. Alternatively, the children of immigrants may come to resent or feel ashamed of the foreign traits of their parents. Socioeconomic success may not soothe, and may indeed exacerbate, such discontents.

Somewhat different problems arise among the grandchildren of immigrants. Here again, as economist Barry Chiswick puts it, an "apparently universal pattern"[142] among immigrant groups to the United States is evident: the third generation on average does less well socioeconomically than the second.[143] Undoubtedly this phenomenon explains why questions about the costs of assimilation become salient among the third generation. The grandchildren who never actually lived in the immigrant enclaves of their forebears may see the past as more appealing than the present. Many such individuals may feel that, in retrospect, the struggle for advancement and acceptance into the mainstream has not been worth the price. As sociologist William Petersen observes: "In the transformation to a modernist, bureaucratic society, much is given up that eventually is regarded as valuable."[144] Indeed, historian Marcus Lee Hansen captured this process of reevaluation in his aphorism: "what the son wishes to forget the grandson wishes to remember."[145] However flawed as a precise predictor of generational cleavages within specific ethnic groups, Hansen's basic insight remains valid: the process of assimilation is a dialectical one, not a neat linear progression.[146]

By and large, Mexican Americans conform to this nonlinear pattern. Mexican immigrants progress such that, after about fifteen years in this country, their earnings equal those of native-born Mexican Americans with similar characteristics.[147] Socioeconomic advancement continues with the second generation.[148] And in keeping with Chiswick's universal pattern, the third generation experiences slippage, obtaining somewhat less education and lower earnings than their parents.[149]

The attitudinal responses to this socioeconomic trajectory similarly reflect the general pattern for immigrant ethnic groups. As we have seen, the evidence is that immigrants themselves are content. As for their children and grandchildren, a good deal of evidence indicates that over time Mexican Americans come to voice positions almost indistinguishable from those of the rest of the population. I have already cited the example of a Mexican-American politician, the child of an immigrant laborer, whose own brother favored immigration restriction and insisted, "Hey, let's take care of the Mexicans who are already here." More systematically, a survey of Latinos in California reports that while 74 percent of the first generation favor amnesty for illegal immigrants, 58 percent of the second and only 49 percent of the third generation do—compared to 44 percent of non-Latino whites. Such data lead Bruce Cain and Roderick Kiewiet to speculate on "the possibility that Latino attitudes, like those of the Irish and Italians before them, may change as Latinos become more established and move up the socio-economic ladder."[150]

Yet equally consistent with the overall pattern of immigrant-group assimilation are signs of disaffection. For example, a study of Mexican-American schoolchildren in El Paso found increasing levels of identification with American political institutions and values until the third generation, at which point there was a discernible falloff, even after controls for intervening variables were introduced.[151] This particular outcome might be explained by the specific circumstances of Mexican Americans in an impoverished border town. Yet similarly troublesome findings emerge from a recent study indicating that Mexican-American mothers of third-generation students in Southern California have "significantly lower educational aspirations than mothers of either second- or first-generation students."[152]

Another indication of problems is complaints of discrimination voiced by a variety of Mexican Americans. Such complaints even come from immigrants themselves. For example, Alejandro Portes and Robert Bach traced the fortunes of a group of legal Mexican immigrants for six years, beginning with their arrival in this country. Although they expressed consistently high levels of satisfaction with and commitment to the United States, these immigrants were also increasingly likely to perceive increased discrimination against their group. Indeed, after three years in the United States, 40 percent of Mexican immigrants reported such discrimination, almost double the figure upon arrival.[153] As Bach and Portes observe: "these perceptions [of discrimination] are consistently associated with greater education, knowledge of English, modernity, and years of residence in the country."[154]

Parallel findings are echoed in other studies. In the Cain and Kiewiet survey of California Latinos, those who had attended college were somewhat more inclined than those who had not to believe that "Latinos get fewer opportunities than they deserve."[155] Even more strikingly, 70 percent of first-generation Latinos said they had personally experienced no discrimination, but only 56 percent of second-generation Latinos so reported.[156]

It is not at all clear how to interpret such findings. On the one hand, Mexican Americans seem increasingly likely to perceive discrimination over time. On the other, they show signs of assimilating, at least attitudinally and socioeconomically, into the mainstream. Of course, it is not implausible that in their generally successful struggle for advancement, Mexican immigrants encounter harsh and unfair treatment. Nor is it implausible that for subsequent generations, a more subtle dynamic may be at work. Analyzing their California survey results, Cain and Kiewiet report that while claims of *economic* discrimination decline steadily from first- to second- to third-generation Latinos, claims of *social* discrimination increase.[157] Presumably, Latino economic advances lead to increased social contacts with non-Latinos and hence more occasions for friction. Once again, we are reminded that assimilation is a multidimensional process in which gains along one dimension may not be neatly paralleled by progress along others.

Another important source of such complaints is the persistent socio-economic gap between Mexican Americans and the general population. Despite the intergenerational gains I have indicated, Mexican Americans continue to lag behind non-Mexican Americans. Educational attainment is a particularly significant indicator in this regard. For example, during the period from 1950 to 1979 even Mexican-American adults with native-born parents had from 15 to almost 20 percent less schooling than non-Hispanic whites.[158] There is a similarly persistent gap in annual earnings (even when other factors are held constant) between third(plus)-generation Mexican Americans and non-Hispanic whites.[159] By contrast, among other immigrants to the United States, Featherman and Hauser report, "the second generation achieves at least parity with (if not excellence over) Americans of native parentage."[160]

Such disparities between Mexican Americans and the rest of American society are definitely cause for concern. And they do appear to support claims that Mexican Americans have suffered racial discrimination. Yet there is considerable evidence challenging this view. After a careful analysis of the determinants of lagging Mexican-American labor market outcomes, economist Barry Chiswick concludes that although discrimination "undoubtedly has reduced opportunities for training and for high wage employment," it "cannot be the full explanation for the disadvantages of the less successful Hispanic groups and may contribute little to the observed differences."[161] Chiswick emphasizes English proficiency, education, and other such human capital factors as critical in explaining much, but by no means all, of the persistent earnings disparity between Mexican Americans and non-Hispanic white males. Of course, racial discrimination presumably plays a role in hindering the development of important skills. But once again, other factors have also been at work. Certainly the legacy of farm or rural ties, which have continued for many Mexican Americans even in this country until rather recently, has some impact.[162] So does the strength of Mexican-American family ties, which (as I argued above) can inhibit individual mobility and achievement. For example, there is evidence that Mexican Americans maximize their current or short-term earnings—and thereby sacrifice individual educational and long-term occupational attainments—by working longer hours and sending more family members into the labor force.[163] In any event, if racial discrimination were the primary explanation for Mexican-American educational deficiencies, we would be at a loss to explain the group's consistently lower education levels relative to blacks.[164]

Another factor in the persistent socioeconomic disadvantage of Mexican Americans may be the competition from recent Mexican immigrants. Due to the political developments I have analyzed here, this factor is not one that Mexican-American leaders have been eager to examine. Social science researchers have similarly avoided or downplayed the topic. Yet the research that has been done confirms the commonsense view that immigration from Mexico has had negative labor market effects on Mexican Americans, particularly on those less skilled and educated.[165] Such effects presumably help explain why, for example, the annual earnings of third(plus)-generation Mexican-American male high school dropouts were only 67 percent of what their Anglo counterparts earned in 1979, down sharply from 87 percent in 1970.[166]

Given the history of Mexican Americans in this country, it would be foolish to argue that these data do not in some way reflect the effects of racial discrimination. On the other hand, the above evidence, along with that cited in chapters 2 and 3 on high levels of Mexican-American intermarriage and residential mobility, indicate that whatever racial barriers Mexican Americans encounter are of a different order of magnitude from those confronting black Americans. In their meticulous analysis of the evidence, Featherman and Hauser conclude:

> It [the persistent socioeconomic disparity between Mexican Americans and non-Mexican Americans] may illustrate the vestiges of ethnic "discrimination" that no longer apply to other groups (except the black minority and Mexicans) but that is a latent feature of American social relations even in the postindustrial decades. It may mark lingering incompatibilities between the sociocultural experiences of this ethnic group and the social organization of the economy and society in which it is a relatively new member.[167]

The media, as I have argued, are incapable of any such subtle conclusions. Our political institutions are almost as incapacitated. In the present context, all disparities across groups are seen as the result of discrimination; all forms of discrimination are treated as equivalent to racial discrimination; and any exposure to racial discrimination is regarded as the basis for claiming the special status that has been afforded to black Americans, the victims of chattel slavery and Jim Crow.

Because contemporary American political institutions and culture encourage Mexican Americans to define all their grievances in racial terms, complaints of increased discrimination by Mexican Americans who have been here the longest, or who are most integrated into mainstream institutions, may not reflect objective conditions so much as changed standards as to what constitutes discrimination. Indeed, I would argue that our post-civil-rights institutions encourage today's Mexican Americans to define discrimination much more broadly than earlier generations did and, at the same time, to interpret an array of problems similar to those experienced by immigrants generally as manifestations of racial prejudice.

How else is one to interpret de la Garza's finding that, unlike their younger colleagues, Mexican-American leaders over the age of 45 "do not see racism as a major issue"?[168] This despite the fact that, as de la Garza and a colleague assert elsewhere: "Older Mexican Americans experienced explicit and harsh discrimination in almost all aspects of their daily lives, while the younger generation has faced real but, in all probability, less severe and less overt discrimination."[169]

BORN AGAIN AT BERKELEY

Critical to the institutional changes I am concerned with here is the role of the contemporary university. As our politics has grown more professionalized, universities and university-trained elites are playing an increasingly visible role. I noted in an earlier chapter how Chicano studies departments at various campuses of California's state university system offer activists important bases from which to pursue their political agendas. More generally, universities today are at the center of the continuing debate over race and ethnicity in American life. Given the university's historic commitment to tolerance and open debate, it is not too much to say that controversies over multiculturalism and political correctness are about the very nature of the institution. More to the point, the politics of ideas and abstractions, and of racial and ethnic identity, come together importantly in the contemporary university. Here again, Janowitz points the way. Analyzing the changing nature of ethnic politics in late twentieth-century America, he observes: "Ethnic groupings emerge more and more as a specialized type of 'interest group' which involves an important emphasis on self-respect."[170] More to the point at hand, Janowitz identifies an "increase in 'intellectual' ethnicity linked to higher education and to the interest of third and subsequent generations in their personal and group heritage."[171]

Such developments are confirmed in the findings of the Diversity Project, a research effort at the University of California at Berkeley concerned to examine "how undergraduate students are experiencing the new ethnic and racial diversity of the campus."[172] What the Project found on the Berkeley campus is "racialization," described as "a development where social relations that were formerly defined in terms of factors other than race come to be defined in racial terms."[173]

It is striking that for Latino as well as other minority students, racialization does *not* begin in high school. Typically, such students are more or less unaware or unmindful of their heritage until they reach the university. As the Berkeley researchers observe:

> One might expect that the predominantly working class backgrounds of many Chicano/Latino students would inculcate a strong sense of ethnic identity and insulate them from the confusing search for identity which confronts other students of color at Berkeley. This, however, is not the case. Like other minority students, Chicano undergraduates also negotiate an array of identity issues that are often exacerbated by their isolated or sheltered secondary education, their "white" appearance, their inability to speak Spanish and, more generally, the corrosive impact of cultural assimilation on their lives. Nevertheless, interviews conducted for this project document the intense ethnic affirmative and solidarity that many Chicano/Latino students experience at Cal.[174]

For students from more middle-class backgrounds, such experiences are even more intense. One undergraduate, who had never thought of herself as "a minority" or "a Mexican" before arriving at Berkeley, recounted her surprise when she got introduced as a classmate's "Mexican friend." Another such student reported that the word "Chicano" was not one that she was familiar with, growing up in a predominantly Anglo community in San Luis Obispo. Another undergraduate, referring to his identity as a Mexican American, described himself as having been "born again here at Berkeley."[175]

Yet another student complained to the Berkeley researchers that the student body at his Jesuit high school in Los Angeles was "pretty white washed," that most of the Chicano students there spoke "perfect English," and that he and they were "pretty much assimilated." Finally, a Chicana who had gone to an ethnically diverse Catholic school in Oakland complained that all the faculty were "white," and that they never "touched upon racism and stuff like that." Indeed, she acknowledged being completely "unaware of all the things that have been going on with our people, all the injustice we've suffered, how the world really is. I thought racism didn't exist and here, you know, it just comes to light."[176]

These young people are typically the first members of their families to go to college. (It is worth noting that Mexican-American students at Berkeley come from families with lower annual incomes than *any* other group on campus.)[177] The issues they are grappling with are real and painful. Their strong family ties dispose Mexican-American students to

feeling particularly uneasy about being separated—physically and emotionally—from home.[178] More than most undergraduates, these students
experience anxieties about failure and the simple anomie of a huge public university.[179]

I am struck that what these Berkeley researchers found echoes what I
heard in the field in Southern California from Mexican-American politicos and activists: frequent complaints that their parents raised them to
be oblivious to their language and culture and that it was not until they
got to college that they realized they were "Chicanos." What such findings, along with the other considerable evidence on Mexican-American
mobility, indicate is that Mexican Americans such as these must grapple
less with *obstacles* to assimilation than with its *consequences*—what the
Diversity Project researchers refer to as "the corrosive impact of cultural
assimilation on their lives."[180] Indeed, though the word "corrosive" is too
polemical, the researchers are right: what these young people are experiencing is the profound sense of loss that historically follows immigrant
assimilation into American life.

Does this mean that Mexican Americans generally experience no obstacles or barriers to their aspirations? Not at all. But it does mean that
as a group Mexican Americans are not exactly the aggrieved racial minority that their leaders claim. To be sure, many Mexican-American undergraduates—the leaders of tomorrow—would disagree with me. How
could they not? In Chicano studies courses they read history that emphasizes the discrimination undeniably experienced by their people.
They go home to visit their parents and are reminded anew of the problems plaguing crowded barrios. They are encouraged by the wider society's elites to define themselves as members of a racial minority. Not
surprisingly, such young people begin to confound the past with the present, and their own prospects with the travails of recent immigrants. Their
sense of loss then gets transformed into a critique of American society
sustained by two contradictory beliefs: first, that this is a racist society that
won't permit Chicanos to assimilate; and second, that assimilation into
the mainstream is an inexorable and insidious process that must be resisted at all costs. The result is confusion of the sort expressed by the Yale
undergraduate from Corpus Christi I described in the opening chapter.

We are reminded, once again, that the social and economic advancement of Mexican Americans does not necessarily result in societal har-
mony. Contrary to the way in which the issue has been framed in public
discourse, the "assimilation" of Mexican Americans is not a question of
social or economic outcomes, but of politics. Indeed, it is a question of
fundamental political importance—of justice—that will inevitably get an-

swered through debate and the weighing of individual and group expectations against concrete realities. The outcome of this political process will in turn be shaped by the institutional context within which it unfolds.

Today, that context notably lacks the mediating institutions that once softened the disruptive effects of immigration. Without political machines or Alinsky community organizations to interpret the immigrants' new and bewildering circumstances, the inevitable insults and injuries experienced by them, and in particular their offspring, don't get moderated. On the contrary, their raw discontents get amplified by such newly powerful institutions as the media and the universities. Especially in the latter, where, in Arthur Schlesinger's pithy observation "ideologues are authority figures,"[181] the blend of politics and youthful identity crisis takes volatile form. But the universities are only part of the picture, because these heightened discontents also get fed directly into today's political system by Chicano activists, Mexican-American politicians, and advocacy groups like MALDEF—all of whose fortunes depend on sustaining the politics of minority grievances. Instead of serving as the starting point for political action, as we see in COPS, the expression and venting of such grievances becomes the goal. To return to Huntington's formulation, it is difficult, if not impossible, to "unlearn" what the group has been taught if political life is dominated by organizations built around the articulation of racially (or ethnically) defined interests. Thus, today's political system lacks the incentives that, in the past, encouraged the transcendence of group discontents and identity.

There is plenty of evidence that Mexican Americans are "assimilating"—in the sense of adopting American language and values, and registering social and economic advances. Indeed, some scholars believe that contemporary mass media, and especially the mass culture purveyed by them, cause Mexicans to assimilate, linguistically for example, more rapidly than immigrant groups that arrived earlier this century.[182] But the more pertinent, and difficult, question is whether such advances will be sufficient to satisfy the expectations of Mexican Americans—or, for that matter, the rest of us. To this question there is simply no definitive answer. What is undeniably clear is that contemporary political institutions and culture encourage many Mexican Americans to "assimilate" precisely by defining themselves as an oppressed racial minority. The fact that this troubling and divisive *political* assimilation is accompanied—even fueled—by social, economic, and cultural assimilation is a paradox that we have yet to comprehend.

◈11◈

Newcomers in a New Nation

The argument of this book—that Mexican Americans are being se-
duced by the new American political system into adopting the not
entirely appropriate, divisive, and counterproductive stance of a racial
minority group—is likely to raise several objections. To some readers, my
interpretation may seem harsh, judgmental, and unduly suspicious of the
motives of Mexican-American leaders. To such charges I can only respond that Mexican-American leaders are no less, and no more, honest
and virtuous than other political actors. Far from impugning their motives or probity, I see them acting as any similarly situated leaders would,
given the constraints and opportunities presented by our political system
today. At the same time, based on scores of interviews and conversations
in which I have heard Mexican-American leaders express admiration and
respect for long-extinct party bosses and machine politicians, I have no
doubt that they would practice a different type of politics if they could.
But they cannot, and they know it.

Perhaps more objectionable, even offensive to some readers, is my
comparison between Mexican Americans and blacks. Such comparisons
strike some liberals as mean-spirited: "a divide-and-conquer strategy," I
have been told. Naturally, I reject this characterization of my efforts. At
the same time, I acknowledge that there is something distasteful about
comparing group histories to determine who has experienced more dis-

367

crimination. Yet this exercise has been forced upon me—indeed, upon us all—by the path our society has embarked upon. Certainly, designating Mexican Americans a racial minority invites, even requires, such comparisons. How can it be otherwise, when substantial benefits hinge upon such categorization?

I would also argue that well-intentioned efforts to de-emphasize or blur salient differences between these two groups can exacerbate tensions. Nevertheless, contrary to my own intentions, the questions I have raised here may be divisive. Such dilemmas are precisely why affirmative action and racial quotas have been criticized as inappropriate for our diverse and individualistic society.

Other readers may sympathize with my argument that the position of Mexican Americans is fundamentally different from that of black Americans. But by the same token, they may also find it implausible that a few Mexican-American leaders committed to racial minority politics will prevail over the powerful forces of social and economic assimilation emphasized in my analysis. Such criticisms are not without merit. After all, as I note in chapter 1, Mexican Americans often present themselves as ethnic immigrants. At the same time, the ambivalence I describe Mexican Americans experiencing over whether to define themselves as an ethnic or a minority group will continue for some time, and could eventually be resolved in favor of the former.

Nevertheless, it is the racial minority perspective that has fundamentally shaped Mexican-American politics—and will continue to do so. There is no reason to believe the Voting Rights Act and other affirmative action programs, which have afforded substantial benefits to an entire generation of Mexican-American leaders, will suddenly cease to exist. On the contrary, it seems certain that the beneficiaries of these programs will comprise a zealous, and growing, constituency for their continuance.

Even more important, the enormous influence of the small but strategically situated Mexican-American political elite over ordinary Mexican Americans must not be underestimated. Here, skeptics should consider the ability of black leaders to define their group's political agenda in the face of a measurable gap between their views and those of the rank and file on a variety of issues.[1] Moreover, the Mexican-American elite fills a vacuum traceable to habits of political passivity, to language barriers, and to persistently high levels of illegal and noncitizenship status.

Further augmenting the influence of this elite is the limited awareness of America's rich ethnic history among even the most assimilated members of the group. Mexican Americans often react with disbelief when told of the discrimination and prejudice encountered by Irish, Polish,

Jewish, and Italian immigrants.] Typical is a political appointee in Mayor Bradley's administration, who observed that the first time he had ever seen "poor white people" was on a trip to Boston. Similarly, a member of the Alatorre-Torres clique acknowledged that when he first arrived in Washington to work in the Carter administration, he had no idea what his new colleagues meant when they spoke of "urban ethnics." Such testimony points to deficiencies in our educational institutions, no doubt. But it also reflects life in the Southwest, where ethnic identity has never been as salient as back East, and where the primary cleavage has been between Anglos on one side; blacks, Mexicans, and Indians on the other.[3]

Of course, those cleavages are precisely why the racial minority perspective strikes such a resonant chord. Indeed, any assessment of the future direction of Mexican-American politics must recognize that the folk wisdom of this group, forged in the rural towns and ranches of the economically backward Southwest, is filled with memories of harsh and unfair treatment at the hands of Anglos. However urbanized and assimilated Mexican Americans have become, such historical grievances against American society will remain powerfully important in their politics.

The influence of Mexican-American leaders on rank-and-file opinion can also be discerned in some of the survey data I have presented. For example, it is worth recalling that coverage under the Voting Rights Act—a quite remarkable and unprecedented development—is almost unanimously supported by Mexican Americans. Equally telling, I believe, is the poll data on bilingual education, where support for Spanish-language retention is arguably the result of the position taken by Mexican-American leaders. Finally, as further evidence of the impact of these leaders, I would once again point out that the overall proportion of Mexican Americans defining themselves racially as "white" is declining.[4]

It is also true that much of the power wielded by Mexican-American leaders derives less from their influence over their own people than from their influence over outsiders. Criticizing separatist-minded leaders among blacks and other groups, Arthur Schlesinger makes the point rather polemically: "They have thus far done better in intimidating the white majority than in converting their own constituencies."[5] He might have had in mind the small group of Mexican-American lawyers, sustained by their foundation sponsors, who transformed the Los Angeles County Board of Supervisors. Or Schlesinger might have been thinking of how even conservative opponents of racial preferences—people like George Will and the editors of the *Wall Street Journal*—routinely use "white, black, and Hispanic" as though they were mutually exclusive racial categories.[6] So successful have been Mexican-American leaders in enforcing the racial minority perspective, "Hispanic" has virtually ceased to be an ethno-cultural designation.[7]

Such examples could be the result of inadvertence or carelessness, but the same cannot be said of the Republican Party's efforts to encourage the creation of Hispanic majority districts under Section 2 of the Voting Rights Act. The Republicans have provided resources to organizations like SVREP and MALDEF in order to maximize Hispanic districts under the 1990 redistricting. Carried out in the name of fighting racial discrimination, such efforts also, by packing Latinos into specified districts, foster the creation of safer Anglo—that is, Republican—seats.[8] However mixed the motives behind this endeavor, it, too, reflects how institutionalized the racial minority perspective on Mexican Americans has become.

only very very far left

The public policy thread weaving through my analysis of Mexican-American politics is, of course, immigration. Here my argument cuts against both the liberal and the conservative perspectives, broadly construed. To take the liberal view first, it has been decidedly laissez-faire—to the point of reluctance to support even the restriction of illegal immigration. This stance has led some observers to argue that liberals see immigrants either as potential members of a revived progressive coalition, or as new clients for social welfare programs. Both arguments have some merit, but I would argue that the more immediate reason is ideological: liberals have opposed immigration restriction because they regard it as a policy pandering to white hostility toward "people of color" from Mexico and other Third World nations. As Robert Reinhold of the *New York Times* has noted, during the 1980s when California's population increased by a "staggering" 6.1 million, "the subject of controlling population was taboo in polite circles, where people feared being accused of racism."[9]

The irony, as we've seen, is that Mexican Americans do not necessarily perceive themselves as "people of color." Nor are they so perceived by blacks. Yet the liberal perspective virtually requires that all differences between these groups be ignored or downplayed. Don't all "people of color" face similar obstacles in contemporary America? In addition to ignoring the obvious sources of economic competition between Mexican immigrants and black Americans (over jobs, housing, public services), liberals have also ignored—almost willfully, it sometimes appears—the intergroup rivalries engendered by their own programs. Certainly affirmative action has set up a direct political competition between blacks and Mexicans, especially as the latter's numbers keep increasing relative to the former's. Finally, liberals are oblivious to the fact that blacks and Mexicans also feel compelled to compete for the attention and support of liberals.[10]

Conservatives have had their own reasons for welcoming the immigrant influx. Clearly, market-oriented conservatives have long looked upon immigrants as a source of cheap labor. And in recent years, traditionalist conservatives have seen immigrants as reinforcements in the battle for mainstream values such as family, religion, and hard work—not to mention ardent anticommunism, in some cases.

But conservatives have been as obtuse as liberals about the transformed political institutions within which immigrants must now make their way in America. Focusing on the evidence of social and economic assimilation, conservatives have assumed that such advancement will, at least in the near term, obviate the need for politics—as it has for various immigrant groups earlier in our history. Quite aside from ignoring the fact that social and economic assimilation generates its own problems, this conservative view also ignores the vacuum created by contemporary political institutions. Today, we have extraordinarily high standards that all groups be formally represented in our major institutions, both private and public. Even the interests of illegal immigrants and noncitizens are deemed worthy of representation, with increasing proposals that they be allowed to vote. Needless to say, such expectations create a demand for leaders that will not go unfilled. Mexican Americans will therefore not eschew politics, because our political institutions and culture will not let them.

All this has quite escaped the attention of conservatives, who seem incapable of recognizing that contemporary immigrants, legal and illegal, bring with them more than the bundles of clothes that earlier immigrants brought. Indeed, newcomers today bring bundles of rights and entitlements, which may not get exercised by them directly, but which will most certainly get exercised on their behalf by "vicarious representatives."[11]

A particularly telling example of the contradictory nature of the conservative perspective can be found on the editorial page of the *Wall Street Journal*, which has simultaneously led the battle against any and all efforts to restrict immigration *and* crusaded against the court suit that culminated in the creation of an Hispanic seat on the Los Angeles County Board of Supervisors. Apparently it has escaped the *Journal* editors' notice that the population figures that made possible the creation of the Hispanic district they opposed so vehemently were driven by the illegal immigrants they welcomed so eagerly. Moreover, the *Journal*'s editors have steadfastly ignored the fact that the new Hispanic district they reviled as "the liberal *barrio*"[12] was, as we have seen, the result of a suit initiated by the Reagan Justice Department.

Given the scale and transformative nature of the immigration this nation has been experiencing over the past decade or more, the perspectives just described add up to a notable conspiracy of silence on this issue among our political elites. To be sure, the Immigration Reform and Control Act of 1986 was debated and finally passed, but as those involved in that battle well understood at the time, its efforts to curtail illegal immigration—by far the largest source of the present influx—were bound to fail. And they have.

It is hardly surprising, therefore, that other voices have broken the silence. With the end of the economic boom of the 1980s, some conservatives have begun having second thoughts about immigration.[13] Many of their concerns have focused on the fiscal impacts of illegal immigration on state and local treasuries. Particularly visible on this front has been Governor Pete Wilson of California, who in the midst of the worst fiscal crisis in the state's history has raised the issue of illegal immigration in a responsible, nonsensational manner. Framing the issue in terms of the federal government's obligation to shoulder more of the burden imposed on states and localities by immigrants, Wilson has perhaps understandably skirted the more fundamental question of what public services immigrants, particularly those here illegally, ought to be entitled to.

More strident and pervasive have been the voices of populists and demagogues who have rushed in where elites fear to tread. Such spokesmen express the nativist impulses of Americans who look with alarm at the steadily growing barrios and conclude that we will never be able to absorb all these Spanish-speaking newcomers, either economically or culturally. Ironically, such fears that Latinos will constitute a new urban underclass merely echo the shrill complaints sounded for the past two decades by Chicano activists, as well as by mainstream Mexican-American leaders and their liberal allies. Yet such fears also express the understandable anxieties of millions of Americans that our nation is undergoing a momentous transformation without much honest or realistic debate about the possible consequences. Unfortunately, such anxieties are often expressed in terms—whether these newcomers will learn English or be loyal Americans—that any fair reading of the evidence reveals to be beside the point. Nevertheless, Americans have reason to wonder out loud if our capacity to absorb newcomers may not become strained, particularly in a harsher economic environment.]

Similarly, there is reason to worry that immigrants from Mexico and other non-European countries are arriving with cultural values that do not, on the whole, help them adapt and prosper in the United States. But once again, such popular concerns miss the point: the cultural values of today's immigrants are not fundamentally different from those brought by earlier generations of newcomers, including many from Europe. This is not to say that the values of earlier groups did not create problems for them—and for the rest of American society. But on balance, these problems were overcome. Moreover, cultural values are hardly immutable. Indeed, the experience of COPS and other IAF community organizations demonstrates that the values of Mexican immigrants can and do change.

But that is exactly the point. Alinsky organizing also teaches that such change does not come about easily—that it has to be coaxed along and nurtured. More broadly, the IAF experience points up the lack, in today's society, of the kind of political institutions that once helped immigrants bridge the gulf between the values they brought with them and the values of their new social and political environment. And it is precisely this deficiency that liberals, conservatives, populists, and nativists ignore when they contemplate—or refuse to contemplate—the impact of contemporary immigration. Indeed, as a self-conscious nation of immigrants, we find it difficult to grapple with the notion that our political institutions are making it harder than ever for newcomers to become fully integrated into American life.

That America was "born modern" has become a social-science cliché, the original insight deriving of course from de Tocqueville. Drawing on his travels in the United States in the 1830s, the brilliant Frenchman nevertheless failed to anticipate the huge influx of premodern peoples soon to engulf the young nation. [How ironic that this "first new nation," to borrow Seymour Martin Lipset's phrase,[14] has since been populated by millions of immigrants from traditional societies who, in order to become Americans, have had to learn how to become modern.] In nations struggling to become modern, Samuel Huntington points out, "the primary problem is not liberty but the creation of a legitimate public order."[15] In the United States today, such a public order is less problematic than the process by which premodern or tradition-oriented groups are integrated into it.

In the past, a critical link in this process was our decidedly premodern political institutions. Lacking a feudal past, the United States never developed the strong, centralized governmental institutions that, in Europe, were necessary in the forging of modern societies. Thus, the distinctive features of the American political system—divided sovereignty, separation of powers, federalism—are actually vestiges of seventeenth-century political institutions that, in Britain, have long since evolved into a unitary parliamentary system. Yet our premodern "Tudor polity," as Huntington calls it,[16] has provided numerous bridges across which immigrants were able to move from their traditional subcultures into the American mainstream. Such bridges were most in evidence at the local level, where weak, fragmented institutions were conducive to the patronage and machine politics so offensive to middle-class Protestant values of economic individualism and republican civic-mindedness. Though never as inclusive as its more romantic defenders assume,[17] this kind of politics served an important assimilative function.

Today, immigrants from Mexico, and elsewhere, must learn lessons similar to those their predecessors learned. But in the twenty-five years since Huntington first offered his insight, our political institutions have been transformed. They have in many respects become more modern. As a result, they offer little help in negotiating the gulf between the traditional values newcomers bring with them and those of contemporary American society. It is central to the argument of this book that these institutional changes impede the political advancement of Mexican Americans more significantly than the racial barriers routinely pointed to by their leaders.

I have identified several possible responses to this state of affairs. One is the community organizing efforts of the IAF. As I have argued, these organizations have considerable appeal as a reformed and reinvigorated variant of the now defunct machines. But it is unclear how widespread such organization politics will be in the future. As I have demonstrated, IAF organizers have been more successful in San Antonio and Texas than in Los Angeles. Since the latter, particularly with its reliance on money and media, appears more indicative of the present and future state of American politics, it follows that such organizing efforts—highly desirable as they are—may not be easily replicated. On the other hand, the IAF has achieved notable success outside of California and Texas—for example, in Baltimore and in New York City. Moreover, because Los Angeles is obviously an extreme example of the developments I have analyzed here, we should be careful about generalizing from it too readily. For that matter, there is nothing preordained about political trends in Los

Angeles itself, which could for example be carved up into much smaller districts or jurisdictions that would then foster the neighborhood-based politics in which the IAF thrives. But this is, after all, another way of saying that the proliferation of such community organizations will require considerable political will and wisdom—perhaps more than we have.

In the absence of successful organization politics, the likely response is what I have called underline{elite-network politics.}Though far less satisfactory as a mechanism of political assimilation than IAF organizing, elite-network politics is far easier to maintain. In this same category, I would place MALDEF, which is not identical to elite-network politics but shares with it many important characteristics. For both reflect the response of Anglo elites to the oft-repeated criticism that pluralism fails to represent the interests of the unorganized. Indeed, what we see here is an ingenious solution to the pluralist dilemma: to "represent" groups that are difficult, perhaps impossible, to organize, we have created interest groups without actual members, but with leaders and spokesmen who are more than prepared to represent them vicariously.

The result is a politics without organization and with weak or non-existent ties between leaders and "members" or "constituents"—what Charles Hamilton calls "patron-recipient politics." And although Hamilton does not cast his argument in such terms, it is quite evident that this kind of politics offers no context for the IAF's "teaching," Huntington's "unlearning," or Janowitz's "bridging." What Hamilton does point out is that because patron-recipient politics is not based on an enduring organizational relationship, it is predicated on servicing "a revolving recipient group."[18] Among Mexican Americans (who are not explicitly addressed in Hamilton's analysis), this aspect of patron-recipient politics is powerfully reinforced by the social and economic mobility I have described. For Mexican-American leaders, faced with the problem of trying to organize a group that has in effect been assimilating out from underneath them, have happened upon an ideal solution: a continuous influx of immigrants to replace those who have assimilated.

This dynamic is the opposite of what critics typically charge—namely, that Mexican-American leaders and advocacy groups seek to control their constituents by isolating them, linguistically and culturally, in barrio enclaves. On the contrary, these leaders know better. They understand firsthand the powerful social, cultural, and economic forces that are drawing Mexicans into the mainstream of American life. They therefore seek not to control constituents, but *to influence agendas*. And because they exercise such influence, they have the ability to shape perceptions and frame public discourse in the media and elsewhere. Moreover, their need to depict the group as a racial minority is abetted by the continuing arrival of relatively poor, uneducated immigrants. Certainly the proliferation of overcrowded barrios where not a word of English is spoken masks the assimilation that has in fact been occurring.

In sum, we have succeeded in incorporating Mexican Americans into our interest group regime. But this is no ordinary interest group. Not only do its "members" share only vaguely defined interests that lack any solid organizational basis, but its competitive edge is based on a presumed moral trump: the group's claim as a victimized racial minority. Mexican-American politics is therefore a curious hybrid of self-interest and self-righteousness. But this may not be as unusual as it first appears: by combining moralism with interest group bargaining, contemporary Mexican-American politics reflects the civil rights era that spawned it.

In *The End of Liberalism* Theodore Lowi laments that the black civil rights movement lost the moral high ground and was "literally demoralized" when it allowed itself to be co-opted into the horse-trading logic of "interest-group liberalism."[19] Yet it would be more accurate to say the reverse has happened: that black leaders have infused interest group politics with the moral fervor of the 1960s civil rights movement. In essence, black leaders have husbanded the moral capital of that righteous cause as a way of enhancing their bargaining position almost three decades later. Mexican Americans are following suit, seeking to bargain as an interest group, but from the moral high ground offered America's designated racial minorities.

Accompanying this moralized interest group politics is a marked impatience. Eager for change, and steeped in the history of the Southwest, Mexican-American leaders are understandably impatient. Much more surprising is the impatience displayed by non-Mexican-American, Anglo elites. Their response may in part reflect a sense of urgency about the need to incorporate a large and growing number of immigrants—quite regardless of their legal status—into our political system. But more fundamentally, these elites are acting on lessons absorbed in the 1960s, long before the present influx. It was during that period that they learned, from the civil rights movement, that if tolerance is a virtue, so is impatience. At least, having once been roundly—and justifiably—criticized for counseling patience to the victims of racial discrimination, these elites are now determined not to make the same mistake again.

Yet impatience may be a mistake when dealing with the problems of recent immigrants. Throughout this book, I have posed the question whether Mexican Americans are in fact a racial minority group entitled to the same special benefits afforded black Americans. My reading of the evidence inclines me to say no. But beyond this specific response lies my broader concern that we have as a society not adequately considered our de facto response to this question. In our impatience with the wrongs suffered by racial minorities, we forget what a long and arduous process it is for immigrants to become full participants in American life. We forget our own history—not just that of Mexicans in the Southwest, but also that of immigrant groups back East. And we indulge our impatience, insisting that newcomers be fully represented and participate in all our institutions, before they have had the time to build up any political institutions or strength of their own. By trying to jump-start the process, we end up short-circuiting it.

Were the recent Los Angeles riots a reflection of this impatience? It is difficult to say. The riots were a complex series of events that we have barely begun to sort out and understand. At a minimum, they would appear to reflect the desperation of Los Angeles blacks, who have felt crowded out of housing and jobs by any number of immigrant groups over the past decade or more. But, contrary to most media portrayals, not all of the rioters were black. Indeed, a majority of those arrested during the disturbances were Latino.[20] Yet it is still not clear what conclusions can be drawn. Much of the rioting and looting occurred west of downtown, in the Pico-Union district, where Central American refugees have crowded into dilapidated apartment buildings. Heavily Mexican-American districts—certainly East LA—were notably calm. Yet some of the rioters were apparently Mexican immigrants. Again, without drawing firm conclusions about a set of circumstances that seems unique to Los Angeles, it is evident that the integration of newcomers into American society is not necessarily smooth or automatic.

Still, the specter of civil unrest does not loom as large as that of an increasingly divisive politics based on the consolidation of Mexican Americans around a racial minority identity. Black Americans will certainly have reason to resent the moral claims made by Mexican Americans—a resentment compounded by the latter's ability to have it both ways, to stake righteous claims while also portraying themselves as an ethnic immigrant group.

Yet blacks will not be the only ones responding negatively to such claims. The resentment of the broader society will take longer to emerge, because, despite the occasional outbursts of Chicano activists and frustrated immigrants, the dominant thrust of Mexican-American politics will be that of the elite-network. As I have explained, this style of politics is dependent upon displays of angry protest. But mainly its goals are pursued through quiet bureaucratic and judicial channels, where the racial minority perspective has been thoroughly institutionalized by governmental and foundation elites. Transformations such as that of the Los Angeles County Board of Supervisors will be wrought with little opposition or notice from the public. Only later, when the leaders installed by this regime advocate policies such as affirmative action and bilingual education, while denying much of the progress their group has made, will the reaction set in. At that point, we may come to appreciate the divisive nature of the approach we are now taking.

In essence, this approach is profoundly antipolitical. It teaches those without political power that it can and should be bestowed on them by elite benefactors, whether Anglo or Latino. This approach also transforms Mexican-American leaders into one more voice of principled disharmony and rigidly defined abstract rights, resistant to compromise in the political arena. In the name of politics, we now have a new source of discord— of antipolitics.

Meanwhile, Mexican immigrants will continue to strive to become Americans. In the absence of the political institutions that historically have assisted in this effort, Mexican-American politics has fixed on race consciousness and resentments. However emotionally and programmatically gratifying this perspective may be to its elite practitioners, Anglo and Mexican, it offers little help to newcomers struggling to make sense of their new lives. Nor does it offer them much hope of appreciating the responsibilities, as well as rights, that await them as participants in the American experiment.

NOTES

1. THE PRIMACY OF POLITICS

1. For a discussion of the Felix Longoria affair and its place in the history of the American G.I. Forum, see Carl Allsup, *The American G.I. Forum: Origins and Evolution* (Austin, TX: Center for Mexican American Studies, The University of Texas at Austin, 1982), 39–49.

2. The same sentiment was found in the 1960s by Leo Grebler et al., *The Mexican-American People: The Nation's Second Largest Minority* (New York: The Free Press, 1970), 545.

3. Richard Mackenzie, "U.S. Culture with a Spanish Accent," *Insight*, 16 December 1985, 14.

4. Morris Janowitz, *The Reconstruction of Patriotism: Education for Civic Consciousness* (Chicago: The University of Chicago Press, 1983), 129, 137.

5. Carlos Muñoz, Jr., and Mario Barrera, "La Raza Unida Party and the Chicano Student Movement in California," *Social Science Journal* 19 (1982): 111; Walker Connor, "Who Are the Mexican-Americans? A Note on Comparability," in Walker Connor, ed., *Mexican-Americans in Comparative Perspective* (Washington, DC: The Urban Institute Press, 1985), 16–18.

6. Over twenty years ago Leo Grebler and his colleagues heard the same complaint in the barrios of Los Angeles. See Leo Grebler et al., *The Mexican-American People*, 429.

7. My field observations on this point are confirmed in Alex M. Saragoza, "The Conceptualization of the History of the Chicano Family," in Armando Valdez et al., eds., *The State of Chicano Research in Family, Labor, and Migration Studies* (Stanford, CA: Stanford Center for Chicano Research, 1983), 126.

8. Yet for evidence that nativist reactions to the current influx of immigrants are not as strong or as negative as some observers assume, see Jack Citrin et al., *American Identity and the Politics of Ethnic Change*, Working Paper 89-1 (Berkeley, CA: Institute of Governmental Studies, University of California, March 1989), 19.

9. It should be noted, however, that for most of the 1980s Buchanan welcomed the immigrant influx and specifically opposed efforts like the Simpson-

Mazzoli bill to curtail immigration. See Patrick Buchanan, "Reagan Should Veto the Mean-Spirited Simpson-Mazzoli Bill," *Los Angeles Herald Examiner*, 27 June 1984, A9. For a conservative treatment of the immigration issue echoing Buchanan's more recent views, see Peter Brimelow, "Time to Rethink Immigration?" *National Review*, 22 June 1992, 30–46.

10. See Anthony King, ed., *The New American Political System* (Washington, DC: American Enterprise Institute, 1978) and Anthony King, ed., *The New American Political System*, second version (Washington, DC: American Enterprise Institute, 1990).

11. For a discussion and analysis of these events, see Abigail M. Thernstrom, *Whose Votes Count? Affirmative Action and Minority Voting Rights* (Cambridge, MA: Harvard University Press, 1987), 43–62.

12. Ibid.

13. Frank D. Bean and Marta Tienda, *The Hispanic Population of the United States* (New York: Russell Sage Foundation, 1987), 18.

14. See "Brutality on the Beat: The Attack by White Cops on a Black Motorist Spotlights the Troubled LAPD," *Newsweek*, 25 March 1991, 32–34; also Haynes Johnson, "A 'Time for Serious Reflection,'" *Washington Post* 22 March 1991, A2.

15. Tracy Wood et al., "Four Officers—Their Paths to Trial," *Los Angeles Times*, 3 February 1992, B1, B6.

16. See, for example, Ronald L. Soble, "FBI to Interview Foothill Officers," *Los Angeles Times*, 25 March 1991, B1; or Bill Boyarsky, "Behind the Scenes, Gates' Position Is Stronger Than It May Appear," *Los Angeles Times*, 23 March 1991, B2.

17. To my knowledge, the only exception to this pattern (other than the one in the *Los Angeles Times* article just cited above) was a brief article written by a Los Angeles police officer. See Susan Yocum, "Why It Happened: An L.A. Cop's View," *Newsweek*, 25 March 1991, 34.

18. Carlos Muñoz, Jr., and Charles Henry, "Rainbow Coalitions in Four Big Cities: San Antonio, Denver, Chicago and Philadelphia," *PS* 19 (1986): 607.

19. Tomás Almaguer et al., *The Diversity Project: An Interim Report to the Chancellor* (Berkeley, CA: Institute for the Study of Social Change, University of California; June 1990), 65.

20. Similar comments about Hispanics by black political leaders are reported by researchers looking at ten Northern California cities during the late 1970s and early 1980s. See Rufus P. Browning et al., *Protest Is Not Enough: The Struggle of Blacks and Hispanics for Equality in the United States* (Berkeley, CA: University of California Press, 1986), 260.

21. Nathan Glazer, "Immigrants and Education," in Nathan Glazer, ed., *Clamor at the Gates: The New American Immigration* (San Francisco: Institute for Contemporary Studies Press, 1985), 226.

22. Indeed, Wirth specifically referred to European immigrants in America as "minorities." See Louis Wirth, "The Problem of Minority Groups," in Ralph

Linton, ed., *The Science of Man in the World Crisis* (New York: Columbia University Press, 1945), 351.

23. Charles Wagley and Marvin Harris, *Minorities in the New World: Six Case Studies* (New York: Columbia University Press, 1958). For a similarly inclusive definition—cultural, linguistic, religious, and racial—of the term, see Arnold M. Rose, "Minorities," in David L. Sills, ed., *The International Encyclopedia of the Social Sciences* (New York: Macmillan and The Free Press, 1968), 365–371.

24. "Although the size of the group may have some effect upon its status and upon its relationship to the dominant group, minorities are not to be judged in terms of numbers." See Wirth, "The Problem of Minority Groups, 349.

25. Lynne Duke and Richard Morin, "Demographic Shift Reshaping Politics," *Washington Post*, 13 August 1991, A7.

26. Almaguer et al., *The Diversity Project*, 15.

27. See, for example, Bruce Cain and Roderick Kiewiet, "California's Coming Minority Majority," *Public Opinion*, February/March 1986, 50–52.

28. Almaguer et al., *The Diversity Project*, 51.

29. See, for example, Robert Blauner, *Racial Oppression in America* (New York: Harper & Row, 1972).

30. Joan W. Moore and Ralph Guzmán, "The Mexican-American: New Wind from the Southwest," *Nation*, 30 May 1966, 645.

31. For a useful discussion of these issues, see William Petersen, "Concepts of Ethnicity," in Stephan Thernstrom, ed., *The Harvard Encyclopedia of American Ethnic Groups* (Cambridge, MA: Harvard University Press, 1980), 234–242.

32. For an example of how a contemporary social scientist uses the distinction highlighted here, see William O'Hare, "Assimilation and Socioeconomic Advancement of Hispanics in the US" (Washington, DC: Population Reference Bureau, 1988), 3–4.

33. Michael Walzer, "Pluralism in Political Perspective," in Walzer et al., eds., *The Politics of Ethnicity* (Cambridge, MA: The Belknap Press of Harvard University Press, 1982), 14–15.

34. John U. Ogbu, "Minority Status and Literacy in Comparative Perspective," *Daedalus* 119 (1990): 150. I am indebted to Paul Peterson for bringing this article to my attention.

35. Ibid. Although Ogbu's terminology—voluntary minorities versus involuntary minorities—adds to the terminological confusion I have identified, the analytic distinction he draws here tracks my own precisely. However, the reader should note that Ogbu actually categorizes Mexican Americans as an involuntary minority. I am not so sure. See ibid., 145–146.

36. The term is from the Voting Rights Act. Under this designation, Hispanics were brought under the Act's coverage in 1975. See Thernstrom, *Whose Votes Count?* 52.

37. William Petersen makes this point in "Concepts of Ethnicity," 236.

38. Among social scientists, the correlation of racial and cultural characteristics has led more to controversy than to confusion. Some scholars argue that minorities constitute a special category of ethnic groups more generally, one segment on an ethnic continuum. Others reject this view as one that perniciously denies the unique barriers experienced by the racially oppressed in the United States. See John Higham, "From Process to Structure: Formulations of American Immigration History," in Peter Kvisto and Dag Blanck, eds., *American Immigrants and Their Generations: Studies and Commentaries on the Hansen Thesis after Fifty Years* (Urbana, IL: University of Illinois Press, 1990), 20.

39. See Thomas Muller et al., *The Fourth Wave: California's Newest Immigrants* (Washington, DC: The Urban Institute Press, 1985), 18–21; and Ronald Takaki, *Strangers from a Different Shore: A History of Asian Americans* (New York: Little, Brown, 1989), 110–111.

40. On the 1922 Ozawa case, see William Petersen, *Japanese Americans: Oppression and Success* (Washington, DC: University Press of America, 1971), 47–48. On the 1924 Immigration Act, see William S. Bernard, "Immigration: History of U.S. Policy," in Thernstrom, *Harvard Encyclopedia of American Ethnic Groups*, 493.

41. See, for example, Arthur S. Hayes, "Asian Americans Go to Court to Fight Bias," *Wall Street Journal*, 3 September 1991, B14. See also Almaguer et al., *The Diversity Project*, 36–48.

42. For a useful analysis of these developments among Asian Americans, see Reed Ueda, "False Modesty: The Curse of Asian American Success," *New Republic*, 3 July 1989, 16–17.

43. Paul E. Peterson, *City Limits* (Chicago, IL: The University of Chicago Press, 1981), 158.

44. The contrasting view is, of course, that minorities have no choices and that their experiences are characterized by pure oppression. For an enlightening discussion and critique of this perspective, see Higham, "From Process to Structure," 19–20.

45. Charles Babington, " 'Minority' Labels in Montgomery Schools Attacked," *Washington Post*, 3 July 1991, C1.

46. See Ben L. Martin, "From Negro to Black to African American," *Political Science Quarterly* 6 (1991): 83–107.

47. Quoted in Diane Ravitch, *The Troubled Crusade: American Education, 1945–1980* (New York: Basic Books, 1983), 271.

48. Stephen R. Graubard, "Preface," *Daedalus* 110 (Spring 1981): vii.

49. I quote here from an advertising circular. For the actual publication, see *Harvard Educational Review* 58 (1988): 265–432.

50. Cain and Kiewiet, "California's Coming Minority Majority," 50.

51. U.S. House of Representatives, Committee on Ways and Means, *1991 Green Book: Overview of Entitlement Programs*, 102nd Cong., 1st sess. (May 7, 1991), 1458.

52. Confirming these data are the findings of the Latino National Political Survey. Conducted around the same time as the 1990 census, the Survey reports that 51 percent of Mexican Americans identify themselves as racially "white." See Rodolfo O. de la Garza et al., "Will the Real American Please Stand Up: A Comparison of Political Values among Mexicans, Cubans, Puerto Ricans and Anglos in the United States," paper presented at the annual meeting of the American Political Science Association (1991), 16.

53. See, for example, Mario Barrera, *Race and Class in the Southwest: A Theory of Racial Inequality* (Notre Dame, IN: University of Notre Dame Press, 1979); or David Montejano, *Anglos and Mexicans in the Making of Texas, 1836–1986* (Austin, TX: University of Texas Press, 1987), passim and especially 261.

54. Rodolfo O. de la Garza, *Public Policy Priorities of Chicano Political Elites*, Working Paper, U.S.–Mexico Project Series, No. 7 (Washington, DC: Overseas Development Council, July 1982), 22.

55. Mario T. García, "Americans All: The Mexican American Generation and the Politics of Wartime Los Angeles, 1941–45," *Social Science Quarterly* 65 (1984): 287.

56. Grebler et al., *The Mexican-American People*, 4–5, 389.

57. García, "Americans All," 285–287.

58. See Onofre di Stefano, " 'Venimos a luchar': A Brief History of *La Prensa*'s Founding," *Aztlán* 16 (1985): 95–118.

59. Grebler et al., *The Mexican-American People*, 325.

60. See de la Garza, *Public Policy Priorities of Chicano Political Elites*, 10–11.

61. Luis Valdez, "Introduction: 'La Plebe,' " in Luis Valdez and Stan Steiner, eds., *Aztlán: An Anthology of Mexican American Literature* (New York: Vintage Books, 1972), xxxiii.

62. See Robert Warren and Ellen Percy Kraly, *The Elusive Exodus: Emigration from the United States* (Washington, DC: The Population Reference Bureau, March 1985), 4–5; and Muller et al., *The Fourth Wave*, 14.

63. Carey McWilliams makes this point in *North from Mexico: The Spanish-Speaking People of the United States* (New York: Greenwood Press, 1968).

64. Connor, "Who Are the Mexican-Americans?" 17.

65. L. H. Gann and Peter J. Duignan, *The Hispanics in the United States: A History* (Boulder, CO: Westview Press, 1986), 17.

66. For a critical view of American cultural influence in Mexico, see Richard Rodriguez, "Lilies That Fester," *Wall Street Journal*, 2 July 1986, A22. See also Alan Riding, *Distant Neighbors: A Portrait of the Mexicans* (New York: Alfred A. Knopf, 1985), 19, 327.

67. A similar point is made by Rodolfo O. de la Garza in "Chicanos and U.S. Foreign Policy: The Future of Chicano-Mexican Relations," *Western Political Quarterly* 33 (1980): 573–575.

68. McWilliams, *North from Mexico*, 179. See also Montejano, *Anglos and Mexicans*, 203–205.

69. Montejano, *Anglos and Mexicans*, 106–128.
70. Quoted in Tony Castro, *Chicano Power: The Emergence of Mexican America* (New York: Saturday Review Press, 1974), 51.
71. Cited by Montejano, *Anglos and Mexicans*, 125.
72. Grebler et al., *The Mexican-American People*, 523–526.
73. See Montejano, *Anglos and Mexicans*, 168–169, 230.
74. These charges are also cited by Joan Moore and Harry Pachon, *Hispanics in the United States* (Englewood Cliffs, NJ: Prentice-Hall, 1985), 30.
75. Grebler et al., *The Mexican-American People*, 521–523.
76. Bean and Tienda, *The Hispanic Population*, 107. Other estimates of the Mexican-origin population in the Southwest in the middle of the nineteenth century are lower. Douglas Massey reports that the 1850 census recorded 13,300 persons of Mexican birth living in the United States. See Douglas S. Massey, *The Demographic and Economic Position of Hispanics in the United States: 1980* (Washington, DC: National Commission for Employment Policy, March 1982), 7.
77. Bean and Tienda, *The Hispanic Population*, 107, 109. A similar emphasis on Mexican Americans as immigrants is found in Saragoza, "The Conceptualization of the History of the Chicano Family," 117.
78. Montejano, *Anglos and Mexicans*, 197–219. I have no doubt that Prof. Montejano would disagree with me that his research supports the immigrant ethnic interpretation of the Mexican-American experience.
79. Edward Murguía, *Chicano Intermarriage: A Theoretical and Empirical Study* (San Antonio, TX: Trinity University Press, 1982), 40–41, 48–49.
80. See Stanley Lieberson and Mary C. Waters, *From Many Strands: Ethnic and Racial Groups in Contemporary America* (New York: Russell Sage Foundation, 1988), 162–203. This pattern was also evident a generation ago. See Grebler et al., *The Mexican-American People*, 405–419.
81. See Douglas S. Massey and Nancy A. Denton, "Trends in the Residential Segregation of Blacks, Hispanics, and Asians: 1970–1980," *American Sociological Review* 52 (1987): 802–825. Also Moore and Pachon, *Hispanics in the United States*, 60.
82. On this point, see Saragoza, "The Conceptualization of the History of the Chicano Family," especially 17–22. On the other hand, more recent research indicates that fewer Mexican immigrants today have rural, peasant origins and more have urban, working-class backgrounds. See Alejandro Portes and Robert L. Bach, *Latin Journey: Cuban and Mexican Immigrants in the United States* (Berkeley, CA: University of California Press, 1985), 4, 121–124, 241.
83. Montejano, *Anglos and Mexicans*, 305.
84. One piece of evidence helping to explain this curious fact is that the Mexican government required American colonists to be or become Roman Catholics. See Dale McLennon, "The Origins of Mexican American Subordination in Texas," *Social Science Quarterly* 53 (1973): 664. On the other

hand, T. R. Fehrenbach reports that this requirement was rarely enforced. See his *Lone Star: A History of Texas and the Texans* (New York: Collier Books, 1980), 137.

85. Grebler et al., *The Mexican-American People*, 385–387.

86. For survey data on how Mexican Americans refer to themselves, see Rodolfo O. de la Garza and Robert R. Brischetto, *The Mexican American Electorate: A Demographic Profile*, the Mexican American Electorate Series, Hispanic Population Studies Program, Occasional Paper No. 1 (San Antonio, TX: Southwest Voter Registration Education Project; and Austin, TX: Center for Mexican American Studies, University of Texas, 1982), 14–15. See also John A. García, "Yo Soy Mexicano . . . : Self-Identity and Sociodemographic Correlates," *Social Science Quarterly* 62 (1981): 88–98; and *Los Angeles Times Poll* No. 65 (March 1983), question 47.

87. On this point, see Grebler et al., *The Mexican-American People*, 578–584.

88. Nancie L. González, *The Spanish-Americans of New Mexico: A Heritage of Pride*, 2nd ed. (Albuquerque, NM: University of New Mexico Press, 1969), 187–188. See also Grebler et al., *The Mexican-American People*, 322.

89. T. R. Fehrenbach, *The San Antonio Story* (Tulsa, OK: Continental Heritage, 1978), 23–39.

90. U.S. Bureau of the Census, Current Population Reports, Series P-20, No. 455, *The Hispanic Population in the United States: March 1991* (Washington, DC: U.S. Government Printing Office, 1991), 16.

91. Alejandro Portes and Rubén G. Rumbaut, *Immigrant America: A Portrait* (Berkeley, CA: University of California Press, 1990), 116–126. See also Bean and Tienda, *The Hispanic Population*, 109.

92. On this point, see James G. March and Johan P. Olsen, *Rediscovering Institutions: The Organizational Basis of Politics* (New York: The Free Press, 1989), especially 1–19. Another critique of this social scientific reductionism is found in Morris Janowitz, *The Last Half-Century: Societal Change and Politics in America* (Chicago, IL: University of Chicago Press, 1978), 78–81.

93. Nathan Glazer and Daniel Patrick Moynihan, *Beyond the Melting Pot: The Negroes, Puerto Ricans, Jews, Italians, and Irish of New York City*, 2nd ed. (Cambridge, MA: MIT Press, 1970), xii–xiii.

94. Morris Janowitz, *The Reconstruction of Patriotism: Education for Civic Consciousness* (Chicago: University of Chicago Press, 1983), 19–21. For an earlier discussion that does not use the term "bridging institutions" but nevertheless develops the concept at some length, see Janowitz, *The Last Half-Century*, 264–319. I, of course, borrow the term "mediating institutions" from Peter L. Berger and Richard John Neuhaus, *To Empower People: The Role of Mediating Structures in Public Policy* (Washington, DC: American Enterprise Institute for Public Policy Research, 1977).

95. See Milton M. Gordon, *Assimilation in American Life: The Role of Race, Religion, and National Origins* (New York: Oxford University Press, 1973), especially 60–83.

2. SAN ANTONIO

1. Thomas A. Baylis, "Leadership Change in Contemporary San Antonio," in David R. Johnson et al., eds., *The Politics of San Antonio: Community, Progress, and Power* (Lincoln, NE: University of Nebraska Press, 1983), 105.

2. Robert R. Brischetto and Rodolfo O. de la Garza, *The Mexican American Electorate: Political Opinions and Behavior across Cultures in San Antonio*, Hispanic Population Studies Program, Occasional Paper No. 5 (San Antonio, TX: Southwest Voter Registration Education Project; and Austin, TX: Center for Mexican American Studies, University of Texas, 1985), 6.

3. Quoted in Kemper Diehl and Jan Jarboe, *Cisneros: Portrait of a New American* (San Antonio, TX: Corona Publishing, 1985), 9.

4. *U.S. Department of Commerce News* (Bureau of the Census), press release #CB91–66, 21 February 1991.

5. T. R. Fehrenbach, *The San Antonio Story* (Tulsa, OK: Continental Heritage, 1978), 169–173.

6. See Robert A. Caro, *The Path to Power: The Years of Lyndon Johnson* (New York: Alfred A. Knopf, 1982), 302.

7. On Cisneros's family, see Diehl and Jarboe, *Cisneros*, 19–26.

8. On Mexican-American versus Anglo values in San Antonio, see Brischetto and de la Garza, *The Mexican American Electorate: Opinions and Behavior*, 13–20.

9. U.S. Bureau of the Census, *1980 Census of Population, Volume 1: Characteristics of the Population, Chapter C: General Social and Economic Characteristics, Part 6: California, PC80-1-C6, Section 1: Tables 56—155* (July 1983), Table 151; and *Part 45: Texas, PC80-1-C45, Section 2: Tables 170—C-3* (July 1983), Table 151. Comparable data at the metropolitan level for 1990 are not yet available. However, state-level data for 1990 are available and confirm my point: in California 44.1 percent of Hispanics in 1990 were foreign-born; in Texas, 25.9 percent. See U.S. Bureau of the Census, *Persons of Hispanic Origin for the United States: 1990* (Washington, DC: mimeograph, undated); U.S. Bureau of the Census; and *The Foreign-Born Population by Place of Birth for the United States: 1990* (Washington, DC: mimeograph, undated).

10. *U.S. Department of Commerce News* (Bureau of the Census), press release #CB91-229, 5 July 1991.

11. U.S. Bureau of the Census, *1980 Census of Population, Vol. 1, Part 45: Texas*, Table 151.

12. Henry Santiestevan and Stina Santiestevan, eds., *The Hispanic Almanac* (New York: Hispanic Policy Development Project, 1984), 121–122. For evidence of this same pattern in previous decades, see Leo Grebler et al., *The Mexican-American People: The Nation's Second Largest Minority* (New York: The Free Press, 1970), 340–341.

13. Thomas Muller et al., *The Fourth Wave: California's Newest Immigrants* (Washington, DC: The Urban Institute Press, 1985), 69.

14. Richard C. Jones, "San Antonio's Spatial Economic Structure, 1955–1980," in Johnson et al., *The Politics of San Antonio*, 28–52.

15. Baylis, "Leadership Change," 98.

16. Cited in Tom Walker, "Dr. Robert V. West, Jr.: Close-Up," *San Antonio Magazine*, March 1978, 39.

17. John A. Booth and David R. Johnson, "Power and Progress in San Antonio Politics, 1836–1970," in Johnson et al., *The Politics of San Antonio*, 20.

18. Diehl and Jarboe, *Cisneros*, 56.

19. *Texas Business*, June 1980.

20. Baylis, "Leadership Change," 109.

21. In the mid-1970s these installations constituted the largest military complex outside Washington. See Fehrenbach, *The San Antonio Story*, 175.

22. Calculated from figures in *Air Force Magazine* 74 (1991): 132–142. In the late 1970s this figure was even higher; see Jones, "San Antonio's Spatial Economic Structure," 33.

23. *Air Force Magazine* 74 (1991): 132–142.

24. Baylis, "Leadership Change," 109.

25. U.S. Department of Labor, *Geographic Profile of Employment and Unemployment, 1987*, Bulletin 2305 (Washington, DC: Bureau of Labor Statistics, April 1988), 130.

26. U.S. Bureau of the Census, *Statistical Abstract of the United States: 1992* (Washington, DC: U.S. Government Printing Office, 1992), 440.

27. David S. Broder, "San Antonio's Uneven Growth Reflected in Wider Income Gap," *Washington Post*, 11 March 1986, A8.

28. Grebler et al., *The Mexican-American People*, 301.

29. Sister Frances Jerome Woods, *Mexican Ethnic Leadership in San Antonio, Texas* (Washington, DC: The Catholic University of America Press, 1949), 28–29.

30. Fehrenbach, *The San Antonio Story*, 169.

31. Richard J. Harris, "Mexican-American Occupational Attainments in San Antonio: Comparative Assessments," in Johnson et al., *The Politics of San Antonio*, 58, 62–70.

32. Grebler et al., *The Mexican-American People*, Table 7–8, 154.

33. Joan Moore and Harry Pachon, *Hispanics in the United States* (Englewood Cliffs, NJ: Prentice-Hall, 1985), 67.

34. Santiestevan and Santiestevan, eds., *Hispanic Almanac*, 122.

35. Harris, "Mexican-American Occupational Attainments," 60–70.

36. U.S. Bureau of the Census, unpublished 1990 census data, Summary Tape File 3.

37. Walker, "Dr. Robert V. West, Jr." 39.

38. Woods, *Mexican Ethnic Leadership in San Antonio*, 18, 44, 50.

39. Booth and Johnson, "Power and Progress," 9.

40. For an analysis of the leadership offered by the middle class, compared to the much more passive Mexican-American upper class in San Antonio, see Woods, *Mexican Ethnic Leadership in San Antonio*, 44–50, 119.

41. On restrictive covenants, see Robert Brischetto et al., "Conflict and Change in the Political Culture of San Antonio in the 1970s," in Johnson et al., *The Politics of San Antonio*, 76. On separate schools and other discriminatory treatment experienced by Mexicans in Texas, see Woods, *Mexican Ethnic Leadership in San Antonio*, 33–36; and David Montejano, *Anglos and Mexicans in the Making of Texas, 1836–1986* (Austin, TX: University of Texas Press, 1987), 191–196. On the burial episode, see Carl Allsup, *The American G.I. Forum: Origins and Evolution* (Austin, TX: Center for Mexican American Studies, The University of Texas, 1982), 39–49.

42. Douglas S. Massey and Nancy A. Denton, "Suburbanization and Segregation in U.S. Metropolitan Areas," *American Journal of Sociology* 94 (1988): 604.

43. Douglas S. Massey and Nancy A. Denton, "Trends in the Residential Segregation of Blacks, Hispanics, and Asians: 1970–1980," *American Sociological Review* 52 (1987): 809, 811–812.

44. Gary Orfield and Franklin Monford, *Racial Change and Desegregation in Large School Districts* (Alexandria, VA: National School Board Association, 1988), 41. If these figures seem extraordinarily high, it is because the San Antonio Independent School District subsumes much of the city's West Side barrio. But there are many other school districts in San Antonio in which the concentration of Mexican-American students is substantial but not so extreme.

45. Edward Murguía, *Chicano Intermarriage: A Theoretical and Empirical Study* (San Antonio, TX: Trinity University Press, 1982), 40–41, 48.

46. Yet it should be noted that even during the 1940s there was enough intermarriage in San Antonio to convince one particularly careful observer that the group cohesion of Mexican Americans there was as a result weakened. See Woods, *Mexican Ethnic Leadership in San Antonio*, 50–51, 117.

47. U.S. Bureau of the Census, unpublished 1990 census data, Summary Tape File 3.

48. For a discussion of the penetration of San Antonio media throughout the region, see Jones, "San Antonio's Spatial Economic Structure," 43–45.

49. Fehrenbach, *The San Antonio Story*, 117.

50. Woods, *Mexican Ethnic Leadership*, 2.

51. Fehrenbach, The San Antonio Story, 47–49.

52. Carey McWilliams, *North from Mexico: The Spanish-Speaking People of the United States* (New York: Greenwood Press, 1968), 151–156.

53. See Ruth Horowitz, *Honor and the American Dream: Culture and Identity in a Chicano Community* (New Brunswick, NJ: Rutgers University Press, 1985), chaps. 4, 5; Alan Riding, *Distant Neighbors: A Portrait of the Mexicans* (New York: Alfred A. Knopf, 1985), esp. chap. 1.

54. Montejano, *Anglos and Mexicans*, 261, 305–307.

55. Diehl and Jarboe, *Cisneros*, 61.

56. Ibid.

57. Harris, "Mexican-American Occupational Attainments," 55. For the position of blacks between Mexican and Anglo voting blocs, see Tucker Gibson, "Mayoralty Politics in San Antonio, 1955–1979," in Johnson et al., *The Politics of San Antonio*, 124.

58. Santiestevan and Santiestevan, eds., *Hispanic Almanac*, 120.

59. Clifton McCleskey et al., *The Government and Politics of Texas*, 7th ed. (Boston, Little, Brown, 1982), 36–40; and Brischetto et al., "Conflict and Change," 86–87. See also Charles L. Cotrell and Jerry Polinard, "Effects of the Voting Rights Act in Texas: Perceptions of County Election Administrators," *Publius* 16 (1986): 68–70.

60. Caro, *Path to Power*, 719–723; and McCleskey et al., *Government and Politics of Texas*, 43. See Brischetto and de la Garza, *The Mexican American Electorate: Political Opinions and Behavior*, 4–5.

61. On the patrón values of the region, see Douglas E. Foley et al., *From Peones to Políticos: Class and Ethnicity in a South Texas Town, 1900–1987* (Austin, TX: University of Texas Press, 1988), 13–17.

62. Caro, *Path to Power*, 720.

63. For Mexican-American registration data in Bexar County (San Antonio) compared to rural South Texas counties in 1950, see José Angel Gutiérrez, "La Raza and Revolution: The Empirical Conditions of Revolution in Four South Texas Counties," M.A. thesis, Department of Political Science, St. Mary's University (1968), 40–41. For more recent evidence on the same point, see Southwest Voter Registration Education Project, "Mexican-American Voting in the 1980 Texas Democratic Primary, May 3, 1980," in Richard Santillan, ed., *The Chicano Community and California Redistricting*, vol. I (Claremont, CA: The Rose Institute of State and Local Government, Claremont Men's College, 1981), 298–304.

64. McCleskey et al., *Government and Politics of Texas*, 54–58.

65. Clifton McCleskey and Bruce Merrill, "Mexican American Political Behavior in Texas," *Social Science Quarterly* 53 (1973): 786.

66. See Booth and Johnson, "Power and Progress," esp. 15–16.

67. Baylis, "Leadership Change," 99.

68. Fehrenbach, *The San Antonio Story*, 181.

69. For a discussion of this direct link being weakened and changed, see Baylis, "Leadership Change," 105–108.

70. Ibid., 99–100, 110.

71. On the GGL's failure to provide new infrastructure and improved city services to Mexican Americans, see Heywood T. Sanders, "Building a New Urban Infrastructure: The Creation of Postwar San Antonio," in Char Miller and Heywood T. Sanders, eds., *Urban Texas: Politics and Development* (College Station, TX: Texas A&M University Press, 1991), 156, 168–169, 172–173. See also Brischetto et al., "Conflict and Change," 76.

72. Diehl and Jarboe, *Cisneros*, 41.

73. Ibid., 52.

74. Ibid., 54–55. But more specifically see Brischetto and de la Garza, *The Mexican American Electorate: Political Opinions and Behavior*, 6.

75. Grebler et al., *The Mexican-American People*, 471. More generally, see Montejano, *Anglos and Mexicans*, 284–285.

76. Diehl and Jarboe, *Cisneros*, 40–42.

77. Karen O'Connor and Lee Epstein, "A Legal Voice for the Chicano Community: The Activities of the Mexican American Legal Defense and Educational Fund, 1968–1982," *Social Science Quarterly* 65 (1984): 245–256.

78. John A. Booth, "Political Change in San Antonio, 1970–82: Toward Decay or Democracy?" in Johnson et al., *The Politics of San Antonio*, 197.

79. For the text of González's remarks, see Luis Valdez and Stan Steiner, eds., *Aztlán: An Anthology of Mexican American Literature* (New York: Vintage Books, 1972), 311–317. For an account of the events, see Tony Castro, *Chicano Power: The Emergence of Mexican America* (New York: Saturday Review Press, 1974), chap. 9.

80. Charles L. Cotrell and R. Michael Stevens, "The 1975 Voting Rights Act and San Antonio, Texas: Toward a Federal Guarantee of a Republican Form of Local Government," *Publius* 8 (1978):, 79–99. See also Diehl and Jarboe, *Cisneros*, 64.

81. For suggestive evidence of a strong parallel between COPS and the GGL, see Joseph D. Sekul, "Communities Organized for Public Service: Citizen Power and Public Policy in San Antonio," in Johnson et al., *The Politics of San Antonio*, 175–190.

82. For a discussion-cum-roadmap of the persistent factions among Texas Democrats generally, see McCleskey et al., *Government and Politics of Texas*, 104–120.

83. Ibid., 169.

84. On the old Democratic South, see V. O. Key, Jr., *Southern Politics in State and Nation* (New York: Alfred A. Knopf, 1949), especially 254–276. On the changes of the past few decades, see Jack Bass and Walter DeVries, *The Transformation of Southern Politics: Social Change and Political Consequences since 1945* (New York: Basic Books, 1976); and William C. Havard, ed., *The Changing Politics of the South* (Baton Rouge, LA: Louisiana State University Press, 1972).

85. On these recent developments in Texas politics, see McCleskey et al., *Government and Politics of Texas*, 79–87.

86. Diehl and Jarboe, *Cisneros*, 86–87.

87. McCleskey et al., *Government and Politics of Texas*, 270–271.

88. Caro, *Path to Power*, 277.

89. Diehl and Jarboe, *Cisneros*, 82.

90. McCleskey et al., *Government and Politics of Texas*, 270.

91. For an amusing and incisive insider's account of Boston and Massachusetts

politics in the late 1950s, see John P. Roche, "The Second Coming
of R.F.K.," *National Review*, 22 July 1988, 32–35. On the lack of a Chicago-
type machine in Boston, see Steven P. Erie, *Rainbow's End: Irish-Americans and the Dilemmas of Urban Machine Politics, 1840–1985* (Berkeley,
CA: University of California Press, 1988), 69–70, 76, 127–128, 176–
179, 224.

3. LOS ANGELES

1. There are no contemporary data on church attendance by Mexican-American Catholics in San Antonio and Los Angeles. Some dated, but nevertheless suggestive evidence is presented by Grebler and his associates, whose
   survey findings led them to conclude in 1970: "San Antonio Mexican Americans score consistently higher on Mass attendance by age and sex groupings than do Los Angeles Mexican Americans." See Grebler et al., *The
   Mexican-American People: The Nation's Second Largest Minority* (New
   York: The Free Press, 1970), 473.
2. Henry Santiestevan and Stina Santiestevan, eds., *The Hispanic Almanac*
   (New York: Hispanic Policy Development Project, 1984), 88–89.
3. Grebler et al., *The Mexican-American People*, 307.
4. Thomas Muller et al., *The Fourth Wave: California's Newest Immigrants*
   (Washington, DC: The Urban Institute Press, 1985), 53.
5. Ibid., 41.
6. "Appellants' Opening Brief on Appeal," Garza, et al. vs. County of Los Angeles, et al. (U.S. Court of Appeals for the Ninth Circuit, No. 90-55944),
   8–9. Muller et al. came up with a similar figure earlier in the 1980s. See *The
   Fourth Wave*, 42.
7. Muller et al., *The Fourth Wave*, 1, 16.
8. U.S. Bureau of the Census, *1980 Census of Population, Volume 1: Characteristics of the Population, Chapter C: General Social and Economic Characteristics, Part 6: California, PC80-1-C6, Section 1: Tables 56—155* (July
   1983), Table 151; and *Part 45: Texas, PC80-1-C45, Section 2: Tables 170—
   C-3* (July 1983), Table 151. For more on the 1990 state-level data on the
   foreign-born, see chapter 2, endnote 9.
9. Ana Veciana-Suarez cites a 1989 study that found more widespread use of
   English among Hispanics in San Antonio than in other large media markets:
   43 percent of San Antonio Hispanics spoke their native tongue (i.e. Spanish) at home most frequently, compared to 75 percent in Los Angeles and
   78 percent nationally. See Ana Veciana-Suarez, *Hispanic Media: Impact and
   Influence* (Washington, DC: The Media Institute, 1990), 56. Similar data
   are presented in Thomas G. Exter, "Focus on Hispanics," *American
   Demographics*, August 1985, 32.
10. Indeed, in her study of Hispanic media, Veciana-Suarez reports that in San
    Antonio the "Spanish-media there are far from strong." She attributes this

in part to the fact that "in San Antonio . . . the retention of Spanish is not as high as in other areas." See Veciana-Suarez, *Hispanic Media*, 19.

11. During the 1960s, Grebler and his colleagues found San Antonio to be "a more 'Mexican' milieu" than Los Angeles. See Grebler et al., *The Mexican-American People*, 398.

12. Ibid., 432–439.

13. Muller et al. stress the rural origins of Mexican immigrants in *The Fourth Wave*, 15. On the other hand, other recent research indicates that fewer Mexican immigrants today have rural, peasant origins and more have urban, working-class backgrounds. See Alejandro Portes and Robert L. Bach, *Latin Journey: Cuban and Mexican Immigrants in the United States* (Berkeley, CA: University of California Press, 1985), 4, 121–124, 241.

14. Eric Heikkila, "Impacts of Urban Growth," in John J. Kirlin and Donald R. Winkler, *California Policy Choices*, Volume 5 (Los Angeles/Sacramento/Washington, DC: School of Public Administration, University of Southern California, 1989), 106–108.

15. For brief historical sketches of various barrios in metropolitan Los Angeles, see Grebler et al., *The Mexican-American People*, 310–312.

16. See Muller et al., *The Fourth Wave*, 70–82.

17. See W. Tim Dagodag, "Illegal Mexican Aliens in Los Angeles: Locational Characteristics," in Richard C. Jones, ed., *Patterns of Undocumented Migration: Mexico and the United States* (Totowa, NJ: Rowman & Allanheld, 1984), 199–217.

18. Grebler et al., *The Mexican-American People*, 310.

19. In their sample of *legal* Mexican immigrants, Portes and Bach found that 65.7 percent had moved at least once within about two years of their arrival; and 30.8 percent had done so twice or more. See Portes and Bach, *Latin Journey*, 93. Illegal immigrants presumably move more frequently.

20. Muller et al., *The Fourth Wave*, 79.

21. Cited in John Nielsen, *Immigration and the Low-cost Housing Crisis: The Los Angeles Area's Experience* (Washington, DC: Center for Immigration Studies, April 1988), 3.

22. U.S. Bureau of the Census and Office of Policy Development and Research, U.S. Department of Housing and Urban Development, *Annual Housing Survey: 1980, Los Angeles-Long Beach, CA*, Report H-170-80-7 (Washington, DC: December 1983), A-22; also *Annual Housing Survey: 1982, San Antonio, TX*, Report H-170-82-36 (October 1984), A-31.

23. U.S. Bureau of the Census, *1980 Census of Population, Volume 1: Characteristics of the Population, Chapter C: General Social and Economic Characteristics, Part 6: California*, PC80-1-C6, Section 1: Tables 56—155 (July 1983), Table 151; and *Part 45: Texas*, PC80-1-C45, Section 2: Tables 170—C-3 (July 1983), Table 151.

24. Ibid., California, Table 151.

25. Ibid., Texas, Table 151. This difference between San Antonio and Los An-

geles has obtained for some time. For evidence of this during the 1960s, see Grebler et al., *The Mexican-American People*, 340.

26. For 1980 census data on this point, see Santiestevan and Santiestevan, eds., *Hispanic Almanac*, 89, 121. A similar pattern during the mid-1960s is reported in Grebler et al., *The Mexican-American People*, 339–341.

27. Muller et al., *The Fourth Wave*, 25.

28. Ricardo Romo, *East Los Angeles: History of a Barrio* (Austin, TX: University of Texas Press, 1983), 124–128.

29. Thomas Hines, "Housing, Baseball and Creeping Socialism: The Battle of Chavez Ravine, Los Angeles, 1949–1959," *Journal of Urban History* 8 (1982): 123–143.

30. Grebler et al., *The Mexican-American People*, 336–337.

31. Ibid., 304–305. For other such comparative data, see Ibid., 154, 235, 327, and 337.

32. Ibid., 312.

33. Ibid., 395.

34. Ibid., 395–398.

35. Ibid., 399.

36. Ibid., 305. For more data on Mexican-American residential patterns, see Ibid., Table II-1, 275.

37. Ibid., 408–409.

38. See Edward Murguía, *Chicano Intermarriage: A Theoretical and Empirical Study* (San Antonio, TX: Trinity University Press, 1982), 49.

39. Grebler et al., *The Mexican-American People*, 407.

40. Such complaints are echoed in Alex M. Saragoza, "The Conceptualization of the History of the Chicano Family," in Armando Valdez et al., *The State of Chicano Research in Family, Labor, and Migration Studies* (Stanford, CA: Stanford Center for Chicano Research, 1983), 125–126.

41. For an economic forecast that raises questions about the continued economic assimilation of Mexican Americans in California, see Kevin F. McCarthy and R. Burciaga Valdez, *Current and Future Effects of Mexican Immigration in California*, Report R-3365-CR (Santa Monica, CA: The Rand Corp., 1986), 67–76.

42. Ibid., 63. See also Douglas S. Massey and Nancy A. Denton, "Trends in the Residential Segregation of Blacks, Hispanics, and Asians: 1970–1980," *American Sociological Review* 52 (1987): 803, 817.

43. Joan Moore and Harry Pachon, *Hispanics in the United States* (Englewood Cliffs, NJ: Prentice-Hall, 1985), 60.

44. Frank D. Bean and Marta Tienda, *The Hispanic Population of the United States* (New York: Russell Sage Foundation, 1987), 176.

45. David E. López, "Chicano Language Loyalty in an Urban Setting," *Sociology and Social Research* 62 (1978): 276.

46. McCarthy and Valdez, *Current and Future Effects of Mexican Immigration*, 61–62. These figures are based on self-reported census data. So they may

be inflated. But the basic thrust of the Rand researchers' conclusion is supported by other research on English-language acquisition among Hispanics. See Calvin Veltman, *The Future of the Spanish Language in the United States* (New York and Washington, DC: Hispanic Policy Development Project, 1988). But such data from 1980 and even earlier may not reflect current realities, and it is possible that the huge and continuing influx since 1980 will prove to have a negative impact on English acquisition among Mexicans.

47. *United States Department of Commerce News*, 11 May 1992, Table 2, "Selected Social Characteristics; Los Angeles County, California."

48. U.S. Bureau of the Census, unpublished 1990 census data, Summary Tape File 3. Figure for San Antonio is Bexar County, and that for Los Angeles is Los Angeles County.

49. See Thomas Muller et al., *The Fourth Wave*, 42–48.

50. Gladwin Hill, *Dancing Bear: An Inside Look at California Politics* (New York: World Publishing, 1968), 211.

51. See, for example, Raymond E. Wolfinger and Steven J. Rosenstone, *Who Votes?* (New Haven, CT: Yale University Press, 1980), 50–54.

52. For evidence that the goals of illegal Mexican immigrants tend to be narrowly economic, see Portes and Bach, *Latin Journey*, 80–81.

53. Tending to confirm this point is Grebler's finding that in the 1960s Mexican Americans in Los Angeles felt less discriminated against than their counterparts in San Antonio. Grebler and his colleagues also found that Mexicans in Los Angeles had much more contact with Anglos. See Grebler et al., *The Mexican-American People*, 378–404.

54. See Portes and Bach, *Latin Journey*, 270–282; Moore and Pachon, *Hispanics in the United States*, 174; and *The National Latino Immigrant Survey* (Washington, DC and Los Angeles: NALEO Educational Fund, 1989), 13, 15, 25. Similar findings about the positive attitudes of immigrant Mexican parents toward their children's school opportunities in the United States are reported in Harriet Romo, "The Mexican Origin Population's Differing Perceptions of Their Children's Schooling," *Social Science Quarterly* 65 (1984): 642–645. A related finding is that Mexican Americans in South Texas tend to be politically conservative because they compare their situation not with that of Anglos, but with that of Mexicans in Mexico. Presumably the same dynamic is at work among recent immigrants from Mexico. See John Staples Shockley, *Chicano Revolt in a Texas Town* (Notre Dame, IN: University of Notre Dame Press, 1974), endnote 63, 290–291.

55. See Hill, *Dancing Bear*, chaps. 3–6.

56. On the civil service ethos in Los Angeles, see Mickey Kaus, "Why California Hates Politics," *Washington Monthly* 17 (1985): 25–30.

57. Alan Citron, "Electoral Logjam: On Westside, Many Politicians Feel Call but Few Are Chosen," *Los Angeles Times*, 30 July 1987, W1. This is an unusually insightful journalistic treatment.

58. The district encompasses 714 square miles. See Dagodag, "Illegal Mexican Aliens," 206.

59. See James A. Regalado, "Latino Representation in Los Angeles" in Roberto E. Villarreal et al., eds., *Latino Empowerment: Progress, Problems, and Prospects* (Westport, CT: Greenwood Press, 1988), 94.

60. In 1982, the median *competitive* assembly candidate (defined by the California Fair Political Practices Commission as a candidate with a reasonable chance of victory) spent $221,000. See *The New Gold Rush: Financing California's Legislative Campaigns*, Report and Recommendations of the California Commission on Campaign Financing (Los Angeles, CA: Center for Responsive Government, 1985), 34.

61. Rob Gurwitt, "California, Here We Come: The Professional Legislature and Its Discontents," *Governing*, August 1991, 67.

62. Carlos Muñoz, Jr., and Charles Henry, "Rainbow Coalitions in Four Big Cities: San Antonio, Denver, Chicago and Philadelphia," *PS* 19 (Summer 1986): 604.

63. J. Morgan Kousser, *How To Determine Intent: Lessons from L.A.*, Social Science Working Paper 741 (Pasadena, CA: Division of Humanities and Social Sciences, California Institute of Technology, June 1990), 18.

64. Tom Waldman, "The Scramble for L.A. County's New Supervisorial Seat," *California Journal*, January 1991, 20.

65. Kousser, *How To Determine Intent*, 18.

66. Finding of fact from Garza v. County of Los Angeles, 756 F.Supp. 1298, 1309 (C.D. Cal. 1990).

67. Kousser, *How To Determine Intent*, 10.

68. Finding of fact in Garza v. County of Los Angeles, 756 F.Supp. 1298, 1309 (C.D. Cal. 1990).

69. Kousser, *How To Determine Intent*, 10.

70. On the problems experienced by Chicano activists with this and other issues, see Carlos Muñoz, Jr., and Mario Barrera, "La Raza Unida Party and the Chicano Student Movement in California," *Social Science Journal* 19 (1982): 101–119.

71. See Roger L. Kemp, *Coping with Proposition 13* (Lexington, MA: Lexington Books, 1980).

72. See Lou Cannon, *Ronnie and Jesse: A Political Odyssey* (Garden City, NY: Doubleday, 1969).

73. Quoted in Walter K. Muir, Jr., *Legislature: California's School for Politics* (Chicago: The University of Chicago Press, 1982), 162.

74. This figure refers to itemized contributions—that is, contributions of $100 or more. See *The New Gold Rush*, 55–56.

75. *The New Gold Rush: Financing California's Legislative Campaigns*, 1987 Update of the Report and Recommendations of the California Commission on Campaign Financing (Los Angeles, CA: Center for Responsive Government, 1987), 16–18.

76. Alan Ehrenhalt et al., eds., *Politics in America: The 100th Congress* (Washington, DC: Congressional Quarterly Press, 1987), 104.

77. On the role of Hollywood money in our politics, see Ronald Brownstein, "The Hollywood Primary," *New Republic*, 23 November 1987, 19–23. See also Fred Barnes, "Flix Mix in Politix: Activism under the Stars," *New Republic*, 30 October 1989, 20–23.

78. Between 1968 and 1982, the average competitive legislative campaign in California increased its direct-mail expenditures by 763 percent, from $15,600 to $134,000. See *The New Gold Rush* (1985), 36–37.

79. On Jewish liberalism in Los Angeles, see Raphe Sonenshein, "Biracial Coalition Politics in Los Angeles," *PS* 19 (1986): 583. On the black-Jewish coalition in Los Angeles generally, see Ibid., 582–590.

80. The figure for blacks is from *United States Department of Commerce* (Bureau of the Census), press release #CB91-229, 5 July 1991. The figure for Jews is from Bruce A. Phillips, "Los Angeles Jewry: A Demographic Profile," *American Jewish Yearbook, 1986* (New York: The American Jewish Committee, 1986), 160.

81. See Donald Haider, "Race in the 1989 Mayoral Races," *Public Opinion*, March/April 1989, 16–18.

82. Raphael Sonenshein reports that in 1982 this low black turnout for Bradley resulted from the mayor's deliberate decision not to mobilize his black base. In any event, Sonenshein also argues that this decision led to disaffection among blacks, which presumably was manifested in 1986. See his "Can Black Candidates Win Statewide Elections?" *Political Science Quarterly* 105 (1990): 232–233.

83. See Alan L. Saltzstein and Raphael J. Sonenshein, "Los Angeles: Transformation of a Governing Coalition," in H. V. Savitch and John Clayton Thomas, eds., *Big City Politics in Transition* (Newbury Park, CA: Sage Publications, 1991), 198–199.

84. Grebler et al., *The Mexican-American People*, 367.

85. On a related issue, for evidence on the relatively strong support for school prayer among Latinos, see Bruce Cain and Roderick Kiewiet, "California's Coming Minority Majority," *Public Opinion*, February/March 1986, 51.

86. On Jews and abortion specifically, see Peter Skerry, "The Class Conflict over Abortion," *The Public Interest* 52 (1978): 74. For comparative data on Jews and Hispanics (not just Mexican Americans), see findings from the National Opinion Research Center's General Social Survey assembled in "Opinion Roundup: Ethnicity in America," *Public Opinion*, October/November 1984, 28–29.

87. See Sonenshein, "Biracial Coalition Politics in Los Angeles," 583.

88. Ralph Chris Carmona, "Language and Ethnic Politics: Bilingualism in Los Angeles City Schools, 1975–1980," Ph.D. diss., Department of Political Science, University of California at Santa Barbara (1984), 125, 169, 170.

89. My findings from the field are borne out by a recent *Los Angeles Times* poll, in which blacks and Latinos in Southern California had almost identical responses to the statement: "There's no excuse for anti-Semitism, but Jews have brought on themselves much of the anti-Jewish feeling that exists in Southern California." Agreeing with this assertion were 27 percent of blacks and 31 percent of Latinos, a statistically insignificant difference. (But it should be noted that this poll reported similar levels of anti-Jewish sentiment among other groups in Los Angeles.) See *Los Angeles Times Poll* January 1989 (No. 172), question 35.

90. Grebler et al., *The Mexican-American People*, 390–394.

91. Cited in Sonenshein, "Biracial Coalition Politics in Los Angeles," 584–585.

92. Ibid., 584–586.

93. "Hispanics Seek More Recognition . . . within the Civil Rights Lobby," *National Journal*, 19 May 1990, 1210–1211. For a discussion of the Leadership Conference episode as part of a lengthy analysis of black-Hispanic relations, see Charles Kamasaki and Raúl Yzaguirre, "Black-Hispanic Tensions: One Perspective," paper delivered at the Annual Meeting of the American Political Science Association (1991).

94. For more on black-Hispanic tensions in Los Angeles, see Peter Skerry, "Borders and Quotas: Immigration and the Affirmative-Action State," *The Public Interest* 96 (1989): 93–94 and Peter Skerry, "On Edge: Blacks and Mexicans in Los Angeles," *American Spectator*, May 1988, 16–18. For specific evidence on black-Hispanic job competition in the public sector, see Susan Welch et al., "Changes in Hispanic Local Public Employment in the Southwest," *Western Political Quarterly* 36 (1983): 660–673; and Rufus P. Browning et al., *Protest Is Not Enough: The Struggle of Blacks and Hispanics for Equality in Urban Politics* (Berkeley, CA: University of California Press, 1984), 194–195.

95. For a useful discussion of this point, see Melvin L. Oliver and James H. Johnson, Jr., "Inter-Ethnic Conflict in an Urban Ghetto: The Case of Blacks and Latinos in Los Angeles," *Research in Social Movements, Conflict and Change* 6 (1984): 57–94.

96. Such complaints could be heard from blacks for some years now. But they have been particularly audible since the 1992 riots. Indeed, blacks in Los Angeles have been staging job-site protests against the employment of Hispanics in postriot rebuilding projects. See, for example, Stephanie Chávez, "Race Tension Grows over South L.A. Employment," *Los Angeles Times*, Washington edition, 22 July 1992, B3.

97. For example, the Urban Institute's study of the impact of immigration on Southern California emphatically minimizes labor market competition between blacks and Mexican immigrants. See Muller et al., *The Fourth Wave*, 101–102. For similar findings, see also McCarthy and Valdez, *Current and Future Effects of Mexican Immigration*, 37–45.

98. My findings from the field are echoed in Oliver and Johnson, "Inter-Ethnic Conflict in an Urban Ghetto," 59 and in Joseph N. Boyce, "Struggle over Hospital in Los Angeles Pits Minority vs. Minority," *Wall Street Journal*, 1 April 1991, A1, A4.

99. Quoted in "Hispanics Wrestle with Life in U.S." *Insight*, 16 December 1985, 10.

100. My emphasis here on political, as opposed to economic, competition is supported by a study of 49 U.S. cities in which the authors identify political—but no socioeconomic—competition between blacks and Hispanics. See Paula D. McClain and Albert K. Karnig, "Black and Hispanic Socioeconomic and Political Outcomes: Is There Competition?" paper delivered at the annual meeting of the American Political Science Association (1988). Unfortunately, this political dimension of the tensions between blacks and Hispanics in Los Angeles is overlooked in an otherwise insightful and indeed courageous article by Jack Miles. See his "Blacks vs. Browns," *Atlantic Monthly*, October 1992, 41–68.

101. Grebler et al., *The Mexican-American People*, 356.

102. See A. G. Block and Robert S. Fairbanks, "The Legislature's Staff—No. 1 Growth Industry in the Capitol," *California Journal*, June 1983, 214–219; Charles G. Bell and Charles M. Price, "20 Years of a Full-time Legislature: Is It Time for Another Reform?" *California Journal*, January 1987, 36–40; Sherry Bebitch Jeffe, "Undermined from Within: For Legislative Staff, Policy Takes a Back Seat to Politics," *California Journal*, January 1987, 42–45.

4. PARADOXICAL POLITICAL OUTCOMES

1. For a critical account of the process by which Congress was persuaded to bring Mexican Americans under the Voting Rights Act, see Abigail M. Thernstrom, *Whose Votes Count? Affirmative Action and Minority Voting Rights* (Cambridge, MA: Harvard University Press, 1987), 43–62.

2. For example, voter turnout is rejected as a political outcome measure in Rufus P. Browning et al., *Protest Is Not Enough: The Struggle of Blacks and Hispanics for Equality in Urban Politics* (Berkeley, CA: University of California Press, 1984), 78, 281–282.

3. Maria Antonia Calvo and Steven J. Rosenstone, *Hispanic Political Participation* (San Antonio, TX: Southwest Voter Research Institute, 1989), 21. It should be noted, however, that Calvo and Rosenstone report that socioeconomic variables have a less pronounced effect on voter turnout among Mexican Americans and other Hispanics than among non-Hispanics.

4. For an earlier elaboration of my point about these districts as rotten boroughs, see Peter Skerry, "Borders and Quotas: Immigration and the Affirmative-Action State," *The Public Interest* 96 (1989): 94–97.

5. Raymond Wolfinger, *Voter Turnout in California, 1974–1986*, unpublished

paper (Berkeley, CA: State Data Program, University of California, 21 February 1988), 4.

6. Ibid., 5.

7. Ibid., 8–9.

8. Carole J. Uhlaner et al., *Political Participation of Ethnic Minorities in the 1980s*, Social Science Working Paper 647 (Pasadena, CA: Division of the Humanities and Social Sciences, California Institute of Technology, June 1987), i.

9. Ibid., 26.

10. For Mexican-origin naturalization rates during the 1950s and 1960s, see Leo Grebler et al., *The Mexican-American People: The Nation's Second Largest Minority* (New York: The Free Press, 1970), 557–560.

11. John A. Booth, "Political Change in San Antonio, 1970–1982: Toward Decay or Democracy?" in David R. Johnson et al., eds., *The Politics of San Antonio: Community, Progress, and Power* (Lincoln, NB: University of Nebraska Press, 1983), 198.

12. Robert R. Brischetto and Rodolfo O. de la Garza, *The Mexican American Electorate: Political Opinions and Behavior across Cultures in San Antonio*, Hispanic Population Studies Program, Occasional Paper No. 5 (San Antonio, TX: Southwest Voter Registration Education Project; and Austin, TX: Center for Mexican American Studies, University of Texas), 5. The historian David Montejano comes up with a similar set of figures for the GGL years, and also shows that in terms of Mexican-American officeholders, the GGL was a big improvement over the mayor-commission form of government in place from 1933 to 1952, during which period there were apparently no Spanish-surnamed mayors or city councillors. See David Montejano, *Anglos and Mexicans in the Making of Texas, 1836–1986* (Austin, TX: University of Texas Press, 1987), 293–294.

13. Such characterizations are common. See, for example, Carlos Muñoz, Jr., and Charles Henry, "Rainbow Coalitions in Four Big Cities: San Antonio, Denver, Chicago and Philadelphia," *PS* 19 (Summer 1986): 598–609.

14. These Hispanic population data are from the 1990 census. The figures on Hispanic elected officials are from *1991 National Roster of Hispanic Elected Officials* (Washington, DC, and Los Angeles, CA: NALEO Educational Fund, 1991), Table 6, viii.

15. These Hispanic population proportions are derived from the 1990 census, and the figures on Hispanic elected officials are calculated from data reported in *1991 National Roster of Hispanic Elected Officials*, Table 4, vii.

16. See John A. García, "The Voting Rights Act and Hispanic Political Representation in the Southwest," *Publius* 16 (1986): 58–59. But there is some confusion on this point. Thus, another study insists that through 1978, no Mexican Americans had been elected to executive offices in Texas at least since Reconstruction. See Charles L. Cotrell, *Status of Civil Rights in Texas, Vol. I: A Report on the Participation of Mexican-Americans, Blacks and Fe-*

males in the Political Institutions and Processes in Texas, 1968–1978 (San Antonio, TX: Texas Advisory Committee to the U.S. Commission on Civil Rights, January 1980), 16.

17. It should be noted, however, that because Raúl González was initially appointed to the bench and because judicial races in Texas are not conducted as conventional electoral contests, his situation was perhaps not typical. See Robert R. Brischetto, *The Political Empowerment of Texas Mexicans, 1974–1988* (San Antonio, TX: Southwest Voter Research Institute, 1988), 10–11.

18. Ibid.

19. See Clifton McCleskey and Bruce Merrill, "Mexican American Political Behavior in Texas," *Social Science Quarterly* 53 (1973): 786.

20. One other such potential statewide candidate is Orange County supervisor Gaddi Vásquez, a Republican.

21. For an analysis demonstrating that the Hispanic caucus in Texas is stronger, more responsive and aggressive than its counterpart in California, see Juan Antonio Sepulveda, Jr., "The Question of Representative Responsiveness for Hispanics: The Roles of Ethnicity, Constituency Influence, and Political Participation," B.A. thesis, Department of Government, Harvard University (1985). See also, Harry Pachon and Louis DeSipio, *Latino Legislators and Latino Caucuses* (Austin, TX: IUP/SSRC Committee for Public Policy Research on Contemporary Hispanic Issues; The Center for Mexican American Studies, University of Texas, 1990).

22. Grebler et al., *The Mexican-American People*, 561.

23. Fernando V. Padilla, "Chicano Representation by Court Order: Impact of Reapportionment," *The Chicano Community and California Redistricting*, vol. I (Claremont, CA: Rose Institute of State and Local Government, Claremont Men's College, 1981), 86.

24. Clifton McCleskey et al., *The Government and Politics of Texas* 7th ed. (Boston: Little, Brown, 1982), 136.

25. Browning et al., *Protest Is Not Enough*, 25.

26. Luis Ricardo Fraga et al., "Hispanic Americans and Educational Policy: Limits to Equal Access," *Journal of Politics* 48 (1986): 860, 869.

27. Peter K. Eisenger, "Black Employment in Municipal Jobs: The Impact of Black Political Power," *American Political Science Review* 76 (1982): 380–392.

28. Quoted in *Los Angeles Reapportionment: Unfinished Business* (Los Angeles: California Advisory Committee to the U.S. Commission on Civil Rights, November 1983), 20.

29. Grebler et al., *The Mexican-American People*, 116, 224.

30. Grace Hall and Alan Saltzstein, "Equal Employment Opportunity for Minorities in Municipal Government," *Social Science Quarterly* 57 (1976): 865–871.

31. *Status of Civil Rights in Texas, Vol. III: A Report on the Status of Minority*

Group Members and Women in Public Employment and Public Education in Texas during 1977 (San Antonio, TX: Texas Advisory Committee to the United States Commission on Civil Rights, January 1980), 181; Appendix F, 89.

32. Grebler et al., *The Mexican-American People*, 222–225.

33. Susan Welch et al., "Changes in Hispanic Local Employment in the Southwest," *Western Political Quarterly* 36 (1983): 660–673.

34. *Los Angeles Reapportionment: Unfinished Business*, 12–13.

35. Data supplied by Terry González, Los Angeles Unified School District.

36. Data supplied by Rene Gaines, Community Information Office, San Antonio Independent School District.

37. Carlos Muñoz, Jr., and Mario Barrera, "La Raza Unida Party and the Chicano Student Movement in California," *Social Science Journal* 19 (1982): 102.

38. In 1978 (the first year for which such data were available), 48.0 percent of eligible Hispanics were registered to vote. By 1984, that figure had jumped to 58.9 percent. By 1990 (the latest year for which data are available), however, Hispanic registrations had dropped back to 51.9 percent. Still, SVREP's enormous success cannot be gainsaid. For these and other voting data, see U.S. Bureau of the Census, Current Population Reports, Series P-20 (Washington, DC: U.S. Government Printing Office): No. 344, *Voting and Registration in the Election of November 1978*, Sept. 1979, 12; No. 405, *Voting and Registration in the Election of November 1984*, March 1986, 17; No. 453, *Voting and Registration in the Election of November 1990*, March 1991, 17.

39. David S. Broder, *Changing of the Guard: Power and Leadership in America* (New York: Simon & Schuster, 1980), 282–283.

40. For an overview of MALDEF, see Karen O'Connor and Lee Epstein, "A Legal Voice for the Chicano Community: The Activities of the Mexican American Legal Defense and Educational Fund, 1968–82," *Social Science Quarterly* 65 (1984): 245–256.

41. Ibid., 249–251.

42. Mario T. García, *Mexican Americans: Leadership, Ideology, & Identity, 1930–1960* (New Haven, CT: Yale University Press, 1989), 25–61. See also Tony Castro, *Chicano Power: The Emergence of Mexican America* (New York: Saturday Review Press, 1974), 188; Joan W. Moore and Harry Pachon, *Mexican Americans* (Englewood Cliffs, NJ: Prentice-Hall, 1970), 145–146; and Juan Gómez-Quiñones, *Chicano Politics: Reality and Promise, 1940–1990* (Albuquerque: University of New Mexico Press, 1990), 62–64.

43. Carl Allsup, *The American G.I. Forum: Origins and Evolution* (Austin, TX: Center for Mexican American Studies, University of Texas, 1982). See also Castro, *Chicano Power*, 188; and Moore and Pachon, *Mexican Americans*, 146–147. For survey data from the 1960s that highlight the Texas origins

and base of these organizations, see Grebler et al., *The Mexican-American People*, 547–548.

44. Kemper Diehl and Jan Jarboe, *Cisneros: Portrait of a New American* (San Antonio, TX: Corona Publishing, 1985), 15–21.

45. For background on *La Prensa*, see Onofre di Stefano, " 'Venimos a luchar': A Brief History of *La Prensa*'s Founding," *Aztlán* 16 (1985): 95–118.

46. Ana Veciana-Suarez, *Hispanic Media, USA: A Narrative Guide to Print and Electronic Hispanic News Media in the United States* (Washington, DC: The Media Institute, 1987), 12–16; and Ana Veciana-Suarez, *Hispanic Media: Impact and Influence* (Washington, DC: The Media Institute, 1990), 29–36.

47. I refer of course to the amended Section 2 provisions of the Voting Rights Act. For a critical analysis of these amendments, see Thernstrom, *Whose Votes Count?*

48. See, for example, Charles L. Cotrell and Jerry Polinard, "Effects of the Voting Rights Act in Texas," *Publius* 16 (1986): 71; and García, "The Voting Rights Act and Hispanic Political Representation," 63–64.

49. Robert D. Thomas and Richard W. Murray, "Applying the VRA in Texas," *Publius* 16 (1986): 81–96.

50. Even in San Antonio, the evidence is that the VRA has been responsible for increased officeholding, but for only modest increases in Mexican-American voting. See Booth, "Political Change in San Antonio," 197.

51. See Garcia, "The Voting Rights Act and Hispanic Political Representation," 49–66.

52. V. O. Key, Jr., *Southern Politics in State and Nation* (New York: Vintage Books, 1949), 513–517.

53. See the aforementioned studies: Eisenger, "Black Employment in Municipal Jobs"; and Fraga et al., "Hispanic Americans and Educational Policy."

54. For a formulation that has helped shape my own thinking in this regard, see Browning et al., *Protest Is Not Enough*, 103–104, 129. See also Kenneth R. Mladenka, "Blacks and Hispanics in Urban Politics," *American Political Science Review* 83 (1989): 165–192.

55. See James Meier, *Expanding Voter Participation: An Assessment of 1984 Non-Partisan Voter Registration Efforts* (New York: Interface Development Project, 1985), 10–11.

56. The irony of the ironing-board approach, which was evident to its originator Marshall Ganz, was apparently lost on columnist Mary McGrory, who praised it in "Dukakis's Ironing-Board Power," *Washington Post*, 6 June 1988, C1.

57. For evidence on the success of voter registration drives in Los Angeles County between 1982 and 1984, see Bruce E. Cain and Ken McCue, "Do Registration Drives Matter? The Realities of Partisan Dreams," paper presented to the annual meeting of the American Political Science Association (1985).

58. Jay Mathews, "Jerry Brown Succeeds Quietly as State Party-Builder," *Washington Post*, 7 April 1990, A6.

59. This is updated from *1989 National Roster of Hispanic Elected Officials* (Los Angeles and Washington: NALEO Educational Fund, 1989), viii.

60. See Grebler et al., *The Mexican-American People*, 317–325.

61. See T. R. Fehrenbach, *The San Antonio Story* (Tulsa, OK: Continental Heritage, 1978), 125.

62. See Sister Frances Jerome Woods, *Mexican Ethnic Leadership in San Antonio, Texas* (Washington, DC: Catholic University of America Press, 1949), 105–116.

63. For Texas elected offices, see *Texas State Directory*, 35th ed. (Austin, TX: Texas State Directory, Inc., 1992). For California offices, see *A Guide to California Government*, 12th ed. (San Francisco: League of Women Voters, 1981).

64. In the field throughout the 1980s, I heard this charge on several occasions. It has also surfaced elsewhere. See, for example, Penn Kimball, *The Disconnected* (New York: Columbia University Press, 1972), 199–200.

65. Ralph Chris Carmona, "Language and Ethnic Politics: Bilingualism in Los Angeles City Schools, 1975–1980," Ph.D. diss., Dept. of Political Science, University of California at Santa Barbara (1984), 125.

66. Quoted in Ibid., 170.

67. Examples from the California legislature during the 1960s and 1970s are discussed in Sepulveda, "The Question of Representative Responsiveness," 39–40.

5. FRIENDS-AND-NEIGHBORS POLITICS AND THE NEED FOR ORGANIZATION

1. See Albert O. Hirschman, *Exit, Voice, and Loyalty: Responses to Decline in Firms, Organizations, and States* (Cambridge, MA: Harvard University Press, 1970).

2. V. O. Key, Jr., *Southern Politics* (New York: Vintage Books, 1949), 37–41, passim.

3. My analysis here obviously draws on the work of James Q. Wilson. See his *Political Organizations* (New York: Basic Books, 1973), especially 30–55.

4. See Leo Grebler et al., *The Mexican-American People* (New York: The Free Press, 1970), 354–355, and Grace Horowitz, *Honor and the American Dream: Culture and Identity in a Chicano Community* (New Brunswick, NJ: Rutgers University Press, 1985), 55–57.

5. Amy Bridges, *A City in the Republic: Antebellum New York and the Origins of Machine Politics* (Cambridge: Cambridge University Press, 1984), 147.

6. See Martin Shefter, "The Emergence of the Political Machine: An Alternative View," in Willis D. Hawley et al., *Theoretical Perspectives on Urban Politics* (Englewood Cliffs, NJ: Prentice-Hall, 1976), 14–44.

7. As recently as the late 1980s, gang activity in San Antonio was minimal. Moreover, the city was noted for its relatively low crime rate. On this latter point, see Thomas Muller et al., *The Fourth Wave: California's Newest Immigrants* (Washington, DC: The Urban Institute Press, 1985), 69.

8. See Clifton McCleskey and Bruce Merrill, "Mexican American Political Behavior in Texas," *Social Science Quarterly* 53 (1973): 786.

9. See Robert R. Brischetto, *The Political Empowerment of Texas Mexicans, 1974–1988* (San Antonio, TX: Southwest Voter Research Institute, 1988), 10–11. See also an interview with Roy Barrera, Jr., "Barrera, We Need Self-Reliance," *Insight*, 16 December 1985, 16–17.

10. David S. Broder, "Cisneros's Hispanic Rival," *Washington Post*, 15 January 1986, 19.

11. Robert A. Caro, *The Path to Power: The Years of Lyndon Johnson* (New York: Knopf, 1982), 166–173.

12. See John Staples Shockley, *Chicano Revolt in a Texas Town* (Notre Dame: University of Notre Dame Press, 1974).

13. San Antonio Independent School District v. Rodriguez, 411 U.S. 1 (1973).

14. Karen O'Connor and Lee Epstein, "A Legal Voice for the Chicano Community: The Activities of the Mexican American Legal Defense and Educational Fund, 1968–82," *Social Science Quarterly* 65 (1984): 250.

15. Wilson, *Political Organizations*, 220.

16. For the classic analysis of the political machines, see Edward C. Banfield and James Q. Wilson, *City Politics* (New York: Vintage Books, 1966), 115–127. While Banfield and Wilson emphasize the primacy of material incentives in the machine, they acknowledge the role of nonmaterial incentives as well. For an analysis that focuses more exclusively on the role of material incentives in the machine, see Raymond E. Wolfinger, "Why Political Machines Have Not Withered Away and Other Revisionist Thoughts," *Journal of Politics* 34 (1972): 365–398.

17. James Q. Wilson, *American Government: Institutions and Policies* (Lexington, MA: D. C. Heath, 1980), 148. Another reason I avoid the term "machine politics" is that it can be distinguished from "political machine." On this point, see Wolfinger, "Why Political Machines Have Not Withered Away," 374–375.

18. One obvious difference between political machines and these Alinsky organizations that will emerge from my analysis is that the latter rely much less on individual material incentives than the former did.

19. Much of this analysis is based on my attendance at a weeklong Industrial Areas Foundation (IAF) training workshop in November 1983, in addition to extensive observation and conversation with IAF organizers and leaders in Los Angeles, San Antonio, and the Rio Grande Valley over the past several years.

20. See Robert Bailey, Jr., *Radicals in Urban Politics: The Alinsky Approach* (Chicago: The University of Chicago Press, 1974).

21. For Saul Alinsky's views on the importance of organizing individuals around their self-interest, see his *Reveille for Radicals*, 2nd ed. (New York: Vintage Books, 1969), 92–93.

22. See Ibid., 223.

23. On welfare rights organizing strategy, see Lawrence N. Bailis, "Bread or Justice: Grassroots Organizing in the Welfare Rights Movement," Ph.D. diss., Department of Government, Harvard University (1972).

24. Alexis de Tocqueville (J. P. Mayer, ed.), *Democracy in America* (Garden City, NY: Anchor Books, 1969), 525–528.

25. See Alinsky, *Reveille for Radicals*, 95–100.

26. On this point, see P. David Finks, *The Radical Vision of Saul Alinsky* (New York: Paulist Press, 1984), 271–272.

27. See Gary Delgado, *Organizing the Movement: The Roots and Growth of ACORN* (Philadelphia: Temple University Press, 1986), 95, 109, 170. For a review essay that is instructive but unfortunately fails to make important distinctions among IAF, ACORN, and other New Left-inspired organizing efforts, see Karen Paget, "Citizen Organizing: Many Movements, No Majority," *American Prospect* 2 (1990): 115–128.

28. Saul Alinsky, "The War on Poverty—Political Pornography," *The Journal of Social Issues* (January 1965): 41–47.

29. On "welfare colonialism," see Alinsky, *Reveille for Radicals*, 211; and Charles E. Silberman, *Crisis in Black and White* (New York: Vintage Books, 1964), chap. 10. For an appreciation of Alinsky's critique of the War on Poverty, see Daniel Patrick Moynihan, *Maximum Feasible Misunderstanding: Community Action in the War on Poverty* (New York: The Free Press, 1969), 185–188.

30. Students of the American labor movement will discern in what I describe here as self-reliance strong parallels with the doctrine of "voluntarism" enunciated by Samuel Gompers. Given Alinsky's origins in the labor movement, the parallel hardly seems coincidental. On voluntarism and the labor movement, see Wilson, *Political Organizations*, 125, and Grant McConnell, *Private Power and American Democracy* (New York: Vintage Books, 1970), 310–311, 332–335.

31. On the CSO, see Finks, *Radical Vision*, 61–72, and Margarite Marín, "Protest in an Urban Barrio: The Chicano Movement in East Los Angeles," Ph.D. diss., University of California at Santa Barbara (1980). On The Woodlawn Organization, see Finks, 132–175, and John Hall Fish, *Black Power/White Control: The Struggle of The Woodlawn Organization in Chicago* (Princeton, NJ: Princeton University Press, 1973).

32. In recent years, the IAF has received foundation support for specific projects, such as conducting seminars for organizers with invited writers and academics. While such activities are obviously perquisites for organizers, the IAF and Cortes appear to be at pains to make sure that the community organizations do not grow dependent on such foundation support.

33. For a discussion of the adbook strategy by a former COPS organizer, see Arnie Graf, *Communities Organized for Public Service: A Case Study of the COPS Adbook* (Washington, DC: The National Center for Citizen Involvement, 1980).

34. A survey of COPS leaders found "personal development" to be one of the most important benefits derived from their participation in the organization. See Joseph Daniel Sekul, "The C.O.P.S. Story: A Case Study of Successful Collective Action," Ph.D. diss., Department of Political Science, University of Texas at Austin (1984), 371–374.

35. Such complications explain why the IAF has tried, whenever possible, to hold organizational meetings in church buildings and other public venues, rather than in members' homes—although there have always been exceptions, such as when the legendary Fred Ross, working among migrant farmworkers who lacked much if any institutional life, relied on house meetings to build up CSO chapters throughout California. See Finks, *Radical Vision*, 61–63. Today, house meetings are increasingly common, but socializing between organizers and leaders remains problematic.

36. See Ernie Cortes, "Reflections on the Catholic Tradition of Family Rights," in John A. Coleman, S.J., ed., *One Hundred Years of Catholic Social Thought: Celebration and Challenge* (Maryknoll, NY: Orbis Books, 1991), 161–164.

37. Here again, this IAF dictum derives from Alinsky. See his *Reveille for Radicals*, 150.

38. Wilson, *Political Organizations*, 185.

39. For more on Alinsky's experience in Rochester, see Finks, *Radical Vision*, 176–228, 216–217.

40. On the strategy on personalization, see Saul Alinsky, *Rules for Radicals: A Practical Primer for Realistic Radicals*, 2nd ed. (New York: Vintage Books, 1972), 130–136.

41. The Alinsky organizers' conception here of "politics as an interpretation of life" contrasts, of course, with that of politics as decision making and resource allocation. For a brief and illuminating discussion of these divergent views of politics, see James G. March and Johan P. Olsen, *Rediscovering Institutions: The Organizational Basis of Politics* (New York: The Free Press, 1989), 47–52.

42. See *Organizing for Family and Congregation* (Huntington, NY: Industrial Areas Foundation, 1978).

43. On this controversial point, see Sanford D. Horwitt, *Let Them Call Me Rebel: Saul Alinsky—His Life and Legacy* (New York: Alfred A. Knopf, 1989). 197, 244, 395.

44. For a sample of the right-wing reaction that Cortes and his colleagues encountered in El Paso, Texas, see Stanley Interrante, *The El Paso Model: A Plan for Revolution through Church Structures and Finance* (St. Paul, MN: The Wanderer Press, 1982). For an account of similarly hostile reactions

to Alinsky organizing efforts in the lower Rio Grande Valley, see Peter Skerry, "Vendetta in the Valley," *New Republic*, 17 and 24 September 1984, 19–21.

45. For a contrasting and in my view ill-informed view of IAF organizers, see Rodolfo Acuña, *Occupied America: A History of Chicanos*, 2nd ed. (New York: Harper & Row, 1981), 407–408.

46. For Alinsky's critique of liberals, see his *Reveille for Radicals*, 19–23.

47. For a similar critique from a decidedly left perspective, see Stuart A. Scheingold, *The Politics of Rights: Lawyers, Public Policy, and Political Change* (New Haven, CT: Yale University Press, 1974).

48. For Alinsky's own elaboration of this perspective, see his *Rules for Radicals*, 77–78, 119–120.

49. For Alinsky's views on power, see ibid., 113–115.

50. David S. Broder, *Changing of the Guard: Power and Leadership in America* (New York: Simon & Schuster, 1980), 476.

51. In contrast, examine the us–them terminology relied on by the youthful organizers working with the New Left-inspired ACORN. See Delgado, *Organizing the Movement*, 123.

52. On the importance of competition within the community organization, see Alinsky, *Reveille for Radicals*, 98.

53. It is in providing organization politics with more purposeful, rational goals that Alinsky community organizations stand in most stark contrast to the classic political machines, which were much more narrowly preoccupied with process and their own survival. Indeed, these community organizations may confirm Theodore Lowi's speculation that had reformers permitted the old machines to survive, they might have evolved into more public-regarding institutions as American society itself became more educated and rationalized. See Theodore Lowi, "Machine Politics—Old and New," *Public Interest* 9 (1967): 91.

54. Finks, *Radical Vision*, 23–24.

55. Horwitt, *Let Them Call Me Rebel*, 85–87.

56. Finks, *Radical Vision*, 139–140.

57. See Horwitt, *Let Them Call Me Rebel*, 197–199, passim; and Charles E. Curran, *Critical Concerns in Moral Theology* (Notre Dame, IN: University of Notre Dame Press, 1984), 189.

58. For a careful comparison of Alinsky's views with liberation theology that identifies some similarities as well as some fundamental differences, see Curran, *Critical Concerns*, 180–188.

59. On BUILD, see Marion Orr, "Urban Regimes and Human Capital Policies: A Study of Baltimore," *Journal of Urban Affairs* 14 (1992): 173–187; on East Brooklyn Congregations, see Jim Sleeper, *The Closest of Strangers: Liberalism and the Politics of Race in New York* (New York: W. W. Norton, 1990), 153–157.

60. See Aldon D. Morris, *The Origins of the Civil Rights Movement: Black Com-*

munities Organizing for Change (New York: The Free Press, 1984), 46–48, 113, 263.

61. Pope Pius XI, "Encyclical Letter on the Reconstruction of the Social Order (Quadragesimo Anno)," in Anton C. Pegis, ed., *The Wisdom of Catholicism* (New York: The Modern Library, 1949), 742. For a brief discussion of subsidiarity, see John Courtney Murray, *We Hold These Truths: Catholic Reflections on the American Proposition* (Kansas City, MO: Sheed and Ward, 1960), 333–334.

62. Robert Nisbet, *The Social Philosophers: Community and Conflict in Western Thought* (New York: Thomas Y. Crowell, 1973), 7, 149, 387–388.

63. In recent years, of course, the flow of CDBG funds from Washington has greatly decreased. This has presumably been one factor in the diminished clout of the organization during this period. Still, the preeminence of COPS as a political force among Mexican Americans in San Antonio and (in association with other IAF organizations in Texas) across the state endures.

64. See Horwitt, *Let Them Call Me Rebel*, 197, 369 and Finks, *Radical Vision*, 30, 49, 114–115.

65. The only writer I am aware of who delves beyond the obvious close personal ties between Alinsky and Maritain to analyze the theological and philosophical ones between them is Curran. See his *Critical Concerns*, 171–199.

66. Max Weber, *The Protestant Ethic and the Spirit of Capitalism* (New York: Charles Scribner's Sons, 1958).

67. Properly identifying this perspective as deriving from Catholicism's natural law tradition, Andrew M. Greeley and Mary Greeley Durkin point out, for example, that Catholic social teaching rejects the ready denunciation of tight-knit neighborhoods as leading to racial segregation and instead leads to an appreciation on the inevitability of such turf-based loyalties and thence to efforts to channel such ties to promote racial integration. See their *How to Save the Catholic Church* (New York: Viking, 1984), 218–219.

6. OBSTACLES TO ORGANIZATION POLITICS

1. See T. R. Fehrenbach, *The San Antonio Story* (Tulsa, OK: Continental Heritage, 1978), 209–210.

2. See Kathy Glasgow, "C.O.P.S.' Job-Training Program Hailed as Model for State, Nation," *San Antonio Express-News*, 18 November 1991, A1, A4. For the IAF perspective on job training, see *Investing in Our Livelihoods: Developing Human Capital in a Global Economy* (Franklin Square, NY: Industrial Areas Foundation, February 1991). Like any astute political organization, COPS and other IAF organizations may propose and even develop various programs, but they do not aspire to operate them. Such responsibilities, the organizers correctly perceive, would enmesh them in activities that would undermine their overall political mission. At the same

time, it is worth noting that as these organizations successfully advocate and then oversee the implementation of various programs, their investments in them necessarily rise and it presumably becomes more difficult for these organizers to assert that "issues don't really matter."

3. COPS is obviously a very different type of effort from the Alinsky organization described by James Q. Wilson more than a generation ago. Based on his observations of The Woodlawn Organization in Chicago in the late 1950s and early 1960s, Wilson depicted an obstructionist organization that fought urban renewal by playing exclusively on the fears and alienation of neighborhood residents. See James Q. Wilson, "Planning and Politics: Citizen Participation in Urban Renewal," in James Q. Wilson, ed., *Urban Renewal: The Record and the Controversy* (Cambridge, MA: The MIT Press, 1967), 415–417.

4. Quoted in John Jacobs, "Grassroots Gardening: The 'New' Campaign Crop," *Golden State Report*, March 1988, 7.

5. See the informative overview of the three organizations at this point in time by Scott Harris, "Community Crusaders: 3 Groups Wage Hard-Nosed Struggle for Social Change," *Los Angeles Times*, 29 November 1987, CC1, CC4, CC5.

6. Jean Merl, "Rally Pushes for School Reforms," *Los Angeles Times*, 22 October 1990, B1.

7. For evidence on the relatively rapid acquisition of English by Hispanics in California, see Kevin F. McCarthy and R. Burciaga Valdez, *Current and Future Effects of Mexican Immigration in California*, Report R-3365-CR (Santa Monica, CA: The Rand Corp., 1986), 61–62. On this process more generally, see Calvin Veltman, *The Future of the Spanish Language in the United States* (New York and Washington: Hispanic Policy Development Project, 1988).

8. In recent years more Mexican-American women in San Antonio have apparently been entering the work force. So, this distinction between the two organizations and the populations from which they draw members and leaders may be diminishing. Yet my more general point that Mexican-American women in Los Angeles enjoy greater opportunities than their counterparts in San Antonio remains indisputably accurate.

9. For survey evidence—albeit dated—that confirms this finding of greater Mexican-American prejudice against non-Mexicans in San Antonio than in Los Angeles, see Leo Grebler et al., *The Mexican-American People: The Nation's Second Largest Minority* (New York: The Free Press, 1970), 390–399.

10. A survey of Hispanic leaders reports that churches topped the list when they were asked what institutions "very well served" their communities. Civil rights institutions and unions trailed well behind. See *Moving Into the Political Mainstream*, vol. I (New York: The Hispanic Policy Development Project, 1984), 14.

11. Yet there are some strong parallels between the relationship of Mexican Americans to the Catholic Church and that of Italian Americans. For one part of

the comparison, see Richard Gambino, *Blood of My Blood: The Dilemma of the Italian-Americans* (Garden City, NY: Anchor Press, 1975), 212–244.

12. See Alan Riding, *Distant Neighbors: A Portrait of the Mexicans* (New York: Alfred A. Knopf, 1985), 89–91.

13. This parallels the weak institutional presence of the Church in Latin America generally. See Harold J. Abramson, *Ethnic Diversity in Catholic America* (New York: John Wiley, 1973), 139–141.

14. On the shortage of Mexican-American priests, see *The Hispanic Presence: Challenge and Commitment* (Washington, DC: National Conference of Catholic Bishops, 1983), 17–18. With regard to the ratio of priests to parishioners, the figure for Los Angeles in 1982 was .0005, and for San Antonio .0007. By contrast that ratio for Boston was .0011. See *The Official Catholic Directory* (Willamett, IL: T. J. Kennedy, 1982), 482, 855.

15. See Joan W. Moore and Harry Pachon, *Mexican Americans* (Englewood Cliffs, NJ: Prentice-Hall, 1970), 89.

16. The same problems of personalism arise for community activists. See Ruth Horowitz, *Honor and the American Dream: Culture and Identity in a Chicano Community* (New Brunswick, NJ: Rutgers University Press, 1983), 215. On the more general question of low levels of involvement with the American Catholic Church among Hispanics, see Roberto O. González and Michael LaVelle, *The Hispanic Catholic in the United States: A Socio-Cultural and Religious Profile* (New York: Northeast Catholic Pastor Center for Hispanics, 1985), 72–75, 126–131.

17. For an account of the effort and expense involved in a *quince años*, see Horowitz, *Honor and the American Dream*, 52–55.

18. I base this observation on a national survey of Hispanics, not on Mexican Americans specifically. See González and LaVelle, *The Hispanic Catholic in the United States*, 127–129.

19. For example, opinion surveys by the *Los Angeles Times* indicate native-born Mexican Americans attend church less frequently than immigrants. See *Los Angeles Times Poll*, No. 65 (March 1983), question no. 65. For a dated but nevertheless useful discussion of the complicated relationship between social and economic mobility and Mexican-American involvement with the Catholic Church—as well as a more general analysis of the ties between Mexican Americans and the Church—see Grebler et al., *The Mexican-American People*, 449–485.

20. Grebler et al., *The Mexican-American People*, 487.

21. Rodolfo O. de la Garza and Robert Brischetto, *The Mexican American Electorate: A Demographic Profile*, Hispanic Population Studies Program, Occasional Paper No. 1 (San Antonio, TX: Southwest Voters Registration Education Project; and Austin, TX: Center for Mexican American Studies, University of Texas, 1982), 10. For the definitive quantitative evidence on Hispanic defection from Catholicism to Protestantism, see Andrew Greeley, "Defection among Hispanics," *America*, 30 July 1988, 61–62. Greeley's

data, which are for Hispanics generally and not Mexican Americans specifically, suggest that defections to Protestantism are even higher than I indicate here. For a broader, cultural appraisal of defections to Protestantism among Latin Americans generally, see Richard Rodriguez, "A Continental Shift," *Los Angeles Times*, 13 August 1989, V-1, V-6.

22. This point is based on my own field observations. But others, particularly Andrew Greeley in the article cited in note 21, argue that converts to Protestantism are the more affluent and upwardly mobile Hispanics. These divergent interpretations may reflect my focus on urban barrios in the Southwest and Greeley's national data set, subsuming Mexican Americans into a broader Hispanic category. It is also possible that both perspectives are correct and that there is a bimodal distribution of Mexican Americans and Hispanics generally defecting to Protestantism. It is worth noting, for example, that in his much-publicized marital problems, one of the sources of tension between Henry Cisneros and his wife, Mary Alice, was her involvement with an evangelical Protestant sect.

23. Roberto Suro, "Hispanic Shift of Allegiance Changes Face of U.S. Religion," *New York Times*, 14 May 1989, 1, 20; John Dart, "U.S. Bishops Endorse Plan to Keep Latinos in the Flock," *Los Angeles Times*, 21 November 1987, II-7. For a more analytical treatment of the challenge to Catholicism from Protestantism, see González and LaVelle, *The Hispanic Catholic in the United States*, 144, 147–152 and Eleace King, *Proselytism and Evangelization: An Exploratory Study* (Washington, DC: Center for Applied Research in the Apostate, Georgetown University, 1991).

24. See Grebler et al., *The Mexican-American People*, 471; and Joseph Daniel Sekul, "The C.O.P.S. Story: A Case Study of Successful Collective Action," Ph.D. diss., Department of Political Science, University of Texas at Austin (1984), 157–161.

25. Grebler et al., *The Mexican-American People*, 470–472.

26. John Gregory Dunne, *True Confessions* (New York: E. P. Dutton, 1970).

27. On McIntyre's emphasis on building parochial schools, see Grebler et al., *The Mexican-American People*, 459–460.

28. See Sekul, "The C.O.P.S. Story," 270–271; and Isidro D. Ortiz, "Chicano Urban Politics and the Politics of Reform in the Seventies," *Western Political Quarterly* 37 (1984): 564–577.

29. Reflecting this activist hostility to UNO is an argument that the organization was used by the Church hierarchy to co-opt Chicano activism. In my view this interpretation overstates the case. To be sure, the hierarchy's acceptance of UNO was in the wake of Chicano activist challenges to its legitimacy. But it is critical to understand that Chicano activists have never had anything to do with UNO—and vice versa. Nevertheless, for an articulation of this view, see Ortiz, "Chicano Urban Politics."

30. Quoted in P. David Finks, *The Radical Vision of Saul Alinsky* (New York: Paulist Press, 1984), 267.

31. Reflecting the extraordinary media attention a priest like Father Olivares attracts in Los Angeles are the many, many articles written about him. A sampling includes: Rodolfo Acuña, "A Uniquely Needy Flock Mustn't Lose Its *Padre*," *Los Angeles Times*, 25 December 1989, B7; Demetria Martinez, "Champion of L.A. Hispanics unhappy to be moved," *National Catholic Reporter*, 22 December 1989, 5; Ruben Martinez and Mike Davis, "The Church," *LA Weekly*, 22–28 December 1989, 14–18, 20–29; Dave McCombs, "The Final Days of Father Olivares," *Downtown News*, 12 March 1990, 1, 8–10.

32. For an analysis of UNO that exaggerates the point made here and concludes, in my view incorrectly, that the organization has been "led by priests," see Rodolfo Acuña, *Occupied America: A History of Chicanos* (New York: Harper & Row, 1981), 407–408. A similarly mistaken interpretation of UNO is offered in Mike Davis, *City of Quartz* (New York: Vintage Books, 1992), 346–348.

33. See Reinhold Niebuhr, *Moral Man and Immoral Society*, 2nd ed. (New York: Charles Scribner's Sons, 1960; first published in 1932).

34. See John Peer Nugent, "Step Father," *Los Angeles*, October 1985, 190–195, 256, and Rubén Castañeda, "Archbishop Roger Mahony of Los Angeles: Activist Pastor for a Diverse Flock," *California Journal*, August 1988, 350–354.

35. Eileen White, "Helping Hand: Catholic Church Plays Role in Implementing New Immigration Law," *Wall Street Journal*, 3 December 1986, 1, 16.

36. For an extremely cynical and undoubtedly exaggerated, but nevertheless intriguing, view of Mahony, see Davis, *City of Quartz*, 340–350, 356–365.

37. I argue this here. But as I pointed out in chapter 4, within COPS there was at the time a debate as to whether single-member districts would help or hinder the political aspirations of Mexican Americans in San Antonio.

38. Mike Davis, characteristically wrong-headed but insightful, refers to Mahony's inclinations in this direction as "papal-Maoism." See his *City of Quartz*, 349.

39. See Tim Ferguson, "Controlling Alcohol—or Koreans—in South Central," *Wall Street Journal*, 9 June 1992, A17.

40. For Waters's criticism of UNO and SCOC, see Rubén Castañeda, "Community Organizers Bring New Clout to Urban Poor," *California Journal*, January 1988, 25. For Ridley-Thomas's comments, see Harris, "Community Crusaders: 3 Groups Wage Hard-Nosed Struggle," CC4.

7. ELITE-NETWORK POLITICS

1. For some illustrative voter registration data for Latinos in the San Gabriel Valley, see *RPC Report* (newsletter of the Southwest Voter Registration Education Project), I–5 (October 1986), 8–9.

2. See Lawrence Harrison, *Underdevelopment Is a State of Mind* (Lanham,

MD: Harvard University Center for International Affairs, 1985); and Alan Riding, *Distant Neighbors: A Portrait of the Mexicans* (New York: Alfred A. Knopf, 1985), especially 238–253.

3. "Case Study: Southwest Voter Registration Education Project," *Expanding Voter Participation: An Assessment of 1984 Non-Partisan Voter Registration Efforts* (New York: New York Interface Development Project, 1985).

4. For a similar analysis in the context of presidential campaigns, see the distinction drawn between the "air war" and the "ground war" by Thomas Byrne Edsall and Mary D. Edsall in their recent book, *Chain Reaction: The Impact of Race, Rights, and Taxes on American Politics* (New York: W. W. Norton, 1991), 208.

5. See James Q. Wilson, *The Amateur Democrat* (Chicago: The University of Chicago Press, 1966). More recently, see John Jacobs, "Grassroots Gardening," *Golden State Report*, March 1988, 7–13.

6. For more on MAPA, see Kenneth C. Burt, "The History of the Mexican American Political Association and Chicano Politics in California," B.A. Honors thesis, Department of Political Science, University of California at Berkeley (1982).

7. For more on Alatorre, see Bill Boyarsky, "Powerbroker of the Barrio," *Los Angeles Times Magazine*, 22 October 1989, 8–18.

8. I draw here on the account of these events in Bruce E. Cain, *The Reapportionment Puzzle* (Berkeley, CA: University of California Press, 1984), 81, 97–98.

9. For more on the redistricting and Alatorre's role in it, see Cain, *The Reapportionment Puzzle*, 81–103.

10. Quoted in Cain, *The Reapportionment Puzzle*, 103.

11. Alan Ehrenhalt, "Reapportionment and Redistricting," in Thomas E. Mann and Norman J. Ornstein, eds., *The American Elections of 1982* (Washington, DC: American Enterprise Institute for Public Policy Research, 1983), 66.

12. Cain, *The Reapportionment Puzzle*, 147–178.

13. Hugh Heclo, "Issue Networks and the Executive Establishment," in Anthony King, ed., *The New American Political System* (Washington, DC: The American Enterprise Institute for Public Policy, 1978), 102.

14. See California Commission on Campaign Financing, *The New Gold Rush: Financing California's Legislative Campaigns* (Los Angeles: Center for Responsive Government, 1985), 55.

15. A similar point about what he calls "the new patronage" is made by Wilbur C. Rich in "The Impact of Public Authorities on Urban Politics: Challenges for Black Politicians and Interest Groups," in Michael B. Preston, Lenneal J. Henderson, and Paul Lionel Puryear, eds., *The New Black Politics: The Search for Political Power* (White Plains, NY: Longman, 1982), 217.

16. See Robert A. Dahl, *Who Governs? Democracy and Power in an American City* (New Haven, CT: Yale University Press, 1961), 39, 45–46.

17. Daniel J. Balz, "Polling the Latino Community: Does Anybody Have the Num-

bers?" in Rodolfo O. de la Garza, ed., *Ignored Voices: Public Opinion Polls and the Latino Community* (Austin, TX: University of Texas Press, 1987), 32.

18. See the *New York Times*/CBS News exit poll, *New York Times*, 10 November 1988, B6 and the Cable News Network-*Los Angeles Times* exit poll, reported in William Schneider, "Solidarity's Not Enough," *National Journal*, 12 November 1988, 2855.

19. For more on Snyder, see Michelle Willens, "California's Most Outrageous Politician: Is It Los Angeles Councilman Art Snyder?" *California Journal*, May 1982, 155–157.

20. For more on Lou Moret and Walter Karabian, see Richard J. Pietschmann, "Real Power," *Los Angeles*, April 1988, 117–118, 127.

21. John Schwada, "Mayor Wants 17 Council Districts," *Los Angeles Herald Examiner*, 23 August 1984, A1, A8.

22. Jay Mathews, "Los Angeles' New Councilwoman Reflects Changing Ethnic Politics," *Los Angeles Times*, 14 April 1987, A4.

23. For more on the advances made by Mexican-American women in California politics, see Robin Kirk, "Viva Latinas," *Golden State Report*, November 1988, 15–18.

24. See Jonathan Peterson, "Ueberroth Names 40 to Help Direct Rebuilding," *Los Angeles Times*, Washington edition, 12 June 1992, A8.

25. Bill Boyarsky, "Molina: Ethics and Relating to Her Colleagues," *Los Angeles Times*, 6 March 1992, B2.

26. Ken Hoover, "In the L.A. Supervisorial Race, Will It Be the Insider or the Outsider?" *Los Angeles Times*, 17 February 1991, M8.

27. See the editorial entitled "Molina for the Council," *Los Angeles Times*, 26 January 1987; and the editorial, "An Election to Make History," *Los Angeles Times*, 19 February 1991.

28. Hector Tobar and Richard Simon, "Molina's First Goal—Expand County Board," *Los Angeles Times*, 21 February 1991, A1, A3.

29. For example, see Tom Waldman, "The Scramble for L.A. County's New Supervisorial Seat," *California Journal*, January 1991, 23.

30. Janet Clayton, "Molina Victory May Give Council More a Tilt Toward Slow-Growth," *Los Angeles Times*, 5 February 1987, CC 1, CC 6; Janet Clayton, "Molina Wins 4-Way Race for 1st District Council Seat," *Los Angeles Times*, 4 February 1987, 1, 3. Some observers have noted that turnouts in such elections have actually been higher than the norm for special elections in California (see Jill Stewart, "1st District Candidates Preparing to Fight an Absentee Ballot War," *Los Angeles Times*, 2 December 1990, B1, B7). Yet it remains unclear whether in such districts, many of which have large numbers of non-Hispanics, Hispanic turnout is above the California norm. It should also be noted that such turnout figures for Hispanics are based on already low Hispanic registration rates.

31. Richard Simon et al., "Torres Leads Molina in Fund Raising," *Los Angeles Times*, 14 February 1991, B1, B4.

32. The most expensive was a 1988 supervisorial race that cost a total of $2.8 million. See Richard Simon et al., "Torres Leads Molina in Fund Raising," B4.

33. On the low turnout, see Lou Cannon, "Hispanic Elected in L.A. County," *Washington Post*, 21 February 1991, 3. On absentee ballots, see Jill Stewart, "1st District Candidates Preparing to Fight an Absentee Ballot War," *Los Angeles Times*, 2 December 1990, B1, B7. On the get-out-the-vote effort more generally, see James Rainey, "Torres, Molina Push to the Last Minute," *Los Angeles Times*, 20 February 1991, B1, B4.

34. Janet Clayton, "Molina, Ex-Rivals Agree on Candidate for Assembly Seat," *Los Angeles Times*, 26 February 1987, B1, B3.

35. George Ramos, "Employment Suit Embroils MALDEF in Controversy," *Los Angeles Times*, 17 February 1987, CC1, CC3; and Marcia Chambers, "Hispanic Rights Leader Gets Post Over Ex-Governor of New Mexico," *New York Times*, 2 March 1987, A15.

36. See Bill Boyarsky, "The Rocky Race of Sarah Flores," *Los Angeles Times*, Nuestro Tiempo section, 11 October 1990, 1, 7. Also Waldman, "The Scramble for L.A. County's New Supervisorial Seat," 23–24. I emphasize here that Flores, a founder of the Los Angeles County Employees Association, is a moderate Republican in contrast to the image of her fostered by the *Wall Street Journal*, whose editorial page waged a crusade on her behalf for several months. See "The Liberal Barrio," *Wall Street Journal*, 13 June 1990, A14; "The Liberal Barrio-II," *Wall Street Journal*, 20 July 1990, A12; "LA's Poodle District," *Wall Street Journal*, 21 August 1990, A14; "Sarah's Hope," *Wall Street Journal*, 16 November 1990, A14.

37. Richard Simon, "Flores Out Front in Crowded 1st District Race for Supervisor," *Los Angeles Times*, 6 June 1990, A3, A25; and Hector Tobar and Mike Ward, "Validity of 1st District Vote in Doubt after Ruling," *Los Angeles Times*, 6 June 1990, A3, A24.

38. Rich Simon and Jill Stewart, "Torres, Molina Woo Ballot Losers," *Los Angeles Times*, 24 January 1991, B1–B2.

39. Quoted in George Ramos, "Assemblyman Becerra to Seek Rep. Roybal's Seat," *Los Angeles Times*, 29 February 1992, B3.

40. For a discussion of the problem of democratic legitimacy in a regime characterized by issue networks, see Heclo, "Issue Networks and the Executive Establishment," 118.

8. PROTEST POLITICS

1. James Q. Wilson, *Political Organizations* (New York: Basic Books, 1973), 282.

2. Ibid., 283.

3. The distinction I draw here between Mexican-American protest in Texas and California obviously parallels the distinction between class and status

politics. Although I choose not to use these categories in my analysis, Texas protest is obviously cognate with class politics, while California protest partakes of status politics. For the classic source on class and status politics, see Daniel Bell, ed., *The New Right* (Garden City, NY: Anchor Books, 1964).

4. Prominent academic expositors of this perspective are Frances Fox Piven and Richard A. Cloward. See in particular their *Poor People's Movements: Why They Succeed and How They Fail* (New York: Vintage Books, 1979), especially xxii, 36–37, 68, 81–82. And for an examination of this question within the context of the ACORN community organizing effort, see Gary Delgado, *Organizing the Movement: The Roots and Growth of ACORN* (Philadelphia: Temple University Press, 1986), 32–34.

5. There is a parallel here with the experience of blacks during the 1960s. As Charles Hamilton observes: "It should not be surprising then that the most violent and prolonged clashes in the streets during the summers of the late 1960s occurred primarily in the North rather than in the South . . . " See his article, "Blacks and the Crisis of Political Participation," *The Public Interest* 34 (1974): 203–204.

6. Joan W. Moore and Ralph Guzmán, "The Mexican-American: New Wind from the Southwest," *Nation*, 30 May 1966, 465.

7. Ibid.

8. Rufus P. Browning et al., *Protest is Not Enough: The Struggle of Blacks and Hispanics for Equality in Urban Politics* (Berkeley, CA: University of California Press, 1984), 93, 133. Given such robust findings, it is no wonder that blacks interviewed by Browning and his colleagues claimed: "Hispanics want us blacks to do it for them" and "The Chicano style was 'me too,' to watch how blacks do it, but hold back until the blacks had won something, and then come in and demand a part of the winnings." See Ibid., 260, footnote 17.

9. For example, in the early 1980s Chávez was the most frequently named national leader in a nationwide survey of Hispanic business and community leaders conducted by the Strategy Research Corporation. See "The Coca-Cola U.S.A. Hispanic Study," reported in *The Coca-Cola U.S.A. Hispanic Business Agenda* (Atlanta, GA: no date), 12–13.

10. See Leo Grebler et al., *The Mexican-American People: The Nation's Second Largest Minority* (New York: The Free Press, 1970), 471. Also John Staples Shockley, *Chicano Revolt in a Texas Town* (Notre Dame, IN: University of Notre Dame, 1974), 216–217. For Connally's dealings with the striking farmworkers, see Tony Castro, *Chicano Power: The Emergence of Mexican America* (New York: Saturday Review Press, 1974), 175–177.

11. David Montejano, *Anglos and Mexicans in the Making of Texas, 1836–1986* (Austin, TX: University of Texas Press, 1987), 284.

12. Shockley, *Chicano Revolt*, 1.

13. Montejano, *Anglos and Mexicans*, 285.

14. Ibid., 289–290.

15. Carlos Muñoz, Jr., and Mario Barrera, "La Raza Unida Party and the Chicano Student Movement in California," *Social Science Journal* 19 (1982): 103–104.

16. For Raza Unida's failure to get on the California ballot, see Ibid., 112. Rodolfo Acuña presents data indicating that in the early 1970s Raza Unida had registered more than twice as many voters in Texas than in California. See his *Occupied America: A History of Chicanos,* second edition (New York: Harper & Row, 1981), 388.

17. Grebler et al., *The Mexican-American People*, 544.

18. For an extremely biased but nevertheless informative account, see David F. Gomez, *Somos Chicanos: Strangers in Our Own Land* (Boston: Beacon Press, 1973), 188–189.

19. Ibid., 130–131.

20. Ibid., 135–136.

21. Ibid., 157–166.

22. For more on activism in Los Angeles, see Muñoz and Barrera, "La Raza Unida Party"; and Acuña, *Occupied America*, 350–383.

23. Muñoz and Barrera, "La Raza Unida Party," 112.

24. See Castro, *Chicano Power*, 168–170. An analysis of the pros and cons of rapid expansion of the ACORN community organizing campaign with parallels to the Raza Unida experience is found in Delgado, *Organizing the Movement*, chap. 5.

25. This perspective, which I heard repeatedly in the field, is also advanced in Montejano, *Anglos and Mexicans*, 288.

26. See the *Los Angeles Times* exit poll results reported in George Skelton, "Democrats Signal Unease About Mondale by Casting Votes for Hart," *Los Angeles Times*, 7 June 1984, 1, 13–14.

27. John Balzar, "Primary: For Once, State Democrats Emerge Unsplit," *Los Angeles Times*, 8 June 1988, 11. For an analysis of the Latino vote for Jackson from the activist perspective, see Antonio H. Rodriguez and Gloria J. Romero, "Latinos Snub Jackson—Is It Racism?" *Los Angeles Times*, 15 July 1988, B7.

28. "Latino Democratic Turnout Tops Texas Average Again," *Southwest Voter Research Notes*, Newsletter of the Southwest Voter Research Institute, II-1 (April 1988), 1, 4.

29. Frank del Olmo, "Chicanos Hit a Nerve in Mexico," *Los Angeles Times*, 5 June 1988, V5.

30. Ron Russell, "Group Calls for Boycott of Dodgers," *Los Angeles Times*, 5 April 1991, B3.

31. Muñoz and Barrera, "La Raza Unida Party," 103–104.

32. Kevin Roderick, "Ferraro, Trias Face Runoff Vote for School Board Seats," *Los Angeles Times*, 13 April 1983, I-14, I-22.

33. See Robert R. Brischetto and Rodolfo O. de la Garza, *The Mexican Ameri-*

can Electorate: Political Participation and Ideology, The Mexican American Electorate Series, Hispanic Population Studies Program, Occasional Paper No. 3 (San Antonio, TX: Southwest Voter Registration Education Project; and Austin, TX: Center for Mexican American Studies, The University of Texas at Austin, 1983), 4.

34. Muñoz and Barrera, "La Raza Unida Party," 107.

35. Ibid., 103.

36. For a brief overview of the condition of Chicano studies in various states, see Acuña, *Occupied America*, 391–394.

37. See Shockley, *Chicano Revolt*, passim.

38. Rodriguez is also a frequent contributor to the *Los Angeles Times*'s op-ed page. See, for example, Rodriguez and Romero, "Latinos Snub Jackson," or Antonio Rodriguez, "Molina's Anti-Union Attack Is Pure Reagan," *Los Angeles Times*, 15 February 1991, B9.

39. For more on the Rose Institute and Republicans, see Bruce E. Cain, *The Reapportionment Puzzle* (Berkeley, CA: University of California Press, 1984), 91. On the Rose Institute and Santillán, see J. Morgan Kousser, *How To Determine Intent: Lessons from L.A.* (Pasadena, CA: California Institute of Technology, Social Science Working Paper 741, June 1990), 32–34.

40. See Grebler et al., *The Mexican-American People*, 544.

41. On Fernando Chávez's takeover of MAPA, see Rick Rodriguez, "Chávez, the Younger," *California Journal*, October 1983, 377–379.

42. See Kenneth C. Burt, "The History of the Mexican American Political Association and Chicano Politics in California," Honors thesis, Department of Political Science, University of California at Berkeley (July 1982).

43. Frank Clifford, "Mondale Barely Edges Jackson in Latino Vote," *Los Angeles Times*, 14 May 1984, A9. On MAPA's role in this episode see Frank del Olmo, "Latino Political Group Has a Last Hurrah," *Los Angeles Times*, 18 May 1984, II-7.

44. Castro, *Chicano Power*, 172.

45. For evidence that sustains my argument here, see Muñoz and Barrera, "La Raza Unida Party," 108. For a related perspective that is based on developments in South Texas and emphasizes the gulf between educated, Anglicized Chicano activist leaders and the much less assimilated, more conservative individuals they claimed to represent, see Shockley, *Chicano Revolt*, endnote 63, 290.

46. Kousser, *How To Determine Intent*, 33–34.

47. Cain, *The Reapportionment Puzzle*, 92.

48. Linda Breakstone, "Mondale alienating Hispanics with non-stand on immigration," *Los Angeles Herald Examiner*, 12 May 1984, A-1, A-6. See also Linda Breakstone, "Mondale wins key Latino endorsements by 4 votes," *Los Angeles Herald Examiner*, 14 May 1984, A-1, A-8.

49. For an exceptionally insightful analysis of these events, see Evan T. Barr, "Borderline Hypocrisy," *New Republic*, 14–21 July 1986, 12–13.

50. On LULAC's obstructionist role in the Simpson-Mazzoli debate, see Christine Marie Sierra, "Mexican Americans and Immigration Reform: Consensus and Fragmentation," paper delivered at the 1989 Annual Meeting of the Western Political Science Association, Salt Lake City, 30 March–1 April 1989.

51. Antonio Rodriguez, Esteban Corral, and Gregorio Román, "The Struggle against the Immigration Control Act," *Chicano Law Review* 8 (1985): 18.

9. THE STATE OF MEXICAN-AMERICAN OPINION

1. Bruce E. Cain and D. Roderick Kiewiet, "California's Coming Minority Majority," *Public Opinion*, February/March 1986, 52.

2. *Southwest Voter Research Notes* (newsletter of the Southwest Voter Research Institute), II-6 (September–December 1988), 1, 4. For a contrary and, in my view, misleading discussion of abortion and Mexican Americans, see Joan Moore and Harry Pachon, *Hispanics in the United States* (Englewood Cliffs, NJ: Prentice-Hall, 1985), 105–106.

3. Seventy-five percent of Mexican Americans surveyed in Los Angeles and San Antonio favored the Equal Rights Amendment. See Rodolfo O. de la Garza and Robert R. Brischetto, with David Vaughn, *The Mexican American Electorate: Information Sources and Policy Orientations*, The Mexican American Electorate Series, Hispanic Population Studies Program, Occasional Paper No. 2 (San Antonio, TX: Southwest Voter Registration Education Project; and Austin, TX: Center for Mexican American Studies, University of Texas, 1983), 9.

4. Seventy-six percent of California Latinos surveyed supported the ERA, compared to 66 percent of "whites." See Bruce E. Cain and D. Roderick Kiewiet, *Minorities in California*, unpublished paper (Pasadena, CA: The California Institute of Technology, March 1986), I-31.

5. Richard Rodriguez, *Hunger of Memory* (Boston: David R. Godine, 1981), 184.

6. *RPC Report* (newsletter of the Southwest Voter Registration Education Project) I-5 (October 1986), 6–7. It is interesting to note that only 3 percent of leaders from Los Angeles favored increased defense spending.

7. *Southwest Voter Research Notes* I-3 (December 1986), 3–4.

8. *Los Angeles Times Poll* No. 156 (Democratic Delegate Survey), question 76.

9. *Southwest Voter Research Notes* II-6 (September–December 1988), 1.

10. *RPC Report* I-5 (October 1986), 6 and *Southwest Voter Research Notes* I-3 (December 1986), 3.

11. *Southwest Voter Research Notes* II-6 (September–December 1988), 1, 4.

12. Antonio González and Richard Nuccio, eds., *Views of Latino Leaders: A Roundtable Discussion on US Policy in Nicaragua and the Central American Peace Plan* (San Antonio, TX: Southwest Voter Research Institute, 1989).

13. De la Garza and Brischetto, *The Mexican American Electorate: Information Sources and Policy Orientations*, 9.

14. See Abigail M. Thernstrom, *Whose Votes Count? Affirmative Action and Minority Voting Rights* (Cambridge, MA: Harvard University Press, 1987).

15. For example, see *1991 National Roster of Hispanic Elected Officials* (Washington, DC: National Association of Latino Elected Officials, 1991), x–xi.

16. On Hispanic attitudes toward crime and drugs as public issues, see F. Chris García et al., "Ethnicity and Ideology: Political Attitudes of Mexican, Puerto Rican and Cuban Origin Populations in the United States," paper delivered at the 1991 Annual Meeting of the American Political Science Association, the Washington Hilton, August 29–September 1, 1991, 13. See also "California Latinos Issue Policy Agenda for the New President," unpublished paper (San Antonio, TX: Southwest Voter Research Institute, December 13, 1988).

17. I use quotation marks here to remind the reader, as I have already done in the overview chapter on Los Angeles, that I regard the word "segregation" as unhelpful and misleading in understanding the situation of Mexican Americans.

18. Gary Orfield and Franklin Monfort, *Change in the Racial Composition and Segregation of Large School Districts, 1967–1986* (Alexandria, VA: National School Boards Association, June 1988).

19. See Ralph Chris Carmona, "Language and Ethnic Politics: Bilingualism in Los Angeles City Schools, 1975–1980," Ph.D. diss., University of California at Santa Barbara (1984), 137–138. For the Mexican-American perspective on busing more generally, see Carlos Manuel Haro, *Mexicano/Chicano Concerns and School Desegregation in Los Angeles* (Los Angeles: Chicano Studies Center, University of California, 1977).

20. Carmona, "Language and Ethnic Politics," 196; and David Armor, unpublished opinion survey (Los Angeles: Los Angeles Unified School District, 1977).

21. In the mid-1980s LAUSD board member Larry González criticized busing Latino kids to underutilized Anglo schools as a solution to the district's overcrowding problem: "What happens to children who miss the bus? What happens when they are transported from their neighborhoods to another school in the San Fernando Valley, and decide they don't belong? Or decide they're isolated and are treated like foreigners or aliens? . . . What's happening is that they're dropping out of school completely because they can't go to a school which is located in their neighborhood." Quoted in Louis Freedberg, "Latinos: Building Power from the Ground Up," *California Journal*, January 1987, 15.

22. Leo Grebler et al., *The Mexican-American People: The Nation's Second Largest Minority* (New York: The Free Press, 1970), 399.

23. Rodolfo O. de la Garza, *Public Policy Priorities of Chicano Political Elites*,

Working Paper, U.S.–Mexico Project Series, No. 7 (Washington, DC: Overseas Development Council, 1982), 13.

24. Keith Melville, *Moving Up to Better Education and Better Jobs*, vol. II (Washington, DC: Hispanic Policy Development Project, 1984), iv, 17.

25. *RPC Report* I-5 (October 1986), 6. See also *Southwest Voter Research Notes* (March 1986), 1; *Southwest Voter Research Notes* (August 1986), 1; *RPC Report* I-1 (December 1985), 4; *RPC Report* I-2 (January 1986), 4. These findings replicated those from earlier leadership meetings polled by SVREP; see Robert Brischetto, "How Mexican American Leaders View the Issues," memorandum to Regional Planning Committees (San Antonio, TX: January 10, 1984), 3.

26. De la Garza and Brischetto, *The Mexican American Electorate: Information Sources and Policy Orientations*, 9.

27. Robert R. Brischetto, "Hispanics in the 1984 Texas Presidential Election: An Analysis of Their Votes and Their Views," unpublished paper (San Antonio, TX: Southwest Voter Registration Education Project, no date), 8; *Southwest Voter Research Notes* I-2 (November 1986), 3.

28. *Southwest Voter Research Notes*, Special Edition: Texas Exit Poll Results, II-9 (September–December 1988), 1–4.

29. *Southwest Voter Research Notes*, Special Edition: California Exit Poll Results, II-7 (September–December 1988), 1–4.

30. Stephen Cole, *Attitudes towards Bilingual Education among Hispanics and a Nationwide Sample* (New York: Center for the Social Sciences at Columbia University, no date), 13.

31. Cain and Kiewiet, *Minorities in California*, I-31.

32. *The Texas Poll Report* 2 (October 1985): 1–3.

33. *California's Latinos, 1988: An Opinion Survey—Full Report* (Claremont, CA: The Rose Institute, Claremont McKenna College, 1988), question 31.

34. Exit poll conducted by the Field Research Corporation, cited in Freedberg, "Latinos: Building Power," *California Journal*, January 1987, 15.

35. *California's Latinos, 1988: An Opinion Survey—Full Report*, question 21.

36. See David S. Broder, *The Changing of the Guard: Power and Leadership in America* (New York: Simon & Schuster, 1980), 285–286.

37. *Los Angeles Times Poll* No. 65 (March 1983), question 78.

38. Joan Baratz-Snowden et al., *Parent Preference Study* (Princeton, NJ: Educational Testing Service, July 1988), 57.

39. Cole, *Attitudes towards Bilingual Education*, 13–14.

40. Ibid., 14–15.

41. Ibid., 14.

42. *Los Angeles Times Poll* No. 65 (March 1983), question 94.

43. Baratz-Snowden et al., *Parent Preference Study*, 49.

44. "Immigration," *California Opinion Index* (San Francisco: The Field Institute, October 1987), 3. Due to a small sample of Hispanics, this figure should be used with caution.

45. Cole, *Attitudes towards Bilingual Education*, 19.

46. Ibid., 46.

47. Baratz-Snowden et al., *Parent Preference Study*, 47–49.

48. Ibid., 38–40.

49. Cole, *Attitudes towards Bilingual Education*, 16.

50. See Kevin F. McCarthy and R. Burciaga Valdez, *Current and Future Effects of Mexican Immigration in California* R-3365-CR (Santa Monica, CA: The Rand Corp., May 1986), 61–62.

51. My interpretation here is supported by recent survey research conducted by the UCLA Chicano Studies Research Center. See Aída Hurtado et al., *Redefining California: Latino Social Engagement in a Multicultural Society* (Los Angeles: UCLA Chicano Studies Research Center, 1992), 37–38.

52. Melville, *Moving Up to Better Education and Better Jobs*, questions 14a and 14b, iv.

53. "California's Expanding Minority Population," *California Opinion Index* (San Francisco: The Field Institute, July 1988), 6. Due to a small sample of Hispanics, this figure must be used with caution.

54. Baratz-Snowden et al., *Parent Preference Study*, 53–54.

55. "Selected Items and Responses to the Phoenix Poll," unpublished paper (San Antonio, TX: SVREP, 1984), question 18, 6.

56. Cole, *Attitudes towards Bilingual Education*, 30–31.

57. Ibid., 88.

58. Baratz-Snowden et al., *Parent Preference Study*, 27–28.

59. Ibid., 41.

60. Ibid., 43.

61. Carmona, "Language and Ethnic Politics," 359.

62. Cain and Kiewiet, *Minorities in California*, I-11, I-12, I-31.

63. Baratz-Snowden et al., *Parent Preference Study*, 49.

64. Ibid., 51–52.

65. Ibid., 56–59.

66. Ibid., 79.

67. Harry P. Pachon, "An Overview of Citizenship in the Hispanic Community," *International Migration Review* 21 (Summer 1987): 300–301. See also Grebler et al., *The Mexican-American People*, 557–560.

68. Baratz-Snowden et al., *Parent Preference Study*, 47, 49, 51–52.

69. *Southwest Voter Research Notes* II-9 (September–December 1988), 4.

70. Cited in Moore and Pachon, *Hispanics in the United States*, 121.

71. See Broder, *The Changing of the Guard*, 285.

72. Quoted in Diane Ravitch, *Troubled Crusade: American Education 1945–1980* (New York: Basic Books, 1983), 273.

73. Ibid.

74. Melville, *Moving Up to Better Education and Better Jobs*, 17.

75. Ibid., questions 14b and 14f, iv.

76. On the basis of a 1969 statewide survey, McCleskey and Merrill emphasized

"the intermediate position of the Mexican Americans" in Texas between Anglos and blacks in terms of their political alienation, ideological orientation, and partisan affiliation. See Clifton McCleskey and Bruce Merrill, "Mexican American Political Behavior in Texas," *Social Science Quarterly* 53 (March 1973): 793.

77. Leo Grebler et al., *The Mexican-American People*, 389–390.

78. John Staples Shockley, *Chicano Revolt in a Texas Town* (Notre Dame, IN: University of Notre Dame Press, 1974), 13.

79. Ibid., 34.

80. Ibid. For a corroborating interpretation of the situation of Mexicans in the Southwest compared to that of blacks in the South, see Joan W. Moore, *Mexican Americans* (Englewood Cliffs, NJ: Prentice-Hall, 1976), 108–109.

81. Clifton McCleskey et al., *The Government and Politics of Texas* (Boston: Little, Brown, 1982), 308.

82. David Montejano, *Anglos and Mexicans in the Making of Texas, 1836–1986* (Austin, TX: University of Texas Press, 1987), 262.

83. Ibid., 235.

84. Ibid.

85. Ibid., 245.

86. Ibid. Yet despite the evidence Montejano adduces to differentiate the historical experience of Mexicans from that of blacks, he nevertheless insists upon characterizing Mexicans in Texas as having lived under "Jim Crow." See, for example, ibid., 262.

87. Ibid., 195, 245.

88. Grebler et al., *The Mexican-American People*, 8–9, 579–580.

89. Strikingly similar accounts of Mexican migrants eating with their Anglo employers are to be found in Montejano, *Anglos and Mexicans*, 151 and Douglas Foley et al., *From Peónes to Políticos: Ethnic Relations in a South Texas Town, 1900 to 1977* (Austin, TX: University of Texas, 1977), 88. For a general discussion of the positive aspects of the migrant experience for Mexican Americans, see Foley et al., *From Peónes to Políticos*, 88–90. An extensive review of the research literature on Mexican-American migrant laborers with evidence confirming my point can be found in Marta Tienda, "Residential Distribution and Internal Migration Patterns of Chicanos: A Critical Assessment," in Armando Valdez et al., *The State of Chicano Research on Family, Labor, and Migration: Proceedings of the First Stanford Symposium on Chicano Research and Public Policy* (Stanford, CA: Stanford Center for Chicano Research, 1983), esp. 174–175.

90. Shockley, *Chicano Revolt*, 16.

91. Grebler et al., *The Mexican-American People*, 201. For a similar comment, again from a businessman, see Foley et al., *From Peónes to Políticos*, 246. And for a similar interpretation of the effects of World War II on Mexican Americans, see Moore and Pachon, *Hispanics in the United States*, 177–178.

92. For a discussion of the negative aspects of the migrant experience, see Foley et al., *From Peónes to Políticos*, 90–91.

93. Grebler et al., *The Mexican-American People*, 389.

94. Rodolfo O. de la Garza and Robert R. Brischetto, *The Mexican American Electorate: A Demographic Profile*, The Mexican American Electorate Series, Hispanic Population Studies Program, Occasional Paper No. 1 (San Antonio, TX: Southwest Voter Registration Education Project; and Austin, TX: Center for Mexican American Studies, University of Texas, 1982), 12.

95. George Atunes and Charles M. Gaitz, "Ethnicity and Participation: A Study of Mexican-Americans, Blacks, and Whites," *American Journal of Sociology* 80 (March 1975): 1192–1211. For a similarly wrong-headed effort, see Nicholas P. Lovrich and Otwin Marenin, "A Comparison of Black and Mexican-American Voters in Denver: Assertive versus Acquiescent Political Orientations and Voting Behavior in an Urban Electorate," *Western Political Quarterly* 29 (1976): 284–294.

96. Cain and Kiewiet, *Minorities in California*, III-100, III-101, III-112.

97. Ibid., III-115, III-104—III-105.

98. Ibid., III-102, III-103, III-114. Confirming this finding is a recent survey of foreign-born Latinos, which reported that only 22 percent of Mexican immigrants reported that they or members of their family had actually experienced discrimination. See *The National Latino Immigrant Survey* (Washington, DC: NALEO Educational Fund, 1989), 25–26.

99. This apparent anomaly for Asians is perhaps resolved when, upon closer inspection, it is found that while two-thirds of the discrimination reported by blacks is economic in nature (not getting a job or the like), about half of that reported by Latinos is economic and half social. By contrast, two-thirds of the discrimination reported by Asians is social and only one-third economic. See Cain and Kiewiet, *Minorities in California*, III-103, III-114.

100. *Los Angeles Times Poll* No. 172 (January 1989), question 10. Note that while the differences between several of the figures cited here are not statistically significant, that between blacks and Latinos is. For further evidence on how blacks perceive more discrimination than Hispanics, see Donald L. Horowitz, "Conflict and Accommodation: Mexican-Americans in the Cosmopolis," in Walker Connor, ed., *Mexican-Americans in Comparative Perspective* (Washington, DC: The Urban Institute Press, 1985).

101. *Los Angeles Times Poll* No. 259 (September 25, 1991), question 56. Virtually the same results on the same question were obtained by the *Los Angeles Times Poll* No. 158 (July 10, 1988).

102. "Ethnicity and the Political Process," *California Opinion Index* (San Francisco: The Field Institute, March 1982), 4. As before, inferences must be drawn with caution from such small sample sizes. But here again, the differences between blacks and Hispanics are in the expected direction. Note

also that in this poll, unlike most, Hispanic and white are mutually exclusive categories.

103. Ibid., 3.

104. Ibid.

105. "California's Expanding Minority Population," 5. Here again, small sample sizes call for interpretive caution. Nevertheless, Hispanics are once again found to be less supportive of affirmative action than blacks, while more supportive than Asians.

106. *Los Angeles Times* No. 156 (Democratic Delegate Survey), questions 51, 107. Here sample sizes are large enough that these differences appear to be statistically significant.

107. Melville, *Moving Up to Better Education and Better Jobs*, question 4s, ii.

108. For more on Mexican-American attitudes toward immigration, see Lawrence W. Miller et al., "Attitudes toward Undocumented Workers: The Mexican American Perspective," *Social Science Quarterly* 65 (June 1984): 482–494. For an overview of American attitudes that include Hispanic views, see Edwin Harwood, "Alienation: American Attitudes toward Immigration," *Public Opinion* 6 (June/July 1983): 49–51; and *A Survey of Public Attitudes toward Refugees and Immigration: Report of Findings* (Washington, DC: U.S. Committee for Refugees, April 1984), esp. 53–54.

109. *Hispanic and Black Attitudes toward Immigration Policy* (Washington, DC: Federation for American Immigration Reform, August 1983), question 8.

110. For example, a 1983 *Los Angeles Times Poll* found that 75 percent of Latinos in California favored amnesty; see *Los Angeles Times Poll* No. 65 (March 1983), question 82. And in November 1986, exit polls indicated that 69 percent of Latinos in California favored "legalization" ; see *Southwest Voter Research Notes*, I-3 (December 1986), 3.

111. Cain and Kiewiet, *Minorities in California*, I-31.

112. *The Texas Poll Report* 2 (October 1985): 1–3. Due to small sample size for Hispanics, this figure should be used with caution.

113. *Southwest Voter Research Notes* I-2 (November 1986), 3; *Southwest Voter Research Notes* I-3 (December 1986), 3.

114. *Hispanic and Black Attitudes*, question 11.

115. Miller et al., "Attitudes toward Undocumented Workers," 491. Moreover, Miller et al. found that first- and second- generation Mexican Americans were more likely to support free education for the children of undocumented workers than third-generation Mexican Americans. Similar findings were reported in a SVREP poll in McAllen-Edinburg, Texas. See Robert Brischetto, "Summary of Findings of McAllen-Edinburg Survey" (San Antonio, TX: Southwest Voter Registration Education Project, no date), 6.

116. *Hispanic and Black Attitudes*, questions 12, 13.

117. Ibid., question 14.

118. Ibid., question 3.
119. Thomas Muller et al., *The Fourth Wave: California's Newest Immigrants* (Washington, DC: The Urban Institute Press, 1985), 201. Blacks and Southern Californians generally felt this same sentiment in even higher proportions.
120. "Immigration," *California Opinion Index*, 1. Two caveats are in order: first, because Field does not employ Spanish-speaking interviewers, their data reflect the views of more assimilated Hispanics, who are arguably less sympathetic to the situation of illegal immigrants; second, because Field does not typically oversample for Hispanics, their Hispanic data are based on small sample sizes and therefore must be cited with caution. Nevertheless, my argument is supported by the fact that five years earlier, in 1982, Field posed the same question and an even higher percentage of California Hispanics (64 percent) felt the overall effect of illegal immigrants on the state to be "unfavorable." See "Immigration," *California Opinion Index* (San Francisco: The Field Institute, June 1982), 5.
121. *Hispanic and Black Attitudes*, questions 2, 15.
122. *Los Angeles Times Poll* No. 65 (March 1983), question 88.
123. "Immigration," *California Opinion Index* (October 1987), 2.
124. "California's Expanding Minority Population," 2. Again, the small sample size should be noted. Yet the consistency of these data is striking.
125. *Los Angeles Times Poll* No. 172 (January 1989), question 42. About a year later the Latino National Political Survey found that 75% of Mexican-American citizens agreed: "There are too many immigrants coming to this country." See Rodolfo de la Garza et al., *Latino Voices* (Boulder: Westview Press, 1992), 101.
126. *Los Angeles Times Poll* No. 174 (February 1989), question 21.
127. *Hispanic and Black Attitudes*, question 7.
128. For a frequently cited (but, in my view, not entirely fair) methodological critique of the FAIR-sponsored survey, see Daniel Melnick, "Analysis of the Poll on Attitudes towards Immigration Conducted by Lance Tarrance and Associates and Peter Hart and Associates," memo to Congressional Hispanic Caucus (Washington, DC: Congressional Research Service, Library of Congress, 27 February 1984).
129. *Los Angeles Times Poll* No. 65 (March 1983), question 81.
130. Reported in Robert Pear, "Rising Public Support for Limits on Immigration Is Found in Poll," *New York Times*, 1 July 1986, 1.
131. Robert R. Brischetto, *Hispanics in the 1984 Texas Presidential Election* (San Antonio, TX: SVREP, 28 November 1984), 8.
132. Cain and Kiewiet, *Minorities in California*, I-31. Two years later, a SVREP exit poll showed California Latinos still split over sanctions: 45 percent favoring them and 41 opposed. See *Southwest Voter Research Notes* I-3 (December 1986), 3.

133. Guillermina Jasso, *Attitudes toward International Migration among Texans: Advance Report*, unpublished preliminary draft (Washington, DC: Immigration and Naturalization Service, 14 February 1979), 18–21. Further from the border, including the metropolitan San Antonio area, 63 percent of Hispanics favored sanctions.

134. Miller et al., "Attitudes toward Undocumented Workers," 490–491.

135. "Immigration," *California Opinion Index* (June 1982), 5–6.

136. Rodolfo de la Garza, "Mexican Americans, Mexican Immigrants, and Immigration Reform," in Nathan Glazer, ed., *Clamor at the Gates: The New American Immigration* (San Francisco: Institute for Contemporary Studies, 1985), 102.

137. *The Texas Poll Report* 2 (October 1985): 1, 4. Once again, the small sample size for Hispanics means these data should be interpreted with caution. Yet it is striking that about one year later, the Texas Poll found about the same level of support for sanctions among Texas Hispanics—59 percent. Cited in "Poll Finds 61% Veto Amnesty," *Houston Post*, 16 December 1986, 1.

138. *Southwest Voter Research Notes* I-2 (November 1986), 3.

139. "Immigration," *California Opinion Index* (October 1987), 2.

140. *Research Report: Texas Immigration and Border Security Study*, report prepared for the Federation for American Immigration Reform (Houston, TX: Tarrance & Associates, May 1989), Table R6.

141. *Research Report: California Immigration Survey*, report prepared for the Federation for American Immigration Reform (Houston, TX: Tarrance & Associates, April 1989), Table R7. In this instance, a very small Hispanic sample counsels extreme caution when interpreting these data.

142. *American Attitudes toward Immigration* (New York: The Roper Organization, April 1992), question 15.

143. Miller et al., "Attitudes toward Undocumented Workers," 490–491.

144. *Los Angeles Times Poll* No. 65 (March 1983), question 81.

145. *Hispanic and Black Attitudes*, question 7.

146. Ibid., question 8.

147. Cain and Kiewiet, *Minorities in California*, I-10, I-40.

148. William C. Velásquez, memorandum to Board of Directors and Supporting Institutions (San Antonio, TX: Southwest Voter Registration Education Project, 1 June 1984), 3–4.

149. William C. Velásquez, memorandum to Board of Directors and Supporting Institutions (San Antonio, TX: Southwest Voter Registration Education Project, 1 May 1984), 4.

150. De la Garza, "Mexican Americans, Mexican Immigrants, and Immigration Reform," 104–105.

151. *Southwest Voter Research Notes* I-3 (December 1986), 3.

152. *RPC Report* I-5 (October 1986), 7. On the other hand, the 1983 poll con-

ducted by Daniel Yankelovich's Public Agenda Foundation for the Hispanic Policy Development Project found that 55 percent of Hispanic leaders nationwide disagreed with the proposition: "Amnesty should be granted to all undocumented Hispanics in the United States"; see Melville, *Moving Up to Better Education and Better Jobs*, question 23e, v. But these data are anomalous, for the preponderance of survey evidence highlights Hispanic leaders' relatively greater enthusiasm for amnesty than the average Hispanic. Nevertheless, the Yankelovich finding points up one difficulty with surveys of elites. Because the criteria for inclusion in this category vary from survey to survey, comparisons must be made with care.

153. *RPC Report* I-1 (December 1985), 4.
154. *RPC Report* I-2 (January 1986), 7.
155. *RPC Report* I-5 (October 1986), 6–7.
156. William C. Velásquez, memorandum to Board of Directors and Supporting Institutions (San Antonio, TX: Southwest Voter Registration Education Project, 1 July 1984), 2–3.
157. Ibid., 2.
158. *RPC Report* I-5 (October 1986), 6–7.
159. De la Garza, *Public Policy Priorities*, 11, 15.
160. Rodolfo O. de la Garza, *Chicano Political Elite Perceptions of the Undocumented Worker: An Empirical Analysis*, Working Papers in U.S.–Mexican Studies, No. 31 (La Jolla, CA: Program in United States–Mexican Studies; University of California, San Diego, 1981), 12–15.
161. Ibid., 22.
162. See McCarthy and Valdez, *Current and Future Effects of Mexican Immigration*, 44–45; and Muller et al., *The Fourth Wave*, 109–113.
163. De la Garza, *Chicano Political Elite Perceptions*, 15.
164. De la Garza, *Public Policy Priorities*, 18, 17.
165. For a discussion of the obstructionist stance of Mexican-American leaders during the Simpson-Mazzoli debate, see Christine Marie Sierra, "Mexican Americans and Immigration Reform: Consensus and Fragmentation," paper delivered at the 1989 Annual Meeting of the Western Political Science Association, Salt Lake City, 30 March–1 April 1989. For an overview of the Simpson-Mazzoli debate, see Harris N. Miller, " 'The Right Thing To Do': A History of Simpson-Mazzoli," in Nathan Glazer, ed., *Clamor at the Gates: The New American Immigration* (San Francisco: Institute for Contemporary Studies, 1985), 49–71.
166. De la Garza, "Mexican Americans, Mexican Immigrants, and Immigration Reform," 100.
167. See Sierra, "Mexican Americans and Immigration Reform," especially pp. 23–27; and Rosanna Perotti, *Resolving Policy Conflict: Negotiating the Immigration Reform and Control Act* (forthcoming).
168. Cited in Dan Balz, "Polling the Latino Community: Does Anybody Have

the Numbers?" in Rodolfo O. de la Garza, ed., *Ignored Voices: Public Opinion Polls and the Latino Community* (Austin, TX: Center for Mexican American Studies, University of Texas, 1987), 32.

169. For example, the *New York Times*/CBS NEWS Poll reported that 69 percent of Hispanics voted for Dukakis, 30 percent Bush (reported in the *New York Times*, 10 November 1988, B6). The Cable News Network–*Los Angeles Times* exit poll indicated that 61 percent of Hispanics supported Dukakis, 38 percent Bush (reported in William Schneider, "Solidarity's Not Enough," *National Journal*, 12 November 1988, 2855).

170. Balz, "Polling the Latino Community," 32.

171. Benjamin Page, "Comment: Why Polls Matter and Why Latinos are Ignored," in de la Garza, ed., *Ignored Voices*, 45–46.

172. Ibid., 45.

173. The 1980 census reported that 91 percent of Hispanics in Texas and 78 percent in California were of Mexican origin.

174. Cited in Balz, "Polling the Latino Community," 32.

175. I. A. Lewis, "Muted Voices—Problems in Polling Latinos," in de la Garza, ed., *Ignored Voices*, 135. The Tarrance-Hart survey of Hispanic and black views on immigration sponsored by FAIR was severely criticized for relying on telephone interviews; see Melnick, "Analysis of the Poll on Attitudes toward Immigration," 6–8.

176. Lewis, "Muted Voices," 134–135.

177. Ibid., 135.

178. Douglas Massey et al., *Return to Aztlán* (Berkeley, CA: University of California Press, 1987).

179. Lewis, "Muted Voices," 135.

180. See Cole, *Attitudes towards Bilingual Education*, 80–84.

181. Maria Antonia Calvo and Steven J. Rosenstone, *Hispanic Political Participation* (San Antonio, TX: Southwest Voter Research Institute, 1989), 2.

182. *The National Latino Immigrant Survey*, 3.

183. Rodolfo O. de la Garza, "Introduction," in de la Garza, ed., *Ignored Voices*, 4.

10. ASSIMILATION AND ITS DISCONTENTS

1. Morris Janowitz, *The Last Half-Century* (Chicago: The University of Chicago Press, 1978), 80.

2. Daniel Bell, *The Coming of Post-Industrial Society* (New York: Basic Books, 1976), 364–367.

3. Samuel P. Huntington, *Political Order in Changing Societies* (New Haven, CT: Yale University Press), 9–10.

4. Samuel P. Huntington and Joan M. Nelson, *No Easy Choice: Political Participation in Developing Countries* (Cambridge, MA: Harvard University Press, 1976), 51.

5. William P. Riordon, ed., *Plunkitt of Tammany Hall* (New York: E. P. Dutton, 1963), 17–20.

6. Daniel P. Moynihan, *Maximum Feasible Misunderstanding: Community Action in the War on Poverty* (New York: The Free Press, 1969), 21–37.

7. Nathan Glazer and Daniel Patrick Moynihan, *Beyond the Melting Pot*, 2nd ed. (Cambridge, MA: The MIT Press, 1970), 229.

8. There is a clear evolution to Moynihan's thinking about the professionalization of reform. Writing in the premier issue of *The Public Interest* in 1965, Moynihan, though not unmindful of potential problems, clearly viewed this development as a positive one. But just three years later, in the immediate aftermath of Robert Kennedy's assassination and in the midst of one of the nation's most tumultuous and unsettling periods, Moynihan was already beginning to rethink his initial enthusiasm for the efforts of reform-oriented professionals. Specifically, he had serious criticisms of their role in arousing the anger and frustrations of poor blacks through Community Action Programs. At this juncture Moynihan took specific aim at the role of philanthropic institutions, the Ford Foundation in particular, in the development of the War on Poverty. By 1973, in *The Politics of a Guaranteed Income*, Moynihan had come to see many of the professionals whom he had formerly identified as promoting reform as actually opposing it—specifically, the Nixon administration's ill-fated Family Assistance Plan. Indeed, by this time Moynihan was arguing that social work professionals had fought Nixon's proposal not on the basis of any expertise, but either out of craven submission to the threats of black militants or out of pure self-interest. See Daniel Patrick Moynihan, "The Professionalization of Reform," *The Public Interest* 1 (1965): 6–16; Daniel Patrick Moynihan, *Maximum Feasible Misunderstanding*, 21–37, 170–172, 190–194; and Daniel Patrick Moynihan, *The Politics of a Guaranteed Income: The Nixon Administration and the Family Assistance Plan* (New York: Vintage Books, 1973), 302–327, 549–550.

9. Samuel P. Hays, "Political Parties and the Community–Society Continuum," in William Nisbet Chambers and Walter Dean Burnham, eds., *The American Party Systems: Stages of Political Development* (New York: Oxford University Press, 1975), 178–181.

10. Benjamin Ginsberg and Martin Shefter, *Politics by Other Means: The Declining Importance of Elections in America* (New York: Basic Books, 1990), 81.

11. Gerald Pomper, "An American Epilogue," in Vernon Bogdanor, ed., *Parties and Democracy in Britain and America* (New York: Praeger, 1984), 271.

12. On the growth of national party bureaucracies, see A. James Reichley, "The Rise of National Parties," in John E. Chubb and Paul E. Peterson, eds., *The New Direction in American Politics* (Washington, DC: The Brookings Institution, 1985), 175–202.

13. Ginsberg and Shefter, *Politics by Other Means*, 10.

14. See Reichley, "The Rise of National Parties," 195–200, and Pomper, "An American Epilogue," 259–262.

15. See Anthony King, ed., *The New American Political System* (Washington, DC: American Enterprise Institute, 1978) and Anthony King, ed., *The New American Political System*, second version (Washington, DC: American Enterprise Institute, 1990). On these developments, see also James Q. Wilson, "American Politics—Then and Now," *Commentary*, February 1979, 39–46.

16. Janowitz, *Last Half-Century*, 312.

17. See Ibid., 303–305.

18. On television's self-conscious role in the civil rights struggle, see Michael J. Robinson, "Television and American Politics: 1956–1976," *The Public Interest* 48 (1977): 28–29.

19. Nancy Gibbs, "Shades of Difference," *Time*, 18 November 1991, 67.

20. Edward T. Kantowicz, "Voting and Parties," in Michael Walzer et al., *Politics of Ethnicity* (Cambridge, MA: The Belknap Press of Harvard University Press, 1982), 46.

21. See, for example, Zbigniew Brzezinski, *Between Two Ages: America's Role in the Technotronic Era* (New York: Penguin Books, 1970), 111–115.

22. As both Thomas Sowell and Nathan Glazer have noted, elite responses to the urban crises of the 1960s typically failed to consider the recent arrival of blacks from the rural South to Northern cities. See Nathan Glazer, "Blacks and Ethnic Groups: The Difference, and the Political Difference It Makes," in Nathan I. Huggins et al., *Key Issues in the Afro-American Experience* (New York: Harcourt Brace Jovanovich, 1971), 193–211; and Thomas Sowell, *Race and Economics* (New York: David McKay, 1975).

23. See William M. Lunch, *The Nationalization of American Politics* (Berkeley, CA: University of California Press, 1987).

24. Leo Grebler et al., *The Mexican-American People: The Nation's Second Largest Minority* (New York: The Free Press, 1970), 4–5.

25. Ibid., 4. One indication of how much this "parochial orientation" of Mexican-American leaders has changed is found in Rodolfo de la Garza's research on Chicano political elites. Identifying a population universe from which to draw a sample of Mexican-American leaders to be interviewed, de la Garza discovered that "very few [Mexican-American] organizations identify themselves as explicitly local in focus." See Rodolfo O. de la Garza, *Public Policy Priorities of Chicano Political Elites*, Working Paper, U.S.–Mexico Project Series, No. 7 (Washington, DC: Overseas Development Council, July 1982), 2.

26. Rufus P. Browning et al., *Protest Is Not Enough: The Struggle of Blacks and Hispanics for Equality in Urban Politics* (Berkeley, CA: University of California Press, 1984), 124–128.

27. On the emergence of "Hispanics" as a political grouping, see Peter Skerry, "E Pluribus Hispanic?" *Wilson Quarterly*, Summer 1992, 62–73.

28. For example, on the important role played by the Ford Foundation and the Carnegie Foundation in support of Chicano activists in South Texas, see

John Staples Shockley, *Chicano Revolt in a Texas Town* (Notre Dame, IN: University of Notre Dame Press, 1974), 125, 204, 221, 291.

29. Tony Castro, *Chicano Power: The Emergence of Mexican America* (New York: Saturday Review Press/E. P. Dutton, 1974), 148–157. For Congressman González's remarks on the House floor, see Henry B. González, "Reverse Racism," in Luiz Valdez and Stan Steiner, eds., *Aztlán: An Anthology of Mexican American Literature* (New York: Vintage Books, 1972), 311–318.

30. Karen O'Connor and Lee Epstein, "A Legal Voice for the Chicano Community: The Activities of the Mexican American Legal Defense and Educational Fund, 1968–1982," *Social Science Quarterly* 65 (1984): 249.

31. It should be pointed out that voter registration drives have been particularly successful examples of post-1960s legal activism. On this point, see Joel Handler, *Social Movements and the Legal System: A Theory of Law Reform and Social Change* (New York: Academic Press, 1978), 118–128.

32. Quoted in O'Connor and Epstein, "A Legal Voice for the Chicano Community," 248.

33. Ibid., 248, 252.

34. Ibid., 253.

35. For an analysis of the structure and incentives of the NAACP and its spin-off, the NAACP Legal Defense and Educational Fund, see James Q. Wilson, *Political Organizations* (New York: Basic Books, 1973), 171–181, 321. See also Joel F. Handler et al., "Public Interest Law and Employment Discrimination," in Burton A. Weisbrod, et al., *Public Interest Law: An Economic and Institutional Analysis* (Berkeley, CA: University of California Press, 1978), 272–273. On MALDEF specifically, see ibid., 273–274.

36. Data compiled from MALDEF and Ford Foundation annual reports.

37. Blanca Facundo, *Responsiveness of U.S. Foundations to Hispanic Needs and Concerns: Results of a Survey on Institutional Policies and Procedures Relevant to Hispanics and an Analysis of Grant Information in the 1977 and 1978 "Foundation Grants Index"* (Reston, VA: Latino Research Institute Division, 1980), 22–24. See also *A Study of Foundation Awards to Hispanic-Oriented Organizations in the U.S.: 1981–1982*, preliminary report (Stanford, CA: Stanford Center for Chicano Research, Stanford University, March 1984), 16–17.

38. For an account of Operation Wetback and the 1930s repatriation efforts, see Grebler et al., *The Mexican-American People*, 521–526.

39. See Walter McManus et al., "Earnings of Hispanic Men: The Role of English Language Proficiency," *Journal of Labor Economics* 1 (1983): 101–130; George J. Borjas and Marta Tienda, "Introduction," in Borjas and Tienda, eds., *Hispanics in the U.S. Economy* (Orlando, FL: Academic Press, 1985), 1–24; and George J. Borjas, "Jobs and Employment for Hispanics," in Pastora San Juan Cafferty and William C. McCready, eds., *Hispanics in the United States: A New Social Agenda* (New Brunswick, NJ: Transaction Books, 1985), 147–157.

40. Patrick Buchanan, "Reagan Should Veto the Mean-Spirited Simpson-Mazzoli Bill," *Los Angeles Herald Examiner*, 27 June 1984, A13.

41. For a statement by MALDEF critical of the amnesty provisions in Simpson-Mazzoli, see Rodolfo O. de la Garza, "Mexican-Americans, Mexican Immigrants, and Immigration Reform," in Nathan Glazer, ed., *Clamor at the Gates: The New American Immigration* (San Francisco: Institute for Contemporary Studies, 1985), 104. By contrast, as I pointed out in the previous chapter on issues, Mexican Americans overwhelmingly supported amnesty. See above, pp. 300–301.

42. O'Connor and Epstein, "A Legal Voice for the Chicano Community," 248.

43. On the activities of such individuals under the banner of a group called Californios for Fair Representation, see J. Morgan Kousser, *How to Determine Intent: Lessons from L.A.*, Social Science Working Paper 741 (Pasadena, CA: Division of Humanities and Social Sciences, California Institute of Technology, June 1990), 30–42.

44. See, for example, Paul Delaney, "A Purge at the Top, Confusion in the Ranks: N.A.A.C.P. Crisis," *New York Times*, 29 March 1992, section 4, 2.

45. See Jeffrey M. Berry, *The Interest Group Society*, 2nd ed. (Glenview, IL: Scott, Foresman/Little, Brown, 1989), 62–63; and James Q. Wilson, *American Government: Institutions and Policies* (Lexington, MA: D. C. Heath, 1980), 215–218.

46. James Q. Wilson, ed., *The Politics of Regulation* (New York: Basic Books, 1980), 370–372. Wilson's discussion of vicarious representation is of course part of his broader analysis of "entrepreneurial politics," which he differentiates from "majoritarian," "client," and "interest group" politics. It is an intriguing—and not readily answered—question as to whether the political dynamics I ascribe to MALDEF are best categorized as entrepreneurial or client politics. See ibid., 367–370.

47. Jay Mathews, *Escalante: The Best Teacher in America* (New York: Henry Holt, 1988), 172–173.

48. Christine Marie Sierra, "Mexican Americans and Immigration Reform: Consensus and Fragmentation," paper presented to the annual meeting of the Western Political Science Association (1989), 24–27.

49. Janowitz, *The Last Half-Century*, 303.

50. Ibid., 27–52, 302.

51. Ibid., 302.

52. Ibid., 301–312.

53. Charles V. Hamilton, "Blacks and the Crisis of Political Participation," *The Public Interest* 34 (1974): 191. Stuart Scheingold makes a similar critique of public interest law strategies, but from a more markedly leftist perspective. See Stuart A. Scheingold, *The Politics of Rights: Lawyers, Public Policy, and Political Change* (New Haven, CT: Yale University Press, 1974).

54. On the Voting Rights Act and its extension to Mexican Americans, see Thernstrom, *Whose Votes Count? Affirmative Action and Minority Voting*

Rights (Cambridge: Harvard University Press, 1987), 43–62. For evidence that the discrimination experienced by Mexicans even in as extreme a context as Texas was less intense than what blacks endured, see Grebler et al., *The Mexican-American People*, 389–390. See also David Montejano, *Anglos and Mexicans in the Making of Texas, 1836–1986* (Austin, TX: University of Texas Press, 1987), though my inferences from Montejano's data differ from his.

55. Quoted in Bruce E. Cain, "Voting Rights and Democratic Theory: Toward a Color-Blind Society?" in Bernard Grofman and Chandler Davidson, eds., *Controversies in Minority Voting: The Voting Rights Act in Perspective* (Washington, DC: The Brookings Institution, 1992), 261.

56. See Robert Brischetto et al., "Conflict and Change in the Political Culture of San Antonio in the 1970s," in David R. Johnson et al., eds., *The Politics of San Antonio: Community, Progress, and Power* (Lincoln, NE: University of Nebraska Press, 1983), 91.

57. See Montejano, *Anglos and Mexicans*, 288–307.

58. Thernstrom, *Whose Votes Count?*, 233.

59. While Mexican-American leaders obviously embrace the Voting Rights Act, there is some evidence that they acknowledge the point I make here, though not publicly. For example, a national survey of Hispanic (not just Mexican-American) leaders that Daniel Yankelovich did for the Hispanic Policy Development Project in 1983 reported that "fewer than a quarter of the respondents considered this [discriminatory voting practices] an important reason for low voter turnout, while almost half appeared to dismiss its importance entirely." See Keith Melville, *Moving into the Political Mainstream*, vol. I (Washington, DC: Hispanic Policy Development Project, 1984), 12.

60. For a similar argument on how the media greatly oversimplified the complex issues involved in the 1981–1982 debates over renewal of the Voting Rights Act, see Thernstrom, *Whose Votes Count?* 117–120.

61. "Ending the Political Shame of L.A.," *Los Angeles Times*, 6 June 1990, B6.

62. Garza v. County of Los Angeles, 756 F.Supp. 1298, 1339–1342 (C.D. Cal. 1990).

63. Garza v. County of Los Angeles, 918 F.2d 763, 778 (9th Cir. 1990) (Kozinski, C. J., concurring and dissenting in part).

64. 756 F.Supp. 1298, at 1304.

65. Ibid.

66. For the election results, see County of Los Angeles, et al. v. Yoland Garza, et al., "Petition for a Writ of Certiorari to the United States Court of Appeals for the Ninth Circuit," Supreme Court of the United States, October Term, 1990; 30 November 1990, 4. For an assessment of Sarah Flores's prospects in what would have been the runoff for the supervisorial seat, see Bill Boyarsky, "The Rocky Race of Sarah Flores," *Los Angeles Times*, Nuestro Tiempo section, 11 October 1990, 1, 7.

67. Richard Simon, "Light Voter Turnout in 1st District Race," *Los Angeles Times*, 23 January 1991, A20.

68. Quoted in Bill Boyarsky, "In 30 Years, History Comes Full Circle from Roybal to Molina," *Los Angeles Times*, 23 February 1991, B2.

69. Kousser, *How to Determine Intent*, 12.

70. Garza v. County of Los Angeles, "Appellants' Opening Brief on Appeal," United States Court of Appeals for the Ninth Circuit, 8–9.

71. I deduce this from the fact that 53 percent of Los Angeles Hispanics told the 1980 census they were citizens. Because we know that these self-reported census data on citizenship are artificially high, it is then entirely possible that less than this 53 percent figure—less than a majority of Los Angeles Hispanics—were citizens in 1980. See Garza v. County of Los Angeles, "Appellants' Opening Brief on Appeal," United States Court of Appeals for the Ninth Circuit, 9.

72. Derived from the data presented in United States of America v. County of Los Angeles, "Declaration of Dr. William P. O'Hare," United States District Court for the Central District of California, 26 October 1989, 10, 12.

73. "An Election to Make History," *Los Angeles Times*, 19 February 1991, B6.

74. Figures derived from data presented in United States of America v. County of Los Angeles, "Declaration of Dr. William P. O'Hare," 8, 12, 14.

75. 756 F.Supp. 1298 at 1318–1319.

76. For the Chicano activists' strategy in 1981, see Nancy D. Kates, *New Kingdoms for the Five Kings: Discriminatory Redistricting and the Los Angeles County Board of Supervisors*, C16-91-1042.0 (Cambridge: Case Program, Kennedy School of Government, Harvard University, 1991), 7–8. See also Kousser, *How to Determine Intent*, 32–41; and 756 F.Supp. 1298 at 1315.

77. 918 F.2d 763 at 769; and Garza v. County of Los Angeles, "Appellants' Opening Brief on Appeal," 14.

78. Richard Simon and Hector Tobar, "Deadline for 1st District Race Passes with No Surprises," *Los Angeles Times*, 1 December 1990, B3.

79. On the strategic choices facing MALDEF in 1981, see Kates, *New Kingdoms for the Five Kings*, 11. For an account, from the activists' perspective, of the events leading up to the MALDEF suit, see Steve Uranga and Marshall Diaz, "For Latinos, a Representative Case," *Los Angeles Times*, 28 July 1988, II-7.

80. This sequence of events is borne out in newspaper accounts of the negotiations culminating in the suit. See Victor Merina and Ron Ostrow, "U.S. Accuses County of Reapportionment Bias," *Los Angeles Times*, 26 May 1988, 1, 34; Victor Merina, "U.S. Vows Suit if Supervisors Don't Revamp to Aid Latinos," *Los Angeles Times*, 20 July 1988, 1, 4; Victor Merina, "Latinos Sue, Charge Bias in Districting by Supervisors," *Los Angeles Times*, 24 August 1988, II-1, II-8; and Victor Merina and Ronald J. Ostrow, "U.S. Sues to Get New Supervisor Districts Drawn," *Los Angeles Times*, 9 September 1988, 1, 28. In the latter article, a senior Justice Department official complained that voting rights division attorneys were caught by surprise "when

MALDEF rushed in and filed suit. They picked up all the work we had done and then threw a hand grenade."

81. Lou Cannon, "Hispanic Elected in L.A. County," *Washington Post*, 21 February 1991, A5.

82. This turnout figure is from the Los Angeles County Office of Public Information. Similarly low turnout figures for a variety of Latino (and black) constituencies in Los Angeles are presented in one of the more thoughtful articles on the 1992 Los Angeles riots. See Tim Rutten, "A New Kind of Riot," *New York Review of Books*, 11 June 1992, 54.

83. 918 F.2d 763 at 779–780 (Kozinski, C. J., concurring and dissenting in part).

84. Ibid. at 781–785.

85. See especially, Kevin F. McCarthy and R. Burciaga Valdez, *Current and Future Effects of Mexican Immigration in California* (Los Angeles: The Rand Corp., 1986), 37–45, 74–75; but also Thomas Muller et al., *The Fourth Wave: California's Newest Immigrants* (Washington, DC: The Urban Institute Press, 1985), 108–123.

86. De la Garza, "Mexican-Americans, Mexican Immigrants, and Immigration Reform," 98.

87. Quoted in Vernon M. Briggs et al., *The Chicano Worker* (Austin, TX: University of Texas Press, 1977), 93. For more on Sanchez's views on immigration and related issues, see Mario T. García, *Mexican Americans: Leadership, Ideology, and Identity, 1930–1960* (New Haven, CT: Yale University Press, 1989), 252–272.

88. On the divisions among Mexican Americans with regard to immigration during the 1960s, see Grebler et al., *The Mexican-American People*, 383.

89. For a critical analysis of efforts by Mexican Americans to maximize their census count, see Peter Skerry, "The Census Wars," *The Public Interest* 106 (1992): 17–31.

90. For a contrasting, but not very persuasive, view, see de la Garza, "Mexican Americans, Mexican Immigrants, and Immigration Reform," 102.

91. For the ambivalent stance toward illegal immigration of Mexican-American agricultural labor organizers in Texas during the last half of the 1960s, see Grebler et al., *The Mexican-American People*, 523.

92. For an elaboration of this point, see Thomas Byrne Edsall, *The New Politics of Inequality* (New York: W. W. Norton, 1984).

93. On the decline of black turnout in Northern cities generally in the pre-Reagan era, see Steven P. Erie, *Rainbow's End: Irish-Americans and the Dilemmas of Urban Machine Politics, 1840–1985* (Berkeley, CA: University of California Press, 1988), 265–266.

94. Charles V. Hamilton, "The Patron-Recipient Relationship and Minority Politics in New York City," *Political Science Quarterly* 94 (1979): 214–215.

95. Ibid., 215–216.

96. Albert O. Hirschman, *Shifting Involvements: Private Interest and Public Action* (Princeton, NJ: Princeton University Press, 1982), 125.

97. See Edward C. Banfield, *The Moral Basis of a Backward Society* (New York: The Free Press, 1958); and Laurence Wylie, *Village in the Vaucluse: An Account of Life in a French Village* (New York: Harper Colophon Books, 1964).

98. See also Ray Gonzales, "Why Chicanos Don't Vote," *California Journal*, July 1975, 245–246.

99. See Alan Riding, *Distant Neighbors: A Portrait of the Mexicans* (New York: Alfred A. Knopf, 1985), 8, 11; and Ruth Horowitz, *Honor and the American Dream: Culture and Identity in a Chicano Community* (New Brunswick, NJ: Rutgers University Press, 1985), 59–66.

100. This conclusion is based on my own observations in the field and is confirmed, for example, by field observations in Horowitz, *Honor and the American Dream*, 55–58, 230. Survey evidence confirming my point is found in de la Garza et al., "Will The Real American Please Stand Up: A Comparison of Political Values among Mexicans, Cubans, Puerto Ricans and Anglos in the United States," paper presented at the annual meeting of the American Political Science Association (1991), 6–8. This paper analyzes data from the Latino National Political Survey and reveals that Mexican Americans, even without controlling for socioeconomic variables, esteem economic self-sufficiency and reject governmental supports as much as Americans generally.

101. For demographic evidence on Mexican-American families, see Frank D. Bean and Marta Tienda, *The Hispanic Population of the United States* (New York: Russell Sage Foundation, 1987), 178–204. While Bean and Tienda cite some evidence that Mexican-American and Hispanic families generally are stronger and more enduring than Anglo and black families, their analysis actually emphasizes that on many indices Hispanic families are not so different from non-Hispanic families. Yet on the level of attitudes and values, Mexican Americans do exhibit enormous attachment to the family as an institution. See Horowitz, *Honor and the American Dream*, 52–76, 230–231.

102. It is intriguing to note that in a recent study of gangs in Los Angeles, Martín Sánchez Jankowski reports that particularly strong family ties and values among Chicanos result in their gangs being less hierarchically organized and less economically rational than black gangs. See Martín Sánchez Jankowski, *Islands in the Street: Gangs and American Urban Society* (Berkeley, CA: University of California Press, 1991), 70–72, 134–135.

103. See Thomas Sowell, *Black Education: Myths and Tragedies* (New York: David McKay, 1972), 25–32. Other observers of the poor have similarly noted how strong family ties—the parents who accuse their ambitious children of abandoning them, the envious siblings, the freeloading relatives—stymie the efforts of the upwardly mobile. See also Richard Sennett, *Families against the City: Middle Class Homes of Industrial Chicago, 1872–1890* (New York: Vintage Books, 1974) and Elmer P. Martin and Joanne Mitchell Martin, *The Black Extended Family* (Chicago: The Uni-

versity of Chicago Press, 1978). For evidence of this dynamic among Mexican Americans specifically, see Horowitz, *Honor and the American Dream*, 208.

104. What I report here from my contemporary field observations is echoed in the 1960s research of Grebler et al., *The Mexican-American People*, 359. Similar findings are reported in recent research on undocumented Mexican immigrants. See Harley L. Browning and Nestor Rodríguez, "The Migration of Mexican Indocumentados as a Settlement Process: Implications for Work," in Borjas and Tienda, *Hispanics in the U.S. Economy*, 291–292, 297.

105. Quoted in Leonard Dinnerstein et al., *Natives and Strangers: Blacks, Indians, and Immigrants in America*, 2nd ed. (New York: Oxford University Press, 1990), 321. Of a Mexican-American father refusing to let his bright teenage daughter go away to college, Los Angeles County Supervisor Gloria Molina observes, "It's a situation that exists in lots of families." See Jay Mathews, "Los Angeles' New Councilwoman Reflects Changing Ethnic Politics," *Washington Post*, 14 April 1987, A4. See also Peter Skerry, "Hispanic Dropouts: A Social Problem, A Political Cause?" *The American Enterprise*, July/August 1990, 20–21. During the 1930s and 1940s similar dynamics were evident among Italian Americans. For more on "the Italian problem," see Glazer and Moynihan, *Beyond the Melting Pot*, 199–202.

106. Mathews, *Escalante*, 128–131. For a brief but particularly insightful discussion of this dynamic, see Briggs et al., *The Chicano Worker*, 22–24. That this tradeoff between the welfare and prosperity of the family and individual mobility is frequent among Mexican Americans is confirmed in David L. Featherman and Robert M. Hauser, *Opportunity and Change* (New York: Academic Press, 1978), 477.

107. Riding, *Distant Neighbors*, 5. On the dialectic between strong family values and individualism, see Ann L. Craig and Wayne A. Cornelius, "Political Culture in Mexico: Continuities and Revisionist Interpretations," in Gabriel A. Almond and Sidney Verba, eds., *The Civic Culture Revisited* (Boston: Little, Brown, 1980), 371–373.

108. George Ramos, "Employment Suit Embroils MALDEF in Controversy," *Los Angeles Times*, 17 February 1987, CC1, CC3; and Marcia Chambers, "Hispanic Rights Leader Gets Post Over Ex-Governor of New Mexico," *New York Times*, 2 March 1987, A15.

109. Morris Janowitz, *The Reconstruction of Patriotism: Education for Civic Consciousness* (Chicago: The University of Chicago Press, 1983), 19.

110. Robert E. Park and Herbert A. Miller, *Old World Traits Transplanted* (New York: Arno Press, 1969), 280.

111. William I. Thomas and Florian Znaniecki, *The Polish Peasant in Europe and America* (New York: Dover Publishers, 1958), 1590.

112. Huntington, *Political Order*, 83.

113. My terminology is borrowed from Peter L. Berger and Richard John Neuhaus, *To Empower People: The Role of Mediating Structures in Public Policy* (Washington, DC: American Enterprise Institute, 1977).

114. Allan Bloom, trans., *The Republic of Plato* (New York: Basic Books, 1968), 13–34.

115. See Jacques Maritain, *Man and the State* (Chicago: The University of Chicago Press, 1951); and John Courtney Murray, *We Hold These Truths: Catholic Reflections on the American Proposition* (Kansas City, MO: Sheed and Ward, 1960). For an analysis that places Alinsky methods in this context, see Charles E. Curran, *Critical Concerns in Moral Theology* (Notre Dame, IN: University of Notre Dame Press, 1984), 171–199.

116. Judith Shklar identifies the same "half-private and half-public" quality in civil society generally and in the institutions of which it is constituted, such as the clubs of apprentices and journeymen organized in colonial Philadelphia by Benjamin Franklin. See Judith Shklar, *American Citizenship: The Quest for Inclusion* (Cambridge, MA: Harvard University Press, 1991), 63, 72.

117. Jane Jacobs, *The Death and Life of Great American Cities* (New York: Vintage Books, 1961), 57.

118. Ibid., 59.

119. Ibid., 62–63.

120. Ibid., 68.

121. Theodore Lowi, "Machine Politics—Old and New," *The Public Interest* 9 (1967): 86.

122. Amy Bridges, *A City in the Republic: Antebellum New York and the Origins of Machine Politics* (Cambridge, UK: Cambridge University Press, 1984), 153–154. For a different but related insight into the role played by the political machine in moderating expectations among urban migrants and their children, see Lloyd E. Ohlin, "Issues in the Development of Indigenous Social Movements among Residents of Deprived Urban Areas," mimeograph, 1960; quoted in Daniel P. Moynihan, *Maximum Feasible Misunderstanding: Community Action in the War on Poverty* (New York: The Free Press, 1969), 119–120.

123. For an analysis of the use of light and shadow in Plato that is pertinent to this point, see Pangle's interpretive essay in Thomas L. Pangle, trans., *The Laws of Plato* (New York: Basic Books, 1980), 381–382.

124. On this point see Grant McConnell, *Private Power and American Democracy* (New York: Vintage Books, 1970), 141–143.

125. For a critical analysis of feminist political theory's casting of the family as a contractual relationship, see Martha Bayles, "Feminism and Abortion," *Atlantic Monthly*, April 1990, 79, 84–88.

126. For an excessively critical but nevertheless useful discussion of how under the Wagner Act trade unions gained recognition at the price of their autonomy, see McConnell, *Private Power and American Democracy*, 146–147.

127. For an analysis and critique of how pluralism has blurred the distinction between the private and the public, see Theodore J. Lowi, *The End of Liberalism*, 2nd ed. (New York: W. W. Norton, 1979), 261, 40, and 50. While my analysis obviously draws on Lowi's, his emphasis is on how this blurring subverts public policy and government. My concern here is with the aggrandizement of government at the expense of private institutional prerogatives.

128. See Peter Skerry, "Christian Schools versus the I.R.S.," *The Public Interest* 61 (1980): 38–41.

129. See Aldon D. Morris, *The Origins of the Civil Rights Movement: Black Communities Organizing for Change* (New York: The Free Press, 1984).

130. For survey data on this point, see Alejandro Portes and Robert L. Bach, *Latin Journey: Cuban and Mexican Immigrants in the United States* (Berkeley, CA: University of California Press, 1985), 277. More generally, on Mexican fears about the corrupting influences of American society, see Richard Rodriguez, "Lilies That Fester," *Wall Street Journal*, 2 July 1986, A25.

131. Nicholas Gage, *A Place for Us* (Boston: Houghton-Mifflin, 1989).

132. See Robert Warren and Ellen Percy Kraly, *The Elusive Exodus: Emigration from the United States* (Washington, DC: The Population Reference Bureau, March 1985), 4–5; and Muller et al., *The Fourth Wave*, 14.

133. Oscar Handlin, *The Uprooted: The Epic Story of the Great Migrations That Made the American People* (New York: Grosset & Dunlap, 1951).

134. William Alfred, "Pride and Poverty: An Irish Integrity," in Thomas C. Wheeler, ed., *The Immigrant Experience* (Baltimore, MD: Penguin Books, 1971), 20.

135. Walter Fogel, "Twentieth-Century Mexican Migration to the United States," in Barry R. Chiswick, ed., *The Gateway: U.S. Immigration Issues and Policies* (Washington, DC: American Enterprise Institute, 1982), 218–219. See also Barry R. Chiswick, "The Labor Market Status of Hispanic Men," *Journal of American Ethnic History* 7 (1987): 30–57.

136. John U. Ogbu, "Minority Status and Literacy in Comparative Perspective," *Daedalus* 119 (1980): 151.

137. Fogel cites evidence confirming that "persons born in the United States who have one or more parents born abroad (the second generation) earn 5 to 10 percent more than immigrants with the same earnings characteristics." See Fogel, "Twentieth-Century Mexican Migration," 218. Fogel's conclusion relies heavily on the research of others. See, in particular, Barry R. Chiswick, "The Economic Progress of Immigrants: Some Apparently Universal Patterns," in William Fellner, ed., *Contemporary Economic Problems 1979* (Washington, DC: American Enterprise Institute, 1979), 357–399.

138. Featherman and Hauser, *Opportunity and Change*, 444.

139. Ibid., 438.

140. For some commentary on this point specific to Mexican Americans, see Grebler et al., *The Mexican-American People*, 293, 342–343. For some insights about upwardly mobile Puerto Ricans that bear on this point, see Joseph P. Fitzpatrick, *Puerto Rican America: The Meaning of Migration to the Mainland* (Englewood Cliffs, NJ: Prentice-Hall, 1987), 35.

141. Alfred, "Pride and Poverty," 20.

142. See Chiswick, "The Economic Progress of Immigrants," 357.

143. Featherman and Hauser, *Opportunity and Change*, 436–444; and Fogel, "Twentieth-Century Mexican Migration," 218. See also Chiswick, "The Labor Market Status of Hispanic Men."

144. William Petersen, "Concepts of Ethnicity," in Stephan Thernstrom, ed., *The Harvard Encyclopedia of American Ethnic Groups* (Cambridge, MA: Harvard University Press, 1980), 239.

145. Marcus Lee Hansen, "The Problem of the Third Generation Immigrant," in Peter Kvisto and Dag Blanck, eds., *American Immigrants and Their Generations: Studies and Commentaries on the Hansen Thesis after Fifty Years* (Urbana, IL: University of Illinois Press, 1990), 195.

146. For an evaluation of Hansen's thesis, see the essays in Kvisto and Blanck, eds., *American Immigrants and Their Generations*.

147. Chiswick, "The Economic Progress of Immigrants," 379–380; Chiswick, "The Labor Market Status of Hispanic Men," 37–41.

148. Ibid.; Featherman and Hauser, *Opportunity and Change*, 464.

149. Featherman and Hauser, *Opportunity and Change*, 462–464, especially 478; and Fogel, "Twentieth-Century Mexican Migration," 219; and Chiswick, "The Labor Market Status of Hispanic Men," 38. This same socioeconomic pattern among Mexican Americans was reported two decades ago in Grebler et al., *The Mexican-American People*, 30–31, 147, 191–192, 219. Linda Chavez presents more recent data than any of the above studies bearing on Mexican-American inter-generational mobility. Chavez notes that while 28 percent of first-generation Mexican-American males aged 25–34 in the late 1980s had completed twelve or more years of schooling, 78 percent of second-generation Mexican-American males in that age cohort had done so. Yet for third-generation Mexican-American males, the figure was 71 percent. See Linda Chavez, *Out of the Barrio: Toward a New Politics of Hispanic Assimilation* (New York: Basic Books, 1991), 113–115. Similar third-generation effects are reported in Frank Bean et al., *Educational and Sociodemographic Incorporation among Hispanic Immigrants to the United States* (Austin, TX: Texas Population Research Center Paper, University of Texas, 1991).

150. Bruce Cain and Roderick Kiewiet, "California's Coming Minority Majority," *Public Opinion*, February/March 1986, 52. For more data and analysis from this survey on this point, see Bruce E. Cain and D. Roderick

Kiewiet, *Minorities in California*, unpublished paper (Pasadena, CA: The California Institute of Technology, March 1986), I-10—I-11.

151. James W. Lamare, "The Political Integration of Mexican American Children: A Generational Analysis," *International Migration Review* 16 (1982): 169–188.

152. Raymond Buriel, *Academic Performance of Foreign- and Native-Born Mexican Americans: A Comparison of First-, Second-, and Third-Generation Students and Parents*, Working Paper No. 14, New Directions for Latino Public Policy Research Series (Austin, TX: IUP/SSRC Committee for Public Policy Research on Contemporary Hispanic Issues Center for Mexican American Studies, University of Texas, 1990), 9–11.

153. Portes and Bach, *Latin Journey*, 277–282. After six years in the United States, 36 percent of Mexican immigrants reported discrimination against their group, a slight but presumably insignificant (statistically) decrease.

154. Ibid., 296.

155. Cain and Kiewiet, *Minorities in California*, III-117. Though in the expected direction, the difference noted here between college-educated and non-college-educated Latinos is apparently not statistically significant.

156. Ibid., III-107, III-118.

157. Ibid. Yet it is not clear how such findings square with the considerable evidence cited in earlier chapters that Mexican Americans and Latinos generally experience considerable intergenerational social mobility, as indicated for example by data on intermarriage and residential patterns.

158. Jorge Chapa, *Are Chicanos Assimilating?* Working Paper 88-8 (Berkeley, CA: Institute of Governmental Studies, University of California, 1988), 4. These data are for adults aged 25–64 and living in California. Similar educational attainment data for second-generation Mexican Americans are presented in Featherman and Hauser, *Opportunity and Change*, 448–452.

159. Barry Chiswick reports: "Other things the same, first-, second-, and later-generation Mexican-Americans earn about 15 to 25 percent less than Anglos, and the difference does not appear to diminish between successive generations." See Chiswick, "Economic Progress of Immigrants," 379. Chiswick reports similar findings for a more recent (1980) data set. See "The Labor Market Status of Hispanic Men," 36–57. Similar earnings data for third(plus)-generation Mexican-American males aged 25–64 in California from 1940–1979 are presented in Chapa, *Are Chicanos Assimilating?*, 5. See also Featherman and Hauser, *Opportunity and Change*, 456–475, 478.

160. Featherman and Hauser, *Opportunity and Change*, 475.

161. Chiswick, "The Labor Market Status of Hispanic Men," 48–54.

162. On farm and rural background as a source of Mexican-American disadvantage, see Featherman and Hauser, *Opportunity and Change*, 445–446, 462. Chiswick makes a related point about the "lingering effects" of human capital formation among Mexican Americans at the turn of the century. See his "The Labor Market Status of Hispanic Men," 54.

163. Featherman and Hauser, *Opportunity and Change*, 477. This finding res-onates with my earlier discussion (see pp. 344–345) of the tension between family values and individual achievement among Mexican Americans. Chiswick similarly hypothesizes that higher fertility and larger families among Mexican Americans generally lead to lower human capital invest-ments per child, which reduce the productivity of schooling, and result in decreased incentives to invest in education. See his "The Labor Market Status of Hispanic Men," 53–54.

164. Featherman and Hauser, *Opportunity and Change*, 464.

165. On this point, I have already cited McCarthy and Valdez, *Current and Future Effects of Mexican Immigration in California*, 37–45, 74–75; and Muller et al., *The Fourth Wave*, 108–123.

166. Chapa, *Are Chicanos Assimilating?*, 5–7.

167. Featherman and Hauser, *Opportunity and Change*, 476.

168. De la Garza, *Public Policy Priorities of Chicano Political Elites*, 10.

169. Rodolfo O. de la Garza and Robert R. Brischetto, *The Mexican American Electorate: A Demographic Profile*, The Mexican American Electorate Se-ries, Hispanic Population Studies Program, Occasional Paper No. 1 (San Antonio, TX: Southwest Voter Registration Education Project; and Austin, TX: Center for Mexican American Studies, University of Texas, 1982), 12.

170. Janowitz, *Last Half-Century*, 312.

171. Ibid., 311. Richard Alba reports a similar positive correlation between eth-nic identity and education in his survey study of residents of metropolitan Albany, New York during the mid-1980s. See Richard D. Alba, *Ethnic Identity: The Transformation of White America* (New Haven, CT: Yale University Press, 1990), 55, 58, 74, 113, 308.

172. Tomás Almaguer et al., *The Diversity Project: An Interim Report to the Chancellor* (Berkeley, CA: Institute for the Study of Social Change, Uni-versity of California, June 1990), 10.

173. Ibid., 81.

174. Ibid., 62.

175. Ibid., 63.

176. Ibid., 65–66.

177. Ibid., 16–17, 62.

178. To my knowledge there is little systematic research on this point, but there is some anecdotal evidence. See, for example, Edward B. Fiske, "Eco-nomic Realities Spur Colleges On Recruiting Hispanics," *New York Times*, 20 March 1988, 1, 28. Certainly, my field interviews and observations con-firm that Mexican-American students who consider going to college are reluctant to remove themselves very far physically from home.

179. For one study touching on this point see M. L. Oliver et al., "Brown and Black in White: The Social Adjustment and Academic Performance of Chi-cano and Black Students in a Predominantly White University," *The Ur-ban Review* 17 (1985): 3–24.

180. Almaguer et al., *Diversity Project*, 62.
181. Arthur M. Schlesinger Jr., *The Disuniting of America: Reflections on a Multicultural Society* (Knoxville, TN: Whittle Books, 1991), 80.
182. For Calvin Veltman's and Benji Wald's views, see David G. Savage, "¿Is the Market Going English?" *Hispanic Business*, December 1982, 20–21.

11. NEWCOMERS IN A NEW NATION

1. See Linda Lichter, "Who Speaks for Black America?," *Public Opinion*, August/September 1985, 41–44, 58.
2. Chicano scholars frequently depict the Mexican-American experience as unique in this respect, overlooking or de-emphasizing the hardships, conflicts, and regrets experienced by European immigrant groups, to say nothing of the persistence of non-Latino ethnic identities in American society. See, for example, David E. Hayes-Bautista et al., *No Longer a Minority: Latinos and Social Policy in California* (Los Angeles: UCLA Chicano Studies Research Center, 1992), 33–34. See also Aída Hurtado et al., *Redefining California: Latino Social Engagement in a Multicultural Society* (Los Angeles: UCLA Chicano Studies Research Center, 1992).
3. I draw here on Nathan Glazer's typology of Northern, Southern, and Western models of group relations in the United States. See his "The Politics of a Multiethnic Society," in Nathan Glazer, *Ethnic Dilemmas, 1964–1982* (Cambridge, MA: Harvard University Press, 1983), 315–336.
4. See above, Table 1.1, p. 17.
5. Arthur M. Schlesinger, Jr., *The Disuniting of America: Reflections on a Multicultural Society* (Knoxville, TN: Whittle Books, 1991), 79.
6. For example, in a recent column on children in poverty, Will notes: "Sixty-three percent of all black babies were born to single women. The figures for Hispanics and whites were 34 percent and 18 percent, respectively." Note the particularly seductive nature of these numbers. On the one hand, they suggest that Hispanics are not as mired in the underclass as blacks. But at the same time, they obscure the fact that most Hispanics actually view themselves as white. See George F. Will, "Harvard's Physicist of Childhood," *Washington Post*, 23 June 1991, A23.

    Even the otherwise immovable *Wall Street Journal* has succumbed. In a recent editorial against the race-norming of employment tests, the *Journal* noted "test results are separated into racial groups, and then whites, blacks, and Hispanics are ranked by percentile against only members of their own race." See "Race-Norming," *Wall Street Journal*, 8 April 1991, A18.
7. For an extended discussion of this point, see Peter Skerry, "E Pluribus Hispanic?," *Wilson Quarterly*, Summer 1992, 62–73.
8. For a critique of this strategy, see Linda Chavez, "Party Lines: The Republicans' Racial Quotas," *New Republic*, 24 June 1991, 14–16. See also Abigail

M. Thernstrom, "A Republican-Civil Rights Conspiracy," *Washington Post*, 23 September 1991, A23.

9. Robert Reinhold, "In California, New Talk of Limits on Immigrants," *New York Times*, 3 December 1991, A20.

10. Bruce Cain and Roderick Kiewiet make a different but related point: "In seeking political allies to support their interests, minority group leaders cannot count on common perceptions of discrimination and justice to foster a natural coalition between their group and other minorities. As a source of political support, liberal Whites would appear to be at least as promising as other minority groups." See Bruce E. Cain and D. Roderick Kiewiet, *Minorities in California*, unpublished paper (Pasadena, CA: The California Institute of Technology, March 1986), III-111.

11. As I noted in the previous chapter, I have elaborated on James Q. Wilson's formulation of "vicarious representation." See James Q. Wilson, ed., *The Politics of Regulation* (New York: Basic Books, 1980), 370–372.

12. "The Liberal Barrio," *Wall Street Journal*, 13 June 1990, A14 and "The Liberal Barrio-II," *Wall Street Journal*, 20 July 1990, A12. See also the *Journal*'s other editorials championing Flores: "Republican Hispanics, Keep Out," *Wall Street Journal*, 7 August 1990, A16; "LA's Poodle District," *Wall Street Journal*, 21 August 1990, A14; and "Sarah's Hope," *Wall Street Journal*, 16 November 1990, A14.

13. See Peter Brimelow, "Time to Rethink Immigration?," *National Review*, 22 June 1992, 30–46; and Tim W. Ferguson, "The Sleeper Issue of the 1990s Awakens," *Wall Street Journal*, 23 June 1992, A21.

14. The phrase of course is from Lipset's classic study, *The First New Nation: The United States in Historical and Comparative Perspective* (Garden City, NY: Anchor Books, 1967).

15. Samuel P. Huntington, *Political Order in Changing Societies* (New Haven, CT: Yale University Press, 1968), 7.

16. Ibid., 93–139.

17. For a recent exploration of this and other limitations of political machines, see Steven P. Erie, *Rainbow's End: Irish Americans and the Dilemmas of Urban Machine Politics, 1840–1985* (Berkeley, CA: University of California Press, 1988).

18. Charles V. Hamilton, "The Patron-Recipient Relationship and Minority Politics in New York City," *Political Science Quarterly* 94 (1979): 215.

19. Theodore J. Lowi, *The End of Liberalism*, 2nd ed. (New York: W. W. Norton, 1979), 234–235.

20. "RAND Analysis Charts L.A. Riot Arrest and Crime Patterns," RAND News Release (Santa Monica, CA: The Rand Corp., 17 June 1992), 1.

INDEX

447